Network+™ 2005 In Depth

Tamara Dean

THOMSON

COURSE TECHNOLOGY

Professional ■ Technical ■ Reference

ISBN: 1-59200-792-9

Library of Congress Catalog Card Number: 2005921045

Printed in the United States of America

06 07 08 09 PH 10 9 8 7 6 5 4 3

Publisher and GM of Course Technology PTR:
Stacy L. Hiquet

Associate Director of Marketing:
Sarah O'Donnell

Marketing Manager:
Heather Hurley

Manager of Editorial Services:
Heather Talbot

Associate Acquisitions Editor:
Megan Belanger

Marketing Coordinator:
Jordan Casey

Technical Reviewers:
Marianne Snow,
Sydney Shewchuk

Developmental Editor:
Ann Shaffer

Contributing Author:
David Klann

Production Editors:
Elena Montillo,
Danielle Slade

PTR Editorial Services Coordinator:
Elizabeth Furbish

Interior Layout Tech:
William Hartman

Cover Designer:
Mike Tanamachi

Indexer:
Kevin Broccoli

Proofreader:
Cathleen Snyder

THOMSON

COURSE TECHNOLOGY
Professional ■ Technical ■ Reference

Thomson Course Technology PTR, a division of Thomson Course Technology
25 Thomson Place ■ Boston, MA 02210 ■ http://www.courseptr.com

Contents

Chapter 6   Topologies and Access Methods 245

Chapter 8   Network Operating Systems and Windows Server 2003-Based Networking 355

Chapter 13 Ensuring Integrity and Availability 565

Chapter 15   Implementing and Managing Networks..... 667

Preface

Knowing how to install, configure, and troubleshoot a computer network is a highly marketable and exciting skill. This book first introduces the fundamental building blocks that form a modern network, such as protocols, topologies, hardware, and network operating systems. It then provides in-depth coverage of the most important concepts in contemporary networking, such as client/server architecture, TCP/IP, Ethernet, wireless transmission, and security. After reading the book, you will be prepared to select the best network design, hardware, and software for your environment. You will also have the skills to build a network from scratch and maintain, upgrade, and troubleshoot an existing network. Finally, you will be well-prepared to pass CompTIA's (the Computing Technology Industry Association's) Network+ certification exam.

Because some technical topics can be difficult to grasp, this book explains concepts logically and in a clear, approachable style. In addition, concepts are reinforced by real-world examples of networking issues from a professional's standpoint. The numerous tables and illustrations, along with the glossaries, appendices, and study questions make the book a valuable reference for any networking professional.

The Network+ CoursePrep Exam Guide, which you can download from http://www.courseptr.com/downloads, offers several hundred multiple choice questions to further prepare you for passing CompTIA's Network+ certification exam.

Intended Audience

This book is intended to serve the needs of students and professionals who are interested in mastering fundamental, vendor-independent networking concepts. No previous networking experience is necessary to begin learning from this book, although knowledge of basic computer principles is helpful. Those seeking to pass CompTIA's Network+ certification exam will find the text's content, approach, and numerous study questions especially helpful. For more information on Network+ certification, visit CompTIA's web site at *www.comptia.org.*

The book's pedagogical features are designed to provide a truly interactive learning experience, preparing you for the challenges of the highly dynamic networking industry.

Chapter Descriptions

Here is a summary of the topics covered in each chapter of this book:

Chapter 1, "An Introduction to Networking," begins by answering the question "What is a network?" Next it presents the fundamental types of networks and describes the elements that constitute the most popular type, the client/server network. This chapter also introduces career options for those interested in mastering networking skills.

Chapter 2, "Networking Standards and the OSI Model," describes the organizations that set standards in the networking industry, including those that oversee wiring codes, network access methods, and Internet addressing. It also discusses, in depth, the OSI Model, which is the industry standard for conceptualizing communication between computers on a network.

Chapter 3, "Transmission Basics and Networking Media," describes signaling techniques used on modern networks, including those used over copper cable, fiber-optic cable, and wireless connections. It also covers the characteristics—including cost, materials, and connector types—for physical and atmospheric media that can be used to carry signals.

Chapter 4, "Network Protocols," explores network protocols in detail, with a particular emphasis on the TCP/IP protocol suite. Functions and interactions between each core protocol and subprotocol are described in the context of the OSI Model. This chapter also explains computer addressing and naming conventions for each major protocol suite.

Chapter 5, "Networking Hardware," examines the hardware associated with a network, including NICs (network interface cards), hubs, routers, bridges, gateways, and switches. In Chapter 5, you will find several photos portraying typical networking equipment.

Chapters 6, "Topologies and Access Methods," discusses the variety of physical and logical topologies used in local area networks. This chapter includes detailed discussions of the popular Ethernet and wireless access methods.

Chapter 7, "WANs, Internet Access, and Remote Connectivity," expands on your knowledge of networks by examining WAN (wide area network) topologies and transmission methods, such as T-carriers, ISDN, DSL, and broadband cable. Here you will also learn about options for accessing networks from remote locations, including dial-up networking and VPNs (virtual private networks).

Chapter 8, "Network Operating Systems and Windows Server 2003-Based Networking," covers the purpose and design of network operating system software. It then provides an overview of the Microsoft Windows Server 2003 network operating system, including Active Directory, the Windows Server 2003 method of organizing network elements. In this chapter you will also learn how to integrate Windows servers with clients and servers running different operating systems.

Chapter 9, "Networking with UNIX-type of Operating Systems," discusses the unique features of UNIX, Linux, and Mac OS X Server network operating systems (collectively termed "UNIX-type of systems"). It enumerates basic commands that can be used on UNIX-type of systems and explains how these operating systems can share resources and communicate over networks.

Chapter 10, "NetWare-Based Networking," describes the unique features of the Novell NetWare network operating system, including eDirectory (or NDS), which is NetWare's method of organizing network elements. You will also learn how to integrate NetWare servers with clients and servers running different operating systems.

Chapter 11, "In-Depth TCP/IP Networking," explores advanced concepts relating to TCP/IP-based networking, such as subnetting and NAT (Network Address Translation). It also details commands useful for evaluating devices and connections that run the TCP/IP protocol suite.

Chapter 12, "Troubleshooting Network Problems," approaches the tasks of troubleshooting and maintaining networks in a logical, practical manner. Once you have learned how networks operate and how to create them, you will need to know how to fix and maintain them.

Chapter 13, "Ensuring Integrity and Availability," explains how to keep network resources available and connections reliable despite threats such as power outages or hardware and software failures. In this chapter you will find information about backup power supplies, redundant disk arrays, and data backup procedures.

Chapter 14, "Network Security," discusses critical network security techniques, including the use of firewalls, encryption, and enterprise-wide security policies. Network security is a major concern when designing and maintaining modern networks, which typically use open protocols and connect to public networks such as the Internet.

Chapter 15, "Implementing and Managing Networks," concludes the book by describing how to approach large network projects including software or hardware updates or an entire network implementation. This chapter builds on all the knowledge you've gained about network fundamentals, design, maintenance, and troubleshooting.

Appendix A, "Network+ Examination Objectives," provides a complete list of the 2005 Network+ certification exam objectives, including the percentage of the exam's content they represent and which chapters in the book cover material associated with each objective.

Appendix B, "Network+ Practice Exam," offers a practice exam containing questions similar in content and presentation to those you will find on CompTIA's Network+ examination.

Appendix C, "Visual Guide to Connectors," provides a visual connector reference chart for quick identification of connectors and receptacles used in contemporary networking.

Appendix D, "Standard Networking Forms," gives examples of forms that you can use while planning, installing, and troubleshooting your network.

Appendix E, "Answers to Chapter Review Questions," provides the answers to the Review Questions at the end of each chapter.

CoursePrep ExamGuide

Available for download from **http://www.courseptr.com/downloads**, you will find PDF files containing the *Network+ CoursePrep ExamGuide*. This certification prep workbook provides the essential information you need to master each exam objective. The Exam-Guide devotes an entire two-page spread to each certification objective from the Comp-TIA Network+ exam, helping you understand the objective, and giving you the bottom line information—what you *really* need to know. Memorize these facts and bulleted points before heading into the exam. In addition, the ExamGuide includes seven practice-test questions for each objective on the right-hand page. That's more than 600 questions total! You can find answers to all the practice test questions in the answer key at the end of the ExamGuide, so that you can practice, drill, and rehearse for the exam.

Features

To aid you in fully understanding networking concepts, this book includes many features designed to enhance your learning experience.

◆ **Chapter Objectives.** Each chapter begins with a list of the concepts to be mastered within that chapter. This list provides you with both a quick reference to the chapter's contents and a useful study aid.

◆ **Illustrations and Tables.** Numerous full-color illustrations of network media, methods of signaling, protocol behavior, hardware, topology, software screens, peripherals, and components help you visualize common network elements, theories, and concepts. In addition, the many tables included provide details and comparisons of both practical and theoretical information.

◆ **Chapter Summaries.** Each chapter's text is followed by a summary of the concepts introduced in that chapter. These summaries provide a helpful way to recap and revisit the ideas covered in each chapter.

◆ **Review Questions.** The end-of-chapter assessment begins with a set of review questions that reinforce the ideas introduced in each chapter. Answering these questions will ensure that you have mastered the important concepts and provide valuable practice for taking CompTIA's Network+ exam.

Text and Graphic Conventions

Wherever appropriate, additional information and exercises have been added to this book to help you better understand the topic at hand. The following icons are used throughout the text to alert you to additional materials:

NOTE

The Note icon draws your attention to helpful material related to the subject being described.

TIP

Tips based on the author's experience provide extra information about how to attack a problem or what to do in real-world situations.

CAUTION

The caution icons draw your attention to warnings about potential problems and explanations of how to avoid them.

All of the content that relates to CompTIA's Network+ Certification exam, whether it's a page or a sentence, is highlighted with a Net+ icon and the relevant objective number. This unique feature highlights the important information at a glance, so you can pay extra attention to the certification material.

Acknowledgments

As with any large undertaking, this book is the result of many contributions and collaborative efforts. It would not exist without the help of friends, family, fellow networking professionals, and Thomson Course Technology staff. Thanks to Kristen Duerr, Publisher and Executive Vice President, for her continued enthusiasm and support for the project and to Will Pitkin, Managing Editor, for his dedication and business expertise. I'm deeply grateful to Amy Lyon, Product Manager, for assembling a top-notch team and maintaining enthusiasm, order, and a steady flow of communication that allowed the project to advance smoothly. Many thanks to Ann Shaffer, Developmental Editor and friend, for handling extreme deadlines with grace and for insisting on coherence, clarity, and precision throughout each draft. With this edition, I am again indebted to Elena Montillo, Senior Production Editor, and Danielle Slade, Production Editor, who guided the book from final edits to finished product. I'm grateful also to Christian Kunciw, Quality Assurance Team Leader, and Marianne Snow, Quality Assurance tester—for scrutinizing every page and alerting me to errors and inconsistencies. Thanks to Copy Editor Karen Annett, whose close attention to details helped make the book clearer, consistent, and more precise. Thanks also to Abby Reip, who researched and obtained photos and permissions.

I'm especially grateful to Technical Editor Sydney Shewchuk who reviewed this edition for technical accuracy and made many valuable suggestions for improvement.

For additional help and advice on technical topics, I'm grateful to networking professionals Jim Berbee, Tom Callaci, Peyton Engel, Michael Grice, Carla Schroeder, Tracy Syslo, Lou Taber, and Ron Young. Special thanks to David Klann, UNIX disciple and contributing author, who generously supplied content, helped with research, and was eager to discuss the implications of non-contiguous subnetting on a Saturday night. Finally, thanks again to Paul and Janet Dean, scientists and teachers both, for their encouragement, support, and continued interest in science and technology.

Photo Credits

Figure 5-23	Courtesy of Enterasys Networks, Inc.; Courtesy of Enterasys Networks, Inc.; Courtesy of NETGEAR
Figure 7-14	Courtesy of NETGEAR
Figure 7-16	Courtesy of Linksys
Figure 12-5	Courtesy of Agilent Technologies
Figure 12-6	Courtesy of Fluke Networks
Figure 12-7	Courtesy of Fluke Networks
Figure 12-8	Courtesy of Network Associates, Inc.
Figure 12-10	Courtesy of Fluke Networks
Figure 13-1	Courtesy of American Power Conversion Corporation
Figure 13-12	Courtesy of Imation
Figure 15-6	Redrawn with permission from SolarWinds.Net

State of the Information Technology (IT) Field

Most organizations today depend on computers and information technology to improve business processes, productivity, and efficiency. Opportunities to become global organizations and reach customers, businesses, and suppliers are a direct result of the widespread use of the Internet. Changing technology further impacts how companies do business. This fundamental shift in business practices has increased the need for skilled and certified IT workers across industries. This transformation moves many IT workers out of traditional IT businesses and into many IT dependent industries such as banking, government, insurance, and healthcare.

In the latest Occupational Outlook Handbook from the Bureau of Labor Statistics (part of the United States Department of Labor), employment of computer support specialist is expected to increase faster than the average increase for all occupations through 2012. Job growth will continue to be driven by the continued expansion of computer system design and related services, which is projected to remain one of the fastest growing industries in the U.S. economy, despite recent job losses.

In any industry, the workforce is important to continually drive business. Having skilled workers in IT is always a struggle with ever-changing technologies. It has been estimated that technologies change approximately every two years. With such a quick product life cycle, IT workers must strive to keep up with these changes to continually bring value to their employers.

Certifications

Different levels of education are required for the many jobs in the IT industry. Additionally, the level of education and type of training required varies from employer to employer, but the need for qualified technicians remains a constant. As technology changes and advances in the industry continue to evolve rapidly, many employers look for employees that possess the skills necessary to implement these new technologies. Traditional degrees and diplomas do not identify the skills that a job applicant possesses. With the growth of the IT industry, companies are relying increasingly on technical certifications to adequately identify a job applicant's skills. Technical certifications are a way for employers to ensure the quality and skill qualifications of their computer professionals, and they can offer job seekers a competitive edge over their competition.

There are two types of certifications, vendor-neutral and vendor-specific. Vendor-neutral certifications are those that test for the skills and knowledge required in specific industry job roles and do not subscribe to a vendor's specific technology solutions. Some examples of vendor-neutral certifications include all of the CompTIA (Computing Technology Industry Association's) certifications, Project Management Institute's certifications, and Security Certified Program certifications. Vendor-specific certifications validate the skills and knowledge necessary to be successful while utilizing a specific vendor's technology solution. Some examples of vendor-specific certifications include those offered by Microsoft, IBM, Novell, and Cisco.

As employers struggle to fill open IT positions with qualified candidates, certifications are a means of validating the skill sets necessary to be successful within organizations. In most careers, salary and compensation is determined by experience and education, but in IT field, the number and type of certifications an employee earns also determine salary and wage increases.

Certification provides job applicants with more than just a competitive edge over their non-certified counterparts applying for the same IT positions. Some institutions of higher education grant college credit to students who successfully pass certification exams, moving them further along in their degree programs. Certification also gives individuals who are interested in careers in the military the ability to move into higher positions more quickly. And many advanced certification programs accept, and sometimes require, entry-level certifications as part of their exams. For example, Cisco and Microsoft accept some CompTIA certifications as prerequisites for their certification programs.

Career Planning

Finding a career that fits a person's personality, skill set, and lifestyle, is challenging and fulfilling, but can often be difficult. What are the steps individuals should take to find that dream career? Is IT interesting to you? Chances are, that if you are reading this book, this question has already been answered. What is it about IT that you like? The world of work in the IT industry is vast. Some questions to ask yourself: Are you a person who likes to work alone, or do you like to work in a group? Do you like speaking directly with customers, or do you prefer to stay behind the scenes? Does your lifestyle encourage a lot of travel, or do you need to stay in one location? All of these factors influence your job decision. Inventory assessments are a good first step to learning more about you, your interests, work values, and abilities. There are a variety of Web sites that offer assistance with career planning and assessments.

CompTIA hosts an informational Web site called the TCC (TechCareer Compass™) that defines careers in the IT industry. The TCC is located at http://tcc.comptia.org. This industry-created Web site outlines over 100 industry jobs. Each defined job includes a job description, alternate job titles, critical work functions, activities and performance indicators, and skills and knowledge required by the job. In other words, it shows exactly what the jobs entail so that you can find one that best fits your interests and abilities. Additionally, the TCC maps over 500 technical certifications to the skills required by each specific job allowing you the ability to research and plan your certification training. The Web site also includes a resource section, which is updated regularly with articles and links to many other career Web sites. The TCC is the one stop location to IT career information.

In addition to CompTIA's TCC, there are many other Web sites that cover components of IT careers and career planning. Many of these sites can also be found in the TCC Resources section. Some of these other career planning sites include: YourITFuture.com, ITCompass.net, and About.com.

CompTIA Authorized Curriculum Program

The logo of the CompTIA Authorized Curriculum Program and the status of this or other training material as "Authorized" under the CompTIA Authorized Curriculum Program signify that, in CompTIA's opinion, such training material covers the content of the CompTIA related certification exam. CompTIA has not reviewed or approved the accuracy of the contents of this training material and specifically disclaims any warranties of merchantability or fitness for a particular purpose. CompTIA makes no guarantee concerning the success of persons using any such "Authorized" or other training material in order to prepare for any CompTIA certification exam.

The contents of this training material were created for the CompTIA Network+ certification exam objectives that were current as of March 2005.

How to Become CompTIA Certified

This training material can help you prepare for and pass a related CompTIA certification exam or exams. To achieve CompTIA certification, you must register for and pass a CompTIA certification exam or exams.

To become CompTIA certified, you must:

1. Select a certification exam provider. For more information, please visit the following Web site:

   www.comptia.org/certification/itprofessionals/get_certified.aspx

2. Register for and schedule a time to take the CompTIA certification exam(s) at a convenient location.

3. Read and sign the Candidate Agreement, which will be presented at the time of the exam(s). The text of the Candidate Agreement can be found at the following Web site:

   www.comptia.org/certification/general_information/candidate_agreement.aspx

4. Take and pass the CompTIA certification exam(s).

For more information about CompTIA's certifications, such as their industry acceptance, benefits, or program news, please visit www.comptia.org/certification/default.aspx

CompTIA is a nonprofit information technology (IT) trade association. CompTIA's certifications are designed by subject matter experts from across the IT industry. Each CompTIA certification is vendor-neutral, covers multiple technologies, and requires demonstration of skills and knowledge widely sought after by the IT industry.

To contact CompTIA with any questions or comments, please contact us at 1-630-678-8300 or email questions@comptia.org.

Chapter 1

An Introduction to Networking

After reading this chapter and completing the exercises, you will be able to:

- List the advantages of networked computing relative to standalone computing

- Distinguish between client/server and peer-to-peer networks

- List elements common to all client/server networks

- Describe several specific uses for a network

- Identify some of the certifications available to networking professionals

- Identify the kinds of nontechnical, or "soft," skills that will help you succeed as a networking professional

Loosely defined, a **network** is a group of computers and other devices (such as printers) that are connected by some type of transmission media. Variations on the elements of a network and the way it is designed, however, are nearly infinite. Networks may be as small as two computers connected by a cable in a home office or as large as several thousand computers connected across the world via a combination of cable, phone lines, and satellite links. In addition to connecting personal computers, networks may link mainframe computers, printers, plotters, fax machines, and phone systems. They may communicate through copper wires, fiber-optic cable, radio waves, infrared, or satellite links. This chapter introduces you to the fundamental characteristics of networks.

Why Use Networks?

All networks offer advantages relative to using a **standalone computer**—that is, a computer that is not connected to other computers and that uses software applications and data stored on its local disks. Most importantly, networks enable multiple users to share devices (for example, printers) and data (for example, spreadsheet files), which are collectively known as the network's **resources**. Sharing devices saves money. For example, rather than buying 20 printers for 20 staff members, a company can buy one printer and have those 20 staff members share it over a network. Sharing devices also saves time. For example, it's faster for coworkers to share data over a network than to copy data to a removable storage device and physically transport the storage device from one computer to another—an outdated file-sharing method commonly referred to as **sneakernet** (presumably because people wore sneakers when walking from computer to computer). Before networks, transferring data via floppy disks was the only possible way to share data.

Another advantage to networks is that they allow you to manage, or administer, resources on multiple computers from a central location. Imagine you work in the Information Technology (IT) department of a multinational bank and must verify that each of 5000 employees around the globe uses the same version of a database program. Without a network you would have to visit every employee's machine to check and install the proper software. With a network, however, you could check the software installed on computers around the world from the computer on your desk. Because they allow you to share devices and administer computers centrally, networks increase productivity. It's not surprising, then, that most businesses depend on their networks to stay competitive.

Types of Networks

Computers can be positioned on a network in different ways relative to each other. They can have different levels of control over shared resources. They can also be made to communicate and share resources according to different schemes. The following sections describe two fundamental network models: peer-to-peer and client/server.

Peer-to-peer Networks

The simplest form of a network is a **peer-to-peer network**. In a peer-to-peer network, every computer can communicate directly with every other computer. By default, no computer on a peer-to-peer network has more authority than another. However, each computer can be configured to share only some of its resources and keep other resources inaccessible to the network. Traditional peer-to-peer networks typically consist of two or more general-purpose personal computers, with modest processing capabilities. Every computer is capable of sending and receiving information to and from every other computer, as shown in Figure 1-1.

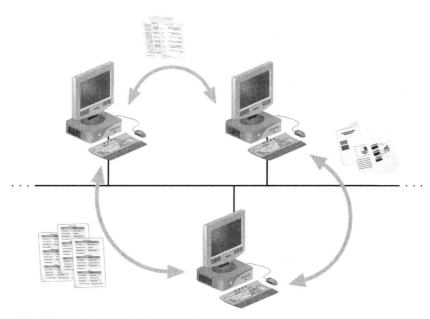

FIGURE 1-1 *Resource sharing on a simple peer-to-peer network*

The advantages of using traditional peer-to-peer networks are:

◆ They are simple to configure. For this reason, they may be used in environments in which time or technical expertise is scarce.

◆ They are typically less expensive to set up and maintain than other types of networks. This fact makes them suitable for environments in which saving money is critical.

The disadvantages of using traditional peer-to-peer networks are:

◆ They are not very flexible. As a peer-to-peer network grows larger, adding or changing significant elements of the network may be difficult.

◆ They are also not necessarily secure—meaning that in simple installations, data and other resources shared by network users can be easily discovered and used by unauthorized people.

◆ They are not practical for connecting more than a handful of computers, because they do not always centralize resources.

For example, if your computer is part of a peer-to-peer network that includes five other computers, and each computer user stores her spreadsheets and word-processing files on her own hard disk, whenever your colleagues want to edit your files, they must access your machine on the network. If one colleague saves a changed version of one of your spreadsheets on her hard disk, you'll find it difficult to keep track of which version is the most current. As you can imagine, the more computers you add to a peer-to-peer network, the more difficult it becomes to find and manage resources.

A common way to share resources on a peer-to-peer network is by modifying the file-sharing controls via the computer's operating system. For example, you could choose to create a directory on your computer's hard disk called "SharedDocs" and then configure the directory to allow all networked computers to read its files. On a peer-to-peer network each user is responsible for configuring her computer to allow access to certain resources and prevent access to others. In other words, resource sharing is not controlled by a central computer or authority. Because access depends on many different users, it typically isn't uniform and may not be secure.

Although traditional peer-to-peer networks are typically small and contained within a home or office, in the last five years large peer-to-peer networks have connected through the Internet. These newer types of peer-to-peer networks (commonly abbreviated **P2P networks**) link computers from around the world to share files between each others' hard disks. Unlike traditional peer-to-peer networks, they require specialized software (besides the computer's operating system) to allow resource sharing. Examples of these networks include Gnutella, Freenet, and the original Napster. In 2001, Napster, which allowed users around the globe to share music files, was forced to cease operation due to charges of copyright infringement from musicians and music producers. Later, the service was redesigned to provide legitimate music file-sharing services.

Client/Server Networks

Another way of designing a network is to use a central computer, known as a **server**, to facilitate communication and resource sharing between other computers on the network, which are known as **clients**. Clients usually take the form of personal computers, also known as **workstations**. A network that uses a server to enable clients to share data, data storage space, and devices is known as a **client/server network**. (The term **client/server architecture** is sometimes used to refer to the design of a network in which clients rely on servers for resource sharing and processing.) In terms of resource sharing and control, you can compare the client/server network to a public library. Just as a librarian manages the use of books and other media by patrons, a server manages the use of shared resources by clients. For example, if a patron does not have the credentials to check out books, the librarian prevents him from doing so. Similarly, a server allows only authorized clients to access its resources.

Every computer on a client/server network acts as a client or a server. (It's possible, but uncommon, for some computers to act as both.) Clients on a network can still run applications from and save data to their local hard disk. But by connecting to a server, they also have the option of using shared applications, data, and devices. Clients on a client/server network do not share their resources directly with each other, but rather use the server as an intermediary. Figure 1-2 illustrates how resources are shared on a client/server network.

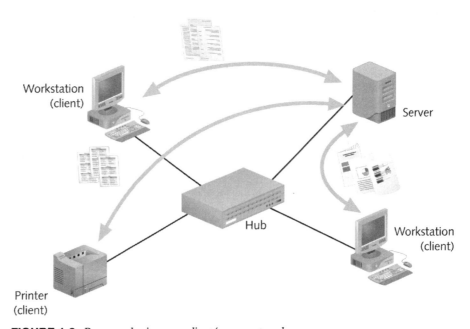

FIGURE 1-2 *Resource sharing on a client/server network*

To function as a server, a computer must be running a **network operating system (NOS)**, a special type of software designed to:

◆ Manage data and other resources for a number of clients

◆ Ensure that only authorized users access the network

◆ Control which type of files a user can open and read

◆ Restrict when and from where users can access the network

◆ Dictate which rules computers will use to communicate

◆ Supply applications to clients

Examples of popular network operating systems include Microsoft Windows Server 2003, Novell NetWare, UNIX, and Linux. (By contrast, a standalone computer, or a client computer, uses a less-powerful operating system, such as Windows XP.)

Usually, servers have more memory, processing, and storage capacity than clients. They may even be equipped with special hardware designed to provide network management functions beyond that provided by the network operating system. For example, a server may contain an extra hard disk and specialized software so that if the primary hard disk fails, the secondary hard disk automatically takes its place.

Although client/server networks are typically more complex in their design and maintenance than peer-to-peer networks, they offer many advantages over peer-to-peer networks, such as:

◆ User logon accounts and passwords for anyone on a server-based network can be assigned in one place.

◆ Access to multiple shared resources (such as data files or printers) can be centrally granted to a single user or groups of users.

◆ Problems on the network can be tracked, diagnosed, and often fixed from one location.

◆ Servers are optimized to handle heavy processing loads and dedicated to handling requests from clients, enabling faster response time.

◆ Because of their efficient processing and larger disk storage, servers can connect more than a handful of computers on a network.

Together, these advantages make client/server networks more easily manageable, more secure, and more powerful than peer-to-peer networks. They are also more **scalable**—that is, they can be more easily added onto and extended—than peer-to-peer networks.

Because client/server networks are the most popular type of network for medium- and large-scale organizations, most of the concepts covered in this book and on the Network+ exam pertain to client/server networks. Next, you will learn how networks are classified according to size.

LANs, MANs, and WANs

As its name suggests, a **local area network (LAN)** is a network of computers and other devices that is confined to a relatively small space, such as one building or even one office. Small LANs first became popular in the early 1980s. At that time LANs might have consisted of a handful of computers connected in a peer-to-peer fashion. Today's LANs are typically much larger and more complex client/server networks.

Often separate LANs are interconnected and rely on several servers running many different applications and managing resources other than data. For example, imagine an office building in which each of a company's departments runs its own LAN and all the LANs are connected. This network may contain many servers, hundreds of workstations, and several shared CD-ROM devices, printers, plotters, and fax machines. Figure 1-3 roughly depicts this type of network (in reality, the network would probably contain many more clients). As you progress through this book, you will learn about every part of this diagram. In the process, you will learn to integrate these pieces so as to create a variety of networks that are reliable, secure, and manageable.

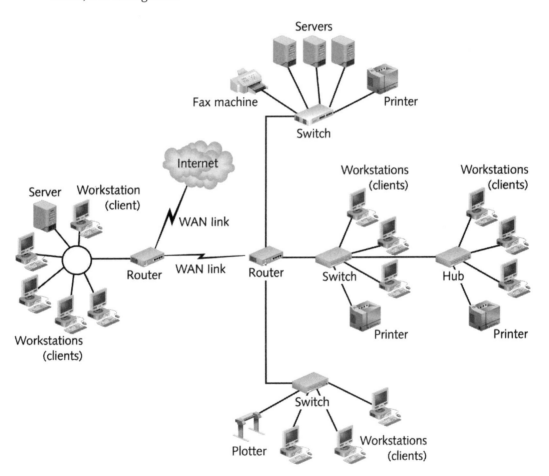

FIGURE 1-3 *A more complex client/server network*

Networks may extend beyond the boundaries of a building. A network that is larger than a LAN and connects clients and servers from multiple buildings—for example, a handful of government offices surrounding a state capitol—is known as a **metropolitan area network (MAN)**. Because of the distance it covers, a MAN may use different transmission technology and media than a LAN.

A network that connects two or more geographically distinct LANs or MANs is called a **wide area network (WAN)**. Because they carry data over longer distances than LANs, WANs require slightly different transmission methods and media and often use a greater variety of technologies than LANs. Most MANs can also be described as WANs; in fact, network engineers are more likely to refer to all networks that cover a broad geographical range as WANs.

WANs commonly connect separate offices in the same organization, whether they are across town or across the world from each other. For example, imagine you work for a nationwide software reseller that keeps its software inventory in warehouses in Topeka, Kansas, and Panama City, Florida. Suppose also that your office is located in New York. When a customer calls and asks whether you have 70 copies of Lotus Notes—an e-mail client/server application—available to ship overnight, you need to check the inventory database located on servers at both the Topeka and Panama City warehouses. To access these servers, you could connect to the warehouses' LANs through a WAN link, then log on to their servers.

WANs are also used to connect LANs that belong to different organizations. For example, all the public universities within a state might combine and share their resources via a WAN. The largest and most varied WAN in the world is the **Internet**. Figure 1-4 depicts a simple WAN.

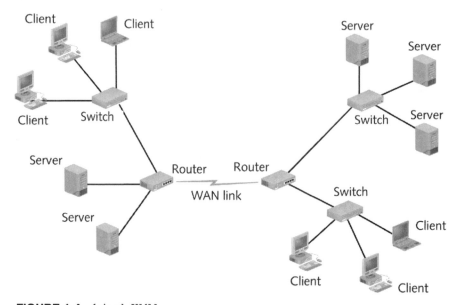

FIGURE 1-4 *A simple WAN*

Elements Common to Client/Server Networks

NET+
3.2

You have learned that networks—no matter how simple or how complex—provide some benefits over standalone computers. They also share terminology and common building blocks, some of which you've already encountered. The following list provides a more complete rundown of basic elements common to all client/server networks. You will learn more about these topics throughout this book.

◆ *Client.* A computer on the network that requests resources or services from another computer on a network. In some cases, a client could also act as a server. The term "client" may also refer to the human **user** of a client workstation or to client software installed on the workstation.

◆ *Server.* A computer on the network that manages shared resources. Servers usually have more processing power, memory, and hard disk space than clients. They run network operating software that can manage not only data, but also users, groups, security, and applications on the network.

◆ *Workstation.* A personal computer (such as a desktop or laptop), which may or may not be connected to a network. Most clients are workstation computers.

NET+
3.2
1.6

◆ *Network interface card (NIC).* The device inside a computer that connects a computer to the network media, thus allowing it to communicate with other computers. Many companies (such as 3Com, IBM, Intel, SMC, and Xircom) manufacture NICs, which come with a variety of specifications that are tailored to the requirements of the workstation and the network. Some connect to the **motherboard**, which is the main circuit that controls the computer, some are integrated as part of the motherboard, and others connect via an external port. NICs are also known as **network adapters**. Figure 1-5 depicts a NIC connected to a computer's motherboard.

FIGURE 1-5 *A network interface card (NIC)*

NET+
3.2
1.6

 NOTE

Because different PCs and network types require different kinds of NICs, you cannot assume that a NIC that works in one workstation will work in another.

NET+
3.2

◆ *Network operating system (NOS).* The software that runs on a server and enables the server to manage data, users, groups, security, applications, and other networking functions. The most popular network operating systems are Microsoft Windows Server 2003, Novell NetWare, UNIX, and Linux.

◆ *Host.* A computer that enables resource sharing by other computers on the same network.

◆ *Node.* A client, server, or other device that can communicate over a network and that is identified by a unique number, known as its network address.

◆ *Connectivity device.* A specialized device that allows multiple networks or multiple parts of one network to connect and exchange data. A client/server network can operate without connectivity devices. However, medium- and large-sized LANs use them to extend the network and to connect with WANs.

◆ *Segment.* A part of a network. Usually, a segment is composed of a group of nodes that use the same communications channel for all their traffic.

◆ *Backbone.* The part of a network to which segments and significant shared devices (such as routers, switches, and servers) connect. A backbone is sometimes referred to as "a network of networks," because of its role in interconnecting smaller parts of a LAN or WAN. Figure 1-6 shows a LAN with its backbone highlighted.

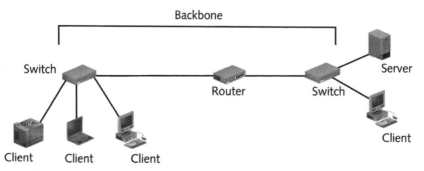

FIGURE 1-6 *A LAN backbone*

◆ *Topology.* The physical layout of a computer network. Topologies vary according to the needs of the organization and available hardware and expertise. Networks are usually arranged in a ring, bus, or star formation; hybrid combinations of these patterns are also possible. Figure 1-7 illustrates the most common network topologies, which you must understand to design and troubleshoot networks.

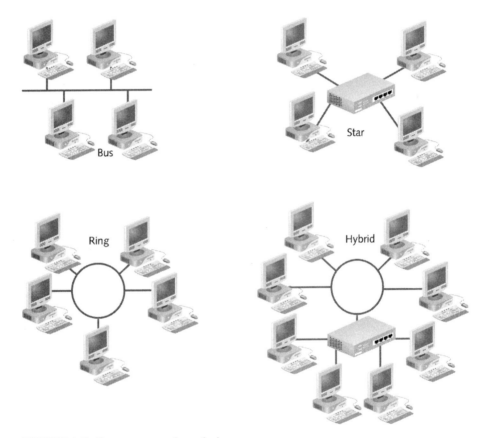

FIGURE 1-7 *Common network topologies*

◆ *Protocol.* A standard method or format for communication between networked devices. Protocols ensure that data are transferred whole, in sequence, and without error from one node on the network to another.

◆ *Data packets.* The distinct units of data that are transmitted from one node on a network to another. Breaking a large stream of data into many packets allows a network to deliver that data more efficiently and reliably.

NET+
3.2

◆ *Addressing*. The scheme for assigning a unique identifying number to every node on the network. The type of addressing used depends on the network's protocols and network operating system. Each network device must have a unique **address** so that data can be transmitted reliably to and from that device.

NET+
3.2
1.5

◆ *Transmission media*. The means through which data is transmitted and received. Transmission media may be physical, such as wire or cable, or atmospheric (wireless), such as radio waves. Figure 1-8 shows several examples of transmission media.

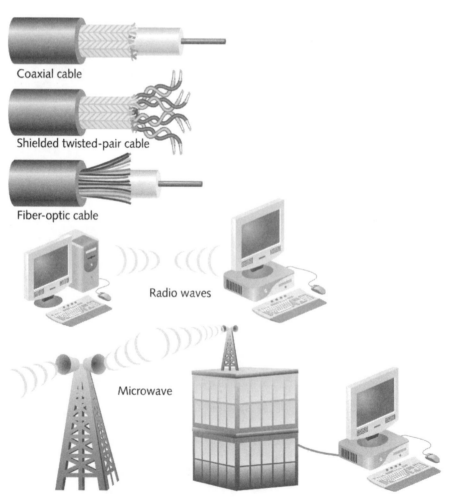

FIGURE 1-8 *Examples of network transmission media*

Now that you are familiar with basic network terminology, you are ready to appreciate the many uses of computer networks.

How Networks Are Used

The functions provided by a network are usually referred to as network services. Any network manager will tell you that the network service with the highest visibility is e-mail. If your company's e-mail system fails, users will notice within minutes—and they will not be shy about informing you of the failure. Although e-mail may be the most visible network service, other services are just as vital. Printer sharing, file sharing, Internet access, remote access capabilities, and management services are all critical business functions provided through networks. In large organizations, separate servers may be dedicated to performing each of these functions. In offices with only a few users and little network traffic, one server may perform all functions.

File and Print Services

File services refer to the capability of a server to share data files, applications (such as word-processing or spreadsheet programs), and disk storage space. A server that provides file services is called a **file server**. File services accounted for the first use of networks and remain the foundation of networking today, for a number of reasons. As mentioned earlier, it's easier and faster to store shared data at a central location than to copy files to disks and then pass the disks around. Data stored at a central location is typically more secure because a network administrator can take charge of backing up this data, rather than relying on individual users to make their own copies. In addition, using a file server to run applications for multiple users requires the purchase of fewer copies of the application and less maintenance work for the network administrator.

Using **print services** to share printers across a network also saves time and money. A high-capacity printer can cost thousands of dollars, but can handle the printing tasks of an entire department, thereby eliminating the need to buy a desktop printer for each worker. With one printer, less time is spent on maintenance and management. If a shared printer fails, the network administrator can diagnose the problem from a workstation anywhere on the network using the network operating system's printer control functions. Often, the administrator can solve the problem without even visiting the printer.

Communications Services

A network's communications services allow remote users to connect to the network. (The term **remote user** refers to a person working on a computer on a different network or in a different geographical location from the LAN's server.) Less frequently, communications services allow network users to connect to machines outside the network. Most network operating systems include built-in communications services that enable users to dial into an **access server**, log on to the network, and take advantage of the network just as if they were logged on to a workstation on the office LAN. A remote access server may also be known as a **communications server** or an **access server**.

Organizations commonly use communications services to provide LAN access for workers at home, workers on the road, and workers at small satellite offices where dedicated WAN connections are not cost-effective. In addition, they may use communications services to allow staff from other organizations (such as a software or hardware vendor) to help diagnose a network problem. For example, suppose you work for a clothing manufacturer that uses embroidery software to control the machines that sew insignias on shirts and hats. You are an expert on networking, but less adept with the automated embroidery software. When the software causes problems, you turn to the software vendor for help. But suppose the vendor's technician can't solve the problem except by logging on to your network. In that case, it's much more efficient and less expensive to allow the technician to dial in to your network through a communications server than to fly the technician to your office.

It's important to remember that remote access servers—no matter which platform (hardware or operating system software) they run on—allow external users to use network resources and devices just as if they were logged on to a workstation in the office. From a remote location, users can print files to shared printers, log on to hosts, retrieve mail from an internal messaging system, or run queries on internal databases. Because they can be accessed by the world outside the local network, remote access servers necessitate strict security measures.

Mail Services

Mail services coordinate the storage and transfer of e-mail between users on a network. The computer responsible for mail services is called a **mail server**. Mail servers may be connected to the Internet or may be isolated within an organization if exchanging e-mail with external users is not necessary.

In addition to simply sending, receiving, and storing mail, mail servers can:

◆ Intercept or filter unsolicited e-mail, known as **spam**

◆ Find objectionable content in e-mails and perform functions (such as user notification) on that content

◆ Route messages according to particular rules—for example, if a technical support representative has not opened a customer's message within 15 minutes of delivery, a mail server could automatically forward the message to a supervisor

◆ Provide a Web-based client for checking e-mail

◆ Notify administrators or users if certain events occur (for example, if a user's mailbox is close to exceeding its maximum amount of space on a server)

◆ Schedule e-mail transmission, retrieval, storage, and maintenance functions

◆ Communicate with mail servers on other networks so that mail can be exchanged between users who do not connect to the same LAN

To supply these services, a mail server runs specialized mail server software, examples of which include Sendmail, Microsoft Exchange Server, and Novell GroupWise. Because of their critical nature and heavy use, maintaining a mail server in any sizable organization requires a significant commitment of technical support and administration resources.

Internet Services

You have probably connected to the Internet without knowing or caring about all of the services running behind the scenes. But in fact, many servers are working together to bring Web pages to your desktop. For example, a **Web server** is a computer installed with the appropriate software to supply Web pages to many different clients upon demand. Supplying Web pages is only one type of Internet service. Other **Internet services** include file transfer capabilities, Internet addressing schemes, security filters, and a means for directly logging on to other computers on the Internet. Internet services are a broad category of network functions; reflecting their growing importance, entire books have been devoted to them.

Management Services

When networks were small, they could be managed easily by a single network administrator and the network operating system's internal functions. For instance, suppose a user called to report a problem logging on to the network. The administrator diagnosed the problem as an addressing conflict (that is, two workstations having the same network address). In a very small network, the conflicting workstations might be located right around the corner from each other, and one address could be changed quickly. In another example, if a manager needed to report the number of copies of Adobe Photoshop in use in a certain department, the network administrator could probably get the desired information by just walking through the department and checking the various workstations.

As networks grow larger and more complex, however, they become more difficult to manage. Using network management services can help you keep track of a large network. Network **management services** centrally administer management tasks on the network, such as ensuring that no more than 20 workstations are using Adobe Photoshop at one time in an organization that purchased a 20-user license for the software. Some organizations dedicate a number of servers to network management functions, with each server performing only one or two unique services.

Numerous services fall under the category of network management. Some of the most important ones include the following:

◆ *Traffic monitoring and control.* Determining how much **traffic** (that is, data transmission activity) is taking place on a network and notifying administrators when the network becomes overloaded. In general, the larger the network, the more critical it is to monitor traffic.

◆ *Load balancing.* Distributing data transfer activity evenly across a network so that no single device becomes overwhelmed. Load balancing is especially important for networks in which it's difficult to predict the number of requests that will be issued to a server, as is the case with Web servers.

◆ *Hardware diagnosis and failure alert*. Determining when a network component fails and automatically notifying the network administrator through e-mail or paging.

◆ *Asset management*. Collecting and storing data on the number and types of software and hardware assets in an organization's network. With asset management software, a server can electronically examine each client's software and hardware and automatically save the data in a database. Before asset management services, this data had to be gathered manually and typed into spreadsheets.

◆ *License tracking*. Determining how many copies of a single application are currently in use on the network and ensuring that number does not exceed the number of licenses purchased. This information is important for legal reasons, as software companies are vigilant about illegally copying software or using more than the authorized number of copies.

◆ *Security auditing*. Evaluating what security measures are currently in force and notifying the network administrator if a security breach occurs.

◆ *Software distribution*. Automatically transferring a file or installing an application from the server to a client on the network. The installation process can be started from either the server or the client. Several options are available when distributing software, such as warning users about updates, writing changes to a workstation's system files, and restarting the workstation after the update.

◆ *Address management*. Centrally managing a finite number of network addresses for an entire network. Usually this task can be accomplished without manually modifying the client workstation configurations.

◆ *Backup and restoration of data*. Copying (or **backing up**) critical data files to a secure storage area and then **restoring** (or retrieving) data if the original files are lost or deleted. Often backups are performed according to a formulaic schedule. Backup and data restoration services provide centralized management of data backup on multiple servers and on-demand restoration of files and directories.

Network management services will be covered in depth later in the book. For now, it is enough to be aware of the variety of services and the importance of this growing area of networking.

Becoming a Networking Professional

Examine the classified ad section of any city newspaper, and you will probably find dozens of ads for computer professionals. Of course, the level of expertise required for each of these jobs differs. Some companies simply need "warm bodies" to ensure that a backup process doesn't fail during the night; other companies are looking for people to plan their information technology strategies. Needless to say, the more extensive your skills, the better your chances for landing a lucrative and interesting job in networking. To prepare yourself to enter this job market, you should master a number of general networking technologies. Only then should you pick a few areas that interest you and study those specialties. Hone your communication and teamwork skills, and stay abreast of emerging technologies. Consider the tremendous advantages of attaining professional certification and getting to know others in your field. The following sections offer suggestions on how to approach a career in networking.

Mastering the Technical Challenges

Although computer networking is a varied field, some general technical skills will serve you well no matter which specialty you choose. Because you are already interested in computers, you probably enjoy an aptitude for logical and analytical thinking. You probably also want to acquire these skills:

◆ Installing, configuring, and troubleshooting network server software and hardware

◆ Installing, configuring, and troubleshooting network client software and hardware

◆ Understanding the characteristics of different transmission media

◆ Understanding network design

◆ Understanding network protocols

◆ Understanding how users interact with the network

◆ Constructing a network with clients, servers, media, and connectivity devices

Because you can expand your networking knowledge in almost any direction, you should pay attention to the general skills that interest you most, then pick one or two of those areas and concentrate on them. The following specialties are currently in high demand:

◆ Network security

◆ Voice/data integration (for example, designing networks to carry both data and telephone signals)

◆ In-depth knowledge about one or more NOSs: UNIX, Linux, Novell NetWare, or Microsoft Windows Server 2003

◆ Network management

◆ Internet and intranet design

◆ Configuration and optimization of routers and switches

◆ Centralized data storage and management for large-scale environments

Determine which method of learning works best for you. A small classroom with an experienced instructor and a hands-on projects lab is an excellent learning environment, because there you can ask questions and learn by doing. Many colleges offer courses or continuing education on networking topics. You may also want to enroll at a computer training center. These training centers can be found in every metropolitan area and in many small towns. If you are pursuing certification, be certain the training center you choose is authorized to provide training for that certification. Most computer training centers also operate a Web site that provides information on their course schedule, fees, and qualifications. Some of these sites even offer online class registration.

Another great way to improve your technical skills is by gaining practical experience. There is no substitute for hands-on experience when it comes to networking hardware and software skills. If you don't already work in an Information Technology department, try to find a position that puts you in that environment, even if it isn't your dream job. Volunteer a few hours a week if necessary. After you are surrounded with other information technology professionals and encounter real-life situations, you will have the opportunity to expand your skills by practicing and asking questions of more experienced staff. On the Web, you can find a number of searchable online job boards and recruiter sites. The placement office at your local college or university can also connect you with job opportunities.

Developing Your "Soft Skills"

Knowing how to configure a router or install UNIX will serve you well, but without advanced soft skills, you cannot excel in the networking field. The term **soft skills** refers to those skills that are not easily measurable, such as customer relations, oral and written communications, dependability, teamwork, and leadership abilities. Some of these soft skills might appear to be advantages in any profession, but they are especially important when you must work in teams, in challenging technical circumstances, and under tight deadlines—requirements that apply to most networking projects. For this reason, soft skills merit closer examination.

◆ *Customer relations.* Perhaps one of the most important soft skills, customer relations involve an ability to listen to customers' frustrations and desires and then empathize, respond, and guide customers to their goals without acting arrogant. Bear in mind that some of your customers will not appreciate or enjoy technology as much as you do, and they will value your patience as you help them. The better your customer relations, the more respected and in demand you will be as a network professional.

◆ *Oral and written communications.* You may understand the most complicated technical details about a network, but if you cannot communicate them to colleagues and clients, the significance of your knowledge is diminished. Imagine that you are a networking consultant who is competing with several other firms to overhaul a metropolitan hospital's network, a project that could generate millions of dollars for your company. You may have designed the best solution and have it clearly mapped out in your head, but your plan is useless if you can't describe it clearly. The hospital's planning committee will accept whichever proposal makes the most sense to them—that is, the proposal whose suggestions and justifications are plainly communicated.

◆ *Dependability.* This characteristic will help you in any career. However, in the field of networking, where breakdowns or glitches can occur at any time of day or night and only a limited number of individuals have the expertise to fix them, being dependable is critical. Your career will benefit when you are the one who is available to address a problem, even if you don't always know the answer immediately.

♦ *Teamwork.* Individual computer professionals often have strong preferences for a certain type of hardware or software. And some technical people like to think that they have all of the answers. For these and other reasons, teamwork in Information Technology departments is sometimes lacking. To be the best networking professional in your department, you must be open to new ideas, encourage cooperation among your colleagues, and allow others to help you and make suggestions.

♦ *Leadership abilities.* As a networking professional, you will sometimes need to make difficult or unpopular decisions under pressure. You may need to persuade opinionated colleagues to try a new product, tell a group of angry users that what they want is not possible, or manage a project with nearly impossible budgetary and time restrictions. In all of these situations, you will benefit from having strong leadership skills.

After your career in networking begins, you will discover which soft skills you already possess and which ones you need to cultivate. The important thing is that you realize the importance of these attributes and are willing to devote the time necessary to develop them.

Pursuing Certification

Certification is the process of mastering material pertaining to a particular hardware system, operating system, programming language, or other software application, then proving your mastery by passing a series of exams. Certification programs are developed and administered either by a manufacturer or a professional organization such as the **Computing Technology Industry Association (CompTIA).** You can pursue a number of different certifications, depending on your specialty interest. For example, if you want to become a PC technician, you should attain **A+** certification. If you want to specialize in Microsoft product support and development, you should pursue **Microsoft Certified Systems Engineer (MCSE)** certification. To specialize in Novell networking product support and administration, you should pursue **Certified NetWare Engineer (CNE)** certification. To prove a mastery of many aspects of networking, you can choose to become Network+ certified. **Network+ (Net+)** is a professional certification established by CompTIA that verifies broad, vendor-independent networking technology skills such as an understanding of protocols, topologies, networking hardware, and network troubleshooting. Network+ may also be a stepping stone to more advanced certifications. For example, Novell now accepts Network+ certification as a substitute for its Networking Technologies exam for candidates pursuing CNE status. The material in this book addresses the knowledge objectives required to qualify for Network+ certification.

Certification is a popular career development tool for job seekers and a measure of an employee's qualifications for employers. Following are a list of benefits to becoming certified:

♦ *Better salary.* Professionals with certification can usually ask for higher salaries than those who aren't certified. Employers will also want to retain certified employees, especially if they helped pay for their training, and will offer incentives to keep certified professionals at the company.

◆ *Greater opportunities.* Certification may qualify you for additional degrees or more advanced technical positions.

◆ *Professional respect.* After you have proven your skills with a product or system, your colleagues and clients will gain great respect for your ability to solve problems with that system or product. They will therefore feel confident asking you for help.

◆ *Access to better support.* Many manufacturers reward certified professionals with less expensive, more detailed, and more direct access to their technical support.

One potential drawback of some certifications is the number of people attaining them—so many that certifications now have less value. Currently, hundreds of thousands of networking professionals have acquired the MCSE certification. When only tens of thousands of people had MCSEs, employers were willing to pay substantially higher salaries to workers with that certification than they are now. Other kinds of certifications, such as Cisco's Certified Internetworking Engineer (CCIE) program, require candidates to pass lab exams. These kinds of certifications, because they require rigorous proof of knowledge, are very highly respected.

Finding a Job in Networking

With the proper credentials and demonstrated technical knowledge, you will qualify for a multitude of positions in networking. For this reason, you can and must be selective when searching for a job. Following are some ways to research your possibilities:

◆ *Search the Web.* Because your job will deal directly with technology, it makes sense that you should use technology to find it. Companies in the computer industry recruit intensively on the Web, either through searchable job databases or through links on their company Web sites. Unlike firms in other industries, these companies typically do not mind (and might prefer) receiving résumés and letters through e-mail. Most job database Web sites do not charge for their services, but may require you to register with them. Some popular Web job databases include Hot Jobs at *hotjobs.yahoo.com*, Dice at *www.dice.com*, Monster at *www.monster.com*, and ComputerJobs.com at *www.computerjobs.com*. A simple Web search could yield dozens more.

◆ *Read the newspaper.* An obvious place to look for jobs is the classified ad section of your local newspaper. Papers with large distributions often devote a section of their classified ads to careers in computing. Highlight the ads that sound interesting to you, even if you don't have all of the qualifications cited by the employer. In some ads, employers will list every skill they could possibly want a new hire to have, but they don't truly expect one person to have all of them.

◆ *Visit a career center.* Regardless of whether you are a registered university or college student, you can use career center services to find a list of job openings in your area. Companies that are hiring pay much attention to the collegiate career centers because of the number of job seekers served by these centers. Visit the college or university campus nearest you and search through its career center listings.

◆ *Network*. Find like-minded professionals with whom you can discuss job possibilities. You may meet these individuals through training classes, conferences, professional organizations, or career fairs. Let them know that you're looking for a job and specify exactly what kind of job you want. If they can't suggest any leads for you, ask these people if they have other colleagues who might.

◆ *Attend career fairs*. Most metropolitan areas host career fairs for job seekers in the information technology field, and some large companies host their own job fairs. Even if you aren't sure you want to work for any of the companies represented at a job fair, attend the job fair to research the market. You can find out which skills are in high demand in your area and which types of companies are hiring the most networking professionals. You can also meet other people in your field who may offer valuable advice based on their employment experience.

◆ *Enlist a recruiter*. With the volume of technical jobs available in the 1990s also came recruiting agencies that deal strictly with clients in the technical fields. By signing up with such a recruiting agency, you may have access to job opportunities that you didn't know existed. You might also take advantage of a temporary assignment, to see if the fit between you and an employer is mutually beneficial, before accepting a permanent job with that employer.

Joining Professional Associations

At some point in your life, you have probably belonged to a club or organization. You know, therefore, that the benefits of joining can vary, depending on many factors. In the best case, joining an organization can connect you with people who have similar interests, provide new opportunities for learning, allow you to access specialized information, and give you more tangible assets such as free goods. Specifically, a networking professional organization might offer its own publications, technical workshops and conferences, free software, pre-release software, and access to expensive hardware labs.

You can choose from several prominent professional organizations in the field of networking. Because the field has grown so quickly and because so many areas in which to specialize exist, however, no single professional organization stands out as the most advantageous or highly respected. You will have to decide whether an organization is appropriate for you. Among other things, you will want to consider the organization's number of members, membership benefits, membership dues, technical emphasis, and whether it hosts a local chapter. Many organizations host student chapters on university campuses. You may also want to find a professional association that caters to your demographic group (such as Women in Technology International, if you are female). Table 1-1 lists some professional organizations and their Web sites.

Table 1-1 Networking organizations

Professional Organization	Web Site
Association for Computing Machinery (ACM)	*www.acm.org*
Association for Information Technology Professionals	*www.aitp.org*
Chinese Information and Networking Association	*www.cina.org*
IEEE Computer Society	*www.computer.org*
Women in Technology International (WITI)	*www.witi.org*

Chapter Summary

◆ A network is a group of computers and other devices (such as printers) that are connected by some type of transmission media, such as copper or fiber-optic cable or the atmosphere, in the case of wireless transmission.

◆ All networks offer advantages relative to using a standalone computer. Networks enable multiple users to share devices and data. Sharing resources saves time and money. Networks also allow you to manage, or administer, resources on multiple computers from a central location.

◆ In a peer-to-peer network, every computer can communicate directly with every other computer. By default, no computer on a peer-to-peer network has more authority than another. However, each computer can be configured to share only some of its resources and keep other resources inaccessible.

◆ Traditional peer-to-peer networks are usually simple and inexpensive to set up. However, they are not necessarily flexible or secure.

◆ Client/server networks rely on a centrally administered server (or servers) to manage shared resources for multiple clients. In this scheme, the server has greater authority than the clients, which are typically desktop or laptop workstations.

◆ Client/server networks are more complex and expensive to install than peer-to-peer networks. However, they are more easily managed, more scalable, and typically more secure. They are also the most popular type of network in use today.

◆ Servers typically possess more processing power, hard disk space, and memory than client computers. To manage access to and use of shared resources, among other centralized functions, a server requires a network operating system.

◆ A local area network (LAN) is a network of computers and other devices that is confined to a relatively small space, such as one building or even one office.

◆ LANs can be interconnected to form wide area networks (WANs), which traverse longer distances, and therefore require slightly different transmission methods and media than LANs. The Internet is the largest example of a WAN.

◆ Client/server networks share some common elements, including clients, servers, workstations, transmission media, connectivity devices, protocols, addressing, topology, NICs, data packets, network operating systems, hosts, backbones, segments, and nodes.

◆ Although e-mail is the most visible network service, networks also provide services for printing, file sharing, Internet access, remote access capabilities, and network management.

◆ File and print services provide the foundation for networking. They enable multiple users to share data, applications, storage areas, and printers.

◆ Networks use communications services to allow remote users to connect to the network or network users to connect to machines outside the network.

◆ Mail services (running on mail servers) allow users on a network to exchange and store e-mail. Most mail packages also provide filtering, routing, scheduling, notification, and connectivity with other mail systems.

◆ Internet services such as World Wide Web servers and browsers, file transfer capabilities, addressing schemes, and security filters enable organizations to connect to and use the global Internet.

◆ Network management services centrally administer and simplify complicated management tasks on the network, such as asset management, security auditing, hardware problem diagnosis, backup and restore services, license tracking, load balancing, and data traffic control.

◆ To prepare yourself for a networking career, you should master a number of broad networking skills, such as installing and configuring client and server hardware and software. Only then should you pick a few areas that interest you, such as network security or voice/data integration, and study those specialties.

◆ Certification is the process of mastering material pertaining to a particular hardware system, operating system, programming language, or other software program, then proving your mastery by passing a series of exams. The benefits of certification can include a better salary, more job opportunities, greater professional respect, and better access to technical support.

◆ To excel in the field of networking, you should hone your soft skills, such as leadership abilities, written and oral communication, a professional attitude, dependability, and customer relations.

◆ Joining an association for networking professionals can connect you with like-minded people, give you access to workshops and technical publications, allow you to receive discounted or free software, and perhaps even help you find a job in the field.

Key Terms

A+—The professional certification established by CompTIA that verifies knowledge about PC operation, repair, and management.

access server—See *remote access server*.

address—A number that uniquely identifies each workstation and device on a network. Without unique addresses, computers on the network could not reliably communicate.

address management—The process of centrally administering a finite number of network addresses for an entire LAN. Usually this task can be accomplished without touching the client workstations.

addressing—The scheme for assigning a unique identifying number to every workstation and device on the network. The type of addressing used on a network depends on its protocols and network operating system.

asset management—The process of collecting and storing data on the number and types of software and hardware assets in an organization's network. The data collection is automated by electronically examining each network client from a server.

backbone—The part of a network to which segments and significant shared devices (such as routers, switches, and servers) connect. A backbone is sometimes referred to as "a network of networks," because of its role in interconnecting smaller parts of a LAN or WAN.

backup—The process of copying critical data files to a secure storage area. Often, backups are performed according to a formulaic schedule.

certification—The process of mastering material pertaining to a particular hardware system, operating system, programming language, or other software program, then proving your mastery by passing a series of exams.

Certified NetWare Engineer—See *CNE*.

client—A computer on the network that requests resources or services from another computer on a network. In some cases, a client could also act as a server. The term "client" may also refer to the user of a client workstation or a client software application installed on the workstation.

client/server architecture—A network design in which clients (typically desktop or laptop computers) use a centrally administered server to share data, data storage space, and devices.

client/server network—A network that uses centrally administered computers, known as servers, to enable resource sharing for and facilitate communication between the other computers on the network.

CNE (Certified NetWare Engineer)—The professional certification established by Novell that demonstrates an in-depth understanding of Novell's networking software, including NetWare.

communications server—See *access server*.

CompTIA (Computing Technology Industry Association)—An association of computer resellers, manufacturers, and training companies that sets industry-wide standards for computer professionals. CompTIA established and sponsors the A+ and Network+ (Net+) certifications.

Computing Technology Industry Association—See *CompTIA*.

connectivity device—One of several types of specialized devices that allows two or more networks or multiple parts of one network to connect and exchange data.

data packet—A discrete unit of information sent from one node on a network to another.

file server—A specialized server that enables clients to share applications and data across the network.

file services—The functions of a file server that allow users to share data files, applications, and storage areas.

host—A computer that enables resource sharing by other computers on the same network.

Internet—A complex WAN that connects LANs and clients around the globe.

Internet services—The services that enable a network to communicate with the Internet, including World Wide Web servers and browsers, file transfer capabilities, Internet addressing schemes, security filters, and a means for directly logging on to other computers.

LAN (local area network)—A network of computers and other devices that is confined to a relatively small space, such as one building or even one office.

license tracking—The process of determining the number of copies of a single application that are currently in use on the network and whether the number in use exceeds the authorized number of licenses.

load balancing—The process of distributing data transfer activity evenly across a network so that no single device is overwhelmed.

local area network—See *LAN*.

mail server—A server that manages the storage and transfer of e-mail messages.

mail services—The network services that manage the storage and transfer of e-mail between users on a network. In addition to sending, receiving, and storing mail, mail services can include filtering, routing, notification, scheduling, and data exchange with other mail servers.

MAN (metropolitan area network)—A network that is larger than a LAN, typically connecting clients and servers from multiple buildings, but within a limited geographic area. For example, a MAN could connect multiple city government buildings around a city's center.

management services—The network services that centrally administer and simplify complicated management tasks on the network. Examples of management services include license tracking, security auditing, asset management, address management, software distribution, traffic monitoring, load balancing, and hardware diagnosis.

MCSE (Microsoft Certified Systems Engineer)—A professional certification established by Microsoft that demonstrates in-depth knowledge about Microsoft products, including Windows 2000, Windows XP, and Windows Server 2003.

metropolitan area network—See *MAN*.

Microsoft Certified Systems Engineer—See *MCSE*.

motherboard—The main circuit board that controls a computer.

network—A group of computers and other devices (such as printers) that are connected by and can exchange data via some type of transmission media, such as a cable, a wire, or the atmosphere.

network adapter—See *NIC*.

Network+ (Net+)—The professional certification established by CompTIA that verifies broad, vendor-independent networking technology skills such as an understanding of protocols, topologies, networking hardware, and network troubleshooting.

network interface card—See *NIC*.

network operating system—See *NOS*.

network services—The functions provided by a network.

NIC (network interface card)—The device that enables a workstation to connect to the network and communicate with other computers. NICs are manufactured by several different companies and come with a variety of specifications that are tailored to the workstation's and the network's requirements. NICs are also called network adapters.

node—A computer or other device connected to a network, which has a unique address and is capable of sending or receiving data.

NOS (network operating system)—The software that runs on a server and enables the server to manage data, users, groups, security, applications, and other networking functions. The most popular network operating systems are Microsoft Windows NT, Windows 2000 Server, and Windows Server 2003, UNIX, Linux, and Novell NetWare.

P2P network—See *peer-to-peer network*.

peer-to-peer network—A network in which every computer can communicate directly with every other computer. By default, no computer on a peer-to-peer network has more authority than another. However, each computer can be configured to share only some of its resources and keep other resources inaccessible to other nodes on the network.

print services—The network service that allows printers to be shared by several users on a network.

protocol—A standard method or format for communication between network devices. Protocols ensure that data are transferred whole, in sequence, and without error from one node on the network to another.

remote access server—A server that runs communications services that enable remote users to log on to a network. Also known as a communications server or access server.

remote user—A person working on a computer on a different network or in a different geographical location from the LAN's server.

resources—The devices, data, and data storage space provided by a computer, whether standalone or shared.

restore—The process of retrieving files from a backup. It is necessary to restore files if the original files are lost or deleted.

scalable—The property of a network that allows you to add nodes or increase its size easily.

security auditing—The process of evaluating security measures currently in place on a network and notifying the network administrator if a security breach occurs.

segment—A part of a network. Usually, a segment is composed of a group of nodes that share the same communications channel for all their traffic.

server—A computer on the network that manages shared resources. Servers usually have more processing power, memory, and hard disk space than clients. They run network operating software that can manage not only data, but also users, groups, security, and applications on the network.

sneakernet—A way of exchanging data between computers that are not connected on a network. Sneakernet requires that data be copied from a computer to a removable storage device such as a floppy disk, carried (presumably by someone wearing sneakers) to another computer, then copied from the storage device onto the second computer.

soft skills—The skills such as customer relations, leadership ability, and dependability, which are not easily measured, but are nevertheless important in a networking career.

software distribution—The process of automatically transferring a data file or installing a software application from the server to a client on the network.

spam—An unsolicited, unwanted e-mail.

standalone computer—A computer that uses applications and data only from its local disks and that is not connected to a network.

topology—The physical layout of computers on a network.

traffic—The data transmission and processing activity taking place on a computer network at any given time.

traffic monitoring—The process of determining how much data transfer activity is taking place on a network or network segment and notifying administrators when a segment becomes overloaded.

transmission media—The means through which data are transmitted and received. Transmission media may be physical, such as wire or cable, or atmospheric (wireless), such as radio waves.

user—A person who uses a computer.

WAN (wide area network)—A network that spans a long distance and connects two or more LANs.

Web server—A computer that manages Web site services, such as supplying a Web page to multiple users on demand.

wide area network—See *WAN*.

workstation—A computer that runs a desktop operating system and connects to a network.

Review Questions

1. A _____ is a group of computers and other devices that are connected by some type of transmission media.
   - **a.** network
   - **b.** data packet
   - **c.** file server
   - **d.** node

2. In a _____ network, every computer can communicate directly with any other computer.
   - **a.** client/server
   - **b.** standalone
   - **c.** file
   - **d.** peer-to-peer

3. Which of the following terms describes a network of computers and other devices that is confined to a relatively small space, such as one building or even one office?
   - **a.** client/server
   - **b.** WAN
   - **c.** LAN
   - **d.** MAN

4. The _____ is the main circuit that controls the computer.
   - **a.** network adapter
   - **b.** motherboard
   - **c.** data packet
   - **d.** CPU

5. _____ ensure that data are transferred whole, in sequence, and without error from one node on the network to another.

   a. Topologies

   b. File servers

   c. Communication servers

   d. Protocols

6. True or false? A network's communication services allow remote users to connect to the network.

7. True or false? To function as a server, the computer must be running a network operating system.

8. True or false? Networks cannot extend beyond the boundaries of a building.

9. True or false? LANs typically connect separate offices in the same organization, whether they are across town or around the world from each other.

10. True or false? Each network device must have a unique address so that data can be transmitted reliably to and from that device.

11. _____ coordinate the storage and transfer of e-mail between users on a network.

12. A(n) _____ is a computer installed with the appropriate software to supply Web pages to many different clients upon demand.

13. The term _____ refers to those skills that are not easily measurable, such as customer relations, oral and written communications, dependability, teamwork, and leadership abilities.

14. _____ is the process of mastering material pertaining to a particular hardware system, operating system, programming language, or other software application, and then proving your mastery by passing a series of exams.

15. _____ refers to the capability of a server to share data files, applications, and disk storage space.

Chapter 2

Networking Standards and the OSI Model

After reading this chapter and completing the exercises, you will be able to:

- Identify organizations that set standards for networking

- Describe the purpose of the OSI Model and each of its layers

- Explain specific functions belonging to each OSI Model layer

- Understand how two network nodes communicate through the OSI Model

- Discuss the structure and purpose of data packets and frames

- Describe the two types of addressing covered by the OSI Model

When trying to grasp a new theoretical concept, it often helps to form a picture of that concept in your mind. In the field of chemistry, for example, even though you can't see a water molecule, you can represent it with a simple drawing of two hydrogen atoms and one oxygen atom. Similarly, in the field of networking, even though you can't see the communication that occurs between two nodes on a network, you can use a model to depict how the communication takes place. The model commonly used to describe network communications is called the OSI (Open Systems Interconnection) Model.

In this chapter, you will learn about the standards organizations that have helped create the various conventions (such as the OSI Model) used in networking. Next, you'll be introduced to the seven layers of the OSI Model and learn how they interact. You will then take a closer look at what goes on in each layer. Finally, you will learn to apply those details to a practical networking environment. Granted, learning the OSI Model is not the most exciting part of becoming a networking expert. Thoroughly understanding it, however, is essential to proficient network design and troubleshooting.

Networking Standards Organizations

Standards are documented agreements containing technical specifications or other precise criteria that stipulate how a particular product or service should be designed or performed. Many different industries use standards to ensure that products, processes, and services suit their purposes. Because of the wide variety of hardware and software in use today, standards are especially important in the world of networking. Without standards, it would be very difficult to design a network because you could not be certain that software or hardware from different manufacturers would work together. For example, if one manufacturer designed a network cable with a 1-centimeter-wide plug and another company manufactured a wall plate with a 0.8-centimeter-wide opening, you would not be able to insert the plug into the wall plate.

When purchasing networking equipment, therefore, you want to verify that equipment meets the standards your network requires. However, bear in mind that standards define the *minimum* acceptable performance of a product or service—not the ideal. So, for example, you might purchase two different network cables that comply with the minimum standard for transmitting at a certain speed, but one cable might exceed that standard, allowing for better network performance. In the case of network cables, exceeding minimum standards often follows from the use of quality materials and careful production techniques.

Because the computer industry grew so quickly out of several technical disciplines, many different organizations evolved to oversee its standards. In some cases, a few organizations are responsible for a single aspect of networking. For example, both ANSI and IEEE are involved in setting standards for wireless networks. Whereas ANSI prescribes the kind of NIC that the consumer needs to accept a wireless connection, IEEE prescribes, among other things, how the network will ensure that different parts of a communication sent through the atmosphere arrive at their destination in the correct sequence.

A complete list of the standards that regulate computers and networking would fill an encyclopedia. Although you don't need to know the fine points of every standard, you should be familiar with the groups that set networking standards and the critical aspects of standards required by your network.

ANSI

ANSI (American National Standards Institute) is an organization composed of more than a thousand representatives from industry and government who together determine standards for the electronics industry and other fields, such as chemical and nuclear engineering, health and safety, and construction. ANSI also represents the United States in setting international standards. This organization does not dictate that manufacturers comply with its standards, but requests voluntarily compliance. Of course, manufacturers and developers benefit from compliance, because compliance assures potential customers that the systems are reliable and can be integrated with an existing infrastructure. New electronic equipment and methods must undergo rigorous testing to prove they are worthy of ANSI's approval.

You can purchase ANSI standards documents online from ANSI's Web site (*www.ansi.org*) or find them at a university or public library. You need not read complete ANSI standards to be a competent networking professional, but you should understand the breadth and significance of ANSI's influence.

EIA and TIA

Two related standards organizations are EIA and TIA. **EIA (Electronic Industries Alliance)** is a trade organization composed of representatives from electronics manufacturing firms across the United States. EIA not only sets standards for its members, but also helps write ANSI standards and lobbies for legislation favorable to the growth of the computer and electronics industries.

In 1988, one of the EIA's subgroups merged with the former United States Telecommunications Suppliers Association (USTSA) to form **TIA (Telecommunications Industry Association)**. TIA focuses on standards for information technology, wireless, satellite, fiber optics, and telephone equipment. Both TIA and EIA set standards, lobby governments and industry, and sponsor conferences, exhibitions, and forums in their areas of interest.

Probably the best known standards to come from the TIA/EIA alliance are its guidelines for how network cable should be installed in commercial buildings, known as the "TIA/EIA 568-B Series." You can find out more about TIA from its Web site: *www.tiaonline.org* and EIA from its Web site: *www.eia.org*.

IEEE

The **IEEE (Institute of Electrical and Electronics Engineers)**, or "I-triple-E," is an international society composed of engineering professionals. Its goals are to promote development and education in the electrical engineering and computer science fields. To this end, IEEE hosts numerous symposia, conferences, and local chapter meetings and publishes papers designed to educate members on technological advances. It also maintains a standards board that establishes its own standards for the electronics and computer industries and contributes to the work of other standards-setting bodies, such as ANSI.

IEEE technical papers and standards are highly respected in the networking profession. Among other places, you will find references to IEEE standards in the manuals that accompany NICs. You can purchase IEEE documents online from IEEE's Web site (*www.ieee.org*) or find them in a university or public library.

ISO

ISO (International Organization for Standardization), headquartered in Geneva, Switzerland, is a collection of standards organizations representing 146 countries. ISO's goal is to establish international technological standards to facilitate global exchange of information and barrier-free trade. Given the organization's full name, you might expect it to be called "IOS," but "ISO" is not meant to be an acronym. In fact, "iso" is the Greek word for "equal." Using this term conveys the organization's dedication to standards.

ISO's authority is not limited to the information-processing and communications industries. It also applies to the fields of textiles, packaging, distribution of goods, energy production and utilization, shipbuilding, and banking and financial services. The universal agreements on screw threads, bank cards, and even the names for currencies are all products of ISO's work. In fact, fewer than 300 of ISO's more than 14,250 standards apply to computer-related products and functions. You can find out more about ISO at its Web site: *www.iso.org*.

ITU

The **ITU (International Telecommunication Union)** is a specialized United Nations agency that regulates international telecommunications, including radio and TV frequencies, satellite and telephony specifications, networking infrastructure, and tariffs applied to global communications. It also provides developing countries with technical expertise and equipment to advance those nations' technological bases.

The ITU was founded in Paris in 1865. It became part of the United Nations in 1947 and relocated to Geneva, Switzerland. Its standards arm contains members from 189 countries and publishes detailed policy and standards documents that can be found on its Web site: *www.itu.int*. Typically, ITU documents pertain more to global telecommunications issues than to industry technical specifications. However, the ITU is deeply involved with the implementation of worldwide Internet services. As in other areas, the ITU cooperates with several different standards organizations, such as ISOC (discussed next), to develop these standards.

ISOC

ISOC (Internet Society), founded in 1992, is a professional membership society that helps to establish technical standards for the Internet. Some current ISOC concerns include rapid growth, security, and the increased need for diverse services over the Internet. ISOC's membership consists of thousands of Internet professionals and companies from over 180 countries.

ISOC oversees groups with specific missions, such as the **IAB (Internet Architecture Board)**. IAB is a technical advisory group of researchers and technical professionals interested in overseeing the Internet's design and management. As part of its charter, IAB is responsible for Internet growth and management strategy, resolution of technical disputes, and standards oversight.

Another ISOC group is the **IETF (Internet Engineering Task Force)**, the organization that sets standards for how systems communicate over the Internet—in particular, how protocols operate and interact. Anyone can submit a proposed standard for IETF approval. The standard then undergoes elaborate review, testing, and approval processes. On an international level, IETF works with the ITU to help give technical standards approved in the United States international acceptance.

You can learn more about ISOC and its member organizations, IAB and IETF, at their Web site: *www.isoc.org*.

IANA and ICANN

You have learned that every computer on a network must have a unique address. On the Internet, this is especially important because millions of different computers must be available to transmit and receive data at any time. Addresses used to identify computers on the Internet and other TCP/IP-based networks are known as **IP (Internet Protocol) addresses**. To ensure that every Internet-connected device has a unique IP address, organizations across the globe rely on centralized authorities.

In early Internet history, a nonprofit group called the **IANA (Internet Assigned Numbers Authority)** kept records of available and reserved IP addresses and determined how addresses were doled out. Starting in 1997, IANA coordinated its efforts with three **RIRs (Regional Internet Registries)**: ARIN (American Registry for Internet Numbers), APNIC (Asia Pacific Network Information Centre), and RIPE (Réseaux IP Européens). An RIR is a not-for-profit agency that manages the distribution of IP addresses to private and public entities. In the late 1990s, the U.S. Department of Commerce (DOC), which funded IANA, decided to overhaul IP addressing and domain name management. The DOC recommended the formation of **ICANN (Internet Corporation for Assigned Names and Numbers)**, a private, nonprofit corporation. ICANN is now ultimately responsible for IP addressing and domain name management. Technically speaking, however, IANA continues to perform the system administration.

Individuals and businesses do not typically obtain IP addresses directly from an RIR or IANA. Instead, they lease a group of addresses from their ISP (Internet Service Provider), a business that provides organizations and individuals with access to the Internet and often other services, such as e-mail and Web hosting. An ISP, in turn, arranges with its RIR for the right to use certain IP addresses on its network. The RIR obtains its right to dole out those addresses from ICANN. In addition, the RIR coordinates with IANA to ensure that the addresses are associated with devices connected to the ISP's network.

You can learn more about IANA and ICANN at their Web sites: *www.iana.org* and *www.icann.org*, respectively.

The OSI Model

NET+
2.2

In the early 1980s, ISO began work on a universal set of specifications that would enable computer platforms across the world to communicate openly. The result was a helpful model for understanding and developing computer-to-computer communications over a network. This model, called the **OSI (Open Systems Interconnection) Model**, divides network communications into seven layers: Physical, Data Link, Network, Transport, Session, Presentation, and Application. At each layer, protocols perform services unique to that layer. While performing those services, the protocols also interact with protocols in the layers directly above and below. In addition, at the top of the OSI Model, Application layer protocols interact with the software you use (such an e-mail or spreadsheet program). At the bottom, Physical layer services act on the networking cables and connectors to issue and receive signals.

You have already learned that protocols are the rules by which computers communicate. A protocol is simply a set of instructions written by a programmer to perform a function or group of functions. Some protocols are included with a computer's operating system. Others are files installed with software programs. Chapter 4 covers protocols in depth; however, some protocols are briefly introduced in the following sections to explain better what happens at each layer of the OSI Model.

The OSI Model is a theoretical representation of what happens between two nodes communicating on a network. It does not prescribe the type of hardware or software that should support each layer. Nor does it describe how software programs interact with other software programs or how software programs interact with humans. Every process that occurs during network communications can be associated with a layer of the OSI Model, so you should be familiar with the names of the layers and understand the key services and protocols that belong to each.

◢ TIP

Networking professionals often devise a mnemonic way of remembering the seven layers of the OSI Model. One strategy is to make a sentence using words that begin with the same first letter of each layer, starting with either the lowest (Physical) or the highest (Application) layer. For example, you might choose to remember the phrase "Programmers Dare Not Throw Salty Pretzels Away." Quirky phrases are often easiest to remember.

NET+
2.2

The path that data takes from one computer to another through the OSI Model is illustrated in Figure 2-1. First, a user or device initiates a data exchange through the Application layer. The Application layer separates data into **PDUs (protocol data units)**, or discrete amounts of data. From there, Application layer PDUs progress down through OSI Model layers 6, 5, 4, 3, 2, and 1 before being issued to the network medium—for example, the wire. The data traverses the network until it reaches the second computer's Physical layer. Then at the receiving computer the data progresses up the OSI Model until it reaches the second computer's Application layer. This transfer of information happens in milliseconds.

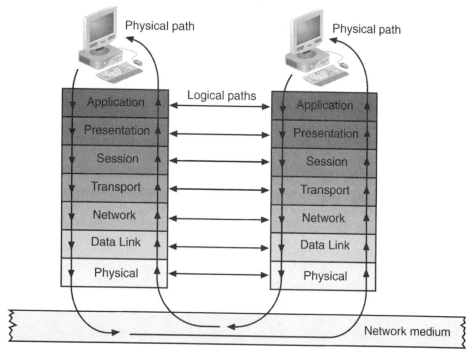

FIGURE 2-1 *Flow of data through the OSI Model*

Logically, however, each layer communicates with the same layer from one computer to another. In other words, the Application layer protocols on one computer exchange information with the Application layer protocols of the second computer. Protocols from other layers do not attempt to interpret Application layer data. In the following sections, the OSI Model layers are discussed from highest to lowest, beginning with the Application layer, where the flow of information is initiated.

Bear in mind that the OSI Model is a generalized and sometimes imperfect representation of network communication. In some cases, network functions can be associated with more than one layer of the model, and in other cases, network operations do not require services from every layer.

Application Layer

The top, or seventh, layer of the OSI Model is the **Application layer**. Contrary to what its name implies, the Application layer does not include software applications, such as Microsoft Word or Netscape. Instead, Application layer services facilitate communication between software applications and lower-layer network services so that the network can interpret an application's request and, in turn, the application can interpret data sent from the network. Through Application layer protocols, software applications negotiate their formatting, procedural, security, synchronization, and other requirements with the network.

For example, when you choose to open a Web page in Netscape, an Application layer protocol called **HTTP (Hypertext Transfer Protocol)** formats and sends your request from your client's browser (a software application) to the server. It also formats and sends the Web server's response back to your client's browser.

Suppose you choose to view the Exhibits page at the Library of Congress's Web site. You type "www.loc.gov/exhibits/index.html" in Netscape and press Enter. At that point Netscape's **API (application program interface)**, a set of routines that make up part of the software, transfers your request to the HTTP protocol. HTTP prompts lower-layer protocols to establish a connection between your computer and the Web server. Next, HTTP formats your request for the Web page and sends the request to the Web server. One part of the HTTP request would include a command that begins with "GET" and tells the server what page you want to retrieve. Other parts of the request would indicate what version of HTTP you're using, what types of graphics and what language your browser can accept, and what browser version you're using, among other things.

After receiving your computer's HTTP request, the Web server responsible for *www.loc.gov* responds, also via HTTP. Its response includes the text and graphics that make up the Web page, plus specifications for the content contained in the page, the HTTP version used, the type of HTTP response, and the length of the page. However, if the Web page is unavailable, the host, *www.loc.gov*, would send an HTTP response containing an error message, such as "Error 404–File Not Found."

After receiving the Web server's response, your workstation uses HTTP to interpret this response so that Netscape can present the *www.loc.gov/exhibits/index.html* Web page in a format you'll recognize, with neatly arranged text and images. Note that the information issued by one node's HTTP protocol is designed to be interpreted by the other node's HTTP protocol. However, as you will learn in later sections, HTTP requests could not traverse the network without the assistance of lower-layer protocols.

Presentation Layer

Protocols at the **Presentation layer** accept Application layer data and format it so that one type of application and host can understand data from another type of application and host. In other words, the Presentation layer serves as a translator. If you have spent any time working with computer graphics, you have probably heard of the GIF, JPG, and TIFF methods of compressing and encoding graphics. MPEG and QuickTime are two popular methods of

NET+
2.2

compressing and encoding audio and video data. Two well-known methods of encoding text are ASCII and EBCDIC. In each of these examples, it is the Presentation layer protocols that perform the coding and compression. They also interpret coded and compressed formats in data received from other computers. In the previous example of requesting a Web page, the Presentation layer protocols would interpret the JPG files transmitted within the Web server's HTTP response.

Presentation layer services also manage data encryption (such as the scrambling of passwords) and decryption. For example, if you look up your bank account status via the Internet, you are using a secure connection, and Presentation layer protocols will encrypt your account data before it is transmitted. On your end of the network, the Presentation layer will decrypt the data as it is received.

Session Layer

Protocols in the **Session layer** coordinate and maintain communications between two nodes on the network. The term **session** refers to a connection for ongoing data exchange between two parties. Historically, it was used in the context of terminal and mainframe communications, in which the **terminal** is a device with little (if any) of its own processing or disk capacity that depends on a host to supply it with software and processing services. Today, the term session is often used in the context of a connection between a remote client and an access server or between a Web browser client and a Web server.

Among the Session layer's functions are establishing and keeping alive the communications link for the duration of the session, keeping the communication secure, synchronizing the dialog between the two nodes, determining whether communications have been cut off, and, if so, figuring out where to restart transmission, and terminating communications. Session layer services also set the terms of communication by deciding which node will communicate first and how long a node can communicate. Finally, the Session layer monitors the identification of session participants, ensuring that only the authorized nodes can access the session.

When you dial your ISP to connect to the Internet, for example, the Session layer services at your ISP's server and on your computer negotiate the connection. If your phone line accidentally falls out of the wall jack, Session layer protocols on your end will detect the loss of a connection and initiate attempts to reconnect. If they cannot reconnect after a certain period of time, they will close the session and inform your dial-up software that communication has ended.

Transport Layer

Protocols in the **Transport layer** accept data from the Session layer and manage end-to-end delivery of data. That means they can ensure that the data is transferred from point A to point B reliably, in the correct sequence, and without errors. Without Transport layer services, data could not be verified or interpreted by its recipient. Transport layer protocols also handle **flow control**, which is the process of gauging the appropriate rate of transmission based on how fast the recipient can accept data. Dozens of different Transport layer protocols exist, but most modern networks, such as the Internet, rely on only a few. In the example of retrieving a Web page, a Transport layer protocol called the Transmission Control Protocol (TCP) takes care of reliably transmitting the HTTP protocol's request from client to server and vice versa. You will learn more about this significant protocol later in this book.

Some Transport layer protocols take steps to ensure that data arrives exactly as it was sent. Such protocols are known as **connection-oriented**, because they establish a connection with another node before they begin transmitting data. TCP is one example of a connection-oriented protocol. In the case of requesting a Web page, the client's TCP protocol first sends a **SYN (synchronization)** packet request for a connection to the Web server. The Web server responds with a **SYN-ACK (synchronization-acknowledgment)** packet, or a confirmation, to indicate that it's willing to make a connection. Then, the client responds with its own **ACK (acknowledgment)**. Through this three-step process a connection is established. Only after TCP establishes this connection does it transmit the HTTP request for a Web page.

Acknowledgments are also used in subsequent communications to ensure that data was properly delivered. For every data unit a node sends, its connection-oriented protocol expects an acknowledgment from the recipient. For example, after a client's TCP protocol issued an HTTP request, it would expect to receive an acknowledgment from the Web server proving that the data arrived. If data isn't acknowledged within a given time period, the client's protocol assumes the data was lost and retransmits it.

To ensure data integrity further, connection-oriented protocols such as TCP use a checksum. A **checksum** is a unique character string that allows the receiving node to determine if an arriving data unit matches exactly the data unit sent by the source. Checksums are added to data at the source and verified at the destination. If at the destination a checksum doesn't match what the source predicted, the destination's Transport layer protocols ask the source to retransmit the data. As you will learn, protocols at other layers of the OSI Model also use checksums.

Not all Transport layer protocols are concerned with reliability. Those that do not establish a connection before transmitting and make no effort to ensure that data is delivered error-free are called **connectionless** protocols. A connectionless protocol's lack of sophistication makes it more efficient than a connection-oriented protocol and renders it useful in situations in which data must be transferred quickly, such as live audio or video transmissions over the Internet. In these cases, connection-oriented protocols—with their acknowledgments, checksums, and flow control mechanisms—would add overhead to the transmission and potentially bog it down. In a video transmission, for example, this could result in pictures that are incomplete or don't update quickly enough to coincide with the audio.

In addition to ensuring reliable data delivery, Transport layer protocols break large data units received from the Session layer into multiple smaller units, called **segments**. This process is known as **segmentation**. On certain types of networks, segmentation increases data transmission efficiency. In some cases, segmentation is necessary for data units to match a network's **MTU (maximum transmission unit)**, the largest data unit it will carry. Every network type specifies a default MTU (though its size can be modified to some extent by a network administrator). For example, by default, Ethernet networks cannot accept packets with data payloads larger than 1500 bytes. Suppose an application wants to send a 6000-byte unit of data. Before

NET+
2.2

this data unit can be issued to an Ethernet network, it must be segmented into units no larger than 1500 bytes. To learn a network's MTU size (and thereby determine whether it needs to segment packets), Transport layer protocols perform a discovery routine upon establishing a connection with the network. Thereafter, the protocols will segment each data unit as necessary until closing the connection.

Segmentation is similar to the process of breaking down words into recognizable syllables that a child uses when learning to read. **Reassembly** is the process of reconstructing the segmented data units. To continue the reading analogy, when a child understands the separate syllables, he can combine them into a word—that is, he can reassemble the parts into a whole. To learn how reassembly works, suppose that you asked this question in history class: "Ms. Jones? How did poor farming techniques contribute to the Dust Bowl?" but that the words arrived at Ms. Jones's ear as "poor farming techniques Ms. Jones? how did to the Dust Bowl? contribute." On a network, the Transport layer recognizes this kind of disorder and rearranges the data pieces so that they make sense.

Sequencing is a method of identifying segments that belong to the same group of subdivided data. Sequencing also indicates where a unit of data begins, as well as the order in which groups of data were issued, and therefore should be interpreted. While establishing a connection, the Transport layer protocols from two devices agree on certain parameters of their communication, including a sequencing scheme. For sequencing to work properly, the Transport layer protocols of two nodes must synchronize their timing and agree on a starting point for the transmission.

Figure 2-2 illustrates the concept of segmentation and reassembly.

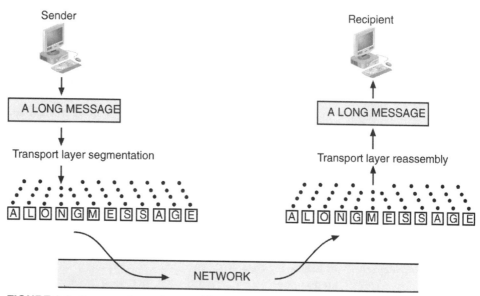

FIGURE 2-2 *Segmentation and reassembly*

Figure 2-3 depicts the information contained in an actual TCP segment used to request the Web page *www.loc.gov/exhibits/index.html*. After reading this section, you should recognize much of the segment's contents. After learning more about protocols later in this book, you will understand the meaning of everything contained in a TCP segment.

```
Transmission Control Protocol, Src Port: http (80), Dst Port: 1958 (1958), Seq: 3043958669, Ack:937013559, Len: 0
Source port: http (80)
   Destination port: 1958 (1958)
   Sequence number: 3043958669
   Acknowledgment number: 937013559
   Header length: 24 bytes
⊟ Flags: 0x0012 (SYN, ACK)
      0... .... = Congestion Window Reduced (CWR): Not set
      .0.. .... = ECN-Echo: Not set
      ..0. .... = Urgent: Not set
      ...1 .... = Acknowledgment: Set
      .... 0... = Push: Not set
      .... .0.. = Reset: Not set
      .... ..1. = Syn: Set
      .... ...0 = Fin: Not set
   Window size: 5840
   Checksum: 0x206a (correct)
⊟ Options: (4 bytes)
      Maximum segment size: 1460 bytes
```

FIGURE 2-3 *A TCP segment*

Network Layer

The primary function of protocols at the **Network layer**, the third layer in the OSI Model, is to translate network addresses into their physical counterparts and decide how to route data from the sender to the receiver. Addressing is a system for assigning unique identification numbers to devices on a network. Each node has two types of addresses.

One type of address is called a network address. **Network addresses** follow a hierarchical addressing scheme and can be assigned through operating system software. They are hierarchical because they contain subsets of data that incrementally narrow down the location of a node, just as your home address is hierarchical because it provides a country, state, ZIP code, city, street, house number, and person's name. Network address formats differ depending on which Network layer protocol the network uses. Network addresses are also called **network layer addresses**, **logical addresses**, or **virtual addresses**. The second type of address assigned to each node is called a physical address, discussed in detail in the next section.

For example, a computer running on a TCP/IP network might have a network layer address of 10.34.99.12 and a physical address of 0060973E97F3. In the classroom example, this addressing scheme is like saying that "Ms. Jones" and "U.S. citizen with Social Security number 123-45-6789" are the same person. Even though there may be other people named "Ms. Jones" in the United States, only one person has the Social Security number 123-45-6789.

NET+
2.2

Within the confines of your classroom, however, there is only one Ms. Jones, so you can be certain the correct person will respond when you say, "Ms. Jones?" There's no need to use her Social Security number.

Network layer protocols accept the Transport layer segments and add logical addressing information in a network header. At this point, the data unit becomes a packet. Network layer protocols also determine the path from point A on one network to point B on another network by factoring in:

◆ Delivery priorities (for example, packets that make up a phone call connected through the Internet might be designated high priority, whereas a mass e-mail message is low priority)

◆ Network congestion

◆ Quality of service (for example, some packets may require faster, more reliable delivery)

◆ Cost of alternative routes

NET+
2.2
2.3

The process of determining the best path is known as routing. More formally, to **route** means to direct data intelligently based on addressing, patterns of usage, and availability. Because the Network layer handles routing, **routers**—the devices that connect network segments and direct data—belong in the Network layer.

NET+
2.2

Although there are numerous Network layer protocols, one of the most common, and the one that underlies most Internet traffic, is the **IP (Internet Protocol)**. In the example of requesting a Web page, IP is the protocol that instructs the network where the HTTP request is coming from and where it should go. Figure 2-4 depicts the data found in an IP packet used to contact the Web site *www.loc.gov/exhibits/index.html*.

```
⊟Internet Protocol, src Addr: 140.147.249.7 (140.147.249.7), Dst Add: 10.11.11.51 (10.11.11.51)
    Version: 4
    Header length: 20 bytes
  ⊞ Differentiated Services Field: 0x00 (DSCP 0x00: Default; ECN: 0x00)
    Total Length: 44
    Identification: 0x0000 (0)
  ⊟ Flags: 0x04
      .1.. = Don't fragment: Set
      ..0. = More fragments: Not Set
    Fragment offset: 0
    Time to live: 64
    Protocol: TCP 0x06
    Header checksum: 0x9ff3 (correct)
    Source: 140.147.249.7 (140.147.249.7)
    Destination: 10.11.11.51 (10.11.11.51)
```

FIGURE 2-4 *An IP packet*

On TCP/IP-based networks, Network layer protocols can perform an additional function called fragmentation. In **fragmentation** a Network layer protocol (such as IP) subdivides the segments it receives from the Transport layer into smaller packets. If this process sounds familiar, it's because fragmentation accomplishes the same task at the Network layer that segmentation performs at the Transport layer. It ensures that packets issued to the network are no larger than the network's maximum transmission unit size. However, if a Transport layer protocol performs segmentation, fragmentation may not be necessary. For greater network efficiency, segmentation is preferred. Not all Transport layer protocols are designed to accomplish segmentation. If a Transport layer protocol cannot perform segmentation, Network layer protocols will perform fragmentation, if needed.

Data Link Layer

The primary function of protocols in the second layer of the OSI Model, the **Data Link layer**, is to divide data they receive from the Network layer into distinct frames that can then be transmitted by the Physical layer. A **frame** is a structured package for moving data that includes not only the raw data, or "payload," but also the sender's and receiver's network addresses, and error checking and control information. The addresses tell the network where to deliver the frame, whereas the error checking and control information ensure that the frame arrives without any problems.

To understand the function of the Data Link layer fully, pretend for a moment that computers communicate as humans do. Suppose you are in Ms. Jones's large classroom, which is full of noisy students, and you need to ask the teacher a question. To get your message through, you might say, "Ms. Jones? Can you explain more about the effects of railroads on commerce in the mid-nineteenth century?" In this example, you are the sender (in a busy network) and you have addressed your recipient, Ms. Jones, just as the Data Link layer addresses another computer on the network. In addition, you have formatted your thought as a question, just as the Data Link layer formats data into frames that can be interpreted by receiving computers.

What happens if the room is so noisy that Ms. Jones hears only part of your question? For example, she might receive "on commerce in the late-nineteenth century?" This kind of error can happen in network communications as well (because of wiring problems, for example). The Data Link layer protocols find out that information has been dropped and ask the first computer to retransmit its message—just as in a classroom setting Ms. Jones might say, "I didn't hear you. Can you repeat the question?" The Data Link layer accomplishes this task through a process called error checking.

Error checking is accomplished by a 4-byte **FCS (Frame Check Sequence)** field, whose purpose is to ensure that the data at the destination exactly matches the data issued from the source. When the source node transmits the data, it performs an algorithm (or mathematical routine) called a **CRC (Cyclic Redundancy Check)**. CRC takes the values of all of the preceding fields in the frame and generates a unique 4-byte number, the FCS. When the destination node

NET+
2.2

receives the frame, its Data Link layer services unscramble the FCS via the same CRC algorithm and ensure that the frame's fields match their original form. If this comparison fails, the receiving node assumes that the frame has been damaged in transit and requests that the source node retransmit the data. Note that the receiving node, and not the sending node, is responsible for detecting errors.

In addition, the sender's Data Link layer waits for acknowledgment from the receiver's Transport layer that data was received correctly. If the sender does not get this acknowledgment within a prescribed period of time, its Data Link layer gives instruction to retransmit the information. The Data Link layer does not try to figure out what went wrong in the transmission. Similarly, as in a busy classroom, Ms. Jones will probably say, "Pardon me?" rather than, "It sounds as if you might have a question about railroads, and I heard only the last part of it, which dealt with commerce, so I assume you are asking about commerce and railroads; is that correct?" Obviously, the former method is more efficient.

Another communications mishap that might occur in a noisy classroom or on a busy network is a glut of communication requests. For example, at the end of class, 20 people might ask Ms. Jones 20 different questions at once. Of course, she can't pay attention to all of them simultaneously. She will probably say, "One person at a time, please," then point to one student who asked a question. This situation is analogous to what the Data Link layer does for the Physical layer. One node on a network (a Web server, for example) may receive multiple requests that include many frames of data each. The Data Link layer controls the flow of this information, allowing the NIC to process data without error.

In fact, the IEEE has divided the Data Link layer into two sublayers, as shown in Figure 2-5. The reason for this change was to allow higher layer protocols (for example, those operating in the Network layer) to interact with Data Link layer protocols without regard for Physical layer specifications.

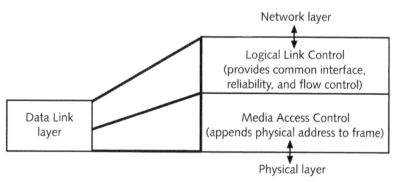

FIGURE 2-5 *The Data Link layer and its sublayers*

The upper sublayer of the Data Link layer, called the **LLC (Logical Link Control)** sublayer, provides an interface to the Network layer protocols, manages flow control, and issues requests for transmission for data that has suffered errors. The **MAC (Media Access Control)** sublayer, the lower sublayer of the Data Link layer, manages access to the physical medium. It appends the **physical address** of the destination computer onto the data frame. The physical address is a fixed number associated with a device's NIC; it is initially assigned at the factory and stored in the NIC's on-board memory. Because this address is appended by the MAC sublayer of the Data Link layer, it is also known as a **MAC address** or a **Data Link layer address**. Sometimes it's also called a **hardware address**.

You can find a NIC's MAC address through your computer's protocol configuration utility or by simply looking at the NIC. The MAC address will be stamped directly onto the NIC's circuit board or on a sticker attached to some part of the NIC, as shown in Figure 2-6. I

MAC addresses contain two parts: a Block ID and a Device ID. The **Block ID** is a six-character sequence unique to each vendor. IEEE manages which Block IDs each manufacturer can use. For example, a series of Ethernet NICs manufactured by the 3Com Corporation begins with the six-character sequence "00608C," while a series of Ethernet NICs manufactured by Intel begins with "00AA00." Some manufacturers have several different Block IDs. The

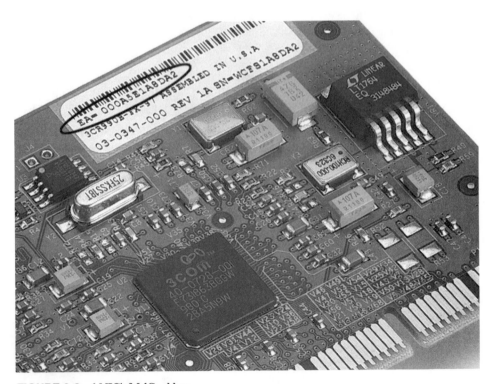

FIGURE 2-6 *A NIC's MAC address*

NET+
2.1

remaining six characters in the MAC address are added at the factory, based on the NIC's model and manufacture date, and collectively form the Device ID. An example of a Device ID assigned by a manufacturer might be 005499. The combination of the Block ID and Device ID result in a unique, 12-character MAC address of 00608C005499. MAC addresses are also frequently depicted in their hexadecimal format—for example, 00:60:8C:00:54:99.

If you know a computer's MAC address, you can determine which company manufactured its NIC by looking up its Block ID. IEEE maintains a database of Block IDs and their manufacturers, which is accessible via the Web. At the time of this writing, the database search page could be found at: *standards.ieee.org/regauth/oui/index.shtml.*

NET+
2.3

Because of their hardware addressing function, NICs can be said to perform in the Data Link layer of the OSI Model. However, they also perform services in the Physical layer, which is described next.

Physical Layer

NET+
2.2

The **Physical layer** is the lowest, or first, layer of the OSI Model. Protocols at the Physical layer accept frames from the Data Link layer and generate voltage so as to transmit signals. (Signals are made of electrical impulses that, when issued in a certain pattern, represent information.) When receiving data, Physical layer protocols detect voltage and accept signals, which they pass on to the Data Link layer. Physical layer protocols also set the data transmission rate and monitor data error rates. However, even if they recognize an error, they cannot perform error correction. When you install a NIC in your desktop PC and connect it to a cable, you are establishing the foundation that allows the computer to be networked. In other words, you are providing a Physical layer.

NET+
2.2
2.3

Connectivity devices such as hubs and repeaters operate at the Physical layer. NICs operate at both the Physical layer and at the Data Link layer. As you would expect, physical network problems, such as a severed wire or a broken connectivity device, affect the Physical layer. Similarly, if you insert a NIC but fail to seat it deeply enough in the computer's main circuit board, your computer will experience network problems at the Physical layer.

NET+
2.2

Most of the functions that network administrators are most concerned with happen in the first four layers of the OSI Model: Physical, Data Link, Network, and Transport. Therefore, the bulk of material in this book and on the Network+ exam relates to these four layers. Software programmers, on the other hand, are more apt to be concerned with what happens at the Application, Presentation, and Session layers.

Applying the OSI Model

NET+
2.2

Now that you have been introduced to the seven layers of the OSI Model, you can take a closer look at exactly how the layers interact. For reference, Table 2-1 summarizes the functions of the seven OSI Model layers.

Table 2-1 Functions of the OSI layers

OSI Model Layer	Function
Application (Layer 7)	Provides interface between applications and network for interpreting application requests and requirements
Presentation (Layer 6)	Allows hosts and applications to use a common language; performs data formatting, encryption, and compression
Session (Layer 5)	Establishes, maintains, and terminates user connections
Transport (Layer 4)	Ensures accurate delivery of data through flow control, segmentation and reassembly, error correction, and acknowledgment
Network (Layer 3)	Establishes network connections; translates network addresses into their physical counterparts and determines routing
Data Link (Layer 2)	Packages data in frames appropriate to network transmission method
Physical (Layer 1)	Manages signaling to and from physical network connections

Communication Between Two Systems

Based on what you've learned about the OSI Model, it should be clear to you that data issued from a software application is not in the same form as the data that your NIC sends to the network. At each layer of the OSI Model, some information—for example, a format specification or a network address—is added to the original data. After it has followed the path from the Application layer to the Physical layer, data is significantly transformed, as shown in Figure 2-7. The following paragraphs describe this process in detail.

To understand how data changes, it is useful to trace the steps in a typical client-server exchange, such as retrieving a mail message from a mail server. Suppose that you dial into your company's network via your home computer's modem, log on, start your e-mail application, and then click a button in the e-mail application to retrieve your mail from the server. At that point, Application layer services on your computer accept data from your mail application and formulate a request meant for the mail server software. They add an application header to the data that the program wants to send. The application header contains information about the e-mail application's requirements, so that the mail server can fulfill its request properly. The Application layer transfers the request to the Presentation layer, in the form of a protocol data unit (PDU).

The Presentation layer first determines whether and how it should format or encrypt the data request received from the Application layer. For example, if your mail client requires encryption, the Presentation layer protocols will add that information to the PDU in a presentation header. If your e-mail message contains graphics or formatted text, that information will also be added.

NET+
2.2

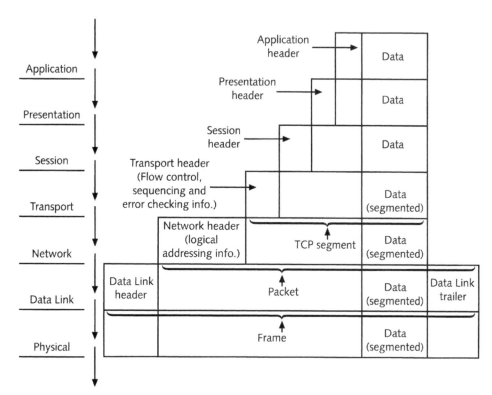

FIGURE 2-7 *Data transformation through the OSI Model*

Then, the Presentation layer sends its PDU to the Session layer, which adds a session header that contains information about how your modem communicates with the network. For example, the session header might indicate that your dial-up connection can only transmit and receive data at 48 Kbps. The Session layer then passes the PDU to the Transport layer.

At the Transport layer, the PDU—your request for mail and the headers added by previous layers—is broken down into smaller pieces of data, or segments. The segments' maximum size is dictated by the type of network transmission method in use (for example, Ethernet). Suppose your mail request PDU is too large to be a single segment. In that case, Transport layer protocols subdivide it into two or more smaller segments and assign sequence identifiers to all of the smaller segments. This information becomes part of the transport header. Protocols also add checksum, flow control, and acknowledgment data to the transport header. The Transport layer then passes these segments, one at a time, to the Network layer.

Next, Network layer protocols add logical addressing information to the segments, so that your request will be properly routed to the mail server and the mail server will respond to your computer. This information is contained in the network header. With the addition of network address information, the pieces of data are called packets. The Network layer then passes the packets to the Data Link layer.

NET+

2.2

At the Data Link layer, protocols add a header to the front of each packet and a trailer to the end of each packet to make frames. (The trailer indicates where a frame ends.) In other words, the Data Link layer protocols **encapsulate** the Network layer packets. Encapsulation is frequently compared to placing an envelope within a larger envelope. This analogy conveys the idea that the Data Link layer does not attempt to interpret any information added in the Network layer, but simply surrounds it.

Using frames reduces the possibility of lost data or errors on the network, because a way of checking for errors is built into each frame. After verifying that the data has not been damaged, the Data Link layer then passes the frames to the Physical layer.

Finally, your request for mail, in the form of many frames, hits the NIC at the Physical layer. The Physical layer does not interpret the frames or add information to the frames; it simply transmits them over the phone line connected to your modem, across your office network, and to the mail server after the binary digits (bits), or ones and zeroes, have been converted to electrical pulses. As the frames arrive at the mail server, the server's Physical layer accepts the frames and transfers them to the Data Link layer. The mail server begins to unravel your request, reversing the process just described, until it responds to your request with its own transmission, beginning from its Application layer.

 NOTE

The terms "frame," "packet," "datagram," and "PDU" are often used interchangeably to refer to a small piece of data formatted for network transmission. Technically, however, a packet is a piece of information that contains network addressing information and a frame is a piece of data enclosed by a Data Link layer header and trailer. "Datagram" is synonymous with "packet." "PDU" generically refers to a unit of data at any layer of the OSI Model. However, networking professionals often use the term "packet" to refer to frames, PDUs, and Transport layer segments alike.

Frame Specifications

NET+

1.2

You have learned that frames are composed of several smaller components, or fields. The characteristics of these components depend on the type of network on which the frames run and on the standards that they must follow. The two major categories of frame types, Ethernet and Token Ring, correspond to the two most commonly used network technologies. You will learn more about these technologies in Chapter 6. The rest of this section tells you just as much as you need to know about these networks in order to discuss Ethernet and Token Ring frames.

Ethernet is a networking technology originally developed at Xerox in the early 1970s and improved by Digital Equipment Corporation, Intel, and Xerox. There are four different types of Ethernet frames. The most popular form of Ethernet is characterized by the unique way in which devices share a common transmission channel, described in the IEEE **802.3** standard.

NET+
1.2

Token Ring is a networking technology developed by IBM in the 1980s. It relies upon direct links between nodes and a ring topology. Nodes pass around **tokens**, special control frames that indicate to the network when a particular node is about to transmit data. Although Token Ring is now less common than Ethernet, there is a chance that you might work on a Token Ring network. The IEEE has defined Token Ring technology in its **802.5** standard.

Ethernet frames are different from Token Ring frames, and the two will not interact with each other on a network. In fact, most LANs do not support more than one frame type, because devices cannot support more than one frame type per physical interface, or NIC. (NICs can, however, support multiple protocols.) Although you can conceivably transmit both Token Ring and Ethernet frames on a network, Ethernet interfaces cannot interpret Token Ring frames, and vice versa. Normally, LANs use *either* Ethernet or Token Ring, and almost all contemporary LANs use Ethernet.

It's important to know what frame type (or types) your network environment requires. You will use this information when installing network operating systems, configuring servers and client workstations, installing NICs, troubleshooting network problems, and purchasing network equipment.

IEEE Networking Specifications

NET+
1.2

In addition to frame types and addressing, IEEE networking specifications apply to connectivity, networking media, error checking algorithms, encryption, emerging technologies, and more. All of these specifications fall under the IEEE's "Project 802," an effort to standardize physical and logical elements of a network. IEEE developed these standards before the OSI Model was standardized by ISO, but IEEE's 802 standards can be applied to the layers of the OSI Model. Table 2-2 describes just some of the IEEE 802 specifications. You should be familiar with the topics that each of these standards covers. The Network+ certification exam includes questions about IEEE 802 specifications.

Table 2-2 IEEE 802 standards

Standard	Name	Topic
802.1	Internetworking	Routing, bridging, and network-to-network communications
802.2	Logical Link Control	Error and flow control over data frames
802.3	Ethernet LAN	All forms of Ethernet media and interfaces
802.4	Token Bus LAN	All forms of Token Bus media and interfaces
802.5	Token Ring LAN	All forms of Token Ring media and interfaces
802.6	Metropolitan Area Network (MAN)	MAN technologies, addressing, and services

Table 2-2 IEEE 802 standards (Continued)

Standard	Name	Topic
802.7	Broadband Technical Advisory Group	Broadband networking media, interfaces, and other equipment
802.8	Fiber Optic Technical Advisory Group	Fiber optic media used in token-passing networks like FDDI
802.9	Integrated Voice/ Data Networks	Integration of voice and data traffic over a single network medium
802.10	Network Security	Network access controls, encryption, certification, and other security topics
802.11	Wireless Networks	Standards for wireless networking for many different broadcast frequencies and usage techniques
802.12	High-Speed Networking	A variety of 100 Mbps-plus technologies, including 100BASE-VG
802.14	Cable broadband LANs and MANs	Standards for designing networks over coaxial cable-based broadband connections
802.15	Wireless Personal Area Networks	The coexistence of wireless personal area networks with other wireless devices in unlicensed frequency bands
802.16	Broadband Wireless Access	The atmospheric interface and related functions associated with Wireless Local Loop (WLL)

Chapter Summary

◆ Standards are documented agreements containing precise criteria that are used as guidelines to ensure that materials, products, processes, and services suit their purpose. Standards also help to ensure interoperability between software and hardware from different manufacturers.

◆ Some of the significant standards organizations are ANSI, EIA/TIA, IEEE, ISO, ITU, ISOC, IANA, and ICANN.

◆ ISO's Open Systems Interconnection (OSI) Model represents communication between two computers on a network. It divides networking architecture into seven layers: Physical, Data Link, Network, Transport, Session, Presentation, and Application. Each layer has its own set of functions and interacts with the layers directly above and below it.

◆ Protocols in the Application layer, the seventh layer of the OSI Model, enable software programs to negotiate their formatting, procedural, security, synchronization, and other requirements with the network.

◆ Protocols in the Presentation layer, the sixth OSI Model layer, serve as translators between the application and the network, using a common language for different hosts and applications to exchange data.

◆ Protocols in the Session layer, the fifth OSI Model layer, coordinate and maintain links between two devices for the duration of their communication. They also synchronize dialogue, determine whether communications have been cut off, and, if so, figure out where to restart transmission.

◆ The primary function of protocols in the Transport layer, the fourth OSI Model layer, is to oversee end-to-end data delivery. In the case of connection-oriented protocols, this means data is delivered reliably. They verify that data is received in the same sequence in which it was sent. They are also responsible for flow control, segmentation, and reassembly of packets. Connectionless Transport layer protocols do not offer such guarantees.

◆ Protocols in the Network layer, the third OSI Model layer, manage logical addressing and determine routes based on addressing, patterns of usage, and availability. Routers belong to the Network layer because they use this information to direct data intelligently from sender to receiver.

◆ Network layer addresses, also called logical or virtual addresses, are assigned to devices through operating system software. They are composed of hierarchical information, so they can be easily interpreted by routers and used to direct data to its destination.

◆ The primary function of protocols at the Data Link layer, the second layer of the OSI Model, is to organize data they receive from the Network layer into frames that contain error checking routines and can then be transmitted by the Physical layer.

◆ The Data Link layer is subdivided into the Logical Link Control and MAC sublayers. The LLC sublayer ensures a common interface for the Network layer protocols. The MAC sublayer is responsible for adding physical address data to frames. MAC addresses are hard-coded into a device's NIC.

◆ Protocols at the Physical layer generate and detect voltage so as to transmit and receive signals carrying data over a network medium. These protocols also set the data transmission rate and monitor data error rates, but do not provide error correction.

◆ A data request from a software program is received by the Application layer protocols and is transferred down through the layers of the OSI Model until it reaches the Physical layer (the network cable, for example). At that point, data is sent to its destination over the wire, and the Physical layer protocols at the destination send it back up through the layers of the OSI Model until it reaches the Application layer.

◆ Data frames are small blocks of data with control, addressing, and handling information attached to them. Frames are composed of several fields. The characteristics of these fields depend on the type of network on which the frames run and the standards that they must follow. Ethernet and Token Ring networks use different frame types, and one type of network cannot interpret the others' frames.

◆ In addition to frame types and addressing schemes, the IEEE networking specifications apply to connectivity, networking media, error checking algorithms, encryption, emerging technologies, and more. All of these specifications fall under the IEEE's Project 802, an effort to standardize the elements of networking.

◆ Significant 802 standards are: 802.3, which describes Ethernet; 802.5, which describes Token Ring; and 802.11, which describes wireless networking.

Key Terms

802.2—The IEEE standard for error and flow control in data frames.

802.3—The IEEE standard for Ethernet networking devices and data handling.

802.5—The IEEE standard for Token Ring networking devices and data handling.

802.11—The IEEE standard for wireless networking.

ACK (acknowledgment)—A response generated at the Transport layer of the OSI Model that confirms to a sender that its frame was received. The ACK packet is the third of three in the three-step process of establishing a connection.

acknowledgment—See *ACK*.

American National Standards Institute—See *ANSI*.

ANSI (American National Standards Institute)—An organization composed of more than 1000 representatives from industry and government who together determine standards for the electronics industry in addition to other fields, such as chemical and nuclear engineering, health and safety, and construction.

API (application program interface)—A set of routines that make up part of a software application.

Application layer—The seventh layer of the OSI Model. Application layer protocols enable software programs to negotiate formatting, procedural, security, synchronization, and other requirements with the network.

application program interface—See *API*.

Block ID—The first set of six characters that make up the MAC address and that are unique to a particular manufacturer.

checksum—A method of error checking that determines if the contents of an arriving data unit match the contents of the data unit sent by the source.

connection-oriented—A type of Transport layer protocol that requires the establishment of a connection between communicating nodes before it will transmit data.

connectionless—A type of Transport layer protocol that services a request without requiring a verified session and without guaranteeing delivery of data.

CRC (Cyclic Redundancy Check)—An algorithm (or mathematical routine) used to verify the accuracy of data contained in a data frame.

Cyclic Redundancy Check—See *CRC*.

Data Link layer—The second layer in the OSI Model. The Data Link layer bridges the networking media with the Network layer. Its primary function is to divide the data it receives from the Network layer into frames that can then be transmitted by the Physical layer.

Device ID—The second set of six characters that make up a network device's MAC address. The Device ID, which is added at the factory, is based on the device's model and manufacture date.

EIA (Electronic Industries Alliance)—A trade organization composed of representatives from electronics manufacturing firms across the United States that sets standards for electronic equipment and lobbies for legislation favorable to the growth of the computer and electronics industries.

Electronic Industries Alliance—See *EIA*.

encapsulate—The process of wrapping one layer's PDU with protocol information so that it can be interpreted by a lower layer. For example, Data Link layer protocols encapsulate Network layer packets in frames.

Ethernet—A networking technology originally developed at Xerox in the 1970s and improved by Digital Equipment Corporation, Intel, and Xerox. Ethernet, which is the most common form of network transmission technology, follows the IEEE 802.3 standard.

FCS (Frame Check Sequence)—The field in a frame responsible for ensuring that data carried by the frame arrives intact. It uses an algorithm, such as CRC, to accomplish this verification.

flow control—A method of gauging the appropriate rate of data transmission based on how fast the recipient can accept data.

fragmentation—A Network layer service that subdivides segments it receives from the Transport layer into smaller packets.

frame—A package for data that includes not only the raw data, or "payload," but also the sender's and recipient's addressing and control information. Frames are generated at the Data Link layer of the OSI Model and are issued to the network at the Physical layer.

Frame Check Sequence—See *FCS*.

hardware address—See *MAC address*.

HTTP (Hypertext Transfer Protocol)—An Application layer protocol that formulates and interprets requests between Web clients and servers.

Hypertext Transfer Protocol—See *HTTP.*

IAB (Internet Architecture Board)—A technical advisory group of researchers and professionals interested in overseeing the Internet's design, growth, standards, and management.

IANA (Internet Assigned Numbers Authority)—A nonprofit, U.S. government-funded group that was established at the University of Southern California and charged with managing IP address allocation and the domain name system. The oversight for many of IANA's functions was given to ICANN in 1998; however, IANA continues to perform Internet addressing and domain name system administration.

ICANN (Internet Corporation for Assigned Names and Numbers)—The nonprofit corporation currently designated by the U.S. government to maintain and assign IP addresses.

IEEE (Institute of Electrical and Electronics Engineers)—An international society composed of engineering professionals. Its goals are to promote development and education in the electrical engineering and computer science fields.

IETF (Internet Engineering Task Force)—An organization that sets standards for how systems communicate over the Internet (for example, how protocols operate and interact).

Institute of Electrical and Electronics Engineers—See *IEEE.*

International Organization for Standardization—See *ISO.*

International Telecommunication Union—See *ITU.*

Internet Architecture Board—See *IAB.*

Internet Assigned Numbers Authority—See *IANA.*

Internet Corporation for Assigned Names and Numbers—See *ICANN.*

Internet Engineering Task Force—See *IETF.*

Internet Protocol—See *IP.*

Internet Protocol address—See *IP address.*

Internet Service Provider—See *ISP.*

Internet Society—See *ISOC.*

IP (Internet Protocol)—A core protocol in the TCP/IP suite that operates in the Network layer of the OSI Model and provides information about how and where data should be delivered. IP is the subprotocol that enables TCP/IP to internetwork.

IP address (Internet Protocol address)—The Network layer address assigned to nodes to uniquely identify them on a TCP/IP network. IP addresses consist of 32 bits divided into four octets, or bytes.

ISO (International Organization for Standardization)—A collection of standards organizations representing 146 countries with headquarters located in Geneva, Switzerland. Its goal is to establish international technological standards to facilitate the global exchange of information and barrier-free trade.

ISOC (Internet Society)—A professional organization with members from more than 180 countries that helps to establish technical standards for the Internet.

ISP (Internet Service Provider)—A business that provides organizations and individuals with Internet access and often other services, such as e-mail and Web hosting.

ITU (International Telecommunication Union)—A United Nations agency that regulates international telecommunications and provides developing countries with technical expertise and equipment to advance their technological bases.

LLC (Logical Link Control) sublayer—The upper sublayer in the Data Link layer. The LLC provides a common interface and supplies reliability and flow control services.

logical address—See *network address*.

Logical Link Control layer—See *LLC (Logical Link Control) sublayer*.

MAC address—A 12-character string that uniquely identifies a network node. The manufacturer hard-codes the MAC address into the NIC. This address is composed of the Block ID and Device ID.

MAC (Media Access Control) sublayer—The lower sublayer of the Data Link layer. The MAC appends the physical address of the destination computer onto the frame.

maximum transmission unit—See *MTU*.

Media Access Control sublayer—See *MAC (Media Access Control) sublayer*.

MTU (maximum transmission unit)—The largest data unit a network (for example, Ethernet or Token Ring) will accept for transmission.

network address—A unique identifying number for a network node that follows a hierarchical addressing scheme and can be assigned through operating system software. Network addresses are added to data packets and interpreted by protocols at the Network layer of the OSI Model.

Network layer—The third layer in the OSI Model. Protocols in the Network layer translate network addresses into their physical counterparts and decide how to route data from the sender to the receiver.

Network layer address—See *network address*.

Open Systems Interconnection Model—See *OSI (Open Systems Interconnection) Model*.

OSI (Open Systems Interconnection) Model—A model for understanding and developing computer-to-computer communication developed in the 1980s by ISO. It divides networking functions among seven layers: Physical, Data Link, Network, Transport, Session, Presentation, and Application.

PDU (protocol data unit)—A unit of data at any layer of the OSI Model.

physical address—See *MAC address*.

Physical layer—The lowest, or first, layer of the OSI Model. Protocols in the Physical layer generate and detect voltage so as to transmit and receive signals carrying data over a network medium. These protocols also set the data transmission rate and monitor data error rates, but do not provide error correction.

Presentation layer—The sixth layer of the OSI Model. Protocols in the Presentation layer translate between the application and the network. Here, data are formatted in a schema that the network can understand, with the format varying according to the type of network used. The Presentation layer also manages data encryption and decryption, such as the scrambling of system passwords.

protocol data unit—See *PDU*.

reassembly—The process of reconstructing data units that have been segmented.

Regional Internet Registry—See *RIR*.

RIR (Regional Internet Registry)—A not-for-profit agency that manages the distribution of IP addresses to private and public entities. ARIN is the RIR for North, Central, and South America and sub-Saharan Africa. APNIC is the RIR for Asia and the Pacific region. RIPE is the RIR for Europe and North Africa.

route—To direct data intelligently between networks based on addressing, patterns of usage, and availability of network segments.

router—A device that connects network segments and directs data based on information contained in the data packet.

segment—A unit of data that results from subdividing a larger protocol data unit.

segmentation—The process of decreasing the size of data units when moving data from a network that can handle larger data units to a network that can handle only smaller data units.

sequencing—The process of assigning a placeholder to each piece of a data block to allow the receiving node's Transport layer to reassemble the data in the correct order.

session—A connection for data exchange between two parties. The term "session" may be used in the context of Web, remote access, or terminal and mainframe communications, for example.

Session layer—The fifth layer in the OSI Model. The Session layer establishes and maintains communication between two nodes on the network. It can be considered the "traffic cop" for network communications.

standard—A documented agreement containing technical specifications or other precise criteria that are used as guidelines to ensure that materials, products, processes, and services suit their intended purpose.

SYN (synchronization)—The packet one node sends to request a connection with another node on the network. The SYN packet is the first of three in the three-step process of establishing a connection.

SYN-ACK (synchronization-acknowledgment)—The packet a node sends to acknowledge to another node that it has received a SYN request for connection. The SYN-ACK packet is the second of three in the three-step process of establishing a connection.

synchronization—See *SYN*.

synchronization-acknowledgement—See *SYN-ACK*.

Telecommunications Industry Association—See *TIA*.

terminal—A device with little (if any) of its own processing or disk capacity that depends on a host to supply it with applications and data-processing services.

TIA (Telecommunications Industry Association)—A subgroup of the EIA that focuses on standards for information technology, wireless, satellite, fiber optics, and telephone equipment. Probably the best known standards to come from the TIA/EIA alliance are its guidelines for how network cable should be installed in commercial buildings, known as the "TIA/EIA 568-B Series."

token—A special control frame that indicates to the rest of the network that a particular node has the right to transmit data.

Token Ring—A networking technology developed by IBM in the 1980s. It relies upon direct links between nodes and a ring topology, using tokens to allow nodes to transmit data.

Transport layer—The fourth layer of the OSI Model. In the Transport layer, protocols ensure that data are transferred from point A to point B reliably and without errors. Transport layer services include flow control, acknowledgment, error correction, segmentation, reassembly, and sequencing.

virtual address—See *network address*.

Review Questions

1. _____ are documented agreements containing technical specifications or other precise criteria that stipulate how a particular product or service should be designed or performed.

   a. Frames

   b. Standards

   c. Tokens

   d. Routers

2. _____ is an organization composed of more than a thousand representatives from industry and government who together determine standards for the electronics industry and other fields, such as chemical and nuclear engineering, health and safety, and construction.

   a. ANSI

   b. IEE

   c. TIA

   d. ITU

3. Protocols at the _____ layer accept Application layer data and format it so that one type of application and host can understand data from another type of application and host.

   a. Network

   b. Transport

   c. Session

   d. Presentation

4. _____ is a networking technology originally developed at Xerox in the early 1970s and improved by Digital Equipment Corporation, Intel, and Xerox.

   a. Token Ring

   b. Internetworking

   c. Ethernet

   d. Logical Link Control

5. _____ is a method of identifying segments that belong to the same group of subdivided data.
   a. Sequencing
   b. Logical addressing
   c. Routing
   d. IP addressing

6. True or false? By default, Ethernet networks cannot accept packets with data payloads larger than 1500 bytes.

7. True or false? At the Network layer, protocols add a header to the front of each packet and a trailer to the end of each packet to make frames.

8. True or false? Using frames reduces the possibility of lost data or errors on the network.

9. True or false? IEEE networking specifications apply to connectivity, networking media, error checking algorithms, encryption, and emerging technologies.

10. True or false? The system that assigns unique identification numbers to devices on a network is known as sequencing.

11. _____ protocols ensure that data arrives exactly as it was sent by establishing a connection with another node before they begin transmitting data.

12. Transport layer protocols break large data units received from the Session layer into multiple smaller units called _____.

13. Network layer addresses are also called _____.

14. The _____ is the lowest, or first, layer of the OSI model.

15. _____ layer services manage data encryption and decryption.

Chapter 3

Transmission Basics and Networking Media

After reading this chapter and completing the exercises, you will be able to:

- Explain basic data transmission concepts, including full duplexing, attenuation, and noise

- Describe the physical characteristics of coaxial cable, STP, UTP, and fiber-optic media

- Compare the benefits and limitations of different networking media

- Identify the best practices for cabling buildings and work areas

- Specify the characteristics of popular wireless transmission methods, including 802.11, infrared, and Bluetooth

Just as highways and streets provide the foundation for automobile travel, networking media provide the physical foundation of data transmission. Media are the physical or atmospheric paths that signals follow. The first networks transmitted data over thick, heavy coaxial cables. Today, data is commonly transmitted over a newer type of cable—one that resembles telephone cords, with their flexible outsides and twisted copper wire insides. For long-distance network connections, fiber-optic cable is preferred. And more and more, organizations are sending signals through the atmosphere to form wireless networks. Because networks are always evolving and demanding greater speed, versatility, and reliability, networking media change rapidly.

Network problems often occur at or below the Physical layer. Therefore, understanding the characteristics of various networking media is critical to designing and troubleshooting networks. You also need to know how data is transmitted over the media. This chapter discusses network media and the details of data transmission. You'll learn what it takes to make data transmission dependable and how to correct some common transmission problems.

Transmission Basics

In data networking, the term **transmit** means to issue signals to the network medium. **Transmission** refers to either the process of transmitting or the progress of signals after they have been transmitted. In other words, you could say, "My NIC transmitted a message, but because the network is slow, the transmission took 10 seconds to reach the server."

Long ago, people transmitted information across distances via smoke or fire signals. Needless to say, many different methods of data transmission have evolved since that time. The transmission techniques in use on today's networks are complex and varied. In the following sections, you will learn about some fundamental characteristics that define today's data transmission. In later chapters, you will learn about more subtle and specific differences between types of data transmission.

Analog and Digital Signaling

One important characteristic of data transmission is the type of signaling involved. On a data network, information can be transmitted via one of two signaling methods: analog or digital. Both types of signals are generated by electrical current, the pressure of which is measured in **volts**. The strength of an electrical signal is directly proportional to its voltage. Thus, when network engineers talk about the strength of an analog or digital signal, they often refer to the signal's **voltage**.

The essential difference between analog and digital signals is the way voltage creates the signal. In **analog** signals, voltage varies continuously and appears as a wavy line when graphed over time, as shown in Figure 3-1. Your speech, a siren, and live music are all examples of analog waves.

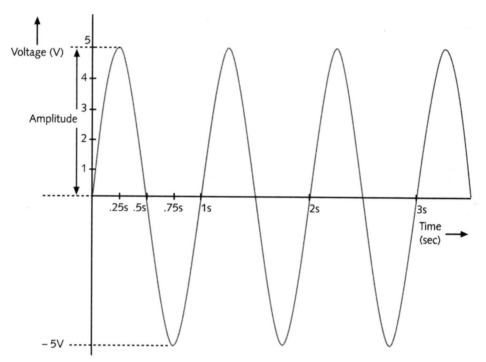

FIGURE 3-1 *An example of an analog signal*

An analog signal, like other waveforms, is characterized by four fundamental properties: amplitude, frequency, wavelength, and phase. A wave's **amplitude** is a measure of its strength at any given point in time. On a wave graph, the amplitude is the height of the wave at any point in time. In Figure 3-1, for example, the wave has an amplitude of 5 volts at .25 seconds, an amplitude of 0 volts at .5 seconds, and an amplitude of -5 volts at .75 seconds.

Whereas amplitude indicates an analog wave's strength, **frequency** is the number of times that a wave's amplitude cycles from its starting point, through its highest amplitude and its lowest amplitude, and back to its starting point over a fixed period of time. Frequency is expressed in cycles per second, or **hertz (Hz)**, named after German physicist Heinrich Hertz, who experimented with electromagnetic waves in the late nineteenth century. For example, in Figure 3-1 the wave cycles to its highest then lowest amplitude and returns to its starting point once in 1 second. Thus, the frequency of that wave would be 1 cycle per second, or 1 Hz—which, as it turns out, is an extremely low frequency.

Frequencies used to convey speech over telephone wires fall in the 300 to 3300 Hz range. Humans can hear frequencies between 20 and 20,000 Hz. An FM radio station may use a frequency between 850,000 Hz (or 850 KHz) and 108,000,000 Hz (or 108 MHz) to transmit its signal through the air. You will learn more about radio frequencies used in networking later in this chapter.

The distance between corresponding points on a wave's cycle is called its **wavelength**. Wavelengths can be expressed in meters or feet. A wave's wavelength is inversely proportional to its frequency. In other words, the higher the frequency, the shorter the wavelength. For example, a radiowave with a frequency of 1,000,000 cycles per second (1 MHz) has a wavelength of 300 meters, while a wave with a frequency of 2,000,000 Hz (2 MHz) has a wavelength of 150 meters.

The term **phase** refers to the progress of a wave over time in relationship to a fixed point. Suppose two separate waves have identical amplitudes and frequencies. If one wave starts at its lowest amplitude at the same time the second wave starts at its highest amplitude, these waves will have different phases. More precisely, they will be 180 degrees out of phase (using the standard assignment of 360 degrees to one complete wave). Had the second wave also started at its lowest amplitude, the two waves would be in phase. Figure 3-2 illustrates waves with identical amplitudes and frequencies whose phases are 90 degrees apart.

One benefit to analog signals is that, because they are more variable than digital signals, they can convey greater subtleties with less energy. For example, think of the difference between your voice and the digital voice of a digital answering machine. The digital voice has a poorer quality than your own voice—that is, it sounds "like a machine." It can't convey the subtle changes in inflection that you expect in a human voice. Only very high-quality digital signals—for example, those used to record music on compact discs—can achieve such accuracy.

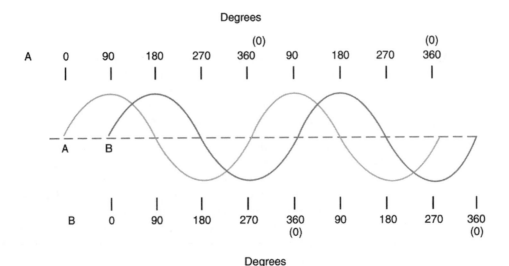

FIGURE 3-2 *Waves with a 90-degree phase difference*

However, because voltage is varied and imprecise in analog signals, analog transmission is more susceptible to transmission flaws such as **noise**, or any type of interference that may degrade a signal, than digital signals. If you have tried to listen to AM radio on a stormy night, you have probably heard the crackle and static of noise affecting the signal.

Now contrast the analog signals pictured in Figures 3-1 and 3-2 to a digital signal, as shown in Figure 3-3. **Digital** signals are composed of pulses of precise, positive voltages and zero voltages. A pulse of positive voltage represents a 1. A pulse of zero voltage (in other words, the lack of any voltage) represents a 0. The use of 1s and 0s to represent information is characteristic of a **binary** system. Every pulse in the digital signal is called a binary digit, or **bit**. A bit can have only one of two possible values: 1 or 0. Eight bits together form a **byte**. In broad terms, one byte carries one piece of information. For example, the byte "01111001" means "121" on a digital network.

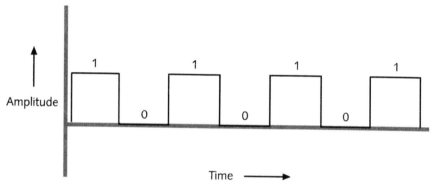

FIGURE 3-3 *An example of a digital signal*

Computers read and write information—for example, program instructions, routing information, and network addresses—in bits and bytes. When a number is represented in binary form (for example, "01111001"), each bit position, or placeholder, in the number represents a specific multiple of 2. Because a byte contains eight bits, it has eight placeholders. When counting placeholders in a byte, you move from right to left. The placeholder farthest to the right is known as the zero position, the one to its left is in the first position, and so on. The placeholder farthest to the left is in the seventh position, as shown in Figure 3-4.

# IP address	host name	alias
132.55.78.109	bingo.games.com	bingo
132.55.78.110	parcheesi.games.com	parcheesi
132.55.78.111	checkers.games.com	checkers
132.55.78.112	darts.games.com	darts

FIGURE 3-4 *Components of a byte*

To find the decimal value of a bit, you multiply the 1 or 0 (whichever the bit is set to) by 2^x, where x equals the bit's position. For example, the 1 or 0 in the zero position must be multiplied by 2 to the 0 power, or 2^0, to determine its value. Any number (other than zero) raised to the power of 0 has a value of 1. Thus, if the zero-position bit is 1, it represents a value of 1 $\times 2^0$, or 1 x 1, which equals 1. If a 0 is in the zero position, its value equals 0 x 2^0, or 0 x 1, which equals 0. In every position, if a bit is 0, that position represents a decimal number of 0.

To convert a byte to a decimal number, determine the value represented by each bit, then add those values together. If a bit in the byte is 1 (in other words, if it's "on"), the bit's numerical equivalent in the coding scheme is added to the total. If a bit is 0, that position has no value and nothing is added to the total. For example, the byte 11111111 equals: $1\times2^7 + 1\times2^6 + 1\times2^5 + 1\times2^4 + 1\times2^3 + 1\times2^2 + 1\times2^1 + 1\times2^0$, or 128 + 64 + 32 + 16 + 8 + 4 + 2 + 1. Its decimal equivalent, then, is 255. In another example, the byte 00100100 equals: $0\times2^7 + 0\times2^6 + 1\times2^5 + 0\times2^4 + 0\times2^3 + 1\times2^2 + 0\times2^1 + 0\times2^0$, or 0 + 0 + 32 + 0 + 0 + 4 + 0 + 0. Its decimal equivalent, then, is 36.

Figure 3-4 illustrates placeholders in a byte, the exponential multiplier for each position, and the different decimal values that are represented by a 1 in each position.

To convert a decimal number to a byte, you reverse this process. For example, the decimal number 8 equals 2^3, which means a single "on" bit would be indicated in the fourth bit position as follows: 00001000. In another example, the decimal number 9 equals 8 + 1, or $2^3 + 2^0$, and would be represented by the binary number 00001001.

The binary numbering scheme may be used with more than eight positions. However, in the digital world, bytes form the building blocks for messages, and bytes always include eight positions. In a data signal, multiple bytes are combined to form a message. If you were to peek at the 1s and 0s used to transmit an entire e-mail message, for example, you might see millions of zeros and ones passing by. A computer can quickly translate these binary numbers into codes, such as ASCII or JPEG, that express letters, numbers, and pictures.

Converting between decimal and binary numbers can be done by hand, as shown previously, or by using a scientific calculator, such as the one available with the Windows XP operating system. Take, for example, the number 131. To convert it to a binary number:

1. On a Windows XP computer, click **Start**, point to **All Programs**, point to **Accessories**, and then click **Calculator**.

2. Click **View**, and then click **Scientific**. Make sure that the **Dec** option button is selected.

3. Type **131**, and then click the **Bin** option button. The binary equivalent of the number 131, 10000011, appears in the display window.

4. Close the Calculator window.

You can reverse this process to convert a binary number to a decimal number.

Because digital transmission involves sending and receiving only a pattern of 1s and 0s, represented by precise pulses, it is more reliable than analog transmission, which relies on variable waves. In addition, noise affects digital transmission less severely. On the other hand, digital transmission requires many pulses to transmit the same amount of information that an analog signal can transmit with a single wave. Nevertheless, the high reliability of digital transmission makes this extra signaling worthwhile. In the end, digital transmission is more efficient than analog transmission because it results in fewer errors and, therefore, requires less overhead to compensate for errors.

Overhead is a term used by networking professionals to describe the nondata information that must accompany data for a signal to be properly routed and interpreted by the network. For example, the Data Link layer header and trailer, the Network layer addressing information, and the Transport layer flow control information added to a piece of data in order to send it over the network are all part of the transmission's overhead.

It is important to understand that in both the analog and digital worlds, a variety of signaling techniques are used. For each technique, standards dictate what type of transmitter, communications channel, and receiver should be used. For example, the type of transmitter (NIC) used for computers on a LAN and the way in which this transmitter manipulates electric current to produce signals is different from the transmitter and signaling techniques used with a satellite link. While not all signaling methods are covered in this book, you will learn about the most common methods used for data networking.

Data Modulation

NET+
1.6

Data relies almost exclusively on digital transmission. However, in some cases the type of connection your network uses may be capable of handling only analog signals. For example, telephone lines are designed to carry analog signals. If you dial into an ISP's network to surf the Internet, the data signals issued by your computer must be converted into analog form before they get to the phone line. Later, they must be converted back into digital form when they arrive at the ISP's access server. A modem accomplishes this translation. The word **modem** reflects this device's function as a *mod*ulator/*dem*odulator—that is, it modulates digital signals into analog signals at the transmitting end, then demodulates analog signals into digital signals at the receiving end.

Data modulation is a technology used to modify analog signals to make them suitable for carrying data over a communication path. In **modulation**, a simple wave, called a carrier wave, is combined with another analog signal to produce a unique signal that gets transmitted from one node to another. The carrier wave has preset properties (including frequency, amplitude, and phase). Its purpose is to help convey information; in other words, it is only a messenger. Another signal, known as the information or data wave, is added to the carrier wave. When the information wave is added, it modifies one property of the carrier wave (for example, the frequency, amplitude, or phase). The result is a new, blended signal that contains properties of both the carrier wave and added data. When the signal reaches its destination, the receiver separates the data from the carrier wave.

Modulation can be used to make a signal conform to a specific pathway, as in the case of **FM (frequency modulation)** radio, in which the data must travel along a particular frequency. In frequency modulation, the frequency of the carrier signal is modified by the application of the data signal. In **AM (amplitude modulation)**, the amplitude of the carrier signal is modified by

NET+
1.6

the application of the data signal. Modulation may also be used to issue multiple signals to the same communications channel and prevent the signals from interfering with one another. Figure 3-5 depicts an unaltered carrier wave, a data wave, and the combined wave as modified through frequency modulation. Later in this book you will learn about networking technologies, such as DSL, that make use of modulation.

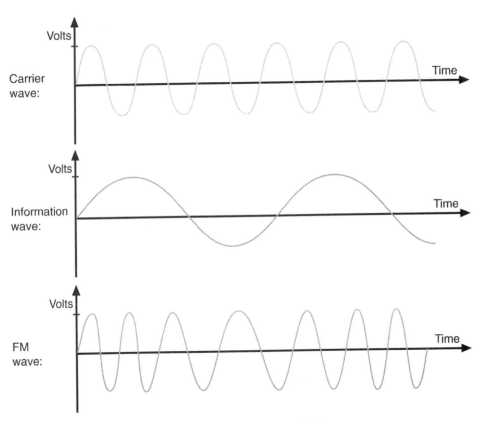

FIGURE 3-5 *A carrier wave modified through frequency modulation*

Transmission Direction

Data transmission, whether analog or digital, may also be characterized by the direction in which the signals travel over the media.

Simplex, Half-Duplex, and Duplex

In cases in which signals may travel in only one direction, the transmission is considered **simplex**. An example of simplex communication is a football coach calling out orders to his team through a megaphone. In this example, the coach's voice is the signal, and it travels in only one direction—away from the megaphone's mouthpiece and toward the team. Simplex is sometimes called one-way, or unidirectional, communication.

In **half-duplex** transmission, signals may travel in both directions over a medium but in only one direction at a time. Half-duplex systems contain only one channel for communication, and that channel must be shared for multiple nodes to exchange information. For example, an apartment's intercom system that requires you to press a "talk" button to allow your voice to be transmitted over the wire uses half-duplex transmission. If you visit a friend's apartment building, you press the "talk" button to send your voice signals to his apartment. When your friend responds, he presses the "talk" button in his apartment to send his voice signal in the opposite direction over the wire to the speaker in the lobby where you wait. If you press the "talk" button while he's talking, you will not be able to hear his voice transmission. In a similar manner, some networks operate with only half-duplex capability.

When signals are free to travel in both directions over a medium simultaneously, the transmission is considered **full-duplex**. Full-duplex may also be called bidirectional transmission or, sometimes, simply **duplex**. When you call a friend on the telephone, your connection is an example of a full-duplex transmission, because your voice signals can be transmitted to your friend at the same time your friend's voice signals are transmitted in the opposite direction to you. In other words, both of you can talk and hear each other simultaneously.

Figure 3-6 compares simplex, half-duplex, and full-duplex transmissions.

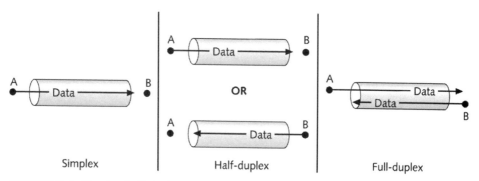

FIGURE 3-6 *Simplex, half-duplex, and full-duplex transmission*

Full-duplex transmission is also used on data networks. For example, modern Ethernet networks are capable of full-duplex. In this situation, full-duplex transmission uses multiple channels on the same medium. A **channel** is a distinct communication path between nodes, much as a lane is a distinct transportation path on a freeway. Channels may be separated either logically or physically. You will learn about logically separate channels in the next section. An example of physically separate channels occurs when one wire within a network cable is used for transmission while another wire is used for reception. In this example, each separate wire in the medium allows half-duplex transmission. When combined in a cable, they form a medium that provides full-duplex transmission. Full-duplex capability increases the speed with which data can travel over a network. In some cases—for example, telephone service over the Internet—full-duplex data networks are a requirement.

Many network devices, such as modems and NICs, allow you to specify whether the device should use half- or full-duplex communication. It's important to know what type of transmission a network supports before installing network devices on that network. If you configure a computer's NIC to use full-duplex while the rest of the network is using half-duplex, for example, that computer will not be able to communicate on the network.

Multiplexing

A form of transmission that allows multiple signals to travel simultaneously over one medium is known as **multiplexing**. To carry multiple signals, the medium's channel is logically separated into multiple smaller channels, or **subchannels**. Many different types of multiplexing are available and the type used in any given situation depends on what the media, transmission, and reception equipment can handle. For each type of multiplexing, a device that can combine many signals on a channel, a **multiplexer (mux)**, is required at the sending end of the channel. At the receiving end, a **demultiplexer (demux)** separates the combined signals and regenerates them in their original form.

Multiplexing is commonly used on networks to increase the amount of data that can be transmitted in a given time span. One type of multiplexing, **TDM (time division multiplexing)**, divides a channel into multiple intervals of time, or time slots. It then assigns a separate time slot to every node on the network and, in that time slot, carries data from that node. For example, if five stations are connected to a network over one wire, five different time slots are established in the communications channel. Workstation A may be assigned time slot 1, workstation B time slot 2, workstation C time slot 3, and so on. Time slots are reserved for their designated nodes regardless of whether the node has data to transmit. If a node does not have data to send, nothing is sent during its time slot. This arrangement can be inefficient if some nodes on the network rarely send data. Figure 3-7 shows a simple TDM model.

Statistical multiplexing is similar to time division multiplexing, but rather than assigning a separate slot to each node in succession, the transmitter assigns slots to nodes according to priority and need. This method is more efficient than TDM, because in statistical multiplexing

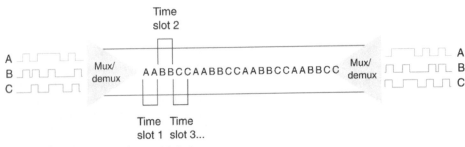

FIGURE 3-7 *Time division multiplexing*

time slots are unlikely to remain empty. To begin with, in statistical multiplexing, as in TDM, each node is assigned one time slot. However, if a node doesn't use its time slot, statistical multiplexing devices recognize that and assign its slot to another node that needs to send data. The contention for slots may be arbitrated according to use or priority or even more sophisticated factors, depending on the network. Most importantly, statistical multiplexing maximizes available bandwidth on a network. Figure 3-8 depicts a simple statistical multiplexing system.

FIGURE 3-8 *Statistical multiplexing*

WDM (wavelength division multiplexing) is a technology used with fiber-optic cable. In fiber-optic transmission, data is represented as pulses of light, rather than pulses of electric current. WDM enables one fiber-optic connection to carry multiple light signals simultaneously. Using WDM, a single fiber can transmit as many as 20 million telephone conversations at one time. WDM can work over any type of fiber-optic cable.

In the first step of WDM, a beam of light is divided into up to 40 different carrier waves, each with a different wavelength (and therefore, a different color). Each wavelength represents a separate transmission channel capable of transmitting up to 10 Gbps. Before transmission, each carrier wave is modulated with a different data signal. Then, through a very narrow beam of light, lasers issue the separate, modulated waves to a multiplexer. The multiplexer combines all of the waves, in the same way that a prism can accept light beams of different wavelengths and concentrate them into a single beam of white light. Next, another laser issues this multiplexed beam to a strand of fiber within a fiber-optic cable. The fiber carries the multiplexed signals to a receiver, which is connected to a demultiplexer. The demultiplexer acts as a prism to separate the combined signals according to their different wavelengths (or colors). Then, the separate waves are sent to their destinations on the network. If the signal risks losing strength between the multiplexer and demultiplexer, an amplifier might be used to boost it. Figure 3-9 illustrates WDM transmission.

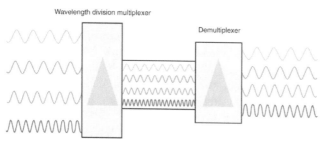

FIGURE 3-9 *Wavelength division multiplexing*

The form of WDM used on most modern fiber-optic networks is **DWDM (dense wave division multiplexing)**. In DWDM, a single fiber in a fiber-optic cable can carry between 80 and 160 channels. It achieves this increased capacity because it uses more wavelengths for signaling. In other words, there is less separation between the usable carrier waves in DWDM than there is in the original form of WDM. Because of its extraordinary capacity, DWDM is typically used on high-bandwidth or long-distance WAN links, such as the connection between a large ISP and its (even larger) network service provider.

Relationships Between Nodes

So far you have learned about two important characteristics of data transmission: the type of signaling (analog or digital) and the direction in which the signal travels (simplex, half-duplex, full-duplex, or multiplex). Another important characteristic is the number of senders and receivers, as well as the relationship between them. In general, data communications may involve a single transmitter with one or more receivers, or multiple transmitters with one or more receivers. The remainder of this section introduces the most common relationships between transmitters and receivers.

When a data transmission involves only one transmitter and one receiver, it is considered a **point-to-point** transmission. An office building in Dallas exchanging data with another office in St. Louis over a WAN connection is an example of point-to-point transmission. In this case, the sender only transmits data that is intended to be used by a specific receiver. By contrast, **broadcast** transmission involves one transmitter and multiple receivers. For example, a TV station indiscriminately transmitting a signal from its tower to thousands of homes with TV antennas uses broadcast transmission. A broadcast transmission sends data to any and all receivers, without regard for which receiver can use it. Broadcast transmissions are frequently used on networks because they are simple and quick. They are used to identify certain nodes, to send data to certain nodes (even though every node is capable of picking up the transmitted data, only the destination node will actually do it), and to send announcements to all nodes. Another example of network broadcast transmission is sending video signals to multiple viewers on a network. When used over the Web, this type of broadcast transmission is called **Webcasting**. Figure 3-10 contrasts point-to-point and broadcast transmissions.

Throughput and Bandwidth

The data transmission characteristic most frequently discussed and analyzed by networking professionals is throughput. **Throughput** is the measure of how much data is transmitted during a given period of time. It may also be called **capacity** or bandwidth (though as you will learn, bandwidth is technically different from throughput). Throughput is commonly expressed as a quantity of bits transmitted per second, with prefixes used to designate different throughput amounts. For example, the prefix "kilo" combined with the word "bit" (as in "kilobit") indicates 1000 bits per second. Rather than talking about a throughput of 1000 bits per second, you typically say the throughput was 1 kilobit per second (1 Kbps). Table 3-1 summarizes the terminology and abbreviations used when discussing different throughput amounts. As an example,

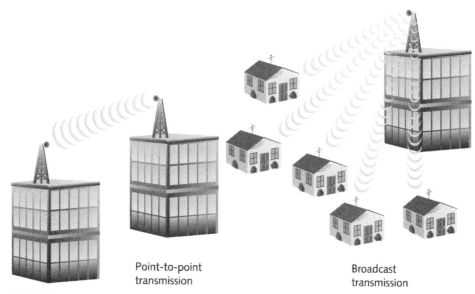

Point-to-point
transmission

Broadcast
transmission

FIGURE 3-10 *Point-to-point versus broadcast transmission*

a typical modem connecting a home PC to the Internet would probably be rated for a maximum throughput of 56.6 Kbps. A fast LAN might transport up to 10 Gbps of data. Contemporary networks commonly achieve throughputs of 10 Mbps, 100 Mbps, or 1 Gbps.

Table 3-1 Throughput measures

Quantity	Prefix	Complete Example	Abbreviation
1 bit per second	n/a	1 bit per second	bps
1000 bits per second	kilo	1 kilobit per second	Kbps
1,000,000 bits per second	mega	1 megabit per second	Mbps
1,000,000,000 bits per second	giga	1 gigabit per second	Gbps
1,000,000,000,000 bits per second	tera	1 terabit per second	Tbps

 NOTE

Be careful not to confuse bits and bytes when discussing throughput. Although data storage quantities are typically expressed in multiples of bytes, data transmission quantities (in other words, throughput) are more commonly expressed in multiples of bits per second. When representing different data quantities, a small "b" represents

> bits, while a capital "B" represents bytes. To put this into context, a modem may transmit data at 56.6 Kbps (kilobits per second); a data file may be 56 KB (kilobytes) in size. Another difference between data storage and data throughput measures is that in data storage the prefix kilo means "2 to the 10th power," or "1024," not "1000."

Often, the term "bandwidth" is used interchangeably with throughput, and in fact, this may be the case on the Network+ certification exam. Bandwidth and throughput are similar concepts, but strictly speaking, **bandwidth** is a measure of the difference between the highest and lowest frequencies that a medium can transmit. This range of frequencies, which is expressed in Hz, is directly related to throughput. For example, if the FCC told you that you could transmit a radio signal between 870 and 880 MHz, your allotted bandwidth (literally, the width of your frequency band) would be 10 MHz.

Baseband and Broadband

Baseband is a transmission form in which (typically) digital signals are sent through direct current (DC) pulses applied to the wire. This direct current requires exclusive use of the wire's capacity. As a result, baseband systems can transmit only one signal, or one channel, at a time. Every device on a baseband system shares the same channel. When one node is transmitting data on a baseband system, all other nodes on the network must wait for that transmission to end before they can send data. Baseband transmission supports half-duplexing, which means that computers can both send and receive information on the same length of wire. In some cases, baseband also supports full duplexing.

Ethernet is an example of a baseband system found on many LANs. In Ethernet, each device on a network can transmit over the wire—but only one device at a time. For example, if you want to save a file to the server, your NIC submits your request to use the wire; if no other device is using the wire to transmit data at that time, your workstation can go ahead. If the wire is in use, your workstation must wait and try again later. Of course, this retrying process happens so quickly that you don't even notice the wait.

Broadband is a form of transmission in which signals are modulated as radiofrequency (RF) analog waves that use different frequency ranges. Unlike baseband, broadband technology does not encode information as digital pulses.

As you may know, broadband transmission is used to bring cable TV to your home. Your cable TV connection can carry at least 25 times as much data as a typical baseband system (like Ethernet) carries, including many different broadcast frequencies on different channels. In traditional broadband systems, signals travel in only one direction—toward the user. To allow users to send data as well, cable systems allot a separate channel space for the user's transmission and use amplifiers that can separate data the user issues from data the network transmits. Broadband transmission is generally more expensive than baseband transmission because of the extra hardware involved. On the other hand, broadband systems can span longer distances than baseband.

In the field of networking, some terms have more than one meaning, depending on their context. "Broadband" is one of those terms. The "broadband" described in this chapter is the transmission system that carries RF signals across multiple channels on a coaxial cable, as used by cable TV. This definition was the original meaning of broadband. However, broadband has evolved to mean any of several different network types that use digital signaling to transmit data at very high transmission rates.

Transmission Flaws

NET+
4.8

Both analog and digital signals are susceptible to degradation between the time they are issued by a transmitter and the time they are received. One of the most common transmission flaws affecting data signals is noise.

Noise

As you learned earlier, noise is any undesirable influence that may degrade or distort a signal. Many different types of noise may affect transmission. A common source of noise is **EMI (electromagnetic interference),** or waves that emanate from electrical devices or cables carrying electricity. Motors, power lines, televisions, copiers, fluorescent lights, manufacturing machinery, and other sources of electrical activity (including a severe thunderstorm) can cause EMI. One type of EMI is **RFI (radiofrequency interference),** or electromagnetic interference caused by radiowaves. (Often, you'll see EMI referred to as EMI/RFI.) Strong broadcast signals from radio or TV towers can generate RFI. When EMI noise affects analog signals, this distortion can result in the incorrect transmission of data, just as if static prevented you from hearing a radio station broadcast. However, this type of noise affects digital signals much less. Because digital signals do not depend on subtle amplitude or frequency differences to communicate information, they are more apt to be readable despite distortions caused by EMI noise.

Another form of noise that hinders data transmission is crosstalk. **Crosstalk** occurs when a signal traveling on one wire or cable infringes on the signal traveling over an adjacent wire or cable. If you have ever been on the phone and heard the conversation on your second line in the background, you have heard the effects of crosstalk. In this example, the current carrying a signal on the second line's wire imposes itself on the wire carrying your line's signal, as shown in Figure 3-11. The resulting noise, or crosstalk, is equal to a portion of the second line's signal. Crosstalk in the form of overlapping phone conversations is bothersome, but does not usually prevent you from hearing your own line's conversation. In data networks, however, crosstalk can be extreme enough to prevent the accurate delivery of data.

In addition to EMI and crosstalk, less obvious environmental influences, including heat, can also cause noise. In every signal, a certain amount of noise is unavoidable. However, engineers have designed a number of ways to limit the potential for noise to degrade a signal. One way is simply to ensure that the strength of the signal exceeds the strength of the noise. Proper cable design and installation are also critical for protecting against noise's effects. Note that all forms of noise are measured in decibels (dB).

NET+
4.8

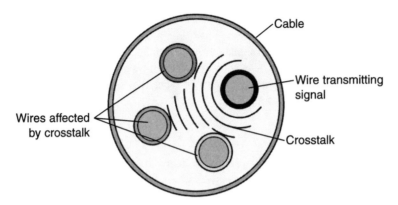

FIGURE 3-11 *Crosstalk between wires in a cable*

Attenuation

Another transmission flaw is **attenuation**, or the loss of a signal's strength as it travels away from its source. To compensate for attenuation, both analog and digital signals are strengthened en route so they can travel farther. However, the technology used to strengthen an analog signal is different from that used to strengthen a digital signal. Analog signals pass through an **amplifier**, an electronic device that increases the voltage, or strength, of the signals. When an analog signal is amplified, the noise that it has accumulated is also amplified. This indiscriminate amplification causes the analog signal to worsen progressively. After multiple amplifications, an analog signal may become difficult to decipher. Figure 3-12 shows an analog signal distorted by noise and then amplified once.

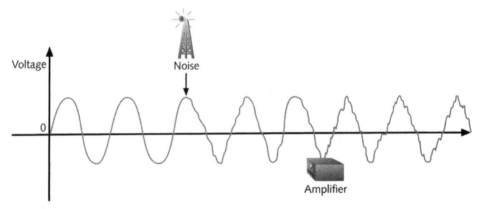

FIGURE 3-12 *An analog signal distorted by noise and then amplified*

NET+
4.8

When digital signals are repeated, they are actually retransmitted in their original form, without the noise they may have accumulated previously. This process is known as **regeneration**. A device that regenerates a digital signal is called a **repeater**. Figure 3-13 shows a digital signal distorted by noise and then regenerated by a repeater.

Amplifiers and repeaters belong to the Physical layer of the OSI Model. Both are used to extend the length of a network. Because most networks are digital, however, they typically use repeaters.

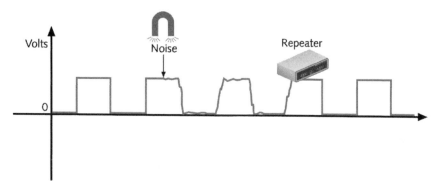

FIGURE 3-13 *A digital signal distorted by noise and then repeated*

Latency

In an ideal world, networks could transmit data instantaneously between sender and receiver, no matter how great the distance between the two. However, in the real world every network is subjected to a delay between the transmission of a signal and its eventual receipt. For example, when you press a key on your computer to save a file to the network, the file's data must travel through your NIC, the network wire, a one or more connectivity devices, more cabling, and the server's NIC before it lands on the server's hard disk. Although electrons travel rapidly, they still have to travel, and a brief delay takes place between the moment you press the key and the moment the server accepts the data. This delay is called **latency**.

The length of the cable involved affects latency, as does the existence of any intervening connectivity device, such as a router. Different devices affect latency to different degrees. For example, modems, which must modulate both incoming and outgoing signals, increase a connection's latency far more than hubs, which simply repeat a signal. The most common way to measure latency on data networks is by calculating a packet's **RTT (round trip time)**, or the length of time it takes for a packet to go from sender to receiver, then back from receiver to sender. RTT is usually measured in milliseconds.

Latency causes problems only when a receiving node is expecting some type of communication, such as the rest of a data stream it has begun to accept. If that node does not receive the rest of the data stream within a given time period, it assumes that no more data is coming. This assumption may cause transmission errors on a network. When you connect multiple

NET+
4.8
network segments and thereby increase the distance between sender and receiver, you increase the latency in the network. To constrain the latency and avoid its associated errors, each type of cabling is rated for a maximum number of connected network segments and each transmission method is assigned a maximum segment length.

Common Media Characteristics

Now that you are familiar with variations in data signaling, you are ready to learn more about the physical and atmospheric paths that these signals traverse. When deciding which kind of transmission media to use, you must match your networking needs with the characteristics of the media. This section describes the characteristics of all types of media, including throughput, cost, size and scalability, connectors, and noise immunity.

Throughput

Perhaps the most significant factor in choosing a transmission method is its throughput. All media are limited by the laws of physics that prevent signals from traveling faster than the speed of light. Beyond that, throughput is limited by the signaling and multiplexing techniques used in a given transmission method. Transmission methods using fiber-optic cables achieve faster throughput than those using copper or wireless connections. Noise and devices connected to the transmission medium can further limit throughput. A noisy circuit spends more time compensating for the noise and, therefore, has fewer resources available for transmitting data.

Cost

The precise costs of using a particular type of cable or wireless connection are often difficult to pinpoint. For example, although a vendor might quote you the cost-per-foot for new network cabling, you might also have to upgrade some hardware on your network to use that type of cabling. Thus, the cost of upgrading your media would actually include more than the cost of the cabling itself. Not only do media costs depend on the hardware that already exists in a network, but they also depend on the size of your network and the cost of labor in your area (unless you plan to install the cable yourself). The following variables can all influence the final cost of implementing a certain type of media:

◆ *Cost of installation*—Can you install the media yourself, or must you hire contractors to do it? Will you need to move walls or build new conduits or closets? Will you need to lease lines from a service provider?

◆ *Cost of new infrastructure versus reusing existing infrastructure*—Can you use existing wiring? In some cases, for example, installing all new Category 7 UTP wiring may not pay off if you can use existing Category 5 UTP wiring. If you replace only part of your infrastructure, will it be easily integrated with the existing media?

◆ *Cost of maintenance and support*—Reuse of an existing cabling infrastructure does not save any money if it is in constant need of repair or enhancement. Also, if you use an unfamiliar media type, it may cost more to hire a technician to service it. Will you be able to service the media yourself, or must you hire contractors to service it?

◆ *Cost of a lower transmission rate affecting productivity*—If you save money by reusing existing slower lines, are you incurring costs by reducing productivity? In other words, are you making staff wait longer to save and print reports or exchange e-mail?

◆ *Cost of obsolescence*—Are you choosing media that may become passing fads, requiring rapid replacement? Will you be able to find reasonably priced connectivity hardware that will be compatible with your chosen media for years to come?

Size and Scalability

Three specifications determine the size and scalability of networking media: maximum nodes per segment, maximum segment length, and maximum network length. In cabling, each of these specifications is based on the physical characteristics of the wire and the electrical characteristics of data transmission. The maximum number of nodes per segment depends on attenuation and latency. Each device added to a network segment causes a slight increase in the signal's attenuation and latency. To ensure a clear, strong, and timely signal, you must limit the number of nodes on a segment.

The maximum segment length depends on attenuation and latency plus the segment type. A network can include two types of segments: populated and unpopulated. A **populated segment** is a part of a network that contains end nodes. For example, a hub connecting users in a classroom is part of a populated segment. An **unpopulated segment**, also known as a **link segment**, is a part of the network that does not contain end nodes, but simply connects two networking devices such as hubs.

Segment lengths are limited because after a certain distance, a signal loses so much strength that it cannot be accurately interpreted. The maximum distance a signal can travel and still be interpreted accurately is equal to a segment's maximum length. Beyond this length, data loss is apt to occur. As with the maximum number of nodes per segment, maximum segment length varies between different cabling types. The same principle of data loss applies to maximum network length, which is the sum of the network's segment lengths.

Connectors and Media Converters

NET+
1.4

Connectors are the pieces of hardware that connect the wire to the network device, be it a file server, workstation, switch, or printer. Every networking medium requires a specific kind of connector. The type of connectors you use will affect the cost of installing and maintaining the network, the ease of adding new segments or nodes to the network, and the technical expertise required to maintain the network. The connectors you are most likely to encounter on modern networks are illustrated throughout this chapter and shown together in Appendix C.

NET+
1.4
1.6

Connectors are specific to a particular media type, but that doesn't prevent one network from using multiple media. Some connectivity devices are designed to accept more than one type of media. If you are working with a connectivity device that can't, you can integrate the two media types by using media converters. A media converter is a piece of hardware that enables networks or segments running on different media to interconnect and exchange signals. For example, suppose a segment leading from your company's data center to a group of workstations uses fiber-optic cable, but the workgroup hub can only accept twisted-pair (copper) cable. In that case, you could use a media converter to interconnect the hub with the fiber-optic cable. The media converter completes the physical connection and also converts the electrical signals from the copper cable to light wave signals that can traverse the fiber-optic cable, and vice versa. Such a media converter is shown in Figure 3-14.

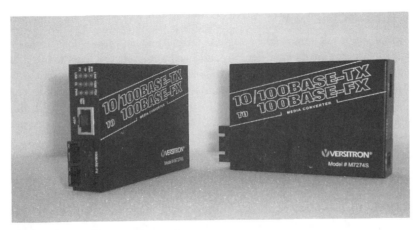

FIGURE 3-14 *UTP-to-fiber media converter*

A media converter is a type of **transceiver**, a device that transmits and receives signals. Because transmitting and receiving signals is also an important function of NICs, NICs can also be considered transceivers.

Noise Immunity

As you learned earlier, noise can distort data signals. The extent to which noise affects a signal depends partly on the transmission media. Some types of media are more susceptible to noise than others. The type of media least susceptible to noise is fiber-optic cable, because it does not use electric current, but light waves, to conduct signals.

On most networks, noise is an ever-present threat, so you should take measures to limit its impact on your network. For example, you should install cabling well away from powerful electromagnetic forces. If your environment still leaves your network vulnerable, you should choose a type of transmission media that helps to protect the signal from noise. For example, wireless signals are more apt to be distorted by EMI/RFI than signals traveling over a cable. It is also possible to use antinoise algorithms to protect data from being corrupted by noise. If these measures don't ward off interference, in the case of wired media, you may need to use a metal **conduit**, or pipeline, to contain and further protect the cabling.

Now that you understand data transmission and the factors to consider when choosing a transmission medium, you are ready to learn about different types of transmission media. To qualify for Network+ certification, you must know the characteristics and limitations of each type of media, how to install and design a network with each type, how to troubleshoot networking media problems, and how to provide for future network growth with each option. The terms "wire" and "cable" are used synonymously in some situations. Strictly speaking, however, "wire" is a subset of "cabling," because the "cabling" category may also include fiber-optic cable, which is almost never called "wire." The exact meaning of the term "wire" depends on context. For example, if you said, in a somewhat casual way, "We had 6 Gigs of data go over the wire last night," you would be referring to whatever transmission media helped carry the data—whether fiber, radio waves, coax, or UTP.

Coaxial Cable

NET+
1.5

Coaxial cable, called "coax" for short, was the foundation for Ethernet networks in the 1970s and remained a popular transmission medium for many years. Over time, however, twisted-pair and fiber-optic cabling have replaced coax in modern LANs. If you work on long-established networks, however, you may have to work with coaxial cable.

Coaxial cable consists of a central copper core surrounded by an insulator, a braided metal shielding, called **braiding**, and an outer cover, called the **sheath** or jacket. Figure 3-15 depicts a typical coaxial cable. The copper core may be constructed of one strand of copper or several thin strands of copper. The core carries the electromagnetic signal, and the braided metal shielding acts as both a shield against noise and a ground for the signal. The insulator layer usually consists of a plastic material such as polyvinyl chloride (PVC) or Teflon. It protects the

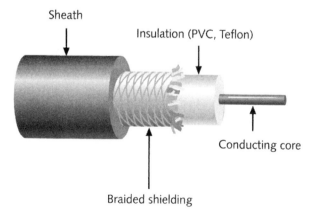

FIGURE 3-15 *Coaxial cable*

copper core from the metal shielding, because if the two made contact, the wire would short-circuit. The sheath, which protects the cable from physical damage, may be PVC or a more expensive, fire-resistant plastic.

Because of its shielding, most coaxial cable has a high resistance to noise. It can also carry signals farther than twisted-pair cabling before amplification of the signals becomes necessary (although not as far as fiber-optic cabling). On the other hand, coaxial cable is more expensive than twisted-pair cable because it requires significantly more raw materials to manufacture.

Coaxial cabling comes in hundreds of specifications, although you are likely to see only two or three types of coax in use on data networks. In any case, all types have been assigned an RG specification number. (RG stands for "radio guide," which is appropriate because coaxial cabling is used to guide radiofrequencies in broadband transmission.) The significant differences between the cable types lie in the materials used for their center cores, which in turn influence their **impedance** (or the resistance that contributes to controlling the signal, as expressed in ohms), throughput, and purpose.

Historically, data networks have used two Physical layer specifications to transmit data over coaxial cable:

◆ **Thicknet (thickwire Ethernet)**—The original Ethernet medium, Thicknet uses RG-8 coaxial cable, which is approximately 1-cm thick and contains a solid copper core. IEEE designates Thicknet as **10BASE-5** Ethernet. The "10" represents its throughput of 10 Mbps, the "Base" stands for baseband transmission, and the "5" represents the maximum segment length of a Thicknet cable, which is 500 meters. Thicknet relies on a bus topology. You will never find Thicknet on new networks, but you may find it on older networks.

◆ **Thinnet (thin Ethernet)**—A popular medium for Ethernet LANs in the 1980s, Thinnet uses RG-58A/U coaxial cable. Its diameter is approximately 0.64 cm, which makes it more flexible and easier to handle and install than Thicknet. Its core is typically made of several thin strands of copper. IEEE has designated Thinnet as **10BASE-2** Ethernet, with the "10" representing its data transmission rate of 10 Mbps, the "Base" representing the fact that it uses baseband transmission, and the "2" representing its maximum segment length of 185 meters (or roughly 200). Thinnet relies on a bus topology. Like Thicknet, Thinnet is almost never on modern networks, although you may encounter it on networks installed in the 1980s.

One situation in which you might still work with coaxial cable is if you are setting up a network that connects to the Internet through a broadband cable carrier (for example, Comcast or Charter). The cable that comes into a house from the carrier is RG-6 coaxial cable. This cable connects to a **cable modem**, a device that modulates and demodulates the broadband cable signals using an F-Type connector. F-Type connectors are threaded and screw together like a nut and bolt assembly. The pin of the connector is the conducting core of the coaxial cable. An F-Type connector is shown in Figure 3-16.

Next, you will learn about the most common media installed on modern LANs, twisted-pair cable.

FIGURE 3-16 *F-Type connector*

Twisted-Pair Cable

NET+
1.5

Twisted-pair cable consists of color-coded pairs of insulated copper wires, each with a diameter of 0.4 to 0.8 mm (approximately the diameter of a straight pin). Every two wires are twisted around each other to form pairs and all the pairs are encased in a plastic sheath, as shown in Figure 3-17. The number of pairs in a cable varies, depending on the cable type.

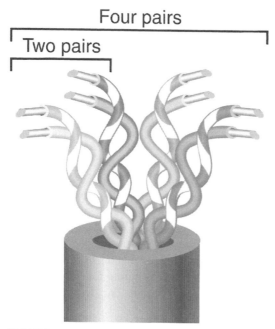

FIGURE 3-17 *Twisted-pair cable*

The more twists per inch in a pair of wires, the more resistant the pair will be to crosstalk. Higher-quality, more expensive twisted-pair cable contains more twists per foot. The number of twists per meter or foot is known as the **twist ratio**. Because twisting the wire pairs more tightly requires more cable, however, a high twist ratio can result in greater attenuation. For optimal performance, cable manufacturers must strike a balance between minimizing crosstalk and reducing attenuation.

Because twisted-pair is used in such a wide variety of environments and for a variety of purposes, it comes in hundreds of different designs. These designs vary in their twist ratio, the number of wire pairs that they contain, the grade of copper used, the type of shielding (if any), and the materials used for shielding, among other things. A twisted-pair cable may contain from 1 to 4200 wire pairs. Modern networks typically use cables that contain four wire pairs, in which one pair is dedicated to sending data and another pair is dedicated to receiving data.

In 1991, two standards organizations, the TIA/EIA, finalized their specifications for twisted-pair wiring in a standard called "TIA/EIA 568." Since then, this body has continually revised the international standards for new and modified transmission media. Its standards now cover cabling media, design, and installation specifications. The TIA/EIA 568 standard divides twisted-pair wiring into several categories. The types of UTP you will hear most about are **Level 1** (the original type of telephone wire) or CAT (category) 3, 4, 5, 5e, 6, 6e, and CAT 7. All of the category cables fall under the TIA/EIA 568 standard. Modern LANs use CAT 5 or higher wiring.

Twisted-pair cable is the most common form of cabling found on LANs today. It is relatively inexpensive, flexible, and easy to install, and it can span a significant distance before requiring a repeater (though not as far as coax). Twisted-pair cable easily accommodates several different topologies, although it is most often implemented in star or star-hybrid topologies. Furthermore, twisted-pair can handle the faster networking transmission rates currently being employed. Due to its wide acceptance, it will probably continue to be updated to handle the even faster rates that will emerge in the future. All twisted-pair cable falls into one of two categories: STP (shielded twisted-pair) or UTP (unshielded twisted-pair).

STP (Shielded Twisted-Pair)

STP (shielded twisted-pair) cable consists of twisted wire pairs that are not only individually insulated, but also surrounded by a shielding made of a metallic substance such as foil. Some STP use a braided copper shielding. The shielding acts as a barrier to external electromagnetic forces, thus preventing them from affecting the signals traveling over the wire inside the shielding. It also contains the electrical energy of the signals inside. The shielding may be grounded to enhance its protective effects. The effectiveness of STP's shield depends on the level and type of environmental noise, the thickness and material used for the shield, the grounding mechanism, and the symmetry and consistency of the shielding. Figure 3-18 depicts an STP cable.

NET+
1.5

Four
twisted
pairs

FIGURE 3-18 *STP cable*

UTP (Unshielded Twisted-Pair)

UTP (unshielded twisted-pair) cabling consists of one or more insulated wire pairs encased in a plastic sheath. As its name implies, UTP does not contain additional shielding for the twisted pairs. As a result, UTP is both less expensive and less resistant to noise than STP. Figure 3-19 depicts a typical UTP cable.

FIGURE 3-19 *UTP cable*

Earlier, you learned that the TIA/EIA consortium designated standards for twisted-pair wiring. To manage network cabling, you need to be familiar with the standards for use on modern networks, particularly CAT 3 and CAT 5 or higher.

◆ **CAT 3 (Category 3)**—A form of UTP that contains four wire pairs and can carry up to 10 Mbps of data with a possible bandwidth of 16 MHz. CAT 3 has typically been used for 10-Mbps Ethernet or 4-Mbps Token Ring networks. Network administrators are replacing their existing CAT 3 cabling with CAT 5 to accommodate higher throughput. (CAT 3 is still used for telephone wiring, however.)

◆ **CAT 4 (Category 4)**—A form of UTP that contains four wire pairs and can support up to 16 Mbps throughput. CAT 4 may be used for 16 Mbps Token Ring or 10 Mbps Ethernet networks. It is guaranteed for signals as high as 20 MHz and provides more protection against crosstalk and attenuation than CAT 1, CAT 2, or CAT 3.

◆ **CAT 5 (Category 5)**—A form of UTP that contains four wire pairs and supports up to 1000 Mbps throughput and a 100-MHz signal rate. Figure 3-20 depicts a typical CAT 5 UTP cable with its twisted pairs untwisted, allowing you to see their matched color coding. For example, the wire that is colored solid orange is twisted around the wire that is part orange and part white to form the pair responsible for transmitting data.

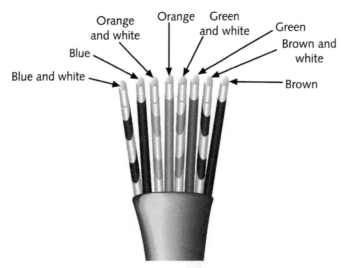

FIGURE 3-20 *A CAT 5 UTP cable with pairs untwisted*

 NOTE

It can be difficult to tell the difference between four-pair CAT 3 cables and four-pair CAT 5 or CAT 5e cables. However, some visual clues can help. On CAT 5 cable, the jacket is usually stamped with the manufacturer's name and cable type, including the CAT 5 specification. A cable whose jacket has no markings is more likely to be CAT 3. Also, pairs in CAT 5 cables have a significantly higher twist ratio than pairs in CAT 3 cables. Although CAT 3 pairs might be twisted as few as three times per foot, CAT 5 pairs are twisted at least 12 times per foot. Other clues, such as the date of installation (old cable is more likely to be CAT 3), looseness of the jacket (CAT 3's jacket is typically looser than CAT 5's), and the extent to which pairs are untwisted before a termination (CAT 5 can tolerate only a small amount of untwisting) are also helpful, though less definitive.

♦ **CAT 5e (Enhanced Category 5)**—A higher-grade version of CAT 5 wiring that contains high-quality copper, offers a high twist ratio, and uses advanced methods for reducing crosstalk. Enhanced CAT 5 can support a signaling rate as high as 350 MHz, more than triple the capability of regular CAT 5.

♦ **CAT 6 (Category 6)**—A twisted-pair cable that contains four wire pairs, each wrapped in foil insulation. Additional foil insulation covers the bundle of wire pairs, and a fire-resistant plastic sheath covers the second foil layer. The foil insulation provides excellent resistance to crosstalk and enables CAT 6 to support a 250-MHz signaling rate and at least six times the throughput supported by regular CAT 5.

♦ **CAT 6e (Enhanced Category 6)**—A higher-grade version of CAT 6 wiring that reduces attenuation and crosstalk, and allows for potentially exceeding traditional network segment length limits. CAT 6e is capable of a 550 MHz signaling rate and can reliably transmit data at multi-Gigabit per second rates.

♦ **CAT 7 (Category 7)**—A twisted-pair cable that contains multiple wire pairs, each surrounded by its own shielding, then packaged in additional shielding beneath the sheath. Although standards have not yet been finalized for CAT 7, cable supply companies are selling it, and some organizations are installing it. One advantage to CAT 7 cabling is that it can support signal rates up to 1 GHz. However, it requires different connectors than other versions of UTP because its twisted pairs must be more isolated from each other to ward off crosstalk. Because of its added shielding, CAT 7 cabling is also larger and less flexible than other versions of UTP cable. CAT 7 is uncommon on modern networks, but it will likely become popular as the final standard is released and network equipment is upgraded.

 NOTE

Technically, because CAT 6 and CAT 7 contain wires that are individually shielded, they are not unshielded twisted-pair. Instead, they are more similar to shielded twisted-pair.

UTP cabling may be used with any one of several IEEE Physical layer networking standards that specify throughput maximums of 10, 100, and 1000 Mbps. Recall that IEEE standards specify how signals are transmitted to the media. The following sections describe these standards, which you must understand to obtain Network+ certification.

 NOTE

In Ethernet technology, the most common theoretical maximum data transfer rates are 10 Mbps, 100 Mbps, and 1 Gbps. Actual data transfer rates on a network will vary, just as you might average 22 miles per gallon (mpg) driving your car to work and back, even though the manufacturer rates the car's gas mileage at 28 mpg.

NET+
1.5

Comparing STP and UTP

STP and UTP share several characteristics. The following list highlights their similarities and differences.

- ◆ *Throughput*—STP and UTP can both transmit data at 10, 100, and 1000 Mbps (1 Gbps), depending on the grade of cabling and the transmission method in use.

- ◆ *Cost*—STP and UTP vary in cost, depending on the grade of copper used, the category rating, and any enhancements. Typically, STP is more expensive than UTP because it contains more materials and it has a lower demand. High-grade UTP, however, can be very expensive. For example, CAT 6 costs more per foot than regular CAT 5 cabling.

NET+
1.4
1.5

- ◆ *Connector*—STP and UTP use **RJ-45 (Registered Jack 45)** modular connectors and data jacks, which look similar to analog telephone connectors and jacks, and which follow the **RJ-11 (Registered Jack 11)** standard. Figure 3-21 shows a close-up of an RJ-45 connector for a cable containing four wire pairs. For comparison, this figure also shows a traditional RJ-11 phone line connector. The section "Installing Cable" later in this chapter describes the use of RJ-45 connectors and data jacks in more detail.

FIGURE 3-21 *RJ-45 and RJ-11 connectors*

NET+
1.5

- ◆ *Noise immunity*—Because of its shielding, STP is more noise-resistant than UTP. On the other hand, signals transmitted over UTP may be subject to filtering and balancing techniques to offset the effects of noise.

- ◆ *Size and scalability*—The maximum segment length for both STP and UTP is 100 m, or 328 feet, on 10BASE-T and 100BASE-T networks (discussed next). These accommodate a maximum of 1024 nodes. (However, attaching so many nodes to a segment is very impractical, as it would slow traffic and make management nearly impossible.)

10BASE-T

NET+
1.2
1.3

10BASE-T is a popular Ethernet networking standard that replaced the older 10BASE-2 and 10BASE-5 technologies. The "10" represents its maximum throughput of 10 Mbps, the "Base" indicates that it uses baseband transmission, and the "T" stands for twisted pair, the medium it uses. On a 10BASE-T network, one pair of wires in the UTP cable is used for transmission, while a second pair of wires is used for reception. These two pairs of wires allow 10BASE-T networks to provide full-duplex transmission. A 10BASE-T network requires CAT 3 or higher UTP.

Nodes on a 10BASE-T Ethernet network connect to a central hub or repeater in a star fashion. As is typical of a star topology, a single network cable connects only two devices. This characteristic makes 10BASE-T networks more fault-tolerant than 10BASE-2 or 10BASE-5, both of which use the bus topology. **Fault tolerance** is the capacity for a component or system to continue functioning despite damage or partial malfunction. Use of the star topology also makes 10BASE-T networks easier to troubleshoot, because you can isolate problems more readily when every device has a separate connection to the LAN.

10BASE-T follows the **5-4-3 rule** of networking. This rule says that, between two communicating nodes, the network cannot contain more than five network segments connected by four repeating devices, and no more than three of the segments may be populated (at least two must be unpopulated). The maximum distance that a 10BASE-T segment can traverse is 100 meters. To go beyond that distance, Ethernet star segments must be connected by additional hubs or switches to form more complex topologies. This arrangement can connect a maximum of five sequential network segments, for an overall distance between communicating nodes of 500 meters. Figure 3-22 depicts a 10BASE-T Ethernet network with maximum segment lengths.

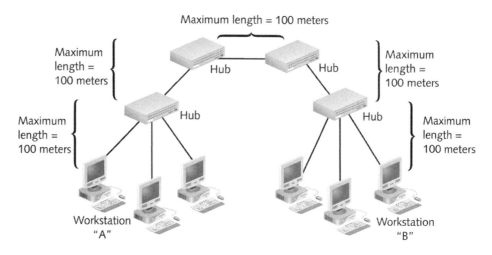

Maximum length between workstation A and B = 500 meters

FIGURE 3-22 *A 10BASE-T network*

NET+
1.2
1.3

100BASE-T (Fast Ethernet)

As networks become larger and handle heavier traffic, Ethernet's long-standing 10-Mbps limitation becomes a bottleneck that detrimentally affects response time. The need for faster LANs that can use the same infrastructure as the popular 10BASE-T technology has been met by **100BASE-T**, also known as **Fast Ethernet**. 100BASE-T, specified in the IEEE **802.3u** standard, enables LANs to run at a 100-Mbps data transfer rate, a tenfold increase from that provided by 10BASE-T, without requiring a significant investment in new infrastructure. 100BASE-T uses baseband transmission and the same star topology as 10BASE-T. It also uses the same RJ-45 modular connectors. Depending on the type of 100BASE-T technology used, it may require CAT 3, CAT 5, or higher UTP.

As with 10BASE-T, nodes on a 100BASE-T network are configured in a star topology. Multiple hubs can be connected to form link segments. However, unlike 10-Mbps Ethernet networks, 100BASE-T networks do not follow the 5-4-3 rule. Because of their faster response requirements, to avoid data errors they require communicating nodes to be even closer. 100BASE-T buses can support a maximum of three network segments connected with two repeating devices. Each segment length is limited to 100 meters. Thus, the overall maximum length between nodes is limited to 300 meters, as shown in Figure 3-23.

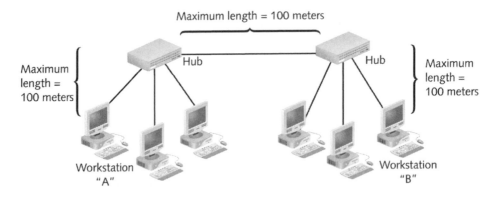

FIGURE 3-23 *A 100BASE-T network*

Two 100BASE-T specifications—100BASE-T4 and 100BASE-TX—have competed for popularity as organizations move to 100-Mbps technology. **100BASE-TX** is the version you are most likely to encounter. It achieves its speed by sending the signal 10 times faster and condensing the time between digital pulses as well as the time a station must wait and listen for a signal. 100BASE-TX requires CAT 5 or higher unshielded twisted-pair cabling. Within the cable, it uses the same two pairs of wire for transmitting and receiving data that 10BASE-T uses. Therefore, like 10BASE-T, 100BASE-TX is also capable of full-duplex transmission. Full duplexing can potentially double the effective bandwidth of a 100BASE-T network to 200 Mbps.

NET+
1.2
1.3

1000BASE-T (Gigabit Ethernet over Twisted-pair)

Because of increasing volumes of data and numbers of users who need to access this data quickly, even 100 Mbps has not met the throughput demands of some networks. Ethernet technologies designed to transmit data at 1 Gbps are collectively known as Gigabit Ethernet. 1000BASE-T is a standard for achieving throughputs 10 times faster than Fast Ethernet over copper cable, described in IEEE's **802.3ab** standard. In "1000BASE-TX," "1000" represents 1000 Megabits per second (Mbps), or 1 Gigabit per second (Gbps). "Base" indicates that it uses baseband transmission, and "T" indicates that it relies on twisted-pair wiring. 1000BASE-T achieves its higher throughput by using all four pairs of wires in a CAT 5 or higher cable to both transmit and receive signals, whereas 100BASE-T uses only two of the four pairs. 1000BASE-T also uses a different data encoding scheme than 100BASE-T networks use. However, the standards can be combined on the same network and you can purchase NICs that support 10 Mbps, 100 Mbps, and 1 Gbps via the same connector jack. Because of this compatibility, and the fact that 1000BASE-T can use existing CAT 5 cabling, the 1-Gigabit technology can be added gradually to an existing 100 Mbps network with minimal interruption of service. The maximum segment length on a 1000BASE-T network is 100 meters. It allows for only one repeater. Therefore, the maximum distance between communicating nodes on a 1000BASE-T network is 200 meters.

1000BASE-CX (Gigabit Ethernet over Twinax)

Another standard that supplies 1-Gigabit throughput is **1000BASE-CX**. This standard uses either STP or **twinaxial cable,** which is a cable similar to the coaxial cable discussed earlier in the chapter, but which contains two copper conductors at its center. With this type of cabling, a specialized connector, called an HSSDC, is required. 1000BASE-CX allows only short segment lengths—up to 25 meters. It was designed for connecting servers or connectivity devices over short distances. However, it is rarely used.

Fiber-Optic Cable

NET+
1.5

Fiber-optic cable, or simply *fiber*, contains one or several glass or plastic fibers at its center, or **core**. Data is transmitted via pulsing light sent from a laser (in the case of 1- and 10-Gigabit technologies) or a light-emitting diode (LED) through the central fibers. Surrounding the fibers is a layer of glass or plastic called **cladding**. The cladding is a different density from the glass or plastic in the strands. It reflects light back to the core in patterns that vary depending on the transmission mode. This reflection allows the fiber to bend around corners without diminishing the integrity of the light-based signal. Outside the cladding, a plastic buffer protects the cladding and core. Because it is opaque, it also absorbs any light that might escape. To prevent the cable from stretching, and to protect the inner core further, strands of Kevlar (an advanced polymeric fiber) surround the plastic buffer. Finally, a plastic sheath covers the strands of Kevlar. Figure 3-24 shows a fiber-optic cable with multiple, insulated fibers.

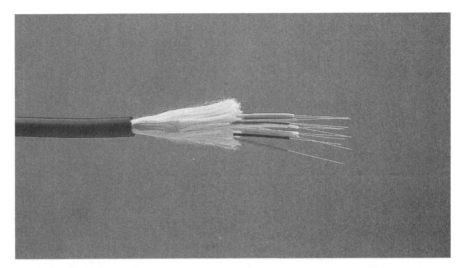

FIGURE 3-24 *A fiber-optic cable*

Like twisted-pair and coaxial cabling, fiber-optic cabling comes in a number of different varieties, depending on its intended use and the manufacturer. For example, fiber-optic cables used to connect the facilities of large telephone and data carriers may contain as many as 1000 fibers and be heavily sheathed to prevent damage from extreme environmental conditions. At the other end of the spectrum, fiber-optic patch cables for use on LANs may contain only two strands of fiber and be pliable enough to wrap around your hand.

However, all fiber cable variations fall into two categories: single-mode and multimode.

SMF (Single-Mode Fiber)

SMF (single-mode fiber) uses a narrow core (less than 10 microns in diameter) through which light generated by a laser travels over one path, reflecting very little. Because it reflects little, the light does not disperse as the signal travels along the fiber. This continuity allows single-mode fiber to accommodate high bandwidths and long distances (without requiring repeaters). Single-mode fiber may be used to connect a carrier's two facilities. However, it costs too much to be considered for use on typical data networks. Figure 3-25 depicts a simplified version of how signals travel over single-mode fiber.

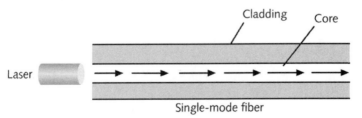

FIGURE 3-25 *Transmission over single-mode fiber-optic cable*

MMF (Multimode Fiber)

MMF (multimode fiber) contains a core with a larger diameter than single-mode fiber (between 50 and 115 microns in diameter; the most common size is 62.5 microns) over which many pulses of light generated by a laser or LED travel at different angles. It is commonly found on cables that connect a router to a switch or a server on the backbone of a network. Figure 3-26 depicts a simplified view of how signals travel over multimode fiber.

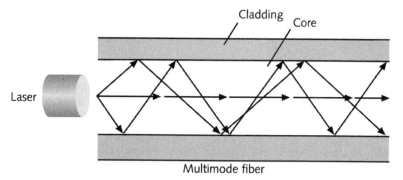

FIGURE 3-26 *Transmission over multimode fiber-optic cable*

Because of its reliability, fiber is currently used primarily as a cable that connects the many segments of a network. Fiber-optic cable provides the following benefits over copper cabling:

◆ Nearly unlimited throughput

◆ Very high resistance to noise

◆ Excellent security

◆ Ability to carry signals for much longer distances before requiring repeaters than copper cable

◆ Industry standard for high-speed networking

The most significant drawback to the use of fiber is its relatively high cost. Also, fiber-optic cable requires special equipment to splice, which means that quickly repairing a fiber-optic cable in the field (given little time or resources) can be difficult. Fiber's characteristics are summarized in the following list:

◆ *Throughput*—Fiber has proved reliable in transmitting data at rates that exceed 10 Gigabits (or 10,000 Megabits) per second. Fiber's amazing throughput is partly due to the physics of light traveling through glass. Unlike electrical pulses traveling over copper, the light experiences virtually no resistance and, therefore, can be reliably transmitted at faster rates than electrical pulses. In fact, a pure glass strand can accept up to 1 billion laser light pulses per second. Its high throughput capability makes it suitable for network backbones and for serving applications that generate a great deal of traffic, such as video or audio conferencing.

◆ *Cost*—Fiber-optic cable is the most expensive transmission medium. Because of its cost, most organizations find it impractical to run fiber to every desktop. Not only is the cable itself more expensive than copper cabling, but fiber-optic NICs and hubs can cost as much as five times more than NICs and hubs designed for UTP networks. In addition, hiring skilled fiber cable installers costs more than hiring twisted-pair cable installers.

◆ *Connector*—With fiber cabling, you can use any of 10 different types of connectors. Figure 3-27 shows four connector types: the **ST (Straight Tip)**, **SC (Subscriber Connector or Standard Connector)**, **LC (Local Connector)**, and **MT-RJ (Mechanical Transfer Registered Jack)** connectors. Each of these connectors can be obtained for single-mode or multimode fiber-optic cable. Existing fiber networks typically use ST or SC connectors. However, MT-RJ connectors are used on the very latest fiber-optic technology. LC and MT-RJ connectors are preferable to ST and SC connectors because of their smaller size, which allows for a higher density of connections at each termination point. The MT-RJ connector is unique because it contains two strands of multimode fiber in a single **ferrule**, which is a short tube within a connector that encircles the fiber and keeps it properly aligned. With two strands in each ferrule, a single MT-RJ connector provides for duplex signaling.

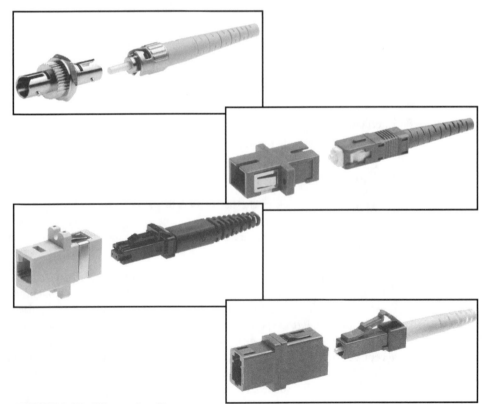

FIGURE 3-27 *Fiber-optic cable connectors*

NET+
1.5

◆ *Noise immunity*—Because fiber does not conduct electrical current to transmit signals, it is unaffected by EMI. Its impressive noise resistance is one reason why fiber can span such long distances before it requires repeaters to regenerate its signal.

◆ *Size and scalability*—Depending on the type of fiber-optic cable used, segment lengths vary from 150 to 40,000 meters. This limit is due primarily to **optical loss**, or the degradation of the light signal after it travels a certain distance away from its source (just as the light of a flashlight dims after a certain number of feet). Optical loss accrues over long distances and grows with every connection point in the fiber network. Dust or oil in a connection (for example, from people handling the fiber while splicing it) can further exacerbate optical loss.

Just as with twisted-pair and coaxial cabling, IEEE has established Physical layer standards for networks that use fiber-optic cable. Commonly used standards are described in the following sections.

10BASE-FL

NET+
1.2
1.3

In the **10BASE-F** standard, the "10" represents its maximum throughput of 10Mbps, "Base" indicates its use of baseband transmission, and "F" indicates that it relies on a medium of fiber-optic cable. In fact, there are at least three different kinds of 10BASE-F. All require two strands of multimode fiber. One strand is used for data transmission and one strand is used for reception, making 10BASE-F a full-duplex technology.

One version of 10BASE-F is **10BASE-FL**. 10BASE-FL is an IEEE 802.3 standard distinguished from other 10 Mbps standards that use fiber-optic cable first by its purpose. 10BASE-FL is designed to connect workstations to a LAN or to connect two repeaters, whereas the other two 10BASE-F standards are designed for backbone connections. 10BASE-FL is also distinguished by its ability to take advantage of fiber-optic repeating technology. Without repeaters, the maximum segment length for 10BASE-FL is 1000 meters. Using repeaters, it is 2000 meters. 10BASE-FL networks may contain no more than two repeaters. Like 10BASE-T, 10BASE-FL makes use of the star topology, with its repeaters connected through a bus.

Because 10BASE-F technologies involve (expensive) fiber and achieve merely 10-Mbps throughput (whereas the fiber medium is capable of much higher throughput), it is not commonly found on modern networks.

100BASE-FX

The **100BASE-FX** standard specifies a network capable of 100-Mbps throughput that uses baseband transmission and fiber-optic cabling. 100BASE-FX requires multimode fiber containing at least two strands of fiber. In half-duplex mode, one strand is used for data transmission, while the other strand is used for reception. In full-duplex implementations, both strands are used for both sending and receiving data. 100BASE-FX has a maximum segment length of 412 meters if half-duplex transmission is used and 2000 meters if full-duplex is used. The standard allows for a maximum of one repeater to connect segments. The 100BASE-FX standard uses a star topology, with its repeaters connected in a bus fashion.

NET+
1.2
1.3

100BASE-FX, like 100BASE-T, is also considered "Fast Ethernet" and is described in IEEE's 802.3u standard. Organizations switching, or migrating, from UTP to fiber media can combine 100BASE-TX and 100BASE-FX within one network. To do this, transceivers in computers and connectivity devices must have both RJ-45 and SC, ST, LC, or MT-RJ ports. Alternatively, a 100BASE-TX to 100BASE-FX media converter may be used at any point in the network to interconnect the different media and convert the signals of one standard to signals that work with the other standard.

1000BASE-LX

IEEE has specified three different types of 1000Base, or 1 Gigabit, Ethernet technologies for use over fiber-optic cable in its **802.3z** standard. Included in this standard is the 1000BASE-CX standard you learned about previously.

Probably the most common 1-Gigabit Ethernet standard in use today is **1000BASE-LX**. The "1000" in 1000BASE-LX stands for 1000-Mbps—or 1 Gbps—throughput. "Base" stands for baseband transmission, and "LX" represents its reliance on "long wavelengths" of 1300 nanometers. (A nanometer equals 0.000000001 meters.) 1000BASE-LX has a longer reach than any other 1-Gigabit technology available today. It relies on either single-mode or multimode fiber. With multimode fiber (62.5 microns in diameter), the maximum segment length is 550 meters. When used with single-mode fiber (8 microns in diameter), 1000BASE-LX can reach 5000 meters. 1000BASE-LX networks can use one repeater between segments. Because of its potential length, 1000BASE-LX is an excellent choice for long backbones—connecting buildings in a MAN, for example, or connecting an ISP with its telecommunications carrier.

1000BASE-SX

1000BASE-SX is similar to 1000BASE-LX in that it has a maximum throughput of 1 Gbps. However, it relies on only multimode fiber-optic cable as its medium. This makes it less expensive to install than 1000BASE-LX. Another difference is that 1000BASE-SX uses short wavelengths of 850 nanometers—thus, the "SX," which stands for "short." The maximum segment length for 1000BASE-SX depends on two things: the diameter of the fiber and the modal bandwidth used to transmit signals. **Modal bandwidth** is a measure of the highest frequency of signal a multimode fiber can support over a specific distance and is measured in MHz-km. It is related to the distortion that occurs when multiple pulses of light, although issued at the same time, arrive at the end of a fiber at slightly different times. The higher the modal bandwidth, the longer a multimode fiber can carry a signal reliably.

When used with fibers whose diameters are 50 microns each, and with the highest possible modal bandwidth, the maximum segment length on a 1000BASE-SX network is 550 meters. When used with fibers whose diameters are 62.5 microns each, and with the highest possible modal bandwidth, the maximum segment length is 275 meters. Only one repeater may be used between segments. Therefore, 1000BASE-SX is best suited for shorter network runs than 1000BASE-LX—for example, connecting a data center with a telecommunications closet in an office building..

10-Gigabit Fiber-Optic Standards

As you have learned, the throughput potential for fiber-optic cable is extraordinary, and scientists continue to push its limits. Now there are standards for transmitting data at 10-Gbps over fiber, all described in IEEE's **802.3ae** standard. All of the 10-Gigabit options rely on a star topology and allow for only one repeater. They differ according to their signaling methods and maximum allowable segment lengths.

One 10-Gigabit option is 10GBASE-SR, in which the "10G" stands for its maximum throughput of 10 Gigabits per second, "base" stands for baseband transmission, and "SR" stands for "short-reach." 10GBASE-SR relies on multimode fiber and transmits signals with wavelengths of 850 nanometers. As with the 1-Gigabit standards, the maximum segment length on a 10GBASE-SR network depends on the diameter of the fibers used. It also depends on the modal bandwidth used. For example, if 50-micron fiber is used, with the maximum possible modal bandwidth, the maximum segment length is 300 meters. If 62.5-micron fiber is used with the maximum possible modal bandwidth, a 10GBASE-SR segment can be 66 meters long.

A second standard defined in IEEE 802.3ae is **10GBASE-LR**, in which the "10G" stands for 10 Gigabits per second, "base" stands for baseband transmission, and "LR" stands for "long-reach." 10GBASE-LR carries signals with wavelengths of 1310 nanometers through single-mode fiber. Its maximum segment length is 10,000 meters.

A third 10-Gigabit option is **10GBASE-ER**, in which "ER" stands for "extended reach." Like 10GBASE-LR, this standard requires single-mode fiber, through which it transmits signals with wavelengths of 1550 nanometers. It allows for segments up to 40,000 meters, or nearly 25 miles.

Summary of Physical Layer Standards

To obtain Network+ certification, you must be familiar with the different characteristics and limitations of each type of network discussed in this chapter. To put this information in context, Table 3-2 summarizes the characteristics and limitations for Physical layer networking standards, including Ethernet networks that use coaxial cable, twisted-pair cable, and fiber-optic cable.

Table 3-2 Physical layer networking standards

Standard	Maximum Transmission Speed (Mbps)	Maximum Distance per Segment (m)	Physical Media	Topology*
10BASE-T	10	100	CAT 3 or higher UTP	Star
10BASE-FL	10	2000	MMF	Star
100BASE-TX	100	100	CAT 5 or higher UTP	Star
1000BASE-T	1000	100	CAT 5 or higher UTP (CAT 5e is preferred)	Star

Table 3-2 Continued

Standard	Maximum Transmission Speed (Mbps)	Maximum Distance per Segment (m)	Physical Media	Topology*
1000BASE-CX	1000	25	Twinaxial cable	Star
100BASE-FX	100	2000	MMF	Star
1000BASE-LX	1000	Up to 550, depending on wavelength and fiber core diameter	MMF	Star
1000BASE-LX	1000	5000	SMF	Star
1000BASE-SX	1000	Up to 500, depending on modal bandwidth and fiber core diameter	MMF	Star
10GBASE-SR	10,000	Up to 300, depending on modal bandwidth and fiber core diameter	MMF	Star
10GBASE-LR	10,000	10,000	SMF	Star
10GBASE-ER	10,000	40,000	SMF	Star

*Although most modern networks use a star-bus hybrid, if you are studying for the Network+ certification exam, you should remember the simple topology on which the network is based.

Cable Design and Management

Organizations that pay attention to their **cable plant**—the hardware that makes up the enterprise-wide cabling system—are apt to experience fewer Physical layer network problems, smoother network expansions, and simpler network troubleshooting. Cable management is a significant element of a sound network management strategy.

In 1991, TIA/EIA released its joint 568 Commercial Building Wiring Standard, also known as **structured cabling**, for uniform, enterprise-wide, multivendor cabling systems. Structured cabling suggests how networking media can best be installed to maximize performance and minimize upkeep. Structured cabling specifies standards without regard for the type of media or transmission technology used on the network. (It does, however assume a network based on the star topology.) In other words, it is designed to work just as well for 10BASE-T networks as it does for 1000BASE-LX networks. Structured cabling is based on a hierarchical design that divides cabling into six subsystems, described in the following list and illustrated in Figure 3-28.

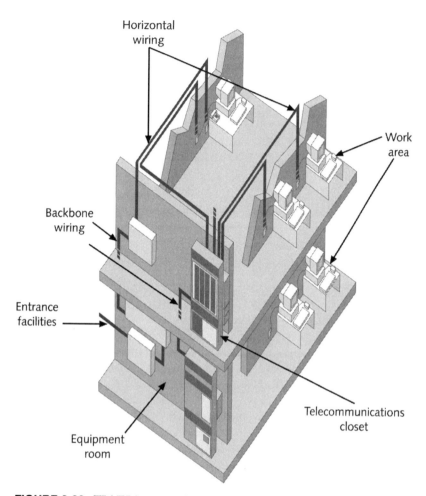

FIGURE 3-28 *TIA/EIA structured cabling subsystems*

♦ *Entrance facilities*—The point at which a building's internal cabling plant begins. The entrance facility separates LANs from WANs and designates where the telecommunications service carrier (whether it's a local phone company, dedicated, or long-distance carrier) accepts responsibility for the (external) wire. The point of division between the service carrier's network and the internal network is also known as the **demarcation point** (or **demarc**).

♦ *Backbone wiring*—The interconnection between telecommunications closets, equipment rooms, and entrance facilities. On a campus-wide network, the backbone includes not only vertical connectors between floors, or **risers**, and cabling between equipment rooms, but also cabling between buildings. The TIA/EIA standard designates distance limitations for backbones of varying cable types, as specified in Table 3-3. On modern networks, backbones are usually composed of fiber-optic or UTP cable. The cross connect is the central connection point for the backbone wiring.

Table 3-3 TIA/EIA specifications for backbone cabling

Cable Type	Cross Connects to Telecommunications Closet	Equipment Room to Telecommunications Closet	Cross Connects to Equipment Room
UTP	800 m (voice specification)	500 m	300 m
Single-mode	3000 m	500 m	1500 m fiber
Multimode	2000 m	500 m	1500 m fiber

◆ *Equipment room*—The location of significant networking hardware, such as servers and mainframe hosts. Cabling to equipment rooms usually connects telecommunications closets. On a campus-wide network, each building may have its own equipment room.

◆ *Telecommunications closet*—A "telco room" that contains connectivity for groups of workstations in its area, plus cross connections to equipment rooms. Large organizations may have several telco rooms per floor. Telecommunications closets typically house patch panels, punch-down blocks, hubs or switches, and possibly other connectivity hardware. A **punch-down block** is a panel of data receptors into which horizontal cabling from the workstations is inserted. If used, a **patch panel** is a wall-mounted panel of data receptors into which patch cables from the punch-down block are inserted. Figure 3-29 shows a patch panel and Figure 3-30 shows a punch-down block. Finally, patch cables connect the patch panel to the hub or switch. Because telecommunications closets are usually small, enclosed spaces, good cooling and ventilation systems are important to maintaining a constant temperature.

◆ *Horizontal wiring*—The wiring that connects workstations to the closest telecommunications closet. TIA/EIA recognizes three possible cabling types for horizontal wiring: STP, UTP, or fiber-optic. The maximum allowable distance for horizontal wiring is 100 m. This span includes 90 m to connect a data jack on the wall to the telecommunications closet plus a maximum of 10 m to connect a workstation to the data jack on the wall. Figure 3-31 depicts a horizontal wiring configuration.

◆ *Work area*—An area that encompasses all patch cables and horizontal wiring necessary to connect workstations, printers, and other network devices from their NICs to the telecommunications closet. A **patch cable** is a relatively short section (usually between 3 and 25 feet long) of cabling with connectors on both ends. The TIA/EIA standard calls for each wall jack to contain at least one voice and one data outlet, as pictured in Figure 3-32. Realistically, you will encounter a variety of wall jacks. For example, in a student computer lab lacking phones, a wall jack with a combination of voice and data outlets is unnecessary.

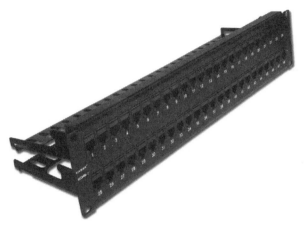

FIGURE 3-29 *Patch panel*

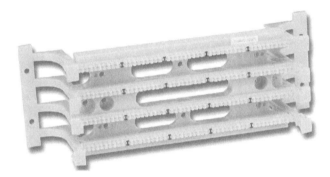

FIGURE 3-30 *Punch–down block*

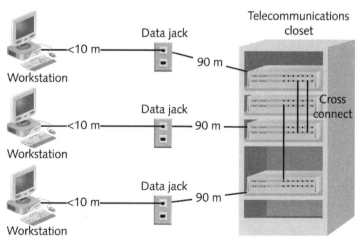

FIGURE 3-31 *Horizontal wiring*

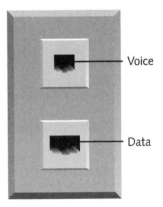

FIGURE 3-32 *A standard TIA/EIA outlet*

Adhering to standard cabling hierarchies is only part of a smart cable management strategy. You or your network manager should also specify standards for the types of cable used by your organization and maintain a list of approved cabling vendors. Keep a supply room stocked with spare parts so that you can easily and quickly replace defective parts.

Create documentation for your cabling plant, including the locations, installation dates, lengths, and grades of installed cable. Label every data jack, punch-down block, and connector. Use color-coded cables for different purposes (cables can be purchased in a variety of sheath colors). For example, you might want to use pink for patch cables, green for horizontal wiring, and gray for vertical (backbone) wiring. Be certain to document your color schemes. Keep your documentation in a centrally accessible location and be certain to update it as you change the network. The more you document, the easier it will be to move or add cable segments.

Finally, plan for how your cabling plant will lend itself to growth. For example, if your organization is rapidly expanding, consider replacing your backbone with fiber and leave plenty of space in your telecommunications closets for more racks.

As you will most likely work with twisted-pair cable, the next section explains how to install this type of cabling from the server to the desktop.

Installing Cable

So far, you have read about the variety of cables used in networking and the limitations inherent in each. You may worry that with hundreds of varieties of cable, choosing the correct one and making it work with your network is next to impossible. The good news is that if you follow both the manufacturers' installation guidelines and the TIA/EIA standards, you are almost guaranteed success. Many network problems can be traced to poor cable installation techniques. For example, if you don't crimp twisted-pair wires in the correct position in an RJ-45 connector, the cable will fail to transmit or receive data (or both—in which case, the cable will not function at all). Installing the wrong grade of cable can either cause your network to fail or render it more susceptible to damage.

With networks moving to faster transmission speeds, adhering to installation guidelines is a more critical concern than ever. A Category 5 UTP segment that flawlessly transmits data at 10 Mbps may suffer data loss when pushed to 100 Mbps. In addition, some cable manufacturers will not honor warranties if their cables were improperly installed. This section outlines the most common method of installing UTP cable and points out cabling mistakes that can lead to network instability.

In the previous section, you learned about the six subsystems of the TIA/EIA structured cabling standard. A typical UTP network uses a modular setup to distinguish between cables at each subsystem. Figure 3-33 provides an overview of a modular cabling installation.

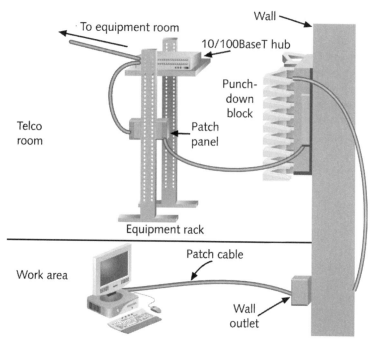

FIGURE 3-33 *A typical UTP cabling installation*

In this example, patch cables connect network devices (such as a workstation) to the wall jacks. Longer cables connect wire from the wall jack to a punch-down block in the telecommunications closet. From the punch-down block, patch cables bring the connection into a patch panel. From the patch panel, more patch cables connect to the hub, switch, or other connectivity device, which in turn connects to the equipment room or to the backbone, depending on the scale of the network. All of these sections of cable make network moves and additions easier. Believe it or not, they also keep the telecommunications closet organized.

NET+
1.4

Although you may never have to make your own patch cables, you might have to replace an RJ-45 connector on an existing cable. TIA/EIA has specified two different methods of inserting UTP twisted pairs into RJ-45 plugs: TIA/EIA 568A and TIA/EIA 568B. Functionally, there is no difference between the standards. You only have to be certain that you use the same standard on every RJ-45 plug and jack on your network, so that data is transmitted and received correctly. Figure 3-34 depicts pin numbers and assignments for the TIA/EIA 568A standard when used on an Ethernet network. Figure 3-35 depicts pin numbers and assignments for the TIA/EIA 568B standard. (Although networking professionals commonly refer to wires in Figures 3-34 and 3-35 as "Transmit" and "Receive," their original "T" and "R" designations stand for "Tip" and "Ring," based on early telephone technology.)

If you terminate the RJ-45 plugs at both ends of a patch cable identically, following one of the TIA/EIA 568 standards, you will create a **straight-through cable**. A straight-through cable is so named because it allows signals to pass "straight through" between terminations. However, in some cases you may want to reverse the pin locations of some wires—for example, when you want to connect two workstations without using a connectivity device or when you want to connect two hubs through their data ports. This can be accomplished through the use of a **crossover cable**, a patch cable in which the termination locations of the transmit and receive wires on one end of the cable are reversed, as shown in Figure 3-36. In this example, the TIA/EIA 568B standard is used on the left side, whereas the TIA/EIA 568A standard is used on the right side. Notice that only pairs 2 and 3 are switched, because those are the pairs sending and receiving data.

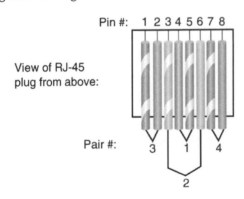

Pin #	Color	Pair #	Function
1	White with green stripe	3	Transmit +
2	Green	3	Transmit -
3	White with orange stripe	2	Receive +
4	Blue	1	Unused
5	White with blue stripe	1	Unused
6	Orange	2	Receive -
7	White with brown stripe	4	Unused
8	Brown	4	Unused

FIGURE 3-34 *TIA/EIA 568A standard terminations*

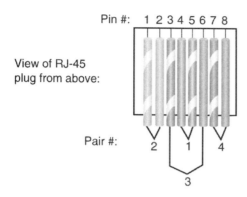

View of RJ-45
plug from above:

Pin #	Color	Pair #	Function
1	White with orange stripe	2	Transmit +
2	Orange	2	Transmit −
3	White with green stripe	3	Receive +
4	Blue	1	Unused
5	White with blue stripe	1	Unused
6	Green	3	Receive −
7	White with brown stripe	4	Unused
8	Brown	4	Unused

FIGURE 3-35 *TIA/EIA 568B standard terminations*

Pin assignments
on Plug A

Pin assignments
on Plug B (reversed)

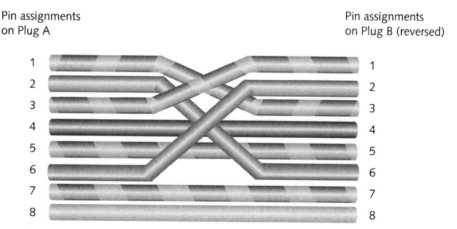

FIGURE 3-36 *RJ-45 terminations on a crossover cable*

The art of proper cabling could fill an entire book. If you plan to specialize in cable installation, design, or maintenance, you should invest in a reference dedicated to this topic. As a network professional, you will likely occasionally add new cables to a room or telecommunications closet, repair defective cable ends, or install a data outlet.

Following are some cable installation tips that will help prevent Physical layer failures:

◆ Do not untwist twisted-pair cables more than one-half inch before inserting them into the punch-down block.

◆ Do not leave more than 1 inch of exposed (stripped) cable before a twisted-pair termination.

◆ Pay attention to the bend radius limitations for the type of cable you are installing. **Bend radius** is the radius of the maximum arc into which you can loop a cable before you will impair data transmission. Generally, a twisted-pair cable's bend radius is equal to or greater than four times the diameter of the cable. Be careful not to exceed it.

◆ Test each segment of cabling as you install it with a cable tester. This practice will prevent you from later having to track down errors in multiple, long stretches of cable.

◆ Avoid cinching cables so tightly that you squeeze their outer covering, a practice that leads to difficult-to-diagnose data errors.

◆ Avoid laying cable across the floor where it might sustain damage from rolling chairs or foot traffic. If you must take this tack, cover the cable with a cable protector.

◆ Install cable at least 3 feet away from fluorescent lights or other sources of EMI.

◆ Always leave some slack in cable runs. Stringing cable too tightly risks connectivity and data transmission problems.

◆ If you run cable in the **plenum**, the area above the ceiling tile or below the subflooring, make sure the cable sheath is plenum-rated and consult with local electric installation codes to be certain you are installing it correctly. A plenum-rated cable is more fire-resistant, and if burned, produces less smoke than other cables.

◆ Pay attention to grounding requirements and follow them religiously.

Wireless Transmission

NET+
1.7

The earth's atmosphere provides an intangible means of transporting data over networks. For decades, radio and TV stations have used the atmosphere to transport information via analog signals. The atmosphere is also capable of carrying digital signals. Networks that transmit signals through the atmosphere via infrared or radiofrequency (RF) waves are known as **wireless networks** or **WLANs (wireless LANs)**. Wireless transmission is now common in business and home networks and are necessary in some specialized network environments. For example, inventory control personnel who drive through large warehouses to record inventory data use wireless networking. In addition to infrared and RF transmission, microwave and satellite links can be used to transport data through the atmosphere.

NET+
1.7

The Wireless Spectrum

All wireless signals are carried through the air along electromagnetic waves. The **wireless spectrum** is a continuum of electromagnetic waves used for data and voice communication. On the spectrum, waves are arranged according to their frequencies. The wireless spectrum (as defined by the FCC, which controls its use) spans frequencies between 9 KHz and 300 GHz. Each type of wireless service can be associated with one area of the wireless spectrum. AM broadcasting, for example, sits near the low frequency end of the wireless communications spectrum, using frequencies between 535 and 1605 KHz. Infrared waves belong to a wide band of frequencies at the high frequency end of the spectrum, between 300 GHz and 300,000 GHz. Most new cordless telephones and wireless LANs use frequencies around 2.4 GHz. Figure 3-37 shows the wireless spectrum and identifies the major wireless services associated with each range of frequencies.

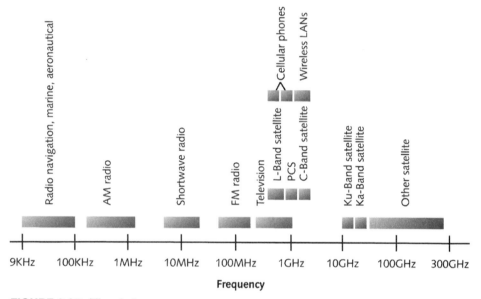

FIGURE 3-37 *The wireless spectrum*

In the United States, the collection of frequencies available for communication—also known as "the airwaves"—is a natural resource available for public use. The FCC grants organizations in different locations exclusive rights to use each frequency. It also determines what frequency ranges can be used for what purposes. Of course, signals propagating through the air do not necessarily remain within one nation. Therefore, it is important for countries across the world to agree on wireless communications standards. ITU is the governing body that sets standards for international wireless services, including frequency allocation, signaling and protocols used by wireless devices, wireless transmission and reception equipment, satellite orbits, and so on. If governments and companies did not adhere to ITU standards, chances are that a wireless device could not be used outside the country in which it was manufactured.

Characteristics of Wireless Transmission

Although **wire-bound** signals (meaning those that travel over a physical medium, such as a cable) and wireless signals share many similarities—including the use of protocols and encoding, for example—the nature of the atmosphere makes wireless transmission vastly different from wire-bound transmission. Because the air provides no fixed path for signals to follow, signals travel without guidance. Contrast this to guided media, such as UTP or fiber-optic cable, which do provide a fixed signal path. The lack of a fixed path requires wireless signals to be transmitted, received, controlled, and corrected differently from wire-bound signals.

Just as with wire-bound signals, wireless signals originate from electrical current traveling along a conductor. The electrical signal travels from the transmitter to an antenna, which then emits the signal, as a series of electromagnetic waves, to the atmosphere. The signal propagates through the air until it reaches its destination. At the destination, another antenna accepts the signal, and a receiver converts it back to current. Figure 3-38 illustrates this process.

FIGURE 3-38 *Wireless transmission and reception*

Notice that antennas are used for both the transmission and reception of wireless signals. As you would expect, to exchange information, two antennas must be tuned to the same frequency. Next, you will learn about some fundamental types of antennas and their properties.

Antennas

Each type of wireless service requires an antenna specifically designed for that service. The service's specifications determine the antenna's power output, frequency, and radiation pattern. An antenna's **radiation pattern** describes the relative strength over a three-dimensional area of all the electromagnetic energy the antenna sends or receives.

A **directional antenna** issues wireless signals along a single direction. This type of antenna is used when the source needs to communicate with one destination, as in a point-to-point link. A satellite downlink (for example, the kind used to receive digital TV signals) uses directional antennas. In contrast, an **omnidirectional antenna** issues and receives wireless signals with equal strength and clarity in all directions. This type of antenna is used when many different receivers must be able to pick up the signal, or when the receiver's location is highly mobile. TV and radio stations use omnidirectional antennas, as do most towers that transmit cellular telephone signals.

The geographical area that an antenna or wireless system can reach is known as its **range**. Receivers must be within the range to receive accurate signals consistently. Even within an antenna's range, however, signals may be hampered by obstacles and rendered unintelligible.

Signal Propagation

Ideally, a wireless signal would travel directly in a straight line from its transmitter to its intended receiver. This type of propagation, known as **LOS (line-of-sight)**, uses the least amount of energy and results in the reception of the clearest possible signal. However, because the atmosphere is an unguided medium and the path between a transmitter and a receiver is not always clear, wireless signals do not usually follow a straight line. When an obstacle stands in a signal's way, the signal may pass through the object or be absorbed by the object, or it may be subject to any of the following phenomena: reflection, diffraction, or scattering. The object's geometry governs which of these three phenomena occurs.

Reflection in wireless signaling is no different from reflection of other electromagnetic waves, such as light. The wave encounters an obstacle and reflects—or bounces back—toward its source. A wireless signal will bounce off objects whose dimensions are large compared to the signal's average wavelength. In the context of a wireless LAN, which may use signals with wavelengths between one and 10 meters, such objects include walls, floors, ceilings, and the earth. In addition, signals reflect more readily off conductive materials, like metal, than insulators, like concrete.

In **diffraction**, a wireless signal splits into secondary waves when it encounters an obstruction. The secondary waves continue to propagate in the direction in which they were split. If you could see wireless signals being diffracted, they would appear to be bending around the obstacle. Objects with sharp edges—including the corners of walls and desks—cause diffraction.

Scattering is the diffusion, or the reflection in multiple different directions, of a signal. Scattering occurs when a wireless signal encounters an object that has small dimensions compared to the signal's wavelength. Scattering is also related to the roughness of the surface a wireless signal encounters. The rougher the surface, the more likely a signal is to scatter when it hits that surface. In an office building, objects such as chairs, books, and computers cause scattering of wireless LAN signals. For signals traveling outdoors, rain, mist, hail, and snow may all cause scattering.

Because of reflection, diffraction, and scattering, wireless signals follow a number of different paths to their destination. Such signals are known as **multipath** signals. Figure 3-39 illustrates multipath signals caused by these three phenomena.

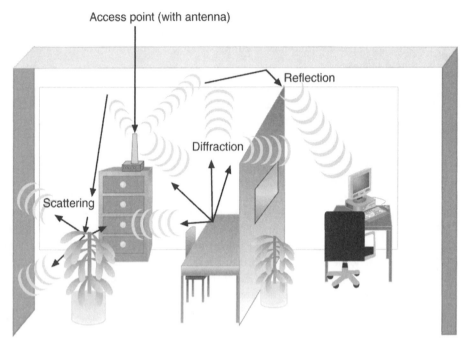

FIGURE 3-39 *Multipath signal propagation*

The multipath nature of wireless signals is both a blessing and a curse. On one hand, because signals bounce off obstacles, they have a better chance of reaching their destination. In environments such as an office building, wireless services depend on signals bouncing off walls, ceilings, floors, and furniture so that they may eventually reach their destination. Imagine how inconvenient and inefficient it would be, for example, to make sure you were standing within clear view of a transmitter to receive a paging signal.

The downside to multipath signaling is that, because of their various paths, multipath signals travel different distances between their transmitter and a receiver. Thus, multiple instances of the same signal can arrive at a receiver at different times, causing signal delay.

Signal Degradation

No matter what paths wireless signals take, they are bound to run into obstacles. When they do, the original signal issued by the transmitter will experience **fading**, or a change in signal strength as a result of some of the electromagnetic energy being scattered, reflected, or diffracted after being issued by the transmitter. After fading, the strength of the signal that reaches the receiver is lower than the transmitted signal's strength. This makes sense because as more waves are reflected, diffracted, or scattered by obstacles, fewer are likely to reach their destination.

As with wire-bound signals, wireless signals also experience attenuation. After a signal is transmitted, the farther it moves away from the transmission antenna the more it weakens.

NET+
1.7

Just as with wire-bound transmission, wireless signals are amplified (if analog) or repeated (if digital) to strengthen the signal so that it can be clearly received. The difference is that the intermediate points through which wireless signals are amplified or repeated are transceivers connected to antennas.

However, attenuation is not the most severe flaw affecting wireless signals. Wireless signals are also susceptible to noise (more often called "interference" in the context of wireless communications). Interference is a significant problem for wireless communications because the atmosphere is saturated with electromagnetic waves. For example, wireless LANs may be affected by cellular phones, mobile phones, or overhead lights.

Interference can distort and weaken a wireless signal in the same way that noise distorts and weakens a wire-bound signal. However, because wireless signals cannot depend on a conduit or shielding to protect them from extraneous EMI, they are more vulnerable to noise. The extent of interference that a wireless signal experiences depends partly on the density of signals within a geographical area. Signals traveling through areas in which many wireless communications systems are in use—for example, the center of a metropolitan area—are the most apt to suffer interference.

Narrowband, Broadband, and Spread Spectrum Signals

Transmission technologies differ according to how much of the wireless spectrum their signals use. An important distinction is whether a wireless service uses narrowband or broadband signaling. In **narrowband**, a transmitter concentrates the signal energy at a single frequency or in a very small range of frequencies. In contrast to narrowband, broadband uses a relatively wide band of the wireless spectrum. Broadband technologies, as a result of their wider frequency bands, offer higher throughputs than narrowband technologies.

The use of multiple frequencies to transmit a signal is known as **spread spectrum** technology (because the signal is spread out over the wireless spectrum). In other words, a signal never stays continuously within one frequency range during its transmission. One result of spreading a signal over a wide frequency band is that it requires less power per frequency than narrowband signaling. This distribution of signal strength makes spread spectrum signals less likely to interfere with narrowband signals traveling in the same frequency band.

Spread spectrum signaling, originally used with military wireless transmissions in World War II, remains a popular way of making wireless transmissions more secure. Because signals are split across several frequencies according to a sequence known only to the authorized transmitter and receiver, it is much more difficult for unauthorized receivers to capture and decode spread spectrum signals. To generic receivers, signals issued via spread spectrum technology appear as unintelligible noise.

One specific implementation of spread spectrum is **FHSS (frequency hopping spread spectrum)**. In FHSS transmission, a signal jumps between several different frequencies within a band in a synchronization pattern known only to the channel's receiver and transmitter. Another type of spread spectrum signaling is called **DSSS (direct sequence spread spectrum)**. In DSSS, a signal's bits are distributed over an entire frequency band at once. Each bit is coded so that the receiver can reassemble the original signal upon receiving the bits.

Fixed versus Mobile

Each type of wireless communication falls into one of two categories: fixed or mobile. In **fixed** wireless systems, the locations of the transmitter and receiver do not move. The transmitting antenna focuses its energy directly toward the receiving antenna. This results in a point-to-point link. One advantage of fixed wireless is that because the receiver's location is predictable, energy need not be wasted issuing signals across a large geographical area. Thus, more energy can be used for the signal. Fixed wireless links are used in some data and voice applications. For example, a service provider may obtain data services through a fixed link with a satellite. In cases in which a long distance or difficult terrain must be traversed, fixed wireless links are more economical than cabling.

Not all communications are suited to fixed wireless, however. For example, a waiter who uses a wireless, handheld computer to transmit orders to the restaurant's kitchen could not use a service that requires him to remain in one spot to send and receive signals. Instead, wireless LANs, along with cellular telephone, paging, and many other services use mobile wireless systems. In **mobile** wireless, the receiver can be located anywhere within the transmitter's range. This allows the receiver to roam from one place to another while continuing to pick up its signal.

Now that you understand some characteristics of wireless transmission, you are ready to learn more about the two types of wireless connections used on computer networks: infrared and wireless LANs.

Infrared Transmission

Infrared signals are transmitted by frequencies in the 300-GHz to 300,000-GHz range, which is just above the top of the wireless spectrum as it is defined by the FCC. Infrared frequencies approach the range of visible light in the electromagnetic spectrum, and in fact, some can be seen. Yet these frequencies can also be used to transmit data through space, just as a television remote control sends signals across the room.

On computer networks, infrared transmission is most often used for communications between devices in the same room. For example, printers can connect to computers using infrared transmission, and two **PDAs (personal digital assistants)**, or handheld computers, can synchronize their data through infrared transmission. This type of exchange relies on the devices being close to each other, and in some cases, with a clear, line-of-sight path between them. Although infrared technology has the potential to transmit data at speeds that rival fiber-optic throughput, it also comes with disadvantages. For example, infrared signaling requires more power, travels shorter distances, and maneuvers around obstacles less successfully than the wireless technique used on most modern networks, which is discussed next.

NET+
1.7

Wireless LAN (WLAN) Architecture

The most common form of WLAN relies on lower frequencies in the 2.4-2.4835 GHz band, more commonly known as the **2.4-GHz band**, to send and receive signals. This set of frequencies is popular for many modern communications services because it is unlicensed in the United States. That is, the FCC does not require users to register their service and reserve sole use of these frequencies.

Because they are not bound by cabling paths between nodes and connectivity devices, wireless networks do not follow the same kind of topologies as wire-bound networks. They have their own, different layouts. Smaller wireless networks, in which a small number of nodes closely positioned need to exchange data, can be arranged in an ad hoc fashion. In an **ad hoc** WLAN, wireless nodes, or **stations**, transmit directly to each other via wireless NICs without an intervening connectivity device, as shown in Figure 3-40.

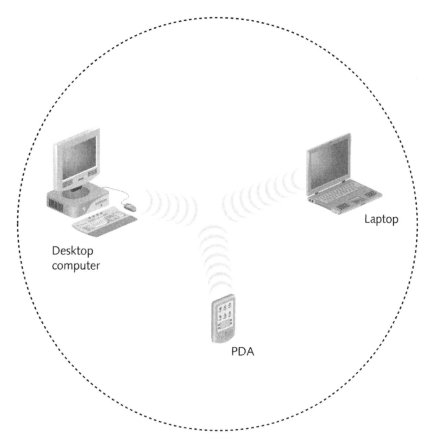

Desktop
computer

Laptop

PDA

FIGURE 3-40 *An ad-hoc WLAN*

NET+
1.6
1.7

However, an ad-hoc arrangement would not work well for a WLAN with many users or whose users are spread out over a wide area, or where obstacles could stand in the way of signals between stations. Instead of communicating directly with each other in ad hoc mode, stations on WLANs can use the infrastructure mode, which depends on an intervening connectivity device called an access point. An **AP (access point)** is a device that accepts wireless signals from multiple nodes and retransmits them to the rest of the network. To cover its intended range, an access point must have sufficient power and be strategically placed so that stations can communicate with it. For instance, if an access point must serve a group of workstations in several offices on one floor in a building, it should probably be located in an open area near the center of that floor. And like other wireless devices, access points contain an antenna connected to their transceivers. An infrastructure WLAN is shown in Figure 3-41 .

It is common for a WLAN to include several access points. The number of access points depends on the number of stations a WLAN connects. The maximum number of stations each access point can serve varies from 10 to 100, depending on the wireless technology used.

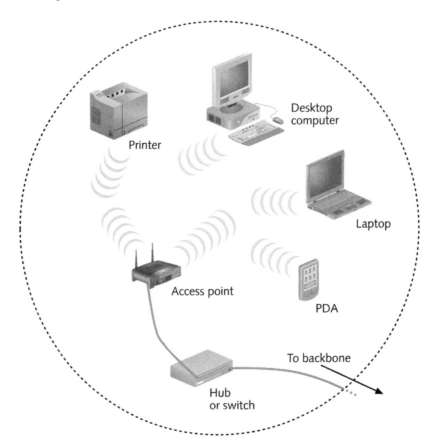

FIGURE 3-41 *An infrastructure WLAN*

NET+
1.6
1.7

Exceeding the recommended maximum leads to a greater incidence of errors and slower over-all transmission.

Mobile networking allows wireless nodes to roam from one location to another within a certain range of their AP. This range depends on the wireless access method, the equipment manufacturer, and the office environment. As with other wireless technologies, WLAN signals are subject to interference and obstruction that cause multipath signaling. Therefore, a building with many thick, concrete walls, for example, will limit the effective range of a WLAN more severely than an office that is divided into a few cubicles. In general, stations must remain within 300 feet of an access point to maintain optimal transmission speeds.

In addition to connecting multiple nodes within a LAN, wireless technology can be used to connect two different parts of a LAN or two separate LANs. Such connections typically use a fixed link with directional antennas between two access points, as shown in Figure 3-42. Because point-to-point links only have to transmit in one direction, they can apply more energy to signal propagation than mobile wireless links. As a result of applying more energy to the signal, their maximum transmission distance is greater. In the case of connecting two WLANs, access points could be as far as 1000 feet apart.

WLANs run over the same protocols and the same operating systems (for example, Unix, Windows, and Novell NetWare) as wire-bound LANs. This compatibility ensures that wireless and wire-bound transmission methods can be integrated on the same network. Only the signaling techniques differ between wireless and wire-bound portions of a LAN. However, techniques for generating and encoding wireless signals vary from one WLAN standard to another. Chapter 6 explains these wireless technologies in detail.

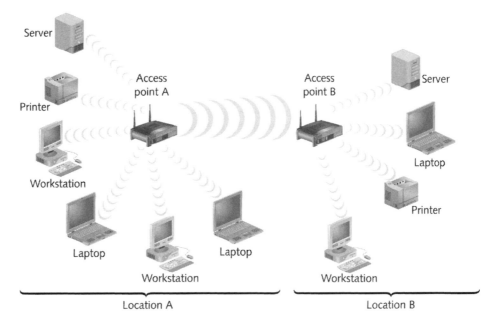

FIGURE 3-42 *Wireless LAN interconnection*

Chapter Summary

◆ Information can be transmitted via two methods: analog or digital. Analog signals are continuous waves that result in variable and inexact transmission. Digital signals are based on electrical or light pulses that represent information encoded in binary form.

◆ In half-duplex transmission, signals may travel in both directions over a medium but in only one direction at a time. When signals may travel in both directions over a medium simultaneously, the transmission is considered full-duplex.

◆ A form of transmission that allows multiple signals to travel simultaneously over one medium is known as multiplexing. In multiplexing, the single medium is logically separated into multiple channels, or subchannels.

◆ Throughput is the amount of data that the medium can transmit during a given period of time. Throughput is usually measured in bits per second and depends on the physical nature of the medium.

◆ Baseband is a form of transmission in which digital signals are sent through direct current pulses applied to the wire. Baseband systems can transmit only one signal, or one channel, at a time. Broadband, on the other hand, uses modulated analog frequencies to transmit multiple signals over the same wire.

◆ Noise is interference that distorts an analog or digital signal. It may be caused by electrical sources, such as power lines, fluorescent lights, copiers, and microwave ovens, or by broadcast signals.

◆ Analog and digital signals both suffer attenuation, or loss of signal, as they travel farther from their sources. To compensate, analog signals are amplified, and digital signals are regenerated through repeaters.

◆ Every network is susceptible to a delay between the transmission of a signal and its receipt. This delay is called latency. The length of the cable contributes to latency, as does the presence of any intervening connectivity device.

◆ Coaxial cable consists of a central copper core surrounded by a plastic insulator, a braided metal shielding, and an outer plastic cover called the sheath. The copper core carries the electromagnetic signal, and the shielding acts as both a protection against noise and a ground for the signal. The insulator layer protects the copper core from the metal shielding. The sheath protects the cable from physical damage.

◆ The type of coaxial cable used to connect cable modems with a broadband cable carrier is RG-6, and it requires an F-Type connector.

◆ Twisted-pair cable consists of color-coded pairs of insulated copper wires, each with a diameter of 0.4 to 0.8 mm, twisted around each other and encased in plastic coating.

◆ STP (shielded twisted-pair) cable consists of twisted wire pairs that are not only individually insulated, but also surrounded by a shielding made of a metallic substance such as foil, to reduce the effects of noise on the signal.

- UTP (unshielded twisted-pair) cabling consists of one or more insulated wire pairs encased in a plastic sheath. As its name suggests, UTP does not contain additional shielding for the twisted pairs. As a result, UTP is both less expensive and less resistant to noise than STP.

- 10BASE-T is a Physical layer specification for an Ethernet network that is capable of 10-Mbps throughput and uses baseband transmission and twisted-pair media. It has a maximum segment length of 100 meters. It follows the 5-4-3 rule, which allows up to five segments between two communicating nodes, permits up to four repeating devices, and allows up to three of the segments to be populated.

- 100BASE-T (also called Fast Ethernet) is a Physical layer specification for an Ethernet network that is capable of 100-Mbps throughput and uses baseband transmission and twisted-pair media. It has a maximum segment length of 100 meters and allows up to three segments connected by two repeating devices.

- 1000BASE-T (also called Gigabit Ethernet) is a Physical layer specification for an Ethernet network that is capable of 1000-Mbps (1-Gbps) throughput and uses baseband transmission and twisted-pair media. It has a maximum segment length of 100 meters and allows only one repeating device between segments.

- Fiber-optic cable contains one or several glass or plastic fibers in its core. Data is transmitted via pulsing light sent from a laser or light-emitting diode through the central fiber(s). Outside the fiber(s), cladding reflects light back to the core in different patterns that vary depending on the transmission mode.

- Fiber-optic cable provides the benefits of very high throughput, very high resistance to noise, and excellent security.

- Fiber cable variations fall into two categories: single-mode and multimode. Single-mode fiber uses a small-diameter core, over which light travels mostly down its center, reflecting very few times. This allows single-mode fiber to accommodate high bandwidths and long distances (without requiring repeaters).

- Multimode fiber uses a core with a larger diameter, over which many pulses of light travel at different angles. Multimode fiber is less expensive than single-mode fiber.

- 10BASE-FL is the most popular of the three 10BASE-F standards, each of which specifies a maximum throughput of 10 Mbps over multimode fiber-optic cable. 10BASE-FL can use repeaters to reach a maximum segment length of 2000 meters.

- 100BASE-FX is a Physical layer specification for a network that can achieve 100-Mbps throughput using baseband transmission running on multimode fiber. Its maximum segment length is 2000 meters.

- 1-Gbps Physical layer standards for fiber-optic networks include 1000BASE-SX and 1000BASE-LX. Because 1000BASE-LX reaches farther and uses a longer wavelength, it is the more popular of the two. 1000BASE-LX can use either single-mode or multimode fiber-optic cable, for which its segments can be up to 550 or 5000 meters, respectively. 1000BASE-SX uses only multimode fiber and can span up to 500 meters.

◆ 1000Base-CX is a Physical layer specification for an Ethernet network that is capable of 1000-Mbps (1-Gbps) throughput and relies on twinaxial cable. It has a maximum segment length of 25 meters and is best suited to short connections within a data center—for example, between two switches or routers.

◆ 10-Gbps Physical layer standards include: 10GBASE-SR ("short reach"), which relies on multimode fiber-optic cable and can span a maximum of 300 meters; 10GBASE-ER ("extended reach"), which relies on single-mode fiber and can span a maximum of 10,000 meters; and 10GBaseLR ("long reach"), which also uses single-mode fiber and can span up to 40,000 meters.

◆ In 1991, TIA/EIA released their joint 568 Commercial Building Wiring Standard, also known as structured cabling, for uniform, enterprise-wide, multivendor cabling systems. Structured cabling is based on a hierarchical design that divides cabling into six subsystems: entrance facility, backbone (vertical) wiring, equipment room, telecommunications closet, horizontal wiring, and work area.

◆ The best practice for installing cable is to follow the TIA/EIA 568 specifications and the manufacturer's recommendations. Be careful not to exceed a cable's bend radius, untwist wire pairs more than one-half inch, or remove more than one inch of insulation from copper wire. Install plenum-rated cable in ceilings and floors, and run cabling far from where it might suffer physical damage.

◆ Wireless transmission requires an antenna connected to a transceiver. Stations can be fixed or mobile within the antenna's range.

◆ Wireless transmission is susceptible to interference from EMI. Signals are also affected by obstacles in their paths, which cause them to reflect, diffract, or scatter. A large number of obstacles can prevent wireless signals from ever reaching their destination.

◆ Infrared transmission, which uses frequencies in the 300- to 300,000-GHz range, can be used for short-distance transmissions such as sending signals between a computer and a nearby printer. Infrared is impractical for longer distances and many users.

◆ Most modern WLANs (wireless LANs) use frequencies in the 2.4-GHz band. They rely on APs (access points) that transmit and receive signals to and from wireless stations and connectivity devices. APs may connect stations to a LAN or multiple network segments to a backbone.

◆ To determine which transmission media are right for a particular networking environment, you must consider the organization's required throughput, cabling distance, noise resistance, security, and plans for growth.

Key Terms

1 gigabit per second (Gbps)—1,000,000,000 bits per second.

1 kilobit per second (Kbps)—1000 bits per second.

1 megabit per second (Mbps)—1,000,000 bits per second.

1 terabit per second (Tbps)—1,000,000,000,000 bits per second.

10BASE-2—See *Thinnet*.

10BASE-5—See *Thicknet*.

10BASE-F—A Physical layer standard for achieving 10-Mbps throughput over multimode fiber-optic cable. Three different kinds of 10BASE-F exist. All require two strands of multimode fiber, in which one strand is used for data transmission and one strand is used for reception, making 10BASE-F a full-duplex technology.

10BASE-FL—The most popular version of the 10BASE-F standard. 10BASE-FL is designed to connect workstations to a LAN or two repeaters and can take advantage of fiber-optic repeating technology to reach its maximum segment length of 2000 meters. 10BASE-FL makes use of the star topology, with its repeaters connected through a bus.

10BASE-T—A Physical layer standard for networks that specifies baseband transmission, twisted-pair media, and 10-Mbps throughput. 10BASE-T networks have a maximum segment length of 100 meters and rely on a star topology.

10GBASE-ER—A Physical layer standard for achieving 10-Gbps data transmission over single-mode, fiber-optic cable. In 10GBASE-ER the "ER" stands for "extended reach." This standard specifies a star topology and segment lengths up to 40 kilometers.

10GBASE-LR—A Physical layer standard for achieving 10-Gbps data transmission over single-mode, fiber-optic cable using wavelengths of 1310 nanometers. In 10GBASE-LR, the "LR" stands for "long reach." This standard specifies a star topology and segment lengths up to 10 kilometers.

10GBASE-SR—A Physical layer standard for achieving 10-Gbps data transmission over multimode fiber using wavelengths of 850 nanometers. The maximum segment length for 10GBASE-SR can reach up to 300 meters, depending on the fiber core diameter and modal bandwidth used.

100BASE-FX—A Physical layer standard for networks that specifies baseband transmission, multimode fiber cabling, and 100-Mbps throughput. 100BASE-FX networks have a maximum segment length of 2000 meters. 100BASE-FX may also be called Fast Ethernet.

100BASE-T—A Physical layer standard for networks that specifies baseband transmission, twisted-pair cabling, and 100-Mbps throughput. 100BASE-T networks have a maximum segment length of 100 meters and use the star topology. 100BASE-T is also known as Fast Ethernet.

100BASE-TX—A type of 100BASE-T network that uses two wire pairs in a twisted-pair cable, but uses faster signaling to achieve 100-Mbps throughput. It is capable of full-duplex transmission and requires CAT 5 or higher twisted-pair media.

1000BASE-CX—A Physical layer standard for achieving 1-Gbps throughput over twinaxial copper wire. 1000BASE-CX segments are limited to 25 meters, and are useful mainly to connect devices such as servers or switches.

1000BASE-LX—A Physical layer standard for networks that specifies 1-Gbps transmission over fiber-optic cable using baseband transmission. 1000BASE-LX can run on either single-mode or multimode fiber. The "LX" represents its reliance on "long wavelengths" of 1300 nanometers. 1000BASE-LX can extend to 5000-meter segment lengths using single-mode, fiber-optic cable. 1000BASE-LX networks can use one repeater between segments.

1000BASE-SX—A Physical layer standard for networks that specifies 1-Gbps transmission over fiber-optic cable using baseband transmission. 1000BASE-SX runs on multimode fiber. Its maximum segment length is 550 meters. The "SX" represents its reliance on "short wavelengths" of 850 nanometers. 1000BASE-SX can use one repeater.

1000BASE-T—A Physical layer standard for achieving 1 Gbps over UTP. 1000BASE-T achieves its higher throughput by using all four pairs of wires in a CAT 5 or higher twisted-pair cable to both transmit and receive signals. 1000BASE-T also uses a different data encoding scheme than that used by other UTP Physical layer specifications.

2.4-GHz band—The range of radiofrequencies from 2.4- to 2.4835-GHz. The 2.4-GHz band is often used for wireless network transmissions.

5-4-3 rule—A guideline for 10-Mbps Ethernet networks stating that between two communicating nodes, the network cannot contain more than five network segments connected by four repeating devices, and no more than three of the segments may be populated.

802.3ab—The IEEE standard that describes 1000BASE-T, a 1-Gigabit Ethernet technology that runs over four pairs of CAT 5 or better cable.

802.3ae—The IEEE standard that describes 10-Gigabit Ethernet technologies, including 10GBASE-SR, 10GBASE-ER, and 10GBASE-LR.

802.3u—The IEEE standard that describes Fast Ethernet technologies, including 100BASE-TX, 100BASE-T4, and 100BASE-FX.

802.3z—The IEEE standard that describes 1000Base (or 1-Gigabit) Ethernet technologies, including 1000BASE-LX, 1000BASE-SX, and 1000BASE-CX.

access point—See *AP*.

ad hoc—A type of wireless LAN in which stations communicate directly with each other (rather than using an access point).

AM (amplitude modulation)—A modulation technique in which the amplitude of the carrier signal is modified by the application of a data signal.

amplifier—A device that boosts, or strengthens, an analog signal.

amplitude—A measure of a signal's strength.

amplitude modulation—See *AM*.

analog—A signal that uses variable voltage to create continuous waves, resulting in an inexact transmission.

AP (access point)—A device used on wireless LANs that transmits and receives wireless signals to and from multiple nodes and retransmits them to the rest of the network segment. Access points can connect a group of nodes with a network or two networks with each other. They may use directional or omni-directional antennas.

attenuation—The extent to which a signal has weakened after traveling a given distance.

bandwidth—A measure of the difference between the highest and lowest frequencies that a medium can transmit.

baseband—A form of transmission in which digital signals are sent through direct current pulses applied to a wire. This direct current requires exclusive use of the wire's capacity, so baseband systems can transmit only one signal, or one channel, at a time. Every device on a baseband system shares a single channel.

bend radius—The radius of the maximum arc into which you can loop a cable before you will cause data transmission errors. Generally, a twisted-pair cable's bend radius is equal to or greater than four times the diameter of the cable.

binary—A system founded on using 1s and 0s to encode information.

bit (binary digit)—A bit equals a single pulse in the digital encoding system. It may have only one of two values: 0 or 1.

braiding—A braided metal shielding used to insulate some types of coaxial cable.

broadband—A form of transmission in which signals are modulated as radiofrequency analog pulses with different frequency ranges. Unlike baseband, broadband technology does not involve binary encoding. The use of multiple frequencies enables a broadband system to operate over several channels and therefore carry much more data than a baseband system.

broadcast—A transmission that involves one transmitter and multiple receivers.

byte—Eight bits of information. In a digital signaling system, broadly speaking, one byte carries one piece of information.

cable modem—A device that modulates and demodulates the broadband cable signals.

cable plant—The hardware that constitutes the enterprise-wide cabling system.

capacity—See *throughput*.

CAT—Abbreviation for the word "category" when describing a type of twisted-pair cable. For example, Category 3 unshielded twisted-pair cable may also be called CAT 3.

CAT 3 (Category 3)—A form of UTP that contains four wire pairs and can carry up to 10 Mbps, with a possible bandwidth of 16 MHz. CAT 3 has typically been used for 10-Mbps Ethernet or 4-Mbps Token Ring networks. Network administrators are gradually replacing CAT 3 cabling with CAT 5 to accommodate higher throughput. CAT 3 is less expensive than CAT 5.

CAT 4 (Category 4)—A form of UTP that contains four wire pairs and can support up to 16-Mbps throughput. CAT 4 may be used for 16-Mbps Token Ring or 10-Mbps Ethernet networks. It is guaranteed for data transmission up to 20 MHz and provides more protection against crosstalk and attenuation than CAT 1, CAT 2, or CAT 3.

CAT 5 (Category 5)—A form of UTP that contains four wire pairs and supports up to 100-Mbps throughput and a 100-MHz signal rate.

CAT 5e (Enhanced Category 5)—A higher-grade version of CAT 5 wiring that contains high-quality copper, offers a high twist ratio, and uses advanced methods for reducing crosstalk. Enhanced CAT 5 can support a signaling rate of up to 350 MHz, more than triple the capability of regular CAT 5.

CAT 6 (Category 6)—A twisted-pair cable that contains four wire pairs, each wrapped in foil insulation. Additional foil insulation covers the bundle of wire pairs, and a fire-resistant plastic sheath covers the second foil layer. The foil insulation provides excellent resistance to crosstalk and enables CAT 6 to support a signaling rate of 250 MHz and at least six times the throughput supported by regular CAT 5.

CAT 6e (Enhanced Category 6)—A higher-grade version of CAT 6 wiring that further reduces attenuation and crosstalk and allows for potentially exceeding traditional network segment length limits. CAT 6e is capable of a 550-MHz signaling rate and can reliably transmit data at multi-Gigabit per second rates.

CAT 7 (Category 7)—A twisted-pair cable that contains multiple wire pairs, each separately shielded then surrounded by another layer of shielding within the jacket. CAT 7 can support up to a 1-GHz signal rate. But because of its extra layers, it is less flexible than other forms of twisted-pair wiring.

Category 3—See _CAT 3_.

Category 4—See _CAT 4_.

Category 5—See _CAT 5_.

Category 6—See _CAT 6_.

Category 7—See _CAT 7_.

channel—A distinct communication path between two or more nodes, much like a lane is a distinct transportation path on a freeway. Channels may be separated either logically (as in multiplexing) or physically (as when they are carried by separate wires).

cladding—The glass or plastic shield around the core of a fiber-optic cable. Cladding reflects light back to the core in patterns that vary depending on the transmission mode. This reflection allows fiber to bend around corners without impairing the light-based signal.

coaxial cable—A type of cable that consists of a central copper core surrounded by an insulator, a braided metal shielding, called braiding, and an outer cover, called the sheath or jacket. Coaxial cable, called "coax" for short, was the foundation for Ethernet networks in the 1980s and remained a popular transmission medium for many years.

conduit—The pipeline used to contain and protect cabling. Conduit is usually made from metal.

connectors—The pieces of hardware that connect the wire to the network device, be it a file server, workstation, switch, or printer.

core—The central component of a cable designed to carry a signal. The core of a fiber-optic cable, for example, consists of one or several glass or plastic fibers. The core of a coaxial copper cable consists of one large or several small strands of copper.

crossover cable—A twisted-pair patch cable in which the termination locations of the transmit and receive wires on one end of the cable are reversed.

crosstalk—A type of interference caused by signals traveling on nearby wire pairs infringing on another pair's signal.

demarcation point (demarc)—The point of division between a telecommunications service carrier's network and a building's internal network.

demultiplexer (demux)—A device that separates multiplexed signals once they are received and regenerates them in their original form.

dense wavelength division multiplexing—See *DWDM*.

diffraction—In the context of wireless signal propagation, the phenomenon that occurs when an electromagnetic wave encounters an obstruction and splits into secondary waves. The secondary waves continue to propagate in the direction in which they were split. If you could see wireless signals being diffracted, they would appear to be bending around the obstacle. Objects with sharp edges—including the corners of walls and desks—cause diffraction.

digital—As opposed to analog signals, digital signals are composed of pulses that can have a value of only 1 or 0.

direct sequence spread spectrum—See *DSSS*.

directional antenna—A type of antenna that issues wireless signals along a single direction, or path.

DSSS (direct sequence spread spectrum)—A transmission technique in which a signal's bits are distributed over an entire frequency band at once. Each bit is coded so that the receiver can reassemble the original signal upon receiving the bits.

duplex—See *full-duplex*.

DWDM (dense wavelength division multiplexing)—A multiplexing technique used over single-mode or multimode fiber-optic cable in which each signal is assigned a different wavelength for its carrier wave. In DWDM, little space exists between carrier waves, in order to achieve extraordinary high capacity.

electromagnetic interference—See *EMI*.

EMI (electromagnetic interference)—A type of interference that may be caused by motors, power lines, televisions, copiers, fluorescent lights, or other sources of electrical activity.

enhanced Category 5—See *CAT 5e.*

enhanced Category 6—See *CAT 6e.*

F-Type connector—A connector used to terminate coaxial cable used for transmitting television and broadband cable signals.

fading—A change in a wireless signal's strength as a result of some of the electromagnetic energy being scattered, reflected, or diffracted after being issued by the transmitter.

Fast Ethernet—A type of Ethernet network that is capable of 100-Mbps throughput. 100BASE-T and 100BASE-FX are both examples of Fast Ethernet.

fault tolerance—The capability for a component or system to continue functioning despite damage or malfunction.

ferrule—A short tube within a fiber-optic cable connector that encircles the fiber strand and keeps it properly aligned.

FHSS (frequency hopping spread spectrum)—A wireless signaling technique in which a signal jumps between several different frequencies within a band in a synchronization pattern known to the channel's receiver and transmitter.

fiber-optic cable—A form of cable that contains one or several glass or plastic fibers in its core. Data is transmitted via pulsing light sent from a laser or light-emitting diode (LED) through the central fiber (or fibers). Fiber-optic cables offer significantly higher throughput than copper-based cables. They may be single-mode or multimode and typically use wave-division multiplexing to carry multiple signals.

fixed—A type of wireless system in which the locations of the transmitter and receiver are static. In a fixed connection, the transmitting antenna focuses its energy directly toward the receiving antenna. This results in a point-to-point link.

FM (frequency modulation)—A method of data modulation in which the frequency of the carrier signal is modified by the application of the data signal.

frequency—The number of times that a signal's amplitude changes over a fixed period of time, expressed in cycles per second, or hertz (Hz).

frequency hopping spread spectrum—See *FHSS.*

frequency modulation—See *FM.*

full-duplex—A type of transmission in which signals may travel in both directions over a medium simultaneously. May also be called, simply, "duplex."

Gigabit Ethernet—A type of Ethernet network that is capable of 1000 Mbps, or 1 Gbps, throughput. Examples of Gigabit Ethernet include 1000BASE-T and 1000BASE-CX.

half-duplex—A type of transmission in which signals may travel in both directions over a medium, but in only one direction at a time.

hertz (Hz)—A measure of frequency equivalent to the number of amplitude cycles per second.

impedance—The resistance that contributes to controlling an electrical signal. Impedance is measured in ohms.

infrared—A type of data transmission in which infrared light signals are used to transmit data through space, similar to the way a television remote control sends signals across the room. Networks may use two types of infrared transmission: direct or indirect.

infrastructure WLAN—A type of WLAN in which stations communicate with an access point and not directly with each other.

latency—The delay between the transmission of a signal and its receipt.

LC (Local Connector)—A connector used with single-mode or multimode fiber-optic cable.

Level 1—A form of UTP that contains two wire pairs. Level 1 is the type of wire used for older voice networks and is unsuitable for transmitting data.

line-of-sight—See *LOS*.

link segment—See *unpopulated segment*.

Local Connector—See *LC*.

LOS (line-of-sight)—A wireless signal or path that travels directly in a straight line from its transmitter to its intended receiver. This type of propagation uses the least amount of energy and results in the reception of the clearest possible signal.

Mechanical Transfer Registered Jack—See *MT-RJ*.

media converter—A device that enables networks or segments using different media to interconnect and exchange signals.

MMF (multimode fiber)—A type of fiber-optic cable that contains a core with a diameter between 50 and 100 microns, through which many pulses of light generated by a light-emitting diode (LED) travel at different angles.

mobile—A type of wireless system in which the receiver can be located anywhere within the transmitter's range. This allows the receiver to roam from one place to another while continuing to pick up its signal.

modal bandwidth—A measure of the highest frequency of signal a multimode fiber-optic cable can support over a specific distance. Modal bandwidth is measured in MHz-km.

modem—A device that modulates analog signals into digital signals at the transmitting end for transmission over telephone lines, and demodulates digital signals into analog signals at the receiving end.

modulation—A technique for formatting signals in which one property of a simple carrier wave is modified by the addition of a data signal during transmission.

MT-RJ (Mechanical Transfer Registered Jack)—A connector used with single-mode or multimode fiber-optic cable.

multimode fiber—See *MMF*.

multipath—The characteristic of wireless signals that follow a number of different paths to their destination (for example, because of reflection, diffraction, and scattering).

multiplexer (mux)—A device that separates a medium into multiple channels and issues signals to each of those subchannels.

multiplexing—A form of transmission that allows multiple signals to travel simultaneously over one medium.

narrowband—A type of wireless transmission in which signals travel over a single frequency or within a specified frequency range.

noise—The unwanted signals, or interference, from sources near network cabling, such as electrical motors, power lines, and radar.

omnidirectional antenna—A type of antenna that issues and receives wireless signals with equal strength and clarity in all directions. This type of antenna is used when many different receivers must be able to pick up the signal, or when the receiver's location is highly mobile.

optical loss—The degradation of a light signal on a fiber-optic network.

overhead—The nondata information that must accompany data in order for a signal to be properly routed and interpreted by the network.

patch cable—A relatively short section (usually between 3 and 25 feet) of cabling with connectors on both ends.

patch panel—A wall-mounted panel of data receptors into which cross-connect patch cables from the punch-down block are inserted.

PDA (personal digital assistant)—A handheld computer. PDAs normally use a stylus for user input and often communicate via infrared or another wireless signaling method.

personal digital assistant—See *PDA*.

phase—A point or stage in a wave's progress over time.

plenum—The area above the ceiling tile or below the subfloor in a building.

point-to-point—A data transmission that involves one transmitter and one receiver.

populated segment—A network segment that contains end nodes, such as workstations.

punch-down block—A panel of data receptors into which horizontal cabling from the workstations is inserted.

radiation pattern—The relative strength over a three-dimensional area of all the electromagnetic energy an antenna sends or receives.

radiofrequency interference—See *RFI*.

range—The geographical area in which signals issued from an antenna or wireless system can be consistently and accurately received.

reflection—In the context of wireless, the phenomenon that occurs when an electromagnetic wave encounters an obstacle and bounces back toward its source. A wireless signal will bounce off objects whose dimensions are large compared to the signal's average wavelength.

regeneration—The process of retransmitting a digital signal. Regeneration, unlike amplification, repeats the pure signal, with none of the noise it has accumulated.

repeater—A device used to regenerate a signal.

RFI (radiofrequency interference)—A kind of interference that may be generated by broadcast signals from radio or TV towers.

RG-6—A type of coaxial cable used for television, satellite, and broadband cable connections.

risers—The backbone cabling that provides vertical connections between floors of a building.

RJ-11 (Registered Jack 11)—The standard connector used with unshielded twisted-pair cabling (usually CAT 3 or Level 1) to connect analog telephones.

RJ-45 (Registered Jack 45)—The standard connector used with shielded twisted-pair and unshielded twisted-pair cabling.

round trip time—See *RTT*.

RTT (round trip time)—The length of time it takes for a packet to go from sender to receiver, then back from receiver to sender. RTT is usually measured in milliseconds.

SC (Subscriber Connector or Standard Connector)—A connector used with single-mode or multimode fiber-optic cable.

scattering—The diffusion of a wireless signal that results from hitting an object that has smaller dimensions compared to the signal's wavelength. Scattering is also related to the roughness of the surface a wireless signal encounters. The rougher the surface, the more likely a signal is to scatter when it hits that surface.

sheath—The outer cover, or jacket, of a cable.

shielded twisted-pair—See *STP*.

simplex—A type of transmission in which signals may travel in only one direction over a medium.

single-mode fiber—See *SMF*.

SMF (single-mode fiber)—A type of fiber-optic cable with a narrow core that carries light pulses along a single path data from one end of the cable to the other end. Data can be transmitted faster and for longer distances on single-mode fiber than on multimode fiber. However, single-mode fiber is more expensive.

spread spectrum—A type of wireless transmission in which lower-level signals are distributed over several frequencies simultaneously. Spread spectrum transmission is more secure than narrowband.

ST (Straight Tip)—A connector used with single-mode or multimode fiber-optic cable.

Standard Connector—See *SC*.

station—An end node on a network; used most often in the context of wireless networks.

statistical multiplexing—A method of multiplexing in which each node on a network is assigned a separate time slot for transmission, based on the node's priority and need.

STP (shielded twisted-pair)—A type of cable containing twisted-wire pairs that are not only individually insulated, but also surrounded by a shielding made of a metallic substance such as foil.

straight-through cable—A twisted-pair patch cable in which the wire terminations in both connectors follow the same scheme.

Straight Tip—See *ST*.

structured cabling—A method for uniform, enterprise-wide, multivendor cabling systems specified by the TIA/EIA 568 Commercial Building Wiring Standard. Structured cabling is based on a hierarchical design using a high-speed backbone.

subchannel—One of many distinct communication paths established when a channel is multiplexed or modulated.

Subscriber Connector—See *SC*.

TDM (time division multiplexing)—A method of multiplexing that assigns a time slot in the flow of communications to every node on the network and, in that time slot, carries data from that node.

Thicknet—An IEEE Physical layer standard for achieving a maximum of 10-Mbps throughput over coaxial copper cable. Thicknet is also known as 10BASE-5. Its maximum segment length is 500 meters, and it relies on a bus topology.

thickwire Ethernet—See *Thicknet*.

thin Ethernet—See *Thinnet*.

Thinnet—An IEEE Physical layer standard for achieving 10-Mbps throughput over coaxial copper cable. Thinnet is also known as 10BASE-2. Its maximum segment length is 185 meters, and it relies on a bus topology.

throughput—The amount of data that a medium can transmit during a given period of time. Throughput is usually measured in megabits (1,000,000 bits) per second, or Mbps. The physical nature of every transmission media determines its potential throughput.

time division multiplexing—See *TDM*.

transceiver—A device that transmits and receives signals.

transmission—In networking, the application of data signals to a medium or the progress of data signals over a medium from one point to another.

transmit—To issue signals to the network medium.

twinaxial cable—A type of cable that consists of two copper conductors at its center surrounded by an insulator, a braided metal shielding, called braiding, and an outer cover, called the sheath or jacket.

twist ratio—The number of twists per meter or foot in a twisted-pair cable.

twisted-pair—A type of cable similar to telephone wiring that consists of color-coded pairs of insulated copper wires, each with a diameter of 0.4 to 0.8 mm, twisted around each other and encased in plastic coating.

unpopulated segment—A network segment that does not contain end nodes, such as workstations. Unpopulated segments are also called link segments.

unshielded twisted-pair—See *UTP*.

UTP (unshielded twisted-pair)—A type of cabling that consists of one or more insulated wire pairs encased in a plastic sheath. As its name implies, UTP does not contain additional shielding for the twisted pairs. As a result, UTP is both less expensive and less resistant to noise than STP.

volt—The measurement used to describe the degree of pressure an electrical current exerts on a conductor.

voltage—The pressure (sometimes informally referred to as the strength) of an electrical current.

WAP (wireless access point)—See *AP*.

wavelength—The distance between corresponding points on a wave's cycle. Wavelength is inversely proportional to frequency.

wavelength division multiplexing—See *WDM*.

WDM (wavelength division multiplexing)—A multiplexing technique in which each signal on a fiber-optic cable is assigned a different wavelength, which equates to its own subchannel. Each wavelength is modulated with a data signal. In this manner, multiple signals can be simultaneously transmitted in the same direction over a length of fiber.

Webcasting—A broadcast transmission from one Internet-attached node to multiple other Internet-attached nodes.

wire-bound—A type of signal that relies on a physical medium, such as a cable, for its transmission.

wireless—The signals made of electromagnetic energy that travel through the atmosphere.

wireless access point—See *WAP*.

wireless LAN—See *WLAN*.

wireless spectrum—A continuum of electromagnetic waves used for data and voice communication. The wireless spectrum (as defined by the FCC, which controls its use) spans frequencies between 9 KHz and 300 GHz. Each type of wireless service can be associated with one area of the wireless spectrum.

WLAN (wireless LAN)—A LAN that uses wireless connections for some or all of its transmissions.

Review Questions

1. A wave's _____ is a measure of its strength at any given point in time.
   a. attenuation
   b. wavelength
   c. latency
   d. amplitude

2. A(n) _____ is a distinct communication path between nodes.
   a. conduit
   b. channel
   c. plenum
   d. amplifier

3. The most common way to measure latency on data networks is by calculating a packet's _____.
   a. round trip time
   b. bend radius
   c. modulation
   d. fault tolerance

4. A(n) _____ issues and receives wireless signals with equal strength and clarity in all directions.
   a. single-mode fiber
   b. omni-directional antenna
   c. subchannel
   d. plenum

5. A(n) _____ is a device that accepts wireless signals from multiple nodes and retransmits them to the rest of the network.

    a. media converter

    b. link segment

    c. access point

    d. diffraction

6. True or false? A noisy circuit spends more time compensating for the noise, and therefore has fewer resources available for transmitting data.

7. True or false? A populated segment is a part of a network that connects two network devices, such as hubs.

8. True or false? 100BASE-FX requires multimode fiber containing at least two strands of fiber.

9. True or false? Backbone wiring provides interconnection between telecommunications closets, equipment rooms, and entrance facilities.

10. True or false? Multiplexing is the diffusion, or the reflection in multiple directions, of a signal.

11. The distance between corresponding points on a wave's cycle is called its _____.

12. _____ is a term used by network professionals to describe the non-data information that must accompany data in order for a signal to be properly routed and interpreted by the network.

13. _____ occurs when a signal traveling on one wire or cable infringes on the signal traveling over an adjacent wire or cable.

14. _____ cable consists of twisted wire pairs that are not only individually insulated, but also surrounded by a shielding made of a metallic substance, such as foil.

15. _____ is the capacity for a component or system to continue functioning despite damage or partial malfunction.

Chapter 4

Network Protocols

After reading this chapter and completing the exercises, you will be able to:

- Identify the characteristics of TCP/IP, IPX/SPX, NetBIOS, and AppleTalk

- Understand how network protocols correlate to layers of the OSI Model

- Identify the core protocols of the TCP/IP suite and describe their functions

- Identify the well-known ports for key TCP/IP services

- Understand addressing schemes for TCP/IP, IPX/SPX, NetBEUI, and AppleTalk

- Describe the purpose and implementation of DNS (Domain Name System) and WINS (Windows Internet Naming Service)

- Install protocols on Windows XP clients

A protocol is a rule that governs how networks communicate. Protocols define the standards for communication between network devices. Without protocols, devices could not interpret the signals sent by other devices, and data would go nowhere. In this chapter, you will learn about the most commonly used networking protocols, their components, and their functions. This chapter is not an exhaustive study of protocols, but rather a practical guide to applying them. At the end of the chapter, you will have the opportunity to read about some realistic networking scenarios pertaining to protocols and devise your own solutions. As protocols form the foundation of network communications, you must fully understand them to manage a network effectively.

Introduction to Protocols

In Chapter 2, you learned about the tasks associated with each layer of the OSI Model, for example, formatting, addressing, and error correction. You also learned that these tasks are performed by protocols, which are sets of instructions designed and coded by programmers. In the networking industry, the term "protocol" is often used to refer to a group, or suite, of individual protocols that work together.

Protocols vary according to their purpose, speed, transmission efficiency, utilization of resources, ease of setup, compatibility, and ability to travel between different LANs. When choosing protocols, you will need to consider these characteristics, plus network interconnection and data security requirements. Also keep in mind the limitations that a network's existing—and sometimes outdated—hardware and software impose. On long-established networks a mix of legacy and new technology might require the use of more than one protocol—for example, IPX/SPX along with TCP/IP. Networks running more than one protocol are called **multiprotocol networks**. To manage a multiprotocol network, it is not only important to know about each protocol suite, but also to understand how they work together.

In the sections that follow, you will learn about the most popular networking protocol suite—TCP/IP—plus other protocol suites—IPX/SPX, NetBIOS, and AppleTalk—that, although once popular, have been replaced by TCP/IP on modern networks. For Network+ certification, you should understand TCP/IP in depth and be familiar with the other protocol suites. Keep in mind that you may occasionally encounter additional protocols (such as SNA or DLC) that are not discussed in this chapter. But if a network was established within the last few years, chances are that it will rely on TCP/IP. TCP/IP is discussed next.

TCP/IP (Transmission Control Protocol/Internet Protocol)

NET+

2.4

TCP/IP (Transmission Control Protocol/Internet Protocol) is not simply one protocol, but rather a suite of specialized protocols—including TCP, IP, UDP, ARP, and many others—called **subprotocols**. Most network administrators refer to the entire group as "TCP/IP," or sometimes simply "IP." For example, a network administrator might say, "Our network only runs IP" when she means that all of the network's services rely on TCP/IP subprotocols.

TCP/IP's roots lie with the U.S. Department of Defense, which developed TCP/IP for its Advanced Research Projects Agency network (ARPAnet, the precursor to today's Internet) in the late 1960s. TCP/IP has grown extremely popular thanks to its low cost, its ability to communicate between a multitude of dissimilar platforms, and its open nature. "Open" means that a software developer, for example, can use and modify TCP/IP's core protocols freely. TCP/IP is a de facto standard on the Internet and has become the protocol of choice on LANs and WANs. UNIX and Linux have always relied on TCP/IP. The most recent versions of Netware and Windows network operating systems also use TCP/IP as their default protocol.

TCP/IP would not have become so popular if it weren't routable. Protocols that can span more than one LAN (or LAN segment) are **routable**, because they carry Network layer addressing information that can be interpreted by a router. Not all protocols are routable, however. For example, NetBEUI is not routable. Protocol suites that are not routable do not enable data to traverse network segments. They are therefore unsuitable for most large networks.

TCP/IP's popularity is also due to its flexibility. It can run on virtually any combination of network operating systems or network media. Because of its flexibility, however, TCP/IP may require more configuration than other protocol suites.

 NOTE

TCP/IP is a broad topic with numerous technical, historical, and practical aspects. If you want to become an expert on TCP/IP, you should invest in a book or study guide solely devoted to this suite of protocols.

NET+

2.4
2.10

The TCP/IP Core Protocols

Certain subprotocols of the TCP/IP suite, called **TCP/IP core protocols**, operate in the Transport or Network layers of the OSI Model and provide basic services to protocols in other layers. As you might guess, TCP and IP are the most significant protocols in the TCP/IP suite. These and other core protocols are introduced in the following sections.

NET+
2.4
2.10

TCP (Transmission Control Protocol)

TCP (Transmission Control Protocol) operates in the Transport layer of the OSI Model and provides reliable data delivery services. TCP is a connection-oriented subprotocol, which means that a connection must be established between communicating nodes before this protocol will transmit data. TCP further ensures reliable data delivery through sequencing and checksums. Without such measures, data would be transmitted indiscriminately, without checking whether the destination node was offline, for example, or whether the data became corrupt during transmission. Finally, TCP provides flow control to ensure that a node is not flooded with data.

Figure 4-1 depicts the format of a TCP segment, the entity that becomes encapsulated by the IP datagram in the Network layer (and thus becomes the IP datagram's "data"). Fields belonging to a TCP segment are described in the following list.

◆ *Source port*—Indicates the port number at the source node. A **port** is the address on a host where an application makes itself available to incoming or outgoing data. One example of a port is port 80, which is typically used to accept Web page requests from the HTTP protocol. The Source port field is 16 bits long.

◆ *Destination port*—Indicates the port number at the destination node. The Destination port field is 16 bits long.

◆ *Sequence number*—Identifies the data segment's position in the stream of data segments already sent. The Sequence number field is 32 bits long.

◆ *Acknowledgment number (ACK)*—Confirms receipt of the data via a return message to the sender. The Acknowledgment number field is 32 bits long.

◆ *TCP header length*—Indicates the length of the TCP header. This field is 4 bits long.

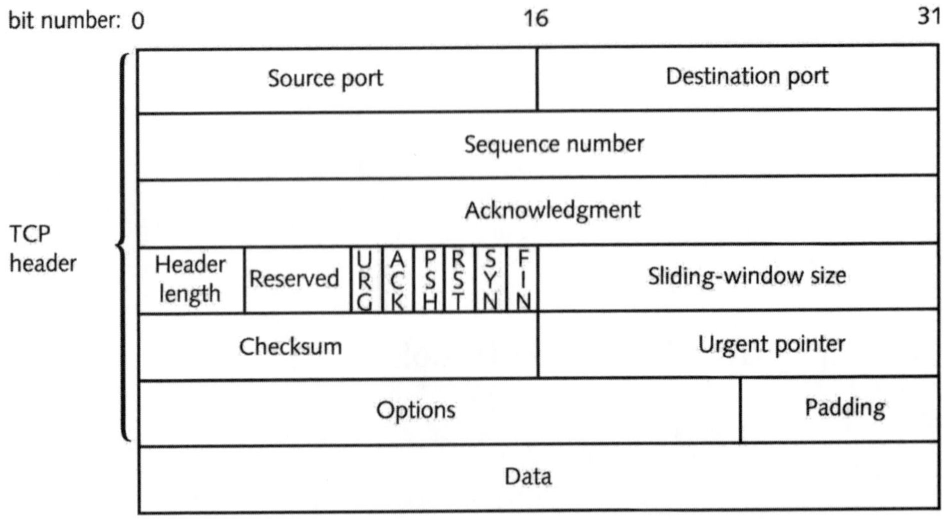

FIGURE 4-1 *A TCP Segment*

NET+
2.4
2.10

- *Reserved*—A 6-bit field reserved for later use.
- *Flags*—A collection of six 1-bit fields that signal special conditions through flags. The following flags are available for the sender's use:
  - URG—If set to "1," the Urgent Pointer field contains information for the receiver.
  - ACK—If set to "1," the Acknowledgment field contains information for the receiver. (If set to "0," the receiver will ignore the Acknowledgment field.)
  - PSH—If set to "1," it indicates that data should be sent to an application without buffering.
  - RST—If set to "1," the sender is requesting that the connection be reset.
  - SYN—If set to "1," the sender is requesting a synchronization of the sequence numbers between the two nodes. This code is used when TCP requests a connection to set the initial sequence number.
  - FIN—If set to "1," the segment is the last in a sequence and the connection should be closed.
- *Sliding-window size (or window)*—Indicates how many bytes the sender can issue to a receiver while acknowledgment for this segment is outstanding. This field performs flow control, preventing the receiver from being deluged with bytes. For example, suppose a server indicates a sliding window size of 4000 bytes. Also suppose the client has already issued 1000 bytes, 250 of which have been received and acknowledged by the server. That means that the server is still buffering 750 bytes. Therefore, the client can only issue 3250 additional bytes before it receives acknowledgment from the server for the 750 bytes. This field is 16 bits long.
- *Checksum*—Allows the receiving node to determine whether the TCP segment became corrupted during transmission. The Checksum field is 16 bits long.
- *Urgent pointer*—Can indicate a location in the data field where urgent data resides. This field is 16 bits long.
- *Options*—Used to specify special options, such as the maximum segment size a network can handle. The size of this field can vary between 0 and 32 bits.
- *Padding*—Contains filler information to ensure that the size of the TCP header is a multiple of 32 bits. The size of this field varies; it is often 0.
- *Data*—Contains data originally sent by the source node. The size of the Data field depends on how much data needs to be transmitted, the constraints on the TCP segment size imposed by the network type, and the limitation that the segment must fit within an IP datagram.

In the Chapter 2 discussion of Transport layer functions you learned how TCP establishes connections for HTTP requests. You also saw an example of TCP segment data from an actual HTTP request. However, you might not have understood what all of the data meant. Now that you know the function of each TCP segment field, you can interpret its contents. Figure 4-2 offers another look at the TCP segment.

NET+
2.4
2.10

Transmission Control Protocol, Src Port: http (80), Dst Port: 1958 (1958), Seq: 3043958669, Ack: 937013559, Len: 0
    Source port : http (80)
    Destination port: 1958 (1958)
    Sequence number: 3043958669
    Acknowledgment number: 937013559
    Header length: 24 bytes
⊟ Flags:_ 0xx0012 (SYN, ACK)
       0... .... = Congestion Window Reduced (CWR): Not set
       .0.. .... = ECN-Echo: Not set
       ..0. .... = Urgent: Not set
       ...1 .... = Acknowledgment: Set
       .... 0... = Push: Not set
       .... .0.. = Reset: Not set
       .... ..1. = Syn: Set
       ....0 = Fin: not set
    window size; 5840
    Checksum: 0x206a (correct)
⊟ Options: (4bytes)
      Maximum segment size: 1460 bytes

FIGURE 4-2 *TCP segment data*

Suppose the segment in Figure 4-2 was sent from Computer B to Computer A. Begin inter-preting the segment at the "Source port" line. Notice the segment was issued from Computer B's port 80, the port assigned to HTTP by default. It was addressed to port 1958 on Com-puter A. The sequence number for this segment is 3043958669. The next segment that Com-puter B expects to receive from Computer A will have the sequence number of 937013559, because this is what Computer B has entered in the Acknowledgment field. By simply having a value, the Acknowledgment field performs its duty of letting a node know that its last com-munication was received. By indicating a sequence number, the Acknowledgment field does double-duty. Next, look at the Header length field. It indicates that the TCP header is 24 bytes long—4 bytes larger than its minimum size—which means that some of the available options were specified or the padding space was used.

In the flags category, notice that there are two unfamiliar flags: Congestion Window Reduced and ECN-Echo. These are optional flags that can be used to help TCP react to and reduce traffic congestion. They are only available when TCP is establishing a connection. However in this segment, they are not set. Of all the possible flags in the Figure 4-2 segment, only the ACK and SYN flags are set. That means that Computer B is acknowledging the last segment it received from Computer A and also negotiating a synchronization scheme for sequencing. The window size is 5840, meaning that Computer B can accept 5840 more bytes of data from Computer A even while this segment remains unacknowledged. The Checksum field indicates the valid outcome of the error-checking algorithm used to verify the segment's header. In this case, the checksum is 0x206a. When Computer A receives this segment, it will perform the same algorithm, and if the result is 0x206a, it will know the TCP header arrived without damage. Finally, this segment uses its option field to specify a maximum TCP segment size of 1460 bytes.

Note that a computer doesn't "see" the TCP segment as it's shown in Figure 4-2. This figure was obtained by using a data analyzer program that translates each packet into a user-friendly

NET+
2.4
2.10

form. From the computer's standpoint, the TCP segment is encoded as hexadecimal characters. (The computer does not need any labels to identify the fields, because as long as TCP/IP protocol standards are followed, it knows exactly where each byte of data is located.)

The TCP segment pictured in Figure 4-2 is part of the process of establishing a connection between Computer B and Computer A. In fact, it is the second segment of three used to establish a TCP connection. In the first step of establishing this connection, Computer A issues a message to Computer B with its SYN bit set, indicating the desire to communicate and synchronize sequence numbers. In its message it sends a random number that will be used to synchronize the communication. In Figure 4-3, for example, this number is 937013558. (Its ACK bit is usually set to 0.) After Computer B receives this message it responds with a segment whose ACK and SYN flags are both set. In Computer B's transmission, the ACK field contains a number that equals the sequence number Computer A originally sent plus 1. As Figure 4-3 illustrates, Computer B sends the number 937013559. In this manner Computer B signals to Computer A that it has received the request for communication and further, it expects Computer A to respond with the sequence number 937013559. In its SYN field, Computer B sends its own random number (in Figure 4-3, this number is 3043958669), which Computer A will use to acknowledge that it received Computer B's transmission. Next, Computer A issues a segment whose sequence number is 937013559 (because this is what Computer B indicated it expected to receive). In the same segment, Computer A also communicates a sequence number via its Acknowledgment field. This number equals the sequence number that Computer B sent plus 1. In the example shown in Figure 4-3, Computer A expects 3043958670 to be the sequence number of the next segment it receives from Computer B. Thus, in its next communication

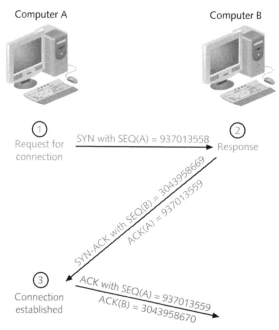

FIGURE 4-3 *Establishing a TCP connection*

NET+
2.4
2.10

(not shown in Figure 4-3), Computer B will respond with a segment whose sequence number is 937013560. The two nodes continue communicating this way until Computer A issues a segment whose FIN flag is set, indicating the end of the transmission.

TCP is not the only core protocol at the Transport layer. A similar but less complex protocol, UDP, is discussed next.

NET+
2.10

UDP (User Datagram Protocol)

UDP (User Datagram Protocol), like TCP, belongs to the Transport layer of the OSI Model. Unlike TCP, however, UDP is a connectionless transport service. In other words, UDP offers no assurance that packets will be received in the correct sequence. In fact, this protocol does not guarantee that the packets will be received at all. Furthermore, it provides no error checking or sequencing. Nevertheless, UDP's lack of sophistication makes it more efficient than TCP. It can be useful in situations where a great volume of data must be transferred quickly, such as live audio or video transmissions over the Internet. In these cases, TCP—with its acknowledgments, checksums, and flow control mechanisms—would only add more overhead to the transmission. UDP is also more efficient for carrying messages that fit within one data packet.

In contrast to a TCP header's 10 fields, the UDP header contains only four fields: Source port, Destination port, Length, and Checksum. Use of the Checksum field in UDP is optional. Figure 4-4 depicts a UDP segment. Contrast its header with the much larger TCP segment header shown in Figure 4-1.

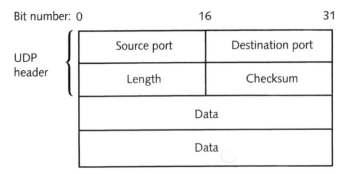

FIGURE 4-4 *A UDP Segment*

Now that you understand the functions of and differences between TCP and UDP, you are ready to learn more about the Internet Protocol (IP).

NET+
2.4
2.10

IP (Internet Protocol)

IP (Internet Protocol) belongs to the Network layer of the OSI Model. It provides information about how and where data should be delivered, including the data's source and destination addresses. IP is the subprotocol that enables TCP/IP to **internetwork**—that is, to traverse more than one LAN segment and more than one type of network through a router.

NET+
2.4
2.10

 NOTE

The following sections describe the IP subprotocol as it is used in **IPv4 (IP version 4)**, the original version that has been used for 20 years and is still used by most networks today.

As you know, at the Network layer of the OSI Model, data is formed into packets. In the context of TCP/IP, a packet is also known as an **IP datagram**. The IP datagram acts as an envelope for data and contains information necessary for routers to transfer data between different LAN segments. IP is an unreliable, connectionless protocol, which means that it does not guarantee delivery of data. Higher-level protocols of the TCP/IP suite, however, use IP to ensure that data packets are delivered to the right addresses. Note that the IP datagram does contain one reliability component, the Header checksum, which verifies only the integrity of the routing information in the IP header. If the checksum accompanying the message does not have the proper value when the packet is received, then the packet is presumed to be corrupt and is discarded; at that point, a new packet is sent.

Figure 4-5 depicts the format of an IP datagram. Its fields are described in the following list.

- ◆ *Version*—Identifies the version number of the protocol—for example, IPv4 or IPv6. The receiving workstation looks at this field first to determine whether it can read the incoming data. If it cannot, it will reject the packet. Rejection rarely occurs, however, because most TCP/IP-based networks use IPv4. This field is 4 bits long.

- ◆ *Internet Header Length (IHL)*—Identifies the number of 4-byte (or 32-bit) blocks in the IP header. The most common header length comprises five groupings, as the

Bit number: 0   16   31

Version	IHL	Differentiated Services	Total length	
Identification			Flags	Fragment offset
Time to live		Protocol	Header checksum	
Source IP address				
Destination IP address				
Options				Padding
Data				

IP header

Data (TCP segment)

FIGURE 4-5 *An IP Datagram*

minimum length of an IP header is 20 4-byte blocks. This field is important because it indicates to the receiving node where data will begin (immediately after the header ends). The IHL field is 4 bits long.

◆ *Differentiated Services (DiffServ) Field*—Informs routers what level of precedence they should apply when processing the incoming packet. This field is 8 bits long. It used to be called the Type of Service (ToS) field, and its purpose was the same as the re-defined Differentiated Services field. However, the ToS specification allowed only eight different values regarding the precedence of a datagram, and the field was rarely used. Differentiated Services allows for up to 64 values and a greater range of priority handling options.

◆ *Total length*—Identifies the total length of the IP datagram, including the header and data, in bytes. An IP datagram, including its header and data, cannot exceed 65,535 bytes. The Total length field is 16 bits long.

◆ *Identification*—Identifies the message to which a datagram belongs and enables the receiving node to reassemble fragmented messages. This field and the following two fields, Flags and Fragment offset, assist in reassembly of fragmented packets. The Identification field is 16 bits long.

◆ *Flags*—Indicates whether a message is fragmented and, if it is fragmented, whether this datagram is the last in the fragment.

◆ *Fragment offset*—Identifies where the datagram fragment belongs in the incoming set of fragments. This field is 13 bits long.

◆ *Time to live (TTL)*—Indicates the maximum time that a datagram can remain on the network before it is discarded. Although this field was originally meant to represent units of time, on modern networks it represents the number of times a datagram has been forwarded by a router, or the number of router **hops** it has endured. The TTL for datagrams is variable and configurable, but is usually set at 32 or 64. Each time a datagram passes through a router, its TTL is reduced by 1. When a router receives a datagram with a TTL equal to 1, it discards that datagram (or more precisely, the frame to which it belongs). The TTL field in an IP datagram is 8 bits long.

◆ *Protocol*—Identifies the type of Transport layer protocol that will receive the datagram (for example, TCP or UDP). This field is 8 bits long.

◆ *Header checksum*—Allows the receiving node to calculate whether the IP header has been corrupted during transmission. This field is 16 bits long.

◆ *Source IP address*—Identifies the full IP address (or Network layer address) of the source node. This field is 32 bits long.

◆ *Destination IP address*—Indicates the full IP address (or Network layer address) of the destination node. This field is 32 bits long.

◆ *Options*—May contain optional routing and timing information. The Options field varies in length.

NET+
2.4
2.10

◆ *Padding*—Contains filler bits to ensure that the header is a multiple of 32 bits. The length of this field varies.

◆ *Data*—Includes the data originally sent by the source node, plus information added by TCP in the Transport layer. The size of the Data field varies.

In the Chapter 2 discussion of the Network layer functions, you were introduced to IP and the data contained in its packets. You also saw an example of IP packet data from an actual HTTP request. However, you might not have understood what all of the data meant. Now that you are familiar with the fields of an IP datagram, you can interpret its contents. Figure 4-6 offers another look at the IP packet, with an interpretation below.

```
⊟Internet Protocol, Src Addr: 140.147.249.7 (140.147.249.7), Dst Addr: 10.11.11.51 (10.11.11.51)
    Version: 4
    Header length: 20 bytes
 ⊞ Differentiated Services Field: 0x00 (DSCP 0x00: Default; ECN 0x00)
    Total Length: 44
    Identification: 0x0000 (0)
 ⊟ Flags: 0x04
       .1.. = Don't fragment: Set
       ..0. = More fragments: Not set
    Fragment offset: 0
    Time to live: 64
    Protocol: TCP (0x06)
    Header checksum: 0x9ff3 (correct)
    Source: 140.147.249.7 (140.147.249.7)
    Destination: 10.11.11.51 (10.11.11.51)
```

FIGURE 4-6 *IP Datagram data*

Begin interpreting the datagram with the Version field, which indicates that this transmission relies on version 4 of the Internet Protocol, which is common for modern networks. Next, notice that the datagram has a header length of 20 bytes. Because this is the minimum size for an IP header, you can deduce that the datagram contains no options or padding. In the Differentiated Services Field no options for priority handling are set, which is not unusual in routine data exchanges such as retrieving a Web page. The total length of the datagram is given as 44 bytes. That makes sense when you consider that its header is 20 bytes, and the TCP segment that it encapsulates (discussed previously) is 24 bytes. Considering that the maximum size of an IP packet is 65,535 bytes, this is a very small packet.

Next in the IP datagram is the Identification field, which uniquely identifies the packet. This packet, the first one issued from Computer B to Computer A in the TCP connection exchange, is identified in hexadecimal notation as 0x0000. In the Flags field, which indicates whether this packet is fragmented, the Don't fragment option is set with a value of 1. So you know that this packet is not fragmented. And because it's not fragmented, the fragment offset field does not apply and is set to 0.

NET+
2.4
2.10

This datagram's TTL (Time to Live) is set to 64. That means that if the packet were to keep traveling across a network, it would be allowed 64 more hops before it was discarded. The Protocol field is next. It indicates that encapsulated within the IP datagram is a TCP segment. TCP is always indicated by the hexadecimal string of "0x06." The next field provides the correct header checksum answer, which is used by the recipient of this packet to determine whether the IP datagram's header was damaged in transit. Finally, the last two fields in the datagram show the logical addresses for the packet's source and destination.

In the next section you learn about another protocol that operates in the Network layer of the OSI Model, ICMP.

NET+
2.10

ICMP (Internet Control Message Protocol)

Whereas IP helps direct data to its correct destination, **ICMP (Internet Control Message Protocol)** is a Network layer protocol that reports on the success or failure of data delivery. It can indicate when part of a network is congested, when data fails to reach its destination, and when data has been discarded because the allotted time for its delivery (its TTL) expired. ICMP announces these transmission failures to the sender, but ICMP cannot correct any of the errors it detects; those functions are left to higher-layer protocols, such as TCP. However, ICMP's announcements provide critical information for troubleshooting network problems.

IGMP (Internet Group Management Protocol)

Another key subprotocol in the TCP/IP suite is **IGMP (Internet Group Management Protocol or Internet Group Multicast Protocol)**. IGMP operates at the Network layer and manages multicasting. **Multicasting** is a transmission method that allows one node to send data to a defined group of nodes (not necessarily the entire network segment, as is the case of a broadcast transmission). Whereas most data transmission occurs on a point-to-point basis, multicasting is a point-to-multipoint method. Multicasting can be used for teleconferencing or videoconferencing over the Internet, for example. Routers use IGMP to determine which nodes belong to a certain multicast group and to transmit data to all nodes in that group. Network nodes use IGMP to join or leave multicast groups at any time.

ARP (Address Resolution Protocol)

ARP (Address Resolution Protocol) is a Network layer protocol that obtains the MAC (physical) address of a host, or node, then creates a database that maps the MAC address to the host's IP (logical) address. If one node needs to know the MAC address of another node on the same network, the first node issues a broadcast message to the network, using ARP, that essentially says, "Will the computer with the IP address 1.2.3.4 please send me its MAC address?" In the context of networking, a broadcast is a transmission that is simultaneously sent to all nodes on a particular network segment. The node that has the IP address 1.2.3.4 then broadcasts a reply that contains the physical address of the destination host.

To make ARP more efficient, computers save recognized MAC-to-IP address mappings on their hard disks in a database known as an **ARP table** (also called an **ARP cache**). After a computer has saved this information, the next time it needs the MAC address for another device, it will find the address in its ARP table and will not need to broadcast another request. Although the precise format of ARP tables may vary from one operating system to another, the essential contents of the table and its purpose remain the same. An example ARP table might look like the following:

```
IP Address          Hardware Address    Type

123.45.67.80        60:23:A6:F1:C4:D2   Static
123.45.67.89        20:00:3D:21:E0:11   Dynamic
123.45.67.73        A0:BB:77:C2:25:FA   Dynamic
```

FIGURE 4-7 *Example ARP table*

An ARP table can contain two types of entries: dynamic and static. **Dynamic ARP table entries** are created when a client makes an ARP request that cannot be satisfied by data already in the ARP table. **Static ARP table entries** are those that someone has entered manually using the ARP utility. The ARP utility, accessed via the arp command from a Windows command prompt or a UNIX or Linux shell prompt, provides a way of obtaining information from and manipulating a device's ARP table. For example, you can view a Windows XP workstation's ARP table by typing arp -a and pressing Enter. ARP can be a valuable troubleshooting tool for discovering the identity of a machine whose IP address you know, or for identifying the problem of two machines trying to use the same IP address.

RARP (Reverse Address Resolution Protocol)

If a device doesn't know its own IP address it cannot use ARP. This is because without an IP address, a device cannot issue an ARP request or receive an ARP reply. One solution to this problem is to allow the client to send a broadcast message with its MAC address and receive an IP address in reply. This process, which is the reverse of ARP, is made possible by **RARP (Reverse Address Resolution Protocol)**. A **RARP server** maintains a table of MAC addresses and their associated IP addresses (similar to an ARP table). After the RARP server receives the client's request, it consults the RARP table to find the IP address that matches the client's MAC address. The RARP server then transmits the IP address information to the client.

RARP was originally developed as a means for **diskless workstations**—workstations that do not contain hard disks, but rely on a small amount of read-only memory to connect to a network—to obtain IP addresses from a server before more sophisticated protocols emerged to perform this function.

NET+
2.4

Addressing in TCP/IP

You have learned that networks recognize two kinds of addresses: logical (or Network layer) and physical (or MAC, or hardware) addresses. MAC addresses are assigned to a device's network interface card at the factory by its manufacturer. Logical addresses can be manually or automatically assigned and must follow rules set by the protocol standards. In the TCP/IP protocol suite, IP is the core protocol responsible for logical addressing. For this reason, addresses on TCP/IP-based networks are often called IP addresses. IP addresses are assigned and used according to very specific parameters.

NET+
2.4
2.5
2.6

Each IP address is a unique 32-bit number, divided into four **octets**, or sets of 8-bits, that are separated by periods. (Because 8 bits equals a byte, each octet is a byte and an IP address is thus composed of 4 bytes.) An example of a valid IP address is 144.92.43.178. An IP address contains two types of information: network and host. From the first octet you can determine the **network class**. Three types of network classes are used on modern LANs: Class A, Class B, and Class C. Table 4-1 summarizes characteristics of the three commonly used classes of TCP/IP-based networks.

Table 4-1 Commonly used TCP/IP classes

Network Class	Beginning Octet	Number of Networks	Maximum Addressable Hosts per Network
A	1–126	126	16,777,214
B	128–191	>16,000	65,534
C	192–223	>2,000,000	254

In addition, Class D and Class E addresses do exist, but are rarely used. Class D addresses, which begin with an octet whose value is between 224 and 239, are reserved for a special type of transmission called multicasting. IETF (Internet Engineering Task Force) reserves Class E addresses, which begin with an octet whose value is between 240 and 254, for experimental use. You should never assign Class D or Class E addresses to devices on your network.

Although 8 bits have 256 possible combinations, only the numbers 1 through 254 can be used to identify networks and hosts in an IP address. The number 0 is reserved to act as a placeholder when referring to an entire group of computers on a network—for example, "10.0.0.0" represents all of the devices whose first octet is "10." The number 255 is reserved for broadcast transmissions. For example, sending a message to the address 255.255.255.255 will send a message to all devices connected to your network segment.

A portion of each IP address contains clues about the network class. An IP address whose first octet is in the range of 1-126 belongs to a Class A network. All IP addresses for devices on a Class A segment share the same first octet, or bits 0 through 7, as shown in Figure 4-8. For example, nodes with the following IP addresses may belong to the same Class A network: 23.78.110.109, 23.164.32.97, 23.48.112.43, and 23.108.37.22. In this example, "23" is the

NET+
2.4
2.5
2.6

network ID. The second through fourth octets (bits 8 through 31) in a Class A address identify the host.

An IP whose first octet is in the range of 128-191 belongs to a Class B network. All IP addresses for devices on a Class B segment share the first two octets, or bits 0 through 15. For example, nodes with the following IP addresses may belong to the same Class B network: 168.34.88.29, 168.34.55.41, 168.34.73.49, and 168.34.205.113. In this example, "168.34" is the network ID. The third and fourth octets (bits 16 through 31) on a Class B network identify the host, as shown in Figure 4-8.

An IP address whose first octet is in the range of 192-223 belongs to a Class C network. All IP addresses for devices on a Class C segment share the first three octets, or bits 0 through 23. For example, nodes with the following addresses may belong to the same Class C network: 204.139.118.7, 204.139.118.54, 204.139.118.14, and 204.139.118.31. In this example, "204.139.118" is the network ID. The fourth octet (bits 24 through 31) on a Class C network identifies the host, as shown in Figure 4-8.

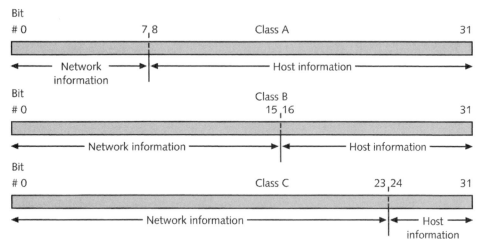

FIGURE 4-8 *IP addresses and their classes*

Internet founders intended the use of network classes to provide easy organization and a sufficient quantity of IP addresses on the Internet. However, their goals haven't necessarily been met. Class A addresses were distributed liberally to large companies and government organizations who were early users of the Internet—for example, IBM. Some organizations reserved many more addresses than they had devices. Class B addresses were distributed to mid-sized organizations and Class C addresses to smaller organizations, such as colleges. Today, many Internet addresses go unused, but cannot be reassigned, because an organization has reserved them. And although potentially more than 4.3 billion Internet addresses are available, the demand for such addresses grows exponentially every year. To respond to this demand, a new addressing scheme has been developed that can supply the world with enough addresses to last well into the twenty-first century. **IP version 6 (IPv6)**, also known as the next-generation IP,

NET+
2.4
2.5
2.6

will incorporate this new addressing scheme. However, because the switch to a new IP addressing scheme will cost billions of dollars in new hardware, software, and training, most organizations are resisting the change.

In addition, some IP addresses are reserved for special functions, like broadcasts, and cannot be assigned to machines or devices. Notice that 127 is not a valid first octet for any IP address. The range of addresses beginning with 127 is reserved for a device communicating with itself, or performing loopback communication. Thus, the IP address 127.0.0.1 is called a **loopback address**. Attempting to contact this IP number—in other words, attempting to contact your own machine—is known as a **loopback test**. (In fact, when you transmit to any IP address beginning with the "127" octet you are communicating with your own machine.) A loopback test can prove useful when troubleshooting problems with a workstation's TCP/IP communications. If you receive a positive response from a loopback test, you know that the TCP/IP core protocols are installed and in use on your workstation.

NET+
4.1
4.2

The command used to view IP information on a Windows XP workstation is **ipconfig**. To view your current IP information on a Windows XP workstation:

1. Click **Start**, point to **All Programs**, point to **Accessories**, then click **Command Prompt**. The Command Prompt window opens.

2. At the command prompt, type **ipconfig /all** and press **Enter**. Your workstation's IP address information is displayed, similar to the information shown in Figure 4-9.

3. Type **exit** and press **Enter** to close the Command Prompt window.

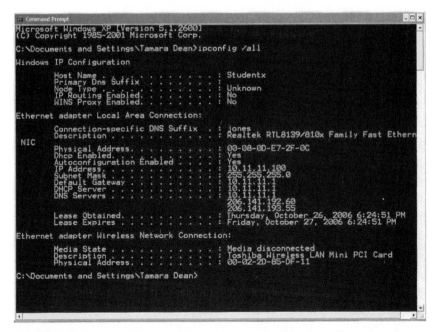

FIGURE 4-9 *Results of the* ipconfig /all *command on Windows XP workstation*

NET+
4.1
4.2

To view and edit IP information on a computer running a version of the UNIX or Linux operating system, use the **ifconfig** command. (Note that ipconfig and ifconfig differ by only one letter.) Simply type ifconfig -a at the shell prompt to view all the information about your TCP/IP connections and addresses, as shown in Figure 4-10. Note that in this figure, the IP address is labeled "inet addr."

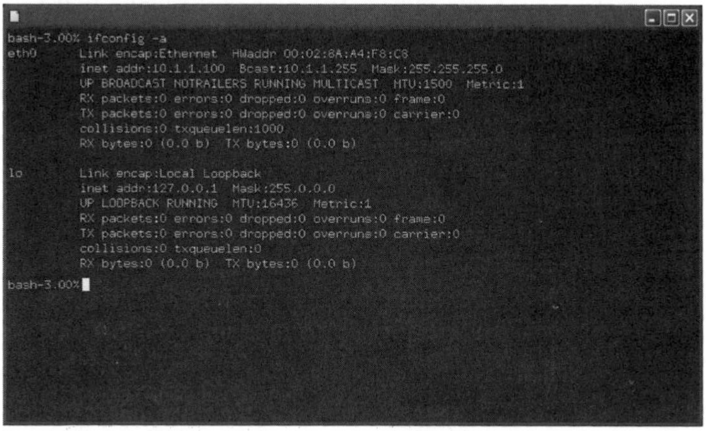

FIGURE 4-10 *Results of the ifconfig -a command on a UNIX workstation*

Now that you have learned the most important characteristics of IP addresses, you are ready to learn more about how computers interpret these addresses.

NET+
2.5

Binary and Dotted Decimal Notation

So far all of the IP addresses in this section have been represented in dotted decimal notation. **Dotted decimal notation**, the most common way of expressing IP addresses, refers to the "shorthand" convention used to represent IP addresses and make them easy for people to read. In dotted decimal notation, a decimal number between 0 and 255 represents each binary octet (for a total of 256 possibilities). A period, or dot, separates each decimal. An example of a dotted decimal IP address is 131.65.10.18.

Each number in a dotted decimal address has a binary equivalent. In Chapter 3 you learned how to convert decimal numbers to their binary equivalents. Converting a dotted decimal address to its binary equivalent is simply a matter of converting each octet and removing the decimal points. For example, in the dotted decimal address 131.65.10.18, the binary equivalent of the first octet, "131," is 10000011, the binary equivalent of the second octet, "65," is 01000001, the binary equivalent of the third octet, "10," is 00001010, and the binary equivalent of the fourth octet, "18," is 00010010. Therefore, the binary value for 131.65.10.18 is 10000011 01000001 00001010 00010010.

NET+
2.4
2.6
2.7

Subnet Mask

In addition to an IP address, every device on a TCP/IP-based network is identified by a sub-net mask. A **subnet mask** is a special 32-bit number that, when combined with a device's IP address, informs the rest of the network about the segment or network to which the device is attached. That is, it identifies the device's **subnet**. Like IP addresses, subnet masks are com-posed of four octets (32 bits) and can be expressed in either binary or dotted decimal notation. Subnet masks are assigned in the same way that IP addresses are assigned—either manually, within a device's TCP/IP configuration, or automatically, through a service such as DHCP (described in detail later in this chapter). A more common term for subnet mask is **net mask**, and sometimes simply **mask** (as in "a device's mask").

You might wonder why a network node even needs a subnet mask, given that the first octet of its IP address indicates its network class. The answer lies with **subnetting**, a process of subdi-viding a single class of network into multiple, smaller logical networks, or segments. Network managers create subnets to control network traffic and to make the best use of a limited num-ber of IP addresses. Methods of subnetting are discussed in detail in Chapter 11. For now, it is enough to know that whether or not a network is subnetted, its devices are assigned a sub-net mask.

On networks that use subnetting, the subnet mask varies depending on the way the network is subnetted. On networks that do not use subnetting, however, the subnet masks take on a default value, as shown in Table 4-2. To qualify for Network+ certification, you should be famil-iar with the default subnet masks associated with each network class.

Table 4-2 Default subnet masks

Network Class	Beginning Octet	Default Subnet Mask
A	1–126	255.0.0.0
B	128–191	255.255.0.0
C	192–223	255.255.255.0

NET+
2.4
2.5
2.9

Assigning IP Addresses

You have learned that several government-sponsored organizations—including IANA, ICANN, and RIRs—cooperate to dole out IP addresses to ISPs and other network providers around the world. You also learned that most companies and individuals obtain IP addresses from their ISPs and not directly from the government's higher authorities. This section describes how an organization assigns its group of IP addresses to networked devices so that they can communicate over the Internet.

Whether connecting to the Internet or to another computer within a LAN, every node on a network must have a unique IP address. If you add a node to a network and its IP address is already in use by another node on the same subnet, an error message will be generated on the new client and its TCP/IP services will be disabled. The existing host may also receive an error message, but can continue to function normally.

 NOTE

Recall that a host is any machine on a network that enables resource sharing. All individual computers connected through a TCP/IP-based network can be called hosts. This idea represents a slightly different interpretation of the term "host," because probably not all computers on a TCP/IP-based network will facilitate resource sharing (though theoretically, they could).

You can assign IP addresses manually, by modifying the client workstation's TCP/IP proper-ties. A manually assigned IP address is called a **static IP address** because it does not change automatically. It changes only when you reconfigure the client's TCP/IP properties. Unfortu-nately, due to human error, static IP addressing can easily result in the duplication of address assignments. So rather than assigning IP addresses manually, most network administrators rely on a network service to automatically assign them. The following sections discuss two meth-ods of automatic IP addressing: BOOTP and DHCP.

BOOTP (Bootstrap Protocol)

On the earliest TCP/IP-based networks, each device was manually assigned a static IP address through a configuration file stored on the hard disk of every computer that needed to com-municate on the network. As networks grew larger, however, these configuration files became more difficult to manage. Imagine the arduous task faced by a network administrator who must visit each of 3000 workstations, printers, and hosts on a company's LAN to assign IP addresses and ensure that no single IP address is used twice. Now imagine how much extra work would be required to revamp the company's IP addressing scheme or to move an entire department's machines to a different or new network.

To facilitate IP address management, a service called the Bootstrap Protocol was developed in the mid-1980s. **BOOTP (Bootstrap Protocol),** an Application layer protocol, uses a central list of IP addresses and their associated devices' MAC addresses to assign IP addresses to clients dynamically. An IP address that is assigned to a device upon request and is changeable is known as a **dynamic IP address**.

When a client that relies on BOOTP first connects to the network, it sends a broadcast mes-sage to the network asking to be assigned an IP address. This broadcast message includes the MAC address of the client's NIC. The BOOTP server recognizes a BOOTP client's request, looks up the client's MAC address in its BOOTP table, and responds to the client with the following information: the client's IP address, the IP address of the server, the host name of the server, and the IP address of a default router. Using BOOTP, a client does not have to remember its own IP address, and therefore network administrators do not have to go to each workstation on a network in order to assign its IP address manually.

You might recognize that the BOOTP process resembles the way RARP issues IP addresses to clients. The main difference between the two protocols is that RARP requests and responses are not routable. Thus, if you wanted to use RARP to issue IP addresses, you would have to install a separate RARP server for every LAN. BOOTP, on the other hand, can traverse LANs. Also, RARP is only capable of issuing an IP address to a client; BOOTP has the potential to issue additional information, such as the client's subnet mask.

In most cases, BOOTP has been surpassed by the more sophisticated IP addressing utility, DHCP (Dynamic Host Configuration Protocol). DHCP requires little intervention, whereas BOOTP requires network administrators to enter every IP and MAC address manually into the BOOTP table. Because of this requirement, the BOOTP table can be difficult to maintain on large networks. You may still encounter BOOTP in existing networks, but most likely it will support only diskless workstations, which are not capable of using DHCP.

DHCP (Dynamic Host Configuration Protocol)

DHCP (Dynamic Host Configuration Protocol) is an automated means of assigning a unique IP address to every device on a network. DHCP, like BOOTP, belongs to the Application layer of the OSI Model. It was developed by the IETF as a replacement for BOOTP. DHCP operates in a similar manner to BOOTP, but unlike BOOTP, DHCP does not require the network administrator to maintain a table of IP and MAC addresses on the server. Thus, the administrative burden of running DHCP is much lower. DHCP does, however, require the network administrator in charge of IP address management to install and configure the DHCP service on a DHCP server.

Reasons for implementing DHCP include the following:

◆ *To reduce the time and planning spent on IP address management.* Central management of IP addresses eliminates the need for network administrators to edit the TCP/IP configuration on every network workstation, printer, or other device.

◆ *To reduce the potential for errors in assigning IP addresses.* With DHCP, almost no possibility exists that a workstation will be assigned an invalid address or that two workstations will attempt to use the same IP address. (Occasionally, the DHCP server software may make a mistake.)

◆ *To enable users to move their workstations and printers without having to change their TCP/IP configuration.* As long as a workstation is configured to obtain its IP address from a central server, the workstation can be attached anywhere on the network and receive a valid address.

◆ *To make IP addressing transparent for mobile users.* A person visiting your office, for example, could attach to your network and receive an IP address without having to change his laptop's configuration.

NET+
2.4
2.5
2.9

 NOTE

In some instances, BOOTP and DHCP may appear together under the same category or service. For example, if you are configuring a Hewlett-Packard LaserJet that uses a JetDirect print server card, you can select "BOOTP/DHCP" from the printer's TCP/IP Configuration menu. BOOTP and DHCP are not always distinguished as separate services, because they appear the same to the client.

DHCP Leasing Process

With DHCP, a device borrows, or **leases**, an IP address while it is attached to the network. In other words, it uses the IP address on a temporary basis for a specified length of time. On most modern networks, a client obtains its DHCP-assigned address as soon as it logs onto a network. The length of time a lease remains in effect depends on DHCP server and client configurations. Leases that expire must be renegotiated in order for the client to remain on the network. Alternatively, users can force a lease termination at the client or a network administrator can force lease terminations at the server.

Configuring the DHCP service involves specifying a range of addresses that can be leased to any network device on a particular segment and a list of excluded addresses (if any). As a network administrator, you configure the duration of the lease to be as short or long as necessary, from a matter of minutes to forever. Once the DHCP server is running, the client and server take the following steps to negotiate the client's first lease. (Note that this example applies to a workstation, but devices such as networked printers may also take advantage of DHCP.)

1. When the client workstation is powered on and its NIC detects a network connection, it sends out a DHCP discover packet in broadcast fashion via the UDP protocol to the DHCP/BOOTP server.

2. Every DHCP server on the same subnet as the client receives the broadcast request. Each DHCP server responds with an available IP address, while simultaneously withholding that address from other clients. The response message includes the available IP address, subnet mask, IP address of the DHCP server, and the lease duration. (Because the client doesn't have an IP address, the DHCP server cannot send the information directly to the client.)

3. The client accepts the first IP address that it receives, responding with a broadcast message that essentially confirms to the DHCP server that it wants to accept the address. Because this message is broadcast, all other DHCP servers that might have responded to the client's original query see this confirmation and hence return the IP addresses they had reserved for the client to their pool of available addresses.

4. When the selected DHCP server receives the confirmation, it replies to the client with an acknowledgment message. It also provides more information, such as DNS, subnet mask, or gateway addresses that the client might have requested.

NET+
2.4
2.5
2.9

The preceding steps involve the exchange of only four packets and therefore do not usually increase the time it takes for a client to log on to the network. Figure 4-11 depicts the DHCP leasing process. The client and server do not have to repeat this exchange until the lease is terminated. The IP address will remain in the client's TCP/IP settings so that even after the client shuts down and reboots, it can use this information and not have to request a new address. However, if the device is moved to another network, it will be assigned different IP address information suited to that network.

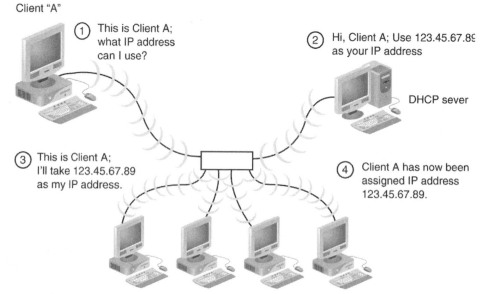

FIGURE 4-11 *The DHCP leasing process*

Terminating a DHCP Lease

A DHCP lease may expire based on the period established for it in the server configuration or it may be manually terminated at any time from either the client's TCP/IP configuration or the server's DHCP configuration. In some instances, a user must terminate a lease. For example, if a DHCP server fails and another is installed to replace it, the clients that relied on the first DHCP server will need to release their old leases (and obtain new leases from the new server). In Windows terms, this event is called a **release** of the TCP/IP settings.

To release TCP/IP settings on a computer running the Windows XP operating system:

1. Click **Start**, point to **All Programs**, point to **Accessories**, then click **Command Prompt**. The Command Prompt window opens.

2. At the command prompt, type **ipconfig /release** and then press **Enter**. Your TCP/IP configuration values will be cleared, and both the IP address and subnet mask will revert to "0.0.0.0."

3. Type **exit** and press **Enter** to close the Command Prompt window.

NET+
2.4
2.5
2.9

Releasing old DHCP information is the first step in the process of obtaining a new IP address. To obtain a new IP address on a Windows XP workstation:

1. If you are not already at a command prompt, click **Start**, point to **All Programs**, point to **Accessories**, then click **Command Prompt**. The Command Prompt window opens.

2. At the command prompt, type `ipconfig /renew` and then press **Enter**. Your client follows the DHCP leasing process, which reestablishes its TCP/IP configuration values. These values will be appropriate for the network to which you are attached.

3. Type exit and press **Enter** to close the Command Prompt window.

With TCP/IP being the protocol of choice on most networks, you will most certainly have to work with DHCP—either at the client, the server, or both. DHCP services run on several types of servers. The installation and configurations for each type of server vary; for specifics, refer to the DHCP server software or NOS manual. To qualify for Network+ certification, you need not know the intricacies of installing and configuring DHCP server software. You do, however, need to know what DHCP does and how it accomplishes it. You also need to understand the advantages of using DHCP rather than other means of assigning IP addresses.

APIPA (Automatic Private IP Addressing)

By now you understand that as long as DHCP is operating correctly, a client will obtain a valid IP address from the DHCP server and use that address to communicate over the network. But what if the DHCP server is unreachable? Even if everything else on the network is functioning properly, a client cannot communicate without a valid IP address. To address the possibility that computer might be configured to use DHCP but be unable to find a DHCP server, Microsoft offers Automatic Private IP Addressing for its Windows 98, Me, 2000, XP client and Windows 2003 server operating systems. As its name implies, **APIPA (Automatic Private IP Addressing)** provides a computer with an IP address automatically. Specifically, it assigns the computer's network adapter an IP address from a pre-defined pool of addresses, 169.254.0.0 through 169.254.255.255, that IANA (Internet Assigned Numbers Authority) has reserved for this purpose. It also assigns a subnet mask of 255.255.0.0, the default subnet mask for a Class B network. Because APIPA is part of a computer's operating software, the assignment happens without the need to register or check with a central authority. In the case of a network whose DHCP is temporarily unavailable, when the DHCP server is available once again APIPA will release its assigned IP address and allow the client to receive a DHCP-assigned address.

After APIPA assigns an address, a computer can then communicate across a LAN. However, it can only communicate with other nodes using addresses in the APIPA range. It cannot communicate with nodes on other subnets. That means, for example, that clients with APIPA-assigned addresses could not send or receive data to or from the Internet or a WAN. Therefore, APIPA is best suited to small networks that do not use DHCP servers, in which case it makes IP address management very easy. But it is unsuitable for networks that must communicate with other subnets or over a WAN.

NET+
2.4
2.5
2.9

APIPA is enabled by default upon installing the operating system software. To check whether a Windows XP, 2000, or 2003 Server computer is using APIPA:

1. Click **Start**, point to **All Programs**, point to **Accessories**, then click **Command Prompt**. The Command Prompt window opens.

2. At the command prompt, type `ipconfig /all` and then press **Enter**. If the "Autoconfiguration Enabled" option is set to Yes, your computer is using APIPA.

Even if your network does not need or use APIPA, leaving it enabled is not necessarily problematic, because APIPA is designed to check for the presence of a DHCP server and allow the DHCP server to assign addresses. And if a computer's IP address has been assigned statically, APIPA will not re-assign a new address. It only works with clients configured to use DHCP. APIPA can be disabled, however, by editing the Windows operating system's registry.

NET+
2.11
2.12

Sockets and Ports

Just as a device requires a unique address to send and receive information over the network, a process also requires a unique address. Every process on a machine is assigned a **port number**. If you compare IP addressing with the addressing system used by the postal service, and you equate a host's IP address to the address of a building, a port number would be similar to an apartment number within that building. A process's port number plus its host machine's IP address equals the process's **socket**. For example, the standard port number for the Telnet service is 23. On a host whose IP address is 10.43.3.87, the socket address for Telnet would be 10.43.3.87:23. In other words, the host assumes that any requests coming into port number 23 are Telnet requests (that is, unless you reconfigure the host to change the default Telnet port). Notice that a port number is expressed as a number following a colon after an IP address. In this example, "23" is not considered an additional octet, but simply a pointer to a port. Sockets form virtual connections between a process on one computer and the same process running on another computer.

The use of port numbers simplifies TCP/IP communications and ensures that data are transmitted to the correct application. When a client requests communications with a server and specifies port 23, for example, the server knows immediately that the client wants a Telnet session. No extra data exchange is necessary to define the session type, and the server can initiate the Telnet service without delay. The server will connect to the client's Telnet port—by default, port 23—and establish a virtual circuit. Figure 4-12 depicts this process.

Port numbers range from 0 to 65535 and are divided by IANA into three types: Well Known Ports, Registered Ports, and Dynamic and/or Private Ports. **Well Known Ports** are in the range of 0 to 1023 and are assigned to processes that only the operating system or an Administrator of the system can access. These were the first ports assigned to processes, and so the earliest TCP/IP protocols, such as TCP, UDP, Telnet, and FTP, use Well Known Ports. Table 4-3 lists some of these Well Known Ports. **Registered Ports** are in the range of 1024 to 49151. These ports are accessible to network users and processes that do not have special administrative privileges. Default assignments of these ports (for example, by a software program) must be registered with IANA. **Dynamic and/or Private Ports** are those from 49152 through 65535 and are open for use without restriction.

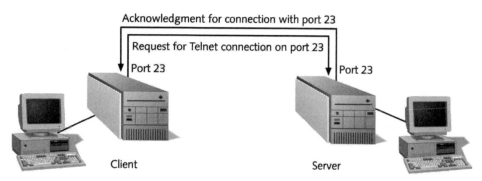

Acknowledgment for connection with port 23

Request for Telnet connection on port 23

Port 23

Port 23

Client

Server

FIGURE 4-12 *A virtual circuit for the Telnet service*

TIP

Although you do not need to memorize every port number for the Network+ certification exam, you may be asked about the port numbers associated with common services, such as Telnet, FTP, and HTTP. Knowing them will also help you in configuring and troubleshooting networks using TCP/IP.

Table 4-3 Commonly used TCP/IP port numbers

Port Number	Process Name	Protocol Used	Description
7	ECHO	TCP and UDP	Echo
20	FTP-DATA	TCP	File Transfer - Data
21	FTP	TCP	File Transfer–Control
22	SSH	TCP	Secure Shell
23	TELNET	TCP	Telnet
25	SMTP	TCP	Simple Mail Transfer Protocol
53	DNS	TCP and UDP	Domain Name System
69	TFTP	UDP	Trivial File Transfer Protocol
80	HTTP	TCP and UDP	World Wide Web HTTP
110	POP3	TCP	Post Office Protocol 3
119	NNTP	TCP	Network News Transport Protocol
143	IMAP	TCP	Internet Message Access Protocol
443	HTTPS	TCP	Secure implementation of HTTP

NET+
2.11
2.12

Port numbers are assigned either by the operating system or by software programs, such as HP Open View, a network management package. Servers maintain an editable, text-based file of port numbers and their associated services. With administrative (unlimited) privileges, you are free to change any port numbers a device uses. For example, you could change the default port number for the Telnet service on your server from 23 to 2330. Changing a default port number is rarely a good idea, however, because it violates the standard and means that processes programmed to use a standard port will not be able to communicate with your machine. Nevertheless, some network administrators who are preoccupied with security may change their servers' port numbers in an attempt to confuse people with malicious intent who try connecting to their devices through conventional sockets.

NET+
2.4
2.5

Addressing in IPv6

Up to this point, you have learned about IP addressing according to the IPv4 scheme. This section introduces you to addressing in IPv6 and the differences between addressing in IPv4 and addressing in IPv6.

As you have learned, IPv6 (IP version 6)—also known as **IP next generation**, or **IPng**—is slated to replace the current IP protocol, IPv4. Some applications, operating systems, and servers already provide support for IPv6, but many organizations have not made the switch due to the anticipated difficulty of changing their addressing scheme. Switching to IPv6 has advantages, however. IPv6 offers a more efficient header, better security, and better prioritization allowances than IPv4, plus automatic IP address configuration. But perhaps the most valuable advantage IPv6 offers is its promise of billions and billions of additional IP addresses through its new addressing scheme.

The most notable difference between IP addresses in IPv4 and IPv6 is their size. While IPv4 addresses are composed of 32 bits, IPv6 addresses are composed of eight 16-bit fields and total 128 bits. The added fields and the larger address size result in an increase of 2^{96} (or 4 billion times 4 billion times 4 billion) available IP addresses in the IPv6 addressing scheme. The addition of more IP addresses not only allows every interface on every Internet-connected device to have a unique number, but also eliminates the need for IP address conservation.

A second difference between IPv4 and IPv6 addresses is the way they are represented. While each octet in an IPv4 address contains binary numbers separated by a period (for example, 123.45.67.89), each field in an IPv6 address contains hexadecimal numbers separated by a colon. An example of a valid IPv6 address is F:F:0:0:0:0:3012:0CE3. Because many IPv6 addresses will contain multiple fields that have values of 0, a shorthand for representing these fields has been established. This shorthand substitutes "::" for any number of multiple, zero-value fields. Thus, the IPv6 address example above could be also be written as F:F::3012:0CE3. An interesting, easily shortened address is the IPv6 loopback address. Recall that in IPv4 the loopback address has a value of 127.0.0.1. In IPv6, however, the loopback address has a value of 0:0:0:0:0:0:0:1. Abbreviated, the IPv6 loopback address becomes ::1. The substitution of multiple zero value fields can only be performed once within an address; otherwise, you would not be able to tell how many fields the "::" symbol represented.

NET+
2.4
2.5

A third difference between the two types of IP addresses is that IPv6 addressing distinguishes between different types of network interfaces. One type of IPv6 address is a **unicast address**, or an address that represents a single interface on a device. A unicast address is the type of address that would be assigned, for example, to a workstation's network adapter. A **multicast address** represents multiple interfaces (often on multiple devices). Multicast addresses are useful for transmitting the same data to many different devices simultaneously. In IPv6, multicast addressing prevents the need for a broadcast address. Thus, there is no such thing as a broadcast address in IPv6. An **anycast address** represents any one interface from a group of interfaces (often on multiple nodes), any one of which (usually the first available) can accept a transmission. Anycast addresses could be useful for identifying all of the routers that belong to one ISP, for example. In this instance, an Internet transmission destined for one of that ISP's servers could be accepted by the first available router in the anycast group. The result is that the transmission finishes faster than if it had to wait for one specific router interface to become available. At this time, anycast addresses are not designed to be assigned to hosts, such as servers or workstations.

A fourth significant difference between IPv4 and IPv6 addressing is that in IPv6, each address contains a **Format Prefix**, or a variable-length field at the beginning of the address that indicates what type of address it is. The Format Prefix also establishes the arrangement of the rest of the address's fields. In the IPv4 addressing scheme, no distinction is made between an address that represents one device or interface and an address that represents multiple devices or interfaces. However, in IPv6, the first field of the IP address would provide a clue as to what type of interface the address represented. A unicast or anycast address begins with one of the two following hexadecimal strings: FEC0 or FE80. A multicast address begins with the following hexadecimal string: FF0*x*, where *x* is a character that corresponds to a group scope ID (for example, a group of addresses that belongs to an entire organization or a group of addresses that belongs to one site on a WAN).

Although IPv6 has been defined since the mid-1990s, organizations have been slow to adopt it. However, the use of IPv6 is predicted to grow rapidly as more and more devices (particularly wireless electronics) are connected to the Internet. During this transition phase, IPv4 and IPv6 will need to coexist. To do so, modern connectivity devices will most likely translate IPv4 addresses into IPv6 addresses for transmission over the Internet by padding the extra fields with zeros to fill the 128-bit address space.

Now that you have learned about core TCP/IP protocols and the way in which hosts are assigned IP addresses, you are ready to learn about how hosts are named.

NET+
2.13

Host Names and DNS (Domain Name System)

Much of TCP/IP addressing involves numbers—often long, complicated numbers. Computers can manage numbers easily. However, most people can remember words better than numbers. Imagine if you had to identify your friends' and families' Social Security numbers whenever you wanted to write a note or talk to them. Communication would be frustrating at the very least, and perhaps even impossible—especially if you're the kind of person who has trouble remembering even your own Social Security number. Similarly, people prefer to associate names with networked devices rather than remember IP addresses. For this reason, the Internet authorities established a naming system for all nodes on the Internet.

Every device on the Internet is technically known as a host. Every host can take a **host name**, a name that describes the device. For example, someone named Peggy McDonald might name her workstation "Peggy." If the computer is reserved for a specific purpose, you may want to name it accordingly. For example, a company that offers free software downloads through the FTP service might call its host machine "ftpserver."

Domain Names

Every host is a member of a **domain**, or a group of computers that belong to the same organization and have part of their IP addresses in common. A domain is identified by its domain name. Usually, a **domain name** is associated with a company or other type of organization, such as a university, government organization, or company. For example, IBM's domain name is ibm.com, and the U.S. Library of Congress's domain name is loc.gov.

Often, when networking professionals refer to a machine's host name, they in fact mean its local host name *plus* its domain name—in other words, its **fully qualified host name**. If you worked at the Library of Congress and gave your workstation the host name "Peggy," your fully qualified host name might be "Peggy.loc.gov."

A domain name is represented by a series of character strings, called **labels**, separated by dots. Each label represents a level in the domain naming hierarchy. In the domain name *www.novell.com*, "com" is the **top-level domain (TLD)**, "novell" is the second-level domain, and "www" is the third-level domain. Each second-level domain can contain multiple third level domains. For instance, in addition to *www.novell.com*, Novell also owns the following domains: *support.novell.com*, *developer.novell.com*, and *ftp.novell.com*.

Domain names must be registered with an Internet naming authority that works on behalf of ICANN. ICANN has established conventions for domain naming so that certain TLDs apply to every type of organization that uses the Internet. Table 4-4 lists ICANN-approved TLDs. The first eight TLDs listed in this table were established in the mid-1980s. Of these, no restrictions exist on the use of the .com, .org, and .net TLDs, but ICANN does restrict what type of hosts can be associated with the .arpa, .mil, .int, .edu, and .gov TLDs. Over the past few years ICANN has responded to requests from various organizations and approved the next seven TLDs in Table 4-4.

In addition to those listed in Table 4-4, ICANN has approved over 240 **country code TLDs** to represent different countries and territories across the globe. For example, .ca is the country code TLD assigned to Canada and .jp is the country code TLD assigned to Japan. Organizations are not required to use country code TLDs. For example, although Cisco's headquarters are located in the United States, the company's domain name is *www.cisco.com*, not *www.cisco.us*. On the other hand, some U.S. organizations do use the .us suffix. For example, the domain name for the Garden City, New York, public school district is *www.gardencity.k12.ny.us*.

Table 4-4 Top-level domains

Domain Suffix	Type of Organization
ARPA	Reverse lookup domain (special Internet function)
COM	Commercial
EDU	Educational
GOV	Government
ORG	Non-commercial Organization (such as a nonprofit agency)
NET	Network (such as an ISP)
INT	International Treaty Organization
MIL	U.S. Military Organization
BIZ	Businesses
INFO	Unrestricted use
AERO	Air-transport industry
COOP	Cooperatives
MUSEUM	Museums
NAME	Individuals
PRO	Professionals such as doctors, lawyers, and engineers

After an organization reserves a domain name, the rest of the world's computers know to associate that domain name with the organization to which it is assigned, and no other organization can legally use it. For example, you might apply for the domain name called "freeflies.com"; not only would the rest of the Internet associate that name with your network, but also, no other parties in the world could use "freeflies.com" in naming computers on their network that connects to the Internet.

Host and domain names are subject to some restrictions. They may consist of any alphanumeric combination up to a maximum of 63 characters, and can include hyphens, underscores, or periods in the name, but no other special characters. The interesting part of host and domain naming relates to how all Internet-connected machines in the world know which names belong to which machines. Before tackling the entire world, however, you can start by thinking about how one company might deal with its local host names, as explained in the following section.

Host Files

The first incarnation of the Internet (ARPAnet) was used by fewer than 1000 hosts. The entire network relied on one ASCII text file called HOSTS.TXT to associate host names with IP addresses. This file was generically known as a **host file**. Growth of the Internet soon made this simple arrangement impossible to maintain—the host file would require constant changes, searching through one file from all over the nation would strain the Internet's bandwidth capacity, and the entire Internet would fail if the file were accidentally deleted.

However, within a company or university, you may still encounter this older system of using a text file to associate (internal) host names with their IP addresses. Figure 4-13 provides an example of such a file. Notice that each host is matched by one line identifying the host's name and IP address. In addition, a third field, called an **alias**, provides a nickname for the host. An alias allows a user within an organization to address a host by a shorter name than the full host name. Typically, the first line of a host file begins with a pound sign and contains comments about the file's columns. A pound sign may precede comments anywhere in the host file.

# IP address	host name	alias
132.55.78.109	bingo.games.com	bingo
132.55.78.110	parcheesi.games.com	parcheesi
132.55.78.111	checkers.games.com	checkers
132.55.78.112	darts.games.com	darts

FIGURE 4-13 *Example host file*

On a UNIX- or Linux-based computer, a host file is called **hosts** and is located in the /etc directory. On a Windows 9x, NT, 2000, or XP computer, a host file is also called **hosts** (with no file extension) and is located in the %systemroot%\system32\drivers\etc folder (where %systemroot% is the directory in which the operating system is installed). If you are using hosts files, you should not only master the syntax of this file, but you should also research the implications of using a static host file on your network.

DNS (Domain Name System)

A simple host file can satisfy the needs of a small organization; however, it is not sufficient for large organizations, much less for the Internet. Instead, a more automated solution has become mandatory. In the mid-1980s, computer scientists responsible for the Internet's growth devised a hierarchical way of associating domain names with IP addresses, called the **DNS (Domain Name System)**. "DNS" refers to both the Application-layer service that accomplishes this association and also to the organized system of computers and databases that makes this association possible. The DNS service does not rely on one file or even one server, but rather on many computers across the globe. These computers are related in a hierarchical manner, with thirteen computers, known as **root servers**, acting as the ultimate authorities. Because it is distributed, DNS will not fail catastrophically if one or a handful of servers experience errors.

To direct traffic efficiently, the DNS service is divided into three components: resolvers, name servers, and name space. **Resolvers** are any hosts on the Internet that need to look up domain name information. The resolver client is built into TCP/IP applications such as HTTP. If you point your Web browser to "*http://www.loc.gov*," your http client software will initiate the

NET+
2.13

resolver service to find the IP address for *www.loc.gov*. If you have visited the site before, the information may exist in temporary memory and may be retrieved very quickly. Otherwise, the resolver service queries your machine's designated name server to find the IP address for *www.loc.gov*.

Name servers (or **DNS servers**) are servers that contain databases of associated names and IP addresses and provide this information to resolvers on request. If one name server cannot resolve the domain name to its IP address, it passes the query to a higher-authority name server. For example, suppose you are trying to open the *www.loc.gov* Web page from a workstation on your company's network. Further, suppose this is the first time you've visited the Library of Congress online. Upon discovering it does not have the information saved locally, your client's resolver service will query the closest name server for the IP address associated with *www.loc.gov*. That name server is probably connected to your LAN. If your LAN's name server cannot supply the IP address for *www.loc.gov*, it will query a higher-level name server. In other words, your company's name server will send a request to the name server at the company's Internet Service Provider (ISP). If that name server does not have the information in its database, it will query a name server elsewhere on the Internet that acts as the ISP's naming authority. This process, depicted in Figure 4-14, continues until the request is granted.

The term **name space** refers to the database of Internet IP addresses and their associated names. Name space is not a database that you can open and view like a store's inventory database. Rather, this abstract concept describes how the name servers of the world share DNS information. Pieces of it are tangible, however, and are stored on a name server in a **resource record**, which is a single record that describes one piece of information in the DNS database. For example, an **address resource record** is a type of resource record that maps the IP address of an Internet-connected device to its domain name. By storing resource records, every name server holds a piece of the DNS name space.

Resource records come in many different types, depending on their function. Each resource record contains a name field to identify the domain name of the machine to which the record refers, a type field to identify the type of resource record involved, a class field to identify the class to which the record belongs (usually "IN" or "Internet"), a time to live field to identify how long the record should be saved in temporary memory, a data length field to identify how much data the record contains, and the actual record data. Approximately 20 types of resource records are currently used.

In the following fictitious address resource record, *knight.chess.games.com* is the host domain name, IN stands for the Internet record class, A identifies the record type as "address," and 203.99.120.76 is the host's IP address:

```
knight.chess.games.com   IN   A   203.99.120.76
```

At one time, network administrators manually maintained resource records for their networks' hosts. Now, however, most modern clients update their resource records dynamically. This saves time and eliminates the possibility for human error in modifying DNS information. Clients can be configured to trigger a DNS update when they receive a new IP address (for example, through DHCP), when their host names change, or when they connect to a network. Alter-

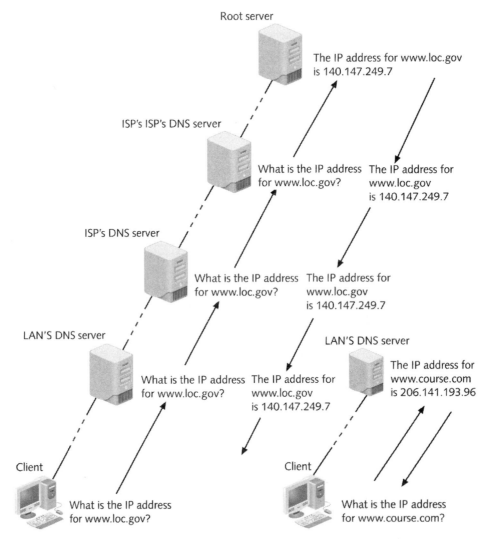

FIGURE 4-14 *Domain name resolution*

natively, a user can force a DNS record update by issuing a command. For example, typing ipconfig /registerdns at the Windows XP command prompt will force an update of the client's registered DNS information.

Configuring DNS

Any host that must communicate with other hosts on the Internet needs to know how to find its name server. Although some organizations use only one name server, large organizations often maintain two name servers—a primary and a secondary name server—to help ensure

Internet connectivity. If the primary name server experiences a failure, all devices on the network will attempt to use the secondary name server. Each device on the network relies on the name server and therefore must know how to find it.

On most networks, the DHCP service automatically assigns clients the appropriate addresses for its primary and secondary name servers. However, on occasion you might need to manually configure these values in a workstation's TCP/IP properties.

To view or change the name server information on a Windows XP workstation:

1. Click **Start**, then click **My Network Places**. The My Network Places window appears.
2. From the Network Tasks list, click **View network connections**. The Network Connections window appears.
3. Right-click the icon that represents your network adapter, and click **Properties** in the shortcut menu. The network adapter's Properties dialog box appears.
4. Under the heading "This connection uses the following items," select **Internet Protocol (TCP/IP),** then click **Properties**. The Internet Protocol (TCP/IP) Properties dialog box appears, as shown in Figure 4-15.

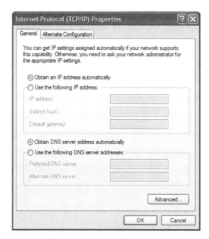

FIGURE 4-15 *The Windows XP Internet Protocol (TCP/IP) Properties dialog box*

5. With the General tab selected, click the **Use the following DNS server addresses** button.
6. Enter the IP address for your primary DNS server in the Preferred DNS Server space and the address for your secondary DNS server in the Alternate DNS Server space.
7. Click **OK**, click **Close** to save your changes, and then close the Network Connections window.

NOTE

For Network+ certification, you should know the purpose of DNS and host files, understand the hierarchical nature of DNS, and be able to specify name servers on a client workstation.

DDNS (Dynamic DNS)

DNS is a reliable way of locating a host as long as the host's IP address remains relatively constant over time—that is, if it's static. However, many Internet users subscribe to a type of Internet service in which their IP address changes periodically. For a user who only wants to send and receive e-mail and surf the Web, frequently changing IP addresses is not problematic. But for a user who wants to host a Web site, for example, it can be. To maintain the association between his Web site's host or domain name and an IP address, such a user must change his computer's DNS record and propagate this change across the Internet each time the IP address changes. When IP addresses change frequently, manually changing DNS records becomes unmanageable.

A solution is to use **DDNS (Dynamic DNS)**. In DDNS, a service provider runs a program on the user's computer that notifies the service provider when the user's IP address changes. Upon notification, the service provider's server launches a routine that automatically updates the DNS record for that user's computer. The DNS record update becomes effective throughout the Internet in a matter of minutes.

Note that DDNS does not take the place of DNS, but is an additional service, available for a small fee. DDNS is a good option for home or small office users who maintain Web sites but do not want to pay the additional (often high) cost of reserving a static IP address. However, because of the slight delay in DNS record propagation caused each time an IP address changes, larger organizations typically prefer to pay more for a statically assigned IP address.

Associating host and domain names with computers on a TCP/IP-based network is performed by the Application layer protocol DNS. The following section describes other important Application layer protocols.

Zeroconf (Zero Configuration)

Zeroconf (Zero Configuration) is a collection of protocols designed by the IETF to simplify the setup of nodes on a TCP/IP network. Zeroconf assigns a node an IP address, resolves the node's host name and IP address without requiring a DNS server, and discovers services, such as print services, available to the node, also without requiring a DNS server. Zeroconf enables two workstations directly connected (using a crossover cable, for example) to communicate without relying on static IP addressing, DHCP servers, or DNS servers. Before Zeroconf, this type of communication could take place among Windows systems using NetBIOS or Macintosh systems using AppleTalk, but not between the two different systems. Zeroconf functions

NET+
2.13

identically on multiple different operating systems, and it comes with Macintosh OS 9 and X, Windows 98, Me, 2000, XP, and Server 2003, and most implementations of Linux. Apple's version of Zeroconf is called **Rendezvous**.

With Zeroconf, IP addresses are assigned through **IPv4LL (IP version 4 Link Local)**, a protocol that manages automatic address assignment among locally connected nodes. In IPv4LL, when Computer A joins the network, it randomly chooses an IP address in the range of 169.254.1.0 to 169.254.254.255, which is reserved for IPv4LL use. Before using its chosen address to communicate, Computer A sends a message, via the ARP protocol, to the rest of its subnet indicating its desire to use that IP address. But suppose Computer B is already using the address. In that case, Computer B will respond to Computer A's message with a broadcast that alerts every other node on the subnet that the IP address is already in use. In that case, Computer A will randomly select a different IP address. However, if, after a brief period of time, no other node responds to the first node's announcement, Computer A will issue a broadcast message that informs the rest of the subnet that it has assigned itself the address it chose initially.

Note that IPv4LL-assigned addresses are reserved for communication among locally linked nodes. Because they are not globally unique, they cannot be used on larger networks, such as the Internet. (Advanced TCP/IP addressing techniques, such as those discussed in Chapter 11, can be used to allow these nodes to communicate with the Internet, however.) IPv4LL is especially useful with network printers. Most printers don't come with interfaces that enable a network administrator to easily configure TCP/IP variables. If they support Zeroconf and use IPv4LL, printers can be connected to the network and ready to communicate with no human intervention. Most printers manufactured today come with Zeroconf support.

NET+
2.10

Some TCP/IP Application Layer Protocols

In addition to the core Transport and Internet layer protocols, the TCP/IP suite encompasses several Application layer protocols. These protocols work over TCP or UDP plus IP, translating user requests into a format the network can read. Earlier you learned about two Application layer protocols used for automatic address assignment, BOOTP and DHCP. The following sections describe some additional Application layer protocols.

Telnet

Telnet is a terminal emulation protocol used to log on to remote hosts using the TCP/IP protocol suite. Using Telnet, a TCP connection is established and keystrokes on the user's machine act like keystrokes on the remotely connected machine. Often Telnet is used to connect two dissimilar systems (such as PCs and UNIX machines). Through Telnet, you can control a remote host over LANs and WANs such as the Internet. For example, network managers can use Telnet to log on to a router from a computer elsewhere on their LAN and modify the router's configuration. Telnet, however, is notoriously insecure (meaning that someone with malicious intent could easily falsify the credentials Telnet requires to log on to a device successfully), so telnetting to a router across a public network would not be wise. Other, more secure methods of remotely connecting to a host have replaced Telnet for that reason.

NET+
2.10

FTP (File Transfer Protocol)

FTP (File Transfer Protocol) is an Application layer protocol used to send and receive files via TCP/IP. In FTP exchanges, a host running the FTP server portion accepts commands from another host running the FTP client portion. FTP clients come with a set of simple commands that make up its user interface. In order to exchange data, the client depends on an FTP server that is always waiting for requests. Once a client connects to the FTP server, FTP data is exchanged via TCP, which means that FTP provides some assurance of delivery.

FTP commands will work from your operating system's command prompt; they do not require special client software. As a network professional, you may need to use these commands to download software (such as NOS patches or client updates) from hosts. For example, if you need to pick up the latest version of the Novell Windows XP client, you can use FTP from your workstation's command prompt to download the compressed software from Novell's FTP server to your hard disk. In order to do so, you can start the FTP utility by typing ftp from your operating system command prompt. The command prompt will turn into the FTP prompt, FTP>. From there you can run FTP commands. Alternatively, if you know what operation you want to perform, you can connect directly to an FTP server. For example, to connect directly to Novell's FTP server, type ftp ftp.novell.com, then press Enter. If the host is running, it will respond with a greeting and a request for you to log on.

Many FTP hosts, especially those whose purpose is to provide software updates, accept anonymous logins. This means that when prompted for a user name, you need only type the word anonymous (in all small letters). When prompted for a password on an anonymous FTP site, you can typically use your e-mail address. The host's login screen should indicate whether this is acceptable. On the other hand, if you are logging on to a private FTP site, you must obtain a valid user name and password from the site's network administrator in order to make a successful connection.

Once you have successfully connected to a host, additional commands allow you to manage the connection and manipulate files. For example, after you have connected to Novell's FTP site, you could type cd pub and press Enter to change your working directory to the pub directory, where files are made available for public access. Then you could type: cd updates and press Enter to change your working directory to the updates directory, where Novell stores software update files. Once in that directory, you could download a file by typing: get *XXX*, where "*XXX*" is the name of the file you want to download. To terminate the connection, simply type quit. The following list summarizes a handful of useful FTP commands and their syntax. To learn more about these and other FTP commands, type help after starting the FTP utility.

♦ ascii—sets the file transfer mode to "ASCII." Most FTP hosts store two types of files: ASCII and binary. Text files are typically ASCII-based and contain formatting characters, such as carriage returns. Binary files (for example, executable programs) typically contain no formatting characters. Before downloading files from an FTP host, you must understand what type of file you are downloading. If you download a file while in the wrong mode (ASCII if the file is binary or vice-versa), your file will appear as gibberish when you open it. If the file you want to download is an ASCII file, type ascii at the FTP prompt and press Enter before starting your file transfer.

♦ binary—sets the file transfer mode to "binary." If the file you want to download from an FTP site is binary (for example, an executable program or a compressed software patch), type binary at the FTP prompt and press Enter before starting your file transfer.

♦ cd—changes your working directory on the host machine.

♦ delete—deletes a file on the host machine (provided you have permissions to do so).

♦ get—transfers a file from the host machine to the client. For example, to transfer the file called update.exe from the host to your workstation, you can type: get update.exe. Unless you specify a target directory and filename, the file will be saved to your hard disk in the directory from where you started the FTP utility. Therefore, if you wanted to save the update.exe file to your C:\download\patches directory, you would type:

get update.exe "c:\download\patches"

(Make sure to include the quotation marks.)

♦ help—provides a list of commands when issued from the FTP prompt. When used in conjunction with a command, help provides information on the purpose of that command. For example, after typing help ls you would learn that the ls command lists the contents of a remote directory.

♦ mget—transfers multiple files from the FTP site to your workstation simultaneously. For example, to transfer all the text files within one directory, you could type: mget *.txt at the FTP> prompt.

♦ mput—transfers multiple files from your workstation to the FTP host.

♦ open—creates a connection with an FTP host.

♦ put—transfers a file from your workstation to the FTP host.

♦ quit—terminates your FTP connection and closes the FTP utility.

Graphical FTP clients, such as MacFTP, WS_FTP, CuteFTP, and SmartFTP, have rendered this command-line method of FTPing files less common. You can also accomplish FTP file transfers directly from a modern Web browser such as Internet Explorer or Netscape Communicator version 6 or higher. In order to do this, you need only point your browser to the FTP host. From there, you can move through directories and exchange files just as you would navigate the files and directories on your desktop or LAN server.

 NOTE

FTP and Telnet share some similarities, including their reliance on TCP and their ability to log on to a remote host and perform commands on that host. However, they differ in that, when you use Telnet, the commands you type require a syntax that is relative to your local workstation. When you use FTP, the commands you type require a syntax that is relative to the remote host that you have logged on to. Also, Telnet has no built-in commands for transferring files between the remote host and your workstation.

TFTP (Trivial File Transfer Protocol)

TFTP (Trivial File Transfer Protocol) is another TCP/IP Application layer protocol that enables file transfers between computers, but it is simpler (or more trivial) than FTP. A significant difference between FTP and TFTP is that TFTP relies on UDP at the Transport layer. Its use of UDP means that TFTP is connectionless and does not guarantee reliable delivery of data. Also, TFTP does not require users to log on to the remote host with an ID and password in order to gain access to a directory and transfer files. Instead, when you enter the TFTP command, your computer issues a simple request to access the host's files. The remote host responds with an acknowledgment, and then the two computers begin transferring data. Each time a packet of data is transmitted to the host, the local workstation waits for an acknowledgment from the host before issuing another packet. In this way, TFTP overcomes some of the limitations of relying on a connectionless Transport layer protocol. A final difference between FTP and TFTP is that the latter does not allow directory browsing. In FTP, you can connect to a host and navigate through all the directories you've been granted access to view.

TFTP is useful when you need to load data or programs on a diskless workstation. For example, suppose a TFTP server holds Microsoft Excel. When a client issues a TFTP request for that program, the server would transmit the program files to the workstation's memory. After the user completes his Excel work, the program files would be released from his workstation's memory. In this situation, the fact that TFTP does not require a user to log on to a host is an advantage. It makes the transfer of program files quick and easy. As you can imagine, however, not requiring a login also presents a security risk, so TFTP servers must be carefully placed and monitored on a network.

NTP (Network Time Protocol)

NTP (Network Time Protocol) is a simple Application layer protocol used to synchronize the clocks of computers on a network. NTP depends on UDP for Transport layer services. Although it is simple, it is also important. Time is critical in routing to determine the most efficient path for data over a network. Time synchronization across a network is also important for time-stamped security methods and maintaining accuracy and consistency between multiple storage systems. NTP is a protocol that benefits from UDP's quick, connectionless nature at the Transport layer. NTP is time-sensitive and cannot wait for the error checking that TCP would require.

NNTP (Network News Transport Protocol)

Another Application layer protocol in the TCP/IP suite is **NNTP (Network News Transport Protocol)**, which facilitates the exchange of newsgroup messages between multiple servers and users. A **newsgroup** is similar to e-mail, in that it provides a means of conveying messages; it differs from e-mail in that it distributes messages to a wide group of users at once rather than from one user to another. Newsgroups have been formed to discuss every conceivable topic, such as political issues, professional affiliations, entertainment interests, or sports clubs. To join a newsgroup, a user subscribes to the server that hosts the newsgroup. From that point forward, the user receives all messages that other newsgroup members post to the group. To

NET+

2.10

send a message to the group, a user only has to address the message to the newsgroup's e-mail address.

Newsgroups require news servers that act as a central collection and distribution point for news-group messages. News servers are organized hierarchically across the Internet, similar to the way DNS servers are organized. Clients can use e-mail, Internet browsers, or special newsgroup reading software to receive newsgroup messages. NNTP supports the process of reading news-group messages, posting new messages, and transferring news files between news servers.

NET+

4.1
4.2

PING (Packet Internet Groper)

PING (Packet Internet Groper) is a utility that can verify that TCP/IP is installed, bound to the NIC, configured correctly, and communicating with the network. It is often employed simply to determine whether a host is responding (or "up"). PING uses ICMP services to send echo request and echo reply messages that determine the validity of an IP address. These two types of messages work in much the same way that sonar operates. First, a signal, called an **echo request**, is sent out to another computer. The other computer then rebroadcasts the signal, in the form of an **echo reply**, to the sender. The process of sending this signal back and forth is known as **pinging**.

You can ping either an IP address or a host name. For example, to determine whether the *www.loc.gov* site is responding, you could type: ping www.loc.gov and press Enter. Alternately, you could type: ping 140.147.249.7 (the IP address of this site at the time this book was written) and press Enter. If the site is operating correctly, you would receive a response that includes multiple replies from that host. If the site is not operating correctly, you will receive a response indicating that the request timed out or that the host was not found. You could also get a "request timed out" message if your workstation is not properly connected to the net-work, or if the network is malfunctioning. Figure 4-16 gives examples of a successful and an unsuccessful ping test.

By pinging the loopback address, 127.0.0.1, you can determine whether your workstation's TCP/IP services are running. By pinging a host on another subnet, you can determine whether the problem lies with a connectivity device between the two subnets.

For example, suppose that you have recently moved your computer from the Accounting Department to the Advertising Department, and now you cannot access the Web. The first test you should perform is pinging the loopback address. If that test is successful, then you know that your workstation's TCP/IP services are running correctly. Next, you might try pinging your neighbor's machine. If you receive a positive response, you know that your network connection is working. You should then try pinging a machine on another subnet that you know is con-nected to the network—for example, a computer in the IT department. If this test is unsuc-cessful, you can safely conclude that you do not have the correct settings in your TCP/IP configuration or that something is wrong with your network's connectivity (for example, a router may be malfunctioning).

```
C:\>ping 140.147.249.7

Pinging 140.147.249.7 with 32 bytes of data:

Reply from 140.147.249.7: bytes=32 time=47ms TTL=243
Reply from 140.147.249.7: bytes=32 time=46ms TTL=243
Reply from 140.147.249.7: bytes=32 time=46ms TTL=243
Reply from 140.147.249.7: bytes=32 time=48ms TTL=243

Ping statistics for 140.147.249.7:
    Packets: Sent = 4, Received = 4, Lost = 0 (0% loss),
Approximate round trip times in milli-seconds:
    Minimum = 46ms, Maximum = 48ms, Average = 46ms

C:\>ping 22.34.129.87

Pinging 22.34.129.87 with 32 bytes of data:

Request timed out.
Request timed out.
Request timed out.
Request timed out.

Ping statistics for 22.34.129.87:
    Packets: Sent = 4, Received = 0, Lost = 4 (100% loss),

C:\>
```

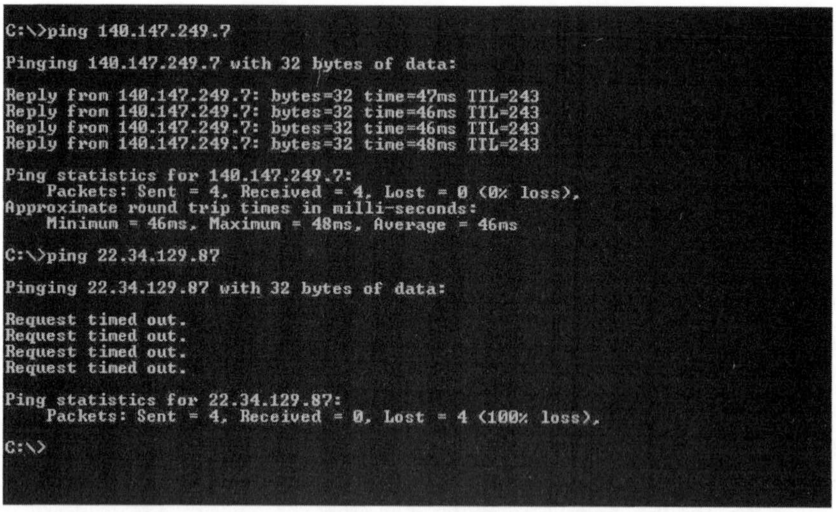

FIGURE 4-16 *Output from successful and unsuccessful PING tests*

As with other TCP/IP commands, PING can be used with a number of different options, or
switches, and the syntax of the command may vary depending on the operating system. But a
ping command always begins with the word "ping" followed by a hyphen (-) and a switch, followed by a variable pertaining to that switch. Below are some useful PING switches:

◆ -?—Displays the help text for the ping command, including its syntax and a full list
of switches.

◆ -a—When used with an IP address, resolves the address to a host name.

◆ -n—Allows you to specify a number of echo requests to send. For example, if you
wanted to ping the Library of Congress site with only two echo requests (rather
than the standard four that a Windows operating system uses), you could type the
following command: ping -n 2 www.loc.gov.

◆ -r—When used with a number from 1 to 9, displays the route taken during ping
hops.

To view the proper syntax and a list of switches available for PING, type ping at the command prompt on a Windows-based computer or at the shell prompt on a UNIX-type system.

IPX/SPX (Internetwork Packet Exchange/Sequenced Packet Exchange)

NET+
2.4

IPX/SPX (Internetwork Packet Exchange/Sequenced Packet Exchange) is a protocol originally developed by Xerox, then modified and adopted by Novell in the 1980s for its NetWare network operating system. IPX/SPX is required to ensure the interoperability of LANs running NetWare versions 3.2 and lower and can be used with LANs running higher versions of the NetWare operating system. On versions 5.0 and higher of NetWare, IPX/SPX has been replaced by TCP/IP as the default protocol. You will probably only use IPX/SPX if your clients must connect with older NetWare systems. To ensure interoperability, other operating systems can use IPX/SPX. Microsoft's implementation of IPX/SPX is called NWLink.

IPX/SPX, like TCP/IP, is a combination of protocols that reside at different layers of the OSI Model. Also like TCP/IP, IPX/SPX carries network addressing information, so it is routable.

The IPX and SPX Protocols

The core protocols of IPX/SPX provide services at the Transport and Network layers of the OSI Model. As you might guess, the most significant core protocols are IPX and SPX.

IPX (Internetwork Packet Exchange) operates at the Network layer of the OSI Model and provides logical addressing and internetworking services, similar to IP in the TCP/IP suite. Like IP, IPX also uses datagrams to transport data and its datagrams also contain source and destination addresses. Furthermore, IPX is a connectionless service because it does not require a session to be established before it transmits, and it does not guarantee that data will be delivered in sequence or without errors. In summary, it is an efficient subprotocol with limited capabilities. All IPX/SPX communication relies upon IPX, however, and upper-layer protocols handle the functions that IPX cannot perform.

SPX (Sequenced Packet Exchange) belongs to the Transport layer of the OSI Model. It works in tandem with IPX to ensure that data are received whole, in sequence, and error free. SPX, like TCP in the TCP/IP suite, is a connection-oriented protocol and therefore must verify that a session has been established with the destination node before it will transmit data. It can detect whether a packet was not received in its entirety. If it discovers a packet has been lost or corrupted, SPX will resend the packet.

The SPX information is encapsulated by IPX. That is, its fields sit inside the data field of the IPX datagram. The SPX packet, like the TCP segment, contains a number of fields to ensure data reliability. An SPX packet consists of a 42-byte header followed by 0 to 534 bytes of data. An SPX packet can be as small as 42 bytes (the size of its header) or as large as 576 bytes.

Addressing in IPX/SPX

Just as with TCP/IP-based networks, IPX/SPX-based networks require that each node on a network be assigned a unique address to avoid communication conflicts. Because IPX is the component of the protocol that handles addressing, addresses on an IPX/SPX network are called **IPX addresses**. IPX addresses contain two parts: the network address (also known as the external network number) and the node address.

Maintaining network addresses for clients running IPX/SPX is somewhat easier than maintaining addresses for TCP/IP-based networks, because IPX/SPX-based networks primarily rely on the MAC address for each workstation. To begin, the network administrator chooses a network address when installing the (older) NetWare operating system on a server. The network address must be an 8-bit hexadecimal address, which means that each of its bits can have a value of either 0–9 or A–F. An example of a valid network address is 000008A2. The network address then becomes the first part of the IPX address on all nodes that use the particular server as their primary server.

> **NOTE**
>
> The address 00000000 is a null value and cannot be used as a network address. The address FFFFFFFF is a broadcast address and also cannot be assigned as a network address.

The second part of an IPX address, the node address, is by default equal to the network device's MAC address. Because every network interface card should have a unique MAC address, no possibility of duplicating IPX addresses exists under this system (unless MAC addresses have been manually altered). In addition, the use of MAC addresses means that you need not configure addresses for the IPX/SPX protocol on each client workstation. Instead, they are already defined by the NIC. Adding a MAC address to the network address example used previously, a complete IPX address for a workstation on the network might be 000008A2:0060973E97F3.

NetBIOS and NetBEUI

NetBIOS (Network Basic Input Output System) is a protocol originally designed for IBM to provide Transport and Session layer services for applications running on small, homogenous networks. Early versions of NetBIOS did not provide a standard Transport layer specification, and networks that used NetBIOS were not necessarily compatible. However, when Microsoft adopted IBM's NetBIOS as its foundation protocol it added a standard Transport layer component called **NetBEUI** (the **NetBIOS Enhanced User Interface**), pronounced, "net-bóo-ee".

On small networks, NetBEUI is an efficient protocol that consumes few network resources, provides excellent error correction, and requires little configuration. It can support only 254 connections, however, and does not allow for good security. Furthermore, because NetBEUI frames include only Data Link layer (or MAC) addresses and not Network layer addresses, it is not routable. On the other hand, because NetBEUI does not use Network layer headers and

NET+
2.4

trailers, it can operate more efficiently. If necessary, NetBEUI can be encapsulated by other protocols, such as TCP/IP, then routed, but in many cases, the preferred method would be to migrate a NetBEUI network to a network running TCP/IP. Thus, this protocol is not suitable for large networks.

Today, NetBEUI might be used in very small Microsoft-based networks to integrate legacy clients. In newer Microsoft-based networks, TCP/IP is the protocol of choice because it is more flexible and scalable than NetBEUI. In fact, with its release of the Windows XP operating system, Microsoft has discontinued its support of NetBEUI. However, the company will provide the necessary tools to communicate with clients that still use NetBEUI and cannot be easily migrated to TCP/IP.

Addressing in NetBEUI

In case you do need to integrate older NetBEUI clients, you should understand how this protocol addresses clients. You have learned that NetBIOS does not contain a Network layer and therefore cannot be routed. To transmit data between network nodes, however, NetBIOS needs to reach each workstation. For this reason, network administrators must assign a NetBIOS name to each workstation. The NetBIOS name can consist of any combination of 16 or fewer alphanumeric characters (the only exception is that you cannot begin a NetBIOS name with an asterisk). Once NetBIOS has found a workstation's NetBIOS name, it will discover the workstation's MAC address and then use this address in further communications with the workstation. For example, a valid NetBIOS name is MY_COMPUTER.

TIP

On networks running both TCP/IP and NetBIOS, it is simplest to make the NetBIOS name identical to the TCP/IP host name.

NET+
2.13

WINS (Windows Internet Naming Service)

WINS (Windows Internet Naming Service) provides a means of resolving NetBIOS names to IP addresses. WINS is used exclusively with systems that use NetBIOS—therefore, it only appears on Windows-based systems. With fewer and fewer networks relying on NetBIOS, however, WINS is becoming less common.

A computer's NetBIOS name and its TCP/IP host name are different entities, though you can choose to use the same name for the NetBIOS name as you use for the TCP/IP name. Earlier, you learned that DNS provides resolutions of TCP/IP host names and IP addresses. WINS, on the other hand, provides resolution of NetBIOS names and IP addresses. Essentially, WINS has the same relationship to NetBIOS as DNS has to TCP/IP. That is, both WINS and DNS associate names with IP addresses.

NET+
2.13

WINS is an automated service that runs on a server. In this sense, it resembles DHCP. WINS may be implemented on servers running Windows NT Server, Windows 2000 Server, or Windows Server 2003. It maintains a database on the server that accepts requests from Windows or DOS clients to register with a particular NetBIOS name. Note that WINS does not assign names or IP addresses, but merely keeps track of which NetBIOS names are linked to which IP addresses.

A distinct advantage to using WINS is that it will guarantee that a unique NetBIOS name is used for each computer on a network. It can also be integrated with DHCP to combine IP address assignment and NetBIOS-to-IP address association. Finally, WINS can offer better network performance because as WINS manages the mappings between IP addresses and NetBIOS names, clients do not have to broadcast their NetBIOS names to the rest of the network. The elimination of this broadcast traffic improves network performance.

Every client workstation that needs to register with the WINS server must know how to find the server. Thus the WINS server cannot use a dynamic IP address (such as one assigned by a DHCP server). Instead, a specific IP address must be assigned to the WINS server. A client's WINS server address is designated in the same way as its other TCP/IP properties.

AppleTalk

NET+
2.4

Businesses and institutions involved in art or education, such as advertising agencies, elementary schools, and graphic designers, often use Apple Macintosh computers. **AppleTalk** is the protocol suite originally designed to interconnect Macintosh computers. Although AppleTalk was meant to support peer-to-peer networking among Macintoshes, it can be routed between network segments and integrated with NetWare-, UNIX-, Linux-, or Microsoft-based networks. Still, it remains impractical for use on large networks. This is just one reason that AppleTalk, as with IPX/SPX and NetBEUI, has been replaced by TCP/IP. An overview of AppleTalk's characteristics is presented here, in case you have to integrate older, AppleTalk-reliant devices with your network.

An AppleTalk network is separated into logical groups of computers called **AppleTalk zones**. Each network can contain multiple zones, but each node can belong to only one zone. AppleTalk zones enable users to share file and printer resources on each other's Macintoshes. Zone names are not subject to the same strict naming conventions that TCP/IP- and IPX/SPX-based networks must follow. Instead, zone names typically describe a department or other group of users who share files. For example, a zone could be named "Sales and Marketing."

In addition to zone names, AppleTalk uses node IDs and network numbers to identify computers on a network. An **AppleTalk node ID** is a unique 8-bit or 16-bit number that identifies a computer on an AppleTalk network. AppleTalk assigns a node ID to each workstation when the workstation first connects to the network. The ID is randomly chosen from a group of currently available addresses. Once a device has obtained an address, it stores it for later use.

NET+
2.4

An **AppleTalk network number** is a unique 16-bit number that identifies the network to which a node is connected. Its use allows nodes from several different networks to communicate. AppleTalk addressing is simple because it allows you to identify a group of shared addresses from the server. When clients attach to that server they pick up an address, thus eliminating the need to configure addresses on each workstation.

Binding Protocols on a Windows XP Workstation

NET+
3.2

The protocols you install will depend on which operating system you are running. This section describes how to bind a protocol suite on a Windows XP client workstation. No equivalent procedure exists on a UNIX- or Linux-based computer, because UNIX and Linux only support the TCP/IP protocol suite, and the TCP/IP protocols are automatically bound to the network interface(or interfaces).

Core Network and Transport layer protocols are normally included with your computer's operating system. When enabled, these protocols attempt to bind with the network interfaces on your computer. **Binding** is the process of assigning one network component to work with another. You can manually bind protocols that are not already associated with a network interface. For optimal network performance, you should bind only those protocols that you absolutely need. For example, a Windows Server 2003 server will attempt to use bound protocols in the order in which they appear in the protocol listing until it finds the correct one for the response at hand. If not all bound protocols are necessary, this approach wastes processing time.

Normally, a workstation running the Windows XP operating system would, by default, have the TCP/IP protocol bound to its network interfaces. The following exercise shows you how to install the NWLink IPX/SPX/NetBIOS Compatible Transport protocol (which is not, by default, bound to interfaces) on a Windows XP workstation:

1. Log on to the workstation as an Administrator.
2. Click **Start**, then click **My Network Places**. The My Network Places window appears.
3. From the Network Tasks list, click **View network connections**. The Network Connections window appears.
4. Right-click the icon that represents your network adapter, and click **Properties** in the shortcut menu. The network adapter's Properties dialog box appears.
5. Click **Install...**. The Select Network Component Type dialog box appears.
6. From the list of network components, select **Protocol**, then click **Add...**. The Select Network Protocol dialog box appears, as shown in Figure 4-17.

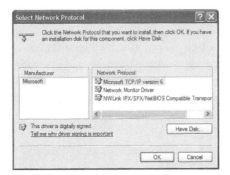

FIGURE 4-17 *The Windows XP Select Network Protocol dialog box*

7. Select **NWLink IPX/SPX/NetBIOS Compatible Transport Protocol**, then click **OK**.

8. Wait a moment while Windows XP adds the protocol to the network components already bound to your NIC. Your network adapter Properties dialog box appears, now with the NWLink NetBIOS and the NWLink IPX/SPX/ NetBIOS Compatible Transport protocols listed under the "This connection uses the following items:" heading.

9. Click **Close** to save your changes, then close the Network Connections window.

On a Windows XP workstation, you can install any other protocol in the same manner as you installed the NWLink protocol.

It is possible to bind multiple protocols to the same network adapter. In fact, this is necessary on networks that use more than one type of protocol. In addition, a workstation may have multiple NICs, in which case several different protocols might be bound to each NIC. What's more, the same protocol may be configured differently on different NICs. For example, let's say you managed a NetWare server that contained two NICs and provided both TCP/IP and IPX/SPX communications to many clients. Using the network operating system's protocol configuration utility, you would need to configure TCP/IP separately for each NIC. Similarly, you would need to configure IPX/SPX separately for each NIC. If you did not configure the protocols for each NIC separately, clients would not know which NIC to address when sending and receiving information to and from the server.

Chapter Summary

◆ Protocols define the standards for communication between nodes on a network. The term protocol can refer to a group, or suite, of individual protocols that work together to accomplish data translation, data handling, error checking, and addressing.

◆ Protocols vary by transmission efficiency, utilization of resources, ease of setup, compatibility, and ability to travel between one LAN segment and another. Protocols that can span more than one LAN are routable, which means they carry Network layer addressing information that can be interpreted by a router.

◆ TCP/IP is the most popular protocol suite, because of its low cost, open nature, ability to communicate between dissimilar platforms, and the fact that it is routable. It is a de facto standard on the Internet and is commonly the protocol of choice on LANs.

◆ TCP (Transmission Control Protocol) belongs to the Transport layer of the OSI Model. TCP is a connection-oriented subprotocol; it requires a connection to be established between communicating nodes before it will transmit data. TCP provides reliability through checksum, flow control, and sequencing information.

◆ UDP (User Datagram Protocol), like TCP, is a Transport layer protocol. UDP is a connectionless service and offers no delivery guarantees. But UDP is more efficient than TCP and useful in applications that require fast data transmission, such as videoconferencing.

◆ IP (Internet Protocol) belongs to the Network layer of the OSI Model and provides information about how and where data should be delivered.

◆ ARP (Address Resolution Protocol) belongs to the Network layer of the OSI Model. It obtains the MAC (physical) address of a host, or node, then creates a local database that maps the MAC address to the host's IP (logical) address. RARP (Reverse Address Resolution Protocol) performs the opposite function; it maps IP addresses to MAC addresses.

◆ In IPv4, each IP address is a unique 32-bit number, divided into four octets (or bytes). Every IP address contains two types of information: network and host.

◆ All nodes on a Class A network share the first octet of their IP numbers, a number between 1 and 126. Nodes on a Class B network share the first two octets, and all their IP addresses begin with a number between 128 and 191. Class C network IP numbers share the first three octets, with their first octet being a number between 192 and 223.

◆ Although computers read IP addresses in binary form, humans usually read them in dotted decimal notation, in which a decimal number represents each octet and every number is separated by a period.

◆ A subnet mask is a 32-bit number that indicates whether and how a network has been subnetted—that is, subdivided into multiple smaller networks—and indicates the difference between network and host information in an IP address. Subnetting is implemented to control network traffic and conserve a limited number of IP addresses.

◆ IP addresses assigned manually are called static IP addresses; however, using static IP addresses allows for the possibility of assigning the same address to more than one device.

◆ Dynamic IP address assignment can be achieved using BOOTP or the more sophisticated DHCP. DHCP, though not foolproof, will essentially eliminate duplicate-addressing problems.

◆ If a computer runs the Windows 98, Me, 2000, 2003, or XP operating system, is configured to use DHCP and cannot locate a DHCP server, it can be assigned an IP address and subnet mask through APIPA (Automatic Private IP Addressing). This configuration allows the computer to communicate with other computers on the same subnet only.

◆ A socket is a logical address assigned to a specific process running on a host. It forms a virtual circuit between the processes on two networked hosts. The socket's address represents a combination of the host's IP address and the port number associated with a process.

◆ IPv6 (IP version 6) is the latest version of IP. Its addresses are composed of eight 16-bit fields and total 128 bits. The larger address size results in up to 2^{96} available IP addresses. IPv6 provides several other benefits over IPv4, including a more efficient header, better overall security, better prioritization allowances, and automatic IP address configuration. IPv6 is not yet widely implemented.

◆ Every host is identified by a host name and belongs to a domain. A domain is a group of hosts that share a domain name and have part of their IP addresses in common.

◆ Every domain is identified by its domain name. Usually, a domain name is associated with a company or other type of organization, such as a university or military unit. Domain names must be reserved with an ICANN-approved domain registrar.

◆ DNS (Domain Name System) is a hierarchical way of tracking domain names and their addresses. The DNS database does not rely on one file or even one server, but rather is distributed over several key computers across the Internet to prevent catastrophic failure if one or a few computers go down.

◆ Name servers (or DNS servers) contain databases of names and their associated IP addresses. If one name server cannot resolve the IP address, the query passes to a higher-level name server. Each name server manages a group of machines called a zone. DNS relies on the hierarchical zones to distribute naming information.

◆ When one host needs to communicate with another host, it must first find its name server. Large organizations often maintain a primary and a secondary name server to help ensure Internet connectivity. You need to specify a name server's IP address in the TCP/IP properties of a workstation so that the workstation will know which machine to query when looking up a name.

Some key TCP/IP Application layer protocols include Telnet (for logging into hosts), FTP and TFTP (for transferring files between hosts), NTP (for synchronizing time between hosts), NNTP (for storage and distribution of newsgroup messages), and PING (for sending echo requests and echo replies that can indicate whether a host is responding).

◆ IPX/SPX (Internetwork Packet Exchange/Sequenced Packet Exchange) was used by Novell for its early versions of the NetWare NOS. IPX/SPX is required for interoperability with LANs running NetWare versions 3.2 and lower. IPX/SPX is a suite of protocols that reside at different layers of the OSI Model. The IPX protocol handles network addressing information, making IPX/SPX routable.

◆ IPX addresses contain two parts: the network address and the node address. The network address must be an 8-bit hexadecimal address. The node address is equal to a device's MAC address.

◆ NetBEUI is a protocol that consumes few network resources, provides error correction, and requires little configuration. But it can support only 254 connections and does not allow for good security. Furthermore, because NetBEUI lacks a Network layer, it is not routable and therefore unsuitable for large networks.

◆ WINS (Windows Internet Naming Service) is a service used on Windows systems to map IP addresses to NetBIOS names.

◆ AppleTalk is the protocol suite originally used to interconnect Macintosh computers. Today's Macintosh computers can still communicate via AppleTalk, but use TCP/IP as their default protocol suite.

Key Terms

Address Resolution Protocol—See *ARP*.

address resource record—A type of DNS data record that maps the IP address of an Internet-connected device to its domain name.

alias—A nickname for a node's host name. Aliases can be specified in a local host file.

anycast address—A type of address specified in IPv6 that represents a group of interfaces, any one of which (and usually the first available of which) can accept a transmission. At this time, anycast addresses are not designed to be assigned to hosts, such as servers or workstations, but rather to routers.

AppleTalk—The protocol suite used to interconnect Macintosh computers. Although AppleTalk was originally designed to support peer-to-peer networking among Macintoshes, it can now be routed between network segments and integrated with NetWare- or Microsoft-based networks.

AppleTalk network number—A unique 16-bit number that identifies the network to which an AppleTalk node is connected.

AppleTalk node ID—A unique 8-bit or 16-bit number that identifies a computer on an AppleTalk network.

AppleTalk zone—A logically defined group of computers on an AppleTalk network.

ARP (Address Resolution Protocol)—A core protocol in the TCP/IP suite that belongs in the Network layer of the OSI Model. ARP obtains the MAC (physical) address of a host, or node, and then creates a local database that maps the MAC address to the host's IP (logical) address.

ARP cache—See *ARP table*.

ARP table—A database of records that map MAC addresses to IP addresses. The ARP table is stored on a computer's hard disk where it is used by the ARP utility to supply the MAC addresses of network nodes, given their IP addresses.

binding—The process of assigning one network component to work with another.

BOOTP (Bootstrap Protocol)—An Application layer protocol in the TCP/IP suite that uses a central list of IP addresses and their associated devices' MAC addresses to assign IP addresses to clients dynamically. BOOTP was the precursor to DHCP.

Bootstrap Protocol—See *BOOTP*.

DHCP (Dynamic Host Configuration Protocol)—An Application layer protocol in the TCP/IP suite that manages the dynamic distribution of IP addresses on a network. Using DHCP to assign IP addresses can nearly eliminate duplicate-addressing problems.

diskless workstation—A workstation that doesn't contain a hard disk, but instead relies on a small amount of read-only memory to connect to a network and to pick up its system files.

DNS (Domain Name System or **Domain Name Service)**—A hierarchical way of tracking domain names and their addresses, devised in the mid-1980s. The DNS database does not rely on one file or even one server, but rather is distributed over several key computers across the Internet to prevent catastrophic failure if one or a few computers go down. DNS is a TCP/IP service that belongs to the Application layer of the OSI Model.

domain name—The symbolic name that identifies a domain. Usually, a domain name is associated with a company or other type of organization, such as a university or military unit.

Domain Name Service—See *DNS*.

Domain Name System—See *DNS*.

dotted decimal notation—The shorthand convention used to represent IP addresses and make them more easily readable by humans. In dotted decimal notation, a decimal number between 0 and 255 represents each binary octet. A period, or dot, separates each decimal.

dynamic address—An IP address that is assigned to a device through DHCP and may change when the DHCP lease expires or is terminated.

dynamic ARP table entry—A record in an ARP table that is created when a client makes an ARP request that cannot be satisfied by data already in the ARP table.

Dynamic Host Configuration Protocol—See *DHCP*

dynamic IP address—An IP address that is assigned to a device upon request and may change over time. BOOTP and DHCP are two ways of assigning dynamic IP addresses.

Dynamic Ports—TCP/IP ports in the range of 49152 through 65535, which are open for use without requiring administrative privileges on a host or approval from IANA.

echo reply—The response signal sent by a device after another device pings it.

echo request—The request for a response generated when one device pings another device.

external network number—Another term for the network address portion of an IPX/SPX address.

File Transfer Protocol—See *FTP*.

Format Prefix—A variable-length field at the beginning of an IPv6 address that indicates what type of address it is (for example, unicast, anycast, or multicast).

FTP (File Transfer Protocol)—An Application layer protocol used to send and receive files via TCP/IP.

hop—A term used to describe each trip a unit of data takes from one connectivity device to another. Typically, "hop" is used in the context of router-to-router communications.

host file—A text file that associates TCP/IP host names with IP addresses.

host name—A symbolic name that describes a TCP/IP device.

hosts—Name of the host file used on UNIX, Linux, and Windows systems. On a UNIX- or Linux-based computer, hosts is found in the /etc directory. On a Windows-based computer, it is found in the %systemroot%\system32\drivers\etc folder.

ICMP (Internet Control Message Protocol)—A core protocol in the TCP/IP suite that notifies the sender that something has gone wrong in the transmission process and that packets were not delivered.

IGMP (Internet Group Management Protocol or **Internet Group Multicast Protocol)**—A TCP/IP protocol used to manage multicast transmissions. Routers use IGMP to determine which nodes use IGMP to join or leave a multicast group.

Internet Control Message Protocol—See *ICMP*.

Internet Group Management Protocol—See *IGMP*.

Internet Group Multicast Protocol—See *IGMP*.

internetwork—To traverse more than one LAN segment and more than one type of network through a router.

Internetwork Packet Exchange—See *IPX*.

Internetwork Packet Exchange/Sequenced Packet Exchange—See *IPX/SPX*.

IP datagram—The IP portion of a TCP/IP frame that acts as an envelope for data, holding information necessary for routers to transfer data between subnets.

IP next generation—See *IPv6*.

IPv4LL (IP version 4 Link Local)—A protocol that manages automatic address assignment among locally connected nodes. IPv4LL is part of the Zeroconf group of protocols.

ifconfig—A TCP/IP configuration and management utility used with UNIX and Linux systems.

ipconfig—The utility used to display TCP/IP addressing and domain name information in the Windows NT, Windows 2000, and Windows XP operating systems.

IPng—See *IPv6*.

IPv4 (IP version 4)—The current standard for IP addressing that specifies 32-bit addresses composed of four octets.

IPv6 (IP version 6)—A newer standard for IP addressing that will replace the current IPv4 (IP version 4). Most notably, IPv6 uses a newer, more efficient header in its packets and allows for 128-bit source and destination IP addresses. The use of longer addresses will allow for many more IP addresses to be in circulation.

IPX (Internetwork Packet Exchange)—A core protocol of the IPX/SPX suite that operates at the Network layer of the OSI Model and provides routing and internetwork services, similar to IP in the TCP/IP suite.

IPX address—An address assigned to a device on an IPX/SPX-based network.

IPX/SPX (Internetwork Packet Exchange/Sequenced Packet Exchange)—A protocol originally developed by Xerox, then modified and adopted by Novell in the 1980s for the NetWare network operating system.

label—A character string that represents a domain (either top-level, second-level, or third-level).

lease—The agreement between a DHCP server and client on how long the client can use a DHCP-assigned IP address. DHCP services can be configured to provide lease terms equal to any amount of time.

loopback address—An IP address reserved for communicating from a node to itself (used mostly for troubleshooting purposes). The loopback address is always cited as 127.0.0.1, although in fact, transmitting to any IP address whose first octet is "127" will contact the originating device.

loopback test—An attempt to contact one's own machine for troubleshooting purposes. In TCP/IP-based networking, a loopback test can be performed by communicating with an IP address that begins with an octet of 127. Usually, this means pinging the address 127.0.0.1.

multicast address—A type of address in the IPv6 that represents multiple interfaces, often on multiple nodes. An IPv6 multicast address begins with the following hexadecimal field: FF0x, where x is a character that identifies the address's group scope.

multicasting—A means of transmission in which one device sends data to a specific group of devices (not necessarily the entire network segment) in a point-to-multipoint fashion. Multicasting can be used for videoconferencing over the Internet, for example.

multiprotocol network—A network that uses more than one protocol.

name server—A server that contains a database of TCP/IP host names and their associated IP addresses. A name server supplies a resolver with the requested information. If it cannot resolve the IP address, the query passes to a higher-level name server.

name space—The database of Internet IP addresses and their associated names distributed over DNS name servers worldwide.

net mask—See *subnet mask.*

NetBEUI (NetBIOS Enhanced User Interface)—The Microsoft adaptation of the IBM Net-BIOS protocol. NetBEUI expands on NetBIOS by adding a Transport layer component. Net-BEUI is a fast and efficient protocol that consumes few network resources, provides excellent error correction, and requires little configuration.

NetBIOS (Network Basic Input Output System)—A protocol designed by IBM to provide Transport and Session layer services for applications running on small, homogeneous networks.

NetBIOS Enhanced User Interface—See *NetBEUI.*

Network Basic Input Output System—See *NetBIOS.*

network class—A classification for TCP/IP-based networks that pertains to the network's potential size and is indicated by an IP address's network ID and subnet mask. Network classes A, B, and C are commonly used by clients on LANs; network classes D and E are reserved for special purposes.

network ID—The portion of an IP address common to all nodes on the same network or subnet.

Network News Transport Protocol—See *NNTP.*

Network Time Protocol—See *NTP.*

newsgroup—An Internet-based forum for exchanging messages on a particular topic. Newsgroups rely on NNTP for the collection and dissemination of messages.

NNTP (Network News Transport Protocol)—An Application layer protocol in the TCP/IP suite which facilitates the exchange of newsgroup messages, or articles, between multiple servers and users.

NTP (Network Time Protocol)—A simple Application layer protocol in the TCP/IP suite used to synchronize the clocks of computers on a network. NTP depends on UDP for Transport layer services.

octet—One of the four 8-bit bytes that are separated by periods and together make up an IP address.

Packet Internet Groper—See *PING.*

ping—To send an echo request signal from one node on a TCP/IP-based network to another, using the PING utility. See also *PING.*

PING (Packet Internet Groper)—A TCP/IP troubleshooting utility that can verify that TCP/IP is installed, bound to the NIC, configured correctly, and communicating with the network. PING uses ICMP to send echo request and echo reply messages that determine the validity of an IP address.

port number—The address on a host where an application makes itself available to incoming data.

RARP (Reverse Address Resolution Protocol)—A core protocol in the TCP/IP suite that belongs in the Network layer of the OSI Model. RARP relies on a RARP table to associate the IP (logical) address of a node with its MAC (physical) address. RARP can be used to supply IP addresses to diskless workstations.

Registered Ports—TCP/IP ports in the range of 1024 to 49151. These ports are accessible to network users and processes that do not have special administrative privileges. Default assignments of these ports must be registered with IANA.

release—The act of terminating a DHCP lease.

Rendezvous—Apple Computer's implementation of the Zeroconf group of protocols.

resolver—Any host on the Internet that needs to look up domain name information.

resource record—The element of a DNS database stored on a name server that contains information about TCP/IP host names and their addresses.

Reverse Address Resolution Protocol—See *RARP*.

root server—A DNS server maintained by ICANN and IANA that is an authority on how to contact the top-level domains, such as those ending with .com, .edu, .net, .us, and so on. ICANN oversees the operation of 13 root servers around the world.

routable—Protocols that can span more than one LAN because they carry Network layer and addressing information that can be interpreted by a router.

Sequenced Packet Exchange—See *SPX*.

socket—A logical address assigned to a specific process running on a computer. Some sockets are reserved for operating system functions.

SPX (Sequenced Packet Exchange)—One of the core protocols in the IPX/SPX suite. SPX belongs to the Transport layer of the OSI Model and works in tandem with IPX to ensure that data are received whole, in sequence, and error free.

static ARP table entry—A record in an ARP table that someone has manually entered using the ARP utility. Static ARP table entries remain the same until someone manually modifies them with the ARP utility.

static IP address—An IP address that is manually assigned to a device and remains constant until it is manually changed.

subnet—A part of a network in which all nodes shares a network addressing component and a fixed amount of bandwidth.

subnet mask—A 32-bit number that, when combined with a device's IP address, indicates what kind of subnet the device belongs to.

subnetting—The process of subdividing a single class of network into multiple, smaller networks.

subprotocols—Small, specialized protocols that work together and belong to a protocol suite.

switch—The letters or words added to a command that allow you to customize a utility's output. Switches are usually preceded by a hyphen or forward slash character.

TCP (Transmission Control Protocol)—A core protocol of the TCP/IP suite. TCP belongs to the Transport layer and provides reliable data delivery services.

TCP/IP (Transmission Control Protocol/Internet Protocol)—A suite of networking protocols that includes TCP, IP, UDP, and many others. TCP/IP provides the foundation for data exchange across the Internet.

TCP/IP core protocols—The major subprotocols of the TCP/IP suite, including IP, TCP, and UDP.

Telnet—A terminal emulation protocol used to log on to remote hosts using the TCP/IP protocol. Telnet resides in the Application layer of the OSI Model.

TFTP (Trivial File Transfer Protocol)—A TCP/IP Application layer protocol that enables file transfers between computers. Unlike FTP, TFTP relies on UDP at the Transport layer and does not require a user to log on to the remote host.

Time to Live—See *TTL*.

TLD (top-level domain)—The highest-level category used to distinguish domain names—for example, .org, .com, .net. A TLD is also known as the domain suffix.

top-level domain—See *TLD*.

Transmission Control Protocol—See *TCP*.

Transmission Control Protocol/Internet Protocol—See *TCP/IP*.

Trivial File Transfer Protocol—See *TFTP*.

TTL (Time to Live)—A number that indicates the maximum time that a datagram or packet can remain on the network before it is discarded. Although this field was originally meant to represent units of time, on modern networks it represents the number of router hops a datagram has endured. The TTL for datagrams is variable and configurable, but is usually set at 32 or 64. Each time a datagram passes through a router, its TTL is reduced by 1. When a router receives a datagram with a TTL equal to 1, the router discards that datagram.

UDP (User Datagram Protocol)—A core protocol in the TCP/IP suite that sits in the Transport layer of the OSI Model. UDP is a connectionless transport service.

unicast address—A type of IPv6 address that represents a single interface on a device. An IPv6 unicast address begins with either FFC0 or FF80.

User Datagram Protocol—See *UDP*.

Well Known Ports—TCP/IP port numbers 0 to 1023, so named because they were long ago assigned by Internet authorities to popular services (for example, FTP and Telnet), and are therefore well known and frequently used.

Windows Internet Naming Service—See *WINS*.

WINS (Windows Internet Naming Service)—A service that resolves NetBIOS names with IP addresses. WINS is used exclusively with systems that use NetBIOS—therefore, it is found on Windows-based systems.

Zeroconf (Zero Configuration)—A collection of protocols designed by the IETF to simplify the setup of nodes on a TCP/IP network. Zeroconf assigns a node an IP address, resolves the node's host name and IP address without requiring a DNS server, and discovers services, such as print services, available to the node, also without requiring a DNS server.

Review Questions

1. A _____ is a rule that governs how networks communicate.
   a. protocol
   b. subnet mask
   c. port
   d. namespace

2. _____ is a Network layer protocol that obtains the MAC address of a host, or node, then creates a database that maps the MAC address to the host's IP address.
   a. Network Time Protocol
   b. File Transfer Protocol
   c. Address Resolution Protocol
   d. Internet Control Message Protocol

3. _____ contain databases of associated names and IP addresses and provide this information to resolvers on request.

   a. Hosts

   b. IP datagrams

   c. Subnets

   d. Name servers

4. The _____ provides a means of resolving NetBIOS names to IP addresses.

   a. Dynamic Host Configuration Protocol

   b. Windows Internet Naming Service

   c. Network News Transport Protocol

   d. Internet Packet Exchange Protocol

5. _____ is the process of assigning one network component to work with another.

   a. Subnetting

   b. Multicasting

   c. Binding

   d. IP addressing

6. True or false? All protocols are routable.

7. True or false? TCP ensures reliable delivery through sequencing and checksums.

8. True or false? TCP is a connectionless transport device.

9. True or false? Every process on a machine is assigned a port number.

10. True or false? IPv6 addresses are composed of eight 16-bit fields and total 32 bits.

11. _____ allows one device to send data to a specific group of devices.

12. A(n) _____ is a special 32-bit number that, when combined with a device's IP address, informs the rest of the network about the segment or network to which it is attached.

13. _____ are any hosts on the Internet that need to look up domain name information.

14. _____ is a terminal emulation protocol used to log on to remote hosts using the TCP/IP protocol suite.

15. The _____ is a simple Application layer protocol used to synchronize the clocks of computers on a network.

Chapter 5

Networking Hardware

After reading this chapter and completing the exercises, you will be able to:

- Identify the functions of LAN connectivity hardware

- Install and configure a network interface card (NIC, or network adapter)

- Identify problems associated with connectivity hardware

- Describe the factors involved in choosing a NIC, hub, switch, or router

- Discuss the functions of repeaters, hubs, bridges, switches, routers, and gateways, and the OSI Model layers at which they operate

- Describe the uses and types of routing protocols

In Chapter 3, you learned how data is transmitted over cable or through the atmosphere. Now you need to know how data arrives at its destination. To understand this process, it's helpful to compare data transmission to the means by which the U.S. Postal Service delivers mail: Mail trucks, airplanes, and delivery staff serve as the transmission system that moves information from place to place. Machines and personnel at the post office interpret addresses on the envelopes and either deliver the mail to a transfer point or to your home. Inefficiencies in mail delivery, such as letters being misdirected to the wrong transfer point, frustrate both the sender and the receiver of the mail and increase the overall cost of delivery.

In data networks, the task of directing information efficiently to the correct destination is handled by hubs, routers, bridges, and switches. In this chapter, you will learn about these devices and their roles in managing data traffic. Material in this chapter relates mostly to functions occurring in the Data Link and Network layers of the OSI Model. Some material also relates to the Physical layer. You will learn the concepts involved in moving data from place to place, including issues related to switching and routing protocols. You will also see pictures of the hardware—hubs, switches, bridges, and routers—that make data transfer possible. (It's important for you to have an accurate mental image of this equipment because, in a cluttered data closet, it may prove difficult to identify the hardware underneath the wiring.) In addition, you will learn all about network interface cards, which serve as the workstation's link to the network and are often the source of connectivity problems.

NICs (Network Interface Cards)

NET+
1.6
2.3

Network interface cards (also called NICs, network adapters, or network cards) are connectivity devices that enable a workstation, server, printer, or other node to receive and transmit data over the network media. Nearly all NICs contain a data transceiver, the device that transmits and receives data signals. NICs belong to both the Physical layer and Data Link layer of the OSI Model, because they apply data signals to the wire and assemble or disassemble data frames. They also interpret physical addressing information to ensure data is delivered to its proper destination. In addition, they perform the routines that determine which node has the right to transmit data over a network at any given instant.

NET+
1.6

Advances in NIC technology are making this hardware smarter than ever. Many can also perform prioritization, network management, buffering, and traffic-filtering functions. On most networks, NICs do not, however, analyze information added by the protocols in Layers 3 through 7 of the OSI Model. For example, they could not determine whether the frames they transmit and receive use IP or IPX datagrams. Nor could they determine whether the Presentation layer has encrypted the data in those frames.

As you learn about installing, configuring, and troubleshooting NICs, you should concentrate first on generalities, then move on to special situations. Because NICs are common to every networking device and every network, knowing as much as possible about them may prove to be the most useful tool you have at your disposal.

NET+
1.6

Types of NICs

Before you order or install a NIC in a network device, you need to know what type of interface the device uses. NICs come in a variety of types depending on:

◆ The access method (for example, Ethernet versus Token Ring)

◆ Network transmission speed (for example, 100 Mbps versus 1 Gbps)

◆ Connector interfaces (for example, RJ-45 versus SC)

◆ Type of compatible motherboard or device (for example, PCI)

◆ Manufacturer (popular NIC manufacturers include 3Com, Adaptec, D-Link, IBM, Intel, Kingston, Linksys, Netgear, SMC, and Western Digital, to name just a few)

The following section describes one category of NICs, those that are installed on an expansion board inside a computer.

Internal Bus Standards

If you have worked with PCs or studied for CompTIA's A+ exam, you are probably familiar with the concept of a bus. A computer's **bus** is the circuit, or signaling pathway, used by the motherboard to transmit data to the computer's components, including its memory, processor, hard disk, and NIC. (A computer's bus may also be called its **system bus** or **main bus**.) Buses differ according to their capacity. The capacity of a bus is defined principally by the width of its data path (expressed in bits) and its clock speed (expressed in MHz). A data path size equals the number of bits that it can transmit in parallel at any given time. In the earliest PCs, buses had an 8-bit data path. Later, manufacturers expanded buses to handle 16 bits of data, then 32 bits. Most new desktop computers use buses capable of exchanging 64 bits of data, and some are even capable of 128 bits. As the number of bits of data that a bus can handle increases, so too does the speed of the devices attached to the bus.

A computer's bus can be expanded to include devices other than those found on the motherboard. The motherboard contains **expansion slots**, or openings with multiple electrical contacts, that allow devices such as NICs, modems, or sound cards to connect to the computer's expanded bus. The devices are found on a circuit board called an **expansion card** or **expansion board**. Inserting an expansion board into an expansion slot establishes an electrical connection between the expansion board and the motherboard. Thus, the device connected to the expansion board becomes connected to the computer's main circuit and part of its bus. With expansion boards connected to its main circuit, a computer can centrally control the device.

Multiple bus types exist, and to become part of a computer's bus, an expansion board must use the same bus type. By far the most popular expansion board NIC is one that uses a PCI bus. **PCI (Peripheral Component Interconnect)** is a 32- or 64-bit bus with a 33- or 66-MHz clock speed whose maximum data transfer rate is 264 MBps. Intel introduced the first version of PCI in 1992. The latest version, 3.0, was released in 2004 and has become the expansion card type used for nearly all NICs in new PCs. It's characterized by a shorter connector length and a much faster data transmission capability than previous bus types such as **ISA (Industry Standard Architecture)**, the original PC bus type, developed in the early 1980s to support an 8-bit and later 16-bit data path and a 4.77-MHz clock speed. Another advantage to PCI adapters is that they work within both PCs and Macintosh computers, allowing an organization to standardize on one type of NIC for use with all of its workstations. Figure 5-1 depicts a typical PCI NIC.

A newer version of the PCI standard is **PCI Express**, which specifies a 64-bit bus with a 133-MHz clock speed capable of transferring data at up to 500 MBps per data path, or lane, in full-duplex transmission. PCI Express, which was introduced in 2002, follows a new type of bus design and offers several advantages over the old PCI: more efficient data transfer, support for quality of service distinctions, error reporting and handling, and compatibility with the current PCI software. Also, PCI Express cards are designed to fit into PCs that currently have older PCI slots. (This requires the addition of a small slot behind each of two existing PCI slots. The PCI Express card is then inserted into both PCI slots.) PCI Express slots vary depending on the number of lanes they support: An x1 slot supports a single lane, an x2 slot supports two lanes, and so on. Each lane offers a full-duplex throughput of 500 Mbps. A PCI Express slot can support up to 16 lanes, and an x16 slot can provide 8 Gbps throughput. Computers such as servers that must perform fast data transfer are already using the PCI Express standard, and manufacturers predict that PCI Express will replace PCI in most PCs in coming years. PCI Express is sometimes referred to as **PCIe** or **PCIx**. Figure 5-2 depicts a PCI Express x1 NIC.

You can easily determine the type of bus your PC uses by reading the documentation that came with the computer. Someday, however, you may need to replace a NIC on a PC whose documentation is missing. To verify the type of bus a PC uses, you can look inside the PC case. (Later in this chapter, you will learn how to open a computer case, check the computer's bus, and install a NIC safely.) Most PCs have at least two different types of bus connections on the same motherboard. Figure 5-3 illustrates a motherboard with ISA, PCI, and PCI Express expansion slots.

If a motherboard supports more than one kind of expansion slot, refer to the NIC and PC manufacturers' guidelines (either in print or on the Web) for information on the preferred type of NIC. If possible, you should choose a NIC that matches the most modern bus on the motherboard. For example, if a PC supports both ISA and PCI, attempt to use a PCI NIC. Although you may be able to use the older bus and NIC types without any adverse effects, some NICs will not work in an older bus if a faster, newer bus is available on the motherboard.

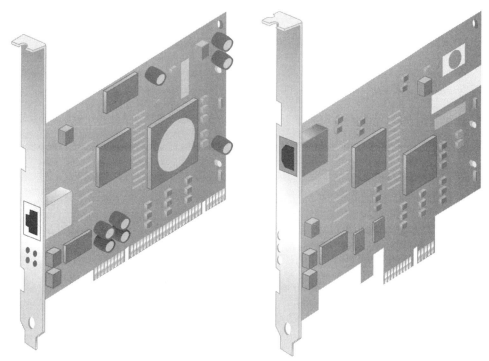

FIGURE 5-1 *PCI NIC*   **FIGURE 5-2** *PCI Express x1 NIC*

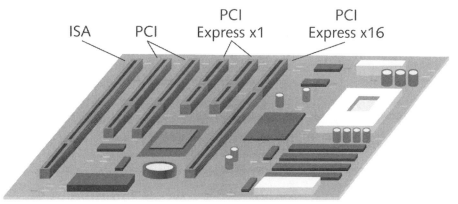

FIGURE 5-3 *A motherboard with multiple expansion slots*

Peripheral Bus Standards

Some peripheral devices, such as modems or NICs, are attached to the computer's bus externally rather than internally. PCMCIA (Personal Computer Memory Card International Association), USB (universal serial bus), CompactFlash, or FireWire (IEEE 1394) slots can all be used to connect peripherals such as NICs. One advantage to externally attached NICs is their simple installation. Typically, an externally attached adapter needs only to be plugged into the port to be physically installed. An expansion board NIC, on the other hand, requires the user to turn off the computer, remove its cover, insert the board into an expansion slot, fasten the board in place, replace the cover, and turn on the computer. The oldest externally attached type of NIC still in use today is the PCMCIA adapter.

In 1989, a group of PC system and computer manufacturers formed the **Personal Computer Memory Card International Association** or **PCMCIA**. The group's original goal was to establish a standard method for connecting external memory to a portable computer. Later, seeing the potential for many other uses, PCMCIA revised the standard and offered cards that could connect virtually any type of external device. Now PCMCIA slots may be used to connect external modems, NICs (for either wire-bound or wireless networks), hard disks, or CD-ROM drives to most laptop computers.

The first standard PCMCIA-standard adapter to be released, called **PC Card**, specified a 16-bit interface running at 8 MHz. However, the PC Card standard was hampered by its slow data transfer rates. In the 1990s, recognizing the need for a faster standard, the PCMCIA group developed CardBus. **CardBus** specifies a 32-bit interface running at 33 MHz, which matches the PCI expansion board standard. Most modern laptops are equipped with CardBus slots. Figure 5-4 depicts a typical CardBus NIC.

As demand for more and faster data transfer grows, PCMCIA has continued to improve its standards. Recently it released the ExpressCard standard. ExpressCard allows many different external devices to connect to portable computers through a 26-pin interface, and offers data transfer rates of 250 MBps in each direction (for a total of 500 MBps). It uses the same data

FIGURE 5-4 *A CardBus NIC*

NET+
1.6

transfer standards as those specified in the PCI Express specification. ExpressCard modules come in two sizes: 34 mm (40% smaller than current CardBus modules) and 54 mm wide (the same width as CardBus modules). The smaller sized module will grow more desirable as devices grow thinner and lighter. This new size is also compatible with smaller devices such as PDAs, Tablet PCs, and digital cameras. Over time, PCMCIA expects the ExpressCard standard to replace the CardBus standard. Figure 5-5 shows examples of the two types of ExpressCard modules.

FIGURE 5-5 *Express Card modules*

> **NOTE**
>
> PCMCIA-standard adapters are often called "credit card adapters" because they are approximately the same size as a credit card.

NET+
1.4
1.6

Another type of externally attached NIC is one that relies on a **USB (universal serial bus) port**. USB is a standard interface used to connect multiple types of peripherals, including modems, mice, audio players, and NICs. The original USB standard was developed in 1995 by a group of computer manufacturers working to make a low-cost, simple-to-install method of connecting peripheral devices to any make or model of computer. Since 1998, USB ports have been supplied on the motherboards of most modern laptop and desktop computers.

USB adapters may follow one of two USB standards: USB 1.1 or USB 2.0. The primary difference between the two standards is speed. The USB 1.1 standard has a maximum data transfer rate of 12 Mbps. The 2.0 standard can reach 480 Mbps, if the correct transfer options are selected and if the attached device is capable of supporting that speed. Most new PCs are shipped with USB 2.0 ports. Figure 5-6 shows an example of a USB NIC, which has a USB connector on one end and an RJ-45 receptacle on the other end.

FIGURE 5-6 *A USB NIC*

Yet another peripheral bus type is called **FireWire**. Apple Computer began developing the FireWire standard in the 1980s, and it was codified by the IEEE as the **IEEE 1394** standard in 1995. It has been included on the motherboards of Macintosh computers for many years, but has become common on PCs only in the last few years. As with PCMCIA and USB standards, FireWire has undergone several improvements since its inception. Traditional FireWire connections support a maximum throughput of 400 Mbps. A newer version of the standard supports potential throughput rates of over 3 Gbps.

FireWire can be used to connect most any type of peripheral, such as a digital camera, VCR, external hard disk, or CD-ROM drive, to a desktop or laptop computer. It can also be used to connect two or more computers on a small network using a bus topology—that is, by linking one computer to another in a daisy-chain fashion. On such a network, FireWire supports a maximum of 63 devices per segment, allows for up to 4.5 meters between nodes, and the chain of FireWire-linked computers can extend no farther than 72 meters from end to end. If your computer doesn't come with a FireWire port, you can install a FireWire NIC, which is a card (usually PCI or PCMCIA) that contains a FireWire port, to allow for this type of network.

FireWire-connected peripherals, such as USB- and PCMCIA-connected peripherals, are simple to install and supported by most modern operating systems. Connectors come in two varieties: 4-pin and 6-pin. The 6-pin connector contains two pins that can be used to supply power to a peripheral. It is also the one most frequently used for interconnecting computers. FireWire has distinctively small connectors and a thin cable, as shown in Figure 5-7.

A fourth external bus standard is the **CompactFlash** standard. The original group of 12 electronics companies that formed the CompactFlash Association (CFA) designed CompactFlash as an ultra-small, removable data and input/output device that would connect to many kinds of peripherals. If you have used a digital camera recently, chances are you've saved photos on a

NET+
1.6

CompactFlash storage card. However, CompactFlash slots can also be used to connect to a network. The latest CompactFlash standard, 2.0, provides a data transfer rate of 16 MBps. Note that this is significantly slower than any of the current external adapter standards discussed previously. Because of their relatively slower speed, CompactFlash NICs are most likely to be found connecting devices too small to handle PCMCIA slots (for example, PDAs or computers embedded into other devices, such as defibrillators or heart monitors). They are often used in wireless connections, although CompactFlash NICs with RJ-45 connectors do exist, as shown in Figure 5-8.

FIGURE 5-7 *FireWire connectors (4-pin and 6-pin)*

FIGURE 5-8 *A CompactFlash NIC*

On-Board NICs

Not all peripheral devices are connected to a computer's motherboard via an expansion slot or peripheral bus. Some are connected directly to the motherboard using **on-board ports**. For example, the electrical connection that controls a computer's mouse operates through an on-board port, as does the connection for its keyboard and monitor. Many new computers also use **on-board NICs,** or NICs that are integrated into the motherboard. The advantage to using an on-board NIC is that it saves space and frees expansion slots for additional peripherals. When a computer contains an on-board network adapter, its RJ-45 port is usually located on the back or, with some laptops, on the side of the computer.

Wireless NICs

NICs are designed for use with either wire-bound or wireless networks. As you have learned, wireless NICs use an antenna (either internal or external) to exchange signals with a base station transceiver or another wireless NIC. Wireless NICs can be found for all of the bus types discussed in this chapter. One disadvantage to using wireless NICs is that currently they are somewhat more expensive than wire-bound NICs. (Other reasons for choosing wire-bound NICs over wireless, if the choices are equally convenient, are the bandwidth and security limitations of wireless transmission. These limitations are discussed elsewhere in the book.) Figure 5-9 depicts wireless PCI, CardBus, and USB NICs.

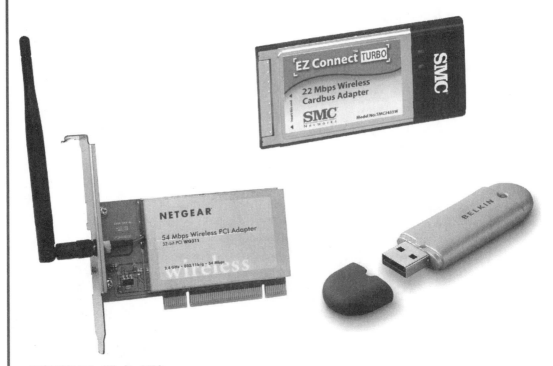

FIGURE 5-9 *Wireless NICs*

NET+
1.6
3.2

Installing NICs

To install a NIC, you must first install the hardware, and then install the software that shipped with it. In some cases, you may also have to perform a third step: configuring the **firmware**, a set of data or instructions that has been saved to a read-only memory (ROM) chip (which is on the NIC). The ROM's data can be changed by a configuration utility program provided with the NIC. Because its data can be erased or changed by applying electrical charges to the chip (via the software program), this particular type of ROM is called **EEPROM (electrically erasable programmable read-only memory)**. You'll learn more about a NIC's firmware later in the chapter. The following sections explain how to install and configure NICs.

Installing and Configuring NIC Hardware

It's always advisable to start by reading the manufacturer's documentation that accompanies the NIC hardware. The following steps generally apply to any kind of expansion card NIC installation in a desktop computer, but your experience may vary.

To install an expansion card NIC:

1. Make sure that your toolkit includes a Phillips-head screwdriver, a ground strap, and a ground mat to protect the internal components from electrostatic discharge. Also, make sure that you have ample space in which to work, whether it be on the floor, a desk, or table.

2. Turn off the computer's power switch, and then unplug the computer. In addition to endangering you, opening a PC while it's turned on can damage the PC's internal circuitry. Also unplug attached peripherals and the network cable, if necessary.

3. Attach the ground strap to your wrist and make sure that it's connected to the ground mat underneath the computer.

4. Open the computer's case. Desktop computer cases are attached in several different ways. They might use four or six Phillips-head screws to attach the housing to the back panel, or they might not use any screws and slide off instead. Remove all necessary screws and then remove the computer's case.

5. Select a slot on the computer's motherboard where you will insert the NIC. Make sure that the slot matches the type of expansion card you have. Remove the metal slot cover for that slot from the back of the PC. Some slot covers are attached with a single Phillips-head screw; after removing the screw, you can lift out the slot cover. Other slot covers are merely metal parts with perforated edges that you can punch or twist out with your hands.

6. Insert the NIC by lining up its slot connector with the slot and pressing it firmly into the slot. Don't be afraid to press down hard, but make sure the expansion card is properly aligned with the slot when you do so. If you have correctly inserted the NIC, it should not wiggle near its base. (Depending on the card's size and thickness, it may have some inherent flexibility, however.) A loose NIC causes connectivity problems. Figure 5-10 shows a closeup of a NIC firmly seated in its slot.

FIGURE 5-10 *A properly inserted NIC*

7. The metal bracket at the end of the NIC should now be positioned where the metal slot cover was located before you removed the slot cover. Attach the bracket with a Phillips-head screw to the back of the computer cover to secure the NIC in place.

8. Make sure that you have not loosened any cables or cards inside the PC or left any screws or debris inside the computer.

9. Replace the cover on the computer and reinsert the screws that you removed in Step 4, if applicable. Also reinsert any cables you removed.

10. Plug in the computer and turn it on. Proceed to configure the NIC's software, as discussed later in this chapter.

Physically installing a PCMCIA-standard NIC is much easier than installing an expansion card NIC. In general, you can simply turn off the machine, insert the card into the PCMCIA slot, as shown in Figure 5-11, then turn on the computer. Most modern operating systems (such as Windows XP) allow you to insert and remove the PCMCIA-standard adapter without restarting the machine. Make sure that the card is firmly inserted. If you can wiggle it, you need to realign it or push it in farther. Installing other types of external NICs, such as USB, Express-Card, and CompactFlash adapters, is similar. All you need to do is insert the device into the computer's port, making sure that it is securely attached.

NET+
1.6
3.2

FIGURE 5-11 *Installing a PCMCIA-standard NIC*

On servers and other high-powered computers, you may need to install multiple NICs. For the hardware installation, you can simply repeat the installation process for the first NIC, choosing a different slot. The trick to using multiple NICs on one machine lies in correctly configuring the software for each NIC. Simple NIC configuration is covered in the following section. The precise steps involved in configuring NICs on servers will depend on the server's networking operating system.

On older expansion board NICs, rather than using firmware utilities to modify settings, you may need to set a jumper or DIP switch. A **jumper** is a small, removable piece of plastic that contains a metal receptacle. This metal receptacle fits over a pair of pins on a circuit board to complete a circuit between those two pins. A **DIP (dual inline package) switch** is a small, plastic toggle switch that can represent an "on" or "off" status that indicates a parameter setting. To set jumpers and DIP switches properly, refer to the documentation for the adapter (typically available at the manufacturer's Web site), which shows how different jumper and DIP switch settings indicate particular NIC configurations.

Installing and Configuring NIC Software

Even if your computer runs an operating system with plug-and-play technology such as Windows XP or Red Hat Linux, you must ensure that the correct device driver is installed for the NIC and that it is configured properly. A **device driver** (sometimes called, simply, a **driver**) is software that enables an attached device to communicate with the computer's operating system. When you purchase a computer that already contains an attached peripheral (such as a

NET+
1.6
3.2

sound card), the device drivers should already be installed. However, when you add hardware, you must install the device drivers. Most operating systems come with a multitude of built-in device drivers. In that case, after you physically install new hardware and reboot, the operating system automatically recognizes the hardware and installs the device's drivers. Each time a computer boots up, the device drivers for all its connected peripherals are loaded into RAM so that the computer can communicate with those devices at any time.

In other cases, the operating system might not contain appropriate device drivers for the hardware you've added. This section describes how to install and configure NIC software on a Windows XP operating system that does not already contain the correct device drivers. For other operating systems with plug-and-play capability, the process will be similar. Regardless of which operating system you use, you should first refer to the NIC's documentation, because your situation may vary. Read the NIC documentation carefully before installing the relevant drivers, and make sure you are installing the appropriate drivers. Installing a device driver designed for Windows 95 on a Windows XP computer, for example, may cause problems.

To install NIC software from a Windows XP interface, you need access to the Windows XP software (via either a Windows XP CD or hard disk) and the device drivers specific to the NIC. These drivers are typically found on CD-ROMs, or in some cases, floppy disks.

If you do not have the CD-ROM or floppy disk that shipped with the NIC and the Windows XP software does not supply device drivers for your NIC, you can probably download the NIC software from the manufacturer's Web site. If you choose this option, make sure that you get the appropriate drivers for your operating system and NIC type. Also, make sure that the drivers you download are the most current version (sometimes called "shipping drivers") and not beta-level (unsupported) drivers.

To install and configure NIC software:

1. Physically install the NIC, and then restart the computer. Log on to the computer as a user with administrator privileges.

2. As long as you haven't disabled the plug-and-play technology in the computer's CMOS settings, Windows XP should automatically detect the new hardware. Upon detecting the NIC, it should also install the NIC's driver. In many cases, you need not install any other software or adjust the configuration for the NIC to operate properly.

3. There are certain situations in which you might want to change or update the device driver that the operating system has chosen. To do this, click **Start** on the task bar, and then click **Control Panel**. The Control Panel window opens.

4. If necessary, switch to Category View. Then click **Performance and Maintenance**. The Performance and Maintenance window appears.

5. Click **System**. The System Properties dialog box opens.

6. Select the **Hardware** tab, and then click the **Device Manager** button. The Device Manager window opens, displaying a list of installed devices.

7. Double-click the **Network adapters** icon. A list of installed NICs appears.

NET+

1.6

3.2

8. Double-click the adapter for which you want to install new device drivers. The NIC's Properties dialog box opens.

9. Select the **Driver** tab. Details about your NIC's current driver opens.

10. Click **Update Driver**. The Windows XP Hardware Update Wizard appears, to walk you through the device driver update process.

11. Select **Install from a list or specific location (Advanced)**, and then click **Next** to continue. Make sure that the CD-ROM or floppy disk with the correct driver on it is inserted.

12. You are prompted to choose your search and installation options. Make sure **Search for the best driver in these locations** and **Search removable media (floppy, CD-ROM...)** are selected, as shown in Figure 5-12, and then click **Next**.

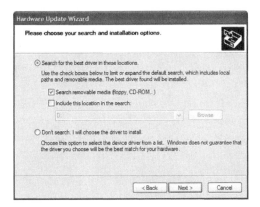

FIGURE 5-12 *Windows XP Hardware Update Wizard*

13. The Windows XP Hardware Update Wizard searches your floppy and CD-ROM drives for a driver that matches your network card. (If the disk sent with the NIC contains drivers for more than one type of NIC, you are asked to select the precise model you are using. After making your choice, click **OK**.)

14. The wizard should find the appropriate driver for your NIC and install it onto your hard disk. Later, it informs you that it has finished. To continue, click **Finish**. Close all open windows.

Procedures in this section work in most situations. Because every situation is different, however, you should always read the manufacturer's documentation and follow the installation instructions. Some manufacturers supply setup programs that automatically install and register NIC software as soon as you run them, thereby eliminating the need to follow the steps outlined previously.

Installing NIC drivers on a UNIX or Linux workstation depends somewhat on the version you're running. For example, a recent version of Linux from Red Hat, which supports plug-and-play technology, normally detects a connected NIC and automatically installs the correct drivers. The first NIC the operating system detects is called, by default, eth0. If a second NIC is present, it will be called eth1. Because they provide the network interface, eth0 and eth1 are called, in UNIX and Linux terminology, simply, interfaces.

As with other operating systems, however, a version of Linux may not always be able to install the proper drivers for your NIC automatically. In that case, you can follow these steps to install NIC software on a client running Fedora Core, a Linux operating system packaged and distributed by Red Hat, Inc. and the GNOME desktop (the default graphical user interface):

1. Log in as root (the default administrator ID) or a user ID with equivalent privileges.

2. Click the **Main Menu** icon in the lower-left corner of the screen (the icon is a red hat). This button reveals the desktop's main menu, similar to the Start button in Windows XP.

3. Point to **System Settings,** and then click **Network**. The Network Configuration window opens, as shown in Figure 5-13. If a NIC is present and installed, it appears in the list of hardware devices in the Devices tab (and also on the Hardware tab).

FIGURE 5-13 *Fedora Core Linux Network Configuration window*

4. To begin adding drivers for a NIC, click **New** on the Network Configuration toolbar. The Add New Device Type window opens.

5. Under the list of device types, click **Ethernet connection,** and then click **Forward**.

6. In the list of Ethernet cards, click **Other Ethernet Card** to add drivers for a new NIC. You are prompted to provide information about the new adapter. Click **Forward**.

7. Supply the adapter information, including adapter name (a drop-down list of common adapter types can help you specify the adapter), device name (for example, eth1), IRQ, memory address, I/O addresses, and DMA addresses. When you have finished, click **Forward**.

NET+
1.6
3.2

8. You are prompted to configure network settings. If your network relies on DHCP (which is most common), simply click **Forward** to continue. (Otherwise, click **Statically set IP addresses**, and enter the NIC's IP address information.) Click **Forward** to continue.

9. A summary of your selections appears under the Create Ethernet Device heading. Click **Apply** to install the drivers and configure network settings for the new NIC.

NET+
1.6
4.3

Interpreting LED Indicators

After you have installed a NIC, you can test it by attempting to transmit data over the network. But even before such a test, you can learn about your NIC's functionality simply by looking at it. Most modern NICs have LEDs that indicate whether they're communicating with the network. The precise location, type, and meaning of LED indicators vary from one manufacturer to another. The following are some general guidelines, but the only way to know for certain what your NIC's LEDs are trying to tell you is to read the documentation. Your NIC may have one or more of the following lights, and they may or may not be labeled:

◆ *ACT*—If blinking, this LED indicates that the NIC is either transmitting or receiving data (in other words, experiencing activity) on the network. If steady, it indicates that the NIC is experiencing heavy traffic volume.

◆ *LNK*—If lit, this LED indicates that the NIC is functional. Further, if the NIC drivers are properly installed, a lit LNK LED indicates that the NIC has a connection to the network (but is not necessarily transmitting or receiving data). In some models, if this LED is blinking, it means the NIC detects the network, but cannot communicate with it (for example, in the case of a 100BASE-TX NIC deployed on a 10BASE-T network).

◆ *TX*—If blinking, this LED indicates that the NIC is functional and transmitting frames to the network.

◆ *RX*—If blinking, this LED indicates that the NIC is functional and receiving frames from the network.

The next sections describe the variable settings you should understand when configuring NICs. Depending on your computer's use of resources, NIC configuration may or may not be necessary after installation. For troubleshooting purposes, however, you need to understand how to view and adjust these variables. If you completed coursework for the A+ certification or have worked with PCs in the past, you should already be familiar with these variables.

NET+
1.6
3.2

IRQ (Interrupt Request)

When a device attached to a computer's bus, such as a keyboard or floppy disk drive, requires attention from the computer's processor, it issues an interrupt request. An **IRQ (interrupt request)** is a message to the computer that instructs it to stop what it is doing and pay attention to something else. An interrupt is the circuit board wire over which a device issues voltage to signal this request. Each interrupt must have a unique IRQ number, a number that

NET+
1.6
3.2

uniquely identifies that component to the main bus. An IRQ number is the means by which the bus understands which device to acknowledge. The term "IRQ" is frequently substituted for "IRQ number" in casual conversation, even though they are technically two different things.

IRQ numbers range from 0 to 15. Many computer devices reserve the same IRQ number by default no matter what type of system they are installed on. For example, on every type of computer, a floppy disk controller claims IRQ 6 and a keyboard controller takes IRQ 1. On the other hand, some IRQ numbers are not reserved by default, but are available to additional devices such as sound cards, graphics cards, modems, and NICs. Most often, NICs use IRQ 9, 10, or 11. To obtain Network+ certification, you should be familiar with the IRQ numbers reserved by common computer devices as well as those most apt to be used by NICs. Table 5-1 lists all of the IRQ numbers and their default device assignments, if they have any.

Table 5-1 IRQ assignments

IRQ Number	Default Device Assignment
0	System timer (only)
1	Keyboard controller (only)
2	Access to IRQs 8–15
3	COM2 (second serial port) or COM4 (fourth serial port)
4	COM1 (first serial port) or COM3 (third serial port)
5	Sound card or LPT2 (second parallel port)
6	Floppy disk drive controller
7	LPT1 (parallel port 1)
8	Real-time clock (only)
9	No default assignment
10	No default assignment
11	No default assignment
12	PS/2 mouse
13	Math coprocessor (only)
14	IDE channel (for example, an IDE hard disk drive)
15	Secondary IDE channel

NET+
1.6
4.4

Normally the BIOS and the operating system manage IRQ assignment without problems. But if two devices attempt to use the same interrupt, resource conflicts and performance problems result. Any of the following symptoms could indicate that two devices are attempting to use the same IRQ:

- ◆ The computer may lock up or "hang" either upon starting or when the operating system is loading.

- ◆ The computer may run much more slowly than usual.

- ◆ Although the computer's NIC may work properly, other devices—such as USB or parallel ports—may stop working.

- ◆ Video or sound card problems may occur. For example, after the operating system loads, you may see an error message indicating that the video settings are incorrect, or your sound card may stop working.

- ◆ The computer may fail to connect to the network (as evidenced by an error message after you attempt to log on to a server, for example).

- ◆ The computer may experience intermittent data errors during transmission.

If IRQ conflicts do occur, you must reassign a device's IRQ. NIC IRQs can be changed through the adapter's EEPROM configuration utility or through the computer's CMOS configuration utility. **CMOS (complementary metal oxide semiconductor)** is a type of microchip that requires very little energy to operate. In a PC, the CMOS stores settings pertaining to a computer's devices, among other things. These settings are saved even after you turn off a PC because the CMOS is powered by a tiny battery in your computer. Information saved in CMOS is used by the computer's **BIOS (basic input/output system)**. The BIOS is a simple set of instructions that enables a computer to initially recognize its hardware. When you turn on a computer, the BIOS performs its start-up tasks. After a computer is up and running, the BIOS provides an interface between the computer's software and hardware, allowing it to recognize which device is associated with each IRQ.

Although you can usually modify IRQ settings in the CMOS configuration utility, whether you can change them via the operating system software depends on the type of NIC involved. For example, on a PCI NIC, which requires a PCI bus controller, the PCI controller's settings will dictate whether this type of modification is possible. The default setting prevents you from changing the NIC's IRQ via the operating system; if you attempt to make this change on a Windows XP computer, for example, on the Resources tab in the PCI NIC's Properties dialog box, the "Use Automatic Settings" option is checked and the "Change Settings" button is disabled.

NET+
1.6
3.2

Memory Range

The **memory range** indicates, in hexadecimal notation, the area of memory that the NIC and CPU use for exchanging, or buffering, data. As with IRQs, some memory ranges are reserved for specific devices—most notably, the motherboard. Reserved address ranges should never be selected for new devices.

NICs typically use a memory range in the high memory area, which in hexadecimal notation equates to the A0000–FFFFF range. As you work with NICs, you will notice that some manufacturers prefer certain ranges. For example, a 3Com PC Card adapter might, by default, choose a range of C8000-C9FFF. An IBM Token Ring adapter might choose a range of D8000-D9FFF.

Memory range settings are less likely to cause resource conflicts than IRQ settings, mainly because there are more available memory ranges than IRQs. Nevertheless, you may run into situations in which you need to change a NIC's memory address. In such an instance, you may or may not be able to change the memory range from the operating system. Refer to the manufacturer's guidelines for instructions.

Base I/O Port

The base I/O port setting specifies, in hexadecimal notation, which area of memory will act as a channel for moving data between the NIC and the CPU. Like its IRQ, a device's base I/O port cannot be used by any other device. Most NICs use two memory ranges for this channel, and the base I/O port settings identify the beginning of each range. Although a NIC's base I/O port varies depending on the manufacturer, some popular addresses (in hexadecimal notation) are 300 (which means that the range is 300–30F), 310, 280, or 2F8.

You will probably not need to change a NIC's base I/O port. If you do, bear in mind that, as with IRQ settings, base I/O port settings for PCI cards can be changed in the computer's CMOS setup utility or sometimes through the operating system.

Firmware Settings

After you have adjusted the NIC's system resources, you may need to modify its transmission characteristics—for example, whether it uses full duplexing, whether it can detect a network's speed, or even its MAC address. These settings are held in the adapter's firmware. As mentioned earlier, firmware constitutes the combination of an EEPROM chip on the NIC and the data it holds. When you change the firmware, you are actually writing to the EEPROM chip on the NIC. You are not writing to the computer's hard disk. Although most configurable settings can be changed in the operating system or NIC setup software, you may encounter complex networking problems that require a change to firmware settings.

To change a NIC's firmware, you need a bootable CD-ROM or floppy disk (DOS version 6.0 or higher) containing the configuration or install utility that shipped with the NIC. If you don't have the utility, you can usually download it from the manufacturer's Web site. To run the utility, you must start the computer with this CD-ROM or floppy disk inserted. The NIC configuration utility may not run if an operating system or memory management program is already running.

Configuration utilities differ slightly, but all should allow you to view the IRQ, I/O port, base memory, and node address. Some may allow you to change settings such as the NIC's CPU

NET+
1.6
3.2

utilization, its ability to handle full duplexing, or its capability to be used with only 10BASE-T or 100BASE-TX media, for example (although many of these can also be changed through the NIC's properties from the operating system interface). The changeable settings vary depending on the manufacturer. Again, read the manufacturer's documentation to find out the details for your hardware.

NIC configuration utilities also allow you to perform diagnostics—tests of the NIC's physical components and connectivity. Most of the tests can be performed without additional hardware. However, to perform the entire group of the diagnostic tests on the NIC's utility disk, you must have a loopback plug. A **loopback plug** (also called a **loopback adapter**) is a connector that plugs into a port, such as a serial or parallel or an RJ-45 port, and crosses over the transmit line to the receive line so that outgoing signals can be redirected into the computer for testing. One connectivity test, called a loopback test, requires you to install a loopback plug into the NIC's media connector. Note that none of the connectivity tests should be performed on a computer connected to a live network. If a NIC fails its connectivity tests, it is probably configured incorrectly. If a NIC fails a physical component test, it may need to be replaced.

 NOTE

The word "loopback" implies that signals are routed back toward their source, rather than toward an external destination. When used in the context of NICs, the loopback test refers to a check of the adapter's ability to transmit and receive signals. Recall that the term "loopback" is also used in the context of TCP/IP protocol testing. In that context, pinging the loopback address provides you with information on TCP/IP functionality.

NET+
1.6

Choosing the Right NIC

You should consider several factors when choosing a NIC for your workstation or server. Of course, the most critical factor is compatibility with your existing system. The adapter must match the network's bus type, access method, connector types, and transmission speed. You also need to ensure that drivers available for that NIC will work with your operating system and hardware.

Beyond these considerations, however, you should examine more subtle differences, such as those that affect network performance. Table 5-2 lists some features available on NICs that specifically influence performance and ease of use. As you review this table, keep in mind that performance is especially important if the NIC will be installed in a server.

Table 5-2 NIC characteristics

NIC Feature	Function	Benefit
Automatic speed selection	Enables NICs to sense and adapt to a network's speed and mode (half- or full-duplex) automatically	Aids configuration and performance
One or more on-board CPUs	Allows the card to perform some data processing independently of the PC's CPU	Improves performance
Direct memory access (DMA)	Enables the card to transfer data to the computer's memory directly	Improves performance
Diagnostic LEDs (lights on the NIC)	Indicates traffic, connectivity, and, sometimes, speed	Aids in troubleshooting
Dual channels	Effectively creates two NICs in one slot	Improves performance; suited to servers
Load balancing	Allows the NIC's processor to determine when to switch traffic between internal cards	Improves performance for heavily-trafficked networks; suited to servers
"Look Ahead" transmit and receive	Allows the NIC's processor to begin processing data before it has received the entire packet	Improves performance
Management capabilities (SNMP)	Allows the NIC to perform its own monitoring and troubleshooting, usually through installed application software	Aids in troubleshooting; can find a problem before it becomes dire
Power management capabilities	Allows a NIC to participate in the computer's power-saving measures; found on PCMCIA-based adapters	Increases the life of the battery for laptop computers
RAM buffering	Provides additional memory on the NIC, which in turn provides more space for data buffering	Improves performance
Upgradeable (flash) ROM	Allows on-board chip memory to be upgraded	Improves ease of use and performance

NET+
1.6

TIP

The quality of the printed documentation that you receive from a manufacturer about its NICs may vary. What's more, this documentation may not apply to the kinds of computers or networking environments you are using. To find out more about the type of NIC you are installing or troubleshooting, visit the manufacturer's Web site.

Repeaters and Hubs

NET+
1.6
2.3

Now that you have learned about the many types of NICs and how to install and configure them, you are ready to learn about connectivity devices. As you'll recall, the telecommunications closet is the area containing the connectivity equipment (usually for a whole floor of a building). Within the telecommunications closet, horizontal cabling from the workstations attaches to punch-down blocks, patch panels, hubs, switches, routers, and bridges. In addition, telecommunications closets may house repeaters. Repeaters are the simplest type of connectivity devices that regenerate a digital signal.

Repeaters operate in the Physical layer of the OSI Model and, therefore, have no means to interpret the data they retransmit. For example, they cannot improve or correct a bad or erroneous signal; they merely repeat it. In this sense, they are not "intelligent" devices. Since they cannot read higher-layer information in the data frames, repeaters cannot direct data to their destination. Instead, repeaters simply regenerate a signal over an entire segment. It is up to the receiver to recognize and accept its data.

NET+
1.6

A repeater is limited not only in function, but also in scope. A repeater contains one input port and one output port, so it is capable only of receiving and repeating a data stream. Furthermore, repeaters are suited only to bus topology networks. The advantage to using a repeater is that it allows you to extend a network inexpensively. However, because of repeaters' limitations and the decreasing costs of other connectivity devices, repeaters are rarely used on modern networks. Instead, clients in a workgroup area are more likely to be connected by hubs.

NET+
1.6
2.3

At its most primitive, a **hub** is a repeater with more than one output port. A hub typically contains multiple **data ports** into which the patch cables for network nodes are connected. Like repeaters, hubs operate at the Physical layer of the OSI Model. A hub accepts signals from a transmitting node and repeats those signals to all other connected nodes in a broadcast fashion. Most hubs also contain one port, called an **uplink port**, that allows the hub to connect to another hub or other connectivity device. On Ethernet networks, hubs can serve as the central connection point for branches of a star or star-based hybrid topology. On Token Ring networks, hubs are called **Multistation Access Units (MAUs)**.

NET+
1.6

In addition to connecting Macintosh and PC workstations, hubs can connect print servers, switches, file servers, or other devices to a network. All devices connected to a hub share the same amount of bandwidth and the same collision domain. A **collision domain** is a logically or physically distinct Ethernet network segment on which all participating devices must detect and accommodate data collisions. You will learn more about data collisions and Ethernet networks in Chapter 6. Suffice it to say that the more nodes participating in the same collision domain, the higher the likelihood of transmission errors and slower performance.

Placement of hubs in a network design can vary. The simplest structure would employ a stand-alone workgroup hub that is connected to another connectivity device, such as a switch or router. Some networks assign a different hub to each small workgroup, thereby benefiting from not having a single point of failure. No matter what the network design, when using hubs, adhering to a network's maximum segment and network length limitations is essential. Figure 5-14 suggests how hubs can fit into the overall design of a network.

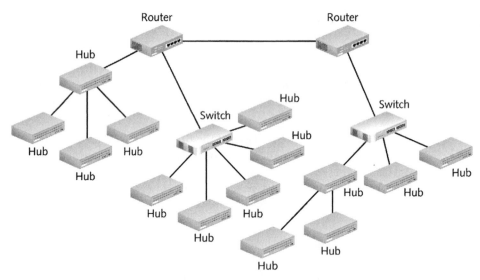

FIGURE 5-14 *Hubs in a network design*

Dozens of types of hubs exist. They vary according to the type of media and data transmission speeds they support. Some hubs allow for multiple media connector types or multiple data transmission speeds. The simplest type of hubs—known as **passive hubs**—do nothing but repeat signals. Like NICs, however, some hubs possess internal processing capabilities. For example, they may permit remote management, filter data, or provide diagnostic information about the network. Hubs that can perform any of these functions are known as **intelligent hubs**. Intelligent hubs are also called **managed hubs**, because they can be managed from anywhere on the network.

Standalone hubs, as their name implies, are hubs that serve a group of computers that are isolated from the rest of the network or that form their own small network. They are best suited to small, organizations or home offices. They can be passive or intelligent, and they are simple to install and connect for a small group of users. Standalone hubs may also be called **workgroup hubs**. Figure 5-15 depicts a small standalone hub.

FIGURE 5-15 *A standalone hub*

Standalone hubs do not follow one design, nor do they contain a standard number of ports (though they usually contain 4, 8, 12, or 24 ports). A small, standalone hub that contains only four ports (primarily used for a small or home office) may be called a "hubby," "hublet," or a "minihub." On the other hand, standalone hubs can provide as many as 200 connection ports. The disadvantage to using a single hub for so many connections is that you introduce a single point of failure on the network. A **single point of failure** is a device or connection on a network that, were it to fail, could cause the entire network or portion of the network to stop functioning. Any sizable network relies on multiple connectivity devices to avoid catastrophic failure.

Stackable hubs resemble standalone hubs, but they are physically designed to be linked with other hubs in a single telecommunications closet. Stackable hubs linked together logically represent one large hub to the network. One benefit to using stackable hubs is that your network or workgroup does not depend on a single hub, which could present a single point of failure. Models vary in the maximum number that can be stacked. For instance, some hub manufacturers restrict the number of their stacked hubs to five; others can be stacked eight units high. Some stackable hubs use a proprietary high-speed cabling system to link the hubs together for better interhub performance.

Like standalone hubs, stackable hubs may support a number of different media connectors and transmission speeds and may come with or without special processing features. The number of ports they provide also varies, although you will most often see 6, 12, or 24 ports on a stackable hub. Figure 5-16 shows three stackable hubs. In a telecommunications closet, these hubs would be rack-mounted one above the other, and interconnected.

Hubs have been a mainstay of network connectivity since the first small networks of the 1980s. However, because of their limited features and the fact that they merely repeat signals within a single collision domain, many network administrators have replaced their hubs with switches. To understand how switches operate, it is helpful to learn about bridges first.

NET+
1.6

FIGURE 5-16 *Stackable hubs*

Bridges

NET+
1.6
2.3

Bridges are devices that connect two network segments by analyzing incoming frames and making decisions about where to direct them based on each frame's MAC address. They operate at the Data Link layer of the OSI Model. Bridges look like repeaters, in that they have a single input and a single output port. They differ from repeaters in that they can interpret physical addressing information.

NET+
1.6

A significant advantage to using bridges over repeaters or hubs is that bridges are protocol-independent. For instance, all bridges can connect an Ethernet segment carrying IP-based traffic with an Ethernet segment carrying IPX-based traffic. Some bridges can also connect two segments using different Data Link and Physical layer protocols—for example, an Ethernet segment with a Token Ring segment, or a wire-bound Ethernet segment (802.3) with a wireless Ethernet segment (802.11).

Because they are protocol-ignorant, bridges can move data more rapidly than traditional routers, for example, which do care about Network layer protocol information. On the other hand, bridges take longer to transmit data than either repeaters or hubs, because bridges actually analyze each packet, whereas repeaters and hubs do not.

Another advantage to using bridges is that they can extend an Ethernet network without further extending a collision domain, or segment. In other words, by inserting a bridge into a network, you can add length beyond the maximum limits that apply to segments. Finally, bridges

NET+
1.6

can help improve network performance because they can be programmed to filter out certain types of frames (for example, unnecessary broadcast frames, whose transmissions squander bandwidth).

To translate between two segment types, a bridge reads a frame's destination MAC address and decides to either forward or filter it. If the bridge determines that the destination node is on another segment on the network, it forwards (retransmits) the packet to that segment. If the destination address belongs to the same segment as the source address, the bridge filters (discards) the frame. As nodes transmit data through the bridge, the bridge establishes a **filtering database** (also known as a **forwarding table**) of known MAC addresses and their locations on the network. The bridge uses its filtering database to determine whether a packet should be forwarded or filtered, as illustrated in Figure 5-17.

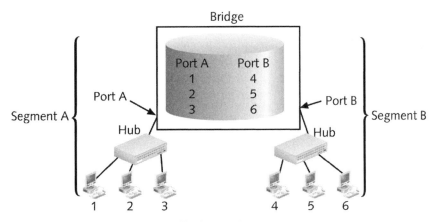

FIGURE 5-17 *A bridge's use of a filtering database*

Using Figure 5-17 as an example, imagine that you sit at workstation 1 on segment A of the LAN, and your colleague Abby sits at workstation 2 on segment A. When you attempt to send data to Abby's computer, your transmission goes through your segment's hub and then to the bridge. The bridge reads the MAC address of Abby's computer. It then searches its filtering database to determine whether that MAC address belongs to the same segment you're on or whether it belongs to a different segment. The bridge can determine only that the MAC address of Abby's workstation is associated with its port A. If the MAC address belongs to a different segment, the bridge forwards the data to that segment, whose corresponding port identity is also in the filtering database. In this case, however, your workstation and Abby's workstation reside on the same LAN segment, so the data would be filtered (that is, ignored) and your message would be delivered to Abby's workstation through segment A's hub.

Conversely, if you wanted to send data to your supervisor's computer, which is workstation 5 in Figure 5-17, your transmission would first pass through segment A's hub and then on to the bridge. The bridge would read the MAC address for your supervisor's machine (the destination address in your data stream) and search for the port associated with that machine. In this case, the bridge would recognize workstation 5 as being connected to port B, and it would forward the data to that port. Subsequently, the segment B hub would ensure delivery of the data to your supervisor's computer.

After you install a new bridge, it uses one of several methods to learn about the network and discover the destination address for each packet it handles. After it discovers this information, it records the destination node's MAC address and its associated port in its filtering database. Over time, it discovers all nodes on the network and constructs database entries for each.

Standalone bridges became popular in the 1980s and early 1990s; since then, bridging technology has evolved to create more sophisticated bridge devices. But devices other than bridges have also evolved. Equipment manufacturers have improved the speed and functionality of routers and switches while lowering their cost, leaving bridges to become nearly extinct.

Now, with the advent of wireless LANs, a new kind of bridge has become popular as an inexpensive way to connect the wireless and wire-bound parts of a network, as shown in Figure 5-18. In fact, you have already learned about these types of bridges, which are also called access points. (An access point without bridging functions could only connect an ad-hoc group of wireless clients with each other. Although such access points exist, they are rare and are generally used to extend wireless segments that at some point connect to a wire-bound portion of the network via a bridge.)

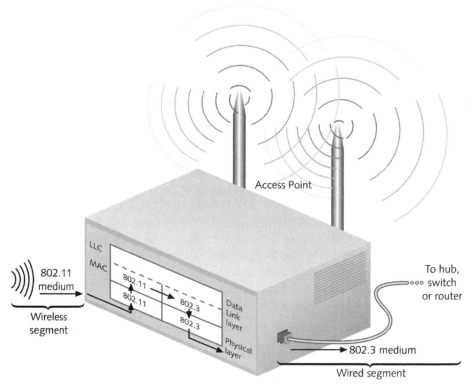

FIGURE 5-18 *A bridge connecting wire-bound and wireless LAN segments*

NET+
1.6

Although bridges are less common than switches on modern wire-bound LANs, understanding the concept of bridging is essential to understanding how switches work. For example, the bridging process pictured in Figure 5-17 applies to every port on a switch. The next section introduces switches and explains their functions.

Switches

NET+
1.6
2.3

Switches are connectivity devices that subdivide a network into smaller logical pieces, or segments. Traditional switches operate at the Data Link layer of the OSI Model, while more modern switches can operate at Layer 3 or even Layer 4. Like bridges, switches interpret MAC address information. In fact, they can be described as multiport bridges. Figure 5-19 depicts two switches. One is a 24-port switch, useful for connecting nodes in a workgroup, and the other is a high-capacity switch that contains multiple redundant features (such as two NICs)

FIGURE 5-19 *Examples of LAN switches*

NET+
1.6
2.3
and even offers routing functions. Switches vary greatly in size and function, so there really is no such thing as a "typical" switch. Most switches have an internal processor, an operating system, memory, and several ports that enable other nodes to connect to it.

NET+
1.6
Because they have multiple ports, switches can make better use of limited bandwidth and prove more cost-efficient than bridges. Each port on the switch acts like a bridge, and each device connected to a switch effectively receives its own dedicated channel. In other words, a switch can turn a shared channel into several channels. From the Ethernet perspective, each dedicated channel represents a collision domain. Because a switch limits the number of devices in a collision domain, it limits the potential for collisions.

Switches have historically been used to replace hubs and ease traffic congestion in LAN workgroups. Some network administrators have replaced backbone routers with switches, because switches provide at least two advantages: better security and better performance. By their nature switches provide better security than many other devices because they isolate one device's traffic from other devices' traffic. And because switches provide separate channels for (potentially) every device, performance stands to gain. Applications that transfer a large amount of traffic and are sensitive to time delays, such as videoconferencing applications, benefit from the full use of the channel's capacity. In addition, hardware and software in a switch are optimized for fast data forwarding.

Switches have their disadvantages, too. Although they contain buffers to hold incoming data and accommodate bursts of traffic, they can become overwhelmed by continuous, heavy traffic. In that event, the switch cannot prevent data loss. Also, although higher-layer protocols, such as TCP, detect the loss and respond with a timeout, others, such as UDP, do not. For packets using such protocols, the number of collisions will mount, and eventually all network traffic grinds to a halt. For this reason, you should plan placement of switches carefully to match backbone capacity and traffic patterns.

Switches have also replaced workgroup hubs on many small and home office networks because their cost has decreased dramatically, they have become easier to install and configure, and they offer the benefit of separating traffic according to port. You might need to install such a switch on a home or office network. The next section describes how to install a simple switch.

Installing a Switch

As with any networking equipment, the best way to ensure that you install a switch properly is to follow the manufacturer's guidelines. Small workgroup switches are normally simple to install. Many operate properly upon being added to a network. The following steps describe, in general, how to connect multiple nodes to a small switch, and then how to connect that switch to another connectivity device.

1. Make sure the switch is situated where you're going to keep it after all the cables are connected.
2. Before connecting any cables to the switch's ports, plug it in and turn it on. Also, when connecting a node to a switch, the node should not be turned on. Otherwise, data irregularities can occur, forcing you to reset the switch.

3. The switch's power light should illuminate. Most switches perform self-tests when turned on, and blinking lights indicate that these tests are in progress. Wait until the tests are completed (as indicated by a steady, green power light).

4. If you are using a small, inexpensive switch, you might not have to configure it and you can skip to Step 5. But if not, you must use a utility that came with the switch (on CD-ROM, for example) to configure the switch. For example, you may need to assign an IP address to the switch, change the administrator password, or set up management functions. Configuring a switch usually requires connecting it to a PC and then running a configuration utility from a CD-ROM. Refer to the instructions that came with your switch to find out how to configure it.

5. Using a straight-through patch cable, connect the node's NIC to one of the switch's ports, as shown in Figure 5-20. If you intend to connect this switch to another connectivity device, do not connect patch cables from nodes to the uplink port or to the port adjacent to the uplink port. On most hubs and switches, the uplink port is directly wired to its adjacent port inside the device.

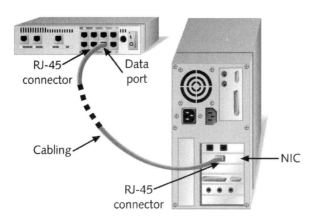

FIGURE 5-20 *Connecting a workstation to a switch*

6. After all the nodes have been connected to the switch, if you do not plan to connect the switch to another connectivity device, you can turn on the nodes. After the nodes connect to the network through the newly installed switch, check to verify that the switch's link and traffic lights for each port act as they should, according to the switch's documentation. Then make sure the nodes can access the network as planned.

7. To connect the switch to a larger network, you can insert one end of a crossover patch cable into the switch's uplink port, then insert the other end of the cable into a data port on the other connectivity device. Alternately, you can insert one end of a straight-through cable into one of the switch's data ports, then insert the other end of the straight-through cable into another device's data port. If you are connecting one switch's uplink port to another switch's uplink port, you must use a crossover cable. After connecting the switch to another device, the switch senses the activity on its uplink port, evidenced by its blinking traffic light.

NET+
1.6

Figure 5-21 illustrates a typical way of using a small switch on a small office or home network. In this example, the switch connects a group of nodes, including workstations, server, and printer, with each other and with an Internet connection.

Switches differ in the method of switching they use—namely, cut-through mode or store and forward mode. These methods of switching are discussed in the next two sections.

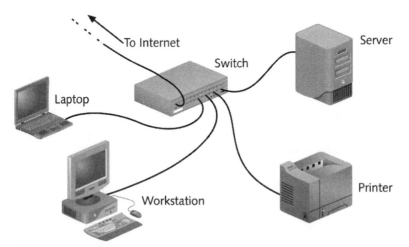

FIGURE 5-21 *A switch on a small network*

Cut-Through Mode

A switch running in **cut-through mode** reads a frame's header and decides where to forward the data before it receives the entire packet. Recall that the first 14 bytes of a frame constitute its header, which contains the destination MAC address. This information is sufficient for the switch to determine which port should get the frame and begin transmitting the frame (without bothering to read the rest of the frame and check its accuracy).

What if the frame becomes corrupt? Because the cut-through mode does not allow the switch to read the frame check sequence before it begins transmitting, it can't verify data integrity in that way. On the other hand, cut-through switches can detect **runts,** or erroneously shortened packets. Upon detecting a runt, the switch waits to transmit that packet until it determines its integrity. It's important to remember, however, that runts are only one type of data flaw. Cut-through switches *cannot* detect corrupt packets; indeed, they may increase the number of errors found on the network by propagating flawed packets.

The most significant advantage of the cut-through mode is its speed. Because it does not stop to read the entire data packet, a cut-through switch can forward information much more rapidly than a store and forward switch can (as described in the next section). The time-saving advantages to cut-through switching become insignificant, however, if the switch is flooded with traffic. In this case, the cut-through switch must buffer (or temporarily hold) data, just like a store

NET+
1.6

and forward switch. Cut-through switches are best suited to small workgroups in which speed is important and the relatively low number of devices minimizes the potential for errors.

Store and Forward Mode

In **store and forward mode**, a switch reads the entire data frame into its memory and checks it for accuracy before transmitting the information. Although this method is more time-consuming than the cut-through method, it allows store and forward switches to transmit data more accurately. Store and forward mode switches are more appropriate for larger LAN environments, because they do not propagate data errors. In contrast, cut-through mode switches do forward errors, so they may contribute to network congestion if a particular segment is experiencing a number of collisions. In large environments, a failure to check for errors can result in problematic traffic congestion.

Store and forward switches can also transfer data between segments running different transmission speeds. For example, a high-speed network printer that serves 50 students could be attached to a 100-Mbps port on the switch, thereby allowing all of the student workstations to connect to 10-Mbps ports on the same switch. With this scheme, the printer can quickly service multiple jobs. This characteristic makes store and forward mode switches preferable in mixed-speed environments.

NET+
3.8

Using Switches to Create VLANs

In addition to improving bandwidth usage, switches can create **virtual local area networks (VLANs)**, logically separate networks within networks, by grouping a number of ports into a broadcast domain. A **broadcast domain** is a combination of ports that make up a Layer 2 segment. Ports in a broadcast domain rely on a Layer 2 device, such as a switch, to forward broadcast frames among them. In contrast to a collision domain, ports in the same broadcast domain do not share a single channel. (Recall that switches separate collision domains.) In the context of TCP/IP networking, a broadcast domain is also known as a subnet. Figure 5-22 illustrates a simple VLAN design.

VLANs can be designed with flexibility. They can include ports from more than one switch or segment. Any type of end node can belong to one or more VLANs. VLANs can link geographically distant users over a WAN, and they can create small workgroups within LANs. Reasons for using VLANs include separating groups of users who need special security or network functions, isolating connections with heavy or unpredictable traffic patterns, identifying groups of devices whose data should be given priority handling, or containing groups of devices that rely on legacy protocols incompatible with the majority of the network's traffic. One case in which a company might want to implement a VLAN is to allow visitors access to minimal network functions—for example, an Internet connection—without allowing the possibility of access to the company's data stored on servers. In another example, companies that use their packet-switched networks to carry telephone calls often group all of the voice traffic on a separate VLAN to prevent this unique and potentially heavy traffic from adversely affecting routine client/server tasks.

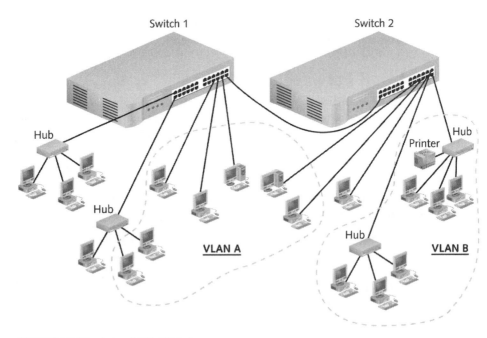

FIGURE 5-22 *A simple VLAN design*

On a wireless network, VLANs allow mobile clients to move from one access point's range to another without losing network functionality or having to reauthenticate with the network. That's because every wireless client's MAC address can be associated with an access point, and each access point can be associated with a port on a switch. When these ports are grouped together in a VLAN, it doesn't matter with which access point a client associates. Because the client stays in the same grouping, it can continue to communicate with the network as if it had remained in one spot.

VLANs are created by properly configuring a switch's software. This can be done manually through the switch's configuration utility or automatically using a VLAN software tool. The critical step is to indicate to which VLAN each port belongs. In addition, network managers can specify security parameters, filtering instructions (if the switch should not forward any frames from a certain segment, for example), performance requirements for certain ports, and network addressing and management options.

One potential problem in creating VLANs is that by grouping together certain nodes, you are not merely including those nodes—you are also excluding another group. This means you can potentially cut off a group from the rest of the network. For example, suppose your company's IT director demands that you assign all executive workstations to their own VLAN, and that you configure the network's switch to group these users' computers into a VLAN. After this change, users would be able to exchange data with each other, but they would not be able to download data from the file server or download mail from the mail server, because these servers are not included in their VLAN.

NET+
3.8

VLAN configuration can be complex. It requires careful planning to ensure that all users and devices that need to exchange data can do so after the VLAN is in operation. It also requires contemplating how the VLAN switch will interact with other devices. For example, in a large office building, you probably would still use hubs or small switches (not configured for a VLAN) as a means of connecting groups of end users to the VLAN switch. If you want users from different VLANs to be able to communicate, you need to connect those VLANs through a Layer 3 device, such as a router or a higher-layer switch, like the ones discussed next.

NET+
1.6
2.3

Higher-Layer Switches

You have learned that switches operate in Layer 2 of the OSI Model, routers operate in Layer 3, and hubs operate in Layer 1. You also learned that the distinctions between bridges, switches, and routers are blurring. Indeed, many networks already use switches that can operate at Layer 3 (Network layer), similar to a router. Manufacturers have also made switches that operate at Layer 4 (Transport layer). A switch capable of interpreting Layer 3 data is called a **Layer 3 switch** (and sometimes called a **routing switch**). Similarly, a switch capable of interpreting Layer 4 data is called a **Layer 4 switch**. These higher-layer switches may also be called **routing switches** or **application switches**.

Among other things, the ability to interpret higher-layer data enables switches to perform advanced filtering, statistics keeping, and security functions. But the features of Layer 3 and Layer 4 switches vary widely depending on the manufacturer and the price. (This variability is exacerbated by the fact that key players in the networking trade have not agreed on standards for these switches.) In fact, it's often hard to distinguish between a Layer 3 switch and a router. In some cases the difference comes down to what the manufacturer has decided to call the device in order to sell more of it. But in general, Layer 3 and Layer 4 switches, like Layer 2 switches, are optimized for fast Layer 2 data handling.

Higher-layer switches can cost three times more than Layer 2 switches, and are typically used as part of a network's backbone. They would not be appropriate for use on a small, contained LAN or to connect a group of end users to the network.

Routers

NET+
1.6
2.3

A **router** is a multiport connectivity device that directs data between nodes on a network. Routers can integrate LANs and WANs running at different transmission speeds and using a variety of protocols. Simply put, when a router receives an incoming packet, it reads the packet's logical addressing information. Based on this, it determines to which network the packet must be delivered. Then it determines the shortest path to that network. Finally it forwards the packet to the next hop in that path. Routers operate at the Network layer (Layer 3) of the OSI Model. They can be devices dedicated to routing, or they can be off-the-shelf computers configured to perform routing services.

Recall that the Network layer directs data from one segment or type of network to another. It's also the layer that manages logical addressing, using protocols such as IP and IPX. Consequently, unlike bridges and Layer 2 switches, routers are protocol-dependent. They must be designed or configured to recognize a certain Network layer protocol before they can forward data transmitted using that protocol. In general, routers are slower than switches or bridges because they take time to interpret information in Layers 3 and higher.

Traditional standalone LAN routers are being replaced by Layer 3 switches that support the routing functions. However, despite competition from Layer 3 switches, routers are finding niches in specialized applications such as linking large Internet nodes or completing digitized telephone calls. The concept of routing, and everything described in the remainder of this section, applies to both routers and Layer 3 switches.

Router Features and Functions

A router's strength lies in its intelligence. Not only can routers keep track of the locations of certain nodes on the network, as switches can, but they can also determine the shortest, fastest path between two nodes. For this reason, and because they can connect dissimilar network types, routers are powerful, indispensable devices on large LANs and WANs. The Internet, for example, relies on a multitude of routers across the world.

A typical router has an internal processor, an operating system, memory, input and output jacks for different types of network connectors (depending on the network type), and, usually, a management console interface. Three examples of routers are shown in Figure 5-23, with most complex on the left and the simplest on the right. High-powered, multiprotocol routers may have several slot bays to accommodate multiple network interfaces (RJ-45, SC, MTRJ, and so on). A router with multiple slots that can hold different interface cards or other devices is called a **modular router**. At the other end of the scale are simple, inexpensive routers often used in small offices and homes called **SOHO (small office-home office) routers**. As with the simple switches described in the previous section, SOHO routers can be added to a network and function properly without significant configuration.

A router is a very flexible device. Although any one can be specialized for a variety of tasks, all routers can do the following:

◆ Connect dissimilar networks.

◆ Interpret Layer 3 addressing and other information (such as quality of service indicators).

◆ Determine the best path for data to follow from point A to point B.

◆ Reroute traffic if a primary path is down but another path is available.

In addition to performing these basic functions, routers may perform any of the following optional functions:

◆ Filter out broadcast transmissions to alleviate network congestion.

FIGURE 5-23 *Routers*

- ◆ Prevent certain types of traffic from getting to a network, enabling customized segregation and security.
- ◆ Support simultaneous local and remote connectivity.
- ◆ Provide high network fault tolerance through redundant components such as power supplies or network interfaces.
- ◆ Monitor network traffic and report statistics.
- ◆ Diagnose internal or other connectivity problems and trigger alarms.

Routers are often categorized according to the scope of the network they serve. A router that directs data between nodes on an autonomous LAN (or one owned and operated by a single organization) is known as an **interior router**. Such routers do not direct data between an employee's workstation and a Web server on the Internet. They can, however, direct data between an employee's workstation and his supervisor's workstation in an office down the hall. Another type of router is an **exterior router**. Exterior routers direct data between nodes external to a given autonomous LAN. Routers that operate on the Internet backbone are exterior routers. Between interior and exterior routers are **border routers** (or **gateway routers**). Such routers connect an autonomous LAN with a WAN. For example, the router that connects a business with its ISP is a border router.

Routers may use one of two methods for directing data on the network: static or dynamic routing. **Static routing** is a technique in which a network administrator programs a router to use specific paths between nodes. Because it does not account for occasional network congestion, failed connections, or device moves, static routing is not optimal. If a router or a segment connected to a router is moved, the network administrator must reprogram the static router's tables. Static routing requires human intervention, so it is less efficient and accurate than dynamic routing. **Dynamic routing**, on the other hand, automatically calculates the best path between two nodes and accumulates this information in a routing table. If congestion or failures affect the network, a router using dynamic routing can detect the problems and reroute data through a different path. As a part of dynamic routing, by default, when a router is added to a network, routing protocols update its routing tables. Most networks primarily use dynamic routing, but may include some static routing to indicate, for example, a router of last resort, the router that accepts all unroutable packets.

Because of their customizability, routers are not simple to install on sizable networks. Typically, an engineer must be very familiar with routing technology to figure out how to place and configure a router to best advantage. Figure 5-24 gives you some idea of how routers fit into a LAN environment. If you plan to specialize in network design or router configuration, you should research router technology further. You might begin with Cisco System's online documentation at *www.cisco.com/univercd/home/home.htm*. Cisco Systems currently provides the majority of networking routers installed in the world.

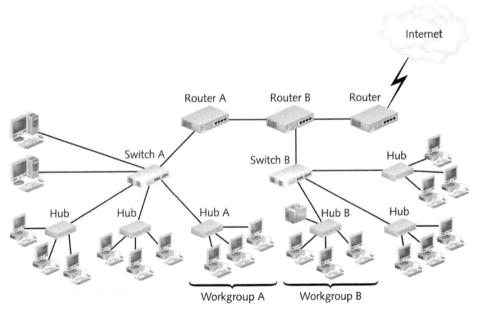

FIGURE 5-24 *The placement of routers on a LAN*

NET+
1.6

In the setup depicted in Figure 5-24, if a workstation in workgroup A wants to print to the printer in workgroup B, it creates a transmission containing the address of the workgroup B printer. Then it sends its packets to hub A. Hub A simply retransmits the message to switch A. When switch A receives the transmission, it checks the MAC address for the printer and determines that the message needs to be forwarded. It forwards the message to router A, which examines the destination network address in each packet and determines the most efficient way of delivering the message. In this example, it sends the data to router B. Before it forwards the data, however, router A increments (increases) the number of hops tallied in all the packets. Each time a packet passes through a router, it makes a hop. Packets can only take a certain number of hops before they are discarded.

After it increments the number of hops tallied in each packet, router A forwards the data to router B. Router B increments each packet's hop count, reads each packet's destination network address, and sends them to switch B. Based on the destination MAC address in the packets, switch B decides to forward the message to hub B, which then broadcasts the transmission to workgroup B. The printer picks up the message, and then begins printing.

Routing Protocols: RIP, OSPF, EIGRP, and BGP

Finding the best route for data to take across the network is one of the most valued and sophisticated functions performed by a router. The term **best path** refers to the most efficient route from one node on a network to another. The best path in a particular situation depends on the number of hops between nodes, the current network activity, the unavailable links, the network transmission speed, and the topology. To determine the best path, routers communicate with each other through **routing protocols**. Keep in mind that routing protocols are *not* the same as routable protocols, such as TCP/IP or IPX/SPX, although routing protocols may piggyback on routable protocols. Routing protocols are used only to collect data about current network status and contribute to the selection of the best paths. From these data, routers create routing tables for use with future packet forwarding.

In addition to its ability to find the best path, a routing protocol can be characterized according to its router **convergence time**, the time it takes for a router to recognize a best path in the event of a change or network outage. Its overhead, or the burden placed on the underlying network to support the routing protocol, is also a distinguishing feature.

Although you do not need to know precisely how routing protocols work to qualify for the Network+ certification, you should be familiar with the most common routing protocols: RIP, OSPF, EIGRP, and BGP. (Several more routing protocols exist, but a discussion of these exceeds the scope of this book.) These four common routing protocols are described in the following list.

◆ *RIP (Routing Information Protocol) for IP and IPX*—The oldest routing protocol, RIP, which is still widely used, factors in only the number of hops between nodes when determining a path from one point to another. It does not consider network congestion or link speed, for example. RIP is an interior routing protocol, meaning that it is used on interior or border routers. Routers using RIP broadcast their routing tables every 30 seconds to other routers, regardless of whether the tables have changed. This broadcasting creates excessive network traffic, especially if a large number of routes exist. If the routing tables change, it may take several minutes before the new information propagates to routers at the far reaches of the network; thus, the convergence time for RIP is poor. However, one advantage to RIP is its stability. For example, RIP prevents routing loops from continuing indefinitely by limiting the number of hops a packet can take between its source and its destination to 15. If the number of hops in a path exceeds 15, the network destination is considered unreachable. Thus, RIP does not work well in very large network environments in which data may have to travel through more than 15 routers to reach their destination (for example, on the Internet). Also, compared with other routing protocols, RIP is slower and less secure.

♦ *OSPF (Open Shortest Path First) for IP*—This routing protocol, also used on interior or border routers, makes up for some of the limitations of RIP and can coexist with RIP on a network. Unlike RIP, OSPF imposes no hop limits on a transmission path. Also, OSPF uses a more complex algorithm for determining best paths than RIP uses. Under optimal network conditions, the best path is the most direct path between two points. If excessive traffic levels or an outage preclude data from following the most direct path, a router may determine that the most efficient path actually goes through additional routers. In OSPF, each router maintains a database of the other routers' links, and if notice is received indicating the failure of a given link, the router can rapidly compute an alternate path. This approach requires more memory and CPU power on the routers, but it keeps network bandwidth to a minimum and provides a very fast convergence time, often invisible to the users. OSPF is supported by all modern routers. Therefore, it is commonly used on LANs that rely on a mix of routers from different manufacturers.

♦ *EIGRP (Enhanced Interior Gateway Routing Protocol) for IP, IPX, and AppleTalk*— This routing protocol, another protocol used on interior or border routers, was developed in the mid-1980s by Cisco Systems. It has a fast convergence time and a low network overhead, and is easier to configure and less CPU-intensive than OSPF. EIGRP also offers the benefits of supporting multiple protocols and limiting unnecessary network traffic between routers. It accommodates very large and heterogeneous networks, but is only supported by Cisco routers. On LANs that use exclusively Cisco routers, EIGRP is generally preferred over OSPF.

♦ *BGP (Border Gateway Protocol) for IP*—BGP is the routing protocol of Internet backbones and is not used to route between nodes on an autonomous LAN—that is, it is used on border and exterior routers. The demands on routers created by Internet growth have driven the development of BGP, the most complex of the routing protocols. The developers of BGP had to contend with not only the prospect of 100,000 potential routes, but also the question of how to route traffic efficiently and fairly through the hundreds of Internet backbones.

NET+
1.6

Brouters

By now it should not surprise you that routers, too, can act like other devices. The networking industry has adopted the term **bridge router**, or **brouter**, to describe routers that take on some characteristics of bridges. The advantage of crossing a router with a bridge is that you can forward nonroutable protocols, such as NetBEUI, plus connect multiple network types through one device. A bridge router offers support at Layers 2 and 3 of the OSI Model. It intelligently handles any packets that contain Layer 3 addressing information and simply forwards the rest.

Gateways

NET+
1.6

Gateways do not fall neatly into any networking hardware category. In broad terms, they are combinations of networking hardware and software that connect two dissimilar kinds of networks. Specifically, they may connect two systems that use different formatting, communications protocols, or architecture. Unlike the connectivity hardware discussed earlier in this chapter, gateways actually repackage information so that it can be read by another system. To accomplish this task, gateways must operate at multiple layers of the OSI Model. They must communicate with an application, establish and manage sessions, translate encoded data, and interpret logical and physical addressing data.

Gateways can reside on servers, microcomputers, connectivity devices (such as routers), or mainframes. They are almost always designed for one category of gateway functions. In addition, they transmit data more slowly than bridges or routers (which are not acting as gateways) because of the complex translations they conduct. Because they are slow, gateways have the potential to cause extreme network congestion. In certain situations, however, only a gateway will suffice.

During your networking career, you will most likely hear gateways discussed in the context of Internet connections and e-mail systems. Popular types of gateways, including e-mail gateways, are described in the following list.

◆ *E-mail gateway*—A gateway that translates messages from one type of e-mail system to another. For example, an e-mail gateway allows networks that use Sendmail mail server software to exchange mail with networks that use Microsoft Exchange Server software.

◆ *IBM host gateway*—A gateway that establishes and manages communication between a PC and an IBM mainframe computer.

◆ *Internet gateway*—A gateway that allows and manages access between LANs and the Internet. An Internet gateway can restrict the kind of access LAN users have to the Internet, and vice versa.

◆ *LAN gateway*—A gateway that allows segments of a LAN running different protocols or different network models to communicate with each other. A router, a single port on a router, or even a server may act as a LAN gateway. The LAN gateway category might also include remote access servers that allow dial-up connectivity to a LAN.

♦ *Voice/data gateway*—A gateway that connects the part of a network that handles data traffic with the part of a network that handles voice traffic. Voice applications have drastically different requirements than data applications. For example, before a voice signal can be transmitted over a data network, it needs to be digitized and compressed. When it reaches a voice receiver, such as a telephone, it has to be uncompressed and regenerated as recognizable speech, without delays. All these functions require specialized protocols and processes. A voice/data gateway can translate between these unique network segments and traditional data network segments.

♦ *Firewall*—A gateway that selectively blocks or filters traffic between networks. As with any other type of gateway, firewalls may be devices optimized for performing their tasks or computers installed with software necessary to accomplish those tasks. Because firewalls are integral to network security, they are discussed in detail in Chapter 14.

Chapter Summary

♦ Network adapters come in a variety of types depending on access method (Ethernet versus Token Ring), network transmission speed (for example, 10 Mbps versus 100 Mbps), connector interfaces (for example, SC versus RJ-45), type of compatible motherboard or device, and manufacturer.

♦ Desktops or tower PCs may use an expansion card NIC, which must match the system's bus. A bus is the type of circuit used by the motherboard to transmit data to components. New desktop computers almost always use PCI buses.

♦ NICs may also be externally attached, through the PCMCIA-standard (PC Card, CardBus, or ExpressCard), USB, FireWire, or CompactFlash peripheral bus types..

♦ Some NICs are integrated into a computer's motherboard. These are also known as on-board NICs.

♦ NICs are designed to be used with either wire-bound or wireless connections. A wireless NIC uses an antenna to exchange signals with the network. This type of connectivity suits environments in which cabling cannot be installed or where roaming clients must be supported.

♦ To install a NIC, you must physically attach it to the bus (or port), install the NIC device drivers, and configure its settings.

♦ Firmware combines hardware and software. The hardware component of firmware is an EEPROM (electrically erasable programmable read-only memory) chip that stores data established at the factory. On a NIC, the EEPROM chip contains information about the adapter's transmission characteristics, plus its MAC address. You can change this data via a configuration utility.

♦ An IRQ is the means by which a device can request attention from the CPU. IRQ numbers range from 0 to 15. The BIOS attempts to assign free IRQ numbers to new devices. Typically, it assigns IRQ numbers 9, 10, or 11 to NICs. If conflicts occur, you must change a device's IRQ number rather than accept the default suggested by the BIOS or operating system.

◆ Repeaters are the connectivity devices that perform the regeneration of a digital signal. They belong to the Physical layer of the OSI Model; therefore, they do not have any means to interpret the data they are retransmitting.

◆ At its most primitive, a hub is a multiport repeater. A hub contains multiple data ports into which the patch cables for network nodes are connected. The hub accepts signals from a transmitting node and repeats those signals to all other connected nodes in a broadcast fashion, thereby creating a single collision domain. Most hubs also contain one port, called an uplink port, that allows the hub to connect to another hub or other connectivity device.

◆ Hubs that merely repeat signals are called passive hubs. Intelligent hubs, also called managed hubs, can provide information about data traffic and can be managed from anywhere on the network.

◆ Bridges resemble repeaters in that they have a single input and a single output port, but they can interpret the data they retransmit. Bridging occurs at the Data Link layer of the OSI Model. Bridges read the destination (MAC) address information and decide whether to forward (retransmit) a packet to another segment on the network or, if the destination address belongs to the same segment as the source address, filter (discard) it.

◆ As nodes transmit data through the bridge, the bridge establishes a filtering database of known MAC addresses and their locations on the network. The bridge uses its filtering database to determine whether a packet should be forwarded or filtered.

◆ Switches subdivide a network into smaller logical pieces. They operate at the Data Link layer (Layer 2) of the OSI Model and can interpret MAC address information. In this respect, switches resemble bridges.

◆ Switches are generally secure because they isolate one device's traffic from other devices' traffic. Because switches provide separate channels for (potentially) every device, they allow applications that transfer a large amount of traffic and that are sensitive to time delays, such as videoconferencing, to make full use of the network's capacity.

◆ A switch running in cut-through mode reads a frame's header and decides where to forward the data before it receives the entire packet. In store and forward mode, switches read the entire data frame into their memory and check it for accuracy before transmitting it. Although this method is more time-consuming than the cut-through method, it allows store and forward switches to transmit data more accurately.

◆ Switches can create VLANs (virtual local area networks) by logically grouping several ports into a broadcast domain. The ports do not have to reside on the same switch or even on the same network segment. VLANs can isolate nodes and their traffic for security, convenience, or better performance.

◆ Manufacturers are producing switches that can operate at Layer 3 (Network layer) and Layer 4 (Transport layer) of the OSI Model, making them act more like routers. The ability to interpret higher-layer data enables switches to perform advanced filtering, statistics keeping, and security functions.

◆ A router is a multiport device that can connect dissimilar LANs and WANs running at different transmission speeds, using a variety of protocols. Routers operate at the Network layer (Layer 3) or higher of the OSI Model. They interpret logical addresses and determine the best path between nodes. The best path depends on the number of hops between nodes, the current network activity, the unavailable links, the network transmission speed, and the topology. To determine the best path, routers communicate with each other through routing protocols.

◆ Unlike bridges and traditional switches, routers are protocol-dependent. They must be designed or configured to recognize a certain protocol before they can forward data transmitted using that protocol.

◆ Static routing is a technique in which a network administrator programs a router to use specific paths between nodes. Dynamic routing automatically calculates the best path between two nodes and accumulates this information in a routing table. If congestion or failures affect the network, a router using dynamic routing can detect the problems and reroute data through a different path. Most modern networks use dynamic routing.

◆ Routing protocols provide rules for communication between routers and help them determine the best path between two nodes. Some popular routing protocols include RIP, OSPF, EIGRP, and BGP.

◆ RIP (Routing Information Protocol) is the slowest and least secure and limits transmissions to 15 hops. OSPF (Open Shortest Path First) is faster than RIP and common on LANs that use routers from different manufacturers. EIGRP (Enhanced Interior Gateway Protocol) is a Cisco standard commonly used on LANs that use exclusively Cisco routers. BGP (Border Gateway Protocol) is used for routing over Internet backbones.

◆ The networking industry has adopted the term "brouter" to describe routers that take on some of the characteristics of bridges. Combining a router with a bridge allows you to forward data using nonroutable protocols, such as NetBEUI, and to connect multiple network types through one device. A brouter offers support at both Layers 2 and 3 of the OSI Model.

◆ Gateways are combinations of networking hardware and software that connect two dissimilar kinds of networks. Specifically, they may connect two systems that use different formatting, communications protocols, or architecture. To accomplish this task, they must operate at multiple layers of the OSI Model.

◆ Several different gateways exist, including e-mail gateways, IBM host gateways, Internet gateways, LAN gateways, firewalls, and voice/data gateways.

Key Terms

application switch—Another term for a Layer 3 or Layer 4 switch.

base I/O port—A setting that specifies, in hexadecimal notation, which area of memory will act as a channel for data traveling between the NIC and the CPU. Like its IRQ, a device's base I/O port cannot be used by any other device.

basic input/output system—See *BIOS*.

best path—The most efficient route from one node on a network to another. Under optimal network conditions, the best path is the most direct path between two points. However, when traffic congestion, segment failures, and other factors create obstacles, the most direct path may not be the best path.

BGP (Border Gateway Protocol)—A complex routing protocol used on border and exterior routers. BGP is the routing protocol used on Internet backbones.

BIOS (basic input/output system)—The firmware attached to a computer's motherboard that controls the computer's communication with its devices, among other things.

Border Gateway Protocol—See *BGP*.

border router—A router that connects an autonomous LAN with an exterior network—for example, the router that connects a business to its ISP.

bridge—A connectivity device that operates at the Data Link layer (Layer 2) of the OSI Model and reads header information to forward packets according to their MAC addresses. Bridges use a filtering database to determine which packets to discard and which to forward. Bridges contain one input and one output port and separate network segments.

bridge router (brouter)—A router capable of providing Layer 2 bridging functions.

broadcast domain—A combination of ports on a switch (or multiple switches) that make up a Layer 2 segment. To be able to exchange data with each other, broadcast domains must be connected by a Layer 3 device, such as a router or Layer 3 switch. A VLAN is one type of broadcast domain.

brouter—See *bridge router*.

bus—The type of circuit used by a computer's motherboard to transmit data to components. Most new Pentium computers use buses capable of exchanging 32 or 64 bits of data. As the number of bits of data a bus handles increases, so too does the speed of the device attached to the bus.

CardBus—A PCMCIA standard that specifies a 32-bit interface running at 33 MHz, similar to the PCI expansion board standard. Most modern laptops are equipped with CardBus slots for connecting external modems and NICs, among other things.

CMOS (complementary metal oxide semiconductor)—A type of microchip that requires very little energy to operate. In a PC, the CMOS stores settings pertaining to a computer's devices, among other things.

collision domain—A portion of a LAN encompassing devices that may cause and detect collisions among their group. Bridges and switches can logically separate collision domains.

CompactFlash—The standard for an ultra-small removable data and input/output device capable of connecting many kinds of external peripherals to workstations, PDAs, and other computerized devices. CompactFlash was designed by the CompactFlash Association (CFA), a consortium of computer manufacturers.

complementary metal oxide semiconductor—See *CMOS*.

convergence time—The time it takes for a router to recognize a best path in the event of a change or network outage.

cut-through mode—A switching mode in which a switch reads a frame's header and decides where to forward the data before it receives the entire packet. Cut-through mode is faster, but less accurate, than the other switching method, store and forward mode.

data port—A port on a connectivity device to which network nodes are connected.

device driver—The software that enables an attached device to communicate with the computer's operating system.

DIP (dual inline package) switch—A small plastic toggle switch on a circuit board that can be flipped to indicate either an "on" or "off" status, which translates into a parameter setting.

driver—See *device driver*.

dynamic routing—A method of routing that automatically calculates the best path between two nodes and accumulates this information in a routing table. If congestion or failures affect the network, a router using dynamic routing can detect the problems and reroute data through a different path. Modern networks primarily use dynamic routing.

EEPROM (electrically erasable programmable read-only memory)—A type of ROM that is found on a circuit board and whose configuration information can be erased and rewritten through electrical pulses.

EIGRP (Enhanced Interior Gateway Routing Protocol)—A routing protocol developed in the mid-1980s by Cisco Systems that has a fast convergence time and a low network overhead, but is easier to configure and less CPU-intensive than OSPF. EIGRP also offers the benefits of supporting multiple protocols and limiting unnecessary network traffic between routers.

electrically erasable programmable read-only memory—See *EEPROM*.

Enhanced Interior Gateway Routing Protocol—See *EIGRP*.

expansion board—A circuit board used to connect a device to a computer's motherboard.

expansion card—See *expansion board*.

expansion slot—A receptacle on a computer's motherboard that contains multiple electrical contacts into which an expansion board can be inserted.

ExpressCard—A PCMCIA standard that allows external devices to connect to portable computers through a 26-pin interface, with data transfer rates of 250 MBps in each direction (for a total of 500 MBps), similar to the PCI Express expansion board specification. ExpressCard modules come in two sizes: 34 mm and 54 mm wide. Over time, PCMCIA expects the ExpressCard standard to replace the CardBus standard.

exterior router—A router that directs data between nodes outside a given autonomous LAN, for example, routers used on the Internet's backbone.

Fedora Core—A popular version of the Linux operating system packaged and distributed by Red Hat, Inc.

filtering database—A collection of data created and used by a bridge that correlates the MAC addresses of connected workstations with their locations. A filtering database is also known as a forwarding table.

firewall—A device (either a router or a computer running special software) that selectively filters or blocks traffic between networks. Firewalls are commonly used to improve data security.

FireWire—A peripheral bus standard developed by Apple Computer and codified by the IEEE as the IEEE 1394 standard. Traditional FireWire connections support a maximum throughput of 400 Mbps, but a newer version supports potential throughput rates of over 3 Gbps. In addition to connecting peripherals, FireWire can be used to network computers directly in a bus fashion.

firmware—A combination of hardware and software. The hardware component of firmware is a ROM (read-only memory) chip that stores data established at the factory and possibly changed by configuration programs that can write to ROM.

forwarding table—See *filtering database*.

gateway—A combination of networking hardware and software that connects two dissimilar kinds of networks. Gateways perform connectivity, session management, and data translation, so they must operate at multiple layers of the OSI Model.

gateway router—See *border router*.

hub—A connectivity device that retransmits incoming data signals to its multiple ports. Typically, hubs contain one uplink port, which is used to connect to a network's backbone.

IEEE 1394—See *FireWire*.

Industry Standard Architecture—See *ISA*.

intelligent hub—A hub that possesses processing capabilities and can therefore monitor network traffic, detect packet errors and collisions, poll connected devices for information, and gather the data in database format.

interior router—A router that directs data between nodes on an autonomous LAN.

interrupt—A circuit board wire through which a device issues voltage, thereby signaling a request for the processor's attention.

interrupt request—See *IRQ.*

interrupt request number—See *IRQ number.*

IRQ (interrupt request)—A message sent to the computer that instructs it to stop what it is doing and pay attention to something else. IRQ is often used (informally) to refer to the interrupt request number.

IRQ number—The unique number assigned to each interrupt in a computer. Interrupt request numbers range from 0 to 15, and many PC devices reserve specific numbers for their use alone.

ISA (Industry Standard Architecture)—The original PC bus type, developed in the early 1980s to support an 8-bit and later 16-bit data path and a 4.77-MHz clock speed.

jumper—A small, removable piece of plastic that contains a metal receptacle that fits over a pair of pins on a circuit board to complete a circuit between those two pins. By moving the jumper from one set of pins to another set of pins, you can modify the board's circuit, thereby giving it different instructions on how to operate.

Layer 3 switch—A switch capable of interpreting data at Layer 3 (Network layer) of the OSI Model.

Layer 4 switch—A switch capable of interpreting data at Layer 4 (Transport layer) of the OSI Model.

loopback adapter—See *loopback plug.*

loopback plug—A connector used for troubleshooting that plugs into a port (for example, a serial, parallel, or RJ-45 port) and crosses over the transmit line to the receive line, allowing outgoing signals to be redirected back into the computer for testing.

main bus—See *bus.*

managed hub—See *intelligent hub.*

MAU (Multistation Access Unit)—A device on a Token Ring network that regenerates signals; equivalent to a hub.

memory range—A hexadecimal number that indicates the area of memory that the NIC and CPU will use for exchanging, or buffering, data. As with IRQs, some memory ranges are reserved for specific devices—most notably, the motherboard.

modular router—A router with multiple slots that can hold different interface cards or other devices so as to provide flexible, customizable network interoperability.

Multistation Access Unit—See *MAU.*

on-board NIC—A NIC that is integrated into a computer's motherboard, rather than connected via an expansion slot or peripheral bus.

on-board port—A port that is integrated into a computer's motherboard.

Open Shortest Path First—See *OSPF.*

OSPF (Open Shortest Path First)—A routing protocol that makes up for some of the limitations of RIP and can coexist with RIP on a network.

passive hub—A hub that simply retransmits signals over the network.

PC Card—A PCMCIA standard that specifies a 16-bit interface running at 8 MHz for externally attached devices. PC Cards' characteristics match those of the ISA expansion card. And like the ISA standard, the PC Card standard suffered from its lower data transfer rates, compared to other PCMCIA standards.

PCI (Peripheral Component Interconnect)—A 32 or 64-bit bus that can run at 33 or 66 MHz, introduced in its original form in the 1990s. The PCI bus is the NIC connection type used for nearly all new PCs. It's characterized by a shorter length than ISA or EISA cards, but has a much faster data transmission capability.

PCIe—See *PCI Express.*

PCI Express—A 64-bit bus standard capable of transferring data at up to 500 MBps in full-duplex transmission. PCI Express was introduced in 2002. It follows a new type of bus design and offers several advantages over the old PCI, and its expansion cards can fit into older PCI slots, with some modifications to the motherboard. Manufacturers predict PCI Express will replace PCI in the coming years.

PCIx—See *PCI Express.*

PCMCIA (Personal Computer Memory Card International Association)—A group of computer manufacturers who developed an interface for connecting any type of device to a portable computer. PCMCIA slots may hold memory, modem, network interface, external hard disk, or CD-ROM cards. PCMCIA-standard cards include PC Card, CardBus, and the newest, ExpressCard.

Peripheral Component Interconnect—See *PCI.*

Personal Computer Memory Card International Association—See *PCMCIA.*

RIP (Routing Information Protocol)—The oldest routing protocol that is still widely used, RIP does not work in very large network environments in which data may have to travel through more than 15 routers to reach their destination (for example, on the Internet). And, compared to other routing protocols, RIP is slower and less secure.

router—A multiport device that operates at Layer 3 of the OSI Model and uses logical addressing information to direct data between networks or segments. Routers can connect dissimilar LANs and WANs running at different transmission speeds and using a variety of Network layer protocols. They determine the best path between nodes based on traffic congestion, available versus unavailable routes, load balancing targets, and other factors.

Routing Information Protocol—See *RIP.*

routing protocols—The means by which routers communicate with each other about network status. Routing protocols determine the best path for data to take between nodes.

routing switch—See *Layer 3 switch*.

runt—An erroneously shortened packet.

single point of failure—A device or connection on a network that, were it to fail, could cause the entire network to stop functioning.

SOHO (small office-home office) router—A router designed for use on small office or home office networks. SOHO routers typically have no more than eight data ports and do not offer advanced features such as traffic prioritization, network management, or hardware redundancy.

stackable hub—A type of hub designed to be linked with other hubs in a single telecommunications closet. Stackable hubs linked together logically represent one large hub to the network.

standalone hub—A type of hub that serves a workgroup of computers that are separate from the rest of the network, also known as a workgroup hub.

static routing—A technique in which a network administrator programs a router to use specific paths between nodes. Because it does not account for occasional network congestion, failed connections, or device moves, static routing is not optimal.

store and forward mode—A method of switching in which a switch reads the entire data frame into its memory and checks it for accuracy before transmitting it. Although this method is more time-consuming than the cut-through method, it allows store and forward switches to transmit data more accurately.

switch—A connectivity device that logically subdivides a network into smaller, individual collision domains. A switch operates at the Data Link layer of the OSI Model and can interpret MAC address information to determine whether to filter (discard) or forward packets it receives.

system bus—See *bus*.

uplink port—A port on a connectivity device, such as a hub or switch, used to connect it to another connectivity device.

USB (universal serial bus) port—A standard external bus that can be used to connect multiple types of peripherals, including modems, mice, and NICs, to a computer. Two USB standards exist: USB 1.1 and USB 2.0. Most modern computers support the USB 2.0 standard.

virtual local area network—See *VLAN*.

VLAN (virtual local area network)—A network within a network that is logically defined by grouping its devices' switch ports in the same broadcast domain. A VLAN can consist of any type of network node in any geographic location and can incorporate nodes connected to different switches.

workgroup hub—See *standalone hub*.

Review Questions

1. _____ are connectivity devices that enable a workstation, server, printer, or other node to receive and transmit data over the network media.

   a. Network interface cards

   b. Adapter cards

   c. Routing protocols

   d. Ports

2. A computer's _____ is the circuit, or signaling pathway, used by the motherboard to transmit data to the computer's components, including its memory, processor, hard disk, and NIC.

   a. port

   b. bus

   c. switch

   d. router

3. _____ is a standard interface used to connect multiple types of peripherals, including modems, mice, audio players, and NICs.

   a. OSPF

   b. PCI

   c. FireWire

   d. USB

4. _____ are physically designed to be linked with other hubs in a single telecommunications closet.

   a. Firewalls

   b. Gateway routers

   c. Stackable hubs

   d. Jumpers

5. _____ are connectivity devices that subdivide a network into smaller logical pieces.

   a. Switches

   b. Segments

   c. Jumpers

   d. Hubs

6. True or false? All peripheral devices are connected to a computer's motherboard via an expansion slot or peripheral bus.

7. True or false? A device's base I/O port cannot be used by any other device.

8. True or false? A repeater is limited in function but not in scope.

9. True or false? A switch running in cut-through mode will read a frame's header and decide where to forward the data before it receives the entire packet.

10. True or false? A router is a multiport connectivity device that directs data between nodes on a network.

11. A(n) _____ is a small, removable piece of plastic that contains a metal receptacle.

12. A(n) _____ is a message to the computer that instructs it to stop what it is doing and pay attention to something else.

13. The _____ indicates, in hexadecimal notation, the area of memory that the NIC and CPU will use for exchanging, or buffering, data.

14. A(n) _____ is a connector that plugs into a port, such as a serial or parallel or an RJ-45 port, and crosses over the transmit line to the receive line so that outgoing signals can be redirected into the computer for testing.

15. A(n) _____ is a logically or physically distinct Ethernet network segment on which all participating devices must detect and accommodate data collisions.

Chapter 6

Topologies and Access Methods

After reading this chapter and completing the exercises, you will be able to:

- Describe the basic and hybrid LAN physical topologies, and their uses, advantages, and disadvantages

- Describe the backbone structures that form the foundation for most LANs

- Compare the different types of switching used in data transmission

- Understand the transmission methods underlying Ethernet, Token Ring, FDDI, and ATM networks

- Describe the characteristics of different wireless network technologies, including Bluetooth and the three IEEE 802.11 standards

Just as an architect of a house must decide where to place walls and doors, where to install electrical and plumbing systems, and how to manage traffic patterns through rooms to make a house more livable, a network architect must consider many factors, both seen and unseen, when designing a network. This chapter details some basic elements of network architecture: physical and logical topologies. These elements are crucial to understanding networking design, troubleshooting, and management, all of which are discussed later in this book.

In this chapter, you will also learn about the most commonly used network access methods: Ethernet, Token Ring, FDDI, ATM, and popular wireless access methods. Once you master the physical and logical fundamentals of network architecture, you will have all the tools necessary to design a network as elegant as the Taj Mahal.

Simple Physical Topologies

NET+
1.1

A **physical topology** is the physical layout, or pattern, of the nodes on a network. It depicts a network in broad scope; that is, it does not specify device types, connectivity methods, or addressing schemes for the network. Physical topologies are divided into three fundamental geometric shapes: bus, ring, and star. These shapes can be mixed to create hybrid topologies. Before you design a network, you need to understand physical topologies, because they are integral to the type of network (for example, Ethernet or Token Ring), cabling infrastructure, and transmission media you use. You must also understand a network's physical topology to troubleshoot its problems or change its infrastructure. A thorough knowledge of physical topologies is necessary to obtain Network+ certification.

TIP

Physical topologies and logical topologies (discussed later) are two different networking concepts. You should be aware that when used alone, the word "topology" often refers to a network's *physical* topology.

Bus

A **bus topology** consists of a single cable connecting all nodes on a network without intervening connectivity devices. The single cable is called the **bus** and can support only one channel for communication; as a result, every node shares the bus's total capacity. Most bus networks—for example, Thinnet and Thicknet—use coaxial cable as their physical medium.

NET+
1.1

On a bus topology network, devices share the responsibility for getting data from one point to another. Each node on a bus network passively listens for data directed to it. When one node wants to transmit data to another node, it broadcasts an alert to the entire network, informing all nodes that a transmission is being sent; the destination node then picks up the transmission. Nodes other than the sending and receiving nodes ignore the message.

For example, suppose that you want to send an instant message to your friend Diane, who works across the hall, asking whether she wants to have lunch with you. You click the Send button after typing your message, and the data stream that contains your message is sent to your NIC. Your NIC then sends a message across the shared wire that essentially says, "I have a message for Diane's computer." The message passes by every NIC between your computer and Diane's computer until Diane's computer recognizes that the message is meant for it and responds by accepting the data.

At the ends of each bus network are 50-ohm resistors known as **terminators**. Terminators stop signals after they have reached the end of the wire. Without these devices, signals on a bus network would travel endlessly between the two ends of the network—a phenomenon known as **signal bounce**—and new signals could not get through. To understand this concept, imagine that you and a partner, standing at opposite sides of a canyon, are yelling to each other. When you call out, your words echo; when your partner replies, his words also echo. Now imagine that the echoes never fade. After a short while, you could not continue conversing because all of the previously generated sound waves would still be bouncing around, creating too much noise for you to hear anything else. On a network, terminators prevent this problem by halting the transmission of old signals. In some cases, a hub provides termination for one end of a segment. A bus network must also be grounded at one end to help remove static electricity that could adversely affect the signal. Figure 6-1 depicts a terminated bus network.

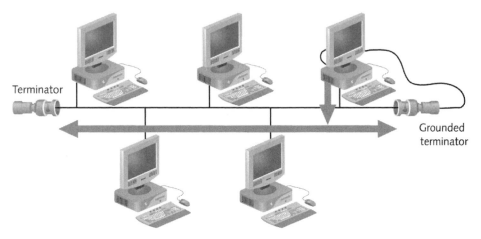

Terminator

Grounded terminator

FIGURE 6-1 *A terminated bus topology network*

NET+
1.1

Although networks based on a bus topology are relatively inexpensive to set up, they do not scale well. As you add more nodes, the network's performance degrades. Because of the single-channel limitation, the more nodes on a bus network, the more slowly the network will transmit and deliver data. For example, suppose a bus network in your small office supports two workstations and a server, and saving a file to the server takes two seconds. During that time, your NIC first checks the communication channel to ensure it is free, then issues data directed to the server. When the data reaches the server, the server accepts it. Suppose, however, that your business experiences tremendous growth, and you add five workstations during one weekend. The following Monday, when you attempt to save a file to the server, the save process might take five seconds, because the new workstations may also be using the communications channel, and your workstation may have to wait for a chance to transmit. As this example illustrates, a bus topology is rarely practical for networks with more than a dozen workstations.

Bus networks are also difficult to troubleshoot, because it is a challenge to identify fault locations. To understand why, think of the game called "telephone," in which one person whispers a phrase into the ear of the next person, who whispers the phrase into the ear of another person, and so on, until the final person in line repeats the phrase aloud. The vast majority of the time, the phrase recited by the last person bears little resemblance to the original phrase. When the game ends, it's hard to determine precisely where in the chain the individual errors cropped up. Similarly, errors may occur at any intermediate point on a bus network, but at the receiving end it's possible to tell only that an error occurred. Finding the source of the error can prove very difficult.

A final disadvantage to bus networks is that they are not very fault-tolerant, because a break or a defect in the bus affects the entire network. As a result, and because of the other disadvantages associated with this topology, you will rarely see a network run on a pure bus topology. You may, however, encounter hybrid topologies that include a bus component.

Ring

In a **ring topology**, each node is connected to the two nearest nodes so that the entire network forms a circle, as shown in Figure 6-2. Data is transmitted clockwise, in one direction (unidirectionally), around the ring. Each workstation accepts and responds to packets addressed to it, then forwards the other packets to the next workstation in the ring. Each workstation acts as a repeater for the transmission. The fact that all workstations participate in delivery makes the ring topology an **active topology**. This is one way a ring topology differs from a bus topology. A ring topology also differs in that it has no "ends" and data stops at its destination. In most ring networks, twisted-pair or fiber-optic cabling is used as the physical medium.

The drawback of a simple ring topology is that a single malfunctioning workstation can disable the network. For example, suppose that you and five colleagues share a pure ring topology LAN in your small office. You decide to send an instant message to Thad, who works three offices away, telling him you found his lost glasses. Between your office and Thad's office are two other offices, and two other workstations on the ring. Your instant message must pass through the two intervening workstations' NICs before it reaches Thad's computer. If one of these workstations has a malfunctioning NIC, your message will never reach Thad.

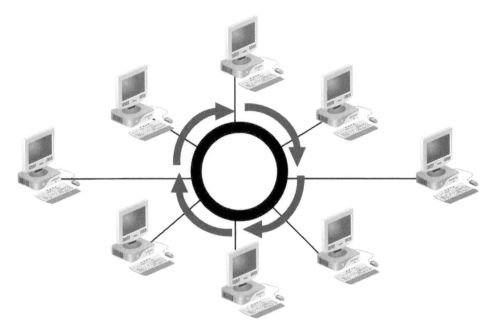

FIGURE 6-2 *A typical ring topology network*

In addition, just as in a bus topology, the more workstations that must participate in data transmission, the slower the response time. Consequently, pure ring topologies are not very flexible or scalable. Contemporary LANs rarely use pure ring topologies.

Star

In a **star topology**, every node on the network is connected through a central device, such as a hub or switch. Figure 6-3 depicts a typical star topology. Star topologies are usually built with twisted-pair or fiber-optic cabling. Any single cable on a star network connects only two devices (for example, a workstation and a hub), so a cabling problem will affect two nodes at most. Devices such as workstations or printers transmit data to the hub, which then retransmits the signal to the network segment containing the destination node.

Star topologies require more cabling than ring or bus networks. They also require more configuration. However, because each node is separately connected to a central connectivity device, they are more fault-tolerant. A single malfunctioning workstation cannot disable an entire star network. A failure in the central connectivity device can take down a LAN segment, though.

Because they include a centralized connection point, star topologies can easily be moved, isolated, or interconnected with other networks; they are therefore scalable. For this reason, and because of their fault tolerance, the star topology has become the most popular fundamental layout used in contemporary LANs. Single star networks are commonly interconnected with other networks through hubs and switches to form more complex topologies. Most Ethernet networks are based on the star topology.

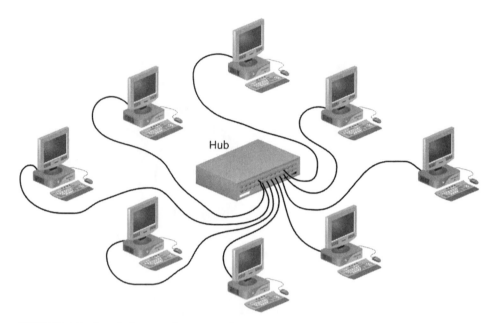

FIGURE 6-3 *A typical star topology network*

Star networks can support a maximum of only 1024 addressable nodes on a logical network. For example, if you have a campus with 3000 users, hundreds of networked printers, and scores of other devices, you must strategically create smaller logical networks. Even if you had 1000 users and *could* put them on the same logical network, you wouldn't, because doing so would result in poor performance and difficult management. Instead, you would use switches to subdivide clients and peripherals into many separate broadcast domains.

Hybrid Physical Topologies

Except in very small networks, you will rarely encounter a network that follows a pure bus, ring, or star topology. Simple topologies are too restrictive, particularly if the LAN must accommodate a large number of devices. More likely, you will work with a complex combination of these topologies, known as a **hybrid topology**. Several kinds of hybrid topologies are explained in the following sections.

Star-Wired Ring

The **star-wired ring topology** uses the physical layout of a star in conjunction with the ring topology's data transmission method. In Figure 6-4, which depicts this architecture, the solid lines represent a physical connection and the dotted lines represent the flow of data. Data is sent around the star in a circular pattern. This hybrid topology benefits from the fault tolerance of the star topology (data transmission does not depend on each workstation to act as a

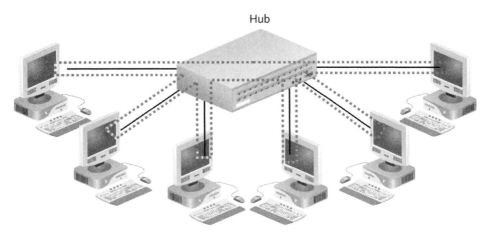

FIGURE 6-4 *A star-wired ring topology network*

repeater) and the reliability of token passing (discussed later in this chapter). Token Ring networks, as specified in IEEE 802.5, use this hybrid topology.

Star-Wired Bus

Another popular hybrid topology combines the star and bus formations. In a **star-wired bus topology**, groups of workstations are star-connected to hubs and then networked via a single bus, as shown in Figure 6-5. With this design, you can cover longer distances and easily interconnect or isolate different network segments. One drawback is that this option is more expensive than using either the star or, especially, the bus topology alone because it requires more cabling and potentially more connectivity devices. The star-wired bus topology forms the basis for modern Ethernet and Fast Ethernet networks.

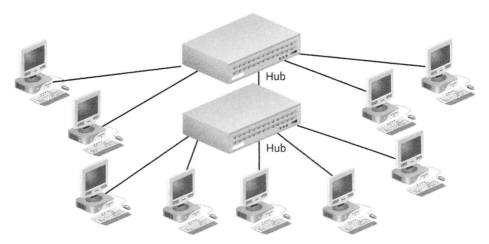

FIGURE 6-5 *A star-wired bus topology network*

Backbone Networks

A network backbone is the cabling that connects the hubs, switches, and routers on a network. Backbones usually are capable of more throughput than the cabling that connects workstations to hubs. This added capacity is necessary because backbones carry more traffic than any other cabling in the network. For example, LANs in large organizations commonly rely on a fiber-optic backbone but continue to use CAT 5 or better UTP to connect hubs or switches with workstations.

Although even the smallest LAN technically has a backbone, on an enterprise-wide network, backbones are more complex and more difficult to plan. In networking, the term **enterprise** refers to an entire organization, including its local and remote offices, a mixture of computer systems, and a number of departments. Enterprise-wide computing must therefore take into account the breadth and diversity of a large organization's computer needs. The backbone is the most significant building block of enterprise-wide networks. It may take one of several different shapes, as described in the following sections.

Serial Backbone

A **serial backbone** is the simplest kind of backbone. It consists of two or more internetworking devices connected to each other by a single cable in a daisy-chain fashion. In networking, a **daisy chain** is simply a linked series of devices. Hubs and switches are often connected in a daisy chain to extend a network. For example, suppose you manage a small star-wired bus topology network in which a single hub serves a workgroup of eight users. When new employees are added to that department and you need more network connections, you could connect a second hub to the first hub in a daisy-chain fashion. The new hub would offer open ports for new users. Because the star-wired hybrids provide for modular additions, daisy chaining is a logical solution for growth. Also, because hubs can easily be connected through cables attached to their ports, a LAN's infrastructure can be expanded with little additional cost.

Hubs are not the only devices that can be connected in a serial backbone. Gateways, routers, switches, and bridges can also form part of the backbone. Figure 6-6 illustrates a serial backbone network, in which the backbone is indicated by a dashed line.

The extent to which you can connect hubs in a serial backbone is limited. For example, in a 10BASE-T network, you may use a maximum of four hubs to connect five network segments in a serial fashion. Using more hubs than the standard suggests (in other words, exceeding the maximum network length) will adversely affect the functionality of a LAN. On a 100BASE-TX network, you may use a maximum of two hubs connecting three network segments. And on most 1-Gbps networks, you can use only one hub to extend the network. If you extend a LAN beyond its recommended size, intermittent and unpredictable data transmission errors will result. Similarly, if you daisy-chain a topology with limited bandwidth, you risk overloading the channel and generating still more data errors.

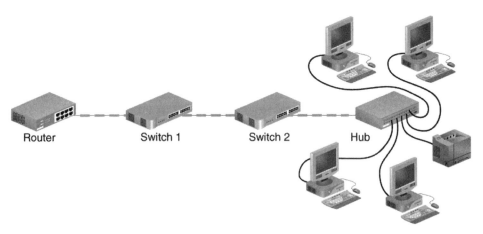

FIGURE 6-6 *A serial backbone*

Distributed Backbone

A **distributed backbone** consists of a number of connectivity devices connected to a series of central connectivity devices, such as hubs, switches, or routers, in a hierarchy, as shown in Figure 6-7. In Figure 6-7, the dashed lines represent the backbone. This kind of topology allows for simple expansion and limited capital outlay for growth, because more layers of devices can be added to existing layers. For example, suppose that you are the network administrator for a small publisher's office. You might begin your network with a distributed backbone consisting

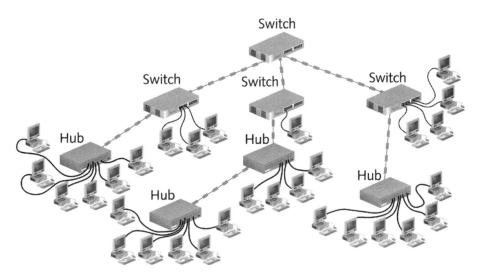

FIGURE 6-7 *A simple distributed backbone*

of two switches that supply connectivity to your 20 users, 10 on each switch. When your company hires more staff, you can connect another switch to one of the existing switches, and use the new switch to connect the new staff to the network.

A more complicated distributed backbone connects multiple LANs or LAN segments using routers, as shown in Figure 6-8. In this example, the routers form the highest layer of the backbone to connect the LANs or LAN segments.

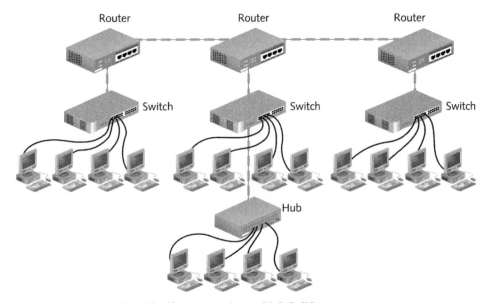

FIGURE 6-8 *A distributed backbone connecting multiple LANs*

A distributed backbone also provides network administrators with the ability to segregate workgroups and therefore manage them more easily. It adapts well to an enterprise-wide network confined to a single building, in which certain hubs or switches can be assigned according to the floor or department. Note that distributed backbones may include hubs linked in a daisy-chain fashion. This arrangement requires the same length considerations that serial backbones demand. Another possible problem in this design relates to the potential single points of failure, such as the devices at the uppermost layers. Despite these potential drawbacks, implementing a distributed backbone network can be relatively simple, quick, and inexpensive.

Collapsed Backbone

The **collapsed backbone** topology uses a router or switch as the single central connection point for multiple subnetworks, as shown in Figure 6-9. Contrast Figure 6-9 with Figure 6-8, in which multiple LANs are connected via a distributed backbone. In a collapsed backbone, a single router or switch is the highest layer of the backbone. The router or switch that makes

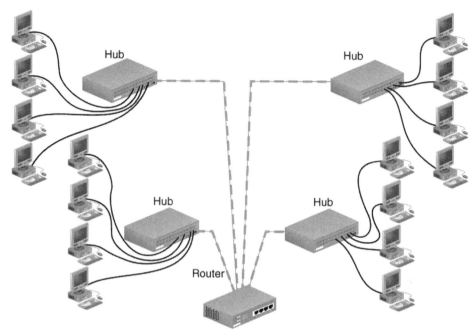

FIGURE 6-9 *A collapsed backbone*

up the collapsed backbone must contain multiprocessors to handle the heavy traffic going through it. This is risky because a failure in the central router or switch can bring down the entire network. In addition, because routers cannot move traffic as quickly as hubs, using a router may slow data transmission.

Nevertheless, a collapsed backbone topology offers substantial advantages. Most significantly, this arrangement allows you to interconnect different types of subnetworks. You can also centrally manage maintenance and troubleshooting chores.

Parallel Backbone

A **parallel backbone** is the most robust type of network backbone. This variation of the collapsed backbone arrangement consists of more than one connection from the central router or switch to each network segment. In a network with more than one router or switch, the parallel backbone calls for duplicate connections between those connectivity devices as well. Figure 6-10 depicts a simple parallel backbone topology. As you can see, each hub is connected to the router or switch by two cables, and the two routers are also connected by two cables. The most significant advantage of using a parallel backbone is that its redundant (duplicate) links ensure network connectivity to any area of the enterprise. Parallel backbones are more expensive than other enterprise-wide topologies because they require much more cabling than the others. However, they make up for the additional cost by offering increased performance and better fault tolerance.

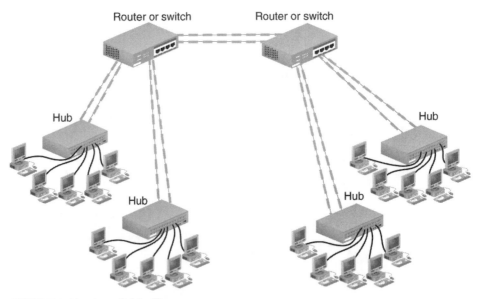

FIGURE 6-10 *A parallel backbone*

As a network administrator, you might choose to implement parallel connections to only some of the most critical devices on your network. For example, if the first and second hubs in Figure 6-10 connected your Facilities and Payroll Departments to the rest of the network, and your organization could never afford to lose connectivity with those departments, you might use a parallel structure for those links. If the third and fourth hubs in Figure 6-10 connected your organization's Recreation and Training Departments to the network, you might decide that parallel connections were unnecessary for these departments. By selectively implementing the parallel structure, you can lower connectivity costs and leave available additional ports on the connectivity devices.

Bear in mind that an enterprise-wide LAN or WAN may include different combinations of simple physical topologies and backbone designs. Now that you understand fundamental physical topologies and backbone networks, you are ready to understand the related concept of logical topologies.

Logical Topologies

NET+
1.1

The term **logical topology** refers to the way in which data is transmitted between nodes, rather than the physical layout of the paths that data takes. A network's logical topology will not necessarily match its physical topology.

The most common logical topologies are bus and ring. In a bus logical topology, signals travel from one network device to all other devices on the network (or network segment). They may or may not travel through an intervening connectivity device (as in a star topology network). A network that uses a bus physical topology also uses a bus logical topology. In addition, networks that use either the star or star-wired bus physical topologies also result in a bus logical topology.

In contrast, in a ring logical topology, signals follow a circular path between sender and receiver. Networks that use a pure ring topology use a ring logical topology. The ring logical topology is also used by the star-wired ring hybrid physical topology because signals follow a circular path, even as they travel through a connectivity device (as shown by the dashed lines in Figure 6-4). Different types of networks are characterized by one of the two main logical topologies. For example, Ethernet networks use the bus logical topology, whereas Token Ring networks use the ring logical topology.

Understanding logical topologies is useful when troubleshooting and designing networks. For example, on Ethernet networks, it is necessary to understand that all of a segment's traffic is transmitted to all nodes in the manner of a bus logical topology. Thus, for example, if one device has a malfunctioning NIC that is issuing bad or excessive packets, those packets will be detected by the NICs of all devices on the same segment. The result is a waste of available bandwidth and potential transmission errors. When network engineers casually refer to topologies, however, they are most often referring to a network's physical topology.

Switching

Switching is a component of a network's logical topology that determines how connections are created between nodes. There are three methods for switching: circuit switching, message switching, and packet switching.

Circuit Switching

In **circuit switching**, a connection is established between two network nodes before they begin transmitting data. Bandwidth is dedicated to this connection and remains available until the users terminate communication between the two nodes. While the nodes remain connected, all data follows the same path initially selected by the switch. When you place a telephone call, for example, your call typically uses a circuit-switched connection.

Because circuit switching monopolizes its piece of bandwidth while the two stations remain connected (even when no actual communication is taking place), it can result in a waste of available resources. However, some network applications benefit from such a "reserved" path. For example, live audio or videoconferencing might not tolerate the time delay it would take to reorganize data packets that have taken separate paths through another switching method. Another example of circuit switching occurs when you connect your home PC via modem to your Internet service provider's access server. WAN technologies, such as ISDN and T1 service, also use circuit switching, as does ATM, a technology discussed later in this chapter.

Message Switching

Message switching establishes a connection between two devices, transfers the information to the second device, and then breaks the connection. The information is stored and forwarded from the second device after a connection between that device and a third device on the path is established. This "store and forward" routine continues until the message reaches its destination. All information follows the same physical path; unlike with circuit switching, however, the connection is not continuously maintained. Message switching requires that each device in the data's path has sufficient memory and processing power to accept and store the information before passing it to the next node. None of the network transmission technologies discussed in this chapter use message switching.

NET+
2.14

Packet Switching

A third and by far the most popular method for connecting nodes on a network is packet switching. **Packet switching** breaks data into packets before they are transported. Packets can travel any path on the network to their destination, because each packet contains the destination address and sequencing information. Consequently, packets can attempt to find the fastest circuit available at any instant. They need not follow each other along the same path, nor must they arrive at their destination in the same sequence as when they left their source.

To understand this technology, imagine that you work in Washington, D.C. and you organized a field trip for 50 colleagues to the National Air and Space Museum. You gave the museum's exact address to your colleagues and told them to leave precisely at 7:00 A.M. from your office building several blocks away. You did not tell your coworkers which route to take. Some might choose the subway, others might hail a taxicab, and still others might choose to drive their own cars or even walk. All of them will attempt to find the fastest route to the museum. But if a group of six decide to take a taxicab and only four people fit in that taxi, the next two people have to wait for a taxi. Or a taxi might get caught in rush hour traffic and be forced to find an alternate route. Thus, the fastest route might not be obvious the moment everyone departs. But no matter which transportation method your colleagues choose, all will arrive at the museum and reassemble as a group. This analogy illustrates how packets travel in a packet-switched network.

When packets reach their destination node, the node reassembles them based on their control information. Because of the time it takes to reassemble the packets into a message, packet switching is not optimal for live audio or video transmission. Nevertheless, it is a fast and efficient mechanism for transporting typical network data, such as e-mail messages, spreadsheet files, or even software programs from a server to client. The greatest advantage to packet switching lies in the fact that it does not waste bandwidth by holding a connection open until a message reaches its destination, as circuit switching does. And unlike message switching, it does not require devices in the data's path to process any information. Ethernet networks and the Internet are the most common examples of packet-switched networks.

Now that you are familiar with the various types of switching, you are ready to investigate specific network technologies that may use switching.

Ethernet

NET+
1.2

As you have learned, Ethernet is a network technology originally developed by Xerox in the 1970s and later improved by Digital Equipment Corporation (DEC), Intel, and Xerox ("DIX"). This flexible technology can run on a variety of network media and offers excellent through-put at a reasonable cost. Ethernet is, by far, the most popular network technology used on mod-ern LANs.

Ethernet has evolved through many variations, and continues to improve. As a result of this history, it supports many different versions—so many, in fact, that you will probably find the many variations a little confusing. However, all Ethernet networks have at least one thing in common—their access method, which is known as CSMA/CD.

CSMA/CD (Carrier Sense Multiple Access with Collision Detection)

A network's **access method** is its method of controlling how network nodes access the com-munications channel. In comparing a network to a highway, the on-ramps would be one part of the highway's access method. A busy highway might use stoplights at each on-ramp to allow only one person to merge into traffic every five seconds. After merging, cars are restricted to lanes and each lane is limited as to how many cars it can hold at one time. All of these high-way controls are designed to avoid collisions and help drivers get to their destinations. On net-works, similar restrictions apply to the way in which multiple computers share a finite amount of bandwidth on a network. These controls make up the network's access method.

The access method used in Ethernet is called **CSMA/CD (Carrier Sense Multiple Access with Collision Detection)**. All Ethernet networks, independent of their speed or frame type, rely on CSMA/CD. To understand Ethernet, you must first understand CSMA/CD. Take a minute to think about the full name "Carrier Sense Multiple Access with Collision Detec-tion." The term "Carrier Sense" refers to the fact that Ethernet NICs listen on the network and wait until they detect (or sense) that no other nodes are transmitting data over the signal (or carrier) on the communications channel before they begin to transmit. The term "Multiple Access" refers to the fact that several Ethernet nodes can be connected to a network and can monitor traffic, or access the media, simultaneously.

In CSMA/CD, when a node wants to transmit data it must first access the transmission media and determine whether the channel is free. If the channel is not free, it waits and checks again after a very brief amount of time. If the channel is free, the node transmits its data. Any node can transmit data after it determines that the channel is free. But what if two nodes simulta-neously check the channel, determine that it's free, and begin to transmit? When this happens, their two transmissions interfere with each other; this is known as a **collision**.

The last part of the term CSMA/CD, "collision detection," refers to the way nodes respond to a collision. In the event of a collision, the network performs a series of steps known as the col-lision detection routine. If a node's NIC determines that its data has been involved in a colli-sion, it immediately stops transmitting. Next, in a process called **jamming**, the NIC issues a special 32-bit sequence that indicates to the rest of the network nodes that its previous trans-mission was faulty and that those data frames are invalid. After waiting, the NIC determines if the line is again available; if it is available, the NIC retransmits its data.

On heavily trafficked networks, collisions are fairly common. It is not surprising that the more nodes there are transmitting data on a network, the more collisions that will take place. (Although a collision rate greater than 5% of all traffic is unusual and may point to a prob-lematic NIC or poor cabling on the network.) When an Ethernet network grows to include a particularly large number of nodes, you may see performance suffer as a result of collisions. This "critical mass" number depends on the type and volume of data that the network regularly trans-mits. Collisions can corrupt data or truncate data frames, so it is important that the network detect and compensate for them. Figure 6-11 depicts the way CSMA/CD regulates data flow to avoid and, if necessary, detect collisions.

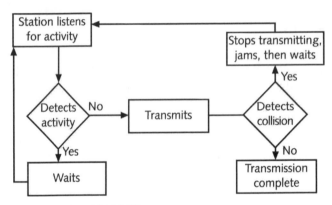

FIGURE 6-11 *CSMA/CD process*

On an Ethernet network, a **collision domain** is the portion of a network in which collisions occur if two nodes transmit data at the same time. When designing an Ethernet network, it's important to note that because repeaters simply regenerate any signal they receive, they repeat collisions just as they repeat data. Thus, connecting multiple parts of a network with repeaters results in a larger collision domain. Higher-layer connectivity devices, such as switches and routers, however, can separate collision domains.

Collision domains play a role in the Ethernet cabling distance limitations. For example, if there is more than 100 meters distance between two nodes on a segment connected to the same 100BASE-TX network bus, data propagation delays will be too long for CSMA/CD to be effective. A **data propagation delay** is the length of time data takes to travel from one point on the segment to another point. When data takes a long time, CSMA/CD's collision detec-tion routine cannot identify collisions accurately. In other words, one node on the segment might begin its CSMA/CD routine and determine that the channel is free even though a sec-ond node has begun transmitting, because the second node's data is taking so long to reach the first node.

NET+
1.2

At rates of 100 or 1000 Mbps, data travels so quickly that NICs can't always keep up with the collision detection and retransmission routines. For example, because of the speed employed on a 100BASE-TX network, the window of time for the NIC to both detect and compensate for the error is much less than that of a 10BASE-T network. To minimize undetected collisions, 100BASE-TX networks can support only a maximum of three network segments connected with two hubs, whereas 10BaseT buses can support a maximum of five network segments connected with four hubs. This shorter path reduces the highest potential propagation delay between nodes.

NET+
1.2
2.14

Switched Ethernet

Traditional Ethernet LANs, called **shared Ethernet**, supply a fixed amount of bandwidth that must be shared by all devices on a segment, and all nodes on that segment belong to the same collision domain. Stations cannot send and receive data simultaneously, nor can they transmit a signal when another station on the same segment is sending or receiving data. This is because they share a segment and a hub or repeater, which merely amplifies and retransmits a signal over the segment. In contrast, a switch can separate a network segment into smaller segments, with each segment being independent of the others and supporting its own traffic. **Switched Ethernet** enables multiple nodes to simultaneously transmit and receive data over different logical network segments. By doing so, each node can individually take advantage of more bandwidth. Figure 6-12 shows how switches can isolate network segments.

Using switched Ethernet increases the effective bandwidth of a network segment because fewer workstations must vie for the same time on the wire. For organizations with existing 10BASE-T infrastructure, switches offer a relatively simple and inexpensive way to augment each node's available bandwidth. Switches can be placed strategically on an organization's network to balance

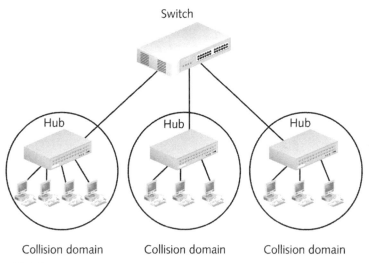

FIGURE 6-12 *A switched Ethernet network*

traffic loads and reduce congestion. Note, however, that switches are not always the best answer to heavy traffic and a need for greater speeds. In a case in which an enterprise-wise Ethernet LAN is generally overtaxed, you should consider upgrading the network's design or infrastructure.

Ethernet Frames

You have already been introduced to data frames, the packages that carry higher-layer data and control information that enable data to reach their destinations without errors and in the correct sequence. Ethernet networks may use one (or a combination) of four kinds of data frames: Ethernet_802.2 ("Raw"), Ethernet_802.3 ("Novell proprietary"), Ethernet_II ("DIX"), and Ethernet_SNAP. This variety of Ethernet frame types came about as different organizations released and revised Ethernet standards during the 1980s, changing as LAN technology evolved. Each frame type differs slightly in the way it codes and decodes packets of data traveling from one device to another.

Physical layer standards, such as 10BASE-T or 100BASE-TX, have no effect on the type of framing that occurs in the Data Link layer. Thus, Ethernet frame types have no relation to the topology or cabling characteristics of the network. Framing also takes place independently of the higher-level layers. Theoretically, all frame types could carry any one of many higher-layer protocols. For example, a single Ethernet_II data frame may carry either TCP/IP or AppleTalk data (but not both simultaneously). But as you'll learn in the following discussion, not all frame types are well suited to carrying all kinds of traffic.

Using and Configuring Frames

You can use multiple frame types on a network, but you cannot expect interoperability between the frame types. For example, in a mixed environment of NetWare 4.11 and UNIX servers, your network might support both Ethernet_802.2 and Ethernet_II frames. A workstation connecting to the NetWare 4.11 server might be configured to use the Ethernet_802.2 frame, whereas a workstation connecting to the UNIX server would likely use the Ethernet_II frame.

A node's Data Link layer services must be properly configured to expect the types of frames it might receive. If a node receives an unfamiliar frame type, it will not be able to decode the data contained in the frame, nor will it be able to communicate with nodes configured to use that frame type. For this reason, it is important for LAN administrators to ensure that all devices use the same, correct frame type. These days almost all networks use the Ethernet_II frame type. But in the 1990s, before this uniformity evolved, the use of different NOSs or legacy hardware often required managing devices to interpret multiple frame types.

Frame types are typically specified through a device's NIC configuration software. To make matters easier, most NICs can automatically sense what types of frames are running on a network and adjust themselves to that specification. This feature is called auto-detect, or autosense. Workstations, networked printers, and servers added to an existing network can all take advantage of auto-detection. Even if your devices use the auto-detect feature, you should nevertheless know what frame types are running on your network so that you can troubleshoot connectivity problems. As easy as it is to configure, the auto-detect feature is not infallible.

Frame Fields

All Ethernet frame types share many fields in common. For example, every Ethernet frame contains a 7-byte preamble and a 1-byte start-of-frame delimiter. The **preamble** signals to the receiving node that data is incoming and indicates when the data flow is about to begin. The **SFD (start-of-frame delimiter)** identifies where the data field begins. Preambles and SFDs are not included, however, when calculating a frame's total size.

Each Ethernet frame also contains a 14-byte header, which includes a destination address, a source address, and an additional field that varies in function and size, depending on the frame type. The destination address and source address fields are each 6 bytes long. The destination address identifies the recipient of the data frame, and the source address identifies the network node that originally sent the data. Recall that any network device can be identified by its physical address, also known as a hardware address or Media Access Control (MAC) address. The source address and destination address fields of an Ethernet frame use the MAC address to identify where data originated and where it should be delivered.

Also, all Ethernet frames contain a 4-byte FCS (Frame Check Sequence) field. Recall that the function of the FCS field is to ensure that the data at the destination exactly matches the data issued from the source using the CRC (Cyclic Redundancy Check) algorithm. Together, the FCS and the header make up the 18-byte "frame" for the data. The data portion of an Ethernet frame may contain from 46 to 1500 bytes of information (and recall that this includes the Network layer datagram). If fewer than 46 bytes of data are supplied by the higher layers, the source node fills out the data portion with extra bytes until it totals 46 bytes. The extra bytes are known as **padding** and have no significance other than to fill out the frame. They do not affect the data being transmitted.

Adding the 18-byte framing portion plus the smallest possible data field of 46 bytes equals the minimum Ethernet frame size of 64 bytes. Adding the framing portion plus the largest possible data field of 1500 bytes equals the maximum Ethernet frame size of 1518 bytes. No matter what frame type is used, the size range of 64 to 1518 total bytes applies to all Ethernet frames.

Because of the overhead present in each frame and the time required to enact CSMA/CD, the use of larger frame sizes on a network generally results in faster throughput. To some extent, you cannot control your network's frame sizes. You can, however, help improve network performance by properly managing frames. For example, network administrators should strive to minimize the number of broadcast frames on their networks, because broadcast frames tend to be very small and, therefore, inefficient. Also, running more than one frame type on the same network can result in inefficiencies, because it requires devices to examine each incoming frame to determine its type. Given a choice, it's most efficient to support only one frame type on a network.

Ethernet_II ("DIX")

Ethernet_II is an Ethernet frame type developed by DEC, Intel, and Xerox (abbreviated as DIX) before the IEEE began to standardize Ethernet. The Ethernet_II frame type is similar to the older Ethernet_802.3 and Ethernet_802.2 frame types, but differs in one field. Where the other types contain a 2-byte length field, the Ethernet_II frame type contains a 2-byte type field. This type field identifies the Network layer protocol (such as IP, ARP, RARP, or IPX) contained in the frame. For example, if a frame were carrying an IP datagram, its type field would contain "0x0800," the type code for IP. Because Ethernet_802.2 and Ethernet_802.3 frames do not contain a type field, they are only capable of transmitting data over a single Network layer protocol (for example, only IP and not both IP and ARP) across the network. For TCP/IP networks, which commonly use multiple Network layer protocols, these frame types are unsuitable.

Like Ethernet_II, the Ethernet_SNAP frame type also provides a type field. However, the Ethernet_SNAP standard calls for additional control fields, so that compared to Ethernet_II frames, the Ethernet_SNAP frames allow less room for data. Therefore, because of its support for multiple Network layer protocols and because it uses fewer bytes as overhead, Ethernet_II is the frame type most commonly used on contemporary Ethernet networks. Figure 6-13 depicts an Ethernet_II frame.

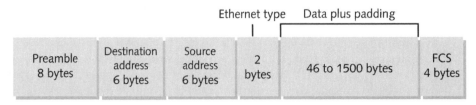

FIGURE 6-13 *Ethernet_II ("DIX") frame*

PoE (Power over Ethernet)

Recently, IEEE has finalized the **802.3af** standard, which specifies a method for supplying electrical power over Ethernet connections, also known as **PoE (Power over Ethernet)**. Although the standard is new, the concept is not. In fact, your home telephone receives power from the telephone company over the lines that come into your home. This power is necessary for dial tone and ringing. On an Ethernet network, carrying power over signaling connections can be useful for nodes that are far from traditional power receptacles or need a constant, reliable power source. For example, a wireless access point at an outdoor theater, a telephone used to receive digitized voice signals, an Internet gaming station in the center of a mall, or a critical router at the core of a network's backbone can all benefit from PoE.

The PoE standard specifies two types of devices: power sourcing equipment (PSE) and PDs (powered devices). **Power sourcing equipment (PSE)** refers to the device that supplies the power; usually this device depends on backup power sources (in other words, not the electrical grid maintained by utilities). **Powered devices (PDs)** are those that receive the power from the PSE. PoE requires CAT 5 or better copper cable. In the cable, electric current may run over an unused pair of wires or over the pair of wires used for data transmission in a 10BASE-T,

100BASE-TX, or 1000BASE-T network. The standard allows for both approaches; however, on a single network, the choice of current-carrying pairs should be consistent between all PSE and PDs. Not all end nodes are capable of receiving PoE. The IEEE standard has accounted for that possibility by requiring all PSE to first determine whether a node is PoE capable before attempting to supply it with power. That means that PoE is compatible with current 802.3 installations. No special modifications need to be made to existing networks before adding this new feature.

Token Ring

NET+
1.2

Now that you have learned about the many forms of Ethernet, you are ready to learn about Token Ring, a less common, but still important network access method. Token Ring is a network technology first developed by IBM in the 1980s. In the early 1990s, the Token Ring architecture competed strongly with Ethernet to be the most popular access method. Since that time, the economics, speed, and reliability of Ethernet have improved, leaving Token Ring behind. Because IBM developed Token Ring, a few IBM-centric IT Departments continue to use it. Other network managers have changed their former Token Ring networks into Ethernet networks.

Token Ring networks have traditionally been more expensive to implement than Ethernet networks. Proponents of the Token Ring technology argue that, although some of its connectivity hardware is more expensive, its reliability results in less downtime and lower network management costs than Ethernet. On a practical level, Token Ring has probably lost the battle for superiority because its developers were slower to develop high-speed standards. Token Ring networks can run at either 4, 16, or 100 Mbps. The 100-Mbps Token Ring standard, finalized in 1999, is known as **HSTR (High-Speed Token Ring)**. HSTR can use either twisted-pair or fiber-optic cable as its transmission medium. Although it is as reliable and efficient, it is still less common than Ethernet because of its higher cost and lagging speed.

Token Ring networks use the token-passing routine and a star-ring hybrid physical topology. In **token passing**, a 3-byte packet, called a token, is transmitted from one node to another in a circular fashion around the ring. When a station has something to send, it picks up the token, changes it to a frame, and then adds the header, information, and trailer fields. The header includes the address of the destination node. All nodes read the frame as it traverses the ring to determine whether they are the intended recipient of the message. If they are, they pick up the data, then retransmit the frame to the next station on the ring. When the frame finally reaches the originating station, the originating workstation reissues a free token that can then be used by another station. The token-passing control scheme avoids the possibility for collisions. This fact makes Token Ring more reliable and efficient than Ethernet. It also does not impose distance limitations on the length of a LAN segment, unlike CSMA/CD.

On a Token Ring network, one workstation, called the active monitor, acts as the controller for token passing. Specifically, the **active monitor** maintains the timing for ring passing, monitors token and frame transmission, detects lost tokens, and corrects errors when a timing error or other disruption occurs. Only one workstation on the ring can act as the active monitor at any given time.

NOTE

The Token Ring architecture is often mistakenly described as a pure ring topology. In fact, its logical topology is a ring. However, its physical topology is a star-ring hybrid in which data circulate in a ring fashion, but the layout of the network is a star.

IEEE standard 802.5 describes the specifications for Token Ring technology. Token Ring networks transmit data at either 4, 16, or 100 Mbps over shielded or unshielded twisted-pair wiring. You may have as many as 255 addressable stations on a Token Ring network that uses shielded twisted-pair or as many as 72 addressable stations on one that uses unshielded twisted-pair. All Token Ring connections rely on a NIC that taps into the network through a MAU (Multistation Access Unit), Token Ring's equivalent of a hub. NICs can be designed and configured to run specifically on 4-, 16-, or 100-Mbps networks, or they can be designed to accommodate all three data transmission rates. In the star-ring hybrid topology, the MAU completes the ring internally with Ring In and Ring Out ports at either end of the unit. In addition, MAUs typically provide eight ports for workstation connections. You can easily expand a Token Ring network by connecting multiple MAUs through their Ring In and Ring Out ports, as shown in Figure 6-14. Unused ports on a MAU, including Ring In and Ring Out ports, have self-shorting data connectors that internally close the loop.

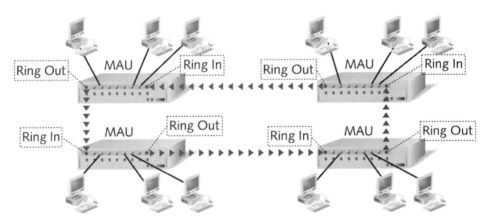

FIGURE 6-14 *Interconnected Token Ring MAUs*

NET+
1.2

The self-shorting feature of Token Ring MAU ports makes Token Ring highly fault-tolerant. For example, if you discover a problematic NIC on the network, you can remove that workstation's cable from the MAU, and the MAU's port will close the ring internally. Similarly, if you discover a faulty MAU, you can remove it from the ring by disconnecting its Ring In and Ring Out cables from its adjacent MAUs and connect the two good MAUs to each other to close the loop.

A Token Ring network may use one of three types of connectors on its cables: RJ-45, DB-9, or type 1 IBM. Modern Token Ring networks with UTP cabling use RJ-45 connectors, which are identical to the RJ-45 connector used on 10BASE-T or 100BASE-T Ethernet networks. Token Ring networks with STP cabling may use a **type 1 IBM connector**, which is depicted in Figure 6-15. Type 1 IBM connectors contain interlocking tabs that snap into an identical connector when one of the connectors is flipped upside-down, making for a secure connection. A **DB-9 connector** (containing nine pins) is another type of connector found on STP Token Ring networks. This connector is also pictured in Figure 6-15.

Type 1 IBM connector   DB-9 connector

FIGURE 6-15 *Type 1 IBM and DB-9 Token Ring connectors*

FDDI (Fiber Distributed Data Interface)

NET+
1.2
2.14

FDDI (Fiber Distributed Data Interface) is a network technology whose standard was originally specified by ANSI in the mid-1980s and later refined by ISO. FDDI (pronounced "fiddy") uses a double ring of multimode or single-mode fiber to transmit data at speeds of 100 Mbps. FDDI was developed in response to the throughput limitations of Ethernet and Token Ring technologies used at the time. In fact, FDDI was the first network technology to reach the 100-Mbps threshold. For this reason, you will frequently find it supporting network backbones that were installed in the late 1980s and early 1990s. FDDI is used on WANs and MANs. For example, FDDI can connect LANs located in multiple buildings, such as those on college campuses. FDDI links can span distances as large as 62 miles. Because Ethernet and Token Ring technologies have developed faster transmission speeds, FDDI is no longer the much-coveted technology that it was in the 1980s.

NET+
1.2
2.14

Nevertheless, FDDI is a stable technology that offers numerous benefits. Its reliance on fiber-optic cable ensures that FDDI is more reliable and more secure than transmission methods that depend on copper wiring. Another advantage of FDDI is that it works well with Ethernet 100BASE-TX technology.

One drawback to FDDI technology is its high cost relative to Fast Ethernet (costing up to 10 times more per switch port than Fast Ethernet). If an organization has FDDI installed, however, it can use the same cabling to upgrade to Fast Ethernet or Gigabit Ethernet, with only minor differences to consider, such as Ethernet's lower maximum segment length.

FDDI is based on ring topologies similar to a Token Ring network, as shown in Figure 6-16. It also relies on the same token-passing routine that Token Ring networks use. However, unlike Token Ring technology, FDDI runs on two complete rings. During normal operation, the primary FDDI ring carries data, while the secondary ring is idle. The secondary ring will assume data transmission responsibilities should the primary ring experience Physical layer problems. This redundancy makes FDDI networks extremely reliable.

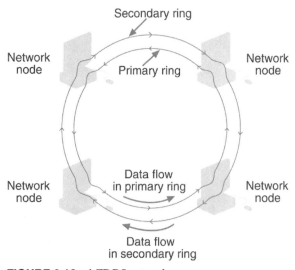

FIGURE 6-16 *A FDDI network*

ATM (Asynchronous Transfer Mode)

ATM (Asynchronous Transfer Mode) is an ITU networking standard describing Data Link layer protocols for both network access and signal multiplexing. It was first conceived by researchers at Bell Labs in 1983 as a higher-bandwidth alternative to FDDI, but it took a dozen years before standards organizations could reach an agreement on its specifications. ATM may run over fiber-optic or CAT 5 or higher UTP or STP cable. It is typically used on WANs, particularly by large public telecommunication carriers.

Like Token Ring and Ethernet, ATM specifies Data Link layer framing techniques. But what sets ATM apart from Token Ring and Ethernet is its fixed packet size. In ATM, a packet is called a **cell** and always consists of 48 bytes of data plus a 5-byte header. This fixed packet size allows ATM to provide predictable network performance. However, recall that a smaller packet size requires more overhead. In fact, ATM's smaller packet size does decrease its potential throughput, but the efficiency of using cells compensates for that loss.

Another unique aspect of ATM technology is that it relies on virtual circuits. **Virtual circuits** are connections between network nodes that, although based on potentially disparate physical links, logically appear to be direct, dedicated links between those nodes. On an ATM network, switches determine the optimal path between the sender and receiver, then establish this path before the network transmits data. One advantage to virtual circuits is their configurable (and therefore, potentially more efficient) use of limited bandwidth. Several virtual circuits can be assigned to one length of cable or even to one channel on that cable. A virtual circuit uses the channel only when it needs to transmit data. Meanwhile, the channel is available for use by other virtual circuits.

Because ATM packages data into cells before transmission, each of which travels separately to its destination, ATM is typically considered a packet-switching technology. At the same time, the use of virtual circuits means that ATM provides the main advantage of circuit switching— that is, a point-to-point connection that remains reliably available to the transmission until it completes, making ATM a connection-oriented technology. Establishing a reliable connection allows ATM to guarantee a specific **QoS (quality of service)** for certain transmissions. QoS is a standard that specifies that data will be delivered within a certain period of time after it is sent. ATM networks can supply four QoS levels, from a "best effort" attempt for noncritical data to a guaranteed, real-time transmission for time-sensitive data. This is important for organizations using networks for time-sensitive applications, such as video and audio transmissions. For example, a company that wants to use its physical connection between two offices located at opposite sides of a state to carry its voice phone calls might choose the ATM network technology with the highest possible QoS to carry that data. On the other hand, they may assign a low QoS to routine e-mail messages exchanged between the two offices. Without QoS guarantees, cells belonging to the same message may arrive in the wrong order or too slowly to be properly interpreted by the receiving node.

ATM's developers have made certain it is compatible with other leading network technologies. Its cells can support multiple types of higher-layer protocols, including TCP/IP, AppleTalk, and IPX/SPX. In addition, the ATM networks can be integrated with Ethernet or Token Ring networks through the use of **LANE (LAN Emulation)**. LANE encapsulates incoming Ethernet or Token Ring frames, then converts them into ATM cells for transmission over an ATM network.

Currently, ATM is expensive and, because of its cost, it is rarely used on small LANs and almost never used to connect typical workstations to a network. Gigabit Ethernet, a faster, cheaper technology, poses a substantial threat to ATM. In addition to its lower cost, Gigabit Ethernet is a more natural upgrade for the multitude of Fast Ethernet users. It overcomes the QoS issue by simply providing a larger pipe for the greater volume of traffic using the network. Although ATM caught on among the very largest carriers in the late 1990s, most networking professionals have followed the Gigabit Ethernet standard rather than spending extra dollars on ATM infrastructure.

Wireless Networks

NET+
1.7

Similar to the development of wire-bound network access technologies, the development of wireless access methods did not follow one direct and cooperative path, but grew from the efforts of multiple vendors and organizations. Now, a handful of different wireless technologies are available. Each wireless technology is defined by a standard that describes unique functions at both the Physical and the Data Link layers of the OSI Model. These standards differ in their specified signaling methods, geographic ranges, and frequency usages, among other things. Such differences make certain technologies better suited to home networks and others better suited to networks at large organizations. The most popular wireless standards used on contemporary LANs are those developed by IEEE's 802.11 committee.

802.11

The IEEE released its first wireless network standard in 1997. Since then, its WLAN (Wireless Local Area Networks) standards committee, also known as the 802.11 committee, has published several distinct standards related to wireless networking. Each IEEE wireless network access standard is named after the 802.11 task group (or subcommittee) that developed it. The three IEEE 802.11 task groups that have generated notable wireless standards are: 802.11b, 802.11a, and 802.11g. These three 802.11 standards share many characteristics. For example, although some of their Physical layer services vary, all three use half-duplex signaling. In other words, a wireless station using one of the 802.11 techniques can either transmit or receive, but cannot do both simultaneously (assuming the station has only one transceiver installed, as is usually the case). In addition, all 802.11 networks follow the same MAC (Media Access Control) sublayer specifications, as described in the following sections.

Access Method

You have learned that the MAC sublayer of the Data Link layer is responsible for appending physical addresses to a data frame and for governing multiple nodes' access to a single medium. As with 802.3 (Ethernet), the 802.11 MAC services append 48-bit (or 6-byte) physical addresses to a frame to identify its source and destination. The use of the same physical addressing scheme allows 802.11 networks to be easily combined with other IEEE 802 networks, including Ethernet networks. However, because wireless devices are not designed to transmit and receive simultaneously (and therefore cannot quickly detect collisions), 802.11 networks use a different access method than Ethernet networks.

802.11 standards specify the use of **CSMA/CA (Carrier Sense Multiple Access with Collision Avoidance)** to access a shared medium. Using CSMA/CA, before a station begins to send data on an 802.11 network, it checks for existing wireless transmissions. If the source node detects no transmission activity on the network, it waits a brief, random amount of time, and then sends its transmission. If the source does detect activity, it waits a brief period of time before checking the channel again. The destination node receives the transmission and, after verifying its accuracy, issues an acknowledgment (ACK) packet to the source. If the source receives this acknowledgment, it assumes the transmission was properly completed. However, interference or other transmissions on the network could impede this exchange. If, after transmitting a message, the source node fails to receive acknowledgment from the destination node, it assumes its transmission did not arrive properly, and it begins the CSMA/CA process anew. Compared to CSMA/CD, CSMA/CA minimizes, but does not eliminate, the potential for collisions.

The use of ACK packets to verify every transmission means that 802.11 networks require more overhead than 802.3 networks. Therefore, a wireless network with a theoretical maximum throughput of 10 Mbps will in fact transmit much less data per second than a wire-bound Ethernet network with the same theoretical maximum throughput. In reality, wireless networks tend to achieve between one-third and one-half of their theoretical maximum throughput. For example, the fastest type of 802.11 network, 802.11g, is rated for a maximum of 54 Mbps; most 802.11g networks achieve between 20 and 25 Mbps.

One way to ensure that packets are not inhibited by other transmissions is to reserve the medium for one station's use. In 802.11 this can be accomplished through the optional **RTS/CTS (Request to Send/Clear to Send)** protocol. RTS/CTS enables a source node to issue an RTS signal to an access point requesting the exclusive opportunity to transmit. If the access point agrees by responding with a CTS signal, the access point temporarily suspends communication with all stations in its range and waits for the source node to complete its transmission. RTS/CTS is not routinely used by wireless stations, but for transmissions involving large packets (those more subject to damage by interference), it can prove more efficient. On the other hand, using RTS/CTS further decreases the overall efficiency of the 802.11 network.

Association

Suppose you have just purchased a new laptop with a wireless NIC and support for one of the 802.11 wireless standards. When you bring your laptop to a local Internet café and turn it on, your laptop soon prompts you to log on to the café's wireless network to gain access to the Internet. This seemingly simple process, known as **association**, involves a number of packet exchanges between the café's access point and your computer. Association is another function of the MAC sublayer described in the 802.11 standard.

As long as a station is on and has its wireless protocols running, it periodically surveys its surroundings for evidence of an access point, a task known as **scanning**. A station can use either active scanning or passive scanning. In **active scanning**, the station transmits a special frame, known as a **probe**, on all available channels within its frequency range. When an access point finds the probe frame, it issues a probe response. This response contains all the information a station needs to associate with the access point, including a status code and station ID number for that station. After receiving the probe response, a station can agree to associate with that access point. The two nodes begin communicating over the frequency channel specified by the access point.

In **passive scanning**, a wireless station listens on all channels within its frequency range for a special signal, known as a **beacon frame**, issued from an access point. The beacon frame contains information that a wireless node requires to associate itself with the access point. For example, the frame indicates the network's transmission rate and the **SSID (Service Set Identifier)**, a unique character string used to identify an access point. After detecting a beacon frame, the station can choose to associate with that access point. The two nodes agree on a frequency channel and begin communicating. When setting up a WLAN, most network administrators use the access point's configuration utility to assign a unique SSID (rather than the default SSID provided by the manufacturer). This can contribute to better security and easier network management. For example, the access point used by employees in the Customer Service Department of a company could be assigned the SSID "CustSvc".

Some WLANs contain multiple access points. If a station detects the presence of several access points, it will choose the one with the strongest signal and the lowest error rate compared to other access points. Notice that a station does not necessarily choose the *closest* access point. For instance, in the previous example, if another user brought his own access point to the Internet café and his access point had a signal twice as strong as the café's access point, your laptop would associate with it instead. Other users' laptops would also associate with his access point (that is, unless those stations were configured to connect to one specific access point, identified by its SSID in the station's wireless connection properties).

Later, a station might choose a different access point through a process called **reassociation**. This can happen if a mobile user moves out of one access point's range and into the range of another, or if the initial access point is experiencing a high rate of errors. On a network with multiple access points, network managers can take advantage of the stations' scanning feature to automatically balance transmission loads between those access points. Figure 6-17 depicts a WLAN with multiple points.

 TIP

The IEEE 802.11 standard specifies communication between two wireless nodes, or stations, and between a station and an access point. However, it does not specify how two access points should communicate. Therefore, when designing an 802.11 network, it is best to use access points manufactured by the same company, to ensure full compatibility.

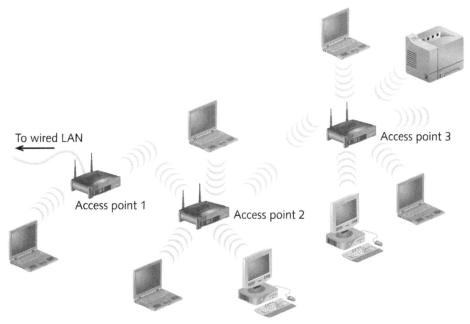

FIGURE 6-17 *A WLAN with multiple access points*

Frames

You have learned about some types of overhead required to manage access to the 802.11 wireless networks—for example, ACKs, probes, and beacons. For each function, the 802.11 standard specifies a frame type at the MAC sublayer. These multiple frame types are divided into three groups: control, management, and data. Management frames are those involved in association and reassociation, such as the probe and beacon frames. Control frames are those related to medium access and data delivery, such as the ACK and RTS/CTS frames. Data frames are those that carry the data sent between stations. An 802.11 data frame is illustrated in Figure 6-18.

Frame Control (2 bytes)	Duration (2 bytes)	Address 1 (6 bytes)	Address 2 (6 bytes)	Address 3 (6 bytes)	Sequence Control (2 bytes)	Address 4 (6 bytes)	Data (0 - 2312 bytes)	Frame Check Sequence (6 bytes)

FIGURE 6-18 *Basic 802.11 MAC frame format*

Compare the 802.11 data frame with the Ethernet_II data frame pictured in Figure 6-13. Notice that the wireless data frame contains four address fields, rather than two. These four addresses are the source address, transmitter address, receiver address, and destination address. The transmitter and receiver addresses refer to the access point or another intermediary device (if used) on the wireless network. The source and destination addresses have the same meaning as they do in the Ethernet_II frame.

Another unique characteristic of the 802.11 data frame is its Sequence Control field. This field is used to indicate how a large packet is fragmented, or subdivided into smaller packets for more reliable delivery. Recall that on wire-bound TCP/IP networks, error checking occurs at the Transport layer of the OSI Model and packet fragmentation, if necessary, occurs at the Network layer. However, in 802.11 networks, error checking and packet fragmentation is handled at the MAC sublayer of the Data Link layer. By handling fragmentation at a lower layer, 802.11 makes its transmission—which is less efficient and more error-prone—transparent to higher layers. This means 802.11 nodes are more easily integrated with 802.3 networks and prevent the 802.11 segments of an integrated network from slowing down the 802.3 segments.

The Frame Control field in an 802.11 data frame holds information about the protocol in use, the type of frame being transmitted, whether the frame is part of a larger, fragmented packet, whether the frame is one that was reissued after an unverified delivery attempt, what type of security the frame uses, and so on. Security is a significant concern with WLANs, because access points are more vulnerable than devices on a wire-bound network. Wireless security is discussed in detail along with other network security later in this book.

Although 802.11b, 802.11a, and 802.11g share all of the MAC sublayer characteristics described in the previous sections, they differ in their coding methods, frequency usage, and ranges. In other words, each varies at the Physical layer. The following sections summarize those differences.

802.11b

In 1999, the IEEE released **802.11b**, also known as "**Wi-Fi**," for Wireless Fidelity. 802.11b uses DSSS (direct sequence spread spectrum) signaling. Recall that in DSSS, a signal is distributed over the entire bandwidth of the allocated spectrum. 802.11b uses the 2.4–2.4835-GHz frequency range (also called the 2.4-GHz band) and separates it into 14 overlapping 22-MHz channels. 802.11b provides a theoretical maximum of 11-Mbps throughput; actual throughput is typically around 5 Mbps. To ensure this throughput, wireless nodes must stay within 100 meters (or approximately 330 feet) of an access point or each other, in the case of an ad-hoc network. Among all the 802.11 standards, 802.11b was the first to take hold and remains the most popular. It is also the least expensive of all the 802.11 WLAN technologies.

802.11a

Although the 802.11a task group began its standards work before the 802.11b group, 802.11a was released after 802.11b. The **802.11a** standard differs from 802.11b and 802.11g in that it uses multiple frequency bands in the 5-GHz frequency range and provides a maximum theoretical throughput of 54 Mbps, though its effective throughput falls generally between 11 and 18 Mbps. 802.11a's high throughput is attributable to its use of higher frequencies, its unique method of encoding data, and more available bandwidth. Perhaps most significant is that the

NET+
1.7

5-GHz band is not as congested as the 2.4-GHz band. Thus, 802.11a signals are less likely to suffer interference from microwave ovens, cordless phones, motors, and other (incompatible) wireless LAN signals. However, higher frequency signals require more power to transmit and travel shorter distances than lower frequency signals. The average geographic range for an 802.11a antenna is 20 meters, or approximately 66 feet. As a result, 802.11a networks require a greater density of access points between the wire-bound LAN and wireless clients to cover the same distance that 802.11b networks cover. The additional access points, as well as the nature of 802.11a equipment, make this standard more expensive than either 802.11b or 802.11g.

802.11g

IEEE's **802.11g** WLAN standard is designed to be just as affordable as 802.11b while increasing its maximum capacity from 11 Mbps to a maximum theoretical throughput of 54 Mbps through different encoding techniques. The effective throughput of 802.11g ranges generally from 20 to 25 Mbps. An 802.11g antenna has a geographic range of 100 meters (or approximately 330 feet).

802.11g, like 802.11b, uses the 2.4-GHz frequency band. In addition to its high throughput, 802.11g benefits from being compatible with 802.11b networks. Thus, if a network administrator installed 802.11b access points on her LAN last year, this year she could add 802.11g access points and laptops, and the laptops could roam between the ranges of the 802.11b and 802.11g access points without an interruption in service. 802.11g's compatibility with the more established 802.11b has caused many network managers to choose it over 802.11a, despite 802.11a's comparative advantages.

Bluetooth

In the early 1990s, Ericsson began developing a wireless networking technology for use between multiple devices, including cordless telephones, PDAs, computers, printers, keyboards, telephone headsets, and pagers, in a home. It was designed to carry voice, video, and data signals over the same communications channels. Besides being compatible with a variety of devices, this technology was also meant to be low-cost and short-range. In 1998, Intel, Nokia, Toshiba, and IBM joined Sony Ericsson to form the **Bluetooth Special Interest Group (SIG)** (its members currently number over 2000 companies), whose aim was to refine and standardize this technology. The resulting standard was named **Bluetooth**. Bluetooth is a mobile wireless networking standard that uses FHSS (frequency hopping spread spectrum) RF signaling in the 2.4-GHz band. Recall that in FHSS, a signal hops between multiple frequencies within a band in a synchronization pattern known only to the channel's receiver and transmitter.

Bluetooth was named after King Harald I of Denmark, who ruled in the tenth century. One legend has it that he was so fond of eating blueberries that his teeth were discolored, earning him the nickname "Bluetooth." This king was also famous for unifying hostile tribes from Denmark, Norway, and Sweden, just as Bluetooth can unify disparate network nodes.

The original Bluetooth standard, version 1.1, was designed to achieve a maximum theoretical throughput of 1 Mbps. However, its effective throughput is 723 Kbps, with error correction and control data consuming the remaining bandwidth. The latest version of the standard, version 2.0, was released in 2004. This version uses different encoding schemes that allow Bluetooth to achieve up to 2.1-Mbps throughput. (The newer version of Bluetooth is backward compatible, meaning that devices running version 2.0 can communicate with devices running earlier versions of Bluetooth.) The Bluetooth 1.1 and 1.2 standards recommend that communicating nodes be spaced no farther than 10 meters (or approximately 33 feet) apart. When using Bluetooth version 2.0, communicating nodes can be as far as 30 meters (or approximately 100 feet) apart.

Bluetooth was designed to be used on small networks composed of personal communications devices, also known as **PANs (personal area networks)**. An example of a **WPAN (wireless PAN)** is shown in Figure 6-19. Bluetooth's relatively low throughput and short range have made it impractical for business LANs. However, due to commercial support from several influential vendors in the Bluetooth SIG, it has become a popular wireless technology for communicating between cellular telephones and PDAs. Bluetooth has been codified by the IEEE in their **802.15.1** standard, which describes WPAN technology.

FIGURE 6-19 *A Wireless personal area network (WPAN)*

A Bluetooth PAN is also known as a **piconet**. The simplest type of piconet is one that contains one master and one slave, which communicate in a point-to-point fashion with each other. The master determines the frequency hopping sequence and synchronizes the communication. A piconet consisting of only two devices requires no setup. As soon as two devices that are running Bluetooth version 1.x (the most common scenario) come within 10 meters of each other, they can communicate. For example, you might use Bluetooth to send your address data from your PDA to another friend's PDA. However, a piconet can be larger. With Bluetooth versions 1.x a piconet can contain one master and up to seven slave stations. With Bluetooth 2.0, the number of slaves is unlimited. Figure 6-20 depicts a piconet with one master and three slaves.

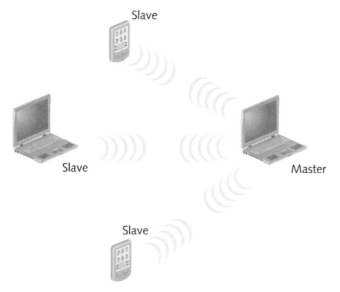

FIGURE 6-20 *A Bluetooth piconet*

Multiple Bluetooth piconets can be combined to form a **scatternet**. In a scatternet, each piconet still requires a single master, but a master from one piconet can act as a slave in another piconet, as shown in Figure 6-21. Also, a slave can participate in more than one piconet.

Bluetooth was designed as a better alternative to an older form of wireless communication also used on PANs, infrared signaling.

Infrared (IR)

Even if you don't run a wireless network in your home, you have probably used infrared (IR) signaling there—for example, to change channels on the TV from your TV remote. You may have noticed that the TV remote works best if you point it directly at the TV and that it doesn't work at all if you are behind a wall in a different room. That's because in general, infrared signals depend on a line-of-sight transmission path between the sender and receiver. Just as light can't pass through a wall, IR signals must follow an unobstructed path between sender

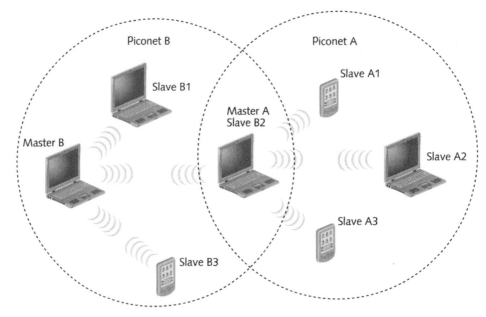

FIGURE 6-21 *A scatternet with two piconets*

and receiver. (However, some IR signals will bounce off of large, angular obstacles and find their way from sender to receiver in a multipath fashion.) Also, IR signals used for communication between computer devices travel only approximately 1 meter (or 3.3 feet). (On the other hand, IR signals from very powerful transmitters could travel hundreds of feet.) Infrared transmission occurs at very high frequencies, in the 300- to 300,000-GHz range, and just above the visible spectrum of light. Like Bluetooth, IR technology is relatively inexpensive. IR requires less power than Bluetooth or the 802.11 transmission technologies. The most recent IR standard allows for a maximum throughput of up to 4 Mbps, significantly faster than Bluetooth. But IR's inability to circumnavigate physical obstacles or travel long distances have limited its uses on modern networks.

Nevertheless, infrared signaling remains an appropriate option for wireless communication in which devices can be positioned close to each other. IR ports are common on computers and peripherals, and IR signaling is used to exchange data between computers, printers, PDAs, cellular telephones, and other devices. For example, you might purchase a wireless keyboard that can communicate with your computer via infrared signaling. In this case, the IR port on the wireless keyboard must be pointed toward the receiving port. In the case of the keyboard shown in Figure 6-22, the wireless keyboard communicates with a wireless keyboard receiver that is attached to the computer's keyboard port with a cable. Specifications for using infrared signaling between devices on a network have been established by the **IrDA (Infrared Data Association),** a nonprofit organization founded in 1994 to develop and promote standards for wireless communication using infrared signals. IrDA is also the term used to refer to the most popular IR networking specifications.

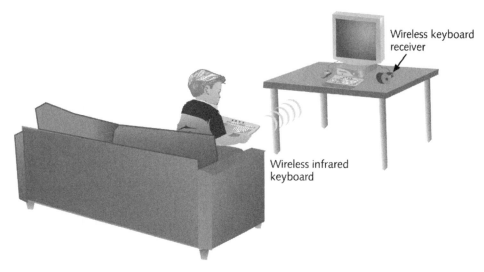

FIGURE 6-22 *Infrared transmission*

To summarize what you have learned about wireless network standards, Table 6-1 lists the significant characteristics of each standard. Table 6-1 offers a comparison of the common wireless networking standards, their ranges, and throughputs.

Table 6-1 Wireless standards

Standard	Frequency Range	Theoretical Maximum Throughput	Effective Throughput (Approximate)	Average Geographic Range
802.11b ("Wi-Fi")	2.4 GHz	11 Mbps	5 Mbps	100 meters (or approximately 330 feet)
802.11a	5 GHz	54 Mbps	11–18 Mbps	20 meters (or approximately 66 feet)
802.11g	2.4 GHz	54 Mbps	20–25 Mbps	100 meters (or approximately 330 feet)
Bluetooth ver. 1.x	2.4 GHz	1 Mbps	723 Kbps	10 meters (or approximately 33 feet)
Bluetooth ver. 2.0	2.4 GHz	2.1 Mbps	1.5 Mbps	30 meters (or approximately 100 feet)
IrDA	300–300,000 GHz	4 Mbps	3.5 Mbps	1 meter (or approximately 3.3 feet)

NOTE

The actual geographic range of any wireless technology depends on several factors, including the power of the antenna, physical barriers or obstacles between sending and receiving nodes, and interference in the environment. Therefore, although a technology is rated for a certain average geographic range, it may actually transmit signals in a shorter or longer range.

Chapter Summary

◆ A physical topology is the basic physical layout of a network; it does not specify devices, connectivity methods, or addresses on the network. Physical topologies are categorized into three fundamental geometric shapes: bus, ring, and star.

◆ A bus topology consists of a single cable connecting all nodes on a network without intervening connectivity devices. At either end of a bus network, 50-ohm resistors (terminators) stop signals after they have reached their destination. Without terminators, signals on a bus network experience signal bounce.

◆ In a ring topology, each node is connected to the two nearest nodes so that the entire network forms a circle. Data is transmitted in one direction around the ring. Each workstation accepts and responds to packets addressed to it, then forwards the other packets to the next workstation in the ring.

◆ In a star topology, every node on the network is connected through a central device, such as a hub. Any single cable on a star network connects only two devices, so a cabling problem will affect only two nodes. Nodes transmit data to the hub, which then retransmits the information to the rest of the network segment where the destination node can pick it up.

◆ Few LANs use the simple physical topologies in their pure form. More often, LANs employ a hybrid of more than one simple physical topology. The star-wired ring topology uses the physical layout of a star and the token-passing data transmission method. Data is sent around the star in a circular pattern. Token Ring networks, as specified in IEEE 802.5, use this hybrid topology.

◆ In a star-wired bus topology, groups of workstations are connected to a hub in a star formation; all the hubs are networked via a single bus. This design can cover longer distances than a simple star topology and easily interconnect or isolate different network segments, although it is more expensive than using either the star or bus topology alone. The star-wired bus topology commonly forms the basis for Ethernet and Fast Ethernet networks.

◆ Hubs that service star-wired bus or star-wired ring topologies can be daisy-chained to form a more complex hybrid topology. However, daisy-chaining can only extend a network so far before data errors are apt to occur. In this case, maximum segment and network length limits must be carefully maintained.

◆ Network backbones may follow serial, distributed, collapsed, or parallel topologies. In a serial topology, two or more internetworking devices are connected to each other by a single cable in a daisy-chain fashion. This is the simplest type of backbone. Hubs or switches are often connected in this way to extend a network.

◆ A distributed backbone consists of a number of connectivity devices connected to a series of central devices in a hierarchy. This topology allows for easy network management and scalability.

◆ The collapsed backbone topology uses a router or switch as the single central connection point for multiple subnetworks. This is risky, because an entire network could fail if the central device fails. Also, if the central connectivity device becomes overtaxed, performance on the entire network suffers.

◆ A parallel backbone is the most fault-tolerant backbone topology. It is a variation of the collapsed backbone arrangement that consists of more than one connection from the central router or switch to each network segment and parallel connections between routers and switches, if more than one is present. Parallel backbones are the most expensive type of backbone to implement.

◆ Network logical topologies describe how signals travel over a network. The two main types of logical topologies are bus and ring. Ethernet networks use a bus logical topology, and Token Ring networks use a ring logical topology.

◆ Switching manages the filtering and forwarding of packets between nodes on a network. Every network relies on one of three types of switching: circuit switching, message switching, or packet switching.

◆ Ethernet employs a network access method called CSMA/CD (Carrier Sense Multiple Access with Collision Detection). All Ethernet networks, independent of their speed or frame type, use CSMA/CD.

◆ On heavily trafficked Ethernet networks, collisions are common. The more nodes that are transmitting data on a network, the more collisions will take place. When an Ethernet network grows to a particular number of nodes, performance may suffer as a result of collisions.

◆ Switching can separate a network segment into smaller logical segments, each independent of the other and supporting its own traffic. The use of switched Ethernet increases the effective bandwidth of a network segment because at any given time fewer workstations vie for the access to a shared channel.

◆ Networks may use one (or a combination) of four kinds of Ethernet data frames. Each frame type differs slightly in the way it codes and decodes packets of data from one device to another. Most modern networks rely on Ethernet_II ("DIX") frames.

◆ Token Ring networks currently run at either 4, 16, or 100 Mbps, as specified by IEEE 802.5. Token Ring networks use the token-passing routine and a star-ring hybrid physical topology. Workstations connect to the network through MAUs (Multistation Access Units). Token Ring networks may use shielded or unshielded twisted-pair cabling.

◆ Token Ring has traditionally been more expensive to implement than Ethernet, but because of its token-passing routine, does not suffer collisions and offers high reliability and fault tolerance. Few Token Ring networks remain, as Ethernet can achieve higher throughput at lower costs.

◆ FDDI (Fiber Distributed Data Interface) is a networking standard originally specified by ANSI in the mid-1980s and later refined by ISO. It uses a dual fiber-optic ring to transmit data at speeds of 100 Mbps. FDDI's fiber-optic cable and dual fiber rings offer greater reliability and security than twisted-pair copper wire. It is much more expensive than Fast Ethernet.

◆ ATM (Asynchronous Transfer Mode) is a Data Link layer standard that relies on fixed packets, called cells, consisting of 48 bytes of data plus a 5-byte header.

◆ ATM is a connection-oriented technology. Its switches establish virtual circuits, or logical point-to-point connections between sender and receiver, and then transmit data. Having a reliable connection enables ATM to guarantee QoS (quality of service) levels for designated transmissions.

◆ Wireless standards vary by frequency, methods of signal, and geographic range. The IEEE 802.11 committee has specified three notable wireless standards: 802.11b, 802.11a, and 802.11g. All three share characteristics at the MAC sublayer level, including the CSMA/CA access method, frame formats, and methods of association between access points and stations.

◆ Currently, 802.11b is the most popular standard used on wireless networks. Its maximum throughput is 11 Mbps (though actual throughput is typically half of that). Home networks might use Bluetooth or Infrared (IR) technology, whose ranges are shorter and throughputs are lower than those of 802.11 networks.

Key Terms

802.11a—The IEEE standard for a wireless networking technique that uses multiple frequency bands in the 5-GHz frequency range and provides a theoretical maximum throughput of 54 Mbps. 802.11a's high throughput, compared with 802.11b, is attributable to its use of higher frequencies, its unique method of encoding data, and more available bandwidth.

802.11b—The IEEE standard for a wireless networking technique that uses DSSS (direct sequence spread spectrum) signaling in the 2.4–2.4835-GHz frequency range (also called the 2.4-GHz band). 802.11b separates the 2.4-GHz band into 14 overlapping 22-MHz channels and provides a theoretical maximum of 11-Mbps throughput. 802.11b is also known as Wi-Fi.

802.11g—The IEEE standard for a wireless networking technique designed to be compatible with 802.11b while using different encoding techniques that allow it to reach a theoretical maximum capacity of 54 Mbps. 802.11g, like 802.11b, uses the 2.4-GHz frequency band.

802.15.1—The IEEE standard for wireless personal area network (WPAN) technology, including Bluetooth.

802.3af—The IEEE standard that specifies a way of supplying electrical power over Ethernet (PoE). 802.3af requires CAT 5 or better UTP or STP cabling and uses power sourcing equipment to supply current over a wire pair to powered devices. PoE is compatible with existing 10BASE-T, 100BASE-TX, and 1000BASE-T implementations.

access method—A network's method of controlling how nodes access the communications channel. CSMA/CD (Carrier Sense Multiple Access with Collision Detection) is the access method specified in the IEEE 802.3 (Ethernet) standard. CSMA/CA (Carrier Sense Multiple Access with Collision Avoidance) is the access method specified by IEEE 802.11 (wireless LAN) standards.

active monitor—On a Token Ring network, the workstation that maintains timing for token passing, monitors token and frame transmission, detects lost tokens, and corrects problems when a timing error or other disruption occurs. Only one workstation on the ring can act as the active monitor at any given time.

active scanning—A method used by wireless stations to detect the presence of an access point. In active scanning, the station issues a probe to each channel in its frequency range and waits for the access point to respond.

active topology—A topology in which each workstation participates in transmitting data over the network.

association—In the context of wireless networking, the communication that occurs between a station and an access point to enable the station to connect to the network via that access point.

Asynchronous Transfer Mode—See *ATM*.

ATM (Asynchronous Transfer Mode)—A Data Link layer technology originally conceived in 1983 at Bell Labs, and standardized by the ITU in the mid-1990s. It relies on fixed packets, called cells, that each consist of 48 bytes of data plus a 5-byte header. ATM relies on virtual circuits and establishes a connection before sending data. Having a reliable connection therefore allows network managers to specify QoS levels for certain types of traffic.

beacon frame—In the context of wireless networking, a frame issued by an access point to alert other nodes of its existence.

Bluetooth—A wireless networking standard that uses FHSS (frequency hopping spread spectrum) signaling in the 2.4-GHz band to achieve a maximum throughput of either 723 Kbps or 2.1 Mbps, depending on the version. Bluetooth was designed for use primarily with small office or home networks in which multiple devices (including cordless phones, computers, and pagers) are connected.

Bluetooth Special Interest Group (SIG)—A consortium of companies, including Sony Ericsson, Intel, Nokia, Toshiba, and IBM, that formally banded together in 1998 to refine and standardize Bluetooth technology.

bus—The single cable connecting all devices in a bus topology.

bus topology—A topology in which a single cable connects all nodes on a network without intervening connectivity devices.

Carrier Sense Multiple Access with Collision Avoidance—See *CSMA/CA*.

Carrier Sense Multiple Access with Collision Detection—See *CSMA/CD*.

cell—A packet of a fixed size. In ATM technology, a cell consists of 48 bytes of data plus a 5-byte header.

circuit switching—A type of switching in which a connection is established between two network nodes before they begin transmitting data. Bandwidth is dedicated to this connection and remains available until users terminate the communication between the two nodes.

collapsed backbone—A type of backbone that uses a router or switch as the single central connection point for multiple subnetworks.

collision—In Ethernet networks, the interference of one network node's data transmission with another network node's data transmission.

collision domain—The portion of an Ethernet network in which collisions could occur if two nodes transmit data at the same time.

CSMA/CA (Carrier Sense Multiple Access with Collision Avoidance)—A network access method used on 802.11 wireless networks. In CSMA/CA, before a node begins to send data it checks the medium. If it detects no transmission activity, it waits a brief, random amount of time, and then sends its transmission. If the node does detect activity, it waits a brief period of time before checking the channel again. CSMA/CA does not eliminate, but minimizes, the potential for collisions.

CSMA/CD (Carrier Sense Multiple Access with Collision Detection)—A network access method specified for use by IEEE 802.3 (Ethernet) networks. In CSMA/CD, each node waits its turn before transmitting data, to avoid interfering with other nodes' transmissions. If a node's NIC determines that its data has been involved in a collision, it immediately stops transmitting. Next, in a process called jamming, the NIC issues a special 32-bit sequence that indicates to the rest of the network nodes that its previous transmission was faulty and that those data frames are invalid. After waiting, the NIC determines if the line is again available; if it is available, the NIC retransmits its data.

daisy chain—A group of connectivity devices linked together in a serial fashion.

data propagation delay—The length of time data takes to travel from one point on the segment to another point. On Ethernet networks, CSMA/CD's collision detection routine cannot operate accurately if the data propagation delay is too long.

DB-9 connector—A connector containing nine pins that is used on STP-based Token Ring networks.

distributed backbone—A type of backbone in which a number of connectivity devices (usually hubs) are connected to a series of central connectivity devices, such as hubs, switches, or routers, in a hierarchy.

enterprise—An entire organization, including local and remote offices, a mixture of computer systems, and a number of departments. Enterprise-wide computing takes into account the breadth and diversity of a large organization's computer needs.

Ethernet_II—The original Ethernet frame type developed by Digital, Intel, and Xerox, before the IEEE began to standardize Ethernet. Ethernet_II contains a 2-byte type field to identify the upper-layer protocol contained in the frame. It supports TCP/IP, AppleTalk, IPX/SPX, and other higher-layer protocols.

FDDI (Fiber Distributed Data Interface)—A networking standard originally specified by ANSI in the mid-1980s and later refined by ISO. FDDI uses a dual fiber-optic ring to transmit data at speeds of 100 Mbps. It was commonly used as a backbone technology in the 1980s and early 1990s, but lost favor as Fast Ethernet technologies emerged in the mid-1990s. FDDI provides excellent reliability and security.

Fiber Distributed Data Interface—See *FDDI*.

High-Speed Token Ring—See *HSTR*.

HSTR (High-Speed Token Ring)—A standard for Token Ring networks that operate at 100 Mbps.

hybrid topology—A physical topology that combines characteristics of more than one simple physical topology.

Infrared Data Association—See *IrDA*.

IrDA (Infrared Data Association)—A nonprofit organization founded in 1994 to develop and promote standards for wireless communication using infrared signals. IrDA is also used to denote the type of wireless technology this group has developed.

jamming—A part of CSMA/CD in which, upon detecting a collision, a station issues a special 32-bit sequence to indicate to all nodes on an Ethernet segment that its previously transmitted frame has suffered a collision and should be considered faulty.

LAN Emulation—See *LANE*.

LANE (LAN Emulation)—A method for transporting Token Ring or Ethernet frames over ATM networks. LANE encapsulates incoming Ethernet or Token Ring frames, then converts them into ATM cells for transmission over an ATM network.

logical topology—A characteristic of network transmission that reflects the way in which data is transmitted between nodes (which may differ from the physical layout of the paths that data takes). The most common logical topologies are bus and ring.

message switching—A type of switching in which a connection is established between two devices in the connection path; one device transfers data to the second device, then breaks the connection. The information is stored and forwarded from the second device after a connection between that device and a third device on the path is established.

network access method—See *access method*.

packet switching—A type of switching in which data is broken into packets before it is transported. In packet switching, packets can travel any path on the network to their destination, because each packet contains a destination address and sequencing information.

padding—The bytes added to the data (or information) portion of an Ethernet frame to ensure this field is at least 46 bytes in size. Padding has no effect on the data carried by the frame.

PAN (personal area network)—A small (usually home) network composed of personal communications devices.

parallel backbone—A type of backbone that consists of more than one connection from the central router or switch to each network segment.

passive scanning—In the context of wireless networking, the process in which a station listens to several channels within a frequency range for a beacon issued by an access point.

PD (powered device)—On a network using Power over Ethernet, a node that receives power from power sourcing equipment.

personal area network—See *PAN*.

physical topology—The physical layout of a network. A physical topology depicts a network in broad scope; it does not specify devices, connectivity methods, or addresses on the network. Physical topologies are categorized into three fundamental geometric shapes: bus, ring, and star. These shapes can be mixed to create hybrid topologies.

piconet—A PAN (personal area network) that relies on Bluetooth transmission technology.

PoE (Power over Ethernet)—A method of delivering current to devices using Ethernet connection cables.

Power over Ethernet—See *PoE*.

power sourcing equipment—See *PSE*.

powered device—See *PD*.

preamble—The field in an Ethernet frame that signals to the receiving node that data is incoming and indicates when the data flow is about to begin.

probe—In 802.11 wireless networking, a type of frame issued by a station during active scanning to find nearby access points.

PSE (power sourcing equipment)—On a network using Power over Ethernet, the device that supplies power to end nodes.

quality of service (QoS)—The result of standards for delivering data within a certain period of time after their transmission. For example, ATM networks can supply four QoS levels, from a "best effort" attempt for noncritical data to a guaranteed, real-time transmission for time-sensitive data.

reassociation—In the context of wireless networking, the process of a station establishing a connection (or associating) with a different access point.

Request to Send/Clear to Send—See *RTS/CTS*.

ring topology—A network layout in which each node is connected to the two nearest nodes so that the entire network forms a circle. Data is transmitted unidirectionally around the ring. Each workstation accepts and responds to packets addressed to it, then forwards the other packets to the next workstation in the ring.

RTS/CTS (Request to Send/Clear to Send)—An exchange in which a wireless station requests the exclusive right to communicate with an access point and the access point confirms that it has granted that request.

scanning—The process a wireless station undergoes to find an access point. See also *active scanning* and *passive scanning*.

scatternet—A network composed of multiple piconets using Bluetooth transmission technology.

serial backbone—A type of backbone that consists of two or more internetworking devices connected to each other by a single cable in a daisy-chain fashion. Hubs are often connected in this way to extend a network.

Service Set Identifier—See *SSID*.

SFD (start-of-frame delimiter)—A 1-byte field that indicates where the data field begins in an Ethernet frame.

shared Ethernet—A version of Ethernet in which all the nodes share a common channel and a fixed amount of bandwidth.

signal bounce—A phenomenon, caused by improper termination on a bus-topology network, in which signals travel endlessly between the two ends of the network, preventing new signals from getting through.

SSID (Service Set Identifier)—A unique character string used to identify an access point on an 802.11 network.

star topology—A physical topology in which every node on the network is connected through a central device, such as a hub. Any single physical wire on a star network connects only two devices, so a cabling problem will affect only two nodes. Nodes transmit data to the hub, which then retransmits the data to the rest of the network segment where the destination node can pick it up.

star-wired bus topology—A hybrid topology in which groups of workstations are connected in a star fashion to hubs that are networked via a single bus.

star-wired ring topology—A hybrid topology that uses the physical layout of a star and the token-passing data transmission method.

start-of-frame delimiter (SFD)—See *SFD*.

switched Ethernet—An Ethernet model that enables multiple nodes to simultaneously transmit and receive data and individually take advantage of more bandwidth because they are assigned separate logical network segments through switching.

switching—A component of a network's logical topology that manages how packets are filtered and forwarded between nodes on the network.

terminator—A resistor that is attached to each end of a bus-topology network and that causes the signal to stop rather than reflect back toward its source.

token passing—A means of data transmission in which a 3-byte packet, called a token, is passed around the network in a round-robin fashion.

type 1 IBM connector—A type of Token Ring connector that uses interlocking tabs that snap into an identical connector when one is flipped upside-down, making for a secure connection. Type 1 IBM connectors are used on STP-based Token Ring networks.

virtual circuit—A connection between network nodes that, although based on potentially disparate physical links, logically appears to be a direct, dedicated link between those nodes.

Wi-Fi—See *802.11b*.

wireless personal area network—See *WPAN*.

WPAN (wireless personal area network)—A small office or home network in which devices such as mobile telephones, PDAs, laptops, and computers are connected via wireless transmission.

Review Questions

1. A _____ topology does not specify device types, connectivity methods, or addressing schemes for the network.

   a. logical

   b. ring

   c. physical

   d. bus

2. The term _____ topology refers to the way in which data is transmitted between nodes, rather than the physical layout of the paths that data takes.

   a. logical

   b. ring

   c. physical

   d. bus

3. In _____, a connection is established between two network nodes before they begin transmitting data.

    a. modular routing

    b. static routing

    c. packet switching

    d. circuit switching

4. _____ is a network technology whose standards were originally specified by ANSI in the mid-1980s and later refined by ISO.

    a. IEEE

    b. FDDI

    c. ISA

    d. IRQ

5. _____ is an ITU networking standard describing Data Link layer protocols for both network access and signal multiplexing.

    a. Cut-Through Mode

    b. Open Shortest Path First

    c. Industry Standard Architecture

    d. Asynchronous Transfer Mode

6. True or false? In a bus topology, every node on the network is connected through a central device, such as a hub or a switch.

7. True or false? Packets need not follow each other along the same path, nor must they arrive at their destination in the same sequence as when they left.

8. True or false? In active scanning, the station transmits a special frame, known as a probe, on all available channels within its frequency range.

9. True or false? 802.11g is a mobile wireless networking standard that uses FHSS RF signaling in the 2.4 GHz band.

10. True or false? Quality of Service is a standard that specifies that data will be delivered within a certain period of time after it is sent.

11. A(n) _____ topology consists of a single cable connecting all nodes on a network without intervening connectivity devices.

12. A(n) _____ consists of a number of connectivity devices connected to a series of central connectivity devices, such as hubs, switches, or routers, in a hierarchy.

13. A network's _____ is its method of controlling how network nodes access the communications channel.

14. _____ enables multiple nodes to simultaneously transmit and receive data over different logical network segments.

15. In _____, a 3-byte packet, called a token, is transmitted from one node to another in a circular fashion around the ring.

Chapter 7

WANs, Internet Access, and Remote Connectivity

After reading this chapter and completing the exercises, you will be able to:

■ Identify a variety of uses for WANs

■ Explain different WAN topologies, including their advantages and disadvantages

■ Describe several WAN transmission and connection methods, including PSTN, ISDN, T-carriers, DSL, broadband cable, SONET, and wireless Internet access technologies

■ Compare the characteristics of WAN technologies, including throughput, security, and reliability

■ Describe the hardware and software requirements for remotely connecting to a network

ow that you understand the basic transmission media, network models, and networking hardware associated with LANs (local area networks), you need to expand that knowledge to encompass WANs (wide area networks). As you have learned, a WAN is a network that connects two or more geographically distinct LANs. You might assume that WANs are the same as LANs, only bigger. Although a WAN is based on the same principles as a LAN, including reliance on the OSI Model, its distance requirements affect its entire infrastructure. As a result, WANs differ from LANs in nearly every respect.

To understand the difference between a LAN and WAN, think of the hallways and stairs of your house as LAN pathways. These interior passages allow you to go from room to room. To reach destinations outside your house, however, you need to use sidewalks and streets. These public thoroughfares are analogous to WAN pathways—except that WAN pathways are not necessarily public.

This chapter discusses the technical differences between LANs and WANs and describes in detail WAN transmission media and methods. It also notes the potential pitfalls in establishing and maintaining WANs. In addition, it introduces you to remote connectivity for LANs—a technology that, in some cases, can be used to extend a LAN into a WAN. Remote connectivity and WANs are significant concerns for organizations attempting to meet the needs of telecommuting workers, global business partners, and Internet-based commerce. To pass the Network+ certification exam, you must be familiar with the variety of WAN and remote connectivity options. You also need to understand the hardware and software requirements for dial-up networking.

WAN Essentials

A WAN is a network that traverses some distance and usually connects LANs, whether across the city or across the nation. You are probably familiar with at least one WAN—the Internet, which is the largest WAN in existence today. However, the Internet is not a typical WAN. Most WANs arise from the simple need to connect one building to another. As an organization grows, the WAN might grow to connect more and more sites, located across the city or around the world. Only an organization's information technology budget and aspirations limit the dimensions of its WAN.

Why might an organization need a WAN? Any business or government institution with sites scattered over a wide geographical area needs a way to exchange data between those sites. Each of the following scenarios demonstrates a need for a WAN:

◆ A bank with offices around the state needs to connect those offices to gather trans-action and account information into a central database.

◆ Regional sales representatives for a national pharmaceutical company need to submit their sales figures to a file server at the company's headquarters and receive e-mail from the company's mail server.

◆ An automobile manufacturer in Detroit contracts out its plastic parts manufacturing to a Delaware-based company. Through WAN links, the auto manufacturer can videoconference with the plastics manufacturer, exchange specification data, and even examine the parts for quality online.

◆ A clothing manufacturer sells its products over the Internet to customers throughout the world.

◆ Although all of these businesses need WANs, they may not need the same kinds of WANs. Depending on the traffic load, budget, geographical breadth, and commercially available technology, each might implement a different transmission method. For every business need, only a few (or possibly only one) appropriate WAN connection types may exist. However, many WAN technologies can coexist on the same network.

WANs and LANs are similar in some fundamental ways. They both are designed to enable communication between clients and hosts for resource sharing. In general, both use the same protocols from Layers 3 and higher of the OSI Model. And both networks typically carry dig-itized data via packet-switched connections.

However, LANs and WANs often differ at Layers 1 and 2 of the OSI Model, in access meth-ods, topologies, and sometimes, media. They also differ in the extent to which the organiza-tion that uses the network is responsible for the network. LANs use a building's internal cabling, such as twisted-pair, that runs from work area to the wall, through plenum areas and to a telecommunications closet. Such wiring is private; it belongs to the building owner. In con-trast, WANs typically send data over publicly available communications networks, which are owned by local and long-distance telecommunications carriers. Such carriers, which are pri-vately owned corporations, are also known as **NSPs (network service providers)**. Some pop-ular NSPs include AT&T, PSInet, Sprintlink, and UUNET (MCI Worldcom). Customers lease connections from these carriers, paying them to use a specified amount of bandwidth on their networks. For better throughput, an organization might lease a **dedicated** line, or a con-tinuously available communications channel, from a telecommunications provider, such as a local telephone company or ISP. Dedicated lines come in a variety of types that are distin-guished by their capacity and transmission characteristics.

The individual geographic locations connected by a WAN are known as WAN sites. A **WAN link** is a connection between one WAN site (or point) and another site (or point). A WAN link is typically described as point-to-point—because it connects one site to only one other site. That is, the link does not connect one site to several other sites, in the way that LAN hubs or switches connect multiple segments or workstations. Nevertheless, one location may be con-nected to more than one location by multiple WAN links. Figure 7-1 illustrates the difference between WAN and LAN connectivity.

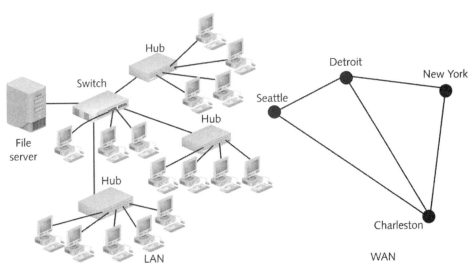

FIGURE 7-1 *Differences in LAN and WAN connectivity*

The following section describes different topologies used on WANs.

WAN Topologies

WAN topologies resemble LAN topologies, but their details differ because of the distance they must cover, the larger number of users they serve, and the heavy traffic they often handle. For example, WAN topologies connect sites via dedicated and, usually, high-speed links. As a consequence, WANs use different connectivity devices. For example, to connect two buildings via high-speed T1 carrier lines, each location must use a special type of terminating device, a multiplexer, plus a router. And because WAN connections require routers or other Layer 3 devices to connect locations, their links are not capable of carrying nonroutable protocols, such as NetBEUI. The following sections describe common WAN topologies and special considerations for using each.

Bus

A WAN in which each site is directly connected to no more than two other sites in a serial fashion is known as a **bus topology WAN**. A bus topology WAN is similar to a bus topology LAN in that each site depends on every other site in the network to transmit and receive its traffic. However, bus topology LANs use computers with shared access to one cable, whereas the WAN bus topology uses different locations, each one connected to another one through point-to-point links.

A bus topology WAN is often the best option for organizations with only a few sites and the capability to use dedicated circuits. Some examples of dedicated circuits include T1, DSL, and

NET+

1.1

ISDN connections. Dedicated circuits make it possible to transmit data regularly and reliably. Figure 7-2 depicts a bus topology WAN using T1 and DSL connections.

Bus WAN topologies are suitable for only small WANs. Because all sites between the sending and receiving location must participate in carrying traffic, this model does not scale well. The addition of more sites can cause performance to suffer. Also, a single failure on a bus topology WAN can take down communications between all sites.

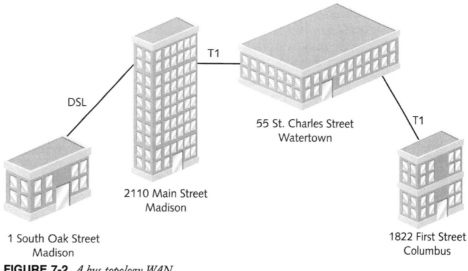

FIGURE 7-2 *A bus topology WAN*

Ring

In a **ring topology WAN**, each site is connected to two other sites so that the entire WAN forms a ring pattern, as shown in Figure 7-3. This architecture is similar to the simple ring topology used on a LAN, except that a WAN ring topology connects locations rather than local nodes and in most WANs, a ring topology uses two parallel paths for data. This means that unlike a ring topology LAN, a ring topology WAN cannot be taken down by the loss of one site; instead, if one site fails, data can be rerouted around the WAN in a different direction. On the other hand, expanding ring-configured WANs can be difficult, and it is more expensive than expanding a bus topology WAN. For these reasons, WANs that use the ring topology are only practical for connecting fewer than four or five locations.

Star

The **star topology WAN** mimics the arrangement of a star topology LAN. A single site acts as the central connection point for several other points, as shown in Figure 7-4. This arrangement provides separate routes for data between any two sites. That means that if a single connection fails, only one location loses WAN access. For example, if the T1 link between the

NET+
1.1

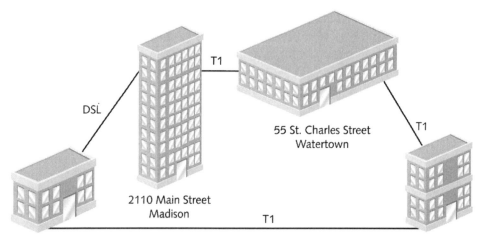

FIGURE 7-3 *A ring topology WAN*

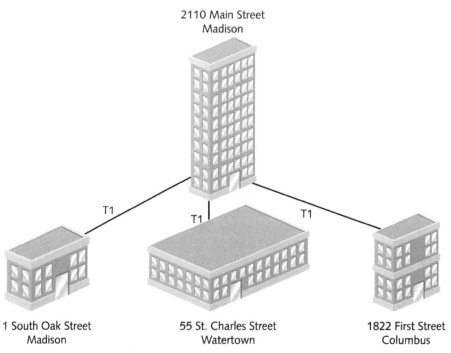

FIGURE 7-4 *A star topology WAN*

NET+
1.1

Oak Street and Main Street locations fails, the Watertown and Columbus locations can still communicate with the Main Street location because they use different routes. In a bus or ring topology, however, a single connection failure would halt all traffic between all sites. Another advantage of a star WAN is that when all of its dedicated circuits are functioning, a star WAN provides shorter data paths between any two sites.

Extending a star WAN is relatively simple and less costly than extending a bus or ring topology WAN. For example, if the organization that uses the star WAN pictured in Figure 7-4 wanted to add a Maple Street, Madison, location to its topology, it could simply lease a new dedicated circuit from the Main Street office to its Maple Street office. None of the other offices would be affected by the change. If the organization were using a bus or ring WAN topology, however, two separate dedicated connections would be required to incorporate the new location into the network.

As with star LAN topologies, the greatest drawback of a star WAN is that a failure at the central connection point can bring down the entire WAN. In Figure 7-4, for example, if the Main Street office suffered a catastrophic fire, the entire WAN would fail. Similarly, if the central connection point is overloaded with traffic, performance on the entire WAN will be adversely affected.

Mesh

A **mesh topology WAN** incorporates many directly interconnected sites. Because every site is interconnected, data can travel directly from its origin to its destination. If one connection suffers a problem, routers can redirect data easily and quickly. Mesh WANs are the most fault-tolerant type of WAN because they provide multiple routes for data to follow between any two points. For example, if the Madison office in Figure 7-5 suffered a catastrophic fire, the Dubuque office could still send and transmit data to and from the Detroit office by going directly to the Detroit office. If both the Madison and Detroit offices failed, the Dubuque and Indianapolis offices could still communicate.

The type of mesh topology in which every WAN site is directly connected to every other site is called a **full mesh WAN**. One drawback to a full mesh WAN is the cost. If more than a few sites are involved, connecting every site to every other requires leasing a large number of dedicated circuits. As WANs grow larger, the expense multiplies. To reduce costs, a network administrator might choose to implement a **partial mesh WAN**, in which only critical WAN sites are directly interconnected and secondary sites are connected through star or ring topologies, as shown in Figure 7-5. Partial mesh WANs are more common in today's business world than full mesh WANs because they are more economical.

Tiered

In a **tiered topology WAN**, sites connected in star or ring formations are interconnected at different levels, with the interconnection points being organized into layers to form hierarchical groupings. Figure 7-6 depicts a tiered WAN. In this example, the Madison, Detroit, and New

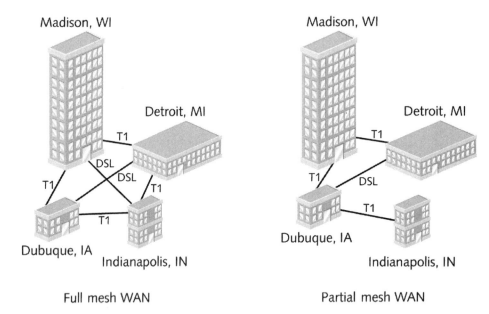

FIGURE 7-5 *Full mesh and partial mesh WANs*

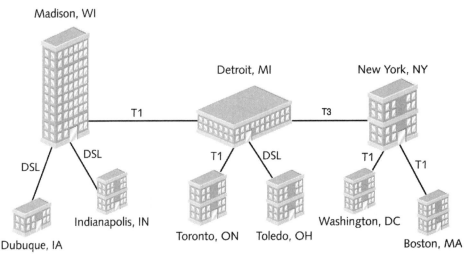

FIGURE 7-6 *A tiered topology WAN*

York offices form the upper tier, and the Dubuque, Indianapolis, Toronto, Toledo, Washington, and Boston offices form the lower tier. If the Detroit office suffers a failure, the Toronto and Toledo offices cannot communicate with any other nodes on the WAN, nor can the Washington, Boston, and New York locations exchange data with the other six locations. Yet the Washington, Boston, and New York locations can still exchange data with each other, as can the Indianapolis, Dubuque, and Madison locations.

Variations on this topology abound. Indeed, flexibility makes the tiered approach quite practical. A network architect can determine the best placement of top-level routers based on traffic patterns or critical data paths. In addition, tiered systems allow for easy expansion and inclusion of redundant links to support growth. On the other hand, their enormous flexibility means that creation of tiered WANs requires careful consideration of geography, usage patterns, and growth potential.

Now that you understand the fundamental shapes that WANs may take, you are ready to learn about specific technologies and types. WAN technologies discussed in the following sections differ in terms of speed, reliability, cost, distance covered, and security. Also, some are defined by specifications at the Data Link layer, whereas others are defined by specifications at the Physical layer of the OSI Model. As you learn about each technology, pay attention to its characteristics and think about its possible applications. To qualify for Network+ certification, you must be familiar with the variety of WAN connection types and be able to identify the networking environments that each suits best.

PSTN

NET+
2.15

PSTN, which stands for **Public Switched Telephone Network**, refers to the network of typical telephone lines and carrier equipment that service most homes. PSTN may also be called **POTS (plain old telephone service)**. It was originally composed of analog lines and designed to handle voice-based traffic. The PSTN comprises the entire telephone system, from the lines that connect homes and businesses to the network centers that connect different regions of a country. Now, except for the lines connecting homes, nearly all of the PSTN uses digital transmission. Its traffic is carried by fiber-optic and copper twisted-pair cable, microwave, and satellite connections. The PSTN is often used by individuals connecting to a WAN (such as the Internet) via a dial-up connection. A **dial-up** connection is one in which a user connects, via a modem, to a distant network from a computer and stays connected for a finite period of time. Most of the time, the term dial-up refers to a connection that uses a PSTN line.

When computers connect via the PSTN, modems are necessary at both the source and destination, because not all of the PSTN is capable of handling digital transmission. A modem converts a computer's digital pulses into analog signals before it issues them to the telephone line, then converts the analog signals back into digital pulses at the receiving computer's end. Unlike other types of WAN connections, dial-up connections provide a fixed period of access to the network, just as the phone call you make to a friend has a fixed length, determined by when you initiate and terminate the call.

Between the two modems, a signal travels through a carrier's network of switches and, possibly, long-distance connections. To understand this network, it's useful to trace the path of a dial-up call. Imagine you dial into your ISP to surf the Web through a 56-Kbps modem. You first initiate a call through your computer's dial-up software, which instructs your modem to dial the number for your ISP's remote access server. Next, your modem attempts to establish a connection. It then converts the digital signal from your computer into an analog signal that travels over the phone line to the local telephone company's network until it reaches the **central office**. A central office is the place where a telephone company terminates lines and switches calls between different locations. Between your house and a central office, the call might go through one or more of the telephone company's remote switching facilities. The portion of the PSTN that connects your house to the nearest central office is known as the **local loop**, or the **last mile**, and is illustrated in Figure 7-7.

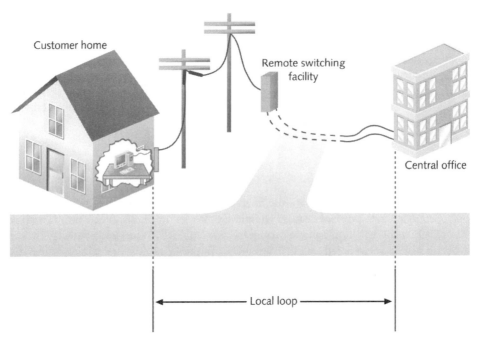

FIGURE 7-7 *Local loop portion of the PSTN*

At either a remote switching facility or at the central office, your signal is converted back to digital pulses. If your home and your ISP share the same central office, the signal is switched from your incoming connection to your ISP's connection. In most cases, the ISP would have a dedicated connection to a central office. If so, your signal is issued over this dedicated connection multiplexed together with many other signals. But suppose you are dialing your ISP from a hotel in another city. The first part of the process is the same as if you were at home—you initiate a call and connect to the local telephone company's central office, where your signal is converted to digital pulses. However, this time your signal cannot go straight to your ISP, because your ISP doesn't have a connection in that carrier's central office. Instead, the local telephone company forwards the signal to a regional central office. This regional office may have to forward the signal to a second regional office, if you are far from the ISP. The closest regional central office to your ISP directs the signal to your ISP's local central office. Finally, the signal is sent to the ISP's location. Figure 7-8 illustrates the path a signal takes in a long-distance dial-up connection.

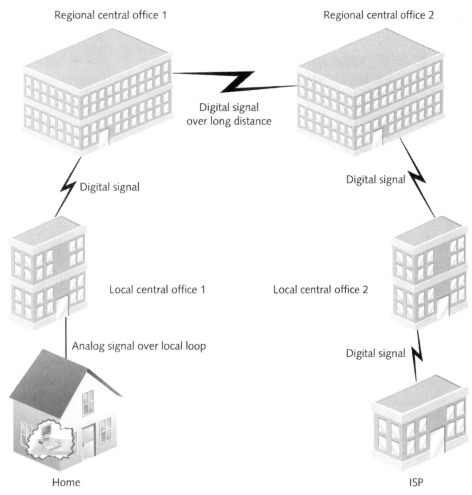

FIGURE 7-8 *A long-distance dial-up connection*

The advantages to using the PSTN are its ubiquity, ease of use, and low cost. A person can travel virtually anywhere in the world and have access to a phone line and, therefore, remote access to a network. Within the United States, the dial-up configuration for one location differs little from the dial-up configuration in another location. And nearly all mobile personal computers contain a modem, the only peripheral hardware a computer requires to establish this type of connection.

But, the PSTN comes with significant disadvantages. Most limiting is its low throughput. Currently, manufacturers of PSTN modems advertise a connection speed of 56 Kbps. However, the 56-Kbps maximum is only a *theoretical* threshold that assumes that the connection between the initiator and the receiver is pristine. Splitters, fax machines, or other devices that a signal

NET+
2.15

must navigate between the sender and receiver all reduce the actual throughput. The number of central offices, switches, and modems through which your phone call travels also affect throughput. Each time the signal passes through a switch or is converted from analog to digital or digital to analog, it loses a little throughput. If you're surfing the Web, for example, by the time a Web page returns to you, the connection may have lost from 5 to 30 Kbps, and your effective throughput might have been reduced to 30 Kbps or less. In addition, the FCC (Federal Communications Commission), the regulatory agency that sets standards and policy for telecommunications transmission and equipment in the United States, limits the use of PSTN lines to 53 Kbps to reduce the effects of crosstalk. Thus, you will never actually achieve full 56-Kbps throughput using a modem over the PSTN.

Nor can the PSTN provide the quality required by many network applications. The quality of a WAN connection is largely determined by how many data packets that it loses or that become corrupt during transmission, how quickly it can transmit and receive data, and whether it drops the connection altogether. To improve this quality, most protocols employ error checking techniques. For example, TCP/IP depends on acknowledgments of the data it receives. In addition, many (though not all) PSTN links are now digital, and digital lines are more reliable than the older analog lines. Such digital lines reduce the quality problems that once plagued purely analog PSTN connections.

Although nearly all central offices in the PSTN handle digitized data, most still use circuit switching rather than the more efficient packet switching. Recall that in circuit switching, data travels over a point-to-point connection that is reserved by a transmission until all of its data has been transferred. You might think that circuit switching makes the PSTN more secure than other types of WAN connections; in fact, the PSTN offers only marginal security. Because it is a public network, PSTN presents many points at which communications can be intercepted and interpreted on their way from sender to receiver. For example, an eavesdropper could easily tap into the connection where your local telephone company's line enters your house.

The PSTN is not limited to servicing workstation dial-up WAN connections. Following sections describe other, more sophisticated WAN technologies that also rely on the public telephone network.

X.25 and Frame Relay

NET+
2.14

X.25 is an analog, packet-switched technology designed for long-distance data transmission and standardized by the ITU in the mid-1970s. The original standard for X.25 specified a maximum of 64-Kbps throughput, but by 1992 the standard was updated to include maximum throughput of 2.048 Mbps. It was originally developed as a more reliable alternative to the voice telephone system for connecting mainframe computers and remote terminals. Later it was adopted as a method of connecting clients and servers over WANs.

The X.25 standard specifies protocols at the Physical, Data Link, and Network layers of the OSI Model. It provides excellent flow control and ensures data reliability over long distances by verifying the transmission at every node. Unfortunately, this verification also renders X.25

NET+
2.14

comparatively slow and unsuitable for time-sensitive applications, such as audio or video. On the other hand, X.25 benefits from being a long-established, well-known, and low-cost technology. X.25 was never widely adopted in the United States, but was accepted by other countries and was for a long time the dominant packet-switching technology used on WANs around the world.

> ### NOTE
>
> Recall that, in packet switching, packets belonging to the same data stream may follow different, optimal paths to their destination. As a result, packet switching uses bandwidth more efficiently and allows for faster transmission than if each packet in the data stream had to follow the same path, as in circuit switching. Packet switching is also more flexible than circuit switching, because packet sizes may vary.

Frame Relay is an updated, digital version of X.25 that also relies on packet switching. ITU and ANSI standardized Frame Relay in 1984. However, because of a lack of compatibility with other WAN technologies at the time, Frame Relay did not become popular in the United States and Canada until the late 1980s. Frame Relay protocols operate at the Data Link layer of the OSI Model and can support multiple different Network and Transport layer protocols (for example, TCP/IP and IPX/SPX). The name is derived from the fact that data is separated into frames, which are then relayed from one node to another without any verification or processing.

An important difference between Frame Relay and X.25 is that Frame Relay does not guarantee reliable delivery of data. X.25 checks for errors and, in the case of an error, either corrects the damaged data or retransmits the original data. Frame Relay, on the other hand, simply checks for errors. It leaves the error correction up to higher-layer protocols. Partly because it doesn't perform the same level of error correction that X.25 performs (and thus has less overhead), Frame Relay supports higher throughput than X.25. It offers throughputs between 64 Kbps and 45 Mbps. A Frame Relay customer chooses the amount of bandwidth he requires and pays for only that amount.

Both X.25 and Frame Relay may be configured as SVCs (switched virtual circuits) or PVCs (permanent virtual circuits). **SVCs** are connections that are established when parties need to transmit, then terminated after the transmission is complete. **PVCs** are connections that are established before data needs to be transmitted and maintained after the transmission is complete. Note that in a PVC, the connection is established only between the two points (the sender and receiver); the connection does not specify the exact route the data will travel. Thus, in a PVC, data may follow any number of paths from point A to point B. For example, a transmission traveling over a PVC from Baltimore to Phoenix might go from Baltimore to Washington, D.C., to Chicago, then to Phoenix; the next transmission over that PVC, however, might go from Baltimore to Boston to St. Louis to Denver to Phoenix.

PVCs are *not* dedicated, individual links. When you lease an X.25 or Frame Relay circuit from your local carrier, your contract reflects the endpoints you specify and the amount of bandwidth you require between those endpoints. The service provider guarantees a minimum amount of bandwidth, called the **CIR (committed information rate)**. Provisions usually account for bursts of traffic that occasionally exceed the CIR. When you lease a PVC, you share bandwidth with the other X.25 and Frame Relay users on the backbone. PVC links are best suited to frequent and consistent data transmission.

On networking diagrams, packet-switched networks such as X.25 and Frame Relay are depicted as clouds, as shown in Figure 7-9, because of the indeterminate nature of their traffic patterns.

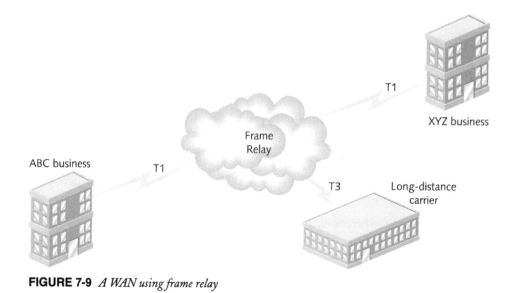

FIGURE 7-9 *A WAN using frame relay*

 NOTE

You may have seen the Internet depicted as a cloud on networking diagrams, similar to the Frame Relay cloud in Figure 7-9. In its early days, the Internet relied largely on X.25 and Frame Relay transmission—hence the similar illustration.

The advantage to leasing a Frame Relay circuit over leasing a dedicated service is that you pay for only the amount of bandwidth required. Another advantage is that Frame Relay is much less expensive than some newer WAN technologies offered today. Also, Frame Relay is a long-established worldwide standard.

On the other hand, because Frame Relay and X.25 use shared lines, their throughput remains at the mercy of variable traffic patterns. In the middle of the night, data over your Frame Relay

NET+
2.14

network may zip along at 1.544 Mbps; during midday, when everyone is surfing the Web, it may slow down to less than your CIR. In addition, Frame Relay circuits are not as private (and potentially not as secure) as dedicated circuits. Nevertheless, because they use the same connectivity equipment as T-carriers, they can easily be upgraded to T-carrier dedicated lines.

ISDN

NET+
2.14

ISDN (Integrated Services Digital Network) is an international standard, originally established by the ITU in 1984, for transmitting digital data over the PSTN. In North America, a standard ISDN implementation wasn't finalized until 1992, because telephone switch manufacturers couldn't agree on compatible technology for supporting ISDN. The technology's uncertain start initially made telephone companies reluctant to invest in it, and ISDN didn't catch on as quickly as predicted. However, in the 1990s ISDN finally became a popular method of connecting WAN locations to exchange both data and voice signals.

ISDN specifies protocols at the Physical, Data Link, and Transport layers of the OSI Model. These protocols handle signaling, framing, connection setup and termination, routing, flow control, and error detection and correction. ISDN relies on the PSTN for its transmission medium. Connections can be either dial-up or dedicated. Dial-up ISDN is distinguished from the workstation dial-up connections discussed previously because it relies exclusively on digital transmission. In other words, it does not convert a computer's digital signals to analog before transmitting them over the PSTN. Also, ISDN is distinguished because it can simultaneously carry as many as two voice calls and one data connection on a single line. Therefore, ISDN can eliminate the need to pay for separate phone lines to support faxes, modems, and voice calls at one location.

All ISDN connections are based on two types of channels: B channels and D channels. The **B channel** is the "bearer" channel, employing circuit-switching techniques to carry voice, video, audio, and other types of data over the ISDN connection. A single B channel has a maximum throughput of 64 Kbps (although it is sometimes limited to 56 Kbps by the ISDN provider). The number of B channels in a single ISDN connection may vary. The **D channel** is the "data" channel, employing packet-switching techniques to carry information about the call, such as session initiation and termination signals, caller identity, call forwarding, and conference calling signals. A single D channel has a maximum throughput of 16 or 64 Kbps, depending on the type of ISDN connection. Each ISDN connection uses only one D channel.

In North America, two types of ISDN connections are commonly used: BRI (Basic Rate Interface) and PRI (Primary Rate Interface). **BRI (Basic Rate Interface)** uses two B channels and one D channel, as indicated by the notation 2B+D. The two B channels are treated as separate connections by the network and can carry voice and data or two data streams simultaneously and separate from each other. In a process called **bonding**, these two 64-Kbps B channels can be combined to achieve an effective throughput of 128 Kbps—the maximum amount of data traffic that a BRI connection can accommodate. Most consumers who subscribe to ISDN from home use BRI, which is the most economical type of ISDN connection.

Figure 7-10 illustrates how a typical BRI link supplies a home consumer with an ISDN link. From the telephone company's lines, the ISDN channels connect to a Network Termination 1 device at the customer's site. The **NT1 (Network Termination 1)** device connects the twisted-pair wiring at the customer's building with the ISDN terminal equipment via RJ-11 (standard telephone) or RJ-45 data jacks. The ISDN **TE (terminal equipment)** may include cards or standalone devices used to connect computers to the ISDN line (similar to a network adapter used on Ethernet or Token Ring networks).

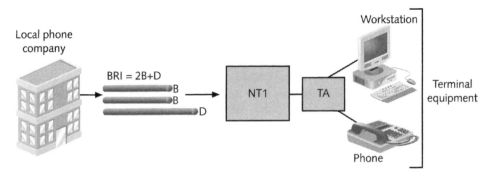

FIGURE 7-10 *A BRI link*

So that the ISDN line can connect to analog equipment, the signal must first pass through a terminal adapter. A **TA (terminal adapter)** converts digital signals into analog signals for use with ISDN phones and other analog devices. (Terminal adapters are sometimes called ISDN modems, though they are not, technically, modems.) Typically, telecommuters who want more throughput than their analog phone line can offer choose BRI as their ISDN connection. For a home user, the terminal adapter would most likely be an ISDN router, whereas the terminal equipment could be an Ethernet card in the user's workstation plus, perhaps, a phone.

 NOTE

The BRI configuration depicted in Figure 7-10 applies to installations in North America only. Because transmission standards differ in Europe and Asia, different numbers of B channels are used in ISDN connections in those regions.

PRI (Primary Rate Interface) uses 23 B channels and one 64-Kbps D channel, as represented by the notation 23B+D. PRI is less commonly used by individual subscribers than BRI is, but it may be selected by businesses and other organizations that need more throughput. As with BRI, the separate B channels in a PRI link can carry voice and data, independently of each other or bonded together. The maximum potential throughput for a PRI connection is 1.544 Mbps.

PRI and BRI connections may be interconnected on a single network. PRI links use the same kind of equipment as BRI links, but require the services of an extra network termination device, called a **NT2 (Network Termination 2)**, to handle the multiple ISDN lines. Figure 7-11 depicts a typical PRI link as it would be installed in North America.

Individual customers who need to transmit more data than a typical modem can handle or who want to use a single line for both data and voice may use ISDN lines. ISDN, although not available in every location of the United States, can be purchased from most local telephone companies. Costs vary depending on the customer's location. PRI and B-ISDN are significantly more expensive than BRI. Dial-up ISDN service is less expensive than dedicated ISDN service. In some areas, ISDN providers charge customers additional usage fees based on the total length of time they remain connected. One disadvantage of ISDN is that it can span a distance of only 18,000 linear feet before repeater equipment is needed to boost the signal. For this reason, it is only feasible to use for the local loop portion of the WAN link.

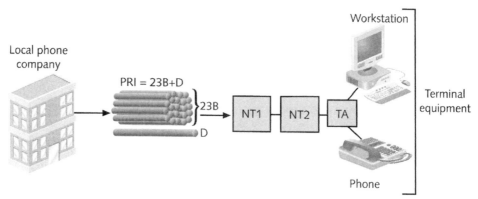

FIGURE 7-11   *A PRI link*

T-Carriers

Another WAN transmission method that grew from a need to transmit digital data at high speeds over the PSTN is T-carrier technology, which includes T1s, fractional T1s, and T3s. **T-carrier** standards specify a method of signaling, which means they belong to the Physical layer of the OSI Model. A T-carrier uses TDM (time division multiplexing) over two wire pairs (one for transmitting and one for receiving) to divide a single channel into multiple channels. For example, multiplexing enables a single T1 circuit to carry 24 channels, each capable of 64-Kbps throughput; thus a T1 has a maximum capacity of 24×64 Kbps, or 1.544 Mbps. Each channel may carry data, voice, or video signals. The medium used for T-carrier signaling can be ordinary telephone wire, fiber-optic cable, or wireless links.

AT&T developed T-carrier technology in 1957 in an effort to digitize voice signals and thereby enable such signals to travel longer distances over the PSTN. Before that time, voice signals, which were purely analog, were expensive to transmit over long distances because of the number of connectivity devices needed to keep the signal intelligible. In the 1970s, many businesses installed T1s to obtain more voice throughput per line. In the 1990s, with increased

NET+
2.14

data communication demands, such as Internet access and geographically dispersed offices, T1s became a popular way to connect WAN sites.

The next section describes the various types of T-carriers, then the chapter moves on to T-carrier connectivity devices.

Types of T-Carriers

A number of T-carrier varieties are available to businesses today, as shown in Table 7-1. The most common T-carrier implementations are T1 and, for higher bandwidth needs, T3. A **T1** circuit can carry the equivalent of 24 voice or data channels, giving a maximum data throughput of 1.544 Mbps. A **T3** circuit can carry the equivalent of 672 voice or data channels, giving a maximum data throughput of 44.736 Mbps (its throughput is typically rounded up to 45 Mbps for the purposes of discussion).

Table 7-1 Carrier specifications

Signal Level	Carrier	Number of T1s	Number of Channels	Throughput (Mbps)
DS0	—	1/24	1	.064
DS1	T1	1	24	1.544
DS1C	T1C	2	24	3.152
DS2	T2	4	96	6.312
DS3	T3	28	672	44.736
DS4	T4	168	4032	274.176

 NOTE

You may hear signal level and carrier terms used interchangeably—for example, DS1 and T1. In fact, T1 is the implementation of the DS1 standard used in North America and most of Asia. In Europe, the standard high-speed carrier connections are **E1** and **E3**. Like T1s and T3s, E1s and E3s use time division multiplexing. However, an E1 allows for 30 channels and offers 2.048-Mbps throughput. An E3 allows for 480 channels and offers 34.368-Mbps throughput. In Japan, the equivalent carrier standards are **J1** and **J3**. Like a T1, a J1 connection allows for 24 channels and offers 1.544-Mbps throughput. A J3 connection allows for 480 channels and offers 32.064-Mbps throughput. Using special hardware, T1s can interconnect with E1s or J1s and T3s with E3s or J3s for international communications.

NET+
2.14

The speed of a T-carrier depends on its signal level. The **signal level** refers to the T-carrier's Physical layer electrical signaling characteristics as defined by ANSI standards in the early 1980s. **DS0 (digital signal, level 0)** is the equivalent of one data or voice channel. All other signal levels are multiples of DS0.

As a networking professional, you are most likely to work with T1 or T3 lines. In addition to knowing their capacity, you should be familiar with their costs and uses. T1s are commonly used by businesses to connect branch offices or to connect to a carrier, such as an ISP. Telephone companies also use T1s to connect their smaller central offices. ISPs may use one or more T1s or T3s, depending on the provider's size, to connect to their Internet carriers.

Because a T3 provides 28 times more throughput than a T1, many organizations may find that multiple T1s—rather than a single T3—can accommodate their throughput needs. For example, suppose a university research laboratory needs to transmit molecular images over the Internet to another university, and its peak throughput need (at any given time) is 10 Mbps. The laboratory would require seven T1s (10 Mbps divided by 1.544 Mbps equals 6.48 T1s). Leasing seven T1s would prove much less expensive for the university than leasing a single T3.

The cost of T1s varies from region to region. On average, leasing a full T1 might cost between $500 and $1500 to install, plus an additional $300 to $1000 per month in access fees. The longer the distance between the provider (such as an ISP or a telephone company) and the subscriber, the higher a T1's monthly charge. For example, a T1 between Houston and New York will cost more than a T1 between Washington, D.C., and New York. Similarly, a T1 from a suburb of New York to the city center will cost more than a T1 from the city center to a business three blocks away.

For organizations that do not need as much as 1.544-Mbps throughput, a fractional T1 might be a better option. A **fractional T1** lease allows organizations to use only some of the channels on a T1 line and be charged according to the number of channels they use. Thus, fractional T1 bandwidth can be leased in multiples of 64 Kbps. A fractional T1 is best suited to businesses that expect their traffic to grow and that may require a full T1 eventually, but can't currently justify leasing a full T1.

T3s are very expensive and are used by the most data-intensive businesses—for example, computer consulting firms that provide online data backups and warehousing for a number of other businesses or large long-distance carriers. A T3 is much more expensive than even multiple T1s. It may cost as much as $3000 to install, plus monthly service fees based on usage. If a customer uses the full T3 bandwidth of 45 Mbps, for example, the monthly charges might be as high as $18,000. Of course, T3 costs will vary depending on the carrier, your location, and the distance covered by the T3. In any event, however, this type of connection is significantly more expensive than a T1. Therefore, only businesses with extraordinary bandwidth requirements should consider using T3s.

T-Carrier Connectivity

The approximate costs mentioned previously include monthly access and installation, but not connectivity hardware. Every T-carrier line requires connectivity hardware at both the customer

NET+
2.14

site and the local telecommunications provider's switching facility. Connectivity hardware may be purchased or leased. If your organization uses an ISP to establish and service your T-carrier line, you will most likely lease the connectivity equipment. If you lease the line directly from the local carrier and you anticipate little change in your connectivity requirements over time, however, you may want to purchase the hardware.

T-carrier lines require specialized connectivity hardware that cannot be used with other WAN transmission methods. In addition, T-carrier lines require different media, depending on their throughput. In the following sections, you will learn about the physical components of a T-carrier connection between a customer site and a local carrier.

Wiring

As mentioned earlier, the T-carrier system is based on AT&T's original attempt to digitize existing long-distance PSTN lines. T1 technology can use UTP or STP (unshielded or shielded twisted-pair) copper wiring—in other words, plain telephone wire—coaxial cable, microwave, or fiber-optic cable as its transmission media. Because the digital signals require a clean connection (that is, one less susceptible to noise and attenuation), STP is preferable to UTP. For T1s using STP, repeaters must regenerate the signal approximately every 6000 feet. Twisted-pair wiring cannot adequately carry the high throughput of multiple T1s or T3 transmissions. Thus, for multiple T1s, coaxial cable, microwave, or fiber-optic cabling may be used. For T3s, microwave or fiber-optic cabling is necessary.

NET+
1.6
2.14

CSU/DSU (Channel Service Unit/Data Service Unit)

Although CSUs (channel service units) and DSUs (data service units) are actually two separate devices, they are typically combined into a single standalone device or an interface card called a **CSU/DSU**. The CSU/DSU is the connection point for a T1 line at the customer's site. The **CSU** provides termination for the digital signal and ensures connection integrity through error correction and line monitoring. The **DSU** converts the T-carrier frames into frames the LAN can interpret and vice versa. It also connects T-carrier lines with terminating equipment. Finally, a DSU usually incorporates a multiplexer. (In some T-carrier installations, the multiplexer can be a separate device connected to the DSU.) For an incoming T-carrier line, the multiplexer separates its combined channels into individual signals that can be interpreted on the LAN. For an outgoing T-carrier line, the multiplexer combines multiple signals from a LAN for transport over the T-carrier. After being demultiplexed, an incoming T-carrier signal passes on to devices collectively known as terminal equipment. Examples of terminal equipment include switches, routers, or telephone exchange devices that accept only voice transmissions (such as a telephone switch).

Figure 7-12 depicts a typical use of a CSU/DSU with a point-to-point T1-connected WAN. In the following sections, you will learn how routers and switches integrate with CSU/DSUs and multiplexers to connect T-carriers to a LAN.

NET+
1.6
2.14

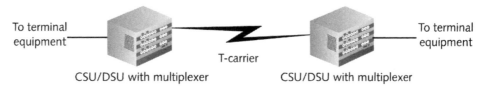

FIGURE 7-12 *A point-to-point T-carrier connection*

Terminal Equipment

On a typical T1-connected data network, the terminal equipment will consist of switches, routers, or bridges. Usually, a router or Layer 3 or higher switch is the best option, because these devices can translate between different Layer 3 protocols that might be used on the WAN and LAN. The router or switch accepts incoming signals from a CSU/DSU and, if necessary, translates Network layer protocols, then directs data to its destination exactly as it does on any LAN.

On some implementations, the CSU/DSU is not a separate device, but is integrated with the router or switch as an expansion card. Compared to a standalone CSU/DSU, which must connect to the terminal equipment via a cable, an integrated CSU/DSU offers faster signal processing and better network performance. In most cases, it is also a less expensive and lower-maintenance solution than using a separate CSU/DSU device. Figure 7-13 illustrates

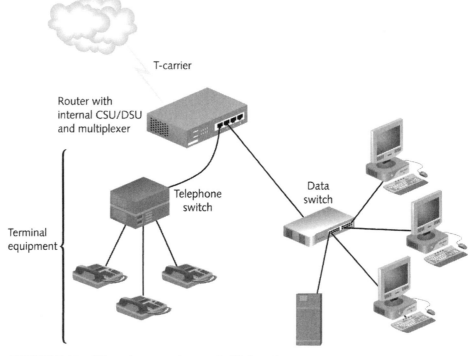

FIGURE 7-13 *A T-carrier connection to a LAN through a router*

NET+
1.6
2.14
one way a router with an integrated CSU/DSU can be used to connect a LAN with a T1 WAN link.

DSL

NET+
2.15
DSL (digital subscriber line) is a WAN connection method introduced by researchers at Bell Laboratories in the mid-1990s. It operates over the PSTN and competes directly with ISDN and T1 services. Like ISDN, DSL can span only limited distances without the help of repeaters and is therefore best suited to the local loop portion of a WAN link. Also, like its competitors, DSL can support multiple data and voice channels over a single line.

DSL uses advanced data modulation techniques (which are Physical layer functions) to achieve extraordinary throughput over regular telephone lines. To understand how DSL and voice signals can share the same line, it's helpful to recall that telephone lines carry voice signals over a very small range of frequencies, between 300 and 3300 Hz. This leaves higher, inaudible frequencies unused and available for carrying data. Also recall that in data modulation, a data signal alters the properties of a carrier signal. Depending on its version, DSL connection may use a modulation technique based on amplitude or phase modulation. However, in DSL, modulation follows more complex patterns than the modulation you learned about earlier in this book. The details of DSL modulation techniques are beyond the scope of this book. However, you should understand that the types of modulation used by a DSL version affect its throughput and the distance its signals can travel before requiring a repeater. The following section describes the different versions of DSL.

Types of DSL

The term **xDSL** refers to all DSL varieties, of which at least eight currently exist. The better-known DSL varieties include ADSL (asymmetric DSL), G.Lite (a version of ADSL), HDSL (High Bit-Rate DSL), SDSL (Symmetric or Single-Line DSL), VDSL (Very High Bit-Rate DSL), and SHDSL (Single-Line High Bit-Rate DSL)—the "x" in "xDSL" is replaced by the variety name. DSL types can be divided into two categories: asymmetrical and symmetrical.

To understand the difference between these two categories, you must understand the concepts of downstream and upstream data transmission. The term **downstream** refers to data traveling from the carrier's switching facility to the customer. **Upstream** refers to data traveling from the customer to the carrier's switching facility. In some types of DSL, the throughput rates for downstream and upstream traffic differ. That is, if you were connected to the Internet via a DSL link, you would be able to download images from the Internet more rapidly than you could send them because the downstream throughput would be greater. A technology that offers more throughput in one direction than in the other is considered **asymmetrical**. In asymmetrical communications, downstream throughput is higher than upstream throughput. Asymmetrical communication is well suited to users who receive more information from the network than they send to it—for example, people watching videoconferences or people surfing the Web. ADSL and VDSL are examples of **asymmetrical DSL**.

NET+
2.15

Conversely, **symmetrical** technology provides equal capacity for data traveling both upstream and downstream. Symmetrical transmission is suited to users who both upload and download significant amounts of data—for example, a bank's branch office, which sends large volumes of account information to the central server at the bank's headquarters and, in turn, receives large amounts of account information from the central server at the bank's headquarters. HDSL, SDSL, and SHDSL are examples of **symmetrical DSL**.

DSL versions also differ in the type of modulation they use. Some, such as the popular full-rate ADSL and VDSL, create multiple narrow channels in the higher frequency range to carry more data. For these versions, a splitter must be installed at the carrier and at the customer's premises to separate the data signal from the voice signal before it reaches the terminal equipment (for example, the phone or the computer). G.Lite, a slower and less expensive version of ADSL, eliminates the splitter but requires the use of a filter to prevent high frequency DSL signals from reaching the telephone. Other types of DSL, such as HDSL and SDSL, cannot use the same wire pair that is used for voice signals. Instead, these types of DSL use the extra pair of wires contained in a telephone cable (that are otherwise typically unused).

The types of DSL also vary in terms of their capacity and maximum line length. A VDSL line that carries as much as 52 Mbps in one direction and as much as 6.4 Mbps in the opposite direction can extend only a maximum of 1000 feet between the customer's premises and the carrier's switching facility. This limitation might suit businesses located close to a telephone company's central office (for example, in the middle of a metropolitan area), but it won't work for most individuals. The most popular form of DSL, ADSL, provides a maximum of 8 Mbps downstream and a maximum of 1.544 Mbps upstream. However, the distance between the customer and the central office affects the actual throughput a customer will experience. Close to the central office, DSL achieves its highest maximum throughput. The farther away the customer's premises, the lower the throughput. In the case of ADSL, a customer 9000 feet from the central office can potentially experience ADSL's maximum potential throughput of 8 Mbps downstream. At 18,000 feet away, the farthest allowable distance, the customer will experience as little as 1.544-Mbps throughput. Still, this throughput and this distance (approximately 3.4 miles) renders ADSL suitable for most telecommuters. Table 7-2 compares current specifications for six DSL types.

Table 7-2 Comparison of DSL types

DSL Type	Maximum Upstream Throughput (Mbps)	Maximum Downstream Throughput (Mbps)	Distance Limitation (Feet)
ADSL "full rate")	1	8	18,000
G.Lite (a type of ADSL)	0.512	1.544	25,000
HDSL or HDSL-2	1.544 or 2.048	1.544 or 2.048	18,000 or 12,000
SDSL	1.544	1.544	12,000
SHDSL	2.36 or 4.7	2.36 or 4.7	26,000 or 18,000
VDSL	1.6, 3.2, or 6.4	12.9, 25.9, or 51.8	1000–4500

NET+
2.15

 NOTE

Published distance limitations and throughput can vary from one service provider to another, depending on how far the provider is willing to guarantee a particular level of service.

In addition to their data modulation techniques, capacity, and distance limitations, DSL types vary according to how they use the PSTN. Next, you will learn about how DSL connects to a business or residence over the PSTN.

DSL Connectivity

This section follows the path of an ADSL connection from a home computer, through the local loop, and to the telecommunications carrier's switching facility. Although variations exist, this describes the most common implementation of DSL.

Suppose you have an ADSL connection at home. One evening you open your Web browser and request the home page of your favorite sports team to find the last game's score. As you know, the first step in this process is establishing a TCP connection with the team's Web server. Your TCP request message leaves your computer's NIC and travels over your home network to a DSL modem. A **DSL modem** is a device that modulates outgoing signals and demodulates incoming DSL signals. Thus, it contains receptacles to connect both to your incoming telephone line and to your computer or network connectivity device. Because you're using ADSL, the DSL modem also contains a splitter to separate incoming voice and data signals. The DSL modem may be external to the computer and connect to a computer's Ethernet NIC via an RJ-45, USB, or wireless interface. If your home network contains more than one computer and you want all computers to share the DSL bandwidth, the DSL modem must connect to a device such as a hub, switch, or router, instead of just one computer. In fact, rather than using two separate devices, you could buy a router that combines DSL modem functionalities with the ability to connect multiple computers and share DSL bandwidth. A DSL modem is shown in Figure 7-14.

FIGURE 7-14 *A DSL modem*

NET+
2.15

When your request arrives at the DSL modem, it is modulated according to the ADSL specifications. Then the DSL modem forwards the modulated signal to your local loop—the lines that connect your home with the rest of the PSTN. For the first stretch of the local loop, the signal continues over four-pair UTP wire. At some distance less than 18,000 feet, it is combined with other modulated signals in a telephone switch. If this switch is not in a central office, it forwards your request—this time over fiber-optic cable or a high-speed wireless link—to another switch at the central office. (To accept DSL signals, your telecommunications carrier must have newer digital switching equipment. In areas of the country where carriers have not updated their switching equipment, DSL service is not available.)

Inside the carrier's switching facility, a splitter separates your line's data signal (the TCP request) from any voice signals that are also carried on the line. Next, your request is sent to a device called a **DSLAM (DSL access multiplexer)**, which aggregates multiple DSL subscriber lines and connects them to a larger carrier or to the Internet backbone, as pictured in Figure 7-15. The request travels over the Internet until it reaches your sports team's Web server. Barring line problems and Internet congestion, the entire journey happens in a fraction of a second. After your team's Web server accepts the connection request, the data follows the same path, but in reverse.

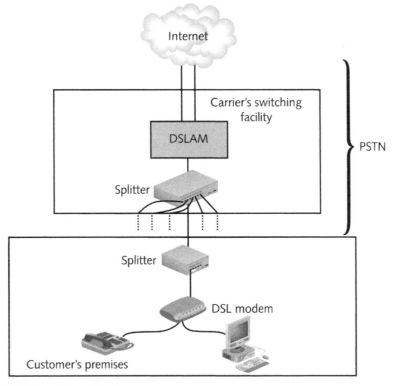

FIGURE 7-15 *A DSL connection*

NET+

2.15

Currently, ADSL is the most common form of DSL, but standards continue to evolve. Telecommunications carriers and manufacturers have positioned DSL as a competitor for T1, ISDN, and broadband cable services. The installation, hardware, and monthly access costs for DSL are slightly less than those for ISDN lines and significantly less than the cost for T1s. (At the time of this writing, ADSL costs approximately $30 per month in the United States.) Considering that DSL technology can provide faster throughput than T1s, it presents a formidable challenge to T-carrier services for business customers.

One drawback to DSL is that it is not available in all areas of the United States, either because carriers have not upgraded their switching equipment or because customers do not reside within the service's distance limitations. In addition, in its early years DSL was more expensive than broadband cable, its main competition among residential customers. For these reasons, two-thirds of consumers in the United States use cable for broadband Internet access service.

Broadband Cable

NET+

2.15

While local and long-distance phone companies strive to make DSL the preferred method of Internet access for consumers, cable companies are pushing their own connectivity option. This option, called **broadband cable** or **cable modem access**, is based on the coaxial cable wiring used for TV signals. Such wiring can theoretically transmit as much as 56 Mbps downstream and as much as 10 Mbps upstream. Thus, broadband cable is an asymmetrical technology. Realistically, however, broadband cable throughput is limited (or throttled) by the cable companies, so that customers are allowed, at most, 3-Mbps downstream and 1-Mbps upstream throughput. The asymmetry of broadband cable makes it a logical choice for users who want to surf the Web or download data from a network. Some companies are also delivering music, videoconferencing, and Internet services over cable infrastructure.

Broadband cable connections require that the customer use a special **cable modem**, a device that modulates and demodulates signals for transmission and reception via cable wiring. Cable modems operate at the Physical and Data Link layer of the OSI Model, and therefore do not manipulate higher-layer protocols such as IP or IPX. The cable modem then connects to a customer's PC via an RJ-45, USB, or wireless interface to a NIC. Alternately, the cable modem could connect to a connectivity device, such as a hub, switch, or router, thereby supplying bandwidth to a LAN rather than to just one computer. It's also possible to use a device that combines cable modem functionality with a router; this single device can then provide both the broadband cable connection and the capability of sharing the bandwidth between multiple nodes. Figure 7-16 provides an example of a cable modem.

Before customers can subscribe to broadband cable, however, their local cable company must have the necessary infrastructure. Traditional cable TV networks supply the infrastructure for downstream communication (the TV programming), but not for upstream communication. To provide Internet access through its network, the cable company must upgrade its existing equipment to support bidirectional, digital communications. For starters, the cable company's network wiring must be replaced with **HFC (hybrid fiber-coax)**, an expensive fiber-optic link that

FIGURE 7-16 *A cable modem*

can support high frequencies. The HFC connects the cable company's offices to a node location near the customer. Most large cable companies, such as Comcast and Charter, long ago upgraded their infrastructure to use HFC. Either fiber-optic or coaxial cable may connect the node to the customer's business or residence via a connection known as a **cable drop**. All cable drops for the cable subscribers in the same neighborhood connect to the local node. These nodes then connect to the cable company's central office, which is known as its **head-end**. At the head-end, the cable company can connect to the Internet through a variety of means (often via fiber-optic cable) or it can pick up digital satellite or microwave transmissions. The head-end can transmit data to as many as 1000 subscribers, in a one-to-many communication system. Figure 7-17 illustrates the infrastructure of a cable system.

Like DSL, broadband cable provides a dedicated, or continuous, connection that does not require dialing up a service provider. Unlike DSL, broadband cable requires many subscribers to share the same local line, thus raising concerns about security and actual (versus theoretical) throughput. For example, if your cable company supplied you and five of your neighbors with broadband cable services, your neighbors could, with some technical prowess, capture the data that you transmit to the Internet. (Modern cable networks provide encryption for data traveling to and from customer premises; however, these encryption schemes can be readily thwarted.) Moreover, the throughput of a cable line is fixed. As with any fixed resource, the more one claims, the less that is left for others. In other words, the greater the number of users sharing a single line, the less throughput available to each individual user. Cable companies counter this perceived disadvantage by rightly claiming that at some point (for example, at a remote switching facility or at the DSLAM interface), a telecommunications carrier's DSL bandwidth is also fixed and shared among a group of customers.

As mentioned earlier, cable broadband access continues to service the majority of residential customers, whereas DSL is more popular among business customers. Now, however, since the cost of DSL has decreased, the rate of new DSL and broadband cable installations is nearly identical. In the United States, broadband cable access costs approximately $45 per month for

NET+
2.15

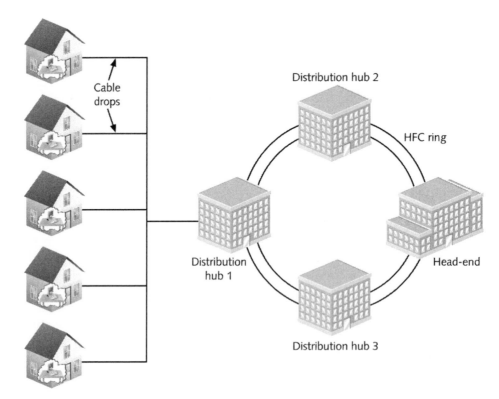

FIGURE 7-17 *Cable infrastructure*

customers who already subscribe to cable TV service. Broadband cable is less often used in businesses than DSL, primarily because most office buildings do not contain a coaxial cable infrastructure.

SONET (Synchronous Optical Network)

NET+
2.14

SONET (Synchronous Optical Network) is a high-bandwidth WAN signaling technique developed by Bell Communications Research in the 1980s, and later standardized by ANSI and ITU. SONET specifies framing and multiplexing techniques at the Physical layer of the OSI Model. Its four key strengths are that it can integrate many other WAN technologies, it offers fast data transfer rates, it allows for simple link additions and removals, and it provides a high degree of fault tolerance. (The word **synchronous** as used in the name of this technology means that data being transmitted and received by nodes must conform to a timing scheme. A clock maintains time for all nodes on a network. A receiving node in synchronous communications recognizes that it should be receiving data by looking at the time on the clock.)

Perhaps the most important SONET advantage is that it provides interoperability. Before SONET, telecommunications carriers that used different signaling techniques (or even the same technique but different equipment) could not be assured that their networks could communicate. Now, SONET is often used to aggregate multiple T1s, T3s, or ISDN lines. SONET is also used as the underlying technology for ATM transmission. Furthermore, because it can work directly with the different standards used in different countries, SONET has emerged as the best choice for linking WANs between North America, Europe, and Asia. Internationally, SONET is known as **SDH (Synchronous Digital Hierarchy)**.

SONET's extraordinary fault tolerance results from its use of a double-ring topology (similar to FDDI) over fiber-optic cable. In this type of layout, one ring acts as the primary route for data, transmitting in a clockwise direction. The second ring acts as a backup, transmitting data counterclockwise around the ring. If, for example, a backhoe operator severs the primary ring, SONET would automatically reroute traffic to the backup ring without any loss of service. This characteristic, known as **self-healing**, makes SONET very reliable. (To lower the potential for a single accident to sever both rings, the cables that make up each ring should not lay adjacent to each other.) Figure 7-18 illustrates a SONET ring and its dual-fiber connections.

A SONET ring begins and ends at the telecommunications carrier's facility. In between, it connects an organization's multiple WAN sites in a ring fashion. It may also connect with multiple carrier facilities for additional fault tolerance. Companies can lease an entire SONET ring from a telecommunications carrier, or they can lease part of a SONET ring—for example, a circuit that offers T1 throughput—to take advantage of SONET's reliability.

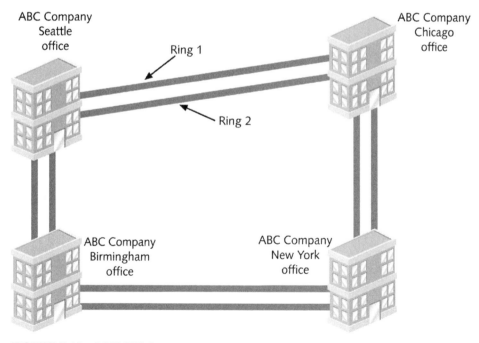

FIGURE 7-18 *A SONET ring*

NET+
2.14

At both the carrier and the customer premises, a SONET ring terminates at a multiplexer. A multiplexer combines individual SONET signals on the transmitting end, and another multiplexer separates combined signals on the receiving end. On the transmitting end, multiplexers accept input from different network types (for example, a T1 or ISDN line) and format the data in a standard SONET frame. That means that many different devices might connect to a SONET multiplexer, including, for example, a private telephone switch, a T1 multiplexer, and an ATM data switch. On the receiving end, multiplexers translate the incoming signals back into their original format. Most SONET multiplexers allow for easy additions or removals of connections to the SONET ring, which makes this technology easily adaptable to growing and changing networks. Figure 7-19 shows the devices necessary to connect a WAN site with a SONET ring. This is the simplest type of SONET connection; however, variations abound.

The data rate of a particular SONET ring is indicated by its **OC (Optical Carrier)** level, a rating that is internationally recognized by networking professionals and standards organizations. OC levels in SONET are analogous to the digital signal levels of T1s. Table 7-3 lists the OC levels and their maximum throughput.

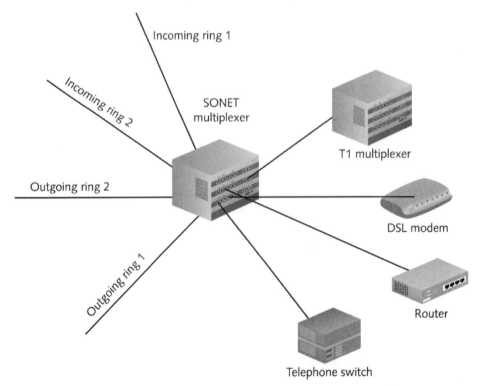

FIGURE 7-19 *SONET connectivity*

Table 7-3 SONET OC levels

OC Level	Throughput (Mbps)
OC1	51.84
OC3	155.52
OC12	622
OC24	1244
OC48	2480
OC96	4976
OC192	9953
OC768	39813

SONET technology is typically not implemented by small or medium-sized businesses, because of its high cost. It is more commonly used by large global companies, long-distance companies linking metropolitan areas and countries, or ISPs that want to guarantee fast, reliable access to the Internet. SONET is particularly suited to audio, video, and imaging data transmission. As you can imagine, given its reliance on fiber-optic cable and its redundancy requirements, SONET technology is expensive to implement.

Wireless WANs and Internet Access

Wireless WANs can be created using many types of transmission technologies. Some of the oldest technologies were developed by telephone companies to provide their customers with an alternative to wire-bound local loops. Other wireless WANs use another technology from the twentieth century—satellite transmission—which was originally developed for TV and radio broadcasts. But the latest wireless WAN technologies, collectively known as **wireless broadband**, are designed specifically for high-throughput, long-distance digital data exchange. The following sections describe a variety of ways wireless clients can access the Internet.

IEEE 802.11 Internet Access

In Chapter 6, you learned how LANs can be created using the IEEE 802.11b ("Wi-Fi"), 802.11a, or 802.11g wireless technology. Wireless access points are also used by airports, libraries, universities, hotels, cafés and restaurants to provide customers or visitors with wireless Internet access. Currently, most use the 802.11b access method. Places where wireless Internet access is available to the public are called **hot spots**. Some organizations, such as T-Mobile, have established a network of hot spots across the nation. Other organizations, such as a local coffee shop, might have only one hot spot. In some cases, Internet access is free. In other cases, the organization running the hot spot requires users to pay based on their usage or subscribe to a service. An average subscription costs $20 to $30 per month.

Organizations that require a service subscription often require users to log on via a Web page to gain access to the service. Alternatively, they might provide users with client software that manages the client's connection to the provider's wireless service. This software allows the user to log on to the network and secures data exchanged between the client computer and the access point, where transmissions are most vulnerable to eavesdropping. As an added security measure, a wireless access provider might configure its access point to accept a user's connection based on his computer's MAC address, in addition to the user's logon id and password. Wireless security measures are discussed in detail in Chapter 14.

At each hot spot, the access point available for public use is connected to the Internet using technology other than 802.11. For example, a local coffee shop might lease a DSL line that terminates at a combined access point and router behind the counter. That device can connect the coffee shop with its ISP while allowing patrons within the access point's range to log on to the Internet, as shown in Figure 7-20. At T-Mobile hot spots, access points are connected (via routers) to T1 links.

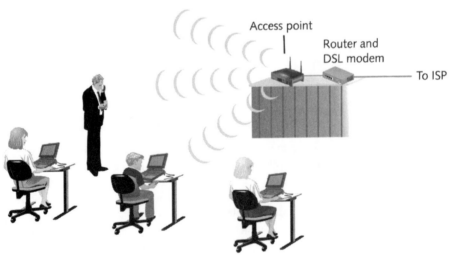

FIGURE 7-20 *A hot spot providing wireless Internet access*

In general, to access the Internet from an 802.11 hot spot, you must:

◆ Configure your wireless connection's TCP/IP properties to use DHCP. (In Windows XP, for example, check the "Obtain an IP address automatically" option in the Internet Protocol TCP/IP Properties dialog box.)

◆ Make sure your computer is not configured to automatically use a dial-up connection.

NET+
2.15

◆ Choose infrastructure mode rather than ad hoc mode. (In Windows XP, for example, in the Wireless Connection Properties dialog box, click the Advanced button and then check one of the following: "Any available network (access point preferred)," "Access point (infrastructure) networks only," or "Computer-to-computer (ad hoc) networks only.")

◆ Use the SSID name for the access point provided by the wireless access service provider.

◆ Follow the service provider's instructions for enabling or disabling wireless encryption; if enabled, specify the encryption key necessary to connect to the provider's access point.

Public 802.11 wireless access hot spots are limited by the same factors that affect 802.11 installations in a home or business. The range of a single access point is limited to approximately 330 feet and signals are susceptible to interference. Throughput depends on the type of 802.11 access used. The most common wireless technology used in hot spots today, 802.11b, offers a theoretical maximum throughput of 11 Mbps and an actual throughput of approximately 5 Mbps. Bear in mind that the throughput supplied by each access point is shared among all users. In a busy coffee shop, this could result in significantly lower throughput for some users.

IEEE created the 802.11 wireless standards for LANs. Next, you will learn about an IEEE wireless transmission that was designed specifically for MANs and WANs.

IEEE 802.16 (WiMAX) Internet Access

In 2001, IEEE standardized a new wireless technology under its **802.16** (wireless MAN) committee. The first version of this standard specified signals operating between 10 GHz and 66 GHz and required antennas with a line-of-sight path between them. Since 2001, IEEE has released additional versions of the 802.16 standard.

The currently favored IEEE 802.16 version is **802.16a**, which was approved in January 2003. 802.16a is also known as **WiMAX**, which stands for **Worldwide Interoperability for Microwave Access**, the name of a group of manufacturers, including Intel and Nokia, who banded together to promote and develop 802.16a products and services. WiMAX operates in frequency ranges between 2 and 11 GHz. As with the 802.11 technologies, WiMAX allows for antennas that do not require a line-of-sight path between them and can exchange signals with multiple stations at once. However, WiMAX is capable of providing much greater throughput than the 802.11 access methods—up to 70 Mbps. Its range is also much greater, at 50 kilometers (or approximately 30 miles). WiMAX is poised to compete with DSL and broadband cable for business and residential customers who want high-speed Internet access. As with any other new technology, WiMAX is more expensive than existing options; its subscriber wireless stations cost approximately $300. However, service providers view WiMAX as an excellent high-speed Internet access option for rural users who are not served by broadband cable or DSL connections. Currently, such rural users depend on dial-up connections over the PSTN or satellite Internet access, which is discussed next.

Satellite Internet Access

In 1945, Arthur C. Clarke (the author of *2001: A Space Odyssey*) wrote an article in which he described the possibility of communication between manned space stations that continually orbited the earth. Other scientists recognized the worth of using satellites to convey signals from one location on earth to another. By the 1960s, the United States was using satellites to transmit telephone and television signals across the Atlantic Ocean. Since then, the proliferation of this technology and reductions in its cost have made satellite transmission appropriate and available for more regional (or even local) consumer voice and data services.

You are probably familiar with satellites used to present live broadcasts of events happening around the world. Satellites are also used to deliver digital television and radio signals, voice and video signals, and cellular and paging signals. And they provide homes and businesses—most notably in rural or hard-to-reach locations—with Internet access. This following sections describe how satellite technology works.

Satellite Orbits

Most satellites circle the earth 22,300 miles above the equator in a geosynchronous orbit. **GEO (geosynchronous orbit** or **geostationary orbit)** means that satellites orbit the earth at the same rate as the earth turns. Consequently, at every point in their orbit, the satellites maintain a constant distance from a specific point on the earth's equator. Because satellites are generally used to relay information from one point on earth to another, information sent to earth from a satellite first has to be transmitted to the satellite from earth in an uplink. An **uplink** is the creation of a communications channel for a transmission from an earth-based transmitter to an orbiting satellite. Often, the uplink signal information is scrambled (in other words, its signal is encoded) before transmission to prevent unauthorized interception. At the satellite, a **transponder** receives the uplink signal, then transmits it to an earth-based receiver in a **downlink**. A typical satellite contains 24 to 32 transponders. Each satellite uses unique frequencies for its downlink. These frequencies, as well as the satellite's orbit location, are assigned and regulated by the FCC (Federal Communications Commission). Back on earth, the downlink is picked up by a dish-shaped antenna. The dish shape concentrates the signal so that it can be interpreted by a receiver. Figure 7-21 provides a simplified view of satellite communication.

An alternative to geosynchronous satellites are **LEO (low earth orbiting)** satellites. LEO satellites orbit the earth with an altitude roughly between 700 and 1400 kilometers, not above the equator but closer to the earth's poles. Because their altitude is lower, LEO satellites cover a smaller geographical range than GEO satellites. However, less power is required to issue signals between earth and an LEO satellite versus a GEO satellite.

In between the altitudes of LEO and GEO satellites lie **MEO (medium earth orbiting)** satellites. MEO satellites orbit the earth between 10,350 and 10,390 kilometers above its surface. As with LEO satellites, MEO satellites are not positioned over the equator, but over a latitude between the equator and the poles. MEOs have the advantage of covering a larger area of the earth's surface than LEO satellites while at the same time using less power and causing less signal delay than GEO satellites.

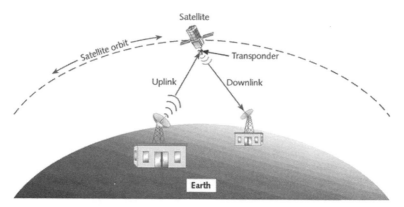

FIGURE 7-21 *Satellite communication*

Geosynchronous orbiting satellites are the type used by the most popular satellite Internet access service providers. This technology is well established, and is the least expensive of all satellite technology. Also, because they remain in a fixed position relative to the earth's surface, stationary receiving dishes on earth can be counted on to receive satellite signals reliably.

Satellite Frequencies

Satellites transmit and receive signals in any of following five frequency bands:

- ◆ **L-band**—1.5–2.7 GHz
- ◆ **S-band**—2.7–3.5 GHz
- ◆ **C-band**—3.4–6.7 GHz
- ◆ **Ku-band**—12–18 GHz
- ◆ **Ka-band**—18–40 GHz

Within each band, frequencies used for uplink and downlink transmissions differ. This variation helps ensure that signals traveling in one direction (for example from a satellite to the earth) do not interfere with signals traveling in the other direction (for example, signals from the earth to a satellite). Satellite Internet access providers typically use frequencies in the C- or Ku-bands. Newer satellite Internet access technologies are currently being developed for the Ka-band.

Satellite Internet Services

A handful of companies offer high-bandwidth Internet access via GEO satellite links. Each subscriber uses a small satellite dish antenna and receiver to exchange signals with the service provider's satellite network. Subscribers can choose one of two types of satellite Internet access service: dial return or satellite return. In a **dial return** arrangement, a subscriber receives data from the Internet via a satellite downlink transmission, but sends data to the satellite via an analog modem (dial-up) connection. With dial return, service providers advertise downstream (or downlink) throughputs of 400–500 Kbps, though in practice, they may be as high as 1 Mbps.

However, upstream (or uplink) throughputs are practically limited to 53 Kbps and are usually lower. Therefore, dial return satellite Internet access is an asymmetrical technology. In a **satellite return** arrangement, a subscriber sends and receives data to and from the Internet using a satellite uplink and downlink. This is a symmetrical technology, in which both upstream and downstream throughputs are advertised to reach 400–500 Kbps. In reality, throughputs are often higher.

To establish a satellite Internet connection, each subscriber must have a dish antenna, which is approximately two feet high by three feet wide, installed in a fixed position. In North America, these dish antennas are pointed toward the southern hemisphere (because the geosynchronous satellites travel over the equator). The dish antenna's receiver is connected, via cable, to a modem. This modem uses either a PCI or USB interface to connect with the subscriber's computer. In a dial return system, an analog modem is also connected to the subscriber's computer to handle upstream communications.

Figure 7-22 illustrates how a home user with dial return satellite Internet access service connects with a satellite Internet service provider.

Costs for popular Internet access services in the United States are approximately $200 for installation (which must be performed by a professional) plus a monthly service fee of $20 to $30.

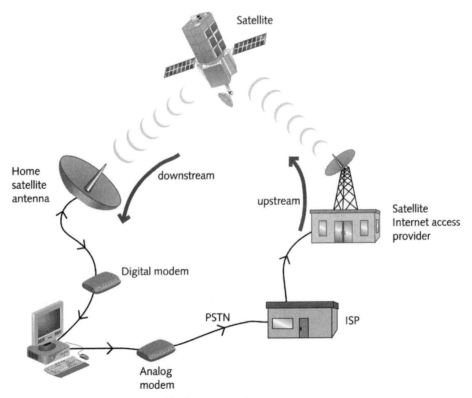

FIGURE 7-22 *Dial return satellite Internet service*

WAN Technologies Compared

NET+
2.14
2.15

You have learned that WAN links offer a wide range of throughputs, from 56 Kbps for a PSTN dial-up connection to potentially 39.8 Gbps for a full-speed SONET connection. Table 7-4 summarizes the media and throughputs offered by each technology discussed in this chapter. Bear in mind that each technology's transmission techniques (for example, switching for Frame Relay versus point-to-point for T1) will affect real throughput, so the maximum transmission speed is a theoretical limit. Actual transmission speeds will vary.

Table 7-4 A comparison of WAN technology throughputs

WAN Technology	Typical Media	Maximum Throughput
Dial-up over PSTN	UTP or STP	56 Kbps theoretical; actual limit is 53 Kbps
X.25	UTP/STP (DS1 or DS3)	64 Kbps or 2.048 Mbps
Frame Relay	UTP/STP (DS1 or DS3)	45 Mbps
BRI (ISDN)	UTP/STP (PSTN)	128 Kbps
PRI (ISDN)	UTP/STP (PSTN)	1.544 Mbps
T1	UTP/STP (PSTN), microwave, or fiber-optic cable	1.544 Mbps
Fractional T1	UTP/STP (PSTN), microwave, or fiber-optic cable	n times 64 Kbps (where n = number of channels leased)
T3	Microwave link or fiber-optic cable	45 Mbps
xDSL	UTP/STP (PSTN)	Theoretically, 1.544 Mbps–52 Mbps (depending on the type), but typical residential DSL throughputs are 1.5 Mbps or lower
Broadband Cable	Hybrid fiber-coaxial cable	Theoretically, 56 Mbps downstream, 10 Mbps upstream, but actual throughputs are approximately 1.5–3 Mbps upstream and 256–768 Kbps downstream
SONET	Fiber-optic cable	51, 155, 622, 1244, 2480, 4976, 9952, or 39813 Mbps (depending on the OC level)
IEEE 802.11b (Wi-Fi)	2.4 GHz RF	Theoretically, 11 Mbps; actual throughput is approximately 5 Mbps
IEEE 802.11g	2.4 GHz RF	Theoretically, 56 Mbps; actual throughput is approximately 20–25 Mbps.

NET+
2.14
2.15

Table 7-4 Continued

WAN Technology	Typical Media	Maximum Throughput
IEEE 802.16a (WiMAX)	2.4–11GHz RF	Up to 70 Mbps
Satellite–Dial Return	C- or Ku-band RF and PSTN	Advertised as 400 Kbps downstream (but often exceeds that); up to 53 Kbps upstream
Satellite–Satellite Return	C- or Ku-band RF	Advertised as 400 Kbps downstream and upstream (but often exceeds that)

Remote Connectivity

NET+
2.16

Most of the connectivity examples you've learned about thus far assume that a WAN site has continuous, dedicated access to the WAN. For example, when a user in Phoenix wants to open a document on a server in Dallas, she needs only to find the Dallas server on her network, open a directory on the Dallas server, and then open the file. The server is available to her at any time, because the Phoenix and Dallas offices are always connected and sharing resources over the WAN. However, this is not the only way to share resources over a WAN. For remote users (such as employees on the road, off-campus students, telecommuters, or staff in small, branch offices), intermittent access with a choice of connectivity methods is often more appropriate.

As a remote user, you must connect to a LAN via **remote access**, a service that allows a client to connect with and log on to a LAN or WAN in a different geographical location. After connecting, a remote client can access files, applications, and other shared resources, such as printers, like any other client on the LAN or WAN. To communicate via remote access the client and host need a transmission path plus the appropriate software to complete the connection and exchange data.

Many remote access methods exist, and they vary according to the type of transmission technology, clients, hosts, and software they can or must use. Popular remote access techniques, including dial-up networking, Microsoft's RAS (Remote Access Service) or RRAS (Routing and Remote Access Service), remote control, terminal services, Web portals, and VPNs (virtual private networks), are described in the following sections. You will also learn about common remote access protocols PPP and SLIP.

Dial-up Networking

Dial-up networking refers to dialing directly into a private network's or ISP's remote access server to log on to a network. Dial-up clients can use PSTN, X.25, or ISDN transmission

NET+
2.16

methods. Most often, however, the term "dial-up networking" refers to a connection between computers using the PSTN—that is, regular telephone lines. To accept client connections, the remote access server is attached to a group of modems, all of which are associated with one phone number. The client must run dial-up software (normally available with the operating system) to initiate the connection. At the same time, the remote access server runs specialized software to accept and interpret the incoming signals. When it receives a request for connection, the remote access server software presents the remote user with a prompt for his **credentials**—typically, his user name and password. The server compares his credentials with those in its database, in a process known as **authentication**. If the credentials match, the user will be allowed to log on to the network. Thereafter, the remote user can perform the same functions she could perform while working at a client computer in the office. With the proper server hardware and software, a remote access server can offer multiple users simultaneous remote access to the LAN. Many Internet subscribers use dial-up networking to connect to their ISP.

Advantages to using dial-up networking are that the technology is well understood and its software comes with virtually every operating system. (On the other hand, this option is more expensive than other options when a client travels far from the network and must dial into the network using a long-distance or 1-800 number supplied by the organization's headquarters.) Connecting to a remote access server can be slow, however, when it relies on the PSTN. Also, it requires a significant amount of maintenance to make sure clients can always connect to a pool of modems. One way to limit the maintenance burden is for an organization to contract with an ISP to supply remote access services. In this arrangement, clients dial into the ISP's remote access server, and then the ISP connects the incoming clients with the organization's network.

The dial-up networking software that Microsoft provided with its Windows 95, 98, NT, and 2000 client operating systems and with its Windows NT and 2000 network operating systems is called **RAS (Remote Access Service)**. For the Network+ exam, you will need to be familiar with the term "RAS" and be aware that, as with other dial-up networking services, RAS requires software installed on both the client and server, a server configured to accept incoming clients, and a client with sufficient privileges (including user name and password) on the server to access its resources. In the Windows XP and Server 2003 operating systems, RAS has been incorporated into a more comprehensive remote access package called the RRAS (Routing and Remote Access Service). RRAS is described in the following section.

Remote Access Servers

The previous section described dial-up networking, a type of remote access method defined by its direct, PSTN-based connection method. However, users who previously depended on dial-up connections are increasingly adopting faster broadband connections, such as DSL and broadband cable technology. This section and following sections describe services that can accept remote access connections from a client, no matter what type of connection it uses.

NET+
2.16

As you have learned, remote access allows a client that is not directly attached to a LAN or WAN to connect and log on to that network. A remote client attempting to connect to a LAN or WAN requires a server to accept its connection and grant it privileges to the network's resources. Many types of remote access servers exist. Some are devices dedicated to this task, such as the Cisco 2500 series routers or the Cisco AS5800 access servers. These devices run software that, in conjunction with their operating system, performs authentication for clients and communicates via dial-up networking protocols. Other types of remote access servers are computers installed with special software that enables them to accept incoming client connections and grant them access to resources.

RRAS (Routing and Remote Access Service) is Microsoft's remote access software available with the Windows Server 2003 network operating system and the Windows XP client operating systems. RRAS enables a Windows Server 2003 computer to accept multiple remote client connections over any type of transmission path. It also enables the server to act as a router, determining where to direct incoming packets across the network. Further, RRAS incorporates multiple security provisions to ensure that data cannot be intercepted and interpreted by anyone other than the intended recipient and to ensure that only authorized clients can connect to the remote access server.

Figure 7-23 illustrates how clients connect with a remote access server to log on to a LAN.

Remote access servers depend on several types of protocols to communicate with clients, as described in the following section.

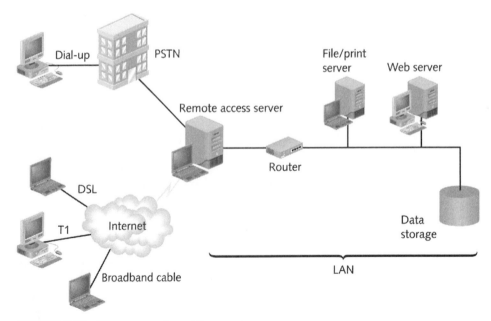

FIGURE 7-23 *Clients connecting with a remote access server*

NET+
2.16

Remote Access Protocols

To exchange data, remote access servers and clients require special protocols. The **SLIP (Serial Line Internet Protocol)** and **PPP (Point-to-Point Protocol)** are two protocols that enable a workstation to connect to another computer using a serial connection (in the case of dial-up networking, "serial connection" refers to a modem). Such protocols are necessary to transport Network layer traffic over serial interfaces, which belong to the Data Link layer of the OSI Model. Both SLIP and PPP encapsulate higher-layer networking protocols, such as TCP and IP, in their lower-layer data frames.

SLIP is an earlier and much simpler version of the protocol than PPP. For example, SLIP can carry only IP packets, whereas PPP can carry many different types of Network layer packets, such as IPX or AppleTalk. Because of its primitive nature, SLIP requires significantly more setup than PPP. When using SLIP, you typically must specify the IP addresses for both your client and for your server in your dial-up networking profile. PPP, on the other hand, can automatically obtain this information as it connects to the server. PPP also performs error correction and data compression, but SLIP does not. In addition, SLIP does not support data encryption, which makes it less secure than PPP. For all these reasons, PPP is the more popular communications protocol for remote access communications.

Another difference between SLIP and PPP is that SLIP supports only asynchronous data transmission, and PPP supports both asynchronous and synchronous transmission. As you learned earlier, in synchronous transmission, data must conform to a timing scheme. **Asynchronous** refers to a communications method in which nodes do not have to conform to any predetermined schemes that specify the timing of data transmissions. In asynchronous communications, a node can transmit at any instant, and the destination node must accept the transmission as it comes. To ensure that the receiving node knows when it has received a complete frame, asynchronous communications provide start and stop bits for each character transmitted. When the receiving node recognizes a start bit, it begins to accept a new character. When it receives the stop bit for that character, it ceases to look for the end of that character's transmission. Asynchronous data transmission therefore occurs in random stops and starts. In fact, asynchronous transmission was designed for communication that happens at random intervals, such as sending the keystrokes of a person typing on a remote keyboard. Thus, it is well suited to use on modem connections.

When PPP is used over an Ethernet network (no matter what the connection type), it is known as **PPPoE (PPP over Ethernet)**. PPPoE is the standard for connecting home computers to an ISP (Internet Service Provider) via DSL or broadband cable. When you sign up for broadband cable or DSL service, the ISP supplies you with connection software that is configured to use PPPoE. Figure 7-24 illustrates the how the protocols discussed in this section and commonly used to establish a broadband Internet connection fit in the OSI Model. (The Application layer protocol RDP is discussed in the following section.)

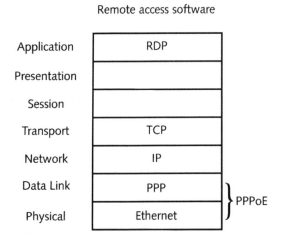

FIGURE 7-24 *Protocols used in a remote access Internet connection*

Remote Control

Remote control allows a remote user on a client computer to control another computer, called the host, across a LAN or WAN connection. This type of remote access first requires a connection between the client and host. The connection could be a dedicated WAN line (such as a T1), an Internet connection, or even a dial-up connection established directly between the client's modem and the host's modem. Also, the host must be configured to allow access from the client by setting user name or computer name and password credentials. A host may allow clients a variety of privileges, from merely viewing the screen to running programs and modifying data files on the host's hard disk. After connecting, if the remote user has sufficient privileges, she can send keystrokes and mouse clicks to the host and receive screen output in return. In other words, to the remote user, it appears as if she is working on the LAN- or WAN-connected host. Remote control software is specially designed to require little bandwidth, which makes it suitable for use over dial-up connections.

One example of such remote control software is Symantec's **pcAnywhere**. Another example of remote control software is the **Remote Desktop** feature that comes with the Windows 95, 98, NT, 2000, XP, and Server 2003 operating systems. Remote Desktop relies on the **RDP (Remote Desktop Protocol)**, which is an Application layer protocol that uses TCP/IP to transmit graphics and text quickly. RDP also carries session, licensing, and encryption information. To enable your Windows XP Professional computer as a Remote Desktop host:

1. First log on to the computer as Administrator or another user name with administrator-level privileges.

2. Click **Start**, and then click **Control Panel**. If necessary, click **Switch to Category View.** The Control Panel window opens in Category view.

NET+
2.16

3. Click **Performance and Maintenance**, and then click the **System** icon. The System Properties dialog box opens.

4. Click the **Remote** tab. Options for remote connections to your computer appear, as shown in Figure 7-25.

FIGURE 7-25 *Remote tab in the Windows XP System Properties window*

5. Check the **Allow remote users to connect remotely to this computer** option.

6. If this is the first time you've enabled remote services, the Remote Sessions window opens, alerting you that accounts used for remote access must have passwords to connect to your computer. Click **OK**.

7. Click **Select Remote Users** to choose from a list of users who you will allow to connect to your computer. The **Remote Desktop Users** dialog box opens.

8. Click **Add** to add a user to the list. The **Select Users** dialog box opens. If you have created multiple user accounts on your computer, these accounts will be listed under "Enter object names to select (examples):"

9. Check the user names that will have access to your computer, and then click **OK**.

10. Click **OK** again to close the Remote Desktop Users dialog box.

11. Click **OK** once more to close the System Properties dialog box and save your changes.

The previous steps describe how to establish your computer as a host. To start a remote desktop session from a Windows XP client:

1. Make sure the remote desktop client software has been installed on the computer. Also make sure that the host and remote computers are connected to networks that can exchange data (for example, the host might be a desktop on a company's office WAN and the remote client might be a home computer that can connect to that WAN over the Internet).

2. Click **Start**, point to **All Programs**, point to **Accessories**, point to **Communications**, and then click **Remote Desktop Connection**. The Remote Desktop Connection window opens, as shown in Figure 7-26.

FIGURE 7-26 *Remote Desktop Connection window*

3. In the Computer: text box, enter the name of the host computer to which you want to connect. The host computer must be running the Remote Desktop software and you must have permission to log on to it.

4. Click **Connect**.

5. In the **Log On to Windows** dialog box, type your user name, password, and domain (if necessary), and then click **OK** to log on to this host.

6. The Remote Desktop window opens, showing you the desktop of the host computer. At this point, your keystrokes and mouse clicks will act on the host computer, not on your client computer.

Although remote control is used less often than other forms of remote access, some situations call for it. For example, suppose a traveling salesperson must submit weekly sales figures to her home office every Friday afternoon. While out of town, she discovers a problem with her spreadsheet program, which should automatically calculate her sales figures (for example, the percentage of a monthly quota she's reached for any given product) after she enters the raw data. She calls the home office, and a support technician attempts to resolve her issue on the phone. When this doesn't work, the technician may decide to run a remote control program and "take over" the salesperson's PC (over a WAN link) to troubleshoot the spreadsheet problem. Every keystroke and mouse click the technician enters on his PC is then issued to the salesperson's PC. After the problem is resolved, the technician can disconnect from the salesperson's PC.

Advantages to using the remote control access method are that it is simple to configure and can run over any type of connection. This benefits telecommuters who must use dial-up connections and who need to work with processing-intensive applications such as databases. In this scenario, the data processing occurs on the host without the data having to traverse the slower modem connection to the remote workstation. Another advantage to remote control connections is that a single host can accept simultaneous connections from multiple clients. A presenter can use this feature to establish a virtual conference, for example, in which several attendees log on to the host and watch the presenter manipulate the host computer's screen and keyboard. However, network managers don't favor remote control connections because they offer minimal security. Although remote control software requires a user to log on with an ID and password, the connection does not go through the network backbone, where stricter security controls are apt to be in place. If frequent remote access to processing-intensive applications is necessary, a better solution would be to use terminal services, as described in the following section.

Terminal Services

A popular method for gaining remote access to LANs is by using terminal services. In **terminal services**, multiple remote computers can connect to a terminal server on the LAN. A **terminal server** is a computer that runs specialized software that allows it to act as a host and supply applications and resource sharing to remote clients. As with remote control, in terminal services remote users send only keystrokes and mouse clicks and receive screen updates from the host. To the remote user, connecting to a LAN from afar appears no different from being a directly connected LAN user. However, terminal services differ from remote control in a few key ways. First, a terminal server allows multiple simultaneous connections. Second, a terminal server is optimized for fast processing and application handling, offering better performance for remote users than could a LAN-connected workstation. Third, implementing terminal services requires more sophisticated software and significant configuration. For example, it allows users to connect via any type of media (not only a modem and phone line). Also, a terminal server can be situated on the network such that remote user connections must pass through firewalls, switches, and routers and be subject to security, addressing, resource access, and VLAN controls, if applicable. As a result, this option offers much greater flexibility and security than remote control.

Many companies have created software to supply terminal services. In fact, the Microsoft version of this solution is called **Terminal Services**. (Windows XP clients connecting to a Microsoft terminal server use the Remote Desktop software described previously.) Another popular option is Citrix System, Inc.'s **Metaframe**. With the Citrix option, remote workstations rely on software known as an **ICA (Independent Computing Architecture) client** to connect with a remote access server and exchange keystrokes, mouse clicks, and screen updates. Citrix's ICA client can work with virtually any operating system or application. Its ease of use and broad compatibility have made the ICA client one of the most popular methods for supplying widespread remote access across an organization. Potential drawbacks to this method include the relatively high cost of Citrix's products and the complex nature of its server software configuration.

A workstation that uses terminal services to access a LAN is often called a **thin client**, because very little hard disk space or processing power is required of the workstation. In fact, the term thin client can apply to any end-user workstation that relies on another networked computer to bear primary processing and disk access responsibilities, including clients that connect through Web portals, as discussed next.

NET+
2.16

Web Portals

Another remote access option that's growing in popularity is running LAN applications from a Web portal. A **Web portal** is simply a secure, Web-based interface to an application. This option is attractive because it places few requirements on the client. Users merely need an Internet connection, Web browser software, and the proper credentials to log on to the application. Any type of Internet connection is sufficient for using Web portals, though of course, a DSL or broadband cable connection performs better than a PSTN connection.

On the host side, a Web server supplies the application to multiple users upon request. However, first an application must be designed for Web-based access. Making applications Web-ready typically requires significant programming. However, more and more applications are being designed this way from the start. In addition, managers must carefully configure the access properties for the Web server hosting the application to make sure only authorized users can access the application. In fact, a company may decide to outsource its Web portal services to an ISP. In that case, the company pays the ISP to provide connectivity, house and maintain the Web server, make sure the application is operating correctly, and prevent unauthorized access to the application.

As you can imagine, making an application accessible via the Web also makes it vulnerable to use by unauthorized individuals. Thus, the use of Web portals calls for secure transmission protocols. Secure transmission protocols are also integral to creating virtual private networks, which are discussed in the following section.

VPNs (Virtual Private Networks)

NET+
2.16

VPNs (virtual private networks) are wide area networks logically defined over public transmission systems. To allow access to only authorized users, traffic on a VPN is isolated from other traffic on the same public lines. For example, a national insurance provider could establish a private WAN that uses Internet connections but serves only its agent offices across the country. By relying on the public transmission networks already in place, VPNs provide a way of constructing a convenient and relatively inexpensive WAN. In the example of a national insurance provider, the company gains significant savings by having each office connect to the Internet separately rather than leasing point-to-point connections between each office and the national headquarters.

The software required to establish VPNs is usually inexpensive, and in some cases is being included with other widely used software. For example, the Windows Server 2003 RRAS allows you to create a simple VPN by turning a Windows server into a remote access server and allowing clients to dial into it. Alternately, clients could dial into an ISP's remote access server, then connect with the VPN managed by RRAS. For Novell-based networks, you can use BorderManager, a NetWare add-on product, to connect nodes and form a VPN. Third-party software companies also provide VPN programs that work with NetWare, Windows, UNIX, Linux, and Macintosh OS X Server network operating systems. Or VPNs can be

NET+
2.16

created simply by configuring special protocols on the routers or firewalls that connect each site in the VPN. This is the most common implementation of VPNs on UNIX-based networks.

Figure 7-27 depicts one possible VPN layout. The beauty of VPNs is that they are tailored to a customer's distance and bandwidth needs, so, of course, every one is different.

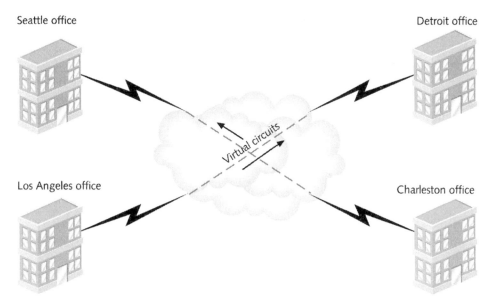

FIGURE 7-27 *An example of a VPN*

Two important considerations when designing a VPN are interoperability and security. To make sure a VPN can carry all types of data in a private manner over any kind of connection, special VPN protocols encapsulate higher-layer protocols in a process known as **tunneling**. You can say that these protocols create the virtual connection, or **tunnel**, between two VPN nodes. One endpoint of the tunnel is the client. The other endpoint may be a connectivity device (for example, a router, firewall, or gateway) or a remote access server that allows clients to log on to the network. As you have learned, encapsulation involves one protocol adding a header to data received from a higher-layer protocol. A VPN tunneling protocol operates at the Data Link layer and encapsulates Network layer packets, be they IP, IPX, or NetBEUI. Two major types of tunneling protocols are used on contemporary VPNs: PPTP or L2TP.

PPTP (Point-to-Point Tunneling Protocol) is a protocol developed by Microsoft that expands on PPP by encapsulating it so that any type of PPP data can traverse the Internet masked as an IP or IPX transmission. PPTP supports the encryption, authentication, and access services provided by the Windows Server 2003 RRAS (and previous versions of this remote access software). Users can either dial directly into an RRAS access server that's part of the VPN, or they can dial into their ISP's remote access server first, then connect to a VPN. Either way, data is transmitted from the client to the VPN using PPTP. Windows, UNIX, Linux, and Macintosh

NET+
2.16

clients are all capable of connecting to a VPN using PPTP. PPTP is easy to install, and is available at no extra cost with Microsoft networking services. However, it provides less stringent security than other tunneling protocols.

Another VPN tunneling protocol is **L2TP (Layer 2 Tunneling Protocol)**, based on technology developed by Cisco and standardized by the IETF. It encapsulates PPP data in a similar manner to PPTP, but differs in a few key ways. Unlike PPTP, L2TP is a standard accepted and used by multiple different vendors, so it can connect a VPN that uses a mix of equipment types—for example, a 3Com router, a Cisco router, and a NetGear router. Also, L2TP can connect two routers, a router and a remote access server, or a client and a remote access server. Another important advantage to L2TP is that tunnel endpoints do not have to reside on the same packet-switched network. In other words, an L2TP client could connect to a router running L2TP on an ISP's network. The ISP could then forward the L2TP frames to another VPN router, without interpreting the frames. This L2TP tunnel, although not direct from node to node, remains isolated from other traffic. Because of its many advantages, L2TP is more commonly used than PPTP.

PPTP and L2TP are not the only protocols that can be used to carry VPN traffic. For networks where security is critical, it is advisable to use protocols that can provide both tunneling and data encryption. Such protocols are discussed in detail in Chapter 14, which focuses on network security.

Chapter Summary

◆ WANs are distinguished from LANs by the fact that WANs traverse a wider geographical area. They usually employ point-to-point, dedicated communications rather than point-to-multipoint communications. They also use different connectivity devices, depending on the WAN technology in use.

◆ A WAN in which each site is connected in a serial fashion to no more than two other sites is known as a bus topology WAN. This topology often provides the best solution for organizations with only a few sites and access to dedicated circuits.

◆ In a ring topology WAN, each site is connected to two other sites so that the entire WAN forms a ring pattern. This architecture is similar to the LAN ring topology, except that most ring topology WANs have the capability to reverse the direction data travels to avoid a failed site.

◆ In the star topology WAN, a single site acts as the central connection point for several other points. This arrangement allows one connection to fail without affecting other connections. Therefore, star topology WANs are more fault-tolerant than bus or ring WANs.

◆ A mesh topology WAN consists of many directly interconnected sites. In partial mesh WANs, only some of the WAN sites are directly interconnected. In full mesh WANs, every site is directly connected to every other site. The full mesh topology is the most fault-tolerant and also the most expensive WAN topology to implement.

◆ A tiered topology WAN is one in which sites that are connected in star or ring formations are interconnected at different levels, with the interconnection points being organized into layers to form hierarchical groupings.

◆ The PSTN (Public Switched Telephone Network) is the network of lines and switching centers that provides traditional telephone service. It was originally composed of analog lines alone, but now also uses digital transmission over fiber-optic and copper twisted-pair cable, microwave, and satellite connections. The local loop portion of the PSTN is still primarily UTP; it is this portion that limits throughput on the PSTN.

◆ A remote user can use the PSTN to access a remote server via a dial-up connection. In a dial-up connection, the user's modem converts the computer's digital pulses into analog signals. These signals travel through PSTN to the receiving computer's modem, which then converts the analog signals back into digital pulses. Unlike other types of WAN connections, dial-up connections provide a fixed period of access to the network. Throughput is limited to a maximum of 53 Kbps.

◆ X.25 is an analog, packet-switched technology optimized for reliable, long-distance data transmission. It can support 2-Mbps throughput. X.25 was originally developed and used for communications between mainframe computers and remote terminals. Though less common in North America, it remains a WAN standard around the world.

◆ Frame Relay, like X.25, relies on packet switching, but carries digital signals. It is digital, and it does not analyze frames to check for errors, but simply relays them from node to node, so Frame Relay supports higher bandwidth than X.25, offering a maximum of 45-Mbps throughput.

◆ Both X.25 and Frame Relay are configured as PVCs (permanent virtual circuits), or point-to-point connections over which data may follow different paths. When leasing an X.25 or Frame Relay circuit from a telecommunications carrier, a customer specifies endpoints and the amount of bandwidth required between them.

◆ ISDN (Integrated Services Digital Network) is an international standard for protocols at the Physical, Data Link, and Transport layers that allows the PSTN to carry digital signals. ISDN lines may carry voice and data signals simultaneously, but require an ISDN phone to carry voice traffic and an ISDN router and ISDN terminal adapter to carry data.

◆ Two types of ISDN connections are commonly used by consumers in North America: BRI (Basic Rate Interface) and PRI (Primary Rate Interface). Both use a combination of bearer channels (B channels) and data channels (D channels). B channels transmit and receive data or voice from point to point. The D channel carries information about the call, such as session initiation and termination signals, caller identity, call forwarding, and conference calling signals.

◆ BRI uses two 64-Kbps circuit-switched B channels and a 16-Kbps D channel. The maximum throughput for a BRI connection is 128 Kbps. PRI uses 23 B channels and one 64-Kbps D channel. The maximum potential throughput for a PRI connection is

1.544 Mbps. Individual subscribers rarely use PRI, preferring BRI instead, but PRI may be used by businesses and other organizations that need more throughput.

◆ T-carrier technology uses TDM (time division multiplexing) to divide a single channel into multiple channels for carrying voice, data, video, or other signals. Devices at the sending end arrange the data streams (multiplex), then devices at the receiving end filter them back into separate signals (demultiplex).

◆ The most common T-carrier implementations are T1 and T3. A T1 circuit can carry the equivalent of 24 voice channels, giving a maximum data throughput of 1.544 Mbps. A T3 circuit can carry the equivalent of 672 voice channels, giving a maximum data throughput of 44.736 Mbps.

◆ The signal level of a T-carrier refers to its Physical layer electrical signaling characteristics, as defined by ANSI standards. DS0 is the equivalent of one data or voice channel. All other signal levels are multiples of DS0.

◆ T1 technology can use UTP or STP. However, twisted-pair wiring cannot adequately carry the high throughput of multiple T1s or T3 transmissions. For T3 transmissions, fiber-optic cable or microwave connections are necessary.

◆ The CSU/DSU is the connection point for a T1 line at the customer's site. The CSU/DSU provides termination for the digital signal, ensures connection integrity through error correction and line monitoring, and converts the T-carrier frames into frames the LAN can interpret, and vice versa. It also connects T-carrier lines with terminating equipment. A CSU/DSU often includes a multiplexer.

◆ DSL uses advanced phase or amplitude modulation in the higher (inaudible) frequencies on a phone line to achieve throughputs of up to 51.8 Mbps. DSL comes in eight different varieties, each of which is either asymmetrical or symmetrical. In asymmetrical transmission, more data can be sent in one direction than in the other direction. In symmetrical transmission, throughput is equal in both directions. The most popular form of DSL is ADSL.

◆ DSL technology creates a dedicated circuit. At the consumer end, a DSL modem connects computers and telephones to the DSL line. At the carrier end, a DSLAM (DSL access multiplexer) aggregates multiple incoming DSL lines before connecting them to the Internet or to larger carriers.

◆ Broadband cable is a dedicated service that relies on the cable wiring used for TV signals. The service can theoretically provide as much as 36-Mbps downstream and 10-Mbps upstream throughput, though actual throughput is much lower. The asymmetry of cable technology makes it a logical choice for users who want to surf the Web or download data from a network.

◆ Broadband cable connections require that the customer use a special cable modem to transmit and receive signals over coaxial cable wiring. In addition, cable companies must have replaced their coaxial cable plant with hybrid fiber-coax cable to support bidirectional, digital communications.

◆ SONET is a high-bandwidth WAN signaling technique that specifies framing and multiplexing techniques at the Physical layer of the OSI Model. Its four key strengths are that it can integrate many other WAN technologies (for example, T-carriers, ISDN, and ATM technology), it offers fast data transfer rates, it allows for simple link additions and removals, and it provides a high degree of fault tolerance. Internationally, SONET is known as SDH.

◆ SONET depends on fiber-optic transmission media and uses multiplexers to connect to network devices (such as routers or telephone switches) at the customer's end. A typical SONET network takes the form of a dual-ring topology. If one ring breaks, SONET technology automatically reroutes traffic along a backup ring. This characteristic, known as self-healing, makes SONET very reliable.

◆ Wireless Internet access can be achieved through one of several technologies. Libraries, universities, coffee shops, and airports might offer access by allowing the public to connect with their IEEE 802.11 (a, b, or g) access points. These organizations, in turn, connect their access points to dedicated, high-speed Internet connections such as T1 links.

◆ IEEE 802.16a (WiMAX) is a wireless Internet access technology designed for MANs. It relies on antennas that do not require line-of-sight paths to exchange data and have ranges up to 20 miles. WiMAX can achieve throughputs of up to 70 Mbps using the 2–10GHz frequency range.

◆ Geosynchronous satellites are used to provide Internet access. This type of setup requires a stationary antenna at the customer's premises, which is connected to a modem connected to the customer's computer. Downstream throughput for satellite Internet access is advertised at throughputs of 400 Kbps, but is often higher. In the case of a dial return arrangement, upstream throughputs are limited by the analog telephone line's 53-Kbps maximum throughput.

◆ As a remote user, you can connect to a LAN or WAN in one of several ways: dial-up networking, connecting to a remote access server, remote control, terminal services, Web portals, or through a VPN (virtual private network).

◆ Dial-up networking involves a remote client dialing into a remote access server and connecting via a PSTN, X.25, or ISDN connection. The client must run dial-up software to initiate the connection and the server runs specialized remote access software to accept and interpret the incoming signals. The Microsoft RAS software provides dial-up connectivity on Windows 95, 98, NT, and 2000 client operating systems and its Windows NT and 2000 network operating systems.

◆ Remote access servers accept incoming connections from remote clients, authenticate users, allow them to log on to a LAN or WAN, and exchange data by encapsulating higher-layer protocols, such as TCP and IP in specialized protocols such as PPP. The Microsoft RRAS (Routing and Remote Access Service) is the remote access software that comes with the Windows XP and Server 2003 operating systems.

◆ To exchange data, remote access servers and clients must communicate through special Data Link layer protocols, such as PPP or SLIP, that encapsulate higher-layer protocols, such as TCP and IP. PPP is the preferred protocol. When PPP is used on an Ethernet network, as is the case with most modern broadband Internet connections, it is called PPP over Ethernet, or PPPoE.

◆ Remote control uses specialized client and host software to allow a remote user to connect via modem to a LAN-attached workstation and control that host. After connecting, the remote user can perform functions just as if she were directly connected to the LAN. Remote Desktop is a remote control client and server package that comes with Windows 95, 98, NT, 2000, XP, and Server 2003 operating systems.

◆ In terminal services, a special terminal server allows simultaneous LAN access for multiple remote users. It requires specialized client and server software. Terminal servers are optimized for fast processing and application handling. They are often connected to the network in such a way as to subject remote users to typical router, firewall, and other access controls.

◆ A Web portal supplies Web-based applications to remote users who gain access through any type of Internet connection. This option requires applications to be designed for Web use and also requires stringent security controls on the Web server.

◆ VPNs (virtual private networks) represent one way to construct a WAN from existing public transmission systems. A VPN offers connectivity only to an organization's users, while keeping the data secure and isolated from other (public) traffic. To accomplish this, VPNs may be software- or hardware-based. Either way, they depend on secure protocols and transmission methods to keep data private.

◆ To make sure a VPN can carry all types of data in a private manner over any kind of connection, special VPN protocols encapsulate higher-layer protocols via tunneling. Common tunneling protocols include PPTP and L2TP.

Key Terms

802.16—An IEEE standard for wireless MANs that specifies the use of frequency ranges between 10 and 66 GHz and requires line-of-sight paths between antennas. 802.16 antennas can cover 50 kilometers (or approximately 30 miles) and connections can achieve a maximum throughput of 70 Mbps.

802.16a—An IEEE standard for wireless MANs that specifies the use of the frequency ranges between 2 and 11 GHz. In IEEE 802.16a, antennas do not require a line-of-sight path between them and can exchange signals with multiple stations at once. 802.16a is capable of achieving up to 70-Mbps throughput and its range is 50 kilometers (or approximately 30 miles).

asymmetrical—The characteristic of a transmission technology that affords greater bandwidth in one direction (either from the customer to the carrier, or vice versa) than in the other direction.

asymmetrical DSL—A variation of DSL that offers more throughput when data travels downstream, downloading from a local carrier's switching facility to the customer, than when it travels upstream, uploading from the customer to the local carrier's switching facility.

asynchronous—A transmission method in which data being transmitted and received by nodes does not have to conform to any timing scheme. In asynchronous communications, a node can transmit at any time and the destination node must accept the transmission as it comes.

authentication—The process of comparing and matching a client's credentials with the credentials in the NOS user database to enable the client to log on to the network.

B channel—In ISDN, the "bearer" channel, so named because it bears traffic from point to point.

Basic Rate Interface—See *BRI*.

bonding—The process of combining more than one bearer channel of an ISDN line to increase throughput. For example, BRI's two 64-Kbps B channels are bonded to create an effective throughput of 128 Kbps.

BRI (Basic Rate Interface)—A variety of ISDN that uses two 64-Kbps bearer channels and one 16-Kbps data channel, as summarized by the notation 2B+D. BRI is the most common form of ISDN employed by home users.

broadband cable—A method of connecting to the Internet over a cable network. In broadband cable, computers are connected to a cable modem that modulates and demodulates signals to and from the cable company's head-end.

bus topology WAN—A WAN in which each location is connected to no more than two other locations in a serial fashion.

cable drop—A fiber-optic or coaxial cable that connects a neighborhood cable node to a customer's house.

cable modem—A device that modulates and demodulates signals for transmission and reception via cable wiring.

cable modem access—See *broadband cable*.

central office—The location where a local or long-distance telephone service provider terminates and interconnects customer lines.

channel service unit—See *CSU*.

CIR (committed information rate)—The guaranteed minimum amount of bandwidth selected when leasing a Frame Relay circuit. Frame Relay costs are partially based on CIR.

committed information rate—See *CIR*.

credentials—A user's unique identifying characteristics that enable him to authenticate with a server and gain access to network resources. The most common type of credentials are a user name and password.

CSU (channel service unit)—A device used with T-carrier technology that provides termination for the digital signal and ensures connection integrity through error correction and line monitoring. Typically, a CSU is combined with a DSU in a single device, a CSU/DSU.

CSU/DSU—A combination of a CSU (channel service unit) and a DSU (data service unit) that serves as the connection point for a T1 line at the customer's site. Most modern CSU/DSUs also contain a multiplexer. A CSU/DSU may be a separate device or an expansion card in another device, such as a router.

D channel—In ISDN, the "data" channel is used to carry information about the call, such as session initiation and termination signals, caller identity, call forwarding, and conference calling signals.

data service unit—See *DSU*.

dedicated—A continuously available link or service that is leased through another carrier. Examples of dedicated lines include ADSL, T1, and T3.

dial return—A satellite Internet access connection in which a subscriber receives data from the Internet via the satellite link, but sends data to the satellite via an analog modem (dial-up) connection. With dial return, downstream throughputs are rated for 400–500 Kbps, whereas upstream throughputs are practically limited to 53 Kbps and are usually lower. Therefore, dial return satellite Internet access is an asymmetrical technology.

dial-up—A type of connection in which a user connects to a distant network from a computer and stays connected for a finite period of time.

dial-up networking—The process of dialing into a remote access server to connect with a network, be it private or public.

digital subscriber line—See *DSL*.

downlink—A connection from an orbiting satellite to an earth-based receiver.

downstream—A term used to describe data traffic that flows from a carrier's facility to the customer. In asymmetrical communications, downstream throughput is usually much higher than upstream throughput. In symmetrical communications, downstream and upstream throughputs are equal.

DS0 (digital signal, level 0)—The equivalent of one data or voice channel in T-carrier technology, as defined by ANSI physical layer standards. All other signal levels are multiples of DS0.

DSL (digital subscriber line)—A dedicated WAN technology that uses advanced data modulation techniques at the Physical layer to achieve extraordinary throughput over regular phone lines. DSL comes in several different varieties, the most common of which is asymmetric DSL (ADSL).

DSL access multiplexer—See *DSLAM*.

DSL modem—A device that demodulates an incoming DSL signal, extracting the information and passing it to the data equipment (such as telephones and computers) and modulates an outgoing DSL signal.

DSLAM (DSL access multiplexer)—A connectivity device located at a telecommunications carrier's office that aggregates multiple DSL subscriber lines and connects them to a larger carrier or to the Internet backbone.

DSU (data service unit)—A device used in T-carrier technology that converts the digital signal used by bridges, routers, and multiplexers into the digital signal used on cabling. Typically, a DSU is combined with a CSU in a single device, a CSU/DSU.

E1—A digital carrier standard used in Europe that offers 30 channels and a maximum of 2.048-Mbps throughput.

E3—A digital carrier standard used in Europe that offers 480 channels and a maximum of 34.368-Mbps throughput.

fractional T1—An arrangement that allows a customer to lease only some of the channels on a T1 line.

Frame Relay—A digital, packet-switched WAN technology whose protocols operate at the Data Link layer. The name is derived from the fact that data is separated into frames, which are then relayed from one node to another without any verification or processing. Frame Relay offers throughputs between 64 Kbps and 45 Mbps. A Frame Relay customer chooses the amount of bandwidth he requires and pays for only that amount.

full mesh WAN—A version of the mesh topology WAN in which every site is directly connected to every other site. Full mesh WANs are the most fault-tolerant type of WAN.

GEO (geosynchronous orbit or **geostationary orbit)**—The term used to refer to a satellite that maintains a constant distance from a point on the equator at every point in its orbit. Geosynchronous satellites are the type used to provide satellite Internet access.

geostationary orbit—See *GEO*.

geosynchronous—See *GEO*.

head-end—A cable company's central office, which connects cable wiring to many nodes before it reaches customers' sites.

HFC (hybrid fiber-coax)—A link that consists of fiber cable connecting the cable company's offices to a node location near the customer and coaxial cable connecting the node to the customer's house. HFC upgrades to existing cable wiring are required before current TV cable systems can provide Internet access.

hot spot—An area covered by a wireless access point that provides visitors with wireless services, including Internet access.

hybrid fiber-coax—See *HFC*.

ICA (Independent Computing Architecture) client—The software from Citrix Systems, Inc. that, when installed on a client, enables the client to connect with a remote access server and exchange keystrokes, mouse clicks, and screen updates. Citrix's ICA client can work with virtually any operating system or application.

Integrated Services Digital Network—See *ISDN*.

ISDN (Integrated Services Digital Network)—An international standard that uses PSTN lines to carry digital signals. It specifies protocols at the Physical, Data Link, and Transport layers of the OSI Model. ISDN lines may carry voice and data signals simultaneously. Two types of ISDN connections are used in North America: BRI (Basic Rate Interface) and PRI (Primary Rate Interface). Both use a combination of bearer channels (B channels) and data channels (D channels).

J1—A digital carrier standard used in Japan that offers 24 channels and 1.544-Mbps throughput.

J3—A digital carrier standard used in Japan that offers 480 channels and 32.064-Mbps throughput.

L2TP (Layer 2 Tunneling Protocol)—A protocol that encapsulates PPP data, for use on VPNs. L2TP is based on Cisco technology and is standardized by the IETF. It is distinguished by its compatibility among different manufacturers' equipment, its ability to connect between clients, routers, and servers alike, and also by the fact that it can connect nodes belonging to different Layer 3 networks.

last mile—See *local loop*.

Layer 2 Tunneling Protocol—See *L2TP*.

LEO (low earth orbiting)—A type of satellite that orbits the earth with an altitude between 700 and 1400 kilometers, closer to the earth's poles than the orbits of either GEO or MEO satellites. LEO satellites cover a smaller geographical range than GEO satellites and require less power.

local loop—The part of a phone system that connects a customer site with a telecommunications carrier's switching facility.

low earth orbiting—See *LEO*.

medium earth orbiting—See *MEO*.

MEO (medium earth orbiting)—A type of satellite that orbits the earth 10,390 kilometers above its surface, positioned between the equator and the poles. MEO satellites can cover a larger area of the earth's surface than LEO satellites while using less power and causing less signal delay than GEO satellites.

mesh topology WAN—A type of WAN in which several sites are directly interconnected. Mesh WANs are highly fault-tolerant because they provide multiple routes for data to follow between any two points.

Metaframe—A software package from Citrix Systems, Inc. that supplies terminal services to remote clients.

network service provider—See *NSP*.

Network Termination 1—See *NT1*.

Network Termination 2—See *NT2*.

NSP (network service provider)—A carrier that provides long-distance (and often global) connectivity between major data-switching centers across the Internet. AT&T, PSINet, Sprint-link, and UUNET (MCI Worldcom) are all examples of network service providers. Customers, including ISPs, can lease dedicated private or public Internet connections from an NSP.

NT1 (Network Termination 1)—A device used on ISDN networks that connects the incoming twisted-pair wiring with the customer's ISDN terminal equipment.

NT2 (Network Termination 2)—An additional connection device required on PRI to handle the multiple ISDN lines between the customer's network termination connection and the local phone company's wires.

OC (Optical Carrier)—An internationally recognized rating that indicates throughput rates for SONET connections.

Optical Carrier—See *OC*.

partial mesh WAN—A version of a mesh topology WAN in which only critical sites are directly interconnected and secondary sites are connected through star or ring topologies. Partial mesh WANs are less expensive to implement than full mesh WANs.

permanent virtual circuit—See *PVC*.

plain old telephone service (POTS)—See *PSTN*.

Point-to-Point Protocol—See *PPP*.

Point-to-Point Protocol over Ethernet—See *PPPoE*.

Point-to-Point Tunneling Protocol—See *PPTP*.

POTS—See *PSTN*.

PPP (Point-to-Point Protocol)—A communications protocol that enables a workstation to connect to a server using a serial connection. PPP can support multiple Network layer protocols and can use both asynchronous and synchronous communications. It performs compression and error correction and requires little configuration on the client workstation.

PPPoE (Point-to-Point Protocol over Ethernet)—PPP running over an Ethernet network.

PPTP (Point-to-Point Tunneling Protocol)—A Layer 2 protocol developed by Microsoft that encapsulates PPP data for transmission over VPN connections. PPTP operates with Windows RRAS access services and can accept connections from multiple different clients. It is simple, but less secure than other modern tunneling protocols.

PRI (Primary Rate Interface)—A type of ISDN that uses 23 bearer channels and one 64-Kbps data channel, represented by the notation 23B+D. PRI is less commonly used by individual subscribers than BRI, but it may be used by businesses and other organizations needing more throughput.

PSTN (Public Switched Telephone Network)—The traditional telephone network, from the lines that connect homes and businesses to the network centers that connect different regions of a country. Now, except for the local loop, nearly all of the PSTN uses digital transmission. Its traffic is carried by fiber-optic and copper twisted-pair cable, microwave, and satellite connections.

Public Switched Telephone Network—See *PSTN*.

PVC (permanent virtual circuit)—A point-to-point connection over which data may follow any number of different paths, as opposed to a dedicated line that follows a predefined path. X.25, Frame Relay, and some forms of ATM use PVCs.

RAS (Remote Access Service)—The dial-up networking software provided with Microsoft Windows 95, 98, NT, and 2000 client operating systems and Windows NT and 2000 network operating systems. RAS requires software installed on both the client and server, a server configured to accept incoming clients, and a client with sufficient privileges (including user name and password) on the server to access its resources. In more recent versions of Windows, RAS has been incorporated into the RRAS (Routing and Remote Access Service).

RDP (Remote Desktop Protocol)—An Application layer protocol that uses TCP/IP to transmit graphics and text quickly over a remote client-host connection. RDP also carries session, licensing, and encryption information.

remote access—A method for connecting and logging on to a LAN from a workstation that is remote, or not physically connected, to the LAN. Remote access can be accomplished by one of many ways, including dial-up connections, terminal services, remote control, or Web portals.

Remote Access Service—See *RAS*.

Remote Desktop—An optional feature in Windows XP operating systems that allows a Windows XP computer to be remotely controlled from a client running the Windows 95, 98, Me, NT, XP, 2000, or Server 2003 operating system. Remote Desktop is also the program Windows XP clients use to connect with computers using Windows Terminal Server.

Remote Desktop Protocol—See *RDP*.

ring topology WAN—A type of WAN in which each site is connected to two other sites so that the entire WAN forms a ring pattern.

Routing and Remote Access service (RRAS)—The software included with Windows NT, Windows 2000 Server, and Windows Server 2003 that enables a server to act as a router, firewall, and remote access server. Using RRAS, a server can provide network access to multiple remote clients.

remote control—A remote access method in which the remote user dials into a workstation that is directly attached to a LAN. Software running on both the remote user's computer and the LAN computer allows the remote user to "take over" the LAN workstation. Only keystrokes, mouse clicks, and screen updates are exchanged between the two computers.

RRAS—See *Routing and Remote Access Service.*

satellite return—A type of satellite Internet access service in which a subscriber sends and receives data to and from the Internet over the satellite link. This is a symmetrical technology, in which both upstream and downstream throughputs are advertised to reach 400–500 Kbps; in reality, throughput is often higher.

SDH (Synchronous Digital Hierarchy)—The international equivalent of SONET.

self-healing—A characteristic of dual-ring topologies that allows them to automatically reroute traffic along the backup ring if the primary ring becomes severed.

Serial Line Internet Protocol—See *SLIP.*

signal level—An ANSI standard for T-carrier technology that refers to its Physical layer electrical signaling characteristics. DS0 is the equivalent of one data or voice channel. All other signal levels are multiples of DS0.

SLIP (Serial Line Internet Protocol)—A communications protocol that enables a workstation to connect to a server using a serial connection. SLIP can support only asynchronous communications and IP traffic, and requires some configuration on the client workstation. SLIP has been made obsolete by PPP.

SONET (Synchronous Optical Network)—A high-bandwidth WAN signaling technique that specifies framing and multiplexing techniques at the Physical layer of the OSI Model. It can integrate many other WAN technologies (for example, T-carriers, ISDN, and ATM technology) and allows for simple link additions and removals. SONET's topology includes a double ring of fiber-optic cable, which results in very high fault tolerance.

star topology WAN—A type of WAN in which a single site acts as the central connection point for several other points. This arrangement provides separate routes for data between any two sites; however, if the central connection point fails, the entire WAN fails.

SVC (switched virtual circuit)—A logical, point-to-point connections that relies on switches to determine the optimal path between sender and receiver. ATM technology uses SVCs.

switched virtual circuit—See *SVC.*

symmetrical—A characteristic of transmission technology that provides equal throughput for data traveling both upstream and downstream and is suited to users who both upload and download significant amounts of data.

symmetrical DSL—A variation of DSL that provides equal throughput both upstream and downstream between the customer and the carrier.

synchronous—A transmission method in which data being transmitted and received by nodes must conform to a timing scheme.

Synchronous Digital Hierarchy—See *SDH*.

Synchronous Optical Network—See *SONET*.

T1—A digital carrier standard used in North America and most of Asia that provides 1.544-Mbps throughput and 24 channels for voice, data, video, or audio signals. T1s rely on time division multiplexing and may use shielded or unshielded twisted-pair, coaxial cable, fiber-optic, or microwave links.

T3—A digital carrier standard used in North America and most of Asia that can carry the equivalent of 672 channels for voice, data, video, or audio, with a maximum data throughput of 44.736 Mbps (typically rounded up to 45 Mbps for purposes of discussion). T3s rely on time division multiplexing and require either fiber-optic or microwave transmission media.

T-carrier—The term for any kind of leased line that follows the standards for T1s, fractional T1s, T1Cs, T2s, T3s, or T4s.

TA (terminal adapter)—A device used to convert digital signals into analog signals for use with ISDN phones and other analog devices. TAs are sometimes called ISDN modems.

TE (terminal equipment)—The end nodes (such as computers and printers) served by the same connection (such as an ISDN, DSL, or T1 link).

terminal adapter—See *TA*.

terminal equipment—See *TE*.

terminal server—A computer that runs specialized software to act as a host and supply applications and resource sharing to remote clients.

terminal services—A remote access method in which a terminal server acts as a host for multiple remote clients. Terminal services requires specialized software on both the client and server. After connecting and authenticating, a client can access applications and data just as if it were directly attached to the LAN.

Terminal Services—The Microsoft software that enables a server to supply centralized and secure network connectivity to remote clients.

thin client—A client that relies on another host for the majority of processing and hard disk resources necessary to run applications and share files over the network.

tiered topology WAN—A type of WAN in which sites that are connected in star or ring formations are interconnected at different levels, with the interconnection points being organized into layers to form hierarchical groupings.

transponder—The equipment on a satellite that receives an uplinked signal from earth, amplifies the signal, modifies its frequency, then retransmits it (in a downlink) to an antenna on earth.

tunnel—A secured, virtual connection between two nodes on a VPN.

tunneling—The process of encapsulating one type of protocol in another. Tunneling is the way in which higher-layer data is transported over VPNs by Layer 2 protocols.

uplink—A connection from an earth-based transmitter to an orbiting satellite.

upstream—A term used to describe data traffic that flows from a customer's site to a carrier's facility. In asymmetrical communications, upstream throughput is usually much lower than downstream throughput. In symmetrical communications, upstream and downstream throughputs are equal.

virtual private network—See *VPN*.

VPN (virtual private network)—A logically constructed WAN that uses existing public transmission systems. VPNs can be created through the use of software or combined software and hardware solutions. This type of network allows an organization to carve out a private WAN through the Internet that serves only its offices, while keeping the data secure and isolated from other (public) traffic.

WAN link—A point-to-point connection between two nodes on a WAN.

Web portal—A secure, Web-based interface to an application or group of applications.

WiMAX—See *802.16a*.

wireless broadband—The term used to describe the recently released standards for high-throughput, long-distance digital data exchange over wireless connections. WiMAX (IEEE 802.16a) is one example of a wireless broadband technology.

Worldwide Interoperability for Microwave Access (WiMAX)—See *802.16a*.

X.25—An analog, packet-switched WAN technology optimized for reliable, long-distance data transmission and standardized by the ITU in the mid-1970s. The X.25 standard specifies protocols at the Physical, Data Link, and Network layers of the OSI Model. It provides excellent flow control and ensures data reliability over long distances by verifying the transmission at every node. X.25 can support a maximum of only 2-Mbps throughput.

xDSL—The term used to refer to all varieties of DSL.

Review Questions

1. A WAN in which each site is directly connected to no more than two other sites in a serial fashion is known as a _____.
   a. bus topology WAN
   b. star topology WAN
   c. ring topology WAN
   d. logical topology WAN

2. _____ is an updated, digital version of X.25 that relies on packet switching.

   a. Remote Access Service

   b. Symmetrical DSL

   c. Frame Relay

   d. xDSL

3. A _____ modulates outgoing signals and demodulates incoming signals.

   a. metaframe

   b. DSL modem

   c. PVC

   d. remote node

4. _____ specifies framing and multiplexing techniques at the Physical layer of the OSI Model.

   a. Switched Virtual Circuit

   b. Routing and Remote Access Service

   c. Terminal Services

   d. Synchronous Optical Network

5. A _____ uses TDM (time division multiplexing) over two wire pairs (one for transmitting and one for receiving) to divide a single channel into multiple channels.

   a. T-carrier

   b. Synchronous Optical Network

   c. terminal adapter

   d. virtual private network

6. True or false? Frame Relay guarantees reliable delivery of packets.

7. True or false? A T1 circuit can carry the equivalent of 672 voice or data channels.

8. True or false? On a typical T1-connected data network, the terminal equipment will consist of switches, routers, or bridges.

9. True or false? Cable modems operate at the Physical and Data Link layer of the OSI Model, and therefore do not manipulate higher-layer protocols, such as IP or IPX.

10. True or false? A SONET ring begins and ends at the telecommunications carrier's facility.

11. A(n) _____ is a network that traverses some distance and usually connects LANs, whether across the city or across the nation.

12. _____ is an analog, packet-switched technology designed for long-distance data transmission and standardized by the ITU in the mid-1970s.

13. A(n) _____ converts digital signals into analog signals for use with ISDN phones and other analog devices.

14. A(n) _____ is the creation of a communications channel for a transmission from an earth-based transmitter to an orbiting satellite.

15. _____ is an international standard, originally established by the ITU in 1984, for transmitting digital signals over the PSTN.

Chapter 8

Network Operating Systems and Windows Server 2003-Based Networking

After reading this chapter and completing the exercises, you will be able to:

- Discuss the functions and features of a network operating system

- Define the requirements for a Windows Server 2003 network environment

- Describe how Windows Server 2003 fits into an enterprise-wide network

- Perform a simple Windows Server 2003 installation

- Manage simple user, group, and rights parameters in Windows Server 2003

- Understand how Windows Server 2003 integrates with other popular network operating systems

Network operating systems enable servers to share resources with clients. They also facilitate other services such as communications, security, and user management. Network operating systems do not fit neatly into one layer of the OSI Model. Some of their functions—those that facilitate communication between computers on a network—belong in the Application layer. However, many of their functions—those that interact with users—take place above the Application layer (that is, above the top layer) of the OSI Model. Consequently, the OSI Model does not completely describe all aspects of network operating systems.

During your career as a networking professional, you will probably work with more than one NOS (network operating system). At the same time, you may work with several versions of the same NOS. To qualify for Network+ certification, you must understand the inner workings of network operating systems in general. In addition, you must be familiar with the major network operating systems: Windows Server 2003, UNIX, Linux, Mac OS X Server (which is based on a UNIX-type of operating system), and NetWare. You must be able to discuss their similarities and differences, and you must be able to integrate the major operating systems, when necessary.

This chapter introduces the basic concepts related to network operating systems and discusses in detail one of the most popular network operating systems, Windows Server 2003. The following two chapters focus on UNIX, Linux, Mac OS X Server, and NetWare.

Introduction to Network Operating Systems

NET+
3.1

Recall that most modern networks are based on a client/server architecture, in which a server enables multiple clients to share resources. Such sharing is managed by the network operating system. However, that's not all an NOS provides. Among other things, an NOS must:

◆ Centrally manage network resources, such as programs, data, and devices (for example, printers)

◆ Secure access to a network

◆ Allow remote users to connect to a network

◆ Allow users to connect to other networks (for example, the Internet)

◆ Back up data and make sure it's always available

◆ Allow for simple additions of clients and resources

◆ Monitor the status and functionality of network elements

NET+
3.1

- ◆ Distribute programs and software updates to clients
- ◆ Ensure efficient use of a server's capabilities
- ◆ Provide fault tolerance in case of a hardware or software problem

Not all of the functions just listed are built into every NOS installation; some are optional. When installing an NOS, you may accept the default settings or customize your configuration to more closely meet your needs. You may also take advantage of special services or enhancements that come with a basic NOS. For example, if you install Linux with only its minimum components, you may later choose to install the clustering service, which enables multiple servers to act as a single server, sharing the burden of NOS functions. The components included in each NOS and every version of a particular NOS vary. This variability is just one reason that you should plan your NOS installation carefully.

 NOTE

> In this chapter, the word "server" refers to the hardware on which a network operating system runs. In the field of networking, the word "server" may also refer to an application that runs on this hardware to provide a dedicated service. For example, although you may use a Compaq server as your hardware, you may run Novell's BorderManager application as your proxy server on that hardware. Some specialized server programs come with an NOS—for example, Novell's NetWare 6.5 includes a Web server program called Apache.

Although each network operating system discussed in this book supports file and print sharing, plus a host of other services, NOSs differ in how they achieve those functions, what type of environment they suit, and how they are administered. In the next section, you will learn how to select an NOS for your network.

Selecting a Network Operating System

Realistically, when designing a network, you can select from only a handful of network operating systems—specifically, Windows 2000 Server, Windows Server 2003, a version of NetWare, UNIX, Linux, or Mac OS X. The only reason not to choose one of these options is if your network is outdated or runs a proprietary, specialized application (for example, a quality control system that measures performance of catalytic converters in a test laboratory) that requires a less familiar NOS (such as Banyan VINES). Some LANs include a mix of NOSs, making interoperability a significant concern.

When choosing an NOS, you should certainly weigh the strengths and weaknesses of the available options before making a choice. Nevertheless, your decision will probably depend largely on the operating systems and applications already running on the LAN. In other words, your choice may be limited by the existing infrastructure.

NET+
3.1

For example, suppose that you are the network manager for a community college that uses 20 NetWare 6.5 servers to manage all IDs, security, and file and print sharing for 4800 users. In addition, you oversee four Windows Server 2003 computers that provide Web development and backup services. You have been asked to select an NOS for a new server for the college's Theater Department. You probably wouldn't choose Windows Server 2003, because a NetWare server would integrate more seamlessly with your existing network and better facilitate administrative tasks, such as adding new users or resources. At another organization, the opposite situation may prevail.

The following list summarizes the questions you should ask when deciding to invest in an NOS. You need to weigh the importance of each factor in your organization's environment separately.

- Is it compatible with my existing infrastructure?
- Will it provide the security required by my resources?
- Can my technical staff manage it effectively?
- Will my applications run smoothly on it?
- Will it accommodate future growth (that is, is it scalable)?
- Does it support the additional services my users require (for example, remote access, Web site development, and messaging)?
- Does it fit my budget?
- What additional training will it require?
- Can I count on competent and consistent support from its manufacturer?

In addition to assessing each NOS according to your needs, you should test an NOS in your environment before making a purchase. You can perform such testing on an extra server, using a test group of typical users and applications with specific test criteria in mind. Bear in mind that trade magazine articles or a vendor's marketing information cannot accurately predict which NOS will best suit your circumstances.

Network Operating Systems and Servers

Most networks rely on servers that exceed the minimum hardware requirements suggested by the software vendor. Every situation will vary, but to determine the optimal hardware for your servers, consider the following issues:

- How many clients will connect to the server?
- What kinds of applications will run on the server?
- How much storage space will each user need?
- How much downtime, if any, is acceptable?
- What can the organization afford?

NET+
3.1

Perhaps the most important question in this list involves the types of applications to be run by the server. For example, you can purchase an inexpensive, low-end server that runs Linux adequately and suffices for resource sharing and simple application services. However, to perform more advanced functions and run resource-intensive applications on your network, you would need to invest in a server that has significantly more processing power and memory. Every application comes with different processor, RAM, and storage requirements. Before purchasing a server, consult the installation guide for each application you intend to run.

The way an application uses resources may also influence your choice of software and hardware. Applications may or may not provide the option of sharing the processing burden between the client and server. For example, you might install a group scheduling and messaging package that requires every client to run executable files from a network drive, thereby almost exclusively using the server's processing resources. Alternately, you may install the program files on each client workstation and use the server only to distribute messages. The latter solution puts the processing burden on the client.

If your server assumes most of the application-processing burden, or if you have a large number of services and clients to support, you will need to add more hardware than the minimum NOS requirements. For example, you might add multiple processors, more RAM, multiple NICs, fault-tolerant hard disks, and a backup drive. Each of these components will enhance network reliability or performance. Carefully analyze your current situation and plans for growth before making a hardware purchasing decision. Whereas high-end servers with massive processing and storage resources plus fault-tolerant components can cost as much as $100,000, your department may need only a $1000 server.

No matter what your needs, you should ensure that your hardware vendor has a reputation for high quality, dependability, and excellent technical support. Although you may be able to trim your costs on workstation hardware by using generic models, you should spend as much as necessary for a very reliable server. A component failure in a server can cause problems for many people, whereas a workstation problem will probably affect only one person.

Network Operating System Services and Features

NET+
3.1

By now, you are familiar with the basic functions that network operating systems provide, including resource sharing, security, and network management. In this section, you will learn more about fundamental NOS functions and the meaning of terms used when comparing NOSs. You will also learn about some advanced features that enable NOSs to service clients more quickly and reliably. These features are available in all of the popular NOSs. However, the degree to which each NOS can support these features may differ. As you read about Windows Server 2003 in this chapter, and UNIX, Linux, Mac OS X Server, and NetWare in later chapters, you will learn more about their differences.

NET+
3.1
3.2

Client Support

The primary reason for using networks is to enable clients to communicate and share resources efficiently. Therefore, client support is one of the most important functions provided by an NOS. For purposes of this discussion, client support includes the following tasks:

◆ Creating and managing client accounts

◆ Enabling clients to connect to the network

◆ Allowing clients to share resources

◆ Managing clients' access to shared resources

◆ Facilitating communication between clients

You are already familiar with the way lower-layer protocols assist clients and servers in communication. The following discussion provides a general view of client/server communication from the higher layers of the OSI Model.

NET+
3.1
3.2
4.5

Client/Server Communication

Both the client software and the NOS participate in logging a client on to the server. Although clients and their software may differ, the process of logging on is similar in all NOSs, no matter what clients are involved. First, the user launches the client software from his desktop. Then, he enters his credentials (normally, a user name and password) and presses the Enter key. At this point, a service on the client workstation, called the **redirector**, intercepts the request to determine whether it should be handled by the client or by the server. A redirector belongs to the Presentation layer of the OSI Model. It is a service of both the NOS and the client's desktop operating system. After the client's redirector decides that the request is meant for the server, the client transmits this data over the network to the server. (If the redirector had determined that the request was meant for the client, rather than the server, it would have issued the request to the client's processor.) For security's sake, most modern clients will encrypt user name and password information before transmitting it to the network media. This is another Presentation layer function.

 NOTE

You should understand the logon process for troubleshooting purposes. For example, if after entering her name and password, a user receives an error message indicating that the server was not found, you can conclude that the request never made it to the server's NOS. In this case, a physical connection problem may be at fault. However, if after entering her name and password, a user receives an error message indicating that the user name or password is invalid, you know that at least the physical connection is working because the request reached the NOS and the NOS attempted to verify the user name. In this case, the password or user name may have been typed incorrectly.

NET+
3.1
3.2
4.5

At the server, the NOS receives the client's request for service and decrypts it, if necessary. Next it attempts to authenticate the user's credentials. If authentication succeeds, the NOS responds to the client by granting it access to resources on the network, according to limitations specified for this client. Figure 8-1 depicts the process of a client connecting to an NOS.

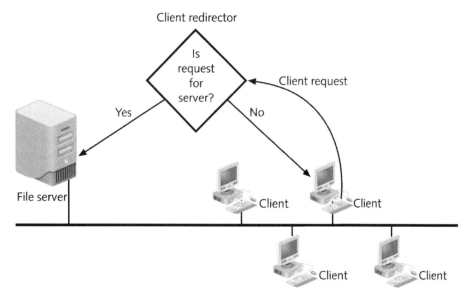

FIGURE 8-1 *A client connecting to a network operating system*

After the client has successfully logged on, the client software communicates with the network operating system each time the client requests services from the server. For example, if you wanted to open a file on the server's hard disk, you would interact with your workstation's operating system to make the file request; the file request would then be intercepted by the redirector and passed to the server via the client software. To expedite access to directories whose files you frequently require, you can **map** a drive to that directory. Mapping involves associating a letter, such as M: or T:, with a disk, directory, or other resource (such as a CD-ROM tower). Logon scripts, which run automatically after a client authenticates, often map drives to directories on the server that contain files required by client applications.

NET+
2.13
3.1
3.2
4.5

In the early days of networking, client software from one manufacturer could not always communicate with network software from another manufacturer. One difference between NOSs is the **file access protocol** that enables one system to access resources stored on another system on the network. For example, Windows Server 2003 and Windows XP clients communicate through the **CIFS (Common Internet File System)** file access protocol. CIFS is a more recent version of an older client/server communications protocol, **SMB (Server Message Block)**, which originated at IBM and then was adopted and further developed by Microsoft. SMB is the native file access protocol for Windows 9x, Me, and NT computers. Macintosh computers use **AFP (AppleTalk Filing Protocol or Apple File Protocol)** to share resources over the network.

NET+
2.13
3.1
3.2
4.5

Now, however, thanks in part to broader support of multiple file access protocols, most every type of client can authenticate and access resources via any NOS. Usually, the NOS manufacturer supplies a preferred client software package for each popular type of client. For example, Novell recommends installing its "Novell Client for Windows NT/2000/XP" on Windows 2000 or Windows XP workstations. Microsoft requires the "Client for Microsoft Networks" for Windows workstations connecting to its Windows Server 2003 NOS. Client software other than that recommended by the NOS manufacturer may work, but it is wise to follow the NOS manufacturer's guidelines.

NET+
3.1
3.2

In some instances, a piece of software called **middleware** is necessary to translate requests and responses between the client and server. Middleware prevents the need for a shared application to function differently for each different type of client. It stands in the middle of the client and the server and performs some of the tasks that an application in a simple client/server relationship would otherwise perform. Typically, middleware runs as a separate service—and often on a separate physical server—from the NOS. To interact with the middleware, a client issues a request to the middleware. Middleware reformats the request in such a way that the application on the server can interpret it. When the application responds, middleware translates the response into the client's preferred format and issues the response to the client. Middleware may be used as a messaging service between clients and servers, as a universal query language for databases, or as a means of coordinating processes between multiple servers that need to work together in servicing clients.

For example, suppose a library's database of materials is contained on a UNIX server. Some library workstations run the Macintosh desktop operating system, while others run Windows 95, Windows XP, and Linux. Each workstation must be able to access the database of materials. Ideally, all client interfaces would look similar, so that a patron who uses a Macintosh workstation one day could use a Linux workstation the next day without even noticing the difference. Further, the library can only manage one large database; it cannot maintain a separate database for each different type of client. In this case, a server running the database middleware can accept the queries from each different type of client. When a Linux workstation submits a query, the database middleware interprets the Linux instruction, reformats it, and then issues the standardized query to the database. The database middleware server might next accept a query from a Macintosh computer, which it then reformats into a standardized query for the database. In this way, the same database can be used by multiple different clients.

A client/server environment that incorporates middleware in this fashion is said to have a **3-tier architecture** because of its three layers: client, middleware, and server. To take advantage of a 3-tier architecture, a client workstation requires the appropriate client software, for example, a Web browser or remote terminal services client. Figure 8-2 illustrates the concept of middleware.

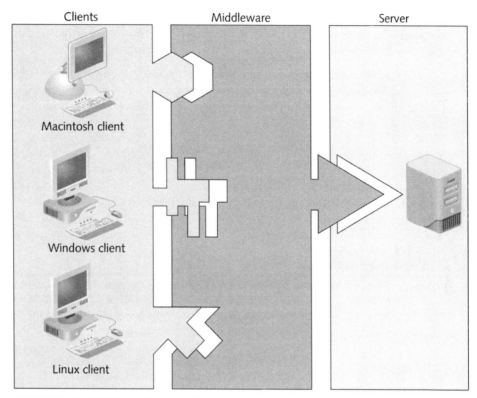

FIGURE 8-2 *Middleware between clients and a server*

Users and Groups

After a client is authenticated by the NOS, it is granted access to services and resources managed by the NOS. The type of access a client (or user) has depends on her user account and the groups to which she's assigned. In this section, you will learn about users and groups of users. Later, you will learn how to create users and groups and give them rights to resources in each of the three common NOSs.

You have probably worked with enough computers and networks to know why user names are necessary: to grant each user on a network access to files and other shared resources. Imagine that you are the network administrator for a large college campus with 20,000 user names. Assigning directory, file, printer, and other resource rights for each user name would consume all of your time, especially if the user population changed regularly. To manage network access more easily, you can combine users with similar needs and restrictions into **groups**.

In every NOS, groups form the basis for resource and account management. Many network administrators create groups according to department or, even more specifically, according to job function within a department. They then assign different file or directory access rights to each group. For example, on a high school's network, the administrator may create a group called Students for the students and a group called Teachers for the teachers. The administrator could then easily grant the Teachers group rights to view all attendance and grade records on the server, but deny the same access to the Students group.

To better understand the role of groups in resource sharing, first consider their use on a relatively small scale. Suppose you are the network administrator for a public elementary school. You might want to give all teachers and students access to run instructional programs from a network directory called PROGRAMS. In addition, you might want to allow teachers to install their own instructional programs in this same directory. Meanwhile, you need to allow teachers and administrators to record grade information in a central database called GRADES. Of course, you don't want to allow students to read information from this database. Finally, you might want administrators to use a shared drive called STAFF to store the teachers' performance review information, which should not be accessible to teachers or students. Table 8-1 illustrates how you can provide this security by dividing separate users into three groups: teachers, students, and administrators.

Table 8-1 Providing security through groups

Group	Rights to PROGRAMS	Rights to GRADES	Rights to STAFF
Teachers	Read, modify	Full control	No access
Students	Read	No access	No access
Administrators	No access	Read, modify	Full control

 TIP

Plan your groups carefully. Creating many groups (for example, a separate group for every job classification in your organization) may impose as much of an administrative burden as not using any groups.

After an NOS authenticates a user, it checks the user name against a list of resources and their access restrictions list. If the user name is part of a group with specific access permissions or restrictions, the system will apply those same permissions and restrictions to the user's account.

For simpler management, groups can be nested (one within another) or arranged hierarchically (multiple levels of nested groups) according to the type of access required by different types of users. The way groups are arranged will affect the permissions granted to each group's members. For example, if you created a group called Temps within the Administrators group for temporary office assistants, the Temps group would be nested within the Administrators

NET+
3.1
3.2
group and would, by default, share the same permissions as the Administrators group. Such permissions are called **inherited** because they are passed down from the parent group (Administrators) to the child group (Temps). If you wanted to restrict the Temps users from seeing the staff performance reviews, you would have to separately assign restrictions to the Temps group for that purpose. After you assign different rights to the Temps group, you have begun creating a hierarchical structure of groups. NOSs differ slightly in how they treat inherited permissions, and enumerating these differences is beyond the scope of this book. However, if you are a network administrator, you must thoroughly understand the implications of hierarchical group arrangements. For the Network+ exam, you should at least understand how groups can be used to efficiently manage permissions and restrict or allow access to resources.

After the user and group restrictions are applied, the client is allowed to share resources on the network, including data, data storage space, applications, and peripherals. To understand how NOSs enable resource sharing, it is useful to first understand how they identify and organize network elements.

NET+
3.1
Identifying and Organizing Network Elements

Modern NOSs follow similar patterns for organizing information about network elements, such as users, printers, servers, data files, and applications. This information is kept in a directory. A **directory** is a list that organizes resources and associates them with their characteristics. One example of a directory is a file system directory, which organizes files and their characteristics, such as file size, owner, type, and permissions. You may be familiar with this type of directory from manipulating or searching for files on a PC. NOSs do use file system directories. However, these directories are different from and unrelated to the directories used to manage network clients, servers, and shared resources.

NET+
2.10
3.1
Recent versions of all popular NOSs use directories that adhere to standard structures and naming conventions set forth by **LDAP (Lightweight Directory Access Protocol)**. LDAP is a protocol used to access information stored in a directory. By following the same directory standard, different NOSs can easily share information about their network elements.

According to the LDAP standard, a thing or person associated with the network is represented by an **object**. Objects may include users, printers, groups, computers, data files, and applications. Each object may have a multitude of **attributes**, or properties, associated with it. For example, a user object's attributes may include a first and last name, location, mail address, group membership, access restrictions, and so on. A printer object's attributes may include a location, model number, printing preferences (for example, double-sided printing), and so on.

NET+
2.10
3.1

In LDAP-compatible directories, a **schema** is the set of definitions of the kinds of objects and object-related information that the database can contain. For example, one type of object is a printer, and one type of information associated with that object is the location of the printer. Thus, "printer" and "location of printer" would be definitions contained within the schema.

A directory's schema may contain two types of definitions: classes and attributes. **Classes** (also known as **object classes**) identify what type of objects can be specified in a directory. User account is an example of an object class. Another object class is Printer. As you learned previously, an attribute is a characteristic associated with an object. For example, Home Directory is the name of an attribute associated with the User account object, whereas Location is an attribute associated with the Printer object. Classes are composed of many attributes. When you create an object, you also create a number of attri-butes that store information about that object. The object class and its attributes are then saved in the directory. Figure 8-3 illustrates some schema elements associated with a User account object.

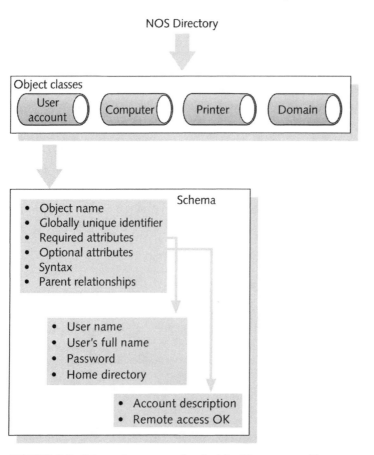

FIGURE 8-3 *Schema elements associated with a User account object*

NET+
2.10
3.1

To better organize and manage objects, a network administrator places objects in **containers,** or **OUs (organizational units)**. OUs are logically defined receptacles that serve only to assemble similar objects. Returning to the example of a school network, suppose each student, teacher, and administrator were assigned a user name and password for the network. Each of these users would be considered an object, and each would require an account. (An **account** is the record of a user that contains all of her properties, including rights to resources, password, name, and so on.) One way of organizing these objects is to put all the user objects in one OU called "Users." But suppose the school provided a server and a room of workstations strictly for student use. The use of these computers would be restricted to applications and Internet access during only certain hours of the day. As the network administrator, you could gather the student user names (or the "Students" group), the student server, the student printers, and the student applications in an OU called "Students." You could associate the restricted network access (an attribute) with this OU so that these students could access the school's applications and the Internet only during certain hours of the day. An OU can hold multiple objects. Also, an OU is a logical construct—that is, a means of organizing other things; it does not represent something real. An OU is different from a group because it can hold and apply parameters for many different types of objects, not only users. In the LDAP standard, directories and their contents form trees. A **tree** is a logical representation of multiple, hierarchical levels within a directory. The term "tree" is drawn from the fact that the whole structure shares a common starting point (the root) and from that point extends **branches** (or containers), which may extend additional branches, and so on. Objects are the last items in the hierarchy connected to the branches and are sometimes called **leaf objects**. Figure 8-4 depicts a simple directory tree.

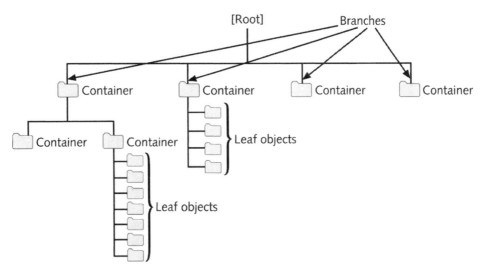

FIGURE 8-4 *A directory tree*

NET+
2.10
3.1

Before you install a network operating system, be sure to plan the directory tree with current and future needs in mind. For example, suppose you work at a new manufacturing firm called Circuits Now that produces high-quality, inexpensive circuit boards. You might decide to create a simple tree that branches into three OUs: users, printers, and computers. But if Circuits Now plans to open new manufacturing facilities sometime in the future (for instance, one devoted to making memory chips and another for transistors), you might want to call the first OU in the tree "circuit boards." This would separate the existing circuit board business from the new businesses, which would employ different people and require different resources. Figure 8-5 shows both possible trees.

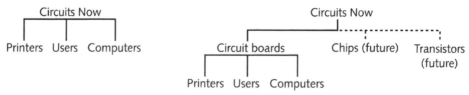

FIGURE 8-5 *Two possible directory trees for the same organization.*

Directory trees are very flexible, and as a result, are usually more complex than the examples in Figure 8-4. Chances are that you will enter an organization that has already established its tree, and you will need to understand the logic of that tree to perform your tasks. Later in this chapter, you will learn about Active Directory, which is the LDAP-compatible directory used by the Windows Server 2003 NOS.

Sharing Applications

NET+
3.1

As you have learned, one of the significant advantages of the client/server architecture is the ability to share resources, thereby reducing costs and the time required to manage the resources. In this section, you will learn how an NOS enables clients to share applications.

Shared applications are often installed on a file server that is specifically designed to run applications. In a small organization, however, they may be installed on the same server that provides other functions, such as Internet, security, and remote access services. As a network administrator, you must be sure to purchase a license for the application that allows it to be shared among clients. In other words, you cannot legally purchase one licensed copy of Microsoft Word, install it on a server, and allow hundreds of your users to share it.

Software licensing practices vary from one vendor to another. A software vendor may sell an organization a fixed quantity of licenses, which allows only that number of clients to use the application simultaneously. This type of licensing is known as **per user** licensing. For example, suppose a life sciences library purchases a 20-user license for a database of full-text articles from a collection of *Biology* journals. If 20 users are running the database, the 21st person who attempts to access the database will receive a message announcing that access to the database is prohibited because all of the licenses are currently in use. Other software vendors sell a separate license for each *potential* user. Regardless of whether the user is accessing an application,

NET+
3.1

a license is reserved so that the user will not be denied access. This practice is commonly known as **per seat** licensing. For example, if the life sciences library wanted to make sure each of its 15 employees could access the *Biology* journal database at any time, it would choose to purchase licenses for each of the employees. The application on the server could verify the user through a logon ID or the workstation's network address, for example. A third licensing option is the **site license**, which for a fixed price allows an unlimited number of users to legally access an application. In general, a site license is most economical for applications shared by many people (for example, if the life sciences library shared its *Biology* journal database with all of the students on a university campus), whereas for small numbers of users, per seat or per user licenses are more economical.

After you have purchased the appropriate type and number of licenses, you are ready to install the application on a server. Before doing so, however, you should make sure your server has enough free hard disk space, memory, and processing power to run the application. Then follow the software manufacturer's guidelines for a server installation. Depending on the application, this process may be the same as installing the application on a workstation or it might be much different.

After installing the software on a server, you are ready to make it available to clients. Through the NOS, you must assign users rights to the directories where the application's files are installed. Users will at least need rights to access and read files in those directories. For some applications, you may also need to give users rights to create, delete, or modify files associated with the application. For example, a database program may create a small temporary file on the server when a user launches the program to indicate to other potential users that the database is open. If this is the case, users must have rights to create files in the directory where this temporary file is kept. An application's installation guidelines will indicate the rights you need to assign users for each of the application's directories.

Next, you will need to provide users with a way to access the application. On Windows-based or Macintosh clients and on some UNIX and Linux clients, you can create an icon on the user's desktop that is associated with the application file. When the user double-clicks the icon, her client software issues a request for the server to open the application. In response, the NOS sends a part of the program to her workstation, where it will be held in RAM. This allows the user to interact with the program quickly, without having to relay every command over the network to the server. As the user works with the application, the amount of processing that occurs on her workstation versus the amount of processing that the server handles will vary according to the network architecture.

You may wonder how an application can operate efficiently or accurately when multiple users are simultaneously accessing its files. After all, an application's program file is a single resource. If two or more network users double-click their application icon simultaneously, how does the application know which client to respond to? In fact, the NOS is responsible for arbitrating access to these files. In the case of multiple users simultaneously launching a network application from their desktop icons, the NOS will respond to one request, then the next, then the next, each time issuing a copy of the program to the client's RAM. In this way, each client is technically working with a separate instance of the application.

NET+
3.1

Shared access becomes more problematic when multiple users are simultaneously accessing the same data files as well as the same program files. For example, consider an online auction site, which accepts bids on many items from many Internet users. Imagine that an auction is nearing a close with three users simultaneously bidding on the same stereo. How does the auction site's database accept bid data for that stereo from multiple sources? One solution to this problem is middleware. The three Internet bidders cannot directly modify the database, located on the auction site's server. Instead, a middleware program on the server accepts data from the clients. If the database is not busy, the middleware passes a bid to the database. If the database is busy (or open), the middleware queues the bids (forces them to wait) until the database is ready to rewrite its existing data, then passes one bid, then another, and another, to the database until its queue is empty. In this way, only one client's data can be written to the database at any point in time.

Sharing Printers

Sharing peripherals, such as printers, can increase the efficiency of managing resources and reduce costs for an organization. In this section, you will learn how networks enable clients to share printers. Sharing other peripheral devices, such as fax machines, works in a similar manner.

In most cases, an organization will designate a server as the print server—that is, as the server in charge of managing print services. A printer may be directly attached to the print server or, more likely, be attached to the network in a location convenient for the users. A printer directly attached to the network requires its own NIC and network address, as with any network node. In other cases, shared printers may be attached to networked workstations. In order for these printers to be accessible, the workstation must be turned on and functioning properly. Figure 8-6 depicts multiple ways to share printers on a network.

After the printer is physically connected to the network, it needs to be recognized and managed by the NOS before users can access it. Different NOSs have different interfaces for managing printers, but all NOSs can:

♦ Create an object that identifies the printer to the rest of the network

♦ Assign the printer a unique name

♦ Install drivers associated with the printer

♦ Set printer attributes, such as location and printing preferences

♦ Establish or limit access to the printer

♦ Remotely test and monitor printer functionality

♦ Update and maintain printer drivers

♦ Manage print jobs, including modifying a job's priority or deleting jobs from the queue

NET+
3.1

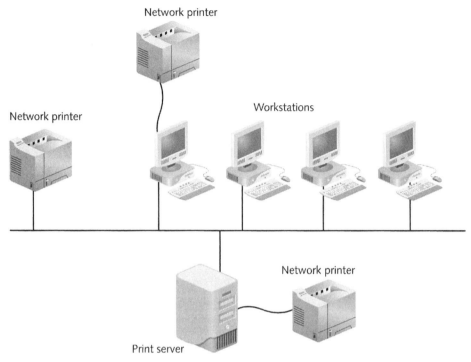

FIGURE 8-6 *Shared printers on a network*

 NOTE

As a network administrator, you should establish a plan for naming printers before you install them. Because the names you assign the printers will appear in lists of printers available to clients, you should choose names that users can easily decipher. For example, an HP LaserJet 5000 in the Engineering Department may be called "ENG_HP5000," or a Xerox Phaser 4400N in the southwest corner of the building may be called "Xe4400_SW." Whatever convention you choose, remain consistent to avoid user confusion and to make your own job easier.

NOSs provide special interfaces for creating new printer objects and assigning them attributes. In Windows Server 2003, the Add Printer Wizard takes you through the process of adding a shared printer step by step. The first step in this process is to indicate whether the printer is local or networked, as shown in Figure 8-7.

In NetWare 6.x, the first step in setting up a shared printer is creating a new object. A series of menu options leads you through the process of creating a new object, beginning with a

FIGURE 8-7 *The Add Printer Wizard*

printer identification screen. With a UNIX or Linux operating system, you can define a printer using the lpd command at the shell prompt or, with many instances of UNIX and Linux, follow a GUI-based tool, similar to the Windows Add Printer Wizard.

As you create the new printer, the NOS will require you to install a printer driver, unless one is already installed on the server. This makes the printer's device driver files accessible to users who want to send jobs to that printer. Before users can access the printer, however, you must ensure that they have proper rights to the printer's queue. The **printer queue** (or share, as it is known in Microsoft terminology) is a logical representation of the printer's input and output. That is, a queue does not physically exist, but rather acts as a sort of virtual "in box" for the printer. When a user prints a document (whether by clicking a button or selecting a menu command), he sends the document to the printer queue. To send it to the printer queue, he must have rights to access that queue. As with shared data, the rights to shared printers can vary. Users may have minimal privileges, which allow them to simply send jobs to the printer, or they may have advanced privileges, which allow them to change the priority of print jobs in the queue, or even (in the case of an administrator) change the name of the queue.

Networked printers appear as icons in the Printers folder on Windows and Macintosh workstations, just as local printers would appear. After they have found a networked printer, users can send documents to that printer just as they would send documents to a local printer. When a user chooses to print, the client redirector determines whether the request should be transmitted to the network or remain at the workstation. On the network, the user's request gets passed to the print server, which puts the job into the appropriate printer queue for transmission to the printer.

Managing System Resources

Because a server's system resources (for example, memory and processor) are limited and are required by multiple users, it is important to make the best use of them. Modern NOSs have capabilities that maximize the use of a server's memory, processor, bus, and hard disk. The result

NET+

3.1

is that a server can accommodate more client requests faster—thus improving overall network performance. In the following sections, you will learn about some NOS techniques for managing a server's resources.

Memory

From working with PCs, you may be familiar with the technique of using virtual memory to boost the total memory available to a system. Servers can use both physical and virtual memory, too, as this section describes.

Before learning about virtual memory, you should understand physical memory. The term **physical memory** refers to the RAM chips that are installed on the computer's system board and whose sole function is to provide memory to that machine. The amount of physical memory required by your server varies depending on the tasks that it performs. For example, the minimum amount of physical memory required to run the Standard Edition of Windows Server 2003 is 256 MB. However, if you intend to run file and print sharing, Internet, and remote access services on one server, additional physical memory will ensure better performance. Windows Server 2003, Standard Edition (the version of Windows Server 2003 designed to meet the needs of most businesses) can support as much as 4 GB of RAM. (When calculating the appropriate amount of physical memory for your server, remember that the ability to process instructions also depends on processing speed.)

Another type of memory may be logically carved out of space on the hard disk for temporary use. In this arrangement, both the space on the hard disk and the RAM together form **virtual memory**. Virtual memory is stored on the hard disk as a **page file** (or **paging file** or **swap file**), the use of which is managed by the operating system. Each time the system exceeds its available RAM, blocks of information, called pages, are moved out of RAM and into virtual memory on disk. This technique is called **paging**. When the processor requires the information moved to the page file, the blocks are moved back from virtual memory into RAM.

Virtual memory is both a blessing and a curse. On the one hand, if your server has plenty of hard disk space, you can use virtual memory to easily expand the memory available to server applications. This is a great advantage when a process temporarily needs more memory than the physical memory can provide. Virtual memory is typically engaged by default; it requires no user or administrator intervention and is accessed without the clients' knowledge. (However, as a network administrator, you can modify the amount of hard disk space available for virtual memory.) On the other hand, using virtual memory slows operations, because accessing a hard disk takes longer than accessing physical memory. Therefore, an excessive reliance on virtual memory will cost you in terms of performance.

Multitasking

Another technique that helps servers use their system resources more efficiently is multitasking. **Multitasking** is the ability of a processor to perform many different operations in a very brief period of time. If you have used multiple programs on a desktop computer, you have taken

NET+
3.1

advantage of your operating system's multitasking capability. All of the major NOSs are capable of multitasking. If they weren't, network performance would be considerably slower, because busy servers are continually receiving and responding to multiple requests.

However, multitasking does not mean performing more than one operation simultaneously. (A computer can only process multiple operations simultaneously if it has more than one processor.) In NetWare, UNIX, Linux, Mac OS X Server, and Windows Server 2003, the server actually performs one task at a time, allowing one program to use the processor for a certain period of time, and then suspending that program to allow another program to use the processor. Thus, each program has to take turns loading and running. Because no two tasks are ever actually performed at one time, this capability is more accurately referred to as **preemptive multitasking**—or, in UNIX terms, **time-sharing**. Preemptive multitasking happens so quickly, however, that the average user would probably think that multiple tasks were occurring simultaneously.

Multiprocessing

Before you learn about the next method of managing system resources, you need to understand the terms used when discussing data processing. A **process** is a routine of sequential instructions that runs until it has achieved its goal. When it is running, a word-processing program's executable file is an example of a process. A **thread** is a self-contained, well-defined task within a process. A process may contain many threads, each of which may run independently of the others. All processes have at least one thread—the main thread. For example, to eliminate the waiting time when you save a file in your word processor, the programmer who wrote the word-processor program might have designed the file save operation as a separate thread. That is, the file save part of the program happens in a thread that is independent of the main thread. This independent execution allows you to continue typing while a document is being written to the disk, for example.

On systems with only one processor, only one thread can be handled at any time. Thus, if a number of programs are running simultaneously, no matter how fast the processor, a number of processes and threads will be left to await execution. Using multiple processors allows different threads to run on different processors. The support and use of multiple processors to handle multiple threads is known as **multiprocessing**. Multiprocessing is often used on servers as a technique to improve response time. To take advantage of more than one processor on a computer, its operating system must be capable of multiprocessing. Depending on the edition, a Windows Server 2003 computer may support up to 32 processors.

Multiprocessing splits tasks among more than one processor to expedite the completion of any single instruction. To understand this concept, think of a busy metropolitan freeway during rush hour. If five lanes are available for traffic, drivers can pick any lane—preferably the fastest lane—to get home as soon as possible. If traffic in one lane slows, drivers may choose another, less congested lane. This ability to move from lane to lane allows all traffic to move faster. If the same amount of traffic had to pass through only one lane, everyone would go slower and get home later. In the same way, multiple processors can handle more instructions more rapidly than a single processor could.

NET+

3.1

Modern NOSs, including the most current versions of NetWare, UNIX, Linux, and Windows Server 2003, support a special type of multiprocessing called **symmetric multiprocessing**, which splits all operations equally among two or more processors. Another type of multiprocessing, **asymmetric multiprocessing**, assigns each subtask to a specific processor. Continuing the freeway analogy, asymmetric multiprocessing would assign all semi trucks to the far-right lane, all pickup trucks to the second-to-the right lane, all compact cars to the far-left lane, and so on. The efficiency of each multiprocessing model is open to debate, but, in general, symmetric processing completes operations more quickly because the processing load is more evenly distributed.

Multiprocessing offers a great advantage to servers with high processor usage—that is, servers that perform numerous tasks simultaneously. If an organization uses its server merely for occasional file and print sharing, however, multiple processors may not be necessary. You should carefully assess your processing needs before purchasing a server with multiple processors. Some processing bottlenecks are not actually caused by the processor—but rather by the time it takes to access the server's hard disks or by problems related to cabling or connectivity devices.

Introduction to Windows Server 2003

NET+

3.1

Windows Server 2003 is the latest version of Microsoft's NOS, released in 2003. Windows Server 2003 is a redesign and enhancement of its predecessors, Windows 2000 Server and Windows NT Server. Windows-based NOSs are known for their intuitive graphical user interface, multitasking capabilities, and compatibility with a huge array of applications. A **GUI (graphical user interface**; pronounced "gooey"**)** is a pictorial representation of computer functions that, in the case of NOSs, enables administrators to manage files, users, groups, security, printers, and so on. Windows Server 2003 carries on many of the advantages of Windows 2000 Server, plus enhances its security, reliability, performance, and ease of administration.

With Windows Server 2003, Microsoft in fact released four different, but related NOSs: Windows Server 2003, Standard Edition; Windows Server 2003, Web Edition; Windows Server 2003, Enterprise Edition; and Windows Server 2003, Datacenter Edition. Differences between the editions can be summarized as follows:

◆ *Standard Edition*—Provides the basic resource sharing and management features necessary for most businesses, including support for up to 4 GB of RAM and four processors performing symmetric multiprocessing.

◆ *Web Edition*—Provides added services for Web site hosting, Web development, and Web-based applications.

◆ *Enterprise Edition*—Provides support for up to eight processors performing symmetric multiprocessing, up to 32 GB of RAM in the 32-bit version (up to 64 GB of RAM in the 64-bit version), and clustering. Designed for environments that need a high level of reliability and performance. (Clustering is a fault-tolerance technique discussed in Chapter 13.)

NET+
3.1

◆ *Datacenter Edition*—Provides support for up to 32 processors performing symmetric multiprocessing in the 32-bit version (up to 64 processors in the 64-bit version), up to 64 GB of RAM in the 32-bit version (512 GB of RAM in the 64-bit version), and clustering. Designed for environments that need the highest degree of reliability and performance.

Windows Server 2003 is a popular network operating system because it addresses most of a network administrator's needs very well. Microsoft is, of course, a well-established vendor, and many devices and programs are compatible with its systems. Its large market share guarantees that technical support—whether through Microsoft, private developer groups, or third-party newsgroups—is readily available. If you become MCSE-certified, you will be eligible to receive enhanced support directly from Microsoft. This enhanced support (including a series of CDs) will help you solve problems more quickly and accurately. Because Windows operating systems are so widely used, you can also search newsgroups on the Web and will probably find someone who has encountered and solved a problem like yours.

Some general benefits of the Windows Server 2003, Standard Edition NOS include:

◆ Support for multiple processors, multitasking, and symmetric multiprocessing

◆ A comprehensive system for organizing and managing network objects, called Active Directory

◆ Simple centralized management of multiple clients, resources, and services through a customizable tool called the MMC (Microsoft Management Console)

◆ Multiple, integrated Web development and delivery services that incorporate a high degree of security and an easy-to-use administrator interface

◆ Support for modern protocols and security standards

 NOTE

Although Windows 2000 Server does support use of the NetBEUI protocol, Windows Server 2003 does not.

◆ Excellent integration with other NOSs and support for many different client operating systems

◆ Integrated remote client services—for example, automatic software updates and client assistance

◆ Provisions for monitoring and improving server performance

◆ Support for high-performance, large-scale storage devices

Although Microsoft NOSs have long been appreciated for their simple user interfaces, some network administrators have criticized their performance and security. With the release of Windows Server 2003, Microsoft has implemented measures to address these criticisms. Bear in

NET+
3.1

mind that performance greatly depends on the type of routines and commands tested. The only sure way to find out how an NOS will perform on your network is to compare it against another NOS using your applications, clients, and infrastructure.

This chapter gives a broad overview of how Windows Server 2003, Standard Edition fits into a network environment. It also provides other information necessary to qualify for Network+ certification. It does not attempt to give exhaustive details of the process of installing, maintaining, or optimizing Windows Server 2003 networks. For this in-depth knowledge (and particularly if you plan to pursue MCSE certification), you should invest in books devoted to Windows Server 2003.

Windows Server 2003 Hardware Requirements

NET+
3.1

You have learned that servers generally require more processing power, memory, and hard disk space than do client workstations. In addition, servers may contain redundant components, self-monitoring firmware, multiple processors and NICs, or peripherals other than the common CD-ROM and floppy disk drives. The type of servers you choose for your network will depend partly on your NOS. Each NOS demands specific server hardware.

An important resource for determining what kind of hardware to purchase for your Windows server is the Microsoft Hardware Compatibility List. The **HCL (Hardware Compatibility List)** lists all computer components proven to be compatible with Windows Server 2003. The HCL is included on the same CD-ROM as your Windows Server 2003 software. If you don't find a hardware component on the HCL that shipped with your software, you can search for it on the Microsoft Web site. At the time of this writing, links to Microsoft's searchable hardware compatibility lists for its Windows 98, Me, 2000, and Server 2003 operating systems could be found at the following Web site: *http://www.microsoft.com/whdc/hcl/default.mspx*. (For Windows Server 2003, the link leads to a catalog of software and hardware that has been certified for use with this operating system.) Always consult this list before buying new hardware. Although hardware that is *not* listed on the HCL may work with Windows Server 2003, Microsoft's technical support won't necessarily help you solve problems related to such hardware.

Table 8-2 lists Microsoft's minimum server requirements for Windows Server 2003, Standard Edition.

Minimum requirements specify the least amount of RAM, hard disk space, and processing power you must have to run the NOS. Your applications and performance demands, however, may require more resources. Some of the minimum requirements listed in Table 8-2 (for example, the 133-MHz Pentium processor) may apply to the smallest test system, but not to a realistic networking environment. Be sure to assess the optimal configuration for your network's server based on your environment's needs before you purchase new hardware. For

NET+
3.1

instance, you should make a list of every application and utility you expect the server to run in addition to the NOS. Then look up the processor, memory, and hard disk requirements for each of those programs and estimate how significantly their requirements will affect your server's overall hardware requirements. It is easier and more efficient to perform an analysis before you install the server than to add hardware after your server is up and running.

Table 8-2 Minimum hardware requirements for Windows Server 2003, Standard Edition

Component	Requirement
Processor	133 MHz or higher Pentium or Pentium-compatible processor; 550 MHz recommended. Windows Server 2003, Standard Edition supports up to four CPUs in one server.
Memory	128 MB of RAM is the absolute minimum, but at least 256 MB is recommended. A computer running Windows Server 2003 may hold a maximum of 4 GB of memory.
Hard disk drive	A hard drive supported by Windows Server 2003 (as specified in the HCL) with a minimum of 1.5 GB of free space available for system files.
NIC	Although a NIC is not required by Windows Server 2003, it is required to connect to a network. Use a NIC found on the HCL. The NOS can support the use of more than one NIC.
CD-ROM	A CD-ROM drive found on the HCL is required unless the installation will take place over the network.
Pointing device	A mouse or other pointing device found on the HCL.
Floppy disk drive	Not required.

A Closer Look at Windows Server 2003

NET+
3.1

By now, you should understand some of the features that are important to all network operating systems. You should also have a sense of the type of organization that might choose Windows Server 2003 as its preferred NOS. Next, you will learn specifically how Windows Server 2003 manages its system resources, data files, and network objects.

Windows Server 2003 Memory Model

Earlier, you learned that Windows Server 2003, Standard Edition can use up to four processors and, further, that it employs a type of multiprocessing called symmetric multiprocessing.

NET+
3.1

In addition, Windows Server 2003 can use virtual memory. This section provides more information on how Windows Server 2003 optimizes its use of a server's memory to juggle many complex tasks.

Some versions of Windows Server 2003 use a 32-bit addressing scheme, whereas others use a 64-bit addressing scheme (which also requires a different type of processor). Essentially, the larger the addressing size, the more efficiently instructions can be processed. For comparison, consider that Microsoft's first NOS used a 16-bit addressing scheme.

The Windows Server 2003, Standard Edition memory model also assigns each application (or process) its own 32-bit memory area. This memory area is a logical subdivision of the entire amount of memory available to the server. Assigning separate areas to processes helps prevent one process from interfering with another's operations, even though the processor is handling both instructions.

Another important feature of the Windows Server 2003 memory model is that it allows you to install more physical memory on the server than previous versions of Windows did, which in turn means that the server can process more instructions faster.

Finally, as you have learned, Windows Server 2003 can use virtual memory. To find out how much virtual memory your Windows Server 2003 computer uses, click Start, click Control Panel, click System, select the Advanced tab, and then click Settings under the Performance heading. The Performance Options dialog box opens. Select the Advanced tab, as shown in Figure 8-8. To change the amount of virtual memory the server uses, click the Change button. This opens the Virtual Memory dialog box, where you can increase or decrease the paging file size. If you suspect that your server's processing is being degraded because it relies on virtual memory too often, you should invest in additional physical memory (RAM).

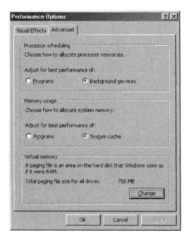

FIGURE 8-8 *Advanced tab in the Performance Options dialog box*

NET+
3.1

Windows Server 2003 File Systems

Windows Server 2003 supports several file systems, or methods of organizing, managing, and accessing its files through logical structures and software routines. Popular file system types include FAT16, FAT32, UDF, CDFS, and NTFS, which are discussed in the following sections. You will also learn when it is most appropriate to use NTFS or FAT32—the two most common file systems for the hard disk—on your Windows Server 2003 computer.

FAT (File Allocation Table)

FAT (file allocation table) is the original PC file system that was designed in the 1970s to support floppy disks and, later, hard disks. To understand FAT, you must first understand the distribution of data on a disk. Disks are divided into allocation units (also known as clusters). Each allocation unit represents a small portion of the disk's space; depending on your operating system, the allocation unit's size may or may not be customizable. A number of allocation units combine to form a **partition**, which is a logically separate area of storage on the hard disk. The actual FAT (that is, the table, which is the basis of the FAT file system) is a hidden file positioned at the beginning of a partition. It keeps track of used and unused allocation units on that partition. The FAT also contains information about the files within each directory, as well as the size of files, their names, and the times that they were created and updated.

 NOTE

When part of a disk uses the FAT method of tracking files, that portion of the disk is called a "FAT partition."

FAT16

One version of FAT, known as **FAT16**, uses 16-bit allocation units. FAT16 was the standard file system for early DOS- and Windows-based computers. But FAT16 has proved inadequate for most modern operating systems because of its partition size limitations, naming limitations, fragmentation, security, and speed issues. Some significant FAT16 characteristics are described in the following list. (Note the differences between Microsoft's version of FAT16 and the standard FAT16.)

◆ A FAT16 partition or file cannot exceed 2 GB (when FAT16 is used with the Windows Server 2003 file system, its maximum size is 4 GB).

◆ FAT16 uses 16-bit fields to store file size information.

◆ FAT16 (without additional utilities) supports only filenames with a maximum of eight characters in the name and three characters in the extension.

◆ FAT16 categorizes files on a disk as Read (a user can read the file), Write (a user can modify or create the file), System (only the operating system can read or write the file), Hidden (a user cannot see the file on the drive without explicitly searching for hidden files), or Archive (used to indicate whether the file has recently been backed up).

NET+
3.1

◆ A FAT16 drive stores data in noncontiguous blocks and uses links between fragments to ensure that data belonging to the same file, for example, can be pieced together when the file is requested by the operating system. This approach is unreliable and inefficient, and it may cause corruption.

◆ Because of FAT16's low overhead, it can write data to a hard disk very quickly.

FAT32

The FAT16 file system was enhanced in the mid-1990s to accommodate longer filenames and to permit faster data access via 32-bit addressing. This version of FAT, called **FAT32**, retains some features of the original FAT, such as the Read, Write, System, Hidden, and Archive file attributes. But in contrast to FAT16, FAT32 reduces the maximum size limit file clusters so that space on a disk is used more efficiently. In some cases, FAT32 can conserve as much as 15% of the space that would be required for the same number of files on a FAT16 partition. These and other FAT32 characteristics are described in the following list:

◆ FAT32 uses 28-bit fields to store file size information (4 of the 32 bits are reserved).

◆ FAT32 supports long filenames.

◆ FAT32 theoretically supports partitions up to 2 Terabytes in size (in Windows Server 2003, however, the maximum FAT32 partition size is 32 Gigabytes).

◆ Unlike FAT16 partitions, FAT32 partitions can be easily resized without damaging data.

◆ FAT32 provides greater security than FAT16.

For these reasons, FAT32 is preferred over FAT16 for modern operating systems.

CDFS (CD-ROM File System) and UDF (Universal Disk Format)

CDFS (CD-ROM File System) is the file system used to read from and write to a CD-ROM disc. Windows Server 2003 supports CDFS so as to allow program installations and CD-ROM file sharing over the network. No intervention is necessary to install or configure the CDFS—it is installed automatically when you install Windows Server 2003. In addition to CDFS, Windows Server 2003 supports the **UDF (Universal Disk Format)**, which is another file system used on CD-ROMs and DVD (digital versatile disc) media. DVDs and CD-ROMs can be used to store large quantities of data in a networking environment.

NTFS (New Technology File System)

Microsoft developed **NTFS (New Technology File System)** expressly for its Windows NT platform, which preceded Windows 2000 Server and Windows Server 2003. NTFS is secure, reliable, and makes it possible to compress files so they take up less space. At the same time, NTFS can handle massive files, and allow fast access to data, programs, and other shared resources. It is used on Windows NT, Windows 2000 Server, Windows XP, and Windows

Server 2003 computers. If you are working with Windows Server 2003, Microsoft recommends choosing NTFS for your server's file system. Therefore, you should familiarize yourself with the following NTFS features:

◆ NTFS filenames can be a maximum of 255 characters long.

◆ NTFS stores file size information in 64-bit fields.

◆ NTFS files or partitions can theoretically be as large as 16 exabytes (2^{64} bytes).

◆ NTFS is required for Macintosh connectivity.

◆ NTFS incorporates sophisticated, customizable compression routines. These compression routines reduce the space taken by files by as much as 40%. A 10-GB database file, for example, could be squeezed into 6 GB of disk space.

◆ NTFS keeps a log of file system activity to facilitate recovery if a system crash occurs.

◆ NTFS is required for encryption and advanced access security for files, user accounts, and processes.

◆ NTFS improves fault tolerance through RAID and system file redundancy. (RAID is discussed in detail in Chapter 13.)

Before installing Windows Server 2003, you should decide which file system (or systems) you will use. Although FAT32 improves on the FAT16 file system and typically appears on Windows 9x workstations, it is not optimal for Windows 2000 Server or Windows Server 2003 computers. Instead, the NTFS file system is preferred because it enables a network administrator to take advantage of security and file compression enhancements.

One drawback to using an NTFS partition is that it cannot be read by older operating systems, such as Windows 95, Windows 2000 Professional, and early versions of UNIX. However, these older OSs—plus Windows NT, 2000 Server, and Server 2003—can read FAT partitions. You should also be aware that you can convert a FAT drive into an NTFS drive on a Windows Server 2003 computer, but you cannot convert an NTFS drive into a FAT drive.

Typically, due to all the benefits listed previously, you should select NTFS whenever you install Windows Server 2003. The only instance in which you should not use NTFS is if one of your server's applications is incompatible with this file system.

MMC (Microsoft Management Console)

For each administrative function, Microsoft's NOS provides a separate tool. For example, a tool is available for creating and managing users and groups, and another tool is available for managing a Web hosting service. Each administrative tool has a unique, but similar, graphical interface. In Windows 2000 Server and Windows Server 2003, all of the administrative tools are integrated into a single interface called the **MMC (Microsoft Management Console)**. This section provides an overview of MMC, its capabilities, and how you can use it in your network environment.

NET+
3.1

An MMC is simply an interface. Its purpose is to gather multiple administrative tools into a convenient console for your network environment. If an MMC doesn't contain the tools you want, you can add or remove administrative tools to suit your situation. The tools you add to the interface are known as **snap-ins**. For example, you may be the network administrator for two servers, one that performs data backup services and another dedicated to Web services, on the same network. On the backup server, your MMC should definitely include the Disk Management snap-in, which allows you to easily manage the hard disk's volumes, and the Event Viewer snap-in, which allows you to view what processes have run on the server and whether they generated any errors. On the Web server, you might want to install the FrontPage Server Extensions, IIS (Internet Information Services), and the IAS (Internet Authentication Service) snap-ins. However, if the first server is only used for data backup, there is no need to add these three Internet-related snap-ins to its MMC. You can create multiple MMCs on multiple servers, or even multiple MMCs on one server.

NOTE

You can find snap-ins either through an MMC or as separate selections from the Administrative Tools menu.

Before using MMCs for the first time, you must create a custom console by running the MMC program and adding your selections. To do so, click Start, click Run, type mmc in the text box in the Run dialog box, and then click OK. The Console1 (MMC) window opens as a window separated into two panes, as shown in Figure 8-9. The left pane lists the administrative tools. The right pane lists specific details for a selected tool.

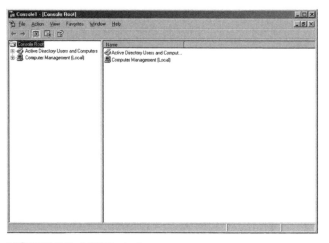

FIGURE 8-9 *MMC window*

When you first open the MMC, it does not contain any snap-ins; the panes of its window are empty. You can customize the MMC by adding administrative tools.

To add administrative tools to your MMC interface:

1. Click **File** in the MMC main menu bar, and then click **Add/Remove Snap-in**. The Add/Remove Snap-in dialog box opens, listing the currently installed snap-ins.

2. Click the **Add** button. The Add Standalone Snap-in dialog box opens with a list of available snap-ins.

3. In the Add Standalone Snap-in dialog box, click the tool you want to add to your console, and then click **Add**. Continue adding snap-ins until you have chosen all that you want to include in your MMC. (When you add some snap-ins, such as Event Viewer and Device Manager, you will be asked to select the computer that you want the snap-in to manage, and to indicate whether the snap-in should manage the local computer or another computer on the network.)

4. After you have added all the snap-ins you want, click **Close**. The Add Standalone Snap-in dialog box closes.

5. Click **OK**. The Add/Remove Snap-in dialog box closes and the new tools are added to the MMC. Notice that the left pane of your MMC window now includes the snap-ins you've added.

After you have customized your MMC, you need to save your settings. When you save your settings, you assign a name to the specific console (or administrative interface) that you have just created. Assign the MMC a name that indicates its function. For example, you might create an MMC specifically for managing users and groups and then name that MMC "My User Tool." Later, you can access this same MMC by choosing Start/All Programs/Administrative Tools/My User Tool.

MMC can operate in two modes—author mode and user mode. Network administrators who have full permissions on the server typically use author mode, which allows full access for adding, deleting, and modifying snap-ins. However, sometimes an administrator may want to delegate certain network management functions to colleagues, without giving them full permissions on the servers. In such a situation, the administrator can create an MMC that runs in user mode—in other words, that provides limited user privileges. For example, the user might be allowed to view administrative information, but not to modify the snap-ins.

Active Directory

Early in this chapter, you learned about directories, the methods for organizing and managing objects on the network. Windows Server 2003 uses a directory service called **Active Directory**, which was originally designed for Windows 2000 Server networks. This section provides an overview of how Active Directory is structured and how it uses standard naming conventions to better integrate with other networks. You'll also learn how Active Directory stores information for Windows domains.

NET+

3.1

Workgroups

A Windows Server 2003 network can be set up in a workgroup model or a domain model. This section describes the workgroup model. In the next section, you will learn about the more popular domain model.

A **workgroup** is a group of interconnected computers that share each other's resources without relying on a central server. In other words, a workgroup is a type of peer-to-peer network. As in any peer-to-peer network, each computer in the workgroup has its own database of user accounts and security privileges.

Because each computer maintains its own database, each user must have a separate account on each computer he wants to access. This decentralized management results in significantly more administration effort than a client/server Windows Server 2003 network would require. In addition, workgroups are only practical for small networks with very few users. On the other hand, peer-to-peer networks such as a Windows Server 2003 workgroup are simple to design and implement and may be the best solution for home or small office networks in which security concerns are minimal.

Domains

In Windows Server 2003 terminology, the term **domain model** refers to a type of client/server network that relies on domains rather than on workgroups. A **domain** is a group of users, servers, and other resources that share a centralized database of account and security information. The database that domains use to record their objects and attributes is contained within Active Directory. Domains are established on a network to make it easier to organize and manage resources and security. For example, a university might create separate domains for each of the following colleges: Life Sciences, Humanities, Communications, and Engineering. Within the Engineering domain, additional domains such as "Chemical Engineering," "Industrial Engineering," "Electrical Engineering," and "Mechanical Engineering" may be created, as shown in Figure 8-10. In this example, all users, workstations, servers, printers, and other resources within the Engineering domain would share a distinct portion of the Active Directory database.

Keep in mind that a domain is not confined by geographical boundaries. Computers and users belonging to the university's Engineering domain may be located at five different campuses across a state, or even across the globe. No matter where they are located, they obtain their object, resource, and security information from the same database and the same portion of Active Directory.

Depending on the network environment, an administrator can define domains according to function, location, or security requirements. For example, if you worked at a large hospital whose WAN connected the city's central healthcare facility with several satellite clinics, you could create separate domains for each WAN location, or you could create separate domains for each clinical department, no matter where they are located. Alternately, you might choose to use only one domain and assign the different locations and specialties to different organizational units within the domain.

NET+
3.1

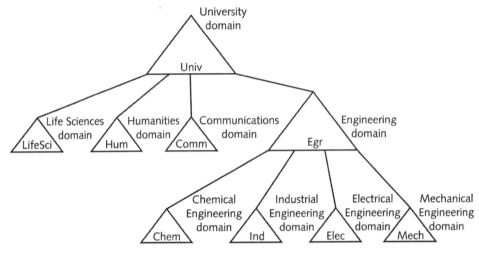

FIGURE 8-10 *Multiple domains in one organization*

The directory containing information about objects in a domain resides on computers called **domain controllers**. A Windows Server 2003 network may use multiple domain controllers. In fact, you should use at least two domain controllers on each network so that if one domain controller fails, the other will continue to retain your domains' databases. Windows Server 2003 computers that do not store directory information are known as **member servers**. Because member servers do not contain a database of users and their associated attributes (such as password or permissions to files), member servers cannot authenticate users. Only domain controllers can do that. Every server on a Windows Server 2003 network is either a domain controller or a member server.

When a network uses multiple domain controllers, a change to the database contained on one domain controller is copied to the databases on other domain controllers so that their databases are always identical. The process of copying directory data to multiple domain controllers is known as **replication**. Replication ensures redundancy so that in case one of the domain controllers fails, another can step in to allow clients to log on to the network, be authenticated, and access resources. Figure 8-11 illustrates a Windows Server 2003 network built using the domain model.

OUs (Organizational Units)

Earlier you learned that NOSs use OUs (organizational units) to hold multiple objects that have similar characteristics. In Windows Server 2003, an OU can contain over 10 million objects. And each OU can contain multiple OUs. For example, suppose you were the network administrator for the university described previously, which has the following domains: Life

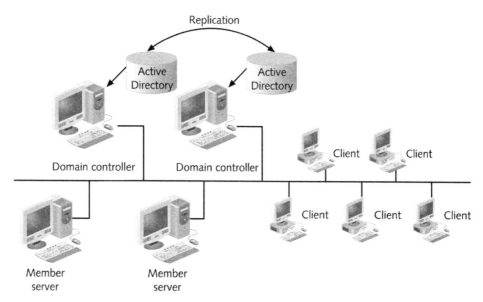

FIGURE 8-11 *Domain model on a Windows Server 2003 network*

Sciences, Humanities, Communications, and Engineering. You could choose to make additional domains within each college's domain. But suppose instead that the colleges weren't diverse or large enough to warrant separate domains. In that case, you might decide to group objects according to organizational units. For the Life Sciences domain, you might create the following OUs that correspond to the Life Sciences departments: Biology, Geology, Zoology, and Botany. In addition, you might want to create OUs for the buildings associated with each department. For example, "Schroeder" and "Randall" for Biology, "Morehead" and "Kaiser" for Geology, "Randall" and "Arthur" for Zoology, and "Thorne" and "Grieg" for Botany. The tree in Figure 8-12 illustrates this example. Notice that "Randall" belongs to both the Biology and Zoology OUs.

Collecting objects in organizational units allows for simpler, more flexible administration. For example, suppose you want to restrict access to the Zoology printers in the Arthur building so that the devices are only available between 8 a.m. and 6 p.m. To accomplish this, you could apply this policy to the OU that contains the Arthur building's printer objects.

Trees and Forests

Now that you understand how an NOS directory can contain multiple levels of domains and organizational units, you are ready to learn the structure of the directory that exists above domains. It is common for large organizations to use multiple domains in their Windows Server 2003 networks. Active Directory organizes multiple domains hierarchically in a **domain tree**

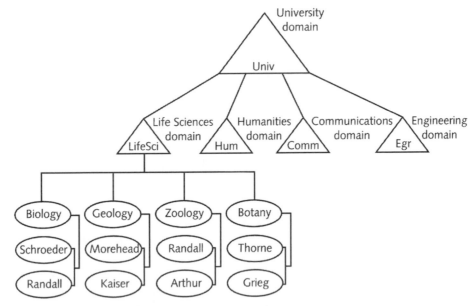

FIGURE 8-12 *A tree with multiple domains and OUs*

(or simply, tree). (Recall that NOS trees were introduced earlier in the chapter. Active Directory's domain tree is an example of a typical NOS tree.) At the base of the Active Directory tree is the **root domain**. From the root domain, **child domains** branch out to separate groups of objects with the same policies, as you saw in Figure 8-10. Underneath the child domains, multiple organizational units branch out to further subdivide the network's systems and objects.

A collection of one or more domain trees is known as a **forest**. All trees in a forest share a common schema. Domains within a forest can communicate, but only domains within the same tree share a common Active Directory database. In addition, objects belonging to different domain trees are named separately, even if they are in the same forest. You will learn more about naming later in this chapter.

Trust Relationships

For your network to work efficiently, you must give some thought to the relationships between the domains in a domain tree. The relationship between two domains in which one domain allows another domain to authenticate its users is known as a **trust relationship**. Active Directory supports two types of trust relationships: two-way transitive trusts and explicit one-way trusts. Each child and parent domain within a domain tree and each top-level domain in a forest share a **two-way transitive trust** relationship. This means that a user in domain A is recognized by and can be authenticated by domain B, and vice versa. In addition, a user in domain A may be granted rights to any of the resources managed by domain B, and vice versa.

NET+
3.1

When a new domain is added to a tree, it immediately shares a two-way trust with the other domains in the tree. These trust relationships allow a user to log on to and be authenticated by a server in any domain within the domain tree. However, this does not necessarily mean that the user has privileges to access any resources in the tree. A user's permissions must be assigned separately for the resources in each different domain. For example, suppose Betty is a research scientist in the Mechanical Engineering Department. Her user account belongs to the Engineering domain at the university. One day, due to construction in her building, she has to temporarily work in an office in the Zoology Department's building across the street. The Zoology Department OU, and all its users and workstations, belong to the Life Sciences domain. When Betty sits down at the computer in her temporary office, she can log on to the network from the Life Sciences domain, which happens to be the default selection on her logon screen. She can do this because the Life Sciences and Engineering domains have a two-way trust. After she is logged on, she can access all her usual data, programs, and other resources in the Engineering domain. But even though the Life Sciences domain authenticated Betty, she will not automatically have privileges for the resources in the Life Sciences domain. For example, she can retrieve her research reports from the Mechanical Engineering Department's server, but unless a network administrator grants her rights to access the Zoology Department's printer, she cannot print the document to the networked printer outside her temporary office.

Figure 8-13 depicts the concept of a two-way trust between domains in a tree.

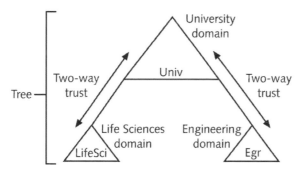

FIGURE 8-13 *Two-way trusts between domains in a tree*

The second type of trust relationship supported by Active Directory is an **explicit one-way trust**. In this scenario, two domains that are not part of the same tree are assigned a trust relationship. The explicit one-way trust does not apply to other domains in the tree, however. Figure 8-14 shows how an explicit one-way trust can enable domains from different trees to share resources. In this figure, notice that the Engineering domain in the University tree and the Research domain in the Science Corporation tree share a one-way trust. However, this trust does not apply to parent or child domains associated with the Engineering or Research domains. In other words, the Research domain could not have access to the entire University domain (including its child domains such as Life Sciences).

NET+
3.1

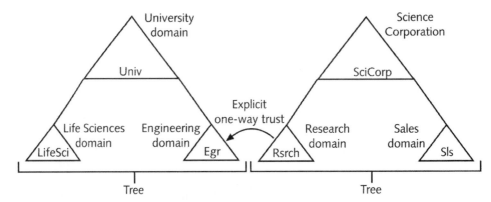

FIGURE 8-14 *Explicit one-way trust between domains in different trees*

This section introduced you to the basic concepts of a Windows Server 2003 network structure. If you are charged with establishing a new network that relies on Windows 2000 Server or Windows Server 2003, you will need to learn a lot more about Active Directory. In that case, you'll want to buy a book on the topic, and perhaps take a class exclusively devoted to Active Directory.

Naming Conventions

In the preceding section, you learned to think about domains in terms of their hierarchical relationships. Getting to know the structure of a network by studying its domain tree is similar to understanding your ancestry by studying a genealogical chart. Another way to look at ancestors is to consider their names and their relationship to you. For example, suppose a man named John Smith walks into a room full of relatives. The various people in the room will refer to him in various ways, depending on their relationship to him. One person might refer to him as "Uncle John," another as "Grandpa John," and another as "My husband, John." In the same way, different types of names, depending on where in the domain they are located, may be used to identify objects in a domain.

NET+
2.10
3.1

Naming (or addressing) conventions in Active Directory are based on the LDAP naming conventions. Because it is a standard, LDAP allows any application to access the directory of any system according to a single naming convention. Naming conventions on the Internet also follow LDAP standards. In Internet terminology, the term **namespace** refers to the complete database of hierarchical names used to map IP addresses to their hosts' names. The Internet namespace is not contained on just one computer. Instead, it is divided into many smaller pieces on computers at different locations on the Internet. In the genealogy analogy, this would be similar to having part of your family records in your home file cabinet, part of them in the state historical archives, part of them in your country's immigration files, and part of them in the municipal records of the country of your ancestors' origins. Somewhere in the Internet's vast, decentralized database of names and IP addresses (its namespace), your office workstation's IP address indicates that it can be located at your organization and, further, that it is associated with your computer.

NET+
3.1

In Active Directory, the term namespace refers to a collection of object names and their associated places in the Windows 2000 Server or Windows Server 2003 network. In the genealogy analogy, this would be similar to having one relative (the Active Directory) who knows the names of each family member and how everyone is related. If this relative recorded the information about every relative in a database (for instance, Mary Smith is the wife of John Smith and the mother of Steve and Jessica Smith), this would be similar to what Active Directory does through its namespace.

Because the Active Directory namespace follows the conventions of the Internet's namespace, when you connect your Windows Server 2003 network to the Internet, these two namespaces are compatible. For example, suppose you work for a company called Trinket Makers, and it contracted with a Web development firm to create a Web site. Further, suppose that the firm chose the Internet domain name "trinketmakers.com" to uniquely identify your company's location on the Internet. When you plan your Windows Server 2003 network, you will want to call your root domain "trinketmakers" to match its existing Internet domain name (the ".com" part is assumed to be a domain). That way, objects within the Active Directory namespace can be assigned names related to the "trinketmakers.com" domain name, and they will match the object's name in the Internet namespace, should that be necessary.

NET+
2.10
3.1

Each object on a Windows Server 2003 network can have three different names. The following list describes the formats for these names, which follow LDAP specifications:

◆ **DN (Distinguished name)**—A long form of the object name that explicitly indicates its location within a tree's containers and domains. A distinguished name includes a **DC (domain component)** name, the names of the domains to which the object belongs, an OU (organizational unit) name, the names of the organizational units to which the object belongs, and a **CN (common name)**, or the name of the object. A common name must be unique within a container. In other words, you could have a user called "Msmith" in the Legal container and a user called "Msmith" in the Accounting container, but you could not have two users called "Msmith" in the Legal container. Distinguished names are expressed with the following notation: DC=domain name, OU=organizational unit name, CN=object name. For example, the user Mary Smith in the Legal OU of the trinket-makers domain would have the following distinguished name: DC=com, DC=trinketmakers, OU=legal, CN=msmith. Another way of expressing this distinguished name would be trinketmakers.com/legal/msmith.

◆ **RDN (Relative distinguished name)**—A name that uniquely identifies an object within a container. For most objects, the relative distinguished name is the same as its CN in the distinguished name convention. A relative distinguished name is an attribute that belongs to the object. This attribute is assigned to the object when the administrator creates the object (as you will learn to do later in this chapter). Figure 8-15 provides an example of an object, its distinguished name, and its relative distinguished name.

NET+
2.10
3.1

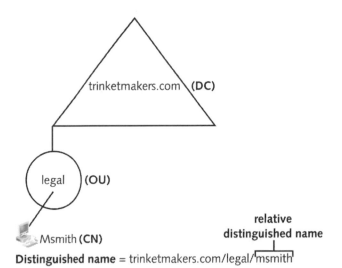

FIGURE 8-15 *Distinguished name and relative distinguished name*

◆ **UPN (user principal name)**—The preferred naming convention for users in e-mail and related Internet services. A user's UPN looks like a familiar Internet address, including the positioning of the domain name after the @ sign. When you create a user account, the user's logon name is added to a **UPN suffix**, the portion of the user's UPN that follows the @ sign. A user's default UPN suffix is the domain name of her root domain. For example, if Mary Smith's user name is msmith and her root domain is trinketmakers.com, her UPN suffix is trinketmakers.com, and her UPN is *msmith@trinketmakers.com.*

In addition to these names, each object has a **GUID (globally unique identifier)**, a 128-bit number that ensures that no two objects have duplicate names. The GUID is generated and assigned to an object upon its creation. Rather than use any of the alphabetical names, network applications and services communicate with an object via the object's GUID.

Now that you have been introduced to the Windows Server 2003 Active Directory structure and naming conventions, you are ready to learn about installing the NOS.

Planning for Installation

NET+
3.1

When installing and configuring an NOS, you must create a plan for your server and its place in your network before you insert the installation CD. You need to consider many factors, including organizational structure, server function, applications, number of users, LAN architecture, and optional services (such as remote access) when developing this plan. After you have installed and configured the NOS, changing its configuration may prove difficult and cause service disruptions for users. To begin, first ensure that your server hardware meets the Windows Server 2003 requirements (see Table 8-2). Next, you must prepare answers to the following list of critical preinstallation decisions.

♦ *How many, how large, and what kind of partitions will the server require?* Windows Server 2003 must be installed on a single partition. When you install it, you will have a choice of:

♦ Creating a new partition on a nonpartitioned portion of a hard disk

♦ Creating a new partition on a partitioned hard disk

♦ Installing Windows Server 2003 on an existing partition

♦ Removing an existing partition and creating a new one for installation

The option you choose will depend on how your server is currently partitioned, whether you want to keep data on existing partitions, and how you want to subdivide your server's hard disk. If you know the number and size of the partitions you need (for example, on a 16-GB hard disk you might want to create a 6-GB system partition and a 10-GB data partition), it is best to create them during installation.

♦ *What type of file system will the server use?* Recall that the optimal file system for a Windows Server 2003 computer is NTFS. Choose NTFS unless your applications require a different file system. NTFS must be used if you intend to use Active Directory and the domain model for centralized resource and client management.

♦ *What will you name the server?* You may use any name that includes a maximum of 15 characters, and that includes numerals, letters, and hyphens, but no spaces, periods, or other special characters (for example, ? or =). Choose a practical, descriptive name that distinguishes the server from others and that is easy for you and your users to remember. For example, you might use geographical server names, such as Boston or Chicago. Alternatively, you might name servers according to their function, such as Marketing or Research. If the server is a member of a large domain, you might identify it in relationship to its domain name. For example, the Marketing server in the Pittsburgh domain might be called Mktg-Pitts.

♦ *Which protocols and network services should the server use?* Before you begin installing Windows Server 2003, you need to know which protocol (or protocols) your network requires. On Windows Server 2003, TCP/IP is the default protocol, and depending on your circumstances, you should probably leave it as such. If your server runs Web services or requires connectivity with UNIX, Linux, or Mac OS X Server systems, you *must* run TCP/IP. If your Windows Server 2003 must communicate with an older NetWare server that relies on IPX/SPX, you should also install the NWLink IPX/SPX Compatible Protocol and Gateway Services for NetWare. For communication with Macintosh computers running the AppleTalk protocol, you need to install AppleTalk.

♦ *What will the Administrator password be?* Use a strong password—in other words, one that is difficult to crack. In Windows Server 2003, network administrators can require users to choose stronger passwords than ever, which means, among other things, they must include a mix of different characters, including numbers, uppercase letters, lowercase letters, and special characters (such as *, & !, @, and so on), and they cannot contain any part of the user's name, nor can they resemble any known English words. The strongest passwords are also the longest. The Administrator password should meet the most stringent criteria.

◆ *Should the network use domains or workgroups, and, if so, what will they be called?* First decide whether your network will use workgroups or domains. During installation you will be asked whether the server should join an existing workgroup, be a new workgroup server, or join an existing domain. As you learned, in a workgroup situation, computers share network access in a peer-to-peer fashion. It is more likely that your environment will require domains, in which the security for clients and resources is centralized. If the server will be joining an existing domain, you must know the domain name, domain controller name, and the DNS server name. Domain names should describe the logical group of servers and users they support. You may use any name that includes numerals, letters, and hyphens, but no spaces, periods, or other special characters (for example, ? or =). Popular schemes for naming domains incorporate geography and function into the names. For example, in a domain model for a WAN spanning several cities, you might want to name your domains Boston, Chicago, Detroit, Pittsburgh, and so on. In a very large organization, you may want to use a less limiting convention. For example, if your company's business is chemical production, you might want to name your domains Hydrocarbons, Resins, Solvents, and so on.

◆ *Will the server support additional services?* During installation, you will be asked to choose which services your server will support. Of course, you must install certain protocols and network services in order for clients to access the server. You may also want to install optional services, such as: Remote Installation Services, Terminal Server, Windows Media Services, and Management and Monitoring Tools. Although it's easiest to include additional services during the original installation, they can be added later as well.

◆ *Which licensing mode will you use?* You may choose one of two licensing modes: per seat or per server. The **per server** licensing mode allows a limited number of clients to access the server simultaneously. (The actual number is determined by your Windows Server 2003 purchase.) In per server mode, any of your organization's clients may be capable of connecting to the server. The number of concurrent connections is restricted. Per server mode is a popular choice in organizations that have a limited number of servers and many users, or where multiple users share workstations (for example, a mail-order catalog's call center). The per seat mode requires a license for every client capable of connecting to the Windows Server 2003. In environments that include multiple Windows Server 2003 computers and in which each user has his own workstation, this choice is probably more economical than per server licensing.

 NOTE

If you are running Windows Server 2003 as a Web or FTP server for anonymous clients (for example, Internet users from anywhere in the world), you do not need separate Windows Server 2003 client licenses for these types of clients.

NET+
3.1

◆ *How can I remember all of this information?* As you make these preinstallation decisions, you should note your choices on a server installation form and keep the form with you during installation. Appendix D offers an example of such a form.

The preceding list describes only the most significant installation options. You should also be prepared to:

◆ Read and accept the license agreement.

◆ Identify your organization.

◆ Provide your Product Key (which can be found on the jacket of your Windows Server 2003 CD-ROM).

◆ Select the appropriate time and date.

◆ Specify display settings.

◆ Identify and supply drivers for hardware components, such as video cards, NICs, printers, and so on.

If you are upgrading a server that currently runs an older Windows NOS, such as Windows NT or Windows 2000 Server, you will have to follow a special upgrade process, as described in the Microsoft documentation. The following section walks you through a new Windows Server 2003 installation.

Installing and Configuring a Windows Server 2003 Server

NET+
3.1

After you have devised a plan for your Windows Server 2003 installation, you can begin the actual installation process. In this section, you will learn about the available options and the decisions you must make when installing and initially configuring your Windows Server 2003 server.

The Installation Process

You can install Windows Server 2003 from a CD-ROM or remotely over the network. If you use the network method, be aware that this type of installation generates a high volume of network traffic and shouldn't be performed while clients are attempting to use the network. You also have the choice of performing a Windows Server 2003 installation in attended or unattended mode. The term "attended mode" simply means that someone is at the computer responding to installation prompts as they appear. Unattended mode relies on a preprogrammed script (which can be customized for different environments) to answer installation prompts. This mode prevents the need for a network administrator to be present during server installation. However, creating the script requires forethought and preparation.

Now that you understand the variables and considerations for a Windows Server 2003 installation, you are prepared to install the NOS. Following is a summary of the process, which

NET+

3.1

assumes an attended installation using a CD-ROM (in other words, somebody will be responding to prompts, rather than allowing a script to respond to prompts automatically). It represents a typical, simple installation for a small or home office. The options you choose and the prompts you see during installation will depend on your network environment and your pre-installation decisions. The time your installation requires will also depend on the options you choose, in addition to your server's processor speed and amount of memory.

Insert the Windows Server 2003 CD-ROM in your server's CD-ROM drive and restart the server (making sure your computer is configured to boot from a CD-ROM). After booting, you may be prompted to press any key to install Windows Server 2003. After you press a key, the Windows Setup screen appears, and installation will proceed, with prompts, to:

♦ Inspect your hardware and load appropriate hardware drivers and other files.

♦ Display the Windows Licensing Agreement, which you should read and then press the F8 key to accept if you want to continue.

♦ Search the hard disk to determine whether any previous versions of Windows are installed.

♦ Scan the hard disk to assess how many partitions and what type of partitions are available.

♦ Select a partition for Windows Server 2003 installation (at this point, you may also create a new partition or delete an existing partition).

♦ Format the disk partition you selected.

♦ Copy files to the Windows installation folders on the hard disk.

After the Windows installation files are copied to your server's hard disk, the Setup process has finished preparing your computer for the Windows Server 2003 installation. Your computer restarts and returns to a graphical user interface screen. During the next part of the process, you are prompted to:

♦ Customize regional and language options, which include how numbers should be formatted and what languages you want Windows Server 2003 to support.

♦ Personalize your software by entering your name and your organization's name.

♦ Enter the 25-character Product Key that appears on your CD-ROM folder.

♦ Select the licensing mode you want to use—either Per Server, Per Device, or Per User.

♦ Assign a name to your server and enter (and confirm) the password associated with the Administrator user account.

♦ Enter modem dialing information.

♦ Enter date and time settings.

♦ Choose whether you want to use typical network settings or manually configure your server's networking components.

♦ Indicate whether the server is part of a workgroup or a domain.

NET+

3.1

After gathering the preceding information, the setup program installs and registers the components you've selected, installs Start menu items, saves settings, and removes the temporary files created during installation. Then, your system restarts (or prompts you to click Finish to restart). Finally, you can log on to the server using the Administrator user name and password.

Initial Configuration

After you have completed the Windows Server 2003 installation, the server still isn't ready to support clients on a network. First, you must configure the software (for instance, assign it a role in the domain, if your network follows the domain model). The first time you log on to the server using the Administrator ID, the Manage Your Server window will open, as shown in Figure 8-16. Here you can establish the server's role. For example, you can designate the server as a file server, print server, mail server, terminal server, and so on.

FIGURE 8-16 *Manage Your Server window*

Suppose you want to assign the role of file server to a newly installed Windows Server 2003 computer. In that case, you would follow these steps:

1. If the Manage Your Server window is not open, click **Start**, and then click **Manage Your Server**. The Manage Your Server window opens.

2. Click **Add or remove a role**. The Configure Your Server Wizard window opens, reminding you to make sure that all of the server's peripherals are installed, that it is connected to the network and to the Internet, if Internet access is desired, and that you have the Windows Server 2003 installation CD handy.

3. Click **Next** to continue.

NET+
3.1

4. The Configure Your Server Wizard detects your network connection settings. Then, it prompts you to select the server's role from a list of possibilities.

5. Click **File server**, then click **Next** to continue.

6. The Configure Your Server Wizard prompts you to set default disk quotas (a limit on how much of the server's hard disk space users' personal files can occupy) for new users, if desired. After you have made your choice, click **Next** to continue.

7. Next, you are prompted to choose whether you want to enable the File Server Indexing Service, which allows users to search indexed files for specific words or characters. (By default, the Indexing Service is turned off.) After making your selection, click **Next** to continue.

8. Finally, you are presented with a summary of your selections. Confirm that the selections are correct, and then click **Next** to continue.

9. The Share a Folder Wizard appears, prompting you to establish shared folders on the server. Click **Next** to continue.

10. Specify a folder path for the folder you want to share. For example, you might want to share the folder called "C:\Documents and Settings\All Users\Documents." Then click **Next** to continue.

11. You are prompted to name the share you have just created and, if you desire, provide a description. For example, you could name the share "Public documents" and enter a description of "A directory available for file sharing among all users." Click **Next** to continue.

12. The Share a Folder Wizard prompts you to indicate users' permissions to the folder. The default selection allows users read-only access to files in the folder, as shown in Figure 8-17. ("Read-only access" means that users can view data files and execute program files within a folder, but they cannot modify, delete, or add files.) If you want users to be able to save files to the folder, you could choose **Administrators have full access; other users have read and write access**. Click **Finish** to continue.

FIGURE 8-17 *Specifying permissions in the Share a Folder Wizard*

13. The next screen announces that "Sharing was Successful." Click **Close** to close the Share a Folder Wizard.

14. The Configure Your Server Wizard announces that "This Server is Now a File Server." Click **Finish** to close the wizard.

15. You have now made it possible for users to share files on this server. In the next section, you will learn how to create user accounts and make users part of a group.

Establishing Users and Groups

The installation process creates two accounts: Guest and Administrator. The **Guest** account is a predefined user account with limited privileges that allows a user to log on to the computer. The **Administrator** account is a predefined user account that has the most extensive privileges for resources both on the computer and on the domain that it controls (if it is a domain controller). These two predefined user accounts are designed primarily to allow you to log on to a computer after installation and before you have created any additional user accounts. The Guest and Administrator accounts cannot be deleted; however, they may be disabled.

CAUTION

To enhance security, at some point you should create a new user account with administrative privileges to perform network administration, and disable the Administrator user account. If you keep the Administrator account active with full privileges, hackers have half the information they need to break into your system.

Additional accounts that you create may be **local accounts**, or those that only have rights on the server they are logged on to, and **domain accounts**, those that have rights throughout the domain. To create domain accounts, you must have Active Directory installed and your domains properly configured. Active Directory is not installed by default when you install Windows Server 2003. To install Active Directory, click Start, and then click Manage Your Server. From the Manage Your Server window, click Add or remove a role, and then select Domain Controller (Active Directory) from the list of server roles that the Configure Your Server Wizard offers. The Active Directory Installation Wizard will lead you through the process of making the computer a domain controller. The following exercise assumes that Active Directory is installed on your Windows Server 2003 computer and that domains have already been configured.

To create a domain user account:

1. Make sure you are logged on as Administrator.

2. Click **Start**, point to **All Programs**, point to **Administrative Tools**, and then click **Active Directory Users and Computers**. The Active Directory Users and Computers snap-in opens.

3. Double-click the Active Directory container in which you want to create the new user. This may be a domain or an OU.

4. Right-click the **Users** folder, point to **New** on the shortcut menu, and then click **User**. The New Object - User dialog box opens, as shown in Figure 8-18.

5. Type the user's last and first name in the appropriate text boxes. You then see the user's full name in the Full name text box.

6. Enter a user name in the User logon name text box. This name uniquely identifies the user in a domain or forest. The domain name is provided automatically. Click **Next** to continue.

7. In the New Object - User dialog box shown in Figure 8-19, enter a password for the user. Enter a strong password (one that consists of at least 10 characters, cannot be found in the dictionary, and contains numbers, letters, and special characters). Retype the password in the Confirm password text box. You may also select from four additional options: User must change password at next logon, User cannot change password, Password never expires, or Account is disabled. It's a good policy to force the user to pick a new password the first time they log on, so that they have a password that is meaningful to them and so that you, as the network administrator, don't know their password. It is also a good policy to allow the password to periodically expire. With this in mind, make certain that the first option, **User must change password at next logon**, is checked, and then click **Next**.

8. The next New Object - User window displays the information you have entered. Click **Finish** to complete the creation of a new domain user account.

FIGURE 8-18 *New Object–User dialog box*

FIGURE 8-19 *Password settings in the New Object–User dialog box*

After you have created a new user, you can configure the properties associated with his account, including his address, telephone number, and e-mail address, his rights to use remote access, his position in the organization, his group memberships, what hours of the day he may log on to the network, and so on. To modify user account properties, you can use the Active Directory Users and Computers snap-in. In the snap-in window, double-click the user account in

NET+

3.1

the right-hand pane. The User Account Properties dialog box opens, with multiple tabs that represent different categories of attributes you may change.

Before you add many users, you will probably want to establish groups into which you can collect user accounts. But before creating a group, you must know what type of scope the group will have. The group's scope identifies how broadly across the Windows Server 2003 network its privileges can reach. The possible scopes are domain local, global, or universal. A **domain local group** is one that allows its members access to resources within a single domain. Domain local groups are used to control access to certain folders, directories, or other resources. They may also contain global groups. A **global group** allows its members access to resources within a single domain also. However, a global group usually contains user accounts and can be inserted (or nested) into a domain local group to gain access to resources in other domains. A **universal group** is one that allows its members access to resources across multiple domains and forests.

To create a group in Windows Server 2003:

1. Make sure you are logged on as Administrator.
2. Click **Start**, point to **All Programs**, point to **Administrative Tools**, and then click **Active Directory Users and Computers**. The Active Directory Users and Computers snap-in starts.
3. Double-click the Active Directory container in which you want to create the new group. This may be a domain or an OU.
4. Click **Action** on the menu bar, click **New**, and then click **Group**. The New Object - Group dialog box appears, as shown in Figure 8-20.

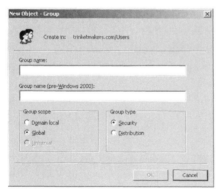

FIGURE 8-20 *New Object–Group dialog box*

5. In the New Object - Group dialog box, enter the name of the group in the Group name text box. In case you are using Windows NT servers on your network, the Group name (pre-Windows 2000) text box is automatically completed.
6. Choose the group scope: Domain local, Global, or Universal.

7. Select the type of group you want to create: Security or Distribution. A Security group is the type you would use to grant a group of users privileges to shared resources, whereas Distribution groups are used solely for sending e-mail messages to a group of users through mail server software such as the Microsoft Exchange Server. After you have made your selection, click **OK** to finish creating the new group.

Modifying the properties of a group account is similar to modifying the properties of a user account. To modify the properties of your newly created group, double-click the group in the right pane of the Active Directory Users and Computers snap-in window. This opens the group's Properties dialog box, which contains four tabs: General, Members, Member Of, and Managed By. Through this dialog box, you can add user accounts to the group, make the group a member of another group, and specify which user account will manage the group.

As mentioned earlier, users and groups are virtually useless unless they have some rights to the server's data and system directories.

Internetworking with Other Network Operating Systems

Windows Server 2003 can communicate with almost any kind of client and, given the proper software and configuration, with the other major NOSs. Interoperability is a major concern, as more organizations face the challenge of dealing with mixed networks. In the interest of the consumer, Microsoft and other NOS vendors have made efforts to close the gap. You will encounter situations in which Windows Server 2003 must coexist on the same network with NetWare, UNIX, Linux, Mac OS X Server, or several of these. This section focuses on Microsoft's solution to the interoperability question.

You might think that establishing communications between two NOSs is simply a matter of installing the same protocol on both systems. For example, you might think that because both NetWare and Windows Server 2003 can run the TCP/IP protocol, the two should be able to communicate directly. In fact, a protocol match is merely one part of the interoperability equation.

To enable clients connected to a NetWare server (version 5.x or 6.x) to view and access resources managed by a Windows Server 2003 server, Microsoft recommends installing its **File and Print Services for NetWare** on the Windows server. After this is installed, the Windows server will appear to NetWare clients as simply another NetWare file or print server; users will not be able to distinguish it from a NetWare server. File and Print Services for NetWare is one application belonging to the **Microsoft Windows Services for NetWare** package, a collection of software that simplifies the integration of Windows Server 2003 servers and NetWare servers on the same network. Another application that belongs to this package is the **MSDSS (Microsoft Directory Synchronization Services)**. When installed on a Windows Server 2003 server, this

NET+
3.1
3.2
3.4

software can synchronize information between an Active Directory database and a NetWare eDirectory database. On a network that runs both Windows and NetWare servers, synchronization means that objects and their attributes are identical across a network, no matter on which type of server they were created or modified. Because both NetWare versions 5.x or 6.x and Windows Server 2003 rely on directories that follow the same LDAP standards, sharing data is simple. To run MSDSS, the Windows server must be configured as a domain controller.

For NetWare clients that rely on the IPX/SPX protocol, additional software is necessary to access a Windows Server 2003 server. One possibility is for clients that depend on the Windows Server 2003 server to run Microsoft's **CSNW (Client Services for NetWare)**. CSNW is a service that in conjunction with NWLink enables the client to log on directly to the NetWare server to access its printers, files, and other resources. If your network includes both Windows Server 2003 and NetWare servers, and both use TCP/IP as their preferred protocol, you do not necessarily have to install CSNW (nor do you need to install NWLink). Instead, on each workstation you could install Novell's recommended client software to access NetWare servers in addition to Microsoft's Client for Networks to access Windows Server 2003 computers. Client Services for NetWare is not supported by the 64-bit versions of Windows Server 2003, such as the Enterprise Edition.

When interconnecting UNIX, Linux, or Mac OS X Server with Windows Server 2003 networks, you can assume that both rely on the TCP/IP protocol. However, you cannot assume both use the same directory structure. If a UNIX type of server does have an LDAP-compatible directory installed, Microsoft provides software for integrating the UNIX-type of directory with Active Directory. This software is installed on the Windows server and allows clients attached to the UNIX-type of server to access Windows Server 2003 resources as if they were resources on the UNIX-type of server. It belongs to Microsoft's **Windows Services for UNIX**.

Another application belonging to the Windows Services for UNIX package allows clients on Windows Server 2003 networks to access UNIX-type of servers and use their files and account privileges. The Windows Services for UNIX include the ability for the client to be recognized by a UNIX-type of server's file system and utilities for manipulating files and directories. There are also other, simpler utilities that Microsoft clients can use to access UNIX-type of servers (for example, a simple FTP client). In the next chapter, you will learn how UNIX-type of clients can connect and act as clients to Windows servers.

Chapter Summary

◆ NOSs are entirely software-based and can run on a number of different hardware platforms and network topologies.

◆ Network administrators choose an appropriate NOS according to what's compatible with the existing infrastructure; whether it supports the applications, services, and security required by the environment; whether it will grow with the organization; whether the vendor will provide reliable technical support; and whether it fits in the budget.

◆ A redirector, which belongs to the Presentation layer of the OSI Model, is inherent in both the NOS and the client operating system. On the client side, it intercepts client communications and decides whether the request is meant for the server or for the client.

◆ When a client attempts to log on, the NOS receives the client's request for service and tries to match the user name and password with the name and password in its user database. If the passwords match, the NOS grants the client access to resources on the network, according to limitations. This process is known as authentication.

◆ A directory is an NOS's method of organizing and managing objects, such as users, printers, server volumes, and applications. It is sometimes compared to a tree, because it has one common starting point and branches into multiple containers, which may branch into additional containers.

◆ A file system is an operating system's method of organizing, managing, and accessing its files through logical structures and software routines. In general, when installing Windows Server 2003, you will want to choose the NTFS file system.

◆ For clients to share a server application, the network administrator must assign users rights to the directories where the application's files are installed. Users will need at least the rights to access and read files in those directories. For some applications, users may also need rights to create, erase, or modify files associated with the application. Users are organized into groups to streamline administration.

◆ For clients to share a network printer, the printer must be created as an object, assigned a name and properties, and then shared among clients. Users or groups may be assigned different levels of privileges to operate printers.

◆ The type of multitasking supported by NetWare, UNIX, Linux, Mac OS X Server, and Windows Server 2003 performs one task at a time, allowing one program to use the processor for a certain period of time, and then suspending that program to allow another program to use the processor. This is called preemptive multitasking.

◆ Multiprocessing splits tasks among multiple processors to expedite the completion of any single instruction. It's a great advantage for servers with high CPU utilization, because it improves performance.

◆ Windows Server 2003 requires the following minimum hardware: Pentium processor with a minimum clock speed of 133 MHz (though at least 550 MHz is recommended), 128 MB of RAM (though at least 256 MB is recommended), at least 1.5 GB free hard disk space for system files, and a pointing device. A CD-ROM and a NIC that are included on the Microsoft HCL (Hardware Compatibility List) are optional.

◆ The Windows Server 2003 memory model assigns each process its own 32-bit (or in some versions, 64-bit) memory area. This memory area is a logical subdivision of the entire amount of memory available to the server. Assigning processes separate areas makes the processes less prone to interfering with each other when they run simultaneously.

◆ The description of object types, or classes, and their required and optional attributes that are stored in Active Directory is known as a schema.

◆ Domains define a group of systems and resources that share common security and management policies. The database that domains use to record their objects and attributes is contained within Active Directory. Domains are established on a network to make it easier to organize and manage resources and security.

◆ To collect domains into logical groups, Windows Server 2003 uses a domain tree (or simply, tree). At the base of the tree is the root domain. From the root domain, child domains branch out to separate objects with the same policies. Underneath the child domains, multiple organizational units branch out to further logically subdivide the network's systems and objects. A collection of domain trees is known as a forest.

◆ Each tree, domain, container, and object has a unique name that becomes part of the namespace. The names of these elements may be used in one of three different ways to uniquely identify an object in a Windows Server 2003 tree: as a distinguished name, as a relative distinguished name, and as a user principal name.

◆ Prior to installation, you need to make a number of decisions regarding your server and network pertaining to the domain or workgroup characteristics, file system, disk partitioning, optional services to be installed, administrator password, protocols to be installed, and server name.

◆ Adding users and groups is accomplished through an administrative tool called Active Directory Users and Computers.

◆ For integrating Windows Server 2003 clients and resources with NetWare 5.x or 6.x clients and server resources, Microsoft provides a suite of applications known as Microsoft Windows Services for NetWare. In this package are tools for synchronizing Active Directory with NetWare's directory database and for allowing NetWare-attached clients to view Windows file and print resources as if they belonged to a NetWare server.

◆ For integrating Windows Server 2003 clients and resources with UNIX-type of clients and server resources, Microsoft provides a suite of applications known as Microsoft Windows Services for UNIX. In this suite are tools for synchronizing data between Active Directory and a UNIX-type of server's directory (if one exists), and for allowing UNIX-attached clients to view Windows file and print resources as if they belonged to a UNIX-type of server.

Key Terms

3-tier architecture—A client/server environment that uses middleware to translate requests between the client and server.

account—A record of a user that contains all of her properties, including rights to resources, password, user name, and so on.

Active Directory—The Windows Server 2003 method for organizing and managing objects associated with the network.

Administrator—A user account that has unlimited privileges to resources and objects managed by a server or domain. The Administrator account is created during NOS installation.

AFP (AppleTalk Filing Protocol or Apple File Protocol)—The native file access protocol used by Macintosh computers.

Apple File Protocol—See *AFP*.

AppleTalk Filing Protocol—See *AFP*.

asymmetric multiprocessing—A multiprocessing method that assigns each subtask to a specific processor.

attribute—A variable property associated with a network object. For example, a restriction on the time of day a user can log on is an attribute associated with that user object.

branch—A part of the organizational structure of an operating system's directory that contains objects or other organizational units.

CDFS (CD-ROM File System)—The read-only file system used to access resources on a CD. Windows Server 2003 supports this file system to allow CD-ROM file sharing.

CD-ROM File System—See *CDFS*.

child domain—A domain established within another domain in a Windows Server 2003 domain tree.

CIFS (Common Internet File System)—A file access protocol. CIFS runs over TCP/IP and is the standard file access protocol used by Windows operating systems.

class—A type of object recognized by an NOS directory and defined in an NOS schema. Printers and users are examples of object classes.

Client Services for NetWare (CSNW)—A Microsoft program that can be installed on Windows clients to enable them to access NetWare servers and make full use of NetWare's eDirectory, its objects, files, directories, and permissions.

CN (common name)—In LDAP naming conventions, the name of an object.

Common Internet File System—See *CIFS*.

common name—See *CN*.

container—See *organizational unit*.

DC (domain component)—In LDAP naming conventions, the name of any one of the domains to which an object belongs.

digital versatile disc—See *DVD*.

directory—In general, a listing that organizes resources and correlates them with their properties. In the context of network operating systems, a method for organizing and managing objects.

distinguished name—See *DN*.

DN (distinguished name)—A long form of an object's name in Active Directory that explicitly indicates the object name, plus the names of its containers and domains. A distinguished name includes a DC (domain component), OU (organizational unit), and CN (common name). A client uses the distinguished name to access a particular object, such as a printer.

domain—A group of users, servers, and other resources that share account and security policies through a Windows Server 2003 network operating system.

domain account—A type of user account on a Windows Server 2003 network that has privileges to resources across the domain onto which it is logged.

domain component—See *DC*.

domain controller—A Windows Server 2003 computer that contains a replica of the Active Directory database.

domain local group—A group on a Windows Server 2003 network that allows members of one domain to access resources within that domain only.

domain model—In Microsoft terminology, the type of client/server network that relies on domains, rather than workgroups.

domain tree—A group of hierarchically arranged domains that share a common namespace in the Windows Server 2003 Active Directory.

DVD (digital versatile disc)—A type of optical disk capable of storing large amounts of data, including audio and video files. Several DVD standards exist, but all have a minimum storage capacity of 4.7 GB.

explicit one-way trust—A type of trust relationship in which two domains that belong to different NOS directory trees are configured to trust each other.

FAT (file allocation table)—The original PC file system designed in the 1970s to support floppy disks and, later, hard disks. FAT is inadequate for most server operating systems because of its partition size limitations, naming limitations, and fragmentation and speed issues.

FAT16 (16-bit file allocation table)—A file system designed for use with early DOS- and Windows-based computers that allocates file system space in 16-bit units. Compared to FAT32, FAT16 is less desirable because of its partition size, file naming, fragmentation, speed, and security limitations.

FAT32 (32-bit file allocation table)—An enhanced version of FAT that accommodates the use of long filenames and smaller allocation units on a disk. FAT32 makes more efficient use of disk space than the original FAT.

file access protocol—A protocol that enables one system to access files on another system.

file allocation table—See *FAT*.

File and Print Services for NetWare—The Microsoft application that, when installed on a Windows Server 2003 server, makes the server's file and print resources appear to NetWare-attached clients as NetWare directory resources. File and Print Services for NetWare is part of the Microsoft Windows Services for NetWare software package.

file system—An operating system's method of organizing, managing, and accessing its files through logical structures and software routines.

forest—In the context of Windows Server 2003, a collection of domain trees that use different namespaces. A forest allows for trust relationships to be established between trees.

global group—A group on a Windows Server 2003 network that allows members of one domain to access resources within that domain as well as resources from other domains in the same forest.

globally unique identifier—See *GUID*.

graphical user interface—See *GUI*.

group—A means of collectively managing users' permissions and restrictions applied to shared resources. Groups form the basis for resource and account management for every type of network operating system, not just Windows Server 2003. Many network administrators create groups according to department or, even more specifically, according to job function within a department.

Guest—A user account with very limited privileges that is created during the installation of a network operating system.

GUI (graphical user interface)—A pictorial representation of computer functions and elements that, in the case of network operating systems, enables administrators to more easily manage files, users, groups, security, printers, and other issues.

GUID (globally unique identifier)—A 128-bit number generated and assigned to an object upon its creation in the Windows Server 2003 Active Directory. Network applications and services use an object's GUID to communicate with it.

Hardware Compatibility List—See *HCL*.

HCL (Hardware Compatibility List)—A list of computer components proven to be compatible with Windows Server 2003. The HCL appears on the same CD as your Windows Server 2003 software and on Microsoft's Web site.

inherited—A type of permission, or right, that is passed down from one group (the parent) to a group within that group (the child).

LDAP (Lightweight Directory Access Protocol)—A standard protocol for accessing network directories.

leaf object—An object in an operating system's directory, such as a printer or user, that does not contain other objects.

Lightweight Directory Access Protocol—See *LDAP*.

local account—A type of user account on a Windows Server 2003 network that has rights to the resources managed by the server the user has logged on to.

map—The action of associating a disk, directory, or device with a drive letter.

member server—A type of server on a Windows Server 2003 network that does not hold directory information and therefore cannot authenticate users.

Microsoft Directory Synchronization Services—See *MSDSS*.

Microsoft Management Console—See *MMC*.

Microsoft Windows Services for NetWare—A suite of tools for integrating Windows 2000 Server or Windows Server 2003 servers with NetWare servers. The suite includes a tool for synchronizing data from NetWare directories with Active Directory, a tool for migrating files from a NetWare server to a Windows Server 2003 server, and File and Print Services for Net-Ware, which allows a Windows Server 2003 computer to appear as a NetWare server to Net-Ware clients.

middleware—The software that sits between the client and server in a 3-tier architecture. Middleware may be used as a messaging service between clients and servers, as a universal query language for databases, or as means of coordinating processes between multiple servers that need to work together in servicing clients.

MMC (Microsoft Management Console)—A customizable, graphical network management interface used with Windows Server 2003.

MSDSS (Microsoft Directory Synchronization Services)—An application that, when installed on a Windows Server 2003 server, can synchronize information between an Active Directory database and a NetWare eDirectory database.

multiprocessing—The technique of splitting tasks among multiple processors to expedite the completion of any single instruction.

multitasking—The ability of a processor to perform multiple activities in a brief period of time (often seeming simultaneous to the user).

namespace—The complete database of hierarchical names (including host and domain names) used to resolve IP addresses with their hosts.

New Technology File System—See *NTFS*.

NTFS (New Technology File System)—A file system developed by Microsoft for use with its Windows NT, Windows 2000 Server, and Windows Server 2003 operating systems. NTFS integrates reliability, compression, the ability to handle massive files, system security, and fast access. Most Windows Server 2003 partitions employ NTFS.

object—A representation of a thing or person associated with the network that belongs in the NOS directory. Objects include users, printers, groups, computers, data files, and applications.

object class—See *class*.

organizational unit—See *OU*.

OU (organizational unit)—A logical receptacle for holding objects with similar characteristics or privileges in an NOS directory. Containers form the branches of the directory tree.

page file—A file on the hard disk that is used for virtual memory.

paging—The process of moving blocks of information, called pages, between RAM and into a page file on disk.

paging file—See *page file*.

partition—An area of a computer's hard disk that is logically defined and acts as a separate disk drive.

per seat—In the context of applications, a licensing mode that limits access to an application to specific users or workstations. In the context of Microsoft's Windows Server 2003, a licensing mode that requires a license for every client capable of connecting to the Windows Server 2003 server.

per server—A Windows Server 2003 licensing mode that allows a limited number of clients to access the server simultaneously. (The number is determined by your Windows Server 2003 purchase agreement.) The restriction applies to the number of concurrent connections, rather than specific clients. Per server mode is the most popular choice for installing Windows Server 2003.

per user—A licensing mode that allows a fixed quantity of clients to use one software package simultaneously.

physical memory—The RAM chips installed on the computer's system board that provide dedicated memory to that computer.

preemptive multitasking—The type of multitasking in which tasks are actually performed one at a time, in very brief succession. In preemptive multitasking, one program uses the processor for a certain period of time, then is suspended to allow another program to use the processor.

printer queue—A logical representation of a networked printer's functionality. To use a printer, clients must have access to the printer queue.

process—A routine of sequential instructions that runs until it has achieved its goal. For example, a spreadsheet program is a process.

RDN (relative distinguished name)—An attribute of an object that identifies the object separately from its related container(s) and domain. For most objects, the relative distinguished name is the same as its common name (CN) in the distinguished name convention.

redirector—A service that runs on a client workstation and determines whether the client's request should be handled by the client or the server.

relative distinguished name—See *RDN*.

replication—The process of copying Active Directory data to multiple domain controllers. This ensures redundancy so that in case one of the domain controllers fails, clients can still log on to the network, be authenticated, and access resources.

root domain—In Windows Server 2003 networking, the single domain from which child domains branch out in a domain tree.

schema—The description of object types, or classes, and their required and optional attributes that are stored in an NOS's directory.

Server Message Block—See *SMB*.

site license—A type of software license that, for a fixed price, allows any number of users in one location to legally access a program.

SMB (Server Message Block)—A protocol for communications and resource access between systems, such as clients and servers. SMB originated at IBM and then was adopted and further developed by Microsoft for use on its Windows operating systems. The current version of SMB is known as the CIFS (Common Internet File System) protocol.

snap-in—An administrative tool, such as Computer Management, that can be added to the MMC (Microsoft Management Console).

swap file—See *page file*.

symmetric multiprocessing—A method of multiprocessing that splits all operations equally among two or more processors. Windows Server 2003 supports this type of multiprocessing.

thread—A well-defined, self-contained subset of a process. Using threads within a process enables a program to efficiently perform related, multiple, simultaneous activities. Threads are also used to enable processes to use multiple processors on SMP systems.

time-sharing—See *preemptive multitasking*.

tree—A logical representation of multiple, hierarchical levels in a directory. It is called a tree because the whole structure shares a common starting point (the root), and from that point extends branches (or containers), which may extend additional branches, and so on.

trust relationship—The relationship between two domains on a Windows Server 2003 network that allows a domain controller from one domain to authenticate users from the other domain.

two-way transitive trust—The security relationship between domains in the same domain tree in which one domain grants every other domain in the tree access to its resources and, in turn, that domain can access other domains' resources. When a new domain is added to a tree, it immediately shares a two-way trust with the other domains in the tree.

UDF (Universal Disk Format)—A file system used on CD-ROMs and DVD (digital video disc) media.

Universal Disk Format—See *UDF*.

universal group—A group on a Windows Server 2003 network that allows members from one domain to access resources in multiple domains and forests.

UPN (user principal name)—The preferred Active Directory naming convention for objects when used in informal situations. This name looks like a familiar Internet address, including the positioning of the domain name after the @ sign. UPNs are typically used for e-mail and related Internet services.

UPN (user principal name) suffix—The portion of a universal principal name (in Windows Server 2003 Active Directory's naming conventions) that follows the @ sign.

user principal name—See *UPN*.

virtual memory—The memory that is logically carved out of space on the hard disk and added to physical memory (RAM).

Windows Services for UNIX—A suite of applications designed to integrate Windows Server 2003 servers with UNIX-type of servers and clients. One application in this suite enables Windows and UNIX-type of servers to share directory information (when the UNIX-type of server has a directory installed). Another application enables UNIX-type of clients to view resources on a Windows Server 2003 server as if they were resources on a UNIX-type of server.

workgroup—A group of interconnected computers that share each others' resources without relying on a central file server.

Review Questions

1. To better organize and manage objects, a network administrator places objects in
   _____.

   a. classes

   b. objects

   c. organizational units

   d. attributes

2. _____ is the ability of a processor to perform many different operations in a very brief period of time.

   a. Multitasking

   b. Paging

   c. Formatting

   d. Replication

3. A _____ is a routine of sequential instructions that runs until it has achieved its goal.

   a. schema

   b. file system

   c. namespace

   d. process

4. _____ is the original PC file system that was designed in the 1970s to support floppy disks and, later, hard disks.

   a. NTFS

   b. FAT

   c. CDFS

   d. DOS

5. _____ is the name that uniquely identifies an object within a container.

   a. Schema

   b. Relative distinguished name

   c. Domain name

   d. Common name

6. True or false? A redirector belongs to the Presentation layer or the OSI Model.

7. True or false? A FAT16 partition or file cannot exceed 2 GB.

8. True or false? FAT is secure, reliable, and makes it possible to compress files so that they take up less space.

9. True or false? NTFS keeps a log file of system activity to facilitate recovery if a system crash occurs.

10. True or false? In Internet terminology, *domain model* refers to the complete database of hierarchical names used to map IP addresses to their hosts' names.

11. _____ involves associating a letter, such as M: or T:, with a disk, directory, or other resource.

12. The _____ account is a predefined user account that has the most extensive privileges for resources both on the computer and on the domain that it controls.

13. The term _____ refers to the RAM chips that are installed on the computer's system board and whose sole function is to provide memory to that machine.

14. The _____ lists all computer components proven to be compatible with Windows Server 2003.

15. The relationship between two domains in which one allows the other to authenticate its users is known as a(n) _____.

Chapter 9

Networking with UNIX-Type of Operating Systems

After reading this chapter and completing the exercises, you will be able to:

■ Describe the origins and history of the UNIX operating system

■ Identify similarities and differences between popular implementations of UNIX

■ Describe the features and capabilities of servers running Solaris, Linux, and Mac OS X Server

■ Explain and execute essential UNIX commands

■ Install and configure Linux on an Intel-based PC

■ Manage users, groups, and file access permissions in Solaris, Linux, and Mac OS X Server

■ Explain how computers running other operating systems can connect to UNIX servers

A long with Microsoft Windows and Novell NetWare, UNIX is one of the most popular network operating systems. All of these operating systems enable servers to provide resource sharing, but UNIX differs in fundamental ways from NetWare and Windows. Researchers at AT&T Bell Laboratories developed UNIX in 1969; thus, it is much older than NetWare and Windows. In fact, UNIX preceded and led to the development of the TCP/IP protocol suite in the early 1970s. Today, most Internet servers run UNIX. Reflecting this operating system's efficiency and flexibility, the number of installed UNIX-type of systems continues to grow. Many local and wide area networks include UNIX servers. You should familiarize yourself with UNIX so you can set up and maintain these networks.

Mastering UNIX can be difficult because, unlike Windows and NetWare, it is not controlled and distributed by a single software manufacturer. Instead, numerous vendors sell their own UNIX varieties. In addition, operating systems that share many of UNIX's characteristics but are nonproprietary and freely distributed are available. The most popular example is **Linux**. Fortunately, the differences between UNIX varieties are relatively minor, and, if you understand how to use one, with a little effort you can understand how to use another. This chapter introduces the UNIX operating system in general and then describes three varieties—Solaris, Mac OS X Server, and Linux—in more detail.

A Brief History of UNIX

In the late 1960s, a few programmers grew dissatisfied with the existing programming environments. In particular, they didn't like the cumbersome nature of systems that required a programmer to write a set of instructions, submit them all at once, and then wait for the results. Instead, programmers desired a more interactive operating environment that allowed them to build and test their programs piece by piece. In addition, the programmers sought a system that imposed as few predetermined structures as possible on the users. For example, they preferred to let programmers decide how data should be formatted within a data file or how to structure filenames. With this in mind, Ken Thompson and Dennis Ritchie, two employees at Bell Labs (which was then part of AT&T) in Murray Hill, New Jersey, decided to create an entirely new programming environment. To properly design this new environment, they decided to start at the lowest level—the operating system. This environment ultimately evolved into the UNIX operating system.

Antitrust law prohibited AT&T from profiting from the sale of computers and software during the 1970s. Thus, for a nominal licensing fee, anyone could purchase the **source code**—that is, the form of a computer program that can be read by people—to the work produced at Bell Labs. The word spread rapidly, and researchers in educational institutions and large corporations all over the world soon had this new software running on their lab computers. Versions of UNIX that come from Bell Labs are known as **System V**. Researchers at the University of

California at Berkeley were among the first enthusiastic supporters of early versions of UNIX. They added many useful features to the operating system, including the TCP/IP network subsystem. Berkeley versions of UNIX are known as **BSD (Berkeley Software Distribution)**.

The 1980s saw the breakup of AT&T and the removal of some of its antitrust restrictions. This enabled the company to begin marketing the UNIX system to other computer manufacturers. However, AT&T eventually sold its rights to the UNIX system, and these rights changed hands a number of times during the early 1990s. Today, ownership of the UNIX system is shared by two organizations—The SCO Group and The Open Group.

The SCO Group is the company that owns the rights to the UNIX source code, or the raw materials for creating a UNIX system. Anyone could try writing a UNIX operating system from scratch, but the effort required to do so is prohibitive. Most organizations choose to start with the existing source code by licensing it from The SCO Group and then make modifications for their specific computer hardware.

In addition, a nonprofit industry association called **The Open Group** owns the UNIX trademark. After a vendor changes the code licensed from The SCO Group, its modified system must pass The Open Group's verification tests before the operating system may be called UNIX. IBM, for example, pays source code licensing fees to The SCO Group and verification and trademark use fees to The Open Group so that it can refer to its AIX operating system as UNIX.

Now that you understand some of the history of UNIX, you are better prepared to learn about its many varieties and how these varieties are related.

Varieties of UNIX

NET+
3.1

Today, the UNIX operating system comes in many varieties, or, as they are more casually called, **flavors**. Before learning about their differences, however, you should know that all flavors of the UNIX operating system share the following features:

◆ The ability to support multiple, simultaneously logged-on users

◆ The ability to coordinate multiple, simultaneously running tasks (or programs)

◆ The ability to **mount**—or to make available—disk partitions upon demand

◆ The ability to apply permissions for file and directory access and modification

◆ A uniform method of issuing data to or receiving data from hardware devices, files, and running programs

◆ The ability to start a program without interfering with a currently running program

◆ Hundreds of subsystems, including dozens of programming languages

◆ Source code portability, or the ability to extract code from one UNIX system and use it on another

◆ Window interfaces that the user can configure, the most popular of which is the **X Window system**

NET+
3.1

Types of the UNIX operating system can be divided into two main categories: proprietary and open source. The following sections describe characteristics of each category and offer examples of UNIX versions in both categories. Note that some flavors of UNIX will operate only on certain types of computers. Examples of such UNIX varieties and their unique hardware requirements are also described next.

Proprietary UNIX

Many companies market both hardware and software based on the UNIX operating system. An implementation of UNIX for which the source code is either unavailable or available only by purchasing a licensed copy from The SCO Group (costing as much as millions of dollars) is known as **proprietary UNIX**. By most counts, the three most popular vendors of proprietary UNIX are Apple Computer, Sun Microsystems, and IBM. Apple's proprietary version of UNIX, **Mac OS X Server**, runs on its **PowerPC**-based computers. Sun's proprietary version of UNIX, called **Solaris**, runs on the company's proprietary **SPARC**-based (the CPU invented by Sun Microsystems) workstations and servers, as well as Intel-based Pentium-class workstations and servers. IBM's proprietary version, **AIX**, runs on its PowerPC-based computers. Apple and IBM use the same central processing unit, the PowerPC, in their computers. But other hardware in their computers is very different, and the software that runs on IBM computers will not run on Apple's computers. Many other organizations have licensed the UNIX source code and created proprietary UNIX versions that run on highly customized computers (that is, computers that are appropriate for very specific tasks).

Choosing a proprietary UNIX system has several advantages:

♦ *Accountability and support*—An organization might choose a proprietary UNIX system so that when something doesn't work as expected, it has a resource on which to call for assistance.

♦ *Optimization of hardware and software*—Workstation vendors who include proprietary UNIX with the computers they sell invest a great deal of time in ensuring that their software runs as well and as fast as possible on their hardware.

♦ *Predictability and compatibility*—Purveyors of proprietary UNIX systems strive to maintain backward-compatibility with new releases. They schedule new releases at somewhat regular, predictable intervals. Customers usually know when and how things will change with proprietary UNIX systems.

One drawback of choosing a proprietary UNIX system, however, relates to the fact that the customer has no access to the system's source code and, thus, cannot customize the operating system. Open source UNIX solves this problem.

Open Source UNIX

An interesting factor in the UNIX marketplace in recent years has been the emergence of UNIX-type of systems that are not owned by any one company. This software is developed and packaged by a few individuals and made available to anyone, without licensing fees. This

NET+
3.1

would be equivalent, in the Windows world, to a large group of people getting together and writing a version of Windows based on the public specifications. (UNIX, however, has been publicly available for much longer than Windows, and Microsoft keeps the specifications to many parts of Windows a closely guarded secret.)

Often referred to as **open source software**, or **freely distributable software**, this category includes UNIX-type of systems such as **GNU** (an acronym that stands for GNU's Not UNIX), BSD, and Linux. These systems, in turn, come in a variety of implementations, each of which incorporates slightly different features and capabilities. As mentioned, these packages are often referred to as the different flavors of the open source software. For example, the different flavors of Linux include Red Hat, Fedora Core, SUSE, Mandrake, and a host of others. Although these packages are available at no cost, it's also possible to purchase the software, thereby gaining a certain amount of convenience. In the case of purchasing Red Hat Enterprise Linux, for example, you are paying for the convenience of a package that includes the software on CD-ROM, documentation, and access to Red Hat's customer support. Choosing to obtain Fedora Core Linux for free from Red Hat means investing a fair amount of time, enough to download more than 2 GB of data, write the software to a DVD-ROM, and learn how to install the software without the aid of printed documentation. Many people find the convenience worth the nominal purchase price of software with a licensing fee.

The key difference between freely distributable UNIX-type of systems and proprietary implementations of UNIX relates to the software license. Proprietary UNIX includes agreements that require payment of royalties for each system sold and that forbid redistribution of the source code. A primary advantage of open source UNIX and Linux is that users can modify their code and thereby add functionality not provided by a proprietary version of UNIX. For example, a manufacturing company that uses computer-controlled robotic spot welders might combine open source UNIX or Linux with custom software to control its robots. In contrast, it might be very difficult or costly to integrate the robotic control software with a proprietary UNIX system.

Another potential advantage of using a freely distributable UNIX-type of system is that these varieties run not only on Intel-based processors, but also on other processor brands, such as the PowerPC used in Apple Macintoshes, the PowerPC used in IBM servers, and SPARC, used in Sun Microsystems workstations. Proprietary UNIX systems cannot be installed on such a wide range of systems.

Three Flavors of UNIX

NET+
3.1

The rest of this chapter focuses on three UNIX or UNIX-type of operating systems: Solaris, Linux, and Mac OS X Server. The following list summarizes some basic information about these three varieties:

◆ Solaris, the UNIX system Sun Microsystems uses on its SPARC-based servers, offers users all the benefits of commercially supported operating systems. It has seen numerous revisions and improvements over the years, and now runs behind the scenes of some of the most intensive applications in the world. Some examples

NET+
3.1

include large multiterabyte databases, weather prediction systems, and large economic modeling applications.

◆ Linux follows standard UNIX conventions, is highly stable, and is free. Linus Torvalds developed it in 1991 when he was a second-year computer science student in Finland. After developing Linux, Torvalds posted it on the Internet and recruited other UNIX aficionados and programmers to help enhance it. Today, Linux is used for file, print, and Web servers across the globe. Its popularity has even convinced large corporations that own proprietary UNIX versions, such as IBM, Hewlett-Packard, and Sun Microsystems, to publicly embrace and support Linux.

◆ Mac OS X Server is a relative newcomer to the UNIX server marketplace. Apple Computer released Mac OS X to the public in the Spring of 2001 to replace its previously released network operating system software, **AppleShare IP**. It includes the traditional Apple Macintosh user interface. Mac OS X Server runs on Apple's **Xserve** line of computers as well as the Power Mac computers. These PowerPC-based servers are used by marketing organizations as well as others requiring high performance hardware and the familiar Macintosh user interface.

All UNIX-type of systems offer a host of features, including the TCP/IP protocol suite and all applications necessary to support the networking infrastructure as a part of the basic operating system. UNIX-type of systems also support non-IP protocols, such as Novell's IPX/SPX and AppleTalk (the original Mac OS network communication protocol). In addition, when you use a UNIX-type of system, you get the programs necessary for routing, firewall protection, DNS services, and DHCP services. Like Windows Server 2003 and NetWare, UNIX also supports many different network topologies and physical media, including Ethernet, Token Ring, FDDI, and wireless LANs. And as described later in this chapter, UNIX-type of systems can also run applications and utilities that make them compatible with other NOSs on the same network.

UNIX-type of systems efficiently and securely handle the growth, change, and stability requirements of today's diverse networks. The source code on which UNIX-type of systems are based is mature, as it has been used and thoroughly debugged by thousands of developers for many years. As with other modern NOSs, UNIX-type of systems allow you to change the server's configuration—for example, assigning a different IP address to an interface—without restarting the server. Similarly, you can easily modify a UNIX-type of system while it is running. When you need to access a backup tape drive, for example, you can enable the tape driver, access the tape, and disable the tape driver without restarting the server. This functionality allows you to use memory on your server very efficiently.

UNIX Server Hardware Requirements

NET+
3.1

Hardware requirements for UNIX-type of systems are very similar to those for Windows Server 2003 servers. One key difference, however, is that any UNIX-type of operating system can act as a workstation or server operating system (whereas Microsoft sells different operating sys-

NET+
3.1

tems for workstations and servers). Therefore, the UNIX computer's minimum hardware requirements depend partly on which version of UNIX-type of operating system you are installing and partly on how you intend to use the system.

A further difference is that in all flavors of UNIX, the use of a GUI (graphical user interface) remains optional—that is, you can choose to use the GUI, a command-line interface, or a combination of the two. By contrast, in Windows Server 2003, you *must* use the GUI for many operations (and so a mouse is required). Many people regard the choice of using a GUI or a command-line interface in UNIX as an advantage. For example, you might choose to use the GUI for operations that require a great deal of interaction, such as adding new users or configuring services. However, for server operations that run unattended, it often makes sense to use the command-line interface (which consumes less of the computer's memory and other resources).

As you learned in Chapter 8, no single "right" server configuration exists. You'll need to add more memory and more disk space according to your networking environment and users' needs. Unfortunately, you sometimes cannot learn the memory requirements of an application until you actually run it on the server. In these instances, it is always better to overestimate your needs than to underestimate them. However, you can get an idea of what additional hardware your server may require by answering the following questions:

◆ How will the server be used (for example, for file and print services or for backups)?

◆ Which applications and services will run on the server?

◆ How many users will this system serve?

◆ Will all users be accessing the server during the same time periods?

◆ What is the maximum amount of downtime the users of this server can tolerate?

The following sections provide rough guidelines for choosing the hardware you will need to run Solaris, Linux, and Mac OS X Server.

Solaris Hardware Requirements

Solaris runs on computers containing Sun SPARC processors or on Intel-based processors. Table 9-1 lists the minimum hardware requirements for the most recent Solaris operating system release, version 10. Components on SPARC workstations and servers have been tested to ensure their compatibility with Solaris. To determine which components on an Intel-based system will be compatible with Solaris, refer to Sun Microsystems' Intel hardware compatibility list at *www.sun.com/software/solaris/specs.html*.

The hardware requirements listed in Table 9-1 reflect the *minimum* amount of memory and hard disk space required to run Solaris 10. However, for better performance, you should consider using more than the minimum requirement. For example, for application support, most systems need at least 10 GB of hard disk space.

Table 9-1 Minimum hardware requirements for Solaris 10

Component	Requirement	Notes
Platform	Sun UltraSPARC 64-bit and Fujitsu SPARC64 or AMD or Intel Pentium class processor	Solaris x86 also supports AMD Opteron and Intel 64-bit processors.
Memory	512 MB RAM	Consider adding more RAM for better system performance.
Hard disk	5 to 7 GB	
NIC	A NIC supported by Solaris (included with SPARC systems)	
CD-ROM/ DVD-ROM	A CD-ROM or DVD-ROM drive supported by Solaris (included with SPARC systems)	

Linux Hardware Requirements

Linux hardware requirements vary to some extent based on the version of Linux you are installing. However, all Linux servers adhere to certain minimum hardware requirements, as shown in Table 9-2. You may find more current lists of supported hardware on the HCL (Hardware Compatibility List) at *www.tldp.org/HOWTO/HOWTO-INDEX/hardware.html*.

Adding high-performance video cards, sound cards, and other I/O devices to your Linux server is also optional.

Table 9-2 Minimum hardware requirements for a Linux server

Component	Requirement	Notes
Processor	Intel-compatible x86	Recent versions of the Linux kernel (2.0 and later) include support for as many as 32 Intel processors.
Memory	64 MB RAM	Consider adding more RAM for better performance; most network administrators opt for 256 MB of RAM or more for servers.
Hard disk	A hard drive supported by Linux with a minimum of 2 GB of free space	Most server implementations require additional free hard drive space; 10 GB of free space is recommended.
NIC	A NIC supported by Linux	

NET+
3.1

Table 9-2 Continued

Component	Requirement	Notes
CD-ROM	A CD-ROM drive listed on the HCL	Recent versions of Linux support SCSI, IDE, and ATAPI CD-ROM drives.
Floppy disk	One or two 3.5-inch floppy disks, if no bootable CD-ROM drive is available	Floppy disks can be useful for creating emergency repair disks during installation.
Pointing device	Optional	A pointing device is only necessary if you install the GUI component.

Mac OS X Server Hardware Requirements

Mac OS X Server runs only on Apple hardware. As with Solaris and Linux, your choices of RAM, secondary storage, and other hardware considerations are driven by the number and type of applications you will run on the server. Table 9-3 shows Apple's recommended hardware for Mac OS X Server.

Table 9-3 Apple hardware recommendations for Mac OS X Server

Component	Requirement	Notes
System	Xserve Power Mac G3, G4, or G5, iMac or eMac	
Memory	256 MB RAM	Consider adding more RAM for servers performing multiple tasks.
Hard disk	4 GB available disk space	Consider using larger hard drives for server applications.
NIC	Included with all Mac servers	
CD-ROM/ DVD-ROM	Included with all Mac servers	

A Closer Look at UNIX

NET+
3.1

UNIX is the second major network operating system discussed in this book. In some ways, it is similar to NetWare (discussed in the next chapter) and Windows Server 2003, and in some ways it differs. This section compares UNIX-type of systems with these other network operating systems.

NET+
3.1

UNIX Multiprocessing

As you have learned, a process represents an instance of a program running in memory (RAM). In addition to processes, UNIX-type of systems also support threads, which are self-contained subsets of a process. Any modern NOS must handle multiple processes and threads in an efficient manner. UNIX-type of systems allocate separate resources (such as memory space) to each process as it is created. They also manage all programs' access to these resources. This approach enables partitioning of processes in memory, thereby preventing one program from disrupting the operation of the entire system. When one program ends unexpectedly on a UNIX-type of system, it doesn't cause the whole computer to crash.

Like Windows Server 2003, modern UNIX-type of systems support SMP (symmetric multiprocessing). Different flavors of UNIX support different numbers of processors:

◆ Solaris supports up to 128 processors per server (although Sun does not make any hardware containing that many processors).

◆ Linux supports SMP using a maximum of 32 processors per server.

◆ Mac OS X Server supports up to two processors per server.

You must know how your servers will be used and plan for multiprocessing servers according to your estimated application-processing loads.

The UNIX Memory Model

From early on, UNIX-type systems were created to use both physical and virtual memory efficiently. Like Windows Server 2003, UNIX-type of systems allocate a memory area for each application. They attempt to decrease the inefficiency of this practice, however, by sharing memory between programs wherever they can. For example, if five people are using FTP on your UNIX server, five instances of the FTP program will run. In reality, only a small part of each FTP program (called the private data region—the part that stores the user name, for example) will receive its own memory space; most of the program will remain in a region of memory shared by all five instances of the program. In this case, rather than using five times the memory required by one instance of the program, a UNIX-type of system sets aside only a little more memory for five FTP users than it does for one FTP user.

Most current UNIX-type of systems use a 32-bit addressing scheme that enables programs to access 4 GB of memory. Most of these systems also run on CPUs that employ 64-bit addresses, enabling programs to access more than 18 exabytes (2^{64} bytes) of memory. That's more than 18 billion billion bytes of data—by one estimate, three times the total number of words ever spoken by human beings! Virtual memory in a UNIX server can take the form of a disk partition, or it can be in a file (much like the virtual memory file pagefile.sys in Windows Server 2003).

The UNIX Kernel

The core of all UNIX-type of systems is called the **kernel**. The kernel is loaded into memory and runs when you turn on your computer. Its primary function is to coordinate access to all

NET+
3.1

your computer's hardware, such as the disks, memory, keyboard, and monitor. You can add or remove functionality on a running UNIX-type of system by loading and unloading kernel modules. A UNIX **kernel module** is a file that contains instructions for performing a specific task such as reading data from and writing data to a hard drive.

The Solaris kernel is derived from the original AT&T UNIX software from Bell Labs. The Linux kernel is the software Linus Torvalds wrote and released to the public in 1991. The Mac OS X Server kernel (called **XNU**) is derived from an operating system called **Mach**, which was developed at Carnegie Mellon University in the 1990s.

UNIX System File and Directory Structure

The UNIX system was one of the first operating systems to implement a **hierarchical file system** (a method of organizing files and directories on a disk in which directories may contain files and other directories). The notion of a file system organized in this way was considered revolutionary at the time of UNIX's inception. Today, most operating systems, including all Microsoft operating systems and Novell NetWare, use hierarchical file systems. Figure 9-1 shows a typical UNIX file system hierarchy.

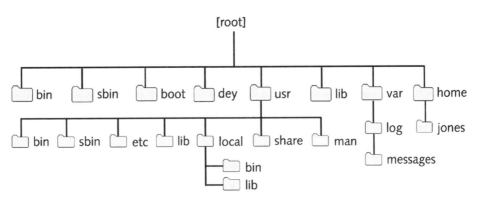

FIGURE 9-1   *UNIX file system hierarchy*

On a UNIX-type of system, the /boot directory contains the kernel and other system initialization files. Applications and services are stored in the /bin and /sbin directories. (The applications and services in the /sbin directory support the system initialization process; you'll rarely use these programs.) The /var directory holds variable data (such as log files, users' unread e-mail, and print jobs waiting to be printed). The file /var/log/messages, for example, stores system log messages, such as a notification of a disk drive that is running out of space. Users' login directories typically appear in /home. Mac OS X Server creates users' login directories in /Users. When you create a new user account, the system assigns a directory in /home to that user (/Users in Mac OS X Server). The login (or home) directory matches the account's user name. Thus, /home/jones is the login (or home) directory for the user name jones on a UNIX system. /Users/jones is the login (or home) directory for the user jones on a Mac OS X Server system.

NET+
2.13
3.1

UNIX System File Services

UNIX file services fall into two broad categories: disk file systems and network file systems. Disk file systems are used to organize the information on a hard drive. Network file systems enable users to access files on other servers via the network.

Disk File Systems

The UNIX disk file system is the operating system's facility for organizing, managing, and accessing files through logical structures and software routines. Just as Windows Server 2003 supports FAT, NTFS, and other file systems, UNIX-type systems also support multiple file system types. The native file system type on Linux, called *ext3*, is the "third extended" file system for Linux. Solaris employs the file system called **UFS** (for "UNIX File System") for its native file system type. Apple's **HFS+** (for hierarchical file system) is the native file system for Mac OS X Server. On UNIX-type of systems, you can access disk partitions formatted with the DOS FAT file system as well as Windows Server 2003 NTFS. This applies to partitions on disks that are physically attached to computers that are running a UNIX or UNIX-type of system. UNIX systems have access to nonnative file system types, such as NTFS, over the network with network file systems.

Network File Systems

UNIX-type of systems also support network file systems, which are analogous to Windows shares or NetWare network volumes. From a UNIX-type of host, the network file system allows you to attach shared file systems (or drives) from Windows, NetWare, or other UNIX servers and share files with users on other computers. Sun Microsystems' **NFS (Network File System)** is a popular remote file system type supported by UNIX. Sun Microsystems published the specification for NFS, and most vendors of UNIX and UNIX-type systems include NFS applications for sharing and accessing files over a network. Another network file system, called **Samba**, is an open source application that implements the Windows SMB and CIFS file system protocols. Samba is included with Solaris, most Linux distributions, and Mac OS X Server systems by default.

Apple's Macintosh computers have long had a built-in network file system called AFP (AppleTalk Filing Protocol or Apple File Protocol). Though Mac OS X Server includes complete support for NFS and Samba network file systems, AFP remains its primary network file system. You must use AFP on a Mac OS X Server system to share files with computers running older versions of the Macintosh operating system.

A UNIX Command Sampler

NET+
3.1

The command line is the primary method of interacting with a UNIX-type of system. Even when you're running a GUI, the GUI actually executes commands in response to your mouse clicks. This section discusses some of the basics of the UNIX user interface, interaction with the UNIX command line, and some fundamental UNIX commands.

NET+
3.1

The program that accepts the commands you type on the keyboard and runs the commands for you is called a **command interpreter**. Also known as a **shell**, a command interpreter translates your typed commands into machine instructions that a UNIX-type of system can understand. In other words, the command interpreter is a program that runs other programs. UNIX command interpreters also perform file globbing (described later) and keep track of what commands you've entered previously. The primary UNIX command interpreter is the file /bin/sh. To use the shell effectively, you should be familiar with at least some basic commands.

Every UNIX-type of system contains full documentation of UNIX commands in the **manual pages** (or **man pages**). The manual pages describe each command's function and proper execution. Although their organization differs slightly in various flavors of UNIX, manual pages are typically arranged in nine sections:

- ◆ *Section 1* covers the commands that you most typically enter while typing in a command window.
- ◆ *Sections 2 through 5* document the programmer's interface to the UNIX system.
- ◆ *Section 6* documents some of the amusements and games that are included in the UNIX system.
- ◆ *Section 7* describes the device drivers for the system.
- ◆ *Section 8* covers the commands used by administrators to manage the system.
- ◆ *Section 9* documents the UNIX kernel functions programmers use when writing device drivers.

You can access manual pages by entering the man command in a UNIX command window. For example, to read the manual page entry for the telnet command, you would type man telnet in a command window, and then press Enter.

Although the UNIX manual pages are accurate and complete, UNIX newcomers often complain that they can't find the appropriate manual page if they don't know the name of the command they want to use. That's why the apropos command exists. It enables you to find possible manual page entries for the command you want to use. For example, you might type apropos list to search for a command that lists files. The apropos command would then display all commands and programming functions that include the keyword *list* in their manual page entries. Type man <command> (where <command> is a command name displayed by apropos), and press Enter when you find a command name that looks like it might do what you want.

Commands function in much the same way as sentences in ordinary language. Some of these sentences are one-word directives to the system requesting that it perform a simple task on your behalf (such as date for "tell me the current date and time"). Other sentences are detailed instructions to the system containing the equivalent of nouns, adjectives, and adverbs and creating a precise description of the task you want the system to perform. For example, to instruct the system to "display the names of all files in the current directory that have been accessed in the past five days," you would type: find . -type f -atime -5 -print.

NET+
3.1

 NOTE

Commands, command options, and filenames in UNIX are all case sensitive. Be certain to use uppercase and lowercase as appropriate each time you type a command in a UNIX command window.

A few rules exist to guide your use of UNIX commands and, as you might expect, exceptions to most of the rules also exist. Most commands (though not all) are lowercase alphabetic characters. Using the analogy of a sentence, the command itself would be the verb—that is, the action you want the system to take (for example, `ls` to list information about files). The things on which you want the system to operate (often files) would be the nouns. (So, for example, you would type `ls index.html` to list a file named index.html.) Options to the commands are analogous to adjectives and adverbs—that is, modifiers that give more specifics about the command. To specify an option, you usually type a hyphen (-) followed by a letter. (For example, if you want to list files in a directory and also list details about the files, such as their size and creation date, you type `ls -l`.) You can make commands even more specific by using **file globbing**—the equivalent to using wildcards in Windows and DOS. On a UNIX-type system, this operation is also called filename substitution. (For example, `ls -la*` would produce a detailed listing of all files beginning with the letter "a".)

A significant (and perhaps initially confusing) difference between the UNIX and Windows command-line interfaces relates to the character you use to separate directory names when you type in a command window. The Windows separator character is "\" (backslash). The equivalent UNIX directory separator character is "/" (forward slash). For example, in a Windows Command Prompt window, you type the `telnet` command as `\windows\system32\telnet.exe`. The `telnet` command in UNIX is `/usr/bin/telnet`.

NET+
2.10
2.13
3.1

Table 9-4 lists some common UNIX commands and provides a brief description of each.

Table 9-4 Commonly used UNIX commands

Command	Function
`date`	Display the current date and time.
`ls -la`	Display with details all the files in the current directory.
`ps -ef`	Display details of the current running programs.
`find dir filename -print`	Search for *filename* in the directory *dir* and display the path to the filename on finding the file.
`cat file`	Display the contents of *file*.
`cd /d1/d2/d3`	Change the current directory to *d3*, located in */d1/d2*.

Table 9-4 Continued

Command	Function
cp *file1 file2*	Make a copy of *file1*, named *file2*.
rm *file*	Remove (delete) *file*. (Note that this is a permanent deletion; there is no trash can or recycle bin from which to recover the deleted file.)
mv *file1 file2*	Move (or rename) *file1* to *file2*.
mkdir *dir*	Make a new directory named *dir*.
rmdir *dir*	Remove the directory named *dir*.
who	Display a list of users currently logged on.
vi *file*	Use the "visual" editor named *vi* to edit *file*.
lpr *file*	Print *file* using the default printer. **lpr** actually places *file* in the printer queue. The file is actually printed by **lpd (line printer daemon)**, the UNIX printer service.
grep "*string*" *file*	Search for the string of characters in *string* in the file named *file*.
ifconfig	Display the network interface configuration, including the IP address, MAC address, and usage statistics for all NICs in the system.
netstat -r	Display the system's TCP/IP network routing table.
sort *filename*	Sort alphabetically the contents of *filename*.
man "*command*"	Display the manual page entry for "*command*".
chmod *rights file*	Change the access rights (the mode) of *file* to *rights*.
chgrp *group file*	Change the group to which the *file* belongs to *group*.
telnet *host*	Start a virtual terminal connection to *host* (where *host* may be an IP address or a host name).
ftp *host*	Start an interactive file transfer to (or from) *host* using the FTP protocol (where *host* may be an IP address or a host name).
startx	Start the X Window system.
kill *process*	Attempt to stop a running program with the process ID *process*.
tail *file*	Display the last 10 lines of *file*.
exit	Stop the current running command interpreter. Log off the system if this is the initial command interpreter started when logging is on.

NOTE

The developers of the original UNIX system worked at AT&T, then the largest public corporation in the world. Two features of communication within large corporations are a tendency to abbreviate words and a reliance on acronyms. The command names in the UNIX system reflect this culture in that they drop vowels and syllables (*cp* for *copy*, *cat* for *concatenate*, and so on), and name commands with the "initials" of their intended use (*grep* for *general regular expression parser* and *ftp* for *File Transfer Protocol*). Refer to the relevant manual pages when you encounter command names that you don't understand. The synopsis section usually indicates the origin of the command name.

The most frequently used UNIX command is ls. By entering ls (and specifying -1, the detailed listing option), you learn everything about a file except its contents. UNIX-type of systems keep quite a bit of information about each file, including:

◆ The filename

◆ The file size (in bytes)

◆ The date and time that the file was created

◆ The date and time that the file was last accessed (viewed or printed)

◆ The date and time that the file contents were last modified (created, edited, or changed in any way)

◆ The number of "aliases" or links to the file

◆ The numeric identifier of the user who owns the file

◆ The numeric identifier of the group to which the file belongs

◆ The access rights for the owner, the group, and all others

For each file, the system stores all of this information (except the filename) in a file **i-node (information node)**. The beginning of each disk partition contains reserved space for all i-nodes on that partition. I-nodes also contain pointers to the actual file contents on the disk. The file's name is stored in the directory that contains the file. To learn about the i-node information, use the ls command. Figure 9-2 shows a sample list generated by ls -1.

In Figure 9-2, the letters in the leftmost column (for example, "drwxr-xr-x") make up the access permissions field. The first character in the access permissions field (on the far left) indicates the file type. Files type designations include the following:

◆ "d" for directories

◆ "-" for regular files, such as word-processing files or spreadsheet files—that is, those which, as far as the operating system is concerned, contain unstructured data

◆ "l" for symbolic link files (much like Windows shortcuts)

◆ "b" for block device files (such as disk partitions)

◆ "c" for character device files (such as serial ports)

The remaining letters in the access permissions field (for example, "rwxr-xr-x") represent the permissions that users and groups have to access each file. The meaning of these letters is described in Figure 9-3's interpretation of the output of ls -l.

Windows and UNIX-type of systems share the powerful ability to direct output from one command to the input of another command. In UNIX, you combine commands using a **pipe**, which is entered as a vertical bar "|". (Think of data "flowing" through a pipe from one command to another.) Two or more commands connected by a pipe are called a **pipeline**. UNIX pipes make it possible to create sequences of commands that might require custom programming on other systems. For example, you can learn the process ID number assigned to a running program by combining two simple UNIX commands as follows: ps-ef|grep "/bin/sh". In UNIX, most commands that display output in a command window allow you to direct the output to another

```
% ls -l
total 154
drwxr-xr-x   2 root root   4096 Nov 14 15:31 bin
drwxr-xr-x   4 root root   1024 Nov 14 15:21 boot
drwxr-xr-x   9 root root   3920 Nov 20 19:55 dev
drwxr-xr-x  74 root root  12288 Nov 20 20:16 etc
drwxr-xr-x   3 root root   4096 Nov 19 15:35 home
drwxr-xr-x   2 root root   4096 Aug 12 12:02 initrd
drwxr-xr-x  11 root root   4096 Nov 14 15:28 lib
drwx------   2 root root  16384 Nov 14 09:03 lost+found
drwxr-xr-x   3 root root   4096 Nov 20 19:55 media
drwxr-xr-x   2 root root   4096 Oct 15 19:21 misc
drwxr-xr-x   2 root root   4096 Aug 12 12:02 mnt
drwxr-xr-x   2 root root   4096 Aug 12 12:02 opt
dr-xr-xr-x  67 root root      0 Nov 20 13:49 proc
drwxr-x---   7 root root   4096 Nov 20 20:11 root
drwxr-xr-x   2 root root  12288 Nov 14 15:26 sbin
drwxr-xr-x   1 root root      0 Nov 20 13:49 selinux
drwxr-xr-x   2 root root   4096 Aug 12 12:02 srv
drwxr-xr-x   9 root root      0 Nov 20 13:49 sys
drwxrwxrwt   5 root root   4096 Nov 20 20:13 tmp
drwxr-xr-x  14 root root   4096 Nov 14 15:19 usr
drwxr-xr-x  20 root root   4096 Nov 14 15:23 var
% _
```

FIGURE 9-2 *Example of output from ls -l*

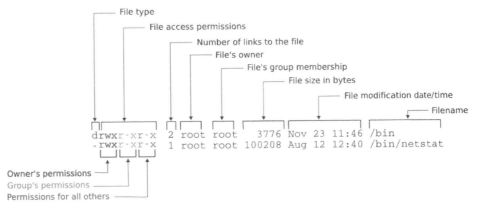

FIGURE 9-3 *Anatomy of ls -l output*

command. Most commands that accept typing from your keyboard also accept input from other commands.

Now that you have learned about commands commonly used by UNIX network administrators, you are ready to plan the installation of a UNIX-type of system. In many cases, you will not need to worry about installing UNIX. For example, Sun Microsystems ships its SPARC servers with Solaris already installed and Apple Computer ships Xserve servers with Mac OS X Server already installed. However, if you are setting up a Linux system, chances are you will have to install and configure it from scratch. The following example of installing Linux uses a popular, free version of Linux called Fedora Core.

Installing Linux

This section describes the prerequisites for and the process of installing **Fedora Core**, the version of Linux packaged and distributed by Red Hat, Inc., on a PC. Most PC manufacturers ship their systems with Windows already installed, so it is usually necessary to install Linux from CD or DVD. As with other network operating systems, a successful Fedora Core installation begins with planning.

Planning a Linux Installation

In the preceding chapter, you learned about the importance of thorough planning in the installation of a new Windows Server 2003 server. These considerations apply to Linux as well. Although making changes to the server setup after you install a Linux system is simple, you should nevertheless plan as carefully as possible to avoid service interruption after a Linux server is running.

Before installing Linux, be prepared to answer the following questions:

◆ *What is the new server's name?* This name is a less important issue for Linux systems than for Windows Server 2003 or NetWare systems, but it's still a good idea to choose it before beginning installation. You can add the server's name to your network name service (DNS, for example) as soon as you choose it. (Using DNS names rather than using IP addresses makes it easier for users to remember how to access computers on the network.) You may use any name containing a maximum of 32 alphanumeric characters, except the following:

> < [ ] . _ : ; | = , + * ´ ?

◆ *What is the server's IP address?* You'll need this address to enable the network on the new server. Network administrators usually configure workstations to obtain an IP address automatically upon start-up. Servers, however, are usually configured with reserved or static IP addresses because some client applications require configuration with a server's IP address rather than a server's name. You'll also need the subnet mask, the IP address of the server's primary gateway (in other words, the default gateway), and the IP address of the new server's domain name server.

NET+
3.1

◆ *What kind of video card is installed in the server?* The Linux setup program (commonly referred to as the "installer") attempts to detect the video card and installs the correct driver if possible. Otherwise, it will prompt you to choose the type of video card from a list. Either way, you should know what kind of video card your server contains.

◆ *What do you want the administrative user's password to be?* Like Windows Server 2003, Linux assigns the system a default administrative user name. In Linux, this user name is called **root**. Choose a difficult-to-guess password for the Linux administrator account. Chapter 14 provides advice on choosing good passwords.

◆ *How can I remember all of this information?* After you have answered these questions, you should create a server installation form and keep the form with you during installation. Appendix D offers an example of such a form.

This list highlights only the most significant installation options. In addition, you should be prepared to identify your keyboard and mouse type, choose a time zone, and specify a new user name. After gathering the information described in this section, you're ready to begin.

Installing and Configuring Fedora Core

Although you can install Fedora Core over the network, this installation summary assumes a typical installation using DVD-ROM. First verify that your computer's BIOS configuration is set to boot from the DVD-ROM, and then boot your system with the Fedora Core 3 disk in your server's DVD-ROM drive. After booting, the system presents you with a welcome screen that prompts you to press Enter to perform a check of the medium, or to skip it and begin the installation. The Fedora Core installation program leads you through the process step-by-step. Help is available in the left-hand panel. Be certain to pay close attention to each option on each screen of the installation process. During this procedure, you're prompted to perform the following:

◆ Select the language the system will use.

◆ Confirm the keyboard layout.

◆ Select Server as the installation type (you could also choose Personal Workstation, Desktop, or Custom).

◆ Select disk drive partitioning options.

◆ Choose booting options (to allow for more than one operating system on the drive).

◆ Configure the network interface (or interfaces).

◆ Configure the network firewall and security level options for the server.

◆ Add support for additional languages.

◆ Set the time and time zone for the server.

◆ Enter (and confirm) the root (administrator) password.

After entering the administrative "root" password, the Fedora Core installer presents you with the Package Group Selection dialog box. This dialog box includes a list of packages in several

NET+
3.1

categories. You may refine your choices by clicking the Details link in the package group selection dialog box. For the purpose of this installation, do not select any of the graphical desktop environments in the Desktops category of the Package Selection Group dialog box.

The Fedora Core installer then formats the hard drive and copies the software to your server. This process may take as long as 60 minutes depending on the speed of your hardware. To complete the installation, the Fedora Core installer prompts you to confirm the server's auto-detected video card and monitor type. When you confirm these settings, the server reboots the new operating system. When it reboots, the server is nearly ready to offer services to network users.

The following section addresses some general system administration tasks common to UNIX-type of systems. These tasks must be completed before users can share resources via the server.

Administering a UNIX-Type of Server

NET+
3.1

Like Windows Server 2003 and NetWare, UNIX-type of systems require the use of user names and passwords to connect clients to the network. Also like these operating systems, UNIX-type of systems assign access rights to groups, and allow users to be members of multiple groups. For example, the UNIX group named *mail* can access the electronic mail programs and electronic mail files. Without user accounts, a UNIX server is little more than a powerful workstation. This section introduces you to the setup process for administering a UNIX-type of system. You'll learn:

◆ The basics of adding users and groups
◆ The basics of modifying file access permissions

To add users and groups to Linux and UNIX systems, you must rely on two commands: groupadd and useradd. Both are explained in their own manual pages. Their names imply their function: groupadd enables you to add a new group to the system, and useradd enables you to add a new user to the system. The process of adding users and groups on a Mac OS X Server system is different. On Mac OS X Server, you use the GUI Workgroup Manager application. The following sections explain how to add users and groups on Linux or Solaris and on Mac OS X Server computers.

Establishing Groups and Users on Linux and Solaris

On a Linux or Solaris system, the groupadd command creates a new group ID and makes the group available for use. Linux and Solaris assign a unique identification number to each group. Note that creating a new group does not automatically assign access rights to that group; you'll learn how to accomplish that task later in this section.

The steps described in this section assume that you are logged on to a Solaris or a Linux system as the administrative user (root) and that your system has presented you with a command prompt.

NET+
3.1

 NOTE

UNIX commands provide no response if they successfully complete the operation. You will see a response only if the command experienced an error.

To add the group *teachers* to your Linux or Solaris system:

1. Type **groupadd teachers** and then press **Enter** at the command prompt. The group *teachers* is added.

You use the useradd command to add a new user ID to a Linux or Solaris system. It creates a new user ID and assigns that user ID to one or more groups. In this example, you'll create a new user, *thomas*, and assign that user to the group *teachers*. The new user will then belong to the general users group as well as the group *teachers*. You must use two options when typing the useradd command: the *-g* option, which specifies the initial (or primary) group for the user, and the *-G* option, which specifies the additional groups to which the new user will belong (*teachers*, in this case). Note that useradd does not assign a password for the new user ID, so you'll use the passwd command to assign a password for *thomas*.

 NOTE

Logon passwords on UNIX-type of systems are case sensitive and can include any of the characters on the keyboard.

To add a new user, add the user to an existing group, and assign the user a password:

1. Type **useradd -m -g users -G teachers thomas** and then press **Enter**.
2. Type **passwd thomas** and then press **Enter**.
3. Linux prompts you to type the new password. As you type the password, notice that the characters do not appear on the screen and the cursor remains stationary. This security precaution prevents people from peering over your shoulder and seeing the password as you type it. After typing the password, press **Enter**.
4. Linux prompts you to retype the user's password. Enter the same password again; this confirmation helps ensure that you type the new password accurately.

To learn more about the passwd command, read the passwd manual page, which you can access by typing man passwd, and press Enter at the shell prompt.

Establishing Groups and Users on Mac OS X Server

You use the **Workgroup Manager** application to add groups and to assign users to groups on a Mac OS X Server system. Workgroup Manager is a GUI application included with Mac OS

X that allows you to manage users and groups. As with Linux and Solaris, creating a new group on a Mac OS X Server does not assign users to that group, but makes it available for use. When you create a new group on Mac OS X Server, you assign a unique name and numeric ID to the group. As with Windows Server 2003, Solaris, and Linux, to manage users and groups in Mac OS X Server, you must be logged on to the system as a user with administrative rights. The following steps use the same example user account and group used in the previous section.

To create the group *teachers* on a Mac OS X Server:

1. Click on the Workgroup Manager icon in the Dock. The Workgroup Manager Connect window opens.

2. Make certain your server's address appears in the Address text box. Enter a user name with administrator-equivalent privileges in the User Name text box and the correct password in the Password text box, then click **Connect**. The Workgroup Manager window opens, with the user account selected by default.

3. Click the group account icon (which depicts three people and is located above the search box). The group account window opens.

4. Click the **New Group** icon.

5. In the Name text box, type **teachers**. By default, the word "teachers" will also appear in the Short Names text box.

6. Click **Save** to save the new group you created.

You also use Workgroup Manager to create new user accounts on a Mac OS X Server.

To create a new user account:

1. If you do not already have Workgroup Manager open, launch it by following Steps 1 and 2 in the previous exercise. The user account window will open by default. If you did not close Workgroup Manager after creating a group in the previous exercise, click the user account icon (the picture of a single person located above the search box).

2. Click the **New User** icon in the Workgroup Manager toolbar. The user options window opens with the Basic pane selected, with default values entered for the Name, User ID, and Short Names text boxes. Delete these default values. Your user options window will look like the one shown in Figure 9-4.

3. In the Name text box, enter the user's full name—for this example, type **Thomas Day**. In Mac OS X Server, long user names are case sensitive when used to log on to the server and can be no longer than 255 characters.

4. In the User ID text box, enter the ID **1025** for this user. In Mac OS X Server, the user ID is a number associated with a user that the NOS uses to identify that user's resources and privileges. It can be any number between 100 and 2,147,483,640 and should be unique for each user.

NET+
3.1

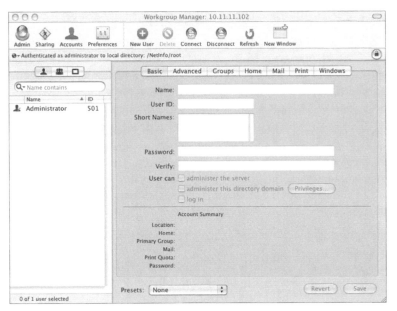

FIGURE 9-4 *User creation in Mac OS X Server's Workgroup Manager*

5. In the Short Name text box, enter **thomas**. The short name will be used to name the user's home directory and identify group memberships on the server. It can also be used to log on to the server.

6. Type a password for the user account called *thomas* in the Password text box, and then type the same password again in the Verify text box.

7. You have the option to enable this user to administer the server, administer the domain, or log in to the server. Click the **log in** check box, if it is not already selected.

8. Click **Save** to save the new user you have created.

To add the user *Thomas Day* to the *teachers* group you just created with Workgroup Manager:

1. In Workgroup Manager, with the user Thomas Day selected, and click the **Groups** tab.

2. Click the add icon, which is represented by a plus sign next to the list of Other Groups. A drawer with a list of groups opens to the right of the main Workgroup Manager window.

3. Double-click **teachers** in the list of groups. The group teachers appears in the list of Other Groups for the user Thomas Day.

4. Click **Save** to save your changes.

5. Close the Workgroup Manager window.

Now that you know how to create users and make them members of a group, you are ready to assign permissions to files that users can share.

NET+
3.1

Changing File Access Permissions

UNIX-type of systems enable you to restrict access to resources by assigning user and group permissions to files and directories. Every file and directory on a UNIX-type of system is owned by exactly one user and is a member of exactly one group. That is, one user and one group have or directory, that user is the file or directory's owner. As an owner, you may assign (or reassign) permissions for yourself, your group, or anyone else.

For example, suppose you are the principal and network administrator for an elementary school. Your user name is *thomas* and you belong to the group *teachers* (both of which were created in the previous section). You want to create a PROGRAMS directory and allow teachers to place new programs in the directory according to the example in Table 9-5. You also want students to be able to run the programs, but not to add new files to the directory or delete existing programs.

The method of creating directories and assigning file access permissions for Linux and UNIX systems, including Solaris, is the same. Mac OS X Server, however, uses a different method. The following two sections describe how to create directories and modify file access permissions on all three types of systems, beginning with Linux and Solaris.

Table 9-5 Providing security through groups

Group	Rights to PROGRAMS	Rights to GRADES	Rights to STAFF
Teachers	Read, modify	Full control	No access
Students	Read	No access	No access
Administrators	No access	Read, modify	Full control

Changing File Access Permissions on Linux and Solaris

To create a directory and assign it to a group on a Linux or Solaris system:

1. If you are still logged on to your UNIX system, log off by typing **exit** and then pressing **Enter**.

2. To log back on to your system as user *thomas*, type **thomas** at the login prompt, and then press **Enter**.

3. Type the password you assigned for *thomas*, and then press **Enter**.

4. You see a command window and a command prompt. To create the new directory, type **mkdir PROGRAMS** and then press **Enter**.

5. Type **ls -l** and then press **Enter**. Notice that the directory belongs to the group *users*. That's because the primary group to which the user *thomas* belongs is *users*.

6. Type **chgrp teachers PROGRAMS** and then press **Enter** to assign ownership of the *PROGRAMS* directory to the group *teachers*.

7. Type **ls -l** and then press **Enter**. Notice that the directory is now assigned to the group *teachers*.

Now that you've created the directory *PROGRAMS* and assigned it to the group *teachers*, you must limit access to the files contained within *PROGRAMS*. Your goal is to enable members of the group *teachers* to create new files in and delete files from *PROGRAMS* and to limit access to all others (including members of the group *students*). To accomplish this task, you must add write permissions to *PROGRAMS* for the *teachers* group and remove write permission for all others.

Changing file and directory permissions requires use of the chmod command. The UNIX chmod command uses a kind of shorthand (made up of two sets of one-letter abbreviations) to specify the permission changes for files. The first set of abbreviations identifies for whom the change will occur: the file's owner (u for "user"), a file's group (g), and all others (o). The second set of abbreviations identifies the access rights for the users in the first set of abbreviations: read (r), write (w), and execute (x). The two sets of abbreviations are separated with a plus sign (+) or a minus sign (-). The plus sign indicates that access rights should be added; the minus sign indicates that access rights should be removed. (You can read more about chmod in its manual page, which you can view by using the command man chmod in a command window on a UNIX-type of host.)

To change the access permissions for the *PROGRAMS* directory:

1. Verify that you are logged on as the user *thomas* (whose primary directory is *teachers*). Type **chmod g+w PROGRAMS** and then press **Enter**. This command adds write access for the *teachers* group to the directory *PROGRAMS*.

2. Next, you will remove read and write access to the *PROGRAMS* directory for all others. To do so, type **chmod o-rw PROGRAMS**, and then press **Enter**.

3. Type **ls -l** and then press **Enter** to view the access permissions assigned to *PROGRAMS*. You should see a line for *PROGRAMS* that includes permissions of drwxrwx--x.

Now, any user who is assigned to the group *teachers* may add files to and remove files from the directory *PROGRAMS*. All other users (users in the group *students*, for example) will be able to run programs that are in the *PROGRAMS* directory, but will not be able to add or delete files in that directory.

Changing File Access Permissions on Mac OS X Server

Creating directories and changing file permissions on a Mac OS X Server is accomplished through the GUI interface. First, make certain you are logged onto the server as a user with administrator privileges, and then:

1. Open a Finder window, and click the icon that represents the server's hard disk.
2. Click on the **Shared Items** folder.
3. Click the **File** menu and then click **Get Info**. The Shared Items Info dialog box opens.
4. Click the triangle to expand Ownership & Permissions, if necessary, and then click the triangle next to Details.

NET+

3.1

5. Click the lock icon to enable changing the group.

6. From the drop-down list next to Owner, select your administrator-equivalent user name.

7. Enter your password in the Authenticate dialog box that opens and then click **OK**.

8. From the drop-down list next to Group, select **teachers**.

9. In the Access drop-down list beneath the Group drop-down list, choose **Read & Write**, if necessary.

10. Close the Shared Items Info dialog box.

You have now created a folder called *PROGRAMS* and allowed only the group *teachers* full access to read, write, modify, execute, or delete files within that folder. Next, you'll learn how to interconnect UNIX-type of servers with computers running different operating systems.

NET+

3.1

3.2

Connecting to UNIX-Type of Servers

Over the years, programmers and network administrators have continually added functionality to UNIX-type systems to make them integrate more easily with other operating systems and with protocols other than TCP/IP. Some of their changes include the addition of Windows networking tools and Windows programming tools. At the same time, as modern operating systems have incorporated the TCP/IP protocol suite, they have gained the ability to communicate with UNIX-type of systems such as Linux servers at some basic level.

However, although UNIX-type of systems and Windows can both communicate via TCP/IP, that doesn't mean their file systems are compatible. One application that bridges this incompatibility is called Samba. When installed on a UNIX-type of system, Samba provides all the networking services necessary to make your UNIX-type of system a fully featured Windows file- and printer-sharing server. Windows users can access resources on UNIX-type of systems as if they were Windows server resources. Users logged on to UNIX-type of hosts can also access Windows drives that have been made available on the network. Printers shared from UNIX-type of systems with Samba appear to Windows users as if they were shared from a Windows server. To achieve this compatibility, Samba communicates with Windows servers using the SMB (server message block) file-sharing protocol and the CIFS (Common Internet File System) protocol, both of which are native to the Windows operating systems. Mac OS X Server includes Samba, but calls it Windows Services. Mac OS X Server also includes the GUI application Server Manager to configure Windows Services.

All modern flavors of UNIX, Linux, and Mac OS X Server support data sharing using directory services based on LDAP. Solaris, for example, implements LDAP in the Sun **Java System Directory Server Enterprise Edition**. Popular Linux distributions include the open source application **OpenLDAP** for directory services. Mac OS X Server includes **Open Directory**, which is Apple's implementation of OpenLDAP.

NET+
2.10
3.1
3.2

As you might guess, UNIX-type of systems also include a full complement of Internet tools. You can use UNIX-type of systems as Web servers, as FTP servers, and as mail servers. One of the most basic Internet services is connecting to a TCP/IP host from a remote computer. This type of connection is provided by the TCP/IP utility, Telnet, which you learned about earlier in this book. Any modern client running the TCP/IP protocol suite will be capable of connecting to a UNIX-type of host via Telnet. Following are steps for accessing a UNIX-type of server from a Windows XP workstation using the Telnet utility. This example uses the user name and password you created earlier in the "Administering a UNIX-type of Server" section of this chapter.

1. To start the Windows Telnet client, click **Start**, point to **All Programs**, point to **Accessories**, and then click **Command Prompt**. The Command Prompt window opens.

2. Type `telnet` in the text box, and press **Enter**. The cursor changes to Microsoft Telnet>.

3. Type `open` followed by the IP address of the UNIX server to which you want to connect, and press **Enter**. Figure 9-5 shows an example of a Windows Telnet session after logging in to a UNIX-type of server and typing `ls`.

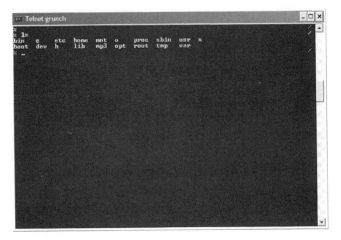

FIGURE 9-5 *Windows Telnet session*

4. Type the user name (in this example, `thomas`) at the login prompt and press **Enter**. A password prompt appears.

5. Enter the password you chose when you added the user *thomas*. You see a shell prompt. You are now logged on to the UNIX server from a remote client via Telnet. You can type commands and view the screen in the Telnet window just as if you were using the keyboard and monitor directly attached to the UNIX server. Type `ls -l /` and then press **Enter**. Figure 9-6 shows the output of the `ls -l /` command.

6. Type `exit` and then press **Enter** to end your Telnet session.

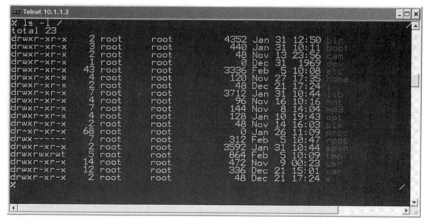

FIGURE 9-6 *Output of* ls -l / *command in a Telnet session*

Chapter Summary

◆ UNIX is a stable, flexible, and efficient network operating system. It relies on TCP/IP and forms the basis of much of the Internet. Despite the preponderance of proprietary implementations of UNIX-type systems, the differences between the various versions—or "flavors"—are relatively minor.

◆ UNIX was developed at AT&T Bell Laboratories, when a few programmers grew dissatisfied with the programming environments available in the late 1960s and decided to devise their own flexible operating system from scratch. Ken Thompson and Dennis Ritchie were the authors of the system.

◆ Currently, The SCO Group owns the copyright to the UNIX source code. The Open Group, a nonprofit trade association, owns the UNIX trademark.

◆ Many varieties of UNIX-type of systems exist, and each of these belong to one of two categories: proprietary and open source. Proprietary UNIX operating systems are those for which the source code is either unavailable or available only by purchasing a licensed copy from The SCO Group. Apple Computer, Sun Microsystems, and IBM sell the three most popular proprietary versions of UNIX—Mac OS X Server, Solaris, and AIX.

◆ In the last few years, open source implementations of UNIX-type of systems have grown in popularity. Open source means that the source code is freely available to anyone. This category includes BSD, GNU, and Linux.

◆ Different flavors of Linux include Fedora Core (a popular Linux packaged and distributed by Red Hat, Inc.), SUSE, and Mandrake.

◆ This chapter focuses on three different UNIX-type of systems: Solaris (from Sun Microsystems), Fedora Core (from Red Hat), and Mac OS X Server (from Apple Computer).UNIX-type of systems make excellent Web servers. UNIX systems underlay the original ARPANET and Internet services, such as FTP, Telnet, gopher, HTTP, and POP. These services are standard with current implementations of most UNIX-type of systems.

◆ Characteristics of UNIX-type of systems include the ability to support multiple, simultaneous users; hierarchical files; a uniform method for interacting with files, devices, and programs; hundreds of subsystems and dozens of programming languages; and source code portability between different implementations of the system.

◆ Minimum hardware requirements for a Solaris 10 server include a SPARC system or Intel-based system with a Pentium-class processor, 512 MB of RAM, 5 to 7 GB of disk space, a Solaris-supported NIC, and a Solaris-supported CD-ROM or DVD-ROM drive.

◆ Minimum hardware requirements for a Linux server include an Intel-compatible x86 processor, 64 MB of RAM, 2 GB of hard disk space, a NIC compatible with the rest of your network, and a CD-ROM drive.

◆ Minimum hardware requirements for Mac OS X Server include a supported PowerPC-based Macintosh computer with 256 MB of RAM and 4 GB of available disk space. The NIC and CD-ROM drive is included with all Macintosh computers. UNIX-type of systems handle multiple processes and multiple threads (self-contained subsets of a process) efficiently and support SMP (symmetric multiprocessing).

◆ Like Windows Server 2003, UNIX-type of systems use virtual memory and also allocate a memory area for each application. UNIX-type of systems attempt to decrease the inefficiency of this practice, however, by sharing memory between programs wherever they can.

◆ Most current UNIX-type of systems use a 32-bit addressing scheme that enables programs to access 4 GB of memory. UNIX-type of systems also run on systems with 64-bit CPUs.

◆ The UNIX kernel, the core of the operating system, is loaded into memory from disk and runs when you turn on your computer. The kernel's primary function is to coordinate access to all the computer's hardware. You can add or remove functionality on a running UNIX-type system by loading and unloading UNIX kernel modules. The Mac OS X Server kernel is based on the operating system kernel named Mach, which was developed at Carnegie Mellon University.

◆ UNIX-type of systems were among the first to include a hierarchical file system, in which directories can hold files and other directories.

◆ Like other NOSs, UNIX-type of systems support multiple file system types. The native file system type for Linux, called *ext3*, is the "third extended" file system for Linux. The default file system for Solaris is UFS (for "UNIX file system"). The default Mac OS X Server file systems is HFS+ (for "hierarchical file system").

◆ UNIX-type of systems support network file systems that are analogous to Windows shares or NetWare network volumes. Common UNIX-type of network file systems include NFS and Samba.

◆ You can liken UNIX commands to ordinary sentences. The command is the action you want to perform, or the verb. The things you want the system to operate on are the nouns—often files. Options to the commands are similar to adjectives and adverbs.

◆ Most UNIX commands are lowercase alphabetic characters. To specify an option, you usually type a hyphen ("-") followed by a letter. The letter is often (but not always) a mnemonic abbreviation for the option (such as -l for a long file listing).

◆ Command names are usually acronyms or abbreviations. Consult the command's manual (man) page by typing man *command* at the shell prompt, and pressing Enter to learn more about a command.

◆ The UNIX ls command is the most frequently used. When you use ls with the -l option, it allows you to learn everything about a file except its contents. ls -l reports the filename, the file size, the date and time that the file was last accessed, the number of "aliases" or links to the file, the user who owns the file, the group to which the file belongs, and the access rights for the owner, the group, and all others.

◆ All the information about a file on a UNIX-type of system (except the file's contents) is stored in an information node (i-node). I-nodes also contain pointers to file contents on the disk.

◆ The useradd command allows you to add new users to your Linux or Solaris system.

◆ The groupadd command allows you to add new groups to your Linux or Solaris system.

◆ The Workgroup Manager application allows you to manage users and groups on a Mac OS X Server system.

◆ The chgrp command assigns a file to a group.

◆ The chmod command changes file access permissions.

◆ Use the Mac OS X Server Finder Info dialog box to assign files and folders to a group and to set file and folder access permissions.

◆ UNIX-type of systems interoperate well with other network operating systems. Installing the Samba application on a UNIX-type of server allows it to exchange information with Windows servers by using Windows file system and file access protocols.

◆ Samba is included with Mac OS X Server and called Windows Services. You use the GUI application Server Manager to configure Windows Services.

◆ All modern flavors of UNIX, Linux, and Mac OS X Server support data sharing using directory services based on LDAP. Solaris uses the Sun Java System Directory Server Enterprise Edition, Linux distributions include OpenLDAP, and Mac OS X Server uses Open Directory (the Apple implementation of OpenLDAP).

◆ Any client that runs the TCP/IP protocol can connect to a UNIX-type of host, such as a Linux server, through the Telnet utility.

Key Terms

AIX—A proprietary implementation of the UNIX system distributed by IBM.

AppleShare IP—A proprietary network operating system from Apple Computer that offers file, print, Web, DNS, and mail services. AppleShare IP was the predecessor to Mac OS X Server.

Berkeley Software Distribution—See *BSD*.

BSD (Berkeley Software Distribution)—A UNIX distribution that originated at the University of California at Berkeley. The BSD suffix differentiates these distributions from AT&T distributions. No longer being developed at Berkeley, the last public release of BSD UNIX was version 4.4.

command interpreter—A (usually text-based) program that accepts and executes system programs and applications on behalf of users. Often, it includes the ability to execute a series of instructions that are stored in a file.

ext3—The name of the primary file system used in most Linux distributions.

Fedora Core—A version of Linux packaged and distributed by Red Hat.

file globbing—A form of filename substitution, similar to the use of wildcards in Windows and DOS.

flavor—The term used to refer to the different implementations of a particular UNIX-type of system. For example, different flavors of Linux include Red Hat's Fedora Core, SUSE, and Mandrake.

freely distributable software—See *open source software*.

GNU—The name given to the public software project to implement a complete, free source code implementation of UNIX. It also refers to the collection of UNIX-inspired utilities and tools that are included with Linux distributions. The term "GNU" is an acronym within an acronym that stands for "GNU's Not UNIX."

HFS+—The primary file system used in Mac OS X Server.

hierarchical file system—The organization of files and directories (or folders) on a disk in which directories may contain files and other directories. When displayed graphically, this organization resembles a treelike structure.

information node—See *i-node*.

i-node (information node)—A UNIX-type file system information storage area that holds all details about a file. This information includes the size, the access rights, the date and time of creation, and a pointer to the actual contents of the file.

Java System Directory Server Enterprise Edition—The Sun Microsystems implementation of LDAP.

kernel—The core of a UNIX-type of system and a NetWare NOS. This part of the operating system is loaded and run when you turn on your computer. It mediates between user programs and the computer hardware.

kernel module—A portion of the kernel that you can load and unload to add or remove functionality on a running UNIX or Linux system.

line printer daemon—See *lpd*.

Linux—A freely distributable implementation of a UNIX-type of system. Finnish computer scientist Linus Torvalds originally developed it.

lpd (line printer daemon)—A UNIX service responsible for printing files placed in the printer queue by the lpr command.

lpr—The UNIX command. This command simply places files in the printer queue. The files are subsequently printed with lpd, the print service.

Mac OS X Server—A proprietary network operating system from Apple Computer that is based on a version of UNIX.

Mach—A UNIX-type of operating system kernel developed by researchers at Carnegie Mellon University in Pittsburgh, PA. Mach is the basis for the kernel in Mac OS X Server.

man pages—See *manual pages*.

manual pages—The online documentation for any variety of the UNIX operating system. This documentation describes the use of the commands and the programming interface.

mount—The process of making a disk partition available.

Network File System—See *NFS*.

NFS (Network File System)—A popular remote file system created by Sun Microsystems, and available for UNIX-type of systems.

OpenLDAP—A popular open source application included with many Linux distributions that implements LDAP.

Open Directory—The version of OpenLDAP by Apple Computer that is included with Mac OS X Server.

open source software—The term used to describe software that is distributed with few restrictions and whose source code is freely available.

pipe—A character that enables you to combine existing commands to form new commands. The pipe symbol is the vertical bar ("|").

pipeline—A series of two or more commands in which the output of prior commands is sent to the input of subsequent commands.

PowerPC—The brand of computer central processing unit invented by Apple Computer, IBM, and Motorola, Inc., and used in Apple computers and IBM servers.

proprietary UNIX—Any implementation of UNIX for which the source code is either unavailable or available only by purchasing a licensed copy from The SCO Group (costing as much as millions of dollars). Redistribution of proprietary UNIX versions requires paying royalties to The SCO Group.

root—A highly privileged user ID that has all rights to create, delete, modify, move, read, write, or execute files on a system. This term may also refer to the network administrator.

Samba—An open source software package that provides complete Windows-style file- and printer-sharing capabilities.

shell—Another term for the UNIX command interpreter.

Solaris—A proprietary implementation of the UNIX operating system by Sun Microsystems.

source code—The computer instructions written in a programming language that is readable by humans. Source code must be translated into a form that is executable by the machine, typically called binary code (for the sequence of zeros and ones) or target code.

SPARC—The brand of computer central processing unit invented by and used in Sun Microsystems servers.

System V—The proprietary version of UNIX that comes from Bell Labs.

The Open Group—A nonprofit industry association that owns the UNIX trademark.

The SCO Group—The company that owns the rights to the UNIX source code.

UFS—The primary file system used in the Solaris operating system.

Workgroup Manager—The application in Mac OS X Server that enables a network administrator to manage users and groups.

XNU—The Mach-based kernel in Mac OS X.

Xserve—The enterprise-class of server computer by Apple Computer, which is based on the PowerPC processor and which runs Mac OS X Server.

X Window system—The GUI environment for UNIX-type of systems.

Review Questions

1. Versions of UNIX that come from Bell Labs are known as
   _____.

   a. AppleShare IP

   b. Linux

   c. System V

   d. Fedora Core

2. On a Linux or Solaris system, the _____ command creates a new group ID and makes the group available for use.

   a. groupadd

   b. ext3

   c. lpr

   d. mount

3. Any modern client running the TCP/IP protocol suite will be capable of connecting to a UNIX-type of host via _____.

   a. Solaris

   b. Samba

   c. DOS

   d. Telnet

4. _____ is equivalent to using wildcards in Windows and DOS.

   a. Pipelining

   b. File globbing

   c. Mounting

   d. Piping

5. Every UNIX-type system contains full documentation of UNIX commands in the _____.

   a. manual pages

   b. pipeline

   c. software

   d. shell

6. True or false? The SCO Group is the company that owns the rights to the UNIX source code.

7. True or false? Any UNIX-type of operating system can act as a workstation or server operating system.

8. True or false? Most current UNIX-type systems use a 16-bit addressing scheme that enables programs to access 4 GB of memory.

9. True or false? Every file and directory on a UNIX-type of system is owned by exactly one user and is a member of exactly one group.

10. True or false? UNIX modules make it possible to create sequences of commands that might require custom programming on other systems.

11. The core of all UNIX-type systems is called the _____.

12. A(n) _____ is a file that contains instructions for performing a specific task, such as reading data from and writing data to a hard drive.

13. Apple's _____ is the native file system for Mac OS X Server.

14. A program that accepts the commands you type on the keyboard and runs the commands for you is called a(n) _____.

15. In UNIX, two or more commands connected by a pipe are called a(n) _____.

Chapter 10

NetWare-Based Networking

After reading this chapter and completing the exercises, you will be able to:

- Identify the advantages of using the NetWare network operating system
- Describe NetWare's server hardware requirements
- Understand NetWare's file system and directory structures
- Plan for and perform a simple NetWare server installation
- Explain how NetWare supports multiple clients and integrates with other network operating systems

You have already learned about two popular network operating systems, or methods for managing resources on a server. In this chapter, you will learn about NetWare, another popular NOS. Novell NetWare shares many characteristics with Windows Server 2003, UNIX, Linux, and Mac OS X Server, such as their use of a hierarchical file system, graphical interfaces for resource management, and server optimization techniques. All provide standard client/server functions, such as file and print sharing, remote access, e-mail, and Internet connectivity. In NetWare 6.5, Novell introduced several open-source components much like those found in UNIX and Linux. Subsequent NetWare releases will be based on a Linux kernel.

This chapter does not attempt to cover all of the details of installing, managing, and optimizing NetWare. For that type of knowledge, and especially if you intend to pursue CNE certification, you should invest in a book devoted to NetWare. This chapter provides an overview of the requirements, characteristics, and basic structure of Novell's popular NOS.

Introduction to NetWare

NET+
3.1

Novell released its first NetWare network operating system in 1983, and it quickly became the NOS of choice for many businesses. In subsequent years, Novell refined NetWare to make it run over TCP/IP (in addition to IPX/SPX) and to provide a graphical user interface for its file and resource management, plus a broad range of Internet services, fault-tolerance techniques, and seamless integration with other operating systems.

NetWare offers excellent answers to a network administrator's questions about ease of use, performance, flexibility, interoperability, and scalability. It has been around for over 20 years and has a faithful following among network administrators. Some veteran networking professionals are more comfortable with NetWare because of its long history and its status as the first NOS designed specifically for file and print sharing. NetWare's popularity arises from an appreciation of its traditional strengths, such as fast performance, reliable services, and strong vendor support. However, in the last decade, NetWare has lost approximately 80% of its previous market share to more popular NOSs, such as Windows Server 2003, UNIX, and Linux.

In your networking career, you may encounter several different versions of NetWare, from NetWare **3.x** (which includes NetWare 3.0, 3.1, and 3.2) and **4.x** (which includes NetWare 4) to **6.x**. If you work on legacy NetWare installations, bear in mind that NetWare versions prior to 4.11 require the IPX/SPX protocol suite. With 4.11, the version sometimes referred to as **intraNetWare**, NetWare began supporting TCP/IP. IntraNetWare was also the first version of NetWare to supply Internet-related services, such as Web server software, IP address management, and FTP hosting. Novell changed the look of its NOS with NetWare **4.x**, which includes versions 4.0, 4.1, and 4.11, in an attempt to make this software more user-friendly, replacing most of the old DOS-based commands with a graphical user interface. NetWare 4.x also provided much better support for enterprise-wide networks containing multiple servers.

In 1998, Novell released version 5.0 of NetWare, and since then has released versions 5.1 and 5.11; collectively, they are known as **NetWare 5.x**. NetWare 5.x was Novell's first NOS wholly based on the IP protocol. This version also offered improved file and print management, plus a graphical interface based on the Java programming language.

With its release of NetWare 6.0 and 6.5—collectively known as the **NetWare 6.x** network operating systems—Novell transformed its NOS once again. NetWare 6.5's key features include the following:

◆ Support for multiple processors, multitasking, and symmetric multiprocessing

◆ Flexible use of virtual and physical memory

◆ eDirectory (formerly called NDS), a comprehensive system for organizing and managing network objects

◆ Simple, centralized management of multiple clients, resources, and services

◆ Multiple, integrated Web development and delivery services

◆ Support for multiple modern protocols

◆ Excellent integration with other NOSs and support for many different clients

◆ Remote client services—for example, remote access and Web-based application services

◆ Built-in clustering services

◆ Provisions for monitoring server performance, automatic backups, and resource utilization

◆ File system specially designed to support high-performance, large-scale storage devices that are accessible from multiple operating systems

With the release of NetWare version 6.5, Novell has made several additions and enhancements to its NOS. Noteworthy changes include the following:

◆ iManager, a browser-based tool for managing eDirectory and its objects

◆ DirXML, a tool for centrally managing and synchronizing NetWare directories with Windows NT domains and Windows 2000 Server and Windows Server 2003 Active Directories

◆ Capability for continuously backing up a server as it runs

◆ Server Consolidation Utility, a utility that makes it possible to share the same data and file information among multiple servers (for example, allowing several servers to share an application located on one server)

◆ Popular open-source Web development tools, such as Apache and MySQL

◆ Virtual Office, a browser-based suite of tools that simplifies the process of synchronizing local files with files on a server, printing to any network printer, and performing e-mail and collaboration tasks

NET+

3.1

◆ Branch Office, a software package that allows remote offices connected to a WAN to maintain independent operation (in case of a failure at headquarters) while belonging to the same NetWare eDirectory

◆ Nterprise Linux Services, a group of network services that allow Linux-based servers and clients to use NetWare's client and network management tools

However, NetWare does not necessarily suit all organizations. For example, if your organization depends heavily on enterprise-wide Microsoft solutions, such as Internet Information Services or Exchange Server, you may want to forego a NetWare purchase. In that case, changing to NetWare might require significant training efforts before technical staff become comfortable with the unfamiliar NOS.

Ideally, you should test your critical applications (including network management functions such as backup and restore services) on several NOSs (NetWare, Windows Server 2003, and Linux, for example) to determine which will work most efficiently in your environment. For evaluation purposes, you can download the NetWare software from Novell's Web site and run it for a limited period of time. Nevertheless, you probably will not have the luxury of designing a network from scratch and picking the NOS. Also, the choice of NOSs your servers run may depend on corporate preferences and technical issues in your environment.

If your organization chooses NetWare, you can count on extensive online support from Novell's support Web site, *support.novell.com.* From there, you can search Novell's knowledgebase, read NetWare documentation, or join a forum in which networking professionals from around the world share their experiences with Novell products. You can also learn about known bugs in different versions of NetWare and find explanations of common problems at the Novell support site. In addition, the company provides enhanced technical support to CNEs (Certified NetWare Engineers) through CDs and discounted calls to Novell's help desk. Alternatively, you can find a number of third-party discussion groups on the Web as well as technical manuals and books that focus on NetWare products.

 NOTE

You do not need to know the specific differences between versions of NetWare to achieve Network+ certification. As a network administrator or technician, however, you will likely encounter environments that use one or several NetWare versions. Therefore, a general understanding of NetWare is essential. This chapter focuses on the most significant, fundamental features of NetWare 6.5.

NetWare Server Hardware Requirements

NET+
3.1

You have learned that servers generally require more hard disk space, memory, and processing power than do client workstations on the network. Servers may also benefit from redundant disk drives, NICs, power supplies, or multiple processors. The more components you install on a server, the more expensive the machine. At the same time, however, the machine will likely operate more reliably and quickly with the added components.

Table 10-1 lists the minimum hardware requirements for NetWare 6.5, as outlined by Novell.

Table 10-1 Minimum hardware requirements for NetWare 6.5 servers

Component	Requirement
Processor	An IBM or IBM-compatible PC with a Pentium II, AMD K7, or better processor. (Out of the box, NetWare 6.5 can support as many as 32 processors.)
Memory	512 MB of RAM (1 GB is recommended)
Hard disk	A hard disk with at least 2 GB of free space available for system files (4 GB is recommended)
NIC	A NIC that supports your network type and for which you have drivers available
CD-ROM	Required
Pointing device	Optional, but necessary if you want to use the GUI console
Floppy disk	Optional

Many networking environments actually require servers that exceed the minimum hardware requirements suggested by the software vendor. Every situation will vary, but to determine the optimal hardware for your server, you should consider the following:

◆ How many clients will connect to the server?
◆ What kinds of applications will run on the server?
◆ Which and how many optional services will the server provide?
◆ How much storage space will each user need?
◆ How much downtime is acceptable?
◆ What can your organization afford?

Perhaps the most important question refers to the types of applications that the server will run. You can purchase a relatively inexpensive server that runs NetWare 6.5 but suffices only for file and print sharing. To run applications and optional services, such as remote access and clustering, you will need a more powerful machine. Every application and service has its own processor, RAM, and storage requirements. In the case of applications, consult the application's installation guide to find out its specific requirements. In the case of optional NetWare services, consult Novell's documentation.

A Closer Look at the NetWare 6.5 Operating System

NET+
3.1

By now, you have probably noticed many similarities between the major features of NetWare and the NOSs described in previous chapters. Next, you'll discover even more similarities, as well as some differences, in their operating system details.

NetWare Integrated Kernel

The core of the NetWare 6.5 operating system is the **NetWare Integrated Kernel**. NetWare's kernel is responsible for overseeing all critical server processes. For example, it manages multiprocessing, multitasking, and access to the server's interrupts, memory, and I/O functions. The kernel is started by the program server.exe, which runs from a server's DOS partition (over the DOS operating system) when a server boots up. Each NetWare 6.5 server must have a DOS partition for this purpose.

NetWare 6.5 takes advantage of symmetric multiprocessing, in which the NetWare Integrated Kernel equally distributes tasks among the processors. In versions 4.x and higher, NetWare supports the use of as many as 32 processors on one server. As you know, multiprocessing increases a server's performance when the server runs several operations simultaneously. For servers performing many processor-intensive activities, having multiple processors is usually worth the investment in the extra hardware. To use NetWare 6.5's multiprocessing capabilities, you simply install multiple processors in the server. The operating system automatically detects and uses these processors, whether 1 or 32 are present, without additional configuration.

The NetWare Integrated Kernel is also responsible for loading and unloading, when necessary, **NLMs (NetWare loadable modules)** used by each application or service. NLMs are routines that enable the server to run a range of programs and offer a variety of services, such as protocol support and Web publishing. Each NLM consumes some of the server's memory and processor resources (at least temporarily). For example, when you install NetWare out of the box, your server will run many critical NLMs. If you install Novell's **GroupWise** e-mail and scheduler software, the server will require an additional set of NLMs. If you install Novell's **BorderManager** software, the server will require still another set of NLMs, and so on. The amount of resources consumed by each NLM depends on the NLM's size and complexity.

During NetWare installation, the appropriate NLMs are selected, based on what services the network administrator chooses for the server. Afterward, each time a server boots up, server.exe loads the critical NLMs that the kernel needs to run the NetWare operating system. In fact, after an NLM loads into memory, it is considered part of the kernel.

A network administrator can also load or unload NLMs through the server's **console**. The console is the server interface, which enables the network administrator to manage disks and volumes and modify server parameters, such as protocols, bindings, system resources, and loaded

NET+
3.1

modules. It provides an administrator with control over the server's operation. Console commands can be accessed at the server or from another computer on the network, and you may use a text-based or graphical menu system to run console commands. The text-based menu that allows a network administrator to view and modify server parameters through console commands is called **Monitor**. The graphical interface that provides access to the same console commands, plus object and directory management, is called **ConsoleOne**. ConsoleOne, which is similar to the Windows Server 2003 MMC, can be used either at the server or from another computer connected to the same network. To run ConsoleOne from the server, choose Novell, and then choose ConsoleOne from the main menu in X Server. **X Server** is a NetWare 6.5 server's graphical desktop, and it is loaded by default when the server starts. To run ConsoleOne from a client computer on the network, you must first install the ConsoleOne client program. A ConsoleOne client window is shown in Figure 10-1.

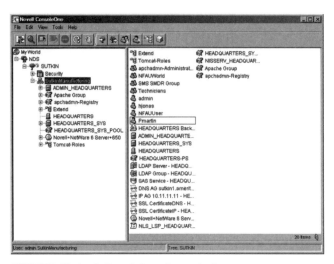

FIGURE 10-1 *A ConsoleOne client window*

To access console commands through a Web browser on another computer on the network, you use the **Remote Manager** tool. For example, suppose you are busy helping a user in one of your company's branch offices. A colleague from your IT Department pages you and when you call back, she asks you to investigate a problem on one of your network's servers. However, the user's workstation doesn't have the ConsoleOne software installed, because this program is typically only used by IT personnel. Instead, you could connect to the Remote Manager utility through a Web browser on the user's desktop workstation. One screen you might be interested in viewing is Remote Manager's Health Monitor window, which is shown in Figure 10-2. If you plan to specialize in NetWare administration (no matter which version of NetWare is involved), you should become very familiar with console commands and how to use them through both graphical and text-based menus.

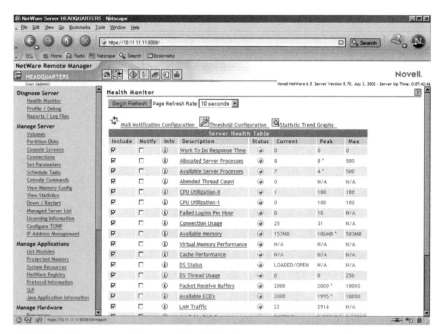

FIGURE 10-2 *Remote Manager Health Monitor*

NetWare File System

As you know, a file system is an operating system's method of organizing, managing, and accessing its files. In NetWare 6.5, the preferred file system is called **NSS (Novell Storage Services)**. NSS is selected by default during NetWare 6.5 installation. Although NetWare 6.5 can run older file systems (such as FAT) through its optional Traditional File Services utility, using traditional file services is less desirable because of the older file systems' many limitations. Benefits of using NSS include the following:

◆ A 64-bit interface, which results in fast data access

◆ Files or directories as large as 8 Terabytes (TB)

◆ Up to a trillion files in a single directory

◆ File compression (enabled by default)

◆ The ability to set user and directory space restrictions

◆ Advanced fault-tolerance techniques

◆ Efficient use of memory

◆ Browser-based volume management

◆ The ability to split volumes over multiple storage devices

A server running NetWare 6.5 and using NSS may have up to four partitions, and one of these must be a DOS partition. The DOS partition is the primary **boot partition**, from which the

NET+

3.1

server.exe file (the NetWare Integrated Kernel) runs. At least one additional partition must be present to hold the NetWare program and data files. On each NetWare 6.5 partition, you may create an unlimited number of volumes.

Like Windows NOSs, NetWare uses volumes as the basis for organizing files and directories on the server. NetWare's installation program automatically creates a volume called SYS. You may choose to create additional volumes such as DATA (for user data) or APPS (for shared applications). (Volume names are best kept short, simple, and descriptive.) Design a volume structure to suit your network's performance, security, growth, and data sharing needs. For example, assigning all user data to its own volume called DATA, separate from the SYS volume that contains system files, can help streamline network management tasks such as backing up files and setting access permissions.

 NOTE

Plan carefully before establishing a server's volume and directory structures—after being established, they are very difficult to change. When installing a NetWare network from scratch, you should consult Novell's NetWare documentation, which can guide you through the process of planning the volume and directory structure for your network.

One unique feature of NSS is the ability to combine free storage space from multiple hard disks (or other storage devices, such as CDs) into a storage **pool**. During installation, NetWare 6.5 creates a default pool, which, like the default volume, is also called SYS and which shares the SYS volume's size. Later, a network administrator can change the characteristics of that pool or create new pools. The primary advantage to using pools is flexibility. For example, if your network grows quickly and you discover that your NetWare 6.5 server is running out of space to store critical system files, you could attach a new server to the network and add its hard disk to the SYS pool. Alternatively, you could add an external hard disk (for example, one attached through a USB port) to increase the size of the pool. This allows you to quickly add storage space without causing downtime and disrupting users. Figure 10-3 illustrates how a pool can

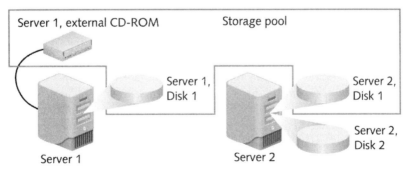

FIGURE 10-3 *A storage pool in Novell Storage Services*

NET+
3.1

be created from multiple storage devices. In this example, one disk from one server, one disk from another server, plus an externally attached CD-ROM drive form a single pool.

In NetWare 6.5, storage devices such as hard disks are considered objects. To manage NSS objects—for instance, to add a new hard disk to an existing pool or create a new pool—a network administrator uses a browser-based tool called **iManager**. In fact, iManager is the primary GUI tool used to manage all objects in NetWare 6.5. Later in this chapter, you will learn how to add users and groups through iManager.

Now that you have been introduced to the NetWare file system, you are ready to learn how NetWare 6.5 organizes its objects.

eDirectory

eDirectory is NetWare 6.5's directory database—its system for organizing and managing multiple servers and their resources, including storage devices, users, volumes, groups, printers, and so on. (In earlier NetWare versions, **NetWare Directory Services**, or **NDS**, contained this information.) The eDirectory model is similar to Active Directory in Windows Server 2003. Both Active Directory and eDirectory treat every networked resource as a separate object with distinct attributes, or properties. Objects belong to certain classes—for example, users or printers. Each object contained in an eDirectory database can be centrally managed from the iManager tool. Figure 10-4 shows a list of some types of objects that are available in eDirectory, as viewed through iManager. eDirectory can store and manage millions of objects.

FIGURE 10-4 *eDirectory objects*

Like Active Directory, eDirectory information is stored in a database that supports LDAP (Lightweight Directory Access Protocol), which makes it compatible with other NOS and Internet directories. Conceptually, eDirectory is not directly associated with one server's hard disk. For example, a server does not store a database file called "eDirectory.DB" containing all of the tree and object information for the network. In fact, NetWare keeps eDirectory information in hidden storage areas, which are usually distributed across multiple servers. For fault tolerance, eDirectory, like Active Directory, can be replicated on (or copied to) multiple servers on a network. This means that if the one server containing eDirectory data fails, clients can still log on to the network and obtain access to resources via a different server.

NET+

3.1

Schema

In eDirectory, as in Active Directory, the word "schema" is used to refer to a defined set of object classes (such as a user or printer) and their properties. In NetWare 6.5, the simplest schema is installed by default with eDirectory, and is called the **base schema**. A base schema consists of the object classes and properties a network typically requires. However, the network administrator can add classes or properties to the schema. After a change is made to the base schema, the new schema is known as an **extended schema**. For example, you may want to add a user's employee number as an optional property for the user object. After doing so, all user objects in your eDirectory database would contain fields in which you could enter employee numbers.

> **NOTE**
>
> Notice that Novell uses the word "properties," whereas Microsoft uses the term "attributes" to refer to the set of characteristics associated with an object.

Trees and OUs (Organizational Units)

When you install the first server in a NetWare 6.5 network, an eDirectory database is created. Later, when adding servers or other resources to the network, you build on this original eDirectory in a hierarchical fashion. Novell uses the analogy of a tree to describe this hierarchical layout. The eDirectory tree is the logical representation of objects in eDirectory. As with Active Directory's domain tree, the eDirectory tree is generally portrayed upside down (compared to a live tree) with a single root at the top and multiple branches at the bottom, as shown in Figure 10-5.

The eDirectory tree can have only one root. In Novell terminology, this root is called the **tree object**, and it bears the name of the tree. For instance, suppose you are establishing a network at your employer, Sutkin Manufacturing. When you install NetWare 6.5 on the server, you might choose to name the tree object "Sutkin."

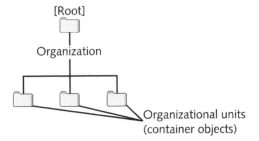

FIGURE 10-5 *A simple eDirectory tree*

NET+

3.1

Below the root is an organization object. The organization object branches out in a hierarchical arrangement of OUs (organizational units, or containers). As in Active Directory, an OU's purpose is to logically subdivide the tree and hold other objects that belong together. OUs can organize users and resources by geographical location, department, professional function, security authorization, or other criteria significant to the particular network. For example, if the organization under the root of the Sutkin Manufacturing Company's eDirectory tree is called "Sutkin," the OUs might be called "Maintenance," "Inventory," "Packing," "Shipping," "Information Services," "Accounting," and so on. On the other hand, if Sutkin Manufacturing is a small company with only a handful of users and other resources in the Maintenance, Inventory, Packing, and Shipping Departments, these users and resources may be grouped in a larger OU called "Operations" and departments within the "Operations" OU may be distinguished through the use of groups.

Figure 10-6 compares two ways of grouping objects. It's usually possible to arrange an eDirectory tree for an organization a number of different ways. The hierarchy of resources and organizational units is something network administrators must plan carefully.

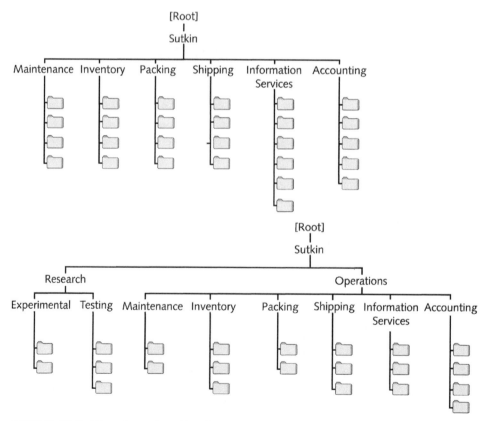

FIGURE 10-6 *Ways of grouping objects in an eDirectory tree*

NET+

3.1

Moving away from the root of the tree, branch objects lead to either more branch objects or leaf objects. As you have learned, a leaf object is an object in the directory tree that does not contain other objects. For example, a printer queue is a leaf object because it handles only the printer queue. A user is a leaf object because it does not contain or manage any objects other than the network user it represents. Several kinds of leaf objects exist. You will typically deal with user-related leaf objects, such as users, groups, profiles, templates, and aliases. You will also deal with printer-related leaf objects, such as printers, queues, and print servers. Some Novell packages, such as GroupWise, introduce other kinds of leaf objects into the tree. Nevertheless, all Novell products integrate with the eDirectory structure to allow easy, centralized administration. Figure 10-7 depicts a more complex eDirectory tree with several branch and leaf objects. (Compared to an eDirectory tree you might find in a large corporation, this example is still greatly simplified.)

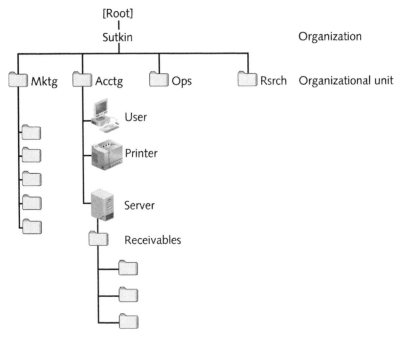

FIGURE 10-7 *A more complex eDirectory tree*

Naming Conventions

Each object in an eDirectory tree has a **context** that indicates where that object belongs in the tree. A context consists of an object's OU names, arranged from most specific to most general, plus the organization name. Periods separate the OU names within the context. You can envision the context as a kind of address for locating an object.

NET+
3.1

Contexts may be expressed in two ways: typeful and typeless. The **typeful** notation is a relatively lengthy way of expressing context that includes identifiers for the organization and OUs. (It is similar to the distinguished name in Windows Server 2003.) For example, a user named Phil who works in the Receivables area of the Accounting ("Acctg") department of Sutkin Manufacturing in Figure 10-7 would have a typeful context of OU=Receivables. OU=Acctg.O=Sutkin. In this typeful context, "OU" stands for "organizational unit" and "O" stands for "organization." The LDAP standard uses typeful names, too, though LDAP notation uses commas rather than periods to separate organization and organizational unit names.

A **typeless** notation eliminates the "OU=" and "O=" symbols. In the preceding example, Phil's typeless context would be Receivables.Acctg.Sutkin. Both the typeful and the typeless contexts indicate that Phil is a member of the Receivables organizational unit, which is located in the Acctg organizational unit, which is part of the Sutkin organization.

In a large corporation with a complex eDirectory tree, a user's context can quickly become very long. Users do not always have to know or provide their context, however. Instead, the workstation support group or network administrator can configure users' client software to assume by default the context and the organization to which each user belongs. Users can then log on to their organizations with only a user name. In the preceding example, a user named Phil with the typeful context of OU=Receivables.OU=Acctg.O=Sutkin would simply type "phil" when prompted for his user name. This is similar to using a relative distinguished name in Windows Server 2003.

Now that you understand the way NetWare 6.5 organizes and manages objects in eDirectory, you are ready to plan and perform a NetWare installation.

Planning for Installation

NET+
3.1

The importance of planning for installation cannot be overemphasized. Poor planning results in more work for the installer, potential downtime for users, and headaches for whomever supports the server after installation. The following list summarizes the critical pre-installation decisions you should make. As you will see, the list is very similar to the decisions that you must make before installing Linux and Windows Server 2003; whereas Windows Server 2003 deals in Active Directory, NetWare focuses on the eDirectory tree.

◆ *Where does the server fit in the eDirectory tree?* The place occupied by the server in your network's eDirectory tree (its context) will depend largely on its function. If this function is merely to allow a group of students to print to a classroom printer, the server might belong to a small organizational unit for that classroom. If the server will provide network access for all of the math instructors at a college, it may belong in the Math organizational unit of your tree. If the server will provide mail services to the entire college, it may have its own organizational unit off the root of the tree called Mail. Clearly, you should develop your organization's tree and its policies for organizational unit and leaf objects before you begin installation. The server's place in the eDirectory tree will affect how easily it can be accessed and managed. After you have established the server's context, you cannot change it.

◆ *What name will the server have?* Choose a practical, descriptive name that distinguishes the server from all other servers. You might use geographical server names, such as Boston or Buffalo. Alternatively, you might name servers according to their function, such as Marketing or Research. Bear in mind that the server name can (and usually will) differ from its eDirectory organizational unit's or organization's name. For example, the Math Department server in a college's eDirectory structure might be called "MATH_DEPT," but it might belong to the "Math" organizational unit, which might in turn belong to a larger organizational unit called "TechCollege" under the root.

◆ *How many and what kinds of NICs will the server use?* Before you begin installing NetWare, you should have driver and diagnostics disks on hand for the server's NICs. The NetWare installation process will usually find your NIC's driver in its own set of software drivers, but it may not always be successful in this quest. You should therefore be prepared to supply the NIC software, and the NIC's IRQ, shared memory address, and I/O base address before beginning the server installation.

◆ *What protocols and network services should the server use?* You need to know which protocols your network requires. By default, NetWare 6.5 will install and run the TCP/IP protocols, which, as you know, are supported by virtually all modern clients and other NOSs. However, if your network supports legacy technology, you may have to install additional protocols.

◆ *What will the Administrator password be?* When you install NetWare, you will be asked to provide an Administrator ID and password. In NetWare 6.5, the default Administrator ID is "Admin." As explained in previous chapters, you should choose a password that is difficult to crack.

◆ *What kind of disk controllers does the server have?* NetWare's installation program will attempt to detect the kind of hard disk and CD-ROM drive your server possesses. If the program can correctly identify the hardware, it will install the drivers. Otherwise, it will prompt you to choose drivers from a list or install a driver from a disk. Either way, you should know what kind of disk controllers your server has (you can find this information in the server's hardware specifications or by viewing BIOS information). Note that the NetWare installation process does not always choose the right controller by default.

◆ *How many, how large, and what kind of volumes will the server require?* NetWare's installation program will ask you to identify the size, number, and names of the server volumes. Initially, the program assigns all free space on the hard disk to its default volume, SYS. To add volumes, you must modify the size of SYS (by subtracting the size of the other volumes you intend to create from SYS's current size).

◆ *What server pattern, or type, will the server be?* In designing the NetWare installation program, Novell has attempted to predict the types of servers users will want to install. Based on these predictions, Novell selected the services that would be necessary for each type and presented each collection of services as server **patterns**. Some patterns you can choose to install include a Basic NetWare File Server, a Customized

NET+

3.1

NetWare Server, or a Pre-Migration Server. If you choose a basic file server, only the key services necessary for sharing, including file system tools and eDirectory, will be installed. If you choose to install a customized server, you can pick any combination of NetWare components to install. A pre-migration server is one that you designate as the recipient of an older server's data and directory information. Other choices include installing a backup server, Web server, and print server. Some components, such as eDirectory, ConsoleOne, and Remote Manager, are installed by default, no matter which server pattern you choose.

◆ *What kind of license do I have?* When you purchased the NetWare operating system, you chose a licensing option for your organization. During the installation of the operating system, you will be prompted for the license disk (or file, if you've copied it to the server's hard disk) that came with your NetWare software. NetWare 6.5 licenses can be purchased on a per site (organization), per server, or per user basis. The per site (or organization) mode requires a license for every organization and authorizes all users (up to 250,000 users) at the organization to connect to the Net-Ware server. The per server licensing mode allows a limited number of clients to access the server simultaneously. In per server mode, any of your organization's clients may be capable of connecting to the server. The number of concurrent connections is restricted. The per user mode requires a license for every user object or client capable of connecting to the NetWare 6.5 server. Licensing restrictions become more complicated if you are using NetWare's clustering services, in which several different servers can act as one large server.

◆ *How can I remember all of this information?* After you have made these decisions, you should create a server installation form and keep it with you during installation. Appendix D offers an example of such a form.

The preceding list highlights only the most significant installation options. You should also be prepared to read and accept the license agreement, identify your time zone, provide IP address information, and choose any optional authentication services the server may use.

Installing and Configuring a NetWare 6.5 Server

NET+

3.1

After you have devised a plan for your NetWare 6.5 installation, you can begin the actual installation process. In this section, you will learn about the available options and the decisions you must make when installing and initially configuring your NetWare 6.5 server.

The Installation Process

After thoroughly planning your installation and obtaining the NetWare 6.5 software from Novell, you are ready to create a NetWare 6.5 server. NetWare can be installed from a CD (the most popular method) or another server on the network. If your computer is configured to boot from the CD-ROM drive, you can merely insert the first NetWare installation CD and start the computer. When the computer boots, it will run the INSTALL program from the CD-ROM. If your computer is not configured to boot from the CD-ROM drive, make sure the server is installed with DOS version 6.22 or higher, and then run the INSTALL program from either a CD-ROM or another server on the network. (Do not attempt to install NetWare from a DOS prompt on a server running a Windows operating system or from the DOS version that comes with Windows.)

The NetWare installation process begins with text-based menus that prompt you to:

◆ Select your language.

◆ Select regional settings.

◆ Accept the Novell Software License Agreement and the JReport Runtime program license agreement from Jinfonet Software (JReport Runtime is a third-party software package used by NetWare).

◆ Choose whether you want to perform a Default or Manual installation. The Default installation preselects standard server settings and simplifies installation. Manual installation allows you to choose settings specific to your network. If you choose the Default installation, you can still change, add, or remove services or settings later.

◆ Prepare the boot partition.

◆ If you have chosen the Default installation, accept default selections of a 4 GB SYS volume, and auto discovery of LAN, disk, and video drivers.

The program copies the NetWare installation files to your server's hard disk. Next, it discovers your hardware and loads the appropriate drivers, then copies the NetWare system files. After that, the installation menus are GUI-based and prompt you to:

◆ Choose a pattern, or select the type of server you are installing.

◆ If you selected a Customized NetWare Server, select the components you want to install.

◆ Review the details of the server you're about to install.

◆ Choose to copy files.

The installation program prompts you to insert a second installation CD-ROM, the NetWare Products CD. After these files have been copied, you need to set up the server. The program will prompt you to:

◆ Name the server.

◆ Enable cryptography.

◆ Specify the network protocols for each network adapter, and in the case of TCP/IP, specify the server's IP addressing information.

◆ Enter the server's host and domain name.

◆ Set the server time zone.

◆ Select whether to create a new eDirectory tree or add the server to an existing eDirectory tree.

◆ Enter eDirectory information (and if desired, create organizational units).

◆ Choose an Administrator ID and password.

◆ License the NetWare server.

◆ Select the login method, or any additional means of authenticating with an eDirectory tree (other than the default method, which is called the NDS login method).

After you provide this information, the installation program copies files necessary for the security services you selected. Then, it closes the installation files and prompts you to remove any installation CDs or disks and reset the server. If you choose to start the server software automatically upon rebooting, the NetWare NOS loads. If you choose to start the server manually, you must type SERVER at the command prompt and then press Enter to load the NetWare NOS.

By default, the NetWare installation program creates the eDirectory tree (if one didn't previously exist), a SYS volume, a SYS pool, an administrator user called Admin who has supervisory rights to all objects in the eDirectory tree and all files in the file system, and a group called [Public] that has Browse rights to view all objects in the tree. The following section describes how to create users and groups in NetWare 6.5.

Establishing Users and Groups

Before users can log in to your NetWare network and share resources, you will need to add objects—including user objects—to the eDirectory tree. After adding objects, you may want to modify their properties or even extend the NetWare schema. Such operations can be accomplished by using one of three tools: ConsoleOne, Remote Manager, or iManager.

 NOTE

Remote Manager and ConsoleOne are installed by default, no matter which NetWare 6.5 server pattern you choose. However, iManager is considered an optional service. You may either choose the Customized NetWare Server pattern during the first installation, and then select iManager as a desired service, or you may install iManager from the server console after installation.

You can run ConsoleOne, Remote Manager, or iManager from any workstation connected to the same network as the NetWare server. To run ConsoleOne, the computer must have the ConsoleOne client installed and be running the same protocols as the server (for example, TCP/IP or IPX/SPX). In the case of Remote Manager and iManager, the workstation must run the TCP/IP protocol and a Web browser—either Internet Explorer version 5.0 or higher or Netscape, version 4.5 or higher. No matter which tool you choose, you need administrator privileges to the server to create users and groups.

NET+

3.1

To run Remote Manager, point your Web browser to the IP address for the NetWare server management interface. By default, this address will be port 8008 on your server. For example, if you gave your NetWare server an IP address of 10.11.11.11, point your browser to the following URL: *https://10.11.11.11:8008*. The NetWare Remote Manager login window opens, prompting you to log on. Enter the administrator ID and password you chose during installation, and then click Login. From there, you can perform server, volume, and limited eDirectory management.

To start iManager, point your browser to the /nps/imanager.html page on your NetWare server. For example, if your NetWare server's IP address is 10.11.11.11, point your browser to the following URL: *https://10.11.11.11/nps/imanager.html*. The NetWare iManager login window opens. Enter the administrator ID and password you chose during installation, and then click Login. After logging on, you can perform unlimited eDirectory management.

The following steps explain how to create a new user object in iManager. Although the same can be accomplished in ConsoleOne or Remote Manager, iManager is the tool Novell recommends for creating and managing user objects.

1. Connect to the iManager URL on your server and log on to the iManager tool as a user with administrator privileges. The iManager window opens, with a list of functions on the left side of the screen.

2. Scroll down the list and click **Create User** under the Users heading. The Create User window opens, as shown in Figure 10-8.

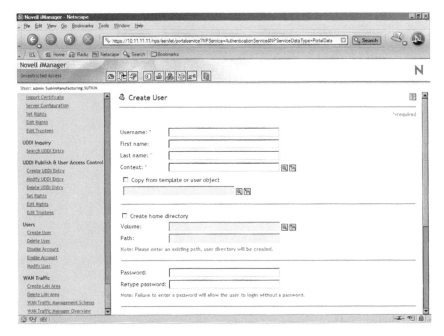

FIGURE 10-8 *The iManager Create User window*

NET+
3.1

3. Enter the user's user name, first name, last name, and context in the text boxes provided. This is the minimum amount of data you must enter. You may enter additional information, such as the user's home directory, password, and personal information. A **home directory** is a directory on the server in which a user can store files. By default, users have full access privileges to files and subdirectories within their home directories. Note that if you do not specify a password for the user name, the user will be able to log on to the network without a password.

4. When you have entered all the user's information, click **OK** to create the user object. iManager responds with a message: "Complete: The Create User request succeeded."

5. Click **OK** to return to the default iManager window.

Creating a group in NetWare 6.5 is similar to creating an object:

1. Connect to the iManager URL on your server and log on to the iManager tool as a user with administrator privileges. The iManager window opens, with a list of functions on the left side of the screen.

2. Scroll down the list of functions and click **Create Group** under the Groups heading. The Create Group window opens, as shown in Figure 10-9.

3. Enter a name and context for the group, and then click **OK**. iManager responds with a message: "Complete: The Create Group request succeeded."

4. Click **Modify** to change the default properties of this group. The Modify Object prompt appears, with a drop-down list and a number of text boxes.

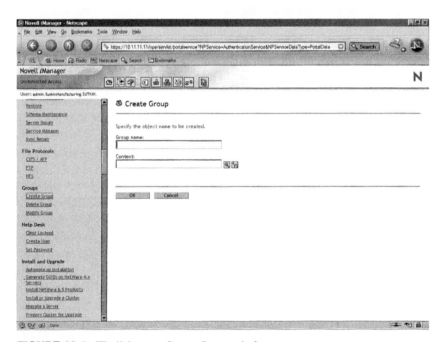

FIGURE 10-9 *The iManager Create Group window*

5. Select **Members** (depending on your browser type, this option might appear as a hyperlink or an item in a drop-down list). A Members prompt appears.

6. To search for objects to be included in this group, click the **Object Selector** icon (which looks like a magnifying glass). The Object Selector window opens.

7. Click the **Browse** button or tab, depending on your browser, to browse through the eDirectory tree until you find the user objects you want to add to this group.

8. Click the user objects you want to add to the group you have created. When you are finished adding users, click **OK** to return to the default iManager window.

After you have created eDirectory objects, you may want to change their properties. For example, if one of your staff members changes her last name, you will want to change the last name property within her User object. Or, when an employee leaves the company, you will want to delete his user object. Changing object properties is simply a matter of choosing the "Modify User" or "Modify Group" option in iManager. These functions represent only a fraction of iManager's capabilities.

TIP

NetWare will not allow you to delete an object that contains leaf objects. If you want to delete an organizational unit, you must first delete all of the objects it contains.

Client Services

NetWare 6.5 provides several ways for different types of clients to access the server and its resources. These access methods can be categorized as follows: traditional client access, native file access, and browser-based access. The following sections briefly describe each method of NetWare 6.5 client connections.

Traditional Client Access

In previous versions of NetWare, clients running Windows, Macintosh, and UNIX-type of operating systems traditionally connected and accessed NetWare resources via a Novell client specifically designed for that client. For example, a Windows 95 client would run the Novell Client for Windows 95/98. A Windows XP client would use the Novell Client for Windows NT/2000/XP. Novell continues to provide these two software packages for Microsoft clients. They are offered at no extra cost with the NetWare NOS, or they can be downloaded from Novell's Web site.

To connect to a NetWare server using traditional client software, the client would also need to have installed the appropriate protocol suite (for example, TCP/IP or IPX/SPX). And depending on the server's configuration, some configuration of the client software may be necessary.

NET+
3.1
3.2
3.4

In most cases, client software is configured to start when a workstation boots up. After the workstation is running, the user is prompted with a Novell Login dialog box, as shown in Figure 10-10. (In Figure 10-10, the Advanced option is selected so that you can see where a user's context and server are specified.)

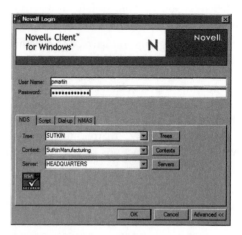

FIGURE 10-10 *Novell Login dialog box*

Client software can be installed individually on each workstation from a CD-ROM or from a file downloaded via Novell's Web site. However, on a large network with many clients (particularly if they are located in different buildings or cities), installing software separately on each workstation becomes burdensome. To streamline the process, Novell provides utilities that automatically install client software (and updates) on all clients. This can occur directly from the NetWare server across a LAN or over the Internet. The network administrator controls how and when automated client installations proceed.

Even simpler than automatically installing client software, however, is not using client software at all. The next two client access methods do not require any special client software.

Native File Access

Earlier in this chapter, you learned that NetWare 6.5 uses NSS (Novell Storage Services), a proprietary file system, to manage its files, directories, and volumes. NetWare is capable of providing clients with direct access to NSS using the clients' native file access protocols—that is, the type of file access protocol that the client expects to use when opening, reading, and saving files. For example, Linux clients can access and share NetWare 6.5 server resources using NFS, the native file access protocol used by UNIX-type of systems. Windows clients can use CIFS (Common Internet File System), the Windows file access protocol, and Macintosh clients can use AFP (AppleTalk Filing Protocol or Apple File Protocol), the file access protocol used on Apple Macintosh systems. Using native file access protocols means that users can browse folders and directories just as if they were connected to a server that runs the same file

NET+
3.1
3.2
3.4

access protocols by default—for example, a Windows XP client connected to a Windows Server 2003 server or a Red Hat Linux client connected to a Linux server.

All file access protocols are installed by default when you install NetWare 6.5. However, before clients can access the server through these protocols, the network administrator has to set up a network share for each protocol. This can be accomplished using the iManager tool. For example, suppose you have installed a NetWare 6.5 server, using the Basic File Server installation choice. Attached to your network are several Windows clients. To make a directory on the server's hard disk appear to the client as a Windows folder, you would log on to iManager, then choose the CIFS/AFP option under the File Protocols heading. You would then specify a directory and share name and possibly change other parameters, such as whether the folder is available to an entire domain or a specific workgroup. After establishing the share, the folder would appear in the client's My Network Places window (in the case of Windows XP).

Although this server access method does not require any special client software, it does impose some requirements on the client. The client must run the same protocols and software it would normally use to connect to a server natively running its file access protocols. For a Windows client, that means that the appropriate network protocols (such as TCP/IP) must be installed and properly configured and the client must run the Client for Microsoft Networks.

NetDrive is software that, when installed on Windows clients, allows them to access directories on a NetWare 6.5 server. Rather than using the Windows native file system access protocol, CIFS, NetDrive uses Internet protocols, such as HTTP and FTP. Before you can use NetDrive, the NetDrive client software must be installed on a workstation. After installation, NetDrive allows users to connect to the NetWare 6.5 server, navigate directories, and manage files through Windows Explorer. If you have ever used FTP client software, you might recognize the look and functioning of a NetDrive client as similar to a GUI FTP client. Figure 10-11 shows the NetDrive connection dialog box.

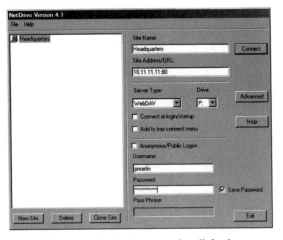

FIGURE 10-11 *NetDrive connection dialog box*

NET+
3.1
3.2
3.4

Browser-Based Access

Perhaps the simplest way for users to access NetWare 6.5 files and directories is through a Web browser. Users can navigate directories and manage their files on a server through Novell's **NetStorage** tool. To use NetStorage, clients need only have the TCP/IP protocols installed and configured. NetStorage uses standard Internet application protocols, such as HTTP. To log on via NetStorage, users connect to a URL on the server. By default, this URL is the server's IP address (or host name) plus /NetStorage. For example, if the server's IP address is 10.11.11.11, a user would connect to the following URL: *https://10.11.11.11/NetStorage*. The NetStorage service would respond with a prompt to log on to the server. After authenticating, the user would see a list of his available folders and files on the server.

From a network administrator's standpoint, however, NetStorage entails more work than providing client access through traditional client services or by using native file access protocols. The network administrator must have installed the optional NetStorage services and configured NetStorage on the server through iManager.

Internetworking with Other Operating Systems

NET+
3.1
3.4

Administration of a network running different network operating systems is much simpler than it was only a few years ago. This is in part a result of Microsoft and Novell both adopting LDAP directory standards. In addition, both companies have offered user-friendly tools for integrating their directory data.

DirXML is Novell's tool for integrating eDirectory and Windows Active Directory or Windows NT domain data. With DirXML installed and configured on both the NetWare and Windows servers in an organization, the servers can share directory data. When data in one directory is updated, DirXML synchronizes the change in the other directory or directories. A network administrator can configure DirXML so that either Active Directory or eDirectory is the authoritative source for directory information. Using DirXML allows users to log on to the network once and gain access to objects from both Active Directory and eDirectory. When DirXML is used in conjunction with the client access tools described in the previous section, users may not even know whether the programs, data, and devices they access are on a NetWare or Windows server.

To simplify NetWare access for users running the Linux NOS, Novell has packaged a group of tools and programs that are collectively known as **Nterprise Linux Services**. Nterprise Linux Services consist of client tools for accessing eDirectory, development tools for integrating Linux servers with DirXML, plus the browser-based file and print services discussed earlier in this chapter. Because Linux operating systems run TCP/IP by default, Linux clients can easily connect to NetWare servers through NetStorage. In addition, Novell has recently purchased two companies that write and distribute Linux software. In Novell's next version of NetWare—NetWare 7.0—the NetWare and Linux kernels will be combined. This means that NetWare

NET+
3.1
3.4
users will have the option of running NetWare on a Linux system (in addition to the option of running it on a DOS-based system, as described in this chapter). As you might expect, running NetWare on a Linux system will eliminate the need for specialized software that enables Linux clients to access a NetWare server. NetWare and Linux servers will also be fully compatible.

Chapter Summary

◆ With NetWare 6.x, Novell has maintained its NOS's traditional file- and print-sharing strengths while adding browser-based management tools, popular open-source Web development tools, a fast, efficient file system, and flexible methods for managing multiple servers, volumes, and storage objects.

◆ The minimum hardware requirements necessary to run a NetWare 6.5 server are: a PC with a Pentium II or AMD K7 or better processor, 512 MB of RAM, at least 2 GB of free hard disk space, a NIC, and a CD-ROM drive. In most cases, a faster processor and additional RAM and hard disk space are preferable. For running additional services, such as Web development or remote access services, such upgrades may be necessary.

◆ The NetWare Integrated Kernel is responsible for overseeing all critical NetWare server processes, such as multiprocessing, multitasking, and access to the server's interrupts, memory, and I/O functions. The kernel is started by the program server.exe, which runs from a server's DOS partition when a server boots up.

◆ NLMs (NetWare loadable modules) are routines that enable the server to run a range of programs and offer a variety of services, such as protocol support and administrative tools. Each NLM consumes some of the server's memory and processor resources.

◆ Using ConsoleOne, administrators can manage servers, volumes, disks, and eDirectory objects. The Remote Manager tool allows an administrator to accomplish the same tasks using a browser interface from any computer on the network.

◆ iManager is the primary means of managing eDirectory objects in NetWare 6.5. iManager is a browser-based utility that runs on any computer connected to the network.

◆ NetWare 6.x's preferred file system is called NSS (Novell Storage Services). NSS offers many advantages over traditional file systems (such as FAT), including faster access, more efficient use of memory, file compression, support of files or directories as large as 8 TB, support for sharing a single application over multiple servers, capability to limit user directory and volume size, and browser-based management tools.

◆ Although NSS is unique to NetWare, NetWare 6.5 allows clients and other NOSs to access NSS files directly, by supporting certain file access protocols native to different clients. For example, it supports the NFS file system access protocol for UNIX or Linux clients and CIFS for Windows clients.

◆ eDirectory is NetWare 6.x's system for organizing and managing multiple servers and their resources, including storage devices, users, volumes, groups, printers, and so on. (In earlier NetWare versions, NetWare Directory Services, or NDS, contained this information.)

◆ eDirectory information is stored in a database that supports LDAP (Lightweight Directory Access Protocol), which makes it compatible with other NOS and Internet directories.

◆ The word "schema" refers to eDirectory's defined set of object classes and their properties. In NetWare 6.5, the simplest schema is the one installed by default with eDirectory, which is called the base schema. If changes are made to the base schema, it becomes an extended schema.

◆ eDirectory follows a tree structure, which is represented by the tree object at the top. From there, organizations and OUs (organizational units) branch out in a hierarchical manner and may contain other OUs or leaf objects, such as users or printers.

◆ Each object has a context that indicates where that object belongs in the eDirectory tree. A context consists of an object's OU names, arranged from most specific to most general, plus the organization name. Periods separate the OU names within the context.

◆ NetWare recognizes two naming conventions for a user's context: typeful and typeless. In typeful notation, the organization and organizational units are designated with the "O=" and "OU=" symbols, respectively. Typeless notation eliminates these symbols. OU=Receivables.OU=Acctg.O=Sutkin is an example of typeful notation, and Receivables.Acctg.Sutkin is an example of typeless notation.

◆ Before you insert the NetWare CD and begin installing the operating system, you should consider many factors, including how you will structure the eDirectory tree, what the server's function will be, what optional services you need to install, what licensing model you need to follow, and what the administrator ID and password will be.

◆ User and Group objects can be created through one of three tools: ConsoleOne, Remote Manager, or iManager. Novell recommends using the iManager tool for this task.

◆ Clients can connect to a NetWare 6.5 server, browse directories, and manage files in one of several different ways. Traditional client software, such as the Novell Client for Windows NT/2000/XP, can be installed on each client workstation to enable logging on. Otherwise, users can connect through native file system access protocols (for example, NFS for Linux and CIFS for Windows), or they may use Novell's browser-based NetStorage tool.

◆ NetWare 6.5 uses the DirXML tool to share data between eDirectory and Active Directory or Windows NT domains. To integrate Linux clients and servers, NetWare 6.5 provides the Nterprise Linux Services collection of client access and development tools.

Key Terms

base schema—The standard set of object classes and attributes installed as the default schema for NetWare's eDirectory. The base schema can be extended through NetWare utilities.

boot partition—A partition on a computer's hard disk from which the operating system software is launched.

BorderManager—An application from Novell that provides proxy and firewall services on NetWare servers.

console—The interface to a NetWare server and its kernel operations.

ConsoleOne—The graphical interface to NetWare server administration tasks. ConsoleOne can be used at the server or from another workstation connected to the same network.

context—The characteristic that indicates where an object belongs in an eDirectory tree. A context is made up of an object's organizational unit names, arranged from most specific to most general, plus the organization name. Periods separate the organizational unit names in context.

DirXML—A Novell tool for integrating eDirectory and Windows Active Directory or Windows NT domain data.

eDirectory—The database of objects and their attributes in NetWare 6.x.

extended schema—In NetWare, a set of object classes and attributes that is different from the base schema.

GroupWise—An application from Novell that runs on NetWare servers and provides e-mail, messaging, scheduling, and collaboration services.

home directory—A directory on a server associated with a particular user account. A user has full access privileges to files and subdirectories within his home directory.

iManager—A browser-based tool for managing eDirectory in NetWare 6.x.

intraNetWare—Another term for NetWare version 4.11, the version in which support for Internet services was first introduced.

Monitor—A NetWare NLM that provides a text-based menu for viewing and modifying server parameters, such as protocols, bindings, system resources, and loaded modules.

NDS (NetWare Directory Services)—In NetWare 4.x and 5.x, the system of managing multiple servers and their resources, including users, volumes, groups, profiles, and printers, used with NetWare versions 4.x and 5.x. The NDS model was the precursor to eDirectory.

NetDrive—The client software that enables Windows workstations to connect to a NetWare 6.5 server using standard Internet protocols, such as FTP and HTTP. After connecting through NetDrive, a user can navigate the server's directories and manage files as if navigating a Windows hard disk.

NetStorage—A TCP/IP-based tool from Novell that allows users to navigate directories and manage files on a NetWare 6.x server.

NetWare 3.x—The group of NetWare versions that includes versions 3.0, 3.1, and 3.2.

NetWare 4.x—The group of NetWare versions that includes versions 4.0, 4.1, and 4.11.

NetWare 5.x—The group of NetWare versions that includes versions 5.0, 5.1, and 5.11.

NetWare 6.x—The group of NetWare versions that includes versions 6.0 and 6.5.

NetWare Directory Services—See *NDS*.

NetWare Integrated Kernel—The core of NetWare 6.x's operating system. The NetWare Integrated Kernel manages multiprocessing, multithreading, and access to the server's interrupts, memory, and I/O address space.

NetWare loadable module—See *NLM*.

NLM (NetWare loadable module)—A routine associated with a particular NetWare application or service. Each NLM consumes some of the server's memory and processor resources (at least temporarily). The kernel requires many NLMs to run NetWare's core operating system.

Novell Storage Services—See *NSS*.

NSS (Novell Storage Services)—The 64-bit file access and storage system installed by default and preferred for use on NetWare 6.x servers. NSS offers several benefits over traditional file systems such as FAT, including faster access, more efficient use of memory, support for files or directories as large as 8 TB, and up to a trillion files in a single directory.

Nterprise Linux Services—A group of tools and programs for integrating Linux computers into a NetWare 6.5 network. Nterprise Linux Services consists of client tools for accessing eDirectory, development tools for use with DirXML, plus browser-based file and print services.

pattern—In the context of installing the NetWare NOS, a choice of server type to install (for example, Basic NetWare File Server). Based on the pattern, the installation program will include files necessary for specific services or, if the Customized NetWare Server pattern is selected, prompt the user to select which services should be installed.

pool—A collection of storage objects in NetWare 6.x.

Remote Manager—A browser-based tool that enables network administrators to perform server and object management in NetWare 6.5.

tree object—In NetWare terminology, the object that represents the root of an eDirectory tree.

typeful—A way of denoting an object's context in which the organization and organizational unit designators ("O=" and "OU=," respectively) are included. For example, OU=Inv.OU=Ops.OU=Corp.O=Sutkin.

typeless—A way of denoting an object's context in which the organization and organizational unit designators ("O=" and "OU=," respectively) are omitted. For example, Inv.Ops.Corp. Sutkin.

X Server—A NetWare 6.x server's graphical desktop. X Server loads by default when the server starts.

Review Questions

1. The _____ tool is used to access console commands through a Web browser on another computer on the network.
   a. iManager
   b. Remote Manager
   c. Console Monitor
   d. NDS

2. A(n) _____ consists of the objects, classes, and properties a network typically needs.
   a. base schema
   b. eDirectory
   c. pool
   d. X Server

3. Each object in an eDirectory has a _____ that indicates where that object belongs in the tree.
   a. pool
   b. monitor
   c. pattern
   d. context

4. _____ is Novell's tool for integrating eDirectory and Windows Active Directory or Windows NT domain data.
   a. Remote Manager
   b. X Server
   c. DirXML
   d. NetDrive

5. Contexts may be expressed in two ways: _____.
   a. typeful and typeless
   b. NetDrive and intraNetWare
   c. DirXML and NetDrive
   d. typeful and tree object

6. True or false? IntraNetWare was the first version of NetWare to supply Internet-related services, such as Web server software, IP address management, and FTP hosting.

7. True or false? Both Active Directory and eDirectory treat every networked resource as a separate object with distinct attributes, or properties.

8. True or false? The eDirectory tree must have at least two roots.

9. True or false? A home directory is a directory on the server where a user can store files.

10. True or false? LDAP notation uses periods to separate organization and organizational unit names.

11. NetWare's _____ is responsible for overseeing all critical server processes.

12. _____ are routines that enable the server to run a range of programs that offer a variety of services, such as protocol support and Web publishing.

13. _____ is a NetWare 6.5 server's graphical desktop that is loaded by default when the server starts.

14. A server running NetWare 6.5 and using NSS may have up to four partitions, and one of them must be a(n) _____ partition.

15. _____ is NetWare 6.5's directory database.

Chapter 11

In-Depth TCP/IP Networking

After reading this chapter and completing the exercises, you will be able to:

■ Understand methods of network design unique to TCP/IP networks, including subnetting, CIDR, NAT, and ICS

■ Explain the differences between public and private networks

■ Describe protocols used between mail clients and mail servers, including SMTP, POP3, and IMAP4

■ Employ multiple TCP/IP utilities for network discovery and troubleshooting

The Internet has become not only a means of communication, but also a means of global commerce, development, and distribution. Industries such as banking, manufacturing, and healthcare depend on the Internet for daily transactions, recordkeeping, and sales. Individuals, too, increasingly rely on the Internet for purchasing and data-gathering operations.

In previous chapters, you learned that the Internet depends on the TCP/IP suite of protocols, as do a number of network operating systems. Because of the increasing popularity of the Internet, having TCP/IP expertise can pave the way to a lucrative, challenging, and rewarding career. In Chapter 4, you learned about core protocols and subprotocols in the TCP/IP protocol suite, addressing schemes, and host and domain naming. You also learned that TCP/IP is a complex and highly customizable protocol suite. This chapter builds on these basic concepts, examining how TCP/IP-based networks are designed and analyzed. It also describes the services and applications that TCP/IP-based networks commonly support. If you are unclear about the concepts related to IP addressing or binary-to-decimal conversion, take time to review Chapter 4 before reading this chapter.

Designing TCP/IP-Based Networks

By now, you understand that most modern networks rely on the TCP/IP protocol suite, not only for Internet connectivity, but also for transmitting data over private connections. Before proceeding with TCP/IP network design considerations, it's useful to briefly review some TCP/IP fundamentals. For example, you have learned that IP is a routable protocol, and that on a network using TCP/IP each interface is associated with a unique IP address. Some nodes may use multiple IP addresses. For example, on a router that contains two NICs, each NIC can be assigned a separate IP address. Or, on a Web server that hosts multiple Web sites—such as one operated by an ISP—each Web service associated with a site can have a different IP address.

IP addresses consist of four 8-bit octets (or bytes) that can be expressed in either binary (for example, 10000011 01000001 00001010 00100100) or dotted decimal (for example, 131.65.10.36) notation. Many networks assign IP addresses and host names dynamically, using DHCP, rather than statically. You also know that every IP address can be associated with a network class—A, B, C, D, or E (though Class D and E addresses are reserved for special purposes). A node's network class provides information about the segment or network to which the node belongs. The following section explains how network and host information in an IP address can be manipulated to subdivide networks into smaller segments.

NET+
2.7

Subnetting

Subnetting separates a network into multiple logically defined segments, or subnets. Networks are commonly subnetted according to geographic locations (for example, the floors of a building connected by a LAN, or the buildings connected by a WAN), departmental boundaries, or technology types (for example, Ethernet or Token Ring). Where subnetting is implemented, each subnet's traffic is separated from every other subnet's traffic. A network administrator might separate traffic to:

◆ *Enhance security*—Subnetworks must be connected via routers or other Layer 3 devices. As you know, these devices do not retransmit incoming frames to all other nodes on the same segment (as a hub does). Instead, they forward frames only as necessary to reach their destination. Because every frame is not indiscriminately retransmitted, the possibility for one node to tap into another node's transmissions is reduced.

◆ *Improve performance*—For the same reason that subnetting enhances security, it also improves performance on a network. When data is selectively retransmitted, unnecessary transmissions are kept to a minimum. In the case of Ethernet networks, subnetting is useful for limiting the amount of broadcast traffic—and therefore the amount of potential collisions—by decreasing the size of each broadcast domain. The more efficient use of bandwidth results in better overall network performance.

◆ *Simplify troubleshooting*—For example, a network administrator might subdivide an organization's network according to geography, assigning a separate subnet to the nodes in the downtown office, west-side office, and east-side office of her company. Suppose one day the network has trouble transmitting data only to a certain group of IP addresses—those located on the west-side office subnet. When troubleshooting, rather than examining the whole network for errors or bottlenecks, the network administrator needs only to see that the faulty transmissions are all associated with addresses on the west-side subnet to know that she should zero in on that subnet.

To understand how subnetting is implemented, it's necessary to first review IP addressing conventions on a network that does not use subnetting.

NET+
2.6

Classful Addressing

In Chapter 4, you learned about the first and simplest type of IP addressing, which is known as **classful addressing** because it adheres to network class distinctions. In classful addressing, only Class A, Class B, and Class C addresses are recognized. Recall that all IP addresses consist of network and host information. In classful addressing, the network information portion of an IP address (the network ID) is limited to the first 8 bits in a Class A address, the first 16 bits in a Class B address, and the first 24 bits in a Class C address. Host information is contained in the last 24 bits for a Class A address, the last 16 bits in a Class B address, and the last 8 bits in a Class C address. Refer to

Figure 4-8 to review the bit separation between network and host information in classful addressing. Figure 11-1 offers some example IP addresses separated into network and host information according to the classful addressing convention.

Example Class A network address: 114.56.204.33
  network information = 114
  host information = 56.204.33

Example Class B network address: 147.12.38.81
  network information = 147.12
  host information = 38.81

Example Class C network address: 214.57.42.7
  network information = 214.57.42
  host information = 7

FIGURE 11-1 *Example IP addresses with classful addressing*

Adhering to a fixed network ID size ultimately limits the number of hosts a network can include. For example, leasing an entire Class C network of addresses gives you only 254 usable IP addresses. In addition, using classful addressing makes it difficult to separate traffic from various parts of a network. As you have learned, separating traffic offers many practical benefits. For example, if an organization used an entire Class B network of addresses, it could have up to 65,534 hosts all on one network segment. Imagine the challenges involved in managing such a highly populated network, not to mention the poor performance that would result. In 1985, because of the difficulty of managing a whole network class of addresses and the dwindling supply of usable IP addresses, computer scientists introduced subnetting.

 NOTE

Depending on the source, you may find the term network ID used interchangeably with the terms **network number** or **network prefix**.

Subnet Masks

Subnetting depends on the use of subnet masks to identify how a network is subdivided. A subnet mask indicates where network information is located in an IP address. The "1" bits in a subnet mask indicate that corresponding bits in an IP address contain network information. The "0" bits in a subnet mask indicate that corresponding bits in an IP address contain host information.

Each network class is associated with a default subnet mask, as shown in Table 11-1. For example, by default, a Class A address's first octet (or 8 bits) represents network information and is composed of all 1s. (Recall that an octet composed of all 1s in binary notation equals 255 in decimal notation. An octet composed of all 0s in binary notation equals 0 in decimal notation.) That means that if you work on a network whose hosts are configured with a subnet mask of 255.0.0.0, you know that the network is using Class A addresses and, furthermore, that it is not using subnetting, because 255.0.0.0 is the default subnet mask for a Class A network.

Table 11-1 Default subnet masks

Network Class	Default Subnet Mask (Binary)	Number of Bits Used for Network Information	Default Subnet Mask (Dotted Decimal)
A	11111111 00000000 00000000 00000000	8	255.0.0.0
B	11111111 11111111 00000000 00000000	16	255.255.0.0
C	11111111 11111111 11111111 00000000	24	255.255.255.0

To calculate a host's network ID given its IP address and subnet mask, you follow a logical process of combining bits known as **ANDing**. In ANDing, a bit with a value of 1 plus another bit with a value of 1 results in a 1. A bit with a value of 0 plus any other bit results in a 0. If you think of 1 as "true" and 0 as "false," the logic of ANDing makes sense. Adding a true statement to a true statement still results in a true statement. But adding a true statement to a false statement results in a false statement. ANDing logic is demonstrated in Table 11-2, which provides every possible combination of having a 1 or 0 bit in an IP address or subnet mask.

Table 11-2 ANDing

IP address bit	1	1	0	0
Subnet mask bit	1	0	1	0
Resulting bit	1	0	0	0

An example host IP address, its default subnet mask, and network ID are shown in Figure 11-2 in both binary and dotted decimal notation. Notice that the IP address's fourth octet could have been composed of any combination of 1s and 0s, and the network ID's fourth octet would still be all 0s.

	IP Address:	11000111	00100010	01011001	01111111	199.34.89.127
and	Subnet Mask:	11111111	11111111	11111111	00000000	255.255.255.0
Equals	Network ID:	11000111	00100010	01011001	00000000	199.34.89.0

FIGURE 11-2 *Example of calculating a host's network ID*

At this point, you should understand how to determine a host's network ID given its IP address and subnet mask. This section explained how to apply ANDing logic to an IP address plus a *default* subnet mask, but it works just the same way for networks that are subnetted and have different subnet masks, as you will soon learn. Before learning how to create subnets, however, it is necessary to understand the types of addresses that cannot be used as subnet masks or host addresses.

Reserved Addresses

Certain types of IP addresses cannot be assigned to a network interface on a node or used as subnet masks. Instead, these IP addresses are reserved for special functions. One type of reserved address should be familiar to you already—that is, the network ID. In a network ID, as you know, bits available for host information are set to 0. Therefore, a workstation on the example network used in Figure 11-2 could not be assigned the IP address 199.34.89.0, because that address is the network ID. When using classful addressing, a network ID always ends with an octet of 0 (and may have additional, preceding octets equal to 0). However, when subnetting is applied and a default subnet mask is no longer used, a network ID may have other decimal values in its last octet(s).

Another reserved IP address is the broadcast address for a network or segment. In a broadcast address, the octet(s) that represent host information are set to equal all 1s, or in decimal notation, 255. In the example in Figure 11-2, the broadcast address would be 199.34.89.255. If a workstation on that network sent a message to the address 199.34.89.255, it would be issued to every node on the segment.

Because the octets equal to 0 and 255 are reserved, only the numbers 1 through 254 can be used for host information in an IP address. Thus, on a network that followed the example in Figure 11-2, the usable host addresses would range from 199.34.89.1 to 199.34.89.254. If you subnetted this network, the range of usable host addresses would be different. The next section describes how subnets are created and how you can determine the range of usable host addresses on a subnet.

Subnetting Techniques

Subnetting breaks the rules of classful addressing. To create subnets, some of an IP address's bits that in classful addressing would represent host information are changed to represent network information instead. By making bits that previously were used for host information represent network information, you reduce the number of bits available for identifying hosts. Consequently, you reduce the number of usable host addresses per subnet. The number of hosts and subnets available after subnetting is related to how many host information bits you use (or borrow, as network professionals like to say) for network information. Table 11-3 illustrates the numbers of subnets and hosts that can be created by subnetting a Class B network. Notice the range of subnet masks that can be used instead of the default Class B subnet mask of 255.255.0.0. Also compare the listed numbers of hosts per subnet to the 65,534 hosts available on a Class B network that does not use subnetting.

Table 11-3 Class B subnet masks

Subnet Mask		Number of Subnets on Network	Number of Hosts per Subnet
255.255.192.0	or 11111111 11111111 11000000 00000000	2	16382
255.255.224.0	or 11111111 11111111 11100000 00000000	6	8190
255.255.240.0	or 11111111 11111111 11110000 00000000	14	4094
255.255.248.0	or 11111111 11111111 11111000 00000000	30	2046
255.255.252.0	or 11111111 11111111 11111100 00000000	62	1022
255.255.254.0	or 11111111 11111111 11111110 00000000	126	510
255.255.255.0	or 11111111 11111111 11111111 00000000	254	254
255.255.255.128	or 11111111 11111111 11111111 10000000	510	126
255.255.255.192	or 11111111 11111111 11111111 11000000	1,022	62
255.255.255.224	or 11111111 11111111 11111111 11100000	2,046	30
255.255.255.240	or 11111111 11111111 11111111 11110000	4,094	14
255.255.255.248	or 11111111 11111111 11111111 11111000	8,190	6
255.255.255.252	or 11111111 11111111 11111111 11111100	16,382	2

Table 11-4 illustrates the numbers of subnets and hosts that can be created by subnetting a Class C network. Notice that a Class C network allows for fewer subnets than a Class B network. This is because Class C addresses have fewer host information bits that can be borrowed for network information. In addition, fewer bits are left over for host information, which leads to a lower number of hosts per subnet than the number available to Class B subnets.

Table 11-4 Class C subnet masks

Subnet Mask	Number of Subnets on Network	Number of Hosts per Subnet
255.255.255.192 or 11111111 11111111 11111111 1100000	2	62
255.255.255.224 or 11111111 11111111 11111111 1110000	6	30
255.255.255.240 or 11111111 11111111 11111111 1111000	14	14
255.255.255.248 or 11111111 11111111 11111111 1111100	30	6
255.255.255.252 or 11111111 11111111 11111111 1111110	62	2

Calculating Subnets

Now that you have seen the results of subnetting, you are ready to try subnetting a network. Suppose you have leased the Class C network whose network ID is 199.34.89.0 and you want to divide it into six subnets to correspond to the six different departments in your company. The formula for determining how to modify a default subnet mask is:

$2^n - 2 = Y$

where n = the number of bits in the subnet mask that must be switched from 0 to 1

and Y = the number of subnets that result

Notice that this formula subtracts 2 from the total number of possible subnets—that is, from the calculation of 2 to the power of the number of the bits that equal 1. That's because in traditional subnetting, bit combinations of all 0s or all 1s are not allowed for identifying subnets; just as host addresses ending in all 0s or all 1s are not allowed because of addresses reserved for the network ID and broadcast transmissions. (However, in the next section of this chapter you learn why this equation doesn't apply to all modern networks.)

Because you want six separate subnets, the equation becomes $6=2^n-2$. Because 6+2 equals 8 and $8=2^3$, you know that the value of n equals 3. Thus, you need to change three additional subnet mask bits from 0 to 1. That means that rather than using the default subnet mask, in which the first 24 bits indicate the position of network information, you would use a subnet mask of 11111111 11111111 11111111 11100000, in which the first 27 bits indicate the position of network information. Converting from binary to the more familiar dotted decimal notation, this subnet mask becomes 255.255.255.224. When you configure the TCP/IP properties of clients on your network, you would specify this subnet mask.

Now that you have calculated the subnet mask, you still need to assign IP addresses to nodes based on your new subnetting scheme. Recall that you have borrowed three bits from what used to be host information in the IP address. That leaves five bits available in the last octet of your Class C addresses to identify hosts. Adding the values of the last five bits, 16 + 8 + 4 + 2 + 1, equals 31, for a total of 32 potential addresses (0 through 31). However, as you have learned, one address is reserved for the network ID and cannot be used. Another address is reserved for the broadcast ID and cannot be used. Thus, using five bits for host information allows a maximum of 30 different host addresses for each of the six subnets. So, in this example, you can have a maximum of 6 x 30, or 180, unique host addresses on the network.

Table 11-5 lists the network ID, broadcast address, and usable host addresses for each of the six subnets in this example Class C network. Together, the additional bits used for subnet information plus the existing network ID are known as the **extended network prefix**. The extended network prefix for each subnet is based on which of the additional (borrowed) network information bits are set to equal 1. For example, in subnet number 1, only the third bit of the three is set to 1, making the last octet of the extended network prefix 00100000, or in decimal notation, 32. In subnet number 2, only the second bit is set to 1, making the last octet of the extended network prefix 01000000, or 64. In Table 11-5, the three bits borrowed from the host information portion of the Class C address (to indicate network information) are underlined.

NET+
2.7

Class A, Class B, and Class C networks can all be subnetted. But because each class reserves a different number of bits for network information, each class has a different number of host information bits that can be used for subnet information. The number of hosts and subnets on your network will vary depending on your network class and the way you use subnetting. Enumerating the dozens of subnet possibilities based on different arrangements and network classes is beyond the scope of this book. However, several Web sites provide excellent tools that help you calculate subnet information. One such site is *www.subnetmask.info*.

If you use subnetting on your LAN, only your LAN's devices need to interpret your devices' subnetting information. Routers external to your LAN, such as those on the Internet, pay attention to only the network portion of your devices' IP addresses when transmitting data to them. As a result, devices external to a subnetted LAN (such as routers on the Internet) can direct data to those LAN devices without interpreting the LAN's subnetting information.

Table 11-5 Subnet information for six subnets in an example Class C network

Subnet Number	Extended Network Prefix	Broadcast Address	Usable Host Addresses
1	199.34.89.32 or 11000111 00100010 01011001 00100000	199.34.89.63 or 11000111 00100010 01011001 00111111	199.34.89.33 through 199.34.89.62
2	199.34.89.64 or 11000111 00100010 01011001 01000000	199.34.89.95 or 11000111 00100010 01011001 01011111	199.34.89.65 through 199.34.89.94
3	199.34.89.96 or 11000111 00100010 01011001 01100000	199.34.89.127 or 11000111 00100010 01011001 01111111	199.34.89.97 through 199.34.89.126
4	199.34.89.128 or 11000111 00100010 01011001 10000000	199.34.89.159 or 11000111 00100010 01011001 10011111	199.34.89.129 through 199.34.89.158
5	199.34.89.160 or 11000111 00100010 01011001 10100000	199.34.89.191 or 11000111 00100010 01011001 10111111	199.34.89.161 through 199.34.89.190
6	199.34.89.192 or 11000111 00100010 01011001 11000000	199.34.89.223 or 11000111 00100010 01011001 11011111	199.34.89.193 through 199.34.89.222

Figure 11-3 illustrates a situation in which a LAN has been granted the Class C range of addresses that begin with 199.34.89. The network administrator has subnetted this Class C network into six smaller networks with the network IDs listed in Table 11-5. As you know, routers connect different network segments via their physical interfaces. In the case of subnetting, a router must interpret IP addresses from different subnets and direct data from one subnet to another. Each subnet corresponds to a different port on the router.

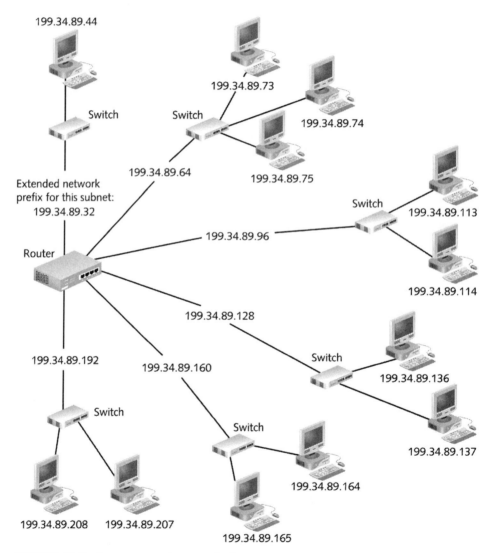

FIGURE 11-3 *A router connecting several subnets*

NET+
2.7

When a router on the internal LAN needs to direct data from a machine with the IP address of 199.34.89.73 to a machine with the IP address of 199.34.89.114, its interpretation of the workstations' subnet masks (255.255.255.224) plus the host information in the IP addresses tells the router that they are on different subnets. The router forwards data between the two subnets (or ports). In this figure, the devices connecting subnets to the router are labeled switches, but they could also be routers, bridges, or hubs. Alternatively, nodes having different extended network prefixes could be directly connected to the router so that each subnet is associated with only one device, though this is an unlikely configuration.

When a server on the Internet attempts to deliver a Web page to the machine with IP address 199.34.89.73, however, the Internet router does not use the subnet mask information. It only knows that the machine is on a Class C network beginning with a network ID of 199.34.89. That's all the information it needs to reach the organization's router. After the data enters the organization's LAN, the LAN's router then interprets the subnet mask information as if it were transmitting data internally to deliver data to the machine with IP address 199.34.89.73. Because subnetting does not affect how a device is addressed by external networks, a network administrator does not need to inform Internet authorities about new segments created via subnetting.

You have learned how to subdivide a network into multiple smaller segments through subnetting. Next, you'll learn about more contemporary variations on this method.

CIDR (Classless Inter-Domain Routing)

By 1993, the Internet was growing exponentially, and the demand for IP addresses was growing with it. The IETF (Internet Engineering Task Force) recognized that additional measures were necessary to increase the availability and flexibility of IP addresses. In response to this need, the IETF devised **CIDR (Classless Inter-Domain Routing**, pronounced *cider*), which is sometimes called **classless routing** or **supernetting**. CIDR is not exclusive of subnetting; it merely provides additional ways of arranging network and host information in an IP address. In CIDR, conventional network class distinctions do not exist.

For example, the previous section described subdividing a Class C network into six subnets of 30 addressable hosts each. To achieve this, the subnet boundary (or length of the extended network prefix) was moved to the right—from the default 24th bit to the 27th bit—into what used to be the host information octet. In CIDR, a subnet boundary can move to the left. Moving the subnet boundary to the left allows you to use more bits for host information and, therefore, generate more usable IP addresses on your network. A subnet created by moving the subnet boundary to the left is known as a **supernet**. Figure 11-4 contrasts examples of a Class C **supernet mask** with a subnet mask.

Notice that in Figure 11-4, 27 bits are used for network information in the subnet mask, whereas only 22 bits are used for network information in the supernet mask.

Suppose that you have leased the Class C range of addresses that shares the network ID 199.34.89.0 and, because of growth in your company, you need to greatly increase the number of host addresses this network allows by default. By changing the default subnet mask of 255.255.255.0 (11111111 11111111 11111111 00000000) to 255.255.252.0 (11111111

```
Example subnet mask:

Bit# 0            8           16          24
     11111111   11111111    11111111    11100000

                       or

               255.255.255.224


Example supernet mask:

Bit# 0            8           16          24
     11111111   11111111    11111100    00000000

                       or

               255.255.252.0
```

FIGURE 11-4 *Subnet mask and supernet mask*

11111111 11111100 00000000), as shown in Figure 11-4, you can make available two extra bits for host information. Adding the values of the last 10 bits, 512 + 256 + 128 + 64 + 32 + 16 + 8 + 4 + 2 + 1, equals 1023, which leads to 1024 (0 through 1023) potential host addresses on each subnet. However, as you know, two addresses are reserved and therefore unusable as host addresses. Thus, the actual number of host addresses available on this subnet is 1022.

In this example, you have subtracted information from the host portion of the IP address. Therefore, the IP addresses that result from this subnetting scheme will be different from the IP addresses you would use if you had left the network ID untouched (as in the subnetting example used in the previous section). The calculation for the new network ID is shown in Figure 11-5. For this example subnetted Class C network, the potential host addresses fall in the range of 199.34.88.1 to 199.34.91.254. The broadcast address is 199.34.91.255.

	IP Address:	11000111	01000100	01011001	01111111	199.34.89.127
and	Subnet Mask:	11111111	11111111	11111100	00000000	255.255.252.0
Equals	Network ID:	11000111	01000100	01011000	00000000	199.34.88.0

FIGURE 11-5 *Calculating a host's network ID on a supernetted network*

With CIDR also came a new shorthand for denoting the position of subnet boundaries, known as **CIDR notation** (or **slash notation**). CIDR notation takes the form of the network ID followed by a forward slash (/), followed by the number of bits that are used for the extended network prefix. For example, for the Class C network whose network ID is 199.34.89.0 and which was divided into six subnets, the slash notation would be 199.34.89.0/27, because 27 bits of the subnets' addresses are used for the extended network prefix. The CIDR notation for the Class C network used as an example of

NET+

2.7

supernetting earlier in this section would be 199.34.89.0/22. In CIDR terminology, the forward slash, plus the number of bits used for the extended network prefix—for example, "/22"—is known as a **CIDR block**.

To take advantage of classless routing, your network's routers must be able to interpret IP addresses that don't adhere to conventional network class parameters. Routers that rely on older routing protocols, such as RIP, are not capable of interpreting classless IP addresses.

NET+

1.6

Internet Gateways

Gateways are a combination of software and hardware that enable two different network segments to exchange data. A gateway facilitates communication between different networks or subnets. Because one device on the network cannot send data directly to a device on another subnet, a gateway must intercede and hand off the information. Every device on a TCP/IP-based network has a **default gateway**—that is, the gateway that first interprets its outbound requests to other subnets, and then interprets its inbound requests from other subnets.

A gateway is analogous to your local post office. Your post office gathers your outbound mail and decides where to forward it. It also handles your inbound mail on its way to your mailbox. Just as a large city has several local post offices, a large organization will have several gateways to route traffic for different groups of devices. Each node on the network can have only one default gateway; that gateway is assigned either manually or automatically (in the latter case, through a service such as DHCP). Of course, if your network includes only one segment and you do not connect to the Internet, your devices would not need a default gateway because traffic would not need to cross the network's boundary.

In many cases, a default gateway is not a separate device, but rather a network interface on a router. For this reason, you may hear the term **default router** used to refer to a default gateway. By using a router's network interfaces as gateways, one router can supply multiple gateways. Each default gateway is assigned its own IP address. In Figure 11-6, workstation 10.3.105.23 (workstation A) uses the 10.3.105.1 gateway to process its requests, and workstation 10.3.102.75 (workstation B) uses the 10.3.102.1 gateway for the same purpose.

 NOTE

An Internet gateway is usually assigned an IP address that ends with an octet of .1.

Default gateways may connect multiple internal networks, or they may connect an internal network with external networks, such as WANs or the Internet. As you have learned, routers that connect multiple networks must maintain a routing table to determine where to forward information. When a router is used as a gateway, it must maintain routing tables as well.

The Internet contains a vast number of routers and gateways. If each gateway had to track addressing information for every other gateway on the Internet, it would be overtaxed. Instead,

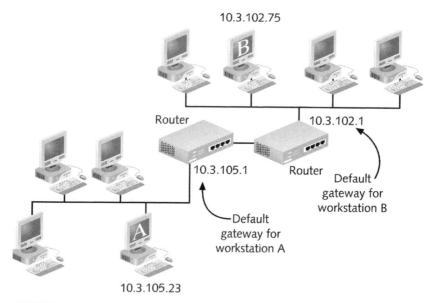

FIGURE 11-6 *The use of default gateways*

each handles only a relatively small amount of addressing information, which it uses to forward data to another gateway that knows more about the data's destination. Like routers on an internal network, Internet gateways maintain default routes to known addresses to expedite data transfer. The gateways that make up the Internet backbone are called **core gateways**.

NAT (Network Address Translation)

Default gateways can also be used to "hide" the IP numbers assigned within an organization and keep its devices' IP addresses secret from a public network (such as the Internet). Hiding IP addresses allows network managers more flexibility in assigning addresses. Clients behind a gateway may use any IP addressing scheme, regardless of whether it is legitimately recognized by the Internet authorities. But once those clients need to connect to the Internet, they must have a legitimate IP address to exchange data. When the client's transmission reaches the default gateway, the gateway assigns the client's transmission a valid IP address. After the transmission has been terminated, that IP address becomes available for another gateway transmission. This process is known as **NAT (Network Address Translation)**.

One reason for hiding IP addresses is to add a marginal amount of security to a private network when it is connected to a public network. Because a transmission is assigned a new IP address each time it reaches the public sphere, those outside an organization cannot trace the origin of the transmission back to the specific network node that sent it. However, the IP address assigned to a transmission by the gateway must be an Internet-authorized IP address; thus, it can be traced back to the organization that leased the address.

NET+
2.13

Another reason for using NAT is to enable a network administrator to develop her own network addressing scheme that does not conform to a scheme dictated by ICANN. For example, suppose you are the network administrator for a private elementary school. You maintain the school's entire network, which, among other things, includes 200 client workstations. Suppose half of these clients are used by students in the classrooms or library and half are used expressly by staff. To make your network management easier, you might decide to assign each student workstation an IP address whose first octet begins with the number 10 and whose second octet is the number of the classroom where the computer is located. For example, a student workstation in room 235 might have an IP address of 10.235.1.12. You might then assign each staff workstation an IP address whose first octet is the number 50 and whose second octet is the number of the employee's office or classroom. For example, the principal's workstation, which is located in his office in Room 135, might have an IP address of 50.135.1.10. These IP addresses would be used strictly for communication between devices on the school's network. When staff or students wanted to access the Internet, however, you would need to have at least some IP addresses that would be legitimate for use on the Internet. Now suppose that, because the school has limited funds and does not require that all clients be connected to the Internet at all times, you decide to lease only 20 IP numbers from your ISP. You then configure a gateway to translate your internal addresses to addresses that can be used on the Internet. Each time a client attempts to reach the Internet, the gateway would replace its source address field in the data packets with one of the 20 legitimate IP addresses. Figure 11-7 depicts how the NAT works.

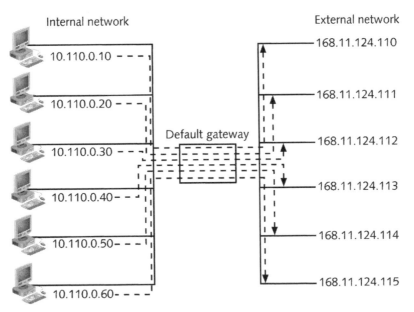

FIGURE 11-7 *NAT through an Internet gateway*

NET+
2.13

You have learned that NAT separates private and public transmissions on a TCP/IP network. In the next section, you will learn about a service of some Windows operating systems that enables one computer to provide NAT for other computers on the same network.

ICS (Internet Connection Sharing)

On a small or home network, multiple computers often share a single Internet connection. In previous chapters, you learned that this can be achieved by using a SOHO router or small switch to which each networked computer is connected. Microsoft offers another alternative for sharing Internet access on computers running the Windows 98, Me, 2000, or 32-bit version of the XP operating system, **ICS (Internet Connection Sharing)**. Using ICS, a computer with Internet access, called the **ICS host**, is configured to translate requests to and from the Internet on behalf of other computers on the network. To do this, it acts as a DHCP server, DNS resolver, and NAT gateway for clients on its LAN. The ICS host requires two network connections: one that connects to the Internet, which could be dial-up, DSL, ISDN, or broadband cable, and one that connects to the LAN. If the network uses a dial-up connection to the Internet, the ICS host connects to the Internet on demand—that is, when other computers on the network issue a request to the Internet.

When ICS is enabled on a LAN, the network adapter on the ICS host that connects to the LAN is assigned an IP address of 192.168.0.1. Clients on the small office or home office LAN must be set up to obtain IP addresses automatically. The ICS host then assigns clients IP addresses in the range of 192.168.0.2 through 192.168.0.255. If you are already using this range of addresses on your network (for example, in a NAT scheme), you might experience problems establishing or using ICS.

To enable ICS on an ICS host:

1. Log on to the ICS host computer as Administrator or as a user with equivalent privileges.

2. Verify that a connection between the ICS host computer and the Internet is operational.

3. Click **Start**, then click **My Network Places**. The My Network Places window opens.

4. Click **View Network Connections**. The Network Connections window opens.

5. Right-click the Local Area Connection icon that represents your ICS host computer's connection to the Internet, and then click **Properties**. The Local Area Connection Properties dialog box opens.

6. Click the **Advanced** tab.

7. Under Internet Connection Sharing, check **Allow other network users to connect through this computer's Internet connection**. By default, the Allow other network users to control or disable the shared Internet connection option is also checked, as shown in Figure 11-8. However, this option can be deselected if you do not want other computers on the network to be able to control the ICS properties on the ICS host.

NET+
2.13

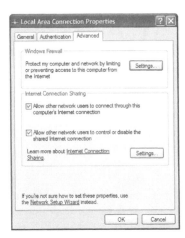

FIGURE 11-8 *Enabling ICS in the Local Area Connection Properties dialog box*

8. You also have the option of specifying which services on your network can be accessed from the Internet. For example, if you hosted a Web site on your LAN, you could configure ICS to allow Internet users to access your LAN's HTTP services. To configure these options, click the **Settings** button. The **Advanced Settings** dialog box opens.

9. After modifying the services available to Internet users, click **OK**.

10. Click **OK** to save your ICS settings and enable ICS on the network.

When designing a network to share an Internet connection, most network administrators prefer using a router or switch rather than ICS because ICS typically requires more configuration. It also requires the ICS host to be available whenever other computers need Internet access. However, if a router or switch is not available, ICS is an adequate alternative for sharing an Internet connection among multiple clients.

NET+
3.9

Intranets and Extranets

You are undoubtedly familiar with TCP/IP-based services such as e-commerce, e-mail, and file sharing. Each of these services can run on private networks as well as the (public) Internet. For example, a network administrator could establish a Web server (or more precisely, an HTTP server) in an organization to supply documents and information to employees in **HTML (Hypertext Markup Language)**, the Web document-formatting language. The HTTP server might or might not be visible to the Internet. In fact, the HTTP server does not even have to be connected to the Internet. A network or part of a network that uses browser-based services to exchange information within an enterprise is known as an **intranet**. In addition to supplying HTTP-accessible documents, intranets are used for e-mail, file sharing, document management (for example, indexing several versions of documents), and collaboration (for example, allowing multiple employees to review and modify messages and files pertaining to a particular project). The flexible, open nature of services and protocols that developed with the Internet and made it popular also makes these services and protocols well-suited to private networks.

NET+
3.9

An intranet is defined by its security policies—that is, by the fact that it allows access only to authorized users who belong to a certain organization. It may extend across an organization's private WAN or it may be accessible only on the LAN. A network that uses Internet-like services and protocols to exchange information within an organization *and* with certain, authorized users outside of that organization is known as an **extranet**. A construction company might use an extranet, for example, to allow its employees to access company documents from home or from a job site and also to allow contractors to submit bids for jobs.

TCP/IP Mail Services

Currently, e-mail is the most frequently used Internet service you will manage as a network administrator. You need to understand how mail services work so that you can set up and support mail clients or install and configure a mail server.

All Internet mail services rely on the same principles of mail delivery, storage, and pickup, though they may use different types of software to accomplish these functions. You have learned that mail servers communicate with other mail servers to deliver messages across the Internet. They send, receive, and store messages. They may also filter messages according to content, route messages according to configurable conditions such as timing or priority, and make available different types of interfaces for different mail clients. Hundreds of different software packages for mail servers exist. The most popular include Sendmail, Microsoft Exchange Server, Lotus Notes, and Novell Groupwise.

Mail clients send messages to and retrieve messages from mail servers. They may also provide ways of organizing messages (using folders or mailboxes), filter messages according to content or sender information, set message priority, create and use distribution lists, send file attachments, and interpret graphic and HTML content. Hundreds of different types of mail clients exist. Examples of popular mail client software include Eudora, Microsoft Outlook, and Pegasus Mail. Many companies that provide Internet access, such as AOL, provide mail client software with their access software. However, in most cases, you can use a mail client other than the package supplied by the Internet access provider.

E-mail servers and clients communicate through special TCP/IP Application layer protocols. These protocols, all of which operate on Macintosh-, NetWare-, Windows-, and UNIX-type of systems, are discussed in the following sections.

NET+
2.10

SMTP (Simple Mail Transfer Protocol)

SMTP (Simple Mail Transfer Protocol) is the protocol responsible for moving messages from one mail server to another over TCP/IP-based networks. SMTP belongs to the Application layer of the TCP/IP Model and relies on TCP at the Transport layer. It operates from port 25. (That is, requests to receive mail and send mail go through port 25 on the SMTP server.) SMTP, which provides the basis for Internet e-mail service, relies on higher-level programs for its instructions. Although SMTP comes with a set of human-readable (text) com-

NET+
2.10

mands that you could conceivably use to transport mail from machine to machine, this method would be laborious, slow, and error-prone. Instead, other services, such as the Sendmail software for UNIX-type of systems, provide more friendly and sophisticated mail interfaces that rely on SMTP as their means of transport.

SMTP is a simple subprotocol, incapable of doing anything more than transporting mail or holding it in a queue. In the post office analogy of data communications, SMTP is like the mail carrier who picks up his day's mail load at the post office and delivers it to the homes on his route. The mail carrier does not worry about where the mail is stored overnight or how it gets from another city's post office to his post office. If a piece of mail is undeliverable, he simply holds onto it; the mail carrier does not attempt to figure out what went wrong. In Internet e-mail transmission, higher-level mail protocols such as POP and IMAP, which are discussed later in this chapter, take care of these functions.

When you configure clients to use Internet e-mail, you need to identify the user's SMTP server. (Sometimes, this server is called the mail server.) Each e-mail program specifies this setting in a different place, though most commonly in the Mail Preferences section. Assuming that your client uses DNS, you do not have to identify the IP address of the SMTP server—only the name. For example, if a user's e-mail address is jdoe@usmail.com, his SMTP server is probably called "usmail.com." You do not have to specify the TCP/IP port number used by SMTP, because both the client workstation and the server assume that SMTP requests and responses flow through port 25.

MIME (Multipurpose Internet Mail Extensions)

The standard message format specified by SMTP allows for lines that contain no more than 1000 ASCII characters. That means if you relied solely on SMTP, you couldn't include pictures or even formatted text in an e-mail message. SMTP sufficed for mail transmissions in the early days of the Internet. However, its limitations prompted IEEE to release **MIME (Multipurpose Internet Mail Extensions)** in 1992. MIME is a standard for encoding and interpreting binary files, images, video, and non-ASCII character sets within an e-mail message. MIME identifies each element of a mail message according to content type. Some content types are: text, graphics, audio, video, and multipart. The multipart content type indicates that a message contains more than non-ASCII element—for example, some of the message's content is formatted as text, some is a binary file, and some is a graphics file.

MIME does not replace SMTP, but works in conjunction with it. It encodes different content types so that SMTP is fooled into thinking it is transporting an ASCII message stream. Most modern e-mail clients and servers support MIME.

NET+
2.10

POP (Post Office Protocol)

POP (Post Office Protocol) is an Application layer protocol used to retrieve messages from a mail server. The most current and commonly used version of the POP protocol is **POP3 (Post Office Protocol, version 3)**. With POP3, mail is delivered and stored on a mail server until a user connects—via an e-mail client—to the server to retrieve his messages. As the user retrieves his messages, the messages are downloaded to his workstation. After they are downloaded, the messages are typically deleted from the mail server. You can think of POP3 as a store-and-forward type of service. Mail is stored on the POP3 server and forwarded to the client on demand. One advantage to using POP3 is that it minimizes the use of server resources because mail is deleted from the server after retrieval. Another advantage is that virtually all mail server and client applications support POP3. However, the fact that POP3 downloads messages rather than keeping them on the server can be a drawback for some users.

POP3's design makes it best suited to users who retrieve their mail from the same workstation all the time. Users who move from machine to machine are at a disadvantage, because POP3 does not normally allow users to keep the mail on the server after they retrieve it. Thus, the mail is not accessible from other workstations. For example, suppose a consultant begins his day at his company's office and retrieves his e-mail on the workstation at his desk. Then, he spends the rest of the day at a client's office, where he retrieves messages on his laptop. When he comes home, he checks his e-mail from his home computer. Using POP3, his messages would be stored on three different computers. A few options exist for circumventing this problem (such as downloading messages from the mail server to a file server on a LAN), but a more thorough solution has been provided by a new, more sophisticated e-mail protocol called IMAP, described next.

IMAP (Internet Message Access Protocol)

IMAP (**Internet Message Access Protocol**) is a mail retrieval protocol that was developed as a more sophisticated alternative to POP3. The most current version of IMAP is version 4, or IMAP4. IMAP4 can replace POP3 without the user having to change e-mail programs. The single biggest advantage IMAP4 has over POP3 is that users can store messages on the mail server, rather than always having to download them to a local machine. This feature benefits users who may check mail from different workstations. In addition, IMAP4 provides the following features:

◆ *Users can retrieve all or only a portion of any mail message.* The remainder can be left on the mail server. This feature benefits users who move from machine to machine and users who have slow connections to the network or minimal free hard disk space.

◆ *Users can review their messages and delete them while the messages remain on the server.* This feature preserves network bandwidth, especially when the messages are long or contain attached files, because the data need not travel over the wire from the server to the client's workstation. For users with a slow modem connection, deleting messages without having to download them represents a major advantage over POP3.

◆ *Users can create sophisticated methods of organizing messages on the server.* A user might, for example, build a system of folders to contain messages with similar content. Also, a user might search through all of the messages for only those that contain one particular keyword or subject line.

◆ *Users can share a mailbox in a central location.* For example, if several maintenance personnel who use different workstations need to receive the same messages from the Facilities Department head but do not need e-mail for any other purpose, they can all log on with the same ID and share the same mailbox on the server. If POP3 were used in this situation, only one maintenance staff member could read the message; she would then have to forward or copy it to her colleagues.

Although IMAP4 provides significant advantages over POP3, it also comes with a few disadvantages. For instance, IMAP4 servers require more storage space and usually more processing resources than POP servers do. By extension, network managers must keep a closer watch on IMAP4 servers to ensure that users are not consuming more than their fair share of space on the server. In addition, if the IMAP4 server fails, users cannot access the mail left there. (IMAP4 does allow users to download messages to their own workstations, however.)

Now that you have learned more about e-mail, the most frequently used TCP/IP service, you are ready to learn about utilities that will help you analyze TCP/IP-based networks.

Additional TCP/IP Utilities

As with any type of communication, many potential points of failure exist in the TCP/IP transmission process, and these points increase with the size of the network and the distance of the transmission. Fortunately, TCP/IP comes with a complete set of utilities that can help you track down most TCP/IP-related problems without using expensive software or hardware to analyze network traffic. You should be familiar with the use of the following tools and their switches, not only because the Network+ certification exam covers them, but also because you will regularly need these diagnostics in your work with TCP/IP networks.

In Chapter 4, you learned about three very important TCP/IP utilities—Telnet, ARP, and PING. The following sections present additional TCP/IP utilities that can help you discover information about your node and network.

Nearly all TCP/IP utilities can be accessed from the command prompt on any type of server or client running TCP/IP. However, the syntax of these commands may differ, depending on your client's operating system. For example, the command that traces the path of packets from one host to another is known as `traceroute` in UNIX-type of operating systems, but as `tracert` in the Windows operating systems. Similarly, the options used with each command may differ according to the operating system. For example, when working on a UNIX-type of system, you can limit the maximum number of router hops the traceroute command allows by typing the `-m` switch. On a Windows-based system, the `-h` switch accomplishes the same thing. The following sections cover the proper command syntax for both Windows- and UNIX-type of systems.

Netstat

The **netstat** utility displays TCP/IP statistics and details about TCP/IP components and connections on a host. Information that can be obtained from the netstat command includes the port on which a particular TCP/IP service is running, regardless of whether a remote node is logged on to a host, which network connections are currently established for a client, how many packets have been handled by a network interface since it was activated, and how many data errors have occurred on a particular network interface. As you can imagine, with so much information available, the netstat utility makes a powerful diagnostic tool.

For example, suppose you are a network administrator in charge of maintaining file, print, Web, and Internet servers for an organization. You discover that your Web server, which has multiple processors, sufficient hard disk space, and multiple NICs, is suddenly taking twice as long to respond to HTTP requests. Of course, you would want to check the server's memory resources as well as its Web server software to determine that nothing is wrong with either of those. In addition, you can use the netstat utility to determine the characteristics of the traffic going into and out of each NIC. You may discover that one network card is consistently handling 80% of the traffic, even though you had configured the server to share traffic equally among the two. This fact may lead you to run hardware diagnostics on the NIC, and perhaps discover that its on-board processor has failed, making it much slower than the other NIC. Netstat provides a quick way to view traffic statistics, without having to run a more complex traffic analysis program, such as Ethereal.

 NOTE

If you use the netstat command without any switches, it will display a list of all the active TCP/IP connections on your machine, including the Transport layer protocol used (UDP or TCP), packets sent and received, IP address, and state of those connections.

However, like other TCP/IP commands, netstat can be used with a number of different switches. A netstat command begins with the word netstat followed by a space, then a hyphen and a switch, followed by a variable pertaining to that switch, if required. For example, netstat -a displays all current TCP and UDP connections from the issuing device to other devices on the network, as well as the source and destination service ports. The netstat -r command allows you to display the routing table on a given machine. The following list describes some of the most common switches used with the netstat utility:

◆ -a—Provides a list of all available TCP and UDP connections, even if they are simply listening and not currently exchanging data

◆ -e—Displays details about all the packets that have been sent over a network interface

◆ -n—Lists currently connected hosts according to their port and IP address (in numerical form)

NET+
4.1
4.2

◆ -p—Allows you to specify what type of protocol statistics to list; this switch must be followed by a protocol specification (TCP or UDP)

◆ -r—Provides a list of routing table information

◆ -s—Provides statistics about each packet transmitted by a host, separated according to protocol type (IP, TCP, UDP, or ICMP)

Figure 11-9 illustrates the output of a netstat -a command run at the command prompt on a Windows XP computer.

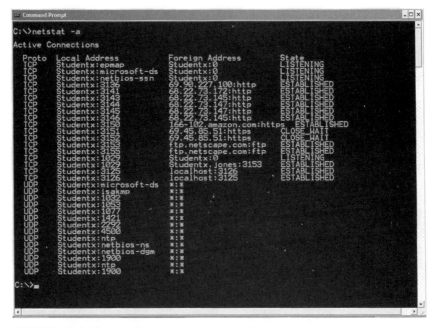

FIGURE 11-9 *Output of a* netstat -a *command*

Nbtstat

As you know, NetBIOS is a protocol that runs in the Session and Transport layers of the OSI Model and associates NetBIOS names with workstations. NetBIOS alone is not routable because it does not contain Network layer information. However, when encapsulated in another protocol such as TCP/IP, it can be routed. On networks that run NetBIOS over TCP/IP, the **nbtstat** utility can provide information about NetBIOS statistics and resolve NetBIOS names to their IP addresses. In other words, if you know the NetBIOS name of a workstation, you can use nbtstat to determine its IP address.

Nbtstat is useful on networks that run Windows-based operating systems and NetBIOS (because Novell and UNIX-type of operating systems do not use NetBIOS, nbtstat is not useful on these types of networks). As more and more networks run pure TCP/IP (and not NetBIOS over TCP/IP), nbtstat is becoming a less-popular TCP/IP diagnostic utility.

As with netstat, nbtstat offers a variety of switches that you can use to tailor the output of the command. For example, you can type `nbtstat -A ip_address` to determine what machine is registered to a given IP address. The following list details popular switches used with the `nbtstat` command. Notice that they are case sensitive; the `-a` switch has a different meaning than the `-A` switch.

◆ `-a`—Displays a machine's name table given its NetBIOS name; the name of the machine must be supplied after the `-a` switch

◆ `-A`—Displays a machine's name table given its IP address; the IP address of the machine must be supplied after the `-A` switch

◆ `-r`—Lists statistics about names that have been resolved to IP addresses by broadcast and by WINS; this switch is useful for determining whether a workstation is resolving names properly or for determining whether WINS is operating correctly

◆ `-s`—Displays a list of all the current NetBIOS sessions for a machine; when used with this switch, the `nbtstat` command attempts to resolve IP addresses to NetBIOS names in the listing; if the machine has no current NetBIOS connections, the result of this command will indicate that fact

Nslookup

The **nslookup** utility allows you to query the DNS database from any computer on the network and find the host name of a device by specifying its IP address, or vice versa. This ability is useful for verifying that a host is configured correctly or for troubleshooting DNS resolution problems. For example, if you wanted to find out whether the host whose name is ftp.netscape.com is operational, you could type: `nslookup ftp.netscape.com` and press Enter. Figure 11-10 shows the result of running a simple `nslookup` command at a Linux shell prompt.

```
% nslookup ftp.netscape.com
Server:  proxy1.mdsn1.wi.home.com
Address:  24.6.204.15

Non-authoritative answer:
Name:    ftp.netscape.com
Address:  64.12.168.249

% 
```

FIGURE 11-10 *Output of a simple nslookup command*

Notice that the command provides not only the host's IP address, but also the primary DNS server name and address that holds the record for this name. To find the host name of a device whose IP address you know, type: `nslookup ip_address` and press Enter. In this case, the response would include not only the host name for that device, but also its IP address and the IP address and host name of its primary DNS server.

Nslookup can reveal much more than just the IP address or host name of a device. Typing just `nslookup` (without any switches), then pressing Enter starts the nslookup utility, and the com-

NET+
4.1
4.2

mand prompt changes to a >. You can then use additional commands to find out more about the contents of the DNS database. For example, on a UNIX-type of system you could view a list of all the host name and IP address correlations on a particular DNS server by typing ls. Or you could specify five seconds as the period to wait for a response by typing timeout=5. (The default is 10 seconds.) Many other nslookup options exist. On a UNIX-type of system, you can find the complete list of the nslookup options in the nslookup man pages. On a Windows-based system, you can view them by typing nslookup ? at the command prompt. To exit the nslookup utility and return to the normal command prompt, type exit.

Dig

A TCP/IP utility similar to nslookup is **dig**, which stands for **domain information groper**. Like nslookup, dig allows you to query a DNS database and find the host name associated with a specific IP address or vice versa. Also like nslookup, dig is useful for helping network administrators diagnose DNS problems. However, both in its simplest form and when used with one or more of its multiple switches, the dig utility can provide more detailed information than nslookup, An example of a simple dig command is dig ftp.netscape.com, the output of which is shown in Figure 11-11. Compare this output to the simple nslookup command output shown in Figure 11-10. Whereas the simple nslookup command returned the IP address for the host name, the simple dig command returned specifics about the resource records associated with the host name ftp.netscape.com. The domain name is in the first column, followed by the record's Time to Live, then its type code (for example, A for an address record or MX for a mail record), and finally, a data field indicating the IP address or other domain name with

```
% dig ftp.netscape.com

; <<>> DiG 9.4.1 <<>> ftp.netscape.com
;; global options:  printcmd
;; Got answer:
;; ->>HEADER<<- opcode: QUERY, status: NOERROR, id: 62444
;; flags: qr rd ra; QUERY: 1, ANSWER: 2, AUTHORITY: 2, ADDITIONAL: 2

;; QUESTION SECTION:
;ftp.netscape.com.                  IN      A

;; ANSWER SECTION:
ftp.netscape.com.        10        IN      CNAME   ftp.gftp.netscape.com.
ftp.gftp.netscape.com.   10        IN      A       205.188.212.121

;; AUTHORITY SECTION:
gftp.netscape.com.       1412      IN      NS      mtc-gdns001.ns.aol.com.
gftp.netscape.com.       1412      IN      NS      dtc-gdns001.ns.aol.com.

;; ADDITIONAL SECTION:
dtc-gdns001.ns.aol.com.  2340      IN      A       205.188.139.67
mtc-gdns001.ns.aol.com.  1464      IN      A       64.12.182.67

;; Query time: 132 msec
;; SERVER: 10.1.1.28#53(10.1.1.28)
;; WHEN: Thu Oct 26 18:34:28 2006
;; MSG SIZE  rcvd: 164

%
```

FIGURE 11-11 *Output of a simple dig command*

NET+

4.1

4.2

which the primary domain name is associated. A summary of this particular query, including the time it took for the dig command to return the data, is shown at the bottom of the output.

The dig utility comes with over two dozen switches, making it much more flexible than nslookup. For example, in a dig command you can specify the DNS server to query and the type of DNS record(s) for which you want to search, a timeout period for the query, a port (other than the default port 53) on the DNS server to query, and many other options. Look for the complete list of dig command switches and the syntax needed to use each in the dig man pages. The dig utility is included with UNIX-type of operating systems. If your computer runs a Windows-based operating system, however, you must obtain the code for the dig utility from a third party and install it on your system.

Whois

You have learned about the process of domain name resolution and how individuals must register domain names with the Internet authority ICANN. When you register a domain name with ICANN, you provide contact information for yourself, the technical person responsible for the domain (for example, an engineer at an ISP who maintains DNS services there), and information about the hosting entity (usually an ISP) and the DNS server addresses. This information is stored in a database maintained by your RIR (Regional Internet Registry). The utility that allows you to query this DNS registration database and obtain information about a domain is called **whois**.

Using whois can help troubleshoot network problems. For example, if you noticed your network received a flood of messages that originated from *www.trinketmakers.com*, you could find out who leases the trinketmakers.com domain and contact them about the problem.

Syntax of the whois command is whois xxx.yy, where xxx.yy is the second-level domain name for which you want to know DNS registration information. For example, you could type whois trinketmakers.com at a UNIX shell prompt to obtain the registration information for *www.trinketmakers.com*. On a computer running one of the Windows operating systems, you first need to install additional network utilities available from Microsoft before you can run the whois command at a command prompt.

 NOTE

A simple whois command does not work with all types of domains, because in some cases, a special server must be queried for some domain information. For example, domains registered with an RIR outside of North America and domains ending in .gov or .mil necessitate querying a server that holds DNS registration information only for these types of domains.

Rather than type whois at the shell or command prompt, however, you might prefer to use one of the many Web sites that provide simple, Web-based interfaces for running the whois command. For example, you could go straight to the source of the whois database, ARIN, at *www.arin.net*. There you will find a whois search prompt on the organization's home page. Many ICANN-authorized domain registrars will also provide whois search capabilities. They may also provide interfaces for running nslookup, PING, and other TCP/IP utilities.

NET+
4.1
4.2

Traceroute (Tracert)

The **traceroute** utility (known as **tracert** on Windows-based systems) uses ICMP to trace the path from one networked node to another, identifying all intermediate hops between the two nodes. This utility is useful for determining router or subnet connectivity problems.

To find the route, the traceroute utility transmits a series of UDP datagrams to a specified destination, using either the IP address or the host name to identify the destination. The first three datagrams that traceroute transmits have their TTL (Time to Live) set to 1. Because the TTL determines how many more network hops a datagram can make, datagrams with a TTL of 1 expire as they hit the first router. When they expire, they are returned to the source—in this case, the node that began the traceroute. In this way, traceroute obtains the identity of the first router. After it learns about the first router in the path, traceroute transmits a series of datagrams with a TTL of 2. The process continues for the next router in the path, and then the third, fourth, and so on, until the destination node is reached. Traceroute also returns the amount of time it took for the datagrams to reach each router in the path.

A traceroute test may stop before reaching the destination, however. This happens for one of two reasons: Either the device that traceroute is attempting to reach is down, or it does not accept ICMP transmissions. The latter is usually the case with firewalls. Therefore, if you are trying to trace a route to a host situated behind a firewall, your efforts will be thwarted. (Because PING uses ICMP transmissions, the same limitations exist for that utility.) Furthermore, traceroute cannot detect router configuration problems or detect whether a router uses different send and receive interfaces. In addition, routers may not decrement the TTL value correctly at each stop in the path. Therefore, traceroute is best used on a network with which you are already familiar. If you are reasonably certain that devices in the path between your host and a destination host do not block ICMP transmissions, traceroute can help you diagnose network congestion or network failures. You can then use your judgment and experience to compare the actual test results with what you anticipate the results should be.

The simplest form of the `traceroute` command (on a UNIX-type of system) is `traceroute ip_address` or `traceroute host_name`. On computers that use a Windows-based operating system, the proper syntax is `tracert ip_address` or `tracert host_name`. When run on a UNIX-type of system the command will return a list as shown in Figure 11-12.

As with other TCP/IP commands, `traceroute` has a number of switches that may be used with the command. The command begins with either `traceroute` or `tracert` (depending on the operating system your computer uses), followed by a hyphen, a switch, and a variable pertaining to a particular switch, if required. For example, on a Windows-based system, `tracert -a` displays all current TCP and UDP connections from the issuing device to other devices on the network, as well as the source and destination service ports.

NET+
4.1
4.2

```
% traceroute www.networksolutions.com
traceroute to www.networksolutions.com (216.168.224.69), 30 hops max, 38 byte packets
 1  * * *

% traceroute -I www.networksolutions.com
traceroute to www.networksolutions.com (216.168.224.69), 30 hops max, 38 byte packets
 1  * * *
 2  10.75.149.1 (10.75.149.1)  21.171 ms  21.026 ms  11.883 ms
 3  bb1-ge2-0.mdsn1.wi.home.net (24.6.204.1)  13.249 ms  14.739 ms  9.679 ms
 4  c2-se3-0-9.chcgil1.home.net (24.7.76.49)  13.511 ms  12.596 ms  18.576 ms
 5  aads.agis.net (206.220.243.19)  18.310 ms  26.789 ms  20.132 ms
 6  at-100100.inindrr01.us.telia.net (206.185.201.6)  68.421 ms  92.255 ms *
 7  at-0001.dcwdcrr01.us.telia.net (206.84.253.14)  97.508 ms  106.618 ms  100.920 ms
 8  ga011.herndon1.us.telia.net (206.84.235.249)  110.407 ms  108.272 ms  106.386 ms
 9  tii-internic.herndon1.us.telia.net (206.84.235.26)  96.980 ms  95.273 ms  92.744 ms
10  www.networksolutions.com (216.168.224.69)  93.718 ms  89.265 ms  88.828 ms
%
```

FIGURE 11-12 *Output of a* `traceroute` *command*

The following list describes some of the popular traceroute switches:

- `-d`—Instructs the `traceroute` command not to resolve IP addresses to host names
- `-h`—Specifies the maximum number of hops the packets should take when attempting to reach a host (the default is 30); this switch must be followed by a specific number of hops (for example, `traceroute -h 12` would indicate a maximum of 12 hops)
- `-w`—Identifies a timeout period for responses; this switch must be followed by a variable to indicate the number of milliseconds the utility should wait for a response

Ipconfig

Earlier in this book, you used the ipconfig utility to determine the TCP/IP configuration of a Windows XP workstation. Ipconfig is the TCP/IP administration utility for use with Windows NT, 2000, XP, and Server 2003 operating systems. If you work with these operating systems, you will frequently use this tool to view a computer's TCP/IP settings. Ipconfig is a command-line utility that provides information about a network adapter's IP address, subnet mask, and default gateway.

To use the ipconfig utility from a Windows XP workstation, for example, click Start, point to All Programs, point to Accessories, and then click Command Prompt to open the Command Prompt window. At the command prompt, type `ipconfig` and press Enter. You should see TCP/IP information for your computer, similar to the output shown in Figure 11-13.

```
Microsoft Windows XP [Version 5.1.2600]
(C) Copyright 1985-2001 Microsoft Corp.

C:\>ipconfig

Windows IP Configuration


Ethernet adapter Local Area Connection:

        Connection-specific DNS Suffix  . : ameritech.net
        IP Address. . . . . . . . . . . . : 10.11.11.54
        Subnet Mask . . . . . . . . . . . : 255.255.255.0
        Default Gateway . . . . . . . . . : 10.11.11.1

C:\>_
```

FIGURE 11-13 *Output of an* `ipconfig` *command on a Windows XP workstation*

NET+
4.1
4.2

In addition to being used alone to list information about the TCP/IP configuration, the ipconfig utility can be used with switches to manage a computer's TCP/IP settings. For example, if you wanted to view complete information about your TCP/IP settings, including your MAC address, when your DHCP lease expires, the address of your WINS server, and so on, you could type: ipconfig /all. Note that the syntax of this command differs slightly from other TCP/IP utilities. With ipconfig, a forward slash (/) precedes the command switches, rather than a hyphen. The following list describes some popular switches that can be used with the ipconfig command.

◆ /?—Displays a list of switches available for use with the ipconfig command

◆ /all—Displays complete TCP/IP configuration information for each network interface on that device

◆ /release—Releases DHCP-assigned addresses for all of the device's network interfaces

◆ /renew—Renews DHCP-assigned addresses for all of the device's network interfaces

Winipcfg

The **winipcfg** utility performs the same TCP/IP configuration and management as the ipconfig utility, but applies to Windows 9x and Me operating systems. It differs also in that it supplies the user with a graphical interface. As with ipconfig, networking technicians frequently use winipcfg when diagnosing TCP/IP problems.

To launch the winipcfg utility from a Windows 9x workstation, click Start, and then click Run to open the Run dialog box. In the Open text box, type winipcfg, and then click OK. The winipcfg dialog box opens, displaying your network adapter's MAC and IP addresses, as well as your subnet mask and default gateway, as shown in Figure 11-14.

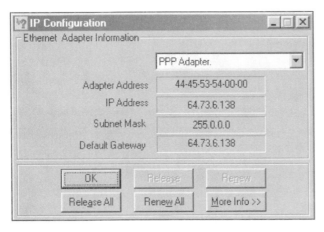

FIGURE 11-14 *Winipcfg dialog box*

NET+
4.1
4.2

As with the ipconfig utility, you can release or renew DHCP-assigned addresses through the winipcfg dialog box. To renew all DHCP-assigned addresses, simply click the Renew All button. To release all DHCP-assigned addresses, simply click the Release All button. You also have the option to view more information about a machine's TCP/IP configuration. By clicking the More Info button, you can also view the host name, node type, WINS server, when your DHCP lease was obtained, when it expires, and other information.

Ifconfig

Ifconfig is the TCP/IP configuration and management utility used on UNIX-type of systems. As with ipconfig on Windows NT/2000/XP/2003 systems and winipcfg on Windows 9x systems, ifconfig enables you to modify TCP/IP settings for a network interface, release and renew DHCP-assigned addresses, or simply check the status of your machine's TCP/IP settings. Ifconfig is also a utility that runs when a UNIX-type of system starts, to establish the TCP/IP configuration for that computer.

As with the other operating systems' TCP/IP configuration utilities, ifconfig can be used alone, or it can be used with switches to reveal more customized information. For example, if you want to view the TCP/IP information associated with every interface on a device, you could type: ifconfig -a. The output would resemble the output shown in Figure 11-15. Notice that the syntax of the ifconfig command uses a hyphen (-) before some of the switches and no preceding character for other switches. The following list describes some of the popular switches you may use with ifconfig. To view a complete list of options, you can read the ifconfig man pages.

◆ -a—Applies the command to all interfaces on a device; can be used with other switches

◆ down—Marks the interface as unavailable to the network

◆ up—Reinitializes the interface after it has been taken "down," so that it is once again available to the network

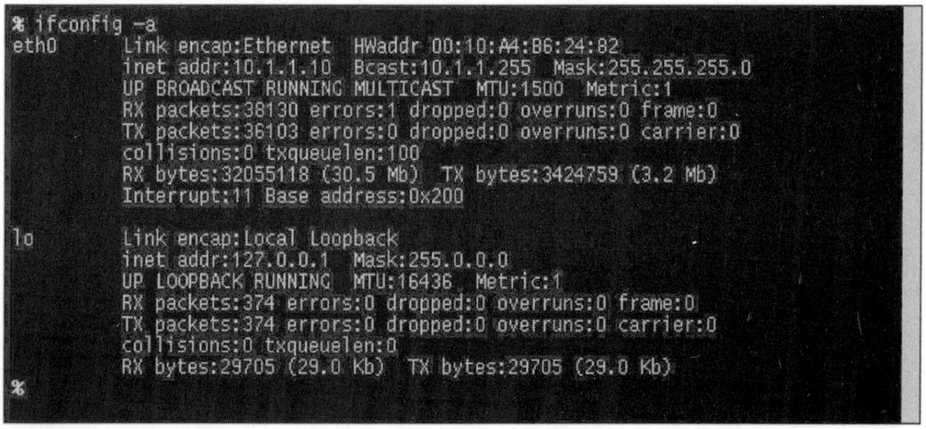

FIGURE 11-15 *Detailed information available through ifconfig*

NOTE

Other ifconfig switches, such as those that apply to DHCP settings, vary according to the type and version of the UNIX-type of operating system you use. Refer to your operating system's help manual (or man pages) for more information.

VoIP (Voice Over IP)

VoIP (voice over IP), also known as **IP telephony**, is the use of packet-switched networks and the TCP/IP protocol to transmit voice conversations. VoIP (pronounced "voyp"), which has existed in various forms for almost a decade, has generated great interest among networking professionals. Although its adoption was slow at first, as technology has matured and become more widely available, use of VoIP has increased dramatically. Objectives for implementing VoIP may include one or more of the following:

◆ *Lower costs for voice calls*—In the case of long-distance calling, using VoIP over a WAN allows an organization to avoid paying long distance telephone charges, a benefit known as **toll bypass**. For example, an organization that already leases T1s between its offices within a region can use the T1s to carry voice traffic between colleagues.

◆ *Supply new or enhanced features and applications*—VoIP runs over TCP/IP, an open protocol suite, whereas the PSTN (Public Switched Telephone Network) runs over proprietary protocols. This means developers with enough skill and interest can develop their own VoIP applications, making the possibilities for new VoIP features and services endless. It also means that off-the-shelf VoIP applications can be modified to suit a particular business's needs.

◆ *Centralize voice and data network management*—When voice and data transmissions use the same infrastructure, a network manager needs only to design, maintain, and troubleshoot a single network. Furthermore, on that network, VoIP devices can provide detailed information about voice transmissions, such as the date, time, and duration of calls, in addition to their originating number and caller names.

 NOTE

Although this section focuses on voice signal transmission, most of the concepts also apply to fax and video transmission. The provision of data, voice, fax, and video services over the same packet-switched network is known as **convergence**.

Voice signals can be carried over TCP/IP networks in a variety of configurations. To converse, VoIP callers can use either a traditional telephone, which uses analog signals, a telephone specially designed for TCP/IP transmission, or a computer equipped with a microphone, speaker, and VoIP client software. And on any VoIP network, a mix of these three types of clients is possible.

If a VoIP caller uses a traditional telephone, signals issued by the telephone must be converted to digital form before being transmitted on a TCP/IP-based network. This conversion can be accomplished in several ways. One way is by using an adapter card within a computer workstation. The traditional telephone line connects to an RJ-11 port on the adapter card. The adapter card, along with its device drivers and software on the computer, converts the voice signals to IP packets, and then issues the packets to the data network.

A second way to achieve this conversion is by connecting the traditional telephone to a switch or router capable of accepting traditional voice signals, converting them into packets, then issuing the packets to a data network. One example of such a switch is a **digital PBX** or, more commonly, an **IP-PBX**. (**PBX** stands for **private branch exchange**, which is the term used to describe a telephone switch used to connect calls within a private organization.) In general, an IP-PBX is a private switch that accepts and interprets both analog and digital voice signals. Thus, it can connect with both traditional PSTN lines and data networks. An IP-PBX transmits and receives IP-based voice signals to and from other network connectivity devices, such as routers or gateways.

In a third scenario, the traditional telephone connects to an analog PBX, which then connects to a voice-data gateway. In this case, the gateway connects the traditional telephone circuits with a TCP/IP network (such as the Internet or a private WAN). The gateway digitizes incoming analog voice signals, compresses the data, assembles the data into packets, and then issues the packets to the packet-switched network. This process relies on special VoIP compression and digitizing protocols. In addition, to translate between the PSTN and VoIP networks, gateways follow special VoIP signaling protocols. A discussion of these protocols is beyond the scope of this book. However, if you choose to specialize in VoIP networking, you need to understand such protocols thoroughly. When transferring calls from a packet-switched network to a circuit-switched network (for example, if you call your home telephone number from your office's IP telephone), a gateway performs the same functions in the reverse order.

Figure 11-16 depicts the different ways traditional telephones can be used to access a VoIP network.

Rather than traditional telephones, most new VoIP installations use **IP telephones** (or **IP phones**), which transmit and receive only digital signals. When a caller uses an IP telephone, his voice is immediately digitized and issued from the telephone to the network in packet form. To communicate on the network, each IP telephone must have a unique IP address, just as any client connected to the network has a unique IP address. The IP telephone looks like a traditional touch-tone phone, but connects to an RJ-45 wall jack, like a computer workstation. Then, its connection may pass through a connectivity device, such as a hub or switch, before reaching the IP-PBX. An IP-PBX may contain its own voice-data gateway, or it may connect to a

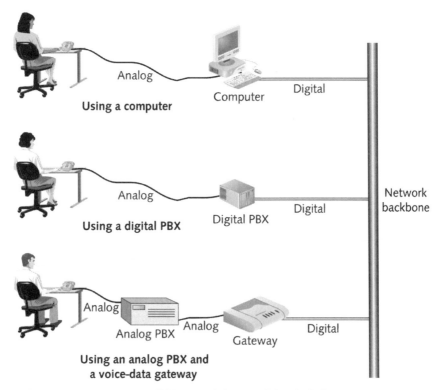

FIGURE 11-16 *Accessing a VoIP network from traditional telephones*

separate voice-data gateway, which is then connected to the network backbone. Figure 11-17 illustrates different ways IP telephones can connect with a data network.

IP telephones act much like traditional telephones. For example, they feature speed-dialing, call hold, transfer, and forwarding buttons, conference calling, voice mail access, speakers and microphones, and an LCD screen that displays caller ID and call hold information. They come in both mobile and wire-bound styles. More sophisticated IP telephones offer features not available with traditional telephones. Because IP telephones are essentially network clients, like workstations, the number and types of customized features that can be programmed for use with these phones is limitless. Makers of IP telephones include Alcatel, Avaya, Cisco, Mitel, NEC, Nortel, and Siemens. In the United States, an IP telephone can cost between $150 and $750.

Rather than using traditional telephones or IP telephones, a third option is to use a computer programmed to act like an IP telephone, otherwise known as a **softphone**. Softphones and IP telephones provide the same calling functions; they simply connect to the network and deliver services in different manners. Before it can be used as a softphone, a computer must meet minimum hardware requirements (which any new workstation purchased at an electronics store would likely meet), be installed with an IP telephony client, and communicate with a digital telephone switch. In addition, softphone computers must have a sound card capable of full-duplex transmission, so that both

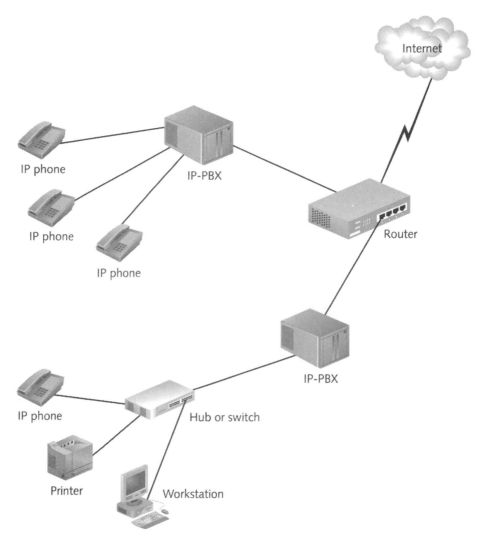

FIGURE 11-17 *Accessing a VoIP network from IP phones*

the caller and the called party can speak at the same time. Finally, a softphone also requires a microphone and speakers or a headset.

Despite all the advantages to using VoIP, it is more difficult to transmit voice signals over a packet-switched network than data signals, which are designed for packet-switched transmission. First, more so than data transmissions, voice conversations can easily be distorted by a connection's quality of service. When you talk with your friend, you need to hear his syllables in the order in which he mouthed them, and preferably, without delay. Therefore, packets carrying voice signals must be received in the same order in which they were issued and reassembled quickly. (In contrast, data packets do not necessarily have to be received in the same order in which they were transmitted, because the destination node will sort the information when it arrives.) Also, voice transmissions are subject to distortion if the connection becomes too noisy. In general, to prevent delays, disorder, and distortion, a voice connection requires more dedicated bandwidth than a data connection.

When VoIP is carried via the Internet, it is often called **Internet telephony**. But not all VoIP calls are carried over the Internet. In fact, VoIP over private lines is an effective and economical method of completing calls between two locations within an organization. And because the line is private, its network congestion can be easily controlled, thus resulting in better sound quality than an Internet telephone call can provide. But given the Internet's breadth and low cost, it is appealing to consider the Internet for carrying conversations that we currently transmit over the PSTN.

Chapter Summary

- ◆ Subnetting separates one network or segment into multiple logically defined segments, or subnets. A network administrator might subnet a network to achieve simpler troubleshooting, enhanced security, improved performance, and easier network management.

- ◆ A subnet mask provides clues about the location of network information in an IP address. Bits in a subnet mask that equal 1 indicate that corresponding bits in an IP address contain network information. Bits in a subnet mask that equal 0 indicate that corresponding bits in an IP address contain host information.

- ◆ To create subnets, some of an IP address's bits that would, by default, represent host information are changed to represent network information instead. The change is indicated by a change in the subnet mask's bits.

- ◆ If you use subnetting on your LAN, only your LAN's devices need to interpret your devices' subnetting information. External routers, such as those on the Internet, pay attention to only the network portion of your devices' IP addresses—not their subnet masks—when transmitting data to them.

- ◆ A newer variation on traditional subnetting is provided by CIDR (Classless Inter-Domain Routing). CIDR offers additional ways of arranging network and host information in an IP address. In CIDR, conventional network class distinctions do not exist.

- ◆ CIDR allows the creation of supernets, or subnets established by using bits that normally would be reserved for network class information. By moving the subnet boundary to the left, more bits are made available for host information, thus increasing the number of usable host addresses on a subnetted network.

- ◆ Gateways facilitate communication between different subnets. Because one device on the network cannot send data directly to a device on another subnet, a gateway (usually in the form of a router interface) must intercede and hand off the information.

◆ Every device on a TCP/IP-based network has a default gateway, the gateway that first interprets its outbound requests to other subnets, and then interprets its inbound requests from other subnets.

◆ Internet gateways maintain default routes to known addresses to expedite data transfer. The gateways that make up the Internet backbone are called core gateways.

◆ NAT (Network Address Translation) allows a network administrator to "hide" IP addresses assigned to nodes on a private network. In NAT, gateways assign transmissions valid Internet IP addresses when the transmission is sent to the Internet.

◆ ICS (Internet Connection Sharing) is a service, included with Windows 98, Me, 2000, and 32-bit versions of XP operating systems, that allows a network of computers to share a single Internet connection through an ICS host computer.

◆ Many private organizations use browser-based services for communication among authorized employees of the organization over an intranet. For communication with authorized personnel both from the organization and external to the organization, they may use an extranet.

◆ All Internet mail services rely on the same principles of mail delivery, storage, and pickup, though they may use different types of software to accomplish these functions.

◆ Mail client software can communicate with various types of mail server software, because the TCP/IP Application layer protocols used for this communication are standard.

◆ SMTP (Simple Mail Transfer Protocol) is responsible for moving messages from one e-mail server to another over TCP/IP-based networks. SMTP operates through port 25, with requests to receive mail and send mail going through that port on the SMTP server. SMTP is used in conjunction with either POP or IMAP. MIME operates over SMTP to enable mail messages to contain non-ASCII content, such as graphics, audio, video, and binary files. Most modern e-mail clients support MIME encoding.

◆ POP (Post Office Protocol) is a mail retrieval protocol. The most current and commonly used version of POP is called POP3. Using POP3, messages are downloaded from the mail server to a client workstation each time the user retrieves messages.

◆ IMAP (Internet Message Access Protocol) is another mail retrieval protocol. Its most current version is IMAP4. IMAP4 differs from POP3 in that it allows users to store messages on the mail server, rather than always having to download them to the local machine. This is an advantage for users who do not always check mail from the same computer.

◆ The netstat utility displays TCP/IP statistics and the state of current TCP/IP components and connections. It also displays ports, which can signal whether services are using the correct ports.

◆ The nbtstat utility provides information about NetBIOS names and their addresses. If you know the NetBIOS name of a workstation, you can use nbtstat to determine the workstation's IP address.

◆ The nslookup utility allows you to look up the DNS host name of a network node by specifying the node's IP address, or vice versa. Nslookup is useful for troubleshooting host configuration and DNS resolution problems.

◆ The dig utility, like nslookup, queries the network's DNS database to return information about a host given its IP address, or vice versa. In its simplest form, or when used with one of its many switches, dig provides more information than nslookup.

◆ The whois utility allows you to obtain DNS registration information for a second-level domain.

◆ The traceroute utility, known as tracert on Windows-based systems, uses ICMP to trace the path from one networked node to another, identifying all intermediate hops between the two nodes. This utility is useful for determining router or subnet connectivity problems.

◆ Typing ipconfig at the command prompt of a system running Windows NT, 2000, XP, or Server 2003 reveals the TCP/IP settings for that computer.

◆ You can view TCP/IP settings on a system that uses the Windows 9x or Me operating system by typing winipcfg at the command prompt.

◆ Ifconfig is the utility that establishes and allows management of TCP/IP settings on a UNIX-type of system.

◆ VoIP (voice over IP) is the use of packet-switched TCP/IP-based networks to carry voice signals. An organization may use VoIP to save money on telephone calls, centralize management of voice and data services, or take advantage of customizable call features.

◆ Many types of clients and network designs are available with VoIP networks. Clients can be traditional telephones, IP telephones, or softphones (a computer running telephony software and connected to a microphone and headphones).

◆ Analog VoIP clients may connect to traditional PBXs (private telephone switches), which then connect to a voice-data gateway that digitizes call information. Digital VoIP clients typically connect to a digital PBX or a router with VoIP capabilities.

Key Terms

ANDing—A logical process of combining bits. In ANDing, a bit with a value of 1 plus another bit with a value of 1 results in a 1. A bit with a value of 0 plus any other bit results in a 0.

CIDR (Classless Inter-domain Routing)—An IP addressing and subnetting method in which network and host information is manipulated without adhering to the limitations imposed by traditional network class distinctions. CIDR is also known as classless routing or supernetting. Older routing protocols, such as RIP, are not capable of interpreting CIDR addressing schemes.

CIDR block—In CIDR notation, the number of bits used for an extended network prefix. For example, the CIDR block for 199.34.89.0/22 is /22.

CIDR notation—In CIDR, a method of denoting network IDs and their subnet boundaries. Slash notation takes the form of the network ID followed by a /, followed by the number of bits that are used for the extended network prefix.

classful addressing—An IP addressing convention that adheres to network class distinctions, in which the first 8 bits of a Class A address, the first 16 bits of a Class B address, and the first 24 bits of a Class C address are used for network information.

Classless Inter-domain Routing—See *CIDR*.

classless routing—See *CIDR*.

convergence—The use of packet-switched networks to carry data, plus video and voice signals.

core gateway—A gateway that operates on the Internet backbone.

default gateway—The gateway that first interprets a device's outbound requests, and then interprets its inbound requests to and from other subnets. In a Postal Service analogy, the default gateway is similar to a local post office.

default router—See *default gateway*.

dig (domain information groper)—A TCP/IP utility that queries the DNS database and provides information about a host given its IP address or vice versa. Dig is similar to the nslookup utility, but provides more information, even in its simplest form, than nslookup can.

digital PBX—See *IP-PBX*.

domain information groper—See *dig*.

extended network prefix—The combination of an IP address's network ID and subnet information. By interpreting the address's extended network prefix, a device can determine the subnet to which an address belongs.

extranet—A network that uses browser-based services to exchange information within an organization *and* with certain, authorized users outside of that organization.

HTML (Hypertext Markup Language)—The language that defines formatting standards for Web documents.

Hypertext Markup Language—See *HTML*.

ICS (Internet Connection Sharing)—A service provided with Windows 98, Me, 2000 and 32-bit versions of XP operating systems that allows one computer, the ICS host, to share its Internet connection with other computers on the same network.

ICS host—On a network using the Microsoft Internet Connection Sharing service, the computer whose Internet connection other computers share. The ICS host must contain two network interfaces: one that connects to the Internet and one that connects to the LAN.

ifconfig—A utility that establishes and allows management of TCP/IP settings on UNIX-type of systems.

IMAP (Internet Message Access Protocol)—A mail retrieval protocol that improves on the shortcomings of POP. The single biggest advantage IMAP4 has relative to POP is that it allows users to store messages on the mail server, rather than always having to download them to the local machine. The most current version of IMAP is version 4 (IMAP4).

IMAP4 (Internet Message Protocol, version 4)—The most commonly used form of the Internet Message Access Protocol (IMAP).

Internet Connection Sharing—See *ICS*.

Internet Message Access Protocol—See *IMAP*.

Internet Message Access Protocol, version 4—See *IMAP4*.

Internet telephony—The provision of telephone service over the Internet.

intranet—A network or part of a network that uses browser-based services to exchange information within an enterprise. Intranets may be contained within a LAN or may be accessible via a WAN or the Internet.

IP-PBX—A private switch that accepts and interprets both analog and digital voice signals (although some IP-PBXs do not accept analog lines). It can connect with both traditional PSTN lines and data networks. An IP-PBX transmits and receives IP-based voice signals to and from other network connectivity devices, such as a router or gateway.

IP phone—See *IP telephone*.

IP telephone—A telephone used for VoIP on a TCP/IP-based network. IP telephones are designed to transmit and receive only digital signals.

IP telephony—See *Voice over IP*.

MIME (Multipurpose Internet Mail Extensions)—A standard for encoding and interpreting binary files, images, video, and non-ASCII character sets within an e-mail message.

Multipurpose Internet Mail Extensions—See *MIME*.

NAT (Network Address Translation)—A technique in which IP addresses used on a private network are assigned a public IP address by a gateway when accessing a public network.

nbtstat—A TCP/IP troubleshooting utility that provides information about NetBIOS names and their addresses. If you know the NetBIOS name of a workstation, you can use nbtstat to determine its IP address.

netstat—A TCP/IP troubleshooting utility that displays statistics and the state of current TCP/IP connections. It also displays ports, which can signal whether services are using the correct ports.

Network Address Translation—See *NAT*.

network number—See *network ID*.

network prefix—See *network ID*.

nslookup—A TCP/IP utility that allows you to look up the DNS host name of a network node by specifying its IP address, or vice versa. This ability is useful for verifying that a host is configured correctly and for troubleshooting DNS resolution problems.

PBX (private branch exchange)—A telephone switch used to connect calls within a private organization.

POP (Post Office Protocol)—An Application layer protocol used to retrieve messages from a mail server. When a client retrieves mail via POP, messages previously stored on the mail server are downloaded to the client's workstation, and then deleted from the mail server.

POP3 (Post Office Protocol, version 3)—The most commonly used form of the Post Office Protocol.

Post Office Protocol—See *POP*.

Post Office Protocol, version 3—See *POP3*.

private branch exchange – See *PBX*.

Simple Mail Transfer Protocol—See *SMTP*.

slash notation—See *CIDR notation*.

SMTP (Simple Mail Transfer Protocol)—The Application layer TCP/IP subprotocol responsible for moving messages from one e-mail server to another.

softphone—A computer programmed to act like an IP telephone. Softphones present the caller with a graphical representation of a telephone dial pad and can connect to a network via a LAN, WAN, PPP dial-up connection, or leased line.

supernet—A type of subnet that is created using bits that normally would be reserved for network class information—by moving the subnet boundary to the left.

supernet mask—A 32-bit number that, when combined with a device's IP address, indicates the kind of supernet to which the device belongs.

supernetting—See *CIDR*.

toll bypass—A cost-savings benefit that results from organizations completing long-distance telephone calls over their packet-switched networks, thus bypassing tolls charged by common carriers on comparable PSTN calls.

traceroute (tracert)—A TCP/IP troubleshooting utility that uses ICMP to trace the path from one networked node to another, identifying all intermediate hops between the two nodes. Traceroute is useful for determining router or subnet connectivity problems. On Windows-based systems, the utility is known as tracert.

Voice over IP (VoIP)—The provision of telephone service over a packet-switched network running the TCP/IP protocol suite. One form of VoIP (pronounced "voyp") is Internet telephony, though VoIP is frequently used over private networks to circumvent long-distance toll charges.

VoIP – See *voice over IP.*

winipcfg—The TCP/IP configuration and management utility for use with Windows 9x and Me systems. Winipcfg differs from ipconfig in that it supplies a graphical user interface.

whois—The utility that allows you to query ICANN's DNS registration database and find the information as a domain.

Review Questions

1. _____ separates a network into multiple logically defined segments.
    a. Classless routing
    b. Subnetting
    c. ANDing
    d. Classful addressing

2. A(n) _____ facilitates communication between different networks or subnets.
    a. gateway
    b. switch
    c. IP telephone
    d. CIDR block

3. _____ is a simple subprotocol, incapable of doing anything more than transporting mail or holding it in a queue.
    a. NAT
    b. VoIP
    c. TCP/IP
    d. SMTP

4. The _____ utility displays TCP/IP statistics and details about TCP/IP components and connections on a host.

   a. nbtstat

   b. ipconfig

   c. netstat

   d. winipcfg

5. On networks that run NetBIOS over TCP/IP, the _____ utility can provide information about NetBIOS statistics and resolve NetBIOS names to their IP addresses.

   a. nbtstat

   b. winnipcfg

   c. ipconfig

   d. netstat

6. True or false? By making bits that previously were used for host information represent network information, you reduce the number of bits available for identifying hosts.

7. True or false? One reason for hiding IP addresses is to add a marginal amount of security to a private network when it is connected to a public network.

8. True or false? A network that uses Internet-like services and protocols to exchange information within an organization and with certain authorized users outside of that organization is known as an intranet.

9. True or false? The Post Office Protocol is a Transport layer protocol used to retrieve messages from a mail server.

10. True or false? Voice over IP is the use of packet-switched networks and the TCP/IP protocol to transmit voice conversations.

11. To calculate a host's network ID given its IP address and subnet mask, you follow a logical process of combining bits known as _____.

12. A network or part of a network that uses browser-based services to exchange information within an enterprise is known as a(n) _____.

13. The utility that allows you to query the DNS registration database and obtain information about a domain name is called _____.

14. The _____ utility uses ICMP to trace the path from one networked node to another, identifying all intermediate hops between the two nodes.

15. On Unix-type systems, the _____ utility allows you to modify TCP/IP settings for a network interface, release and renew DHCP-assigned addresses, or simply check the status of your machine's TCP/IP settings.

Chapter 12

Troubleshooting Network Problems

After reading this chapter and completing the exercises, you will be able to:

■ Describe the steps involved in an effective troubleshooting methodology

■ Follow a systematic troubleshooting process to identify and resolve networking problems

■ Document symptoms, solutions, and results when troubleshooting network problems

■ Use a variety of software and hardware tools to diagnose problems

By now, you know how networks should work. Like other complex systems, however, they don't always work as planned. Many things can go wrong on a network, just as many things can go wrong with your car, your house, or a project at work. In fact, a network professional probably spends more time fixing network problems than designing or upgrading a network. Some breakdowns (such as an overtaxed processor) come with plenty of warning, but others (such as a hard disk controller failure) can strike instantly.

The best defense against problems is prevention. Just as you maintain your car regularly, you should monitor the health of your network regularly. Of course, even the most well-monitored network will sometimes experience unexpected problems. For example, a utility company could dig a new hole for its cable and accidentally cut your dedicated link to the Internet. In such a situation, your network can go from perfect to disastrous performance in an instant. In this chapter, you learn how to diagnose and solve network problems in a logical, step-by-step fashion, using a variety of tools.

Troubleshooting Methodology

NET+
4.9

Successful troubleshooters proceed logically and methodically. This section introduces a basic troubleshooting methodology, leading you through a series of general problem-solving steps. These steps follow the recommendations specified in CompTIA's Network+ exam objectives. Bear in mind that experience in your network environment may prompt you to follow the steps in a different order or to skip certain steps entirely. For example, if you know that one segment of your network is poorly cabled, you may try replacing a section of cable in that area to solve a connectivity problem before attempting to verify the physical and logical integrity of the workstation's NIC. In general, however, it is best to follow each step in the order shown. Such a logical approach can save you from undertaking wasteful, time-consuming efforts such as unnecessary software or hardware replacements.

Steps for troubleshooting network problems are as follows:

1. Identify the symptoms and potential causes. Record what you learn from people or systems that alerted you to the problem and keep that documentation handy.

2. Identify the affected area. Are users across the entire network experiencing the problem at all times? Or, is the problem limited to a specific geographic area of the network, to a specific demographic group of users, or to a particular period of time? Are all of the symptoms related to a single problem, or are you dealing with multiple problems?

NET+
4.9

3. Establish what has changed. Recent hardware or software changes may be causing the symptoms.

4. Select the most probable cause. To find the probable cause, you may need to complete the following:

   a. Verify user competency.

   b. Recreate the problem, and ensure that you can reproduce it reliably.

   c. Verify the physical integrity of the network connection (such as cable connections, NIC installations, and power to devices), starting at the affected nodes and moving outward toward the backbone.

   d. Verify the logical integrity of the network connection (such as addressing, protocol bindings, software installations, and so on).

5. Implement an action plan and solution and be prepared for all potential effects. For example, if you have to reassign IP addresses, how will the change of an IP address on a server affect its clients? Or, in another case, if you upgrade the type of client software used on a workstation, how will that affect a user's daily routine?

6. Test the result. Has your solution been implemented successfully?

7. Identify the results and effects of the solution.

8. Document the solution and process. Make sure that both you and your colleagues understand the cause of the problem and how you solved it. This information should be kept in a centrally available repository, such as an online database.

TIP

In addition to the organized method of troubleshooting described in this section, a good, general rule for troubleshooting can be stated as follows: Pay attention to the obvious! Although some questions may seem too simple to bother asking, don't discount them. You can often save much time by checking cable connections first. Every networking professional can tell a story about spending half a day trying to figure out why a computer wouldn't connect to the network, only to discover that the network cable was not plugged into the wall jack or the device's NIC.

NET+
4.9

Identify the Symptoms and Potential Causes

When troubleshooting a network problem, your first step is to identify the specific symptoms of the problem. After you identify the problem's symptoms, you can begin to deduce its cause. For example, suppose you have identified a user's inability to access a network drive as a symptom. At that point, you can list several potential causes, including a faulty NIC, cable, hub, or router; an incorrect client software configuration; a server failure; or a user error. On the other hand, you can probably rule out a power failure, a printer failure, an Internet connectivity failure, an e-mail server failure, and a host of other problems.

NET+
4.9

Answering the following questions may help you identify symptoms of a network problem that aren't immediately obvious:

◆ Is access to the network affected?

◆ Is network performance affected?

◆ Are data or programs affected? Or are both affected?

◆ Are only certain network services (such as printing) affected?

◆ If programs are affected, does the problem include one local application, one networked application, or multiple networked applications?

◆ What specific error messages do users report?

◆ Is one user or are multiple users affected?

◆ Do the symptoms manifest themselves consistently?

One danger in troubleshooting technical problems is jumping to conclusions about the symptoms. For example, you might field 12 questions from users one morning about a problem printing to the network printer in the Facilities Department. You might have already determined that the problem is an addressing conflict with the printer and be in the last stages of resolving the problem. Minutes later, when a 13th caller says, "I'm having problems printing," you might immediately conclude that she is another Facilities staff member and that her inability to print results from the same printer addressing problem. In fact, this user may be in the Administration Department, and her inability to print could represent a symptom of a larger network problem.

Take time to pay attention to the users, system and network behaviors, and any error messages. Treat each symptom as unique (but potentially related to others). In this way, you avoid the risk of ignoring problems or—even worse—causing more problems.

TIP

Take note of the error messages reported by users. If you aren't near the users, ask them to read the messages to you directly off their screens or, better yet, print the screens that contain the error messages. (On some computers, pressing the Print Screen button—which is sometimes labeled "Print Scrn" or "PrtSc"—will issue a copy of what's on the screen to the computer's clipboard, after which it can be printed or saved as a file. On other computers, you can use the Shift+Print Screen or Alt+Print Screen keystroke combinations.) Keep a record of these error messages along with your other troubleshooting notes for that problem.

Identify the Affected Area

After you have identified the problem's symptoms, you should determine whether the problem affects only a certain group of users or certain areas of the organization, or if the problem occurs

NET+
4.9

at certain times. For example, if a problem affects only users on a wireless network segment, you may deduce that the problem lies with that segment's access point. On the other hand, if symptoms are limited to one user, you can typically narrow down the cause of the problem to a single piece of hardware (for example, a workstation's NIC), software configuration, or user.

To begin, you must ascertain how many users or network segments are affected. For example, do the symptoms apply to:

◆ One user or workstation?

◆ A workgroup?

◆ A department?

◆ One location within an organization?

◆ An entire organization?

In addition, it is useful to narrow down the time frame during which the problem occurred. The following questions can help you determine the chronological scope of a problem:

◆ When did the problem begin?

◆ Has the network, server, or workstation ever worked properly?

◆ Did the symptoms appear in the last hour or day?

◆ Have the symptoms appeared intermittently for a long time?

◆ Do the symptoms appear only at certain times of the day, week, month, or year?

Like identifying symptoms, narrowing down the area affected by a problem can eliminate some causes and point to others. In particular, it can help distinguish workstation (or user) problems from network problems. If the problem affects only a department or floor of your organization, for example, you probably need to examine that network segment, its router interface, its cabling, or a server that provides services to those users. Or, you might trace a problem to a single user in that area—for example, an employee who watches video news reports from the Internet on his lunch hour, thereby consuming most of that segment's shared bandwidth. If a problem affects users at a remote location, you should examine the WAN link or its router interfaces. If a problem affects all users in all departments and locations, a catastrophic failure has occurred, and you should assess critical devices such as central switches and backbone connections.

With all network problems, including catastrophic ones, you should take the time to troubleshoot them correctly, by asking specific questions designed to identify their scope. For example, suppose a user complains that his mail program isn't picking up e-mail. You should begin by asking when the problem began, whether it affects only that user or everyone in his department, and what error message (or messages) the user receives when he attempts to pick up mail. In answering your questions, he might say, "The problem began about 10 minutes ago. Both my neighbors are having problems with e-mail, too. And as a matter of fact, a network technician was working on my machine this morning and installed a new graphics program."

As you listen to the user's response, you may need to politely filter out information that is unlikely to be related to the problem. In this situation, the user relayed two significant pieces of information: (1) The scope of the problem includes a group of users, and (2) the problem

NET+
4.9

began 10 minutes ago. With this knowledge, you can then delve further in your troubleshooting. In this example, you would proceed by focusing on the network segment rather than on one workstation.

Discovering the time or frequency with which a problem occurs can reveal more subtle network problems. For example, if multiple users throughout the organization experience poor performance when attempting to log on to the server at 8:05 A.M., you may deduce that the server needs additional resources to handle the processing burden of accepting so many requests. If a network fails at noon every Tuesday, you may be able to correlate this problem with a test of your building's power system, which causes a power dip that affects the servers, routers, and other devices.

Identifying the affected area of a problem leads you to your next troubleshooting steps. The path may not always be clear-cut, but as the flowcharts in Figures 12-1 and 12-2 illustrate, some direction can be gained from narrowing both the demographic (or geographic) and the chronological scopes of a problem. Notice that these flowcharts end with the process of further troubleshooting. In the following sections, you will learn more about these subsequent troubleshooting steps.

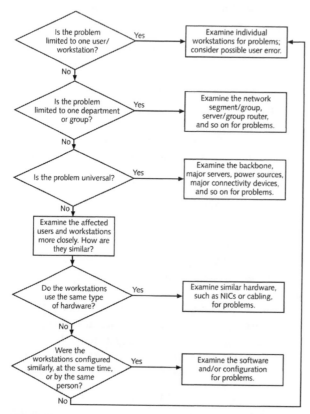

FIGURE 12-1 *Identifying the area affected by a problem*

NET+
4.9

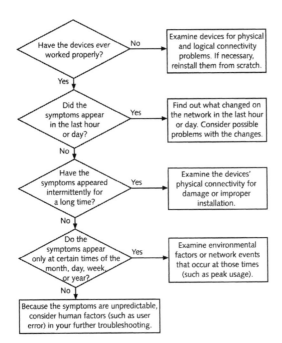

FIGURE 12-2 *Identifying the chronological scope of a problem*

 NOTE

One fascinating example of troubleshooting that began with determining a problem's chronological scope was experienced by a wireless networking engineer working on a small metropolitan area network. His spread-spectrum RF network links, which connected businesses to a carrier's facility via a transmitter and receiver on a hospital's roof, worked perfectly all day, but failed when the sun went down. When the sun came up the next morning, the wireless links worked again. The engineer confirmed that the equipment was fully operational (as he suspected), then talked with the hospital personnel. The hospital's director informed him that the hospital had installed security cameras on the outside of the building. The cameras used the same RF frequency as the network's wireless links. When the security cameras were activated at sunset, their signals interfered with the wireless network's signals, preventing data from reaching its destination.

Establish What Has Changed

One could argue that considering recent network changes is not a separate step, but rather a continual and integral part of the troubleshooting process. As you begin troubleshooting, you should be aware of any recent changes to your network. The following questions may help you pinpoint a problem that results from a network change:

- ◆ Did the operating system or configuration on a server, workstation, or connectivity device change?
- ◆ Were new components added to a server, workstation, or connectivity device?
- ◆ Were old components removed from a server, workstation, or connectivity device?
- ◆ Were new users or segments added to the network?
- ◆ Was a server, workstation, or connectivity device moved from its previous location to a new location?
- ◆ Was a server, workstation, or connectivity device replaced?
- ◆ Was new software installed on a server, workstation, or connectivity device?
- ◆ Was old software removed from a server, workstation, or connectivity device?

If you suspect that a network change has generated a problem, you can react in two ways: you can attempt to correct the problem that resulted from the change, or you can attempt to reverse the change and restore the hardware or software to its previous state. Both options come with hazards. Of the two, reverting to a previous state is probably less risky and less time-consuming.

However, correcting the problem is sometimes the best solution. For example, if you immediately suspect that a change-related problem can be fixed easily, try correcting the problem first. If it is impossible to restore a software or hardware configuration to its previous state, your only choice is to solve the problem.

 TIP

Before changing a network device or configuration, develop a plan and gather the proper resources for reversing the change in case things go wrong. For example, if you upgrade the memory module in a server, you should keep the old memory module handy in case the new one has flaws. In another situation, you might keep a backup of device or application configurations—perhaps by making a copy of the directory that stores the target configuration.

To track what has changed on a network, you and your colleagues in the IT Department should keep complete network change records. The more precisely you describe a change, its purpose, and the time and date when it occurred in your records, the easier your troubleshooting will be if the change subsequently causes problems.

NET+
4.9

In addition to keeping thorough records, you must make them available to staff members who might need to reference them. For example, you might want to keep a record of changes in a database on a file server, and then use a Web-based form to retrieve and submit information from and to the database. That way, no matter where a network technician works in the organization, she can retrieve the information from any Web-enabled workstation. A simpler alternative is to keep a clipboard in the computer room with notes about changes.

Often, network changes cause unforeseen problems. For example, if you have narrowed a connectivity problem to a group of six users in the Marketing Department, you might refer to your network's change log and find that a switch in the Marketing Department's telecommunications closet was recently moved from one end of the closet to another. Reviewing the record of this change can help you more quickly pinpoint the switch as a possible cause of the problem. Perhaps the switch was incorrectly reconnected to the backbone after the move, or perhaps it became damaged in the move or lost its configuration.

Select the Most Probable Cause

After you have identified the scope of the problem and analyzed recent changes to the network, you are close to determining the problem's cause. The following sections provide techniques on how to zero in on the most likely cause among several plausible scenarios.

Verify User Competency

You have probably experienced a moment in your dealings with computers in which you were certain you were doing everything correctly, but still couldn't access the network, save a file, or pick up your e-mail. For example, you may have typed your case-sensitive network password without realizing that the Caps Lock function was turned on. Even though you were certain that you typed the right password, you received a "password incorrect" error message each time you tried to enter it. All users experience such problems from time to time.

It's natural for human beings to make mistakes. Thus, as a troubleshooter, one of your first steps is to ensure that human error is not the source of the problem. This approach saves you time and worry. In fact, a problem caused by human error is usually simple to solve. It's much quicker and easier to assist a user in remapping a network drive, for example, than to perform diagnostics on the file server.

Sometimes, an inability to log on to the network results from a user error. Users become so accustomed to typing their passwords every morning and logging on to the network that, if something changes in the logon process, they don't know what to do. In fact, some users might never log out, so they don't know how to log on properly. Although these kinds of problems may seem simple to solve, unless a user receives training in the proper procedures and understands what might go wrong, she will never know how to solve a logon problem without assistance. Even if the user took a computer class that covered logging on, she may not remember what to do in unfamiliar situations.

NET+
4.9

The best way to verify that a user is performing network tasks correctly is to watch the user. If this tactic isn't practical, the next best way is to talk with the user by phone while she tries to replicate the error. At every step, calmly ask the user to explain what appears on the screen and what, exactly, she is doing. Urge the user to proceed slowly, according to your prompts, so that she doesn't rush ahead. After every keystroke or command, ask the user again what appears on the screen. With this methodical approach, you will have a good chance at catching user-generated mistakes. At the same time, if the problem does not result from human error, you will gain important clues for further troubleshooting.

Recreate the Problem

An excellent way to learn more about the causes of a problem is to try to recreate the symptoms yourself. If you cannot reproduce the symptoms, you may suspect that a problem was a one-time occurrence or that a user performed an operation incorrectly.

You should try to reproduce symptoms both while logged on as the user who reported the problem and while logged on under a privileged account (such as an administrator-equivalent user name). If the symptoms appear only when you're logged on as the user, you may suspect that the problem relates to the user's limited rights on the network. For example, a user may complain that he could edit a particular spreadsheet in the Accounting directory on the file server on Friday, but was unable to open the file on Monday. When you visit his workstation, you can verify this sequence of events while logged on with his user name. When you then log on as Administrator, however, you may be able to open and edit the file. The difference in your experiences points to a user rights problem. At that point, you should check the user's privileges—especially whether they have changed since he could last retrieve the file. Perhaps someone removed him from a group that had Read and Modify rights to the Accounting directory.

Answering the following questions may help you determine whether a problem's symptoms are truly reproducible and, if so, to what extent:

- ◆ Can you make the symptoms recur every time? If symptoms recur, are they consistent?
- ◆ Can you make the symptoms recur some of the time?
- ◆ Do the symptoms happen only under certain circumstances? For instance, if you log on under a different user name or try the operation from a different machine, do the symptoms still appear?
- ◆ In the case of software malfunctions, are the symptoms consistent no matter how many and which programs or files the user has open?
- ◆ Do the symptoms *ever* happen when you try to repeat them?

When attempting to reproduce the symptoms of a problem, you should follow the same steps that the person reporting the symptoms followed. As you know, many computer functions can be achieved through different means. For example, in a word-processing program, you might save a file by using the menu bar, using a keystroke combination, or clicking a button on a toolbar. All three methods result in the same outcome. Similarly, you might log on to the net-

NET+
4.9
work from a command prompt, from a predefined script inside a batch file, or from a window presented by the client software. If you attempt to reproduce a problem by performing different functions than those employed by the user, you may not be able to reproduce a legitimate problem and thus might assume that the symptoms resulted from user error. In fact, you may be missing a crucial clue to solving the problem.

To reproduce a symptom reliably, ask the user precisely what she did before the error appeared. For example, if a user complains that her network connection mysteriously drops when she's in the middle of surfing the Web, try to replicate the problem at her workstation; also, find out what else was running on the user's workstation or what kind of Web sites she was surfing.

CAUTION

Use good judgment when attempting to reproduce problems. In some cases, reproducing a problem could wreak havoc on the network, its data, and its devices; you should not attempt to reproduce such a problem. An obvious example involves a power outage in which your backup power source failed to supply power. After your network equipment comes back online, you would not cut the power again simply to verify that the problem derived from a faulty backup power source.

NET+
4.8
4.9

Verify Physical Connectivity

By some estimates, more than half of all network problems occur at the Physical layer of the OSI Model, which includes cabling, network adapters, repeaters, and hubs. The Physical layer also controls signaling—both wire-bound and wireless. Because Physical layer faults are so common (and are often easily fixed), you should be thoroughly familiar with the symptoms of such problems.

Symptoms of Physical Layer Problems

Often, physical connectivity problems manifest as a continuous or intermittent inability to connect to the network and perform network-related functions. Causes of unreliable network connectivity may include the following:

- ◆ Segment or network lengths that exceed the IEEE maximum standards (for example, an Ethernet 100BASE-TX segment that exceeds 100 meters)
- ◆ Noise affecting a wireless or wire-bound signal (from EMI sources, improper grounding, or crosstalk)
- ◆ Improper terminations, faulty connectors, loose connectors, or poorly crimped connections
- ◆ Damaged cables (for example, crushed, bent, nicked, or partially severed)
- ◆ Faulty NICs

NET+

4.8

4.9

Physical connectivity problems do not typically (but occasionally can) result in software application anomalies, the inability to use a single application, poor network performance, protocol errors, software licensing errors, or software usage errors. Some software errors, however, point to a physical connectivity problem. For example, a user might be able to log on to his file server without problems. When he chooses to run a query on a database, however, his report software might produce an error message indicating that the database is unavailable or not found. If the database resides on a separate server, this symptom could point to a physical connectivity problem with the database server.

Diagnosing Physical Layer Problems

Answering the following questions may help you identify a problem pertaining to physical connectivity:

◆ Is the device turned on?

◆ Is the NIC properly inserted?

◆ In the case of wireless NICs, is the antenna turned on?

◆ Is a device's network cable properly (that is, not loosely) connected to both its NIC and the wall jack?

◆ Do patch cables properly connect punch-down blocks to patch panels and patch panels to hubs or switches?

◆ Is the hub, router, or switch properly connected to the backbone?

◆ Are all cables in good condition (without signs of wear or damage)?

◆ Are all connectors (for example, RJ-45) in good condition and properly seated?

◆ Do network (maximum and segment) lengths conform to the IEEE 802 specifications?

◆ Are all devices configured properly to work with your network type or speed?

 TIP

A first step in verifying the physical integrity of a connection is to follow that connection from one endpoint on the network to the other. For example, if a workstation user cannot log on to the network, and you have verified that he is typing his password correctly, check the physical connectivity from his workstation's NIC and patch cable. Follow his connection all the way through the network to the server that he cannot reach.

In addition to verifying the connections between devices, you must verify the soundness of the hardware used in those connections. A sound connection means that cables are inserted firmly in ports, NICs, and wall jacks; NICs are seated firmly in the system board; connectors are not broken; and cables are not damaged. Damaged or improperly inserted connectivity elements may result in only occasional (and therefore difficult-to-troubleshoot) errors.

NET+
4.8
4.9

Swapping Equipment

If you suspect a problem lies with a network component, one of the easiest ways to test your theory is to exchange that component for a functional one. In many cases, such a swap resolves the problem very quickly, so you should try this tactic early in your troubleshooting process. It won't always work, of course, but with experience you will learn what types of problems are most likely due to component failure.

For example, if a user cannot connect to the network, and you have checked to make sure all the connections are secure and the logical connectivity elements are sound, you might consider swapping the user's network cable with a functional one. As you know, network cables must meet specific standards to operate properly. If one becomes damaged (for example, by a chair repeatedly rolling over it), it will prevent a user from connecting to the network. Swapping an old network cable with a new one is a quick test that may save you further troubleshooting.

In addition to swapping network cables, you might need to change a patch cable from one port in a switch to another, or from one data jack to another. Ports and data jacks can be operational one day and faulty the next. You might also swap a network adapter from one machine to another, or try installing a new network adapter, making sure it's compatible with the client. Obviously, it's more difficult to swap a switch or router because of the number of nodes serviced by these components and the potentially significant configuration they require; if network connectivity has failed for an entire segment or network, however, this approach may provide a quicker answer than attempting to troubleshoot the faulty device.

NOTE

A better—albeit more expensive—alternative to swapping parts is to have redundancy built into your network. For example, you might have a server that contains two network adapters, allowing one network adapter to take over for the other if one adapter should fail. If properly installed and configured, this arrangement results in no downtime; in contrast, swapping parts requires at least a few minutes of service disruption. In the case of swapping a router, the downtime might last for several hours.

CAUTION

Before swapping any network component, make sure that the replacement has exactly the same specifications as the original part. By installing a component that doesn't match the original device, you risk thwarting your troubleshooting efforts because the new component might not work in the environment. In the worst case, you may damage existing equipment by installing a component that isn't rated for it.

NET+
4.8
4.9

The flowchart in Figure 12-3 illustrates how logically assessing Physical layer elements can help you solve a network problem. The steps in this flowchart apply to a typical problem: a user's inability to log on to the network. They assume that you have already ruled out user error and that you have successfully reproduced the problem under both your and the user's logon ID.

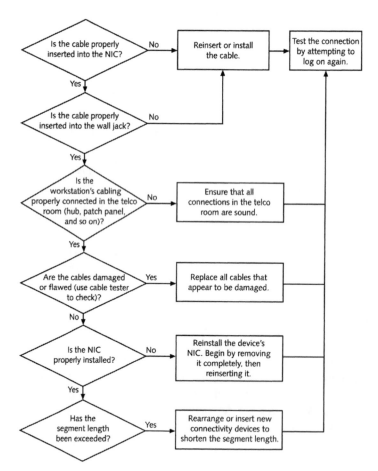

FIGURE 12-3 *Verifying physical connectivity*

NET+
4.6
4.9

Verify Logical Connectivity

After you have verified the physical connections, you must examine the firmware and software configurations, settings, installations, and privileges. Depending on the type of symptoms, you may need to investigate networked applications, the network operating system, or hardware configurations, such as NIC IRQ settings. All of these elements belong in the category of "logical connectivity."

Answering the following questions may help you identify a problem with logical connectivity:

◆ Do error messages reference damaged or missing files or device drivers?

◆ Do error messages reference malfunctioning or insufficient resources (such as memory)?

◆ Has an operating system, configuration, or application been recently changed, introduced, or deleted?

◆ Does the problem occur with only one application or a few, similar applications?

◆ Does the problem happen consistently?

◆ Does the problem affect a single user or one group of users?

Logical connectivity problems often prove more difficult to isolate and resolve than physical connectivity problems because they can be more complex. For example, a user might complain that she has been unable to connect to the network for the last two hours. After you go to her workstation and find that you can reproduce the symptoms while logged on under both her user name and your user name, you check the physical connections. Everything seems to be in order. Next, you may ask the user whether anything changed on her machine approximately two hours ago. She tells you that she didn't do a thing to the machine—it just stopped working.

At this point, you may investigate the workstation's logical connectivity. Some possible software-based causes for a failure to connect to the network include (but are not limited to) the following: resource conflicts with the NIC's configuration, an improperly configured NIC (for example, it may be set to the wrong data rate), improperly installed or configured client software, and improperly installed or configured network protocols or services. In this example, you may take another look at the client logon screen and notice that the wrong server is selected as the default. After you change the default server setting in the user's client software, she will likely be able to log on to the network.

Implement an Action Plan and Solution Including Potential Effects

After you have thoroughly analyzed a network problem, you will be able to devise an action plan and implement your solution. First, however, you must consider how your solution might affect users and network functionality.

Scope

One of the most important aspects to consider is the breadth, or scope, of your change. For example, replacing a cable that connects a workstation to a hub may affect only one user, but replacing a cable that connects a server to a switch affects all users who access that server. Assess the scope of your solution—whether it is a single workstation, a workgroup, a location, or the entire network—before implementing that solution. If the problem does not pose an emergency, wait until no one is on the network before implementing solutions that affect many users.

That way, you will have time to assess the solution's effects systematically and fix any new problems that might arise.

Tradeoffs

Along with the scope, another factor to consider is the tradeoff your solution might impose. In other words, your solution may restore functionality for one group of users, but remove it for others. For example, let's say you are a network technician at a stationery company that uses specialized software to program custom logos and control its embossing machines. When you add a group of new Windows XP workstations to your network, you discover that these new workstations can't run the embossing control software properly. The software vendor tells you that to be compatible with Windows XP, you must install a new, XP-compatible version of the software on your file server. You may be thrilled to hear of such a simple solution and install the updated embossing control software immediately. In the next half hour, you receive numerous phone calls from employees using Windows 2000 workstations who cannot properly use the embossing control software. Now you have solved one problem, but created another. In this situation, it would have been wise to ask the software vendor about their upgrade's compatibility with all the other operating systems your company uses. If the vendor told you about a problem with Windows 2000 workstations, you could have kept the old installation on the server for these users, then installed the new version of the software in another directory for use by Windows XP users.

Security

Be aware of the security implications of your solution because it may inadvertently result in the addition or removal of network access or resource privileges for a user or group of users. One consequence may be that a user can no longer access a data file or application he is used to accessing. But a worse consequence is that you could create a security vulnerability that allows unauthorized people to access your network.

Scalability

Also consider the scalability of the solution you intend to implement. Does it position the network for additions and enhancements later on, or is it merely a temporary fix that the organization will outgrow in a year? Ideally, your solution would be perfectly suited to your network and allow for future growth. But a temporary fix is not necessarily wrong, depending on the scenario. For example, you might walk into the office one day to find that none of your users can access the network. You may track down the problem as an internal hardware problem with your Internet gateway. Because the gateway is under warranty, you quickly call the manufacturer to get the gateway replaced or fixed immediately. The manufacturer may tell you that although they don't have the identical gateway available in their local office, they can substitute a different, smaller model to get your users reconnected today, and meanwhile order the identical gateway that you can install when you have more time. In this situation, it is preferable to take the temporary gateway and restore functionality than to wait for the ideal solution.

NET+

4.9

Cost

Another factor to consider when implementing your solution is cost. Obviously, replacing one patch cable or faulty network adapter is a fairly inexpensive proposition, and you don't need to analyze cost in these cases. But if the solution you have proposed requires significant dollars for either software or hardware, weigh your options carefully. For example, you may discover a problem with performance on your network. After some investigation, you may determine that the best solution is to replace all of your 400 workstations' network adapters with newer, faster network adapters. If you purchase quality NICs, this solution could cost over $8,000 for the hardware alone, not to mention the time it will take technicians to replace the devices, which may cost more. Also you should consider when these workstations will be replaced and if you will have to either discard or remove the network adapters you just installed. It may be more prudent to identify where the network's performance is poor and address those areas separately—for example, by adding a switch to a busy segment or adding a more powerful server for a heavily used application.

Use Vendor Information

Some networking professionals pride themselves in being able to install, configure, and troubleshoot devices without reading the instructions—or at least exhausting all possibilities before they submit to reading a manual. Although some manufacturers provide better documentation than others, you have nothing to lose by referring to the manual, except a little time. Chances are you will find exactly what you need—jumper settings for a NIC, configuration commands and their arguments for a router, and troubleshooting tips for a network operating system function.

In addition to the printed documentation that comes with a networking component, most network software and hardware vendors provide free online troubleshooting information. For example, Microsoft, Novell, Red Hat, and Apple offer searchable databases in which you can type your error message or a description of your problem and receive lists of possible solutions. Reputable equipment manufacturers, such as 3Com, Compaq, Cisco, IBM, and Intel, also offer sophisticated Web interfaces for troubleshooting their equipment. If you cannot find the documentation for a networking component, you should try looking for information on the Web.

Call the vendor's technical support phone number only after you have read the manual and searched the vendor's Web page. With some manufacturers, you can talk to a technical support agent only if you have established and paid for a support agreement. With others, you must pay per phone call. Each vendor has a different pricing structure for technical support, so before you agree to pay for technical support, you should find out whether the vendor charges on a per-hour or per-problem basis.

If you are uncertain whether your proposed solution is the *best* solution, even after your thorough diagnosis and research, you should consult with others, either within or outside your organization. Colleagues or consultants may share an experience that leads you to prefer one solution to another.

TIP

Keep a list handy of the hardware and software vendors for your networking equipment; the list should include the company's name, its technical support phone number, a contact name (if available), its technical support Web site address, its policies for technical support, and the type of agreement you currently have with the vendor. You can find an example of such a form in Appendix D. Make sure the list is updated regularly and available to all IT personnel who might need it.

Implement the Solution

Finally, after you have researched the effects of your proposed solution, you are ready to implement the solution. This step may be very brief (such as correcting the default server designation in a user's client logon screen) or it may take a long time (such as replacing the hard disk of a server). In either case, implementing a solution requires foresight and patience. As with finding the problem, the more methodically and logically you can approach the solution, the more efficient the correction process will be. If a problem is causing catastrophic outages, however, you should solve it as quickly as possible.

The following steps will help you implement a safe and reliable solution:

1. Collect all the documentation you have about a problem's symptoms from your investigation and keep it handy while solving the problem.

2. If you are reinstalling software on a device, make a backup of the device's existing software installation. If you are changing hardware on a device, keep the old parts handy in case the solution doesn't work. If you are changing the configuration of a program or device, take the time to print the program or device's current configuration. Even if the change seems minor, jot down notes about the original state. For example, if you intend to add a user to a privileged group to allow her to access the Accounting spreadsheets, first write down the groups to which she currently belongs.

3. Perform the change, replacement, move, or addition that you believe will solve the problem. Record your actions in detail so that you can later enter the information into a database.

4. Test your solution (see the following section).

5. Before leaving the area in which you were working, clean it up. For instance, if you created a new patch cable for a telecommunications room, remove the debris left from cutting and crimping the cable.

6. If the solution fixes the problem, record the details you have collected about the symptoms, the problem, and the solution in your organization's troubleshooting database.

7. If your solution involved a significant change or addressed a significant problem (one that affected more than a few users), revisit the solution a day or two later to verify that the problem has, indeed, been solved and that it hasn't created additional problems.

NET+
4.9

In the case of large-scale fixes—for example, applying new configurations on a global VPN's routers because of a security threat—you should roll out changes in stages. This approach allows you to find and correct any problem that occurs during the upgrade before it affects all users. It also allows you to test whether you're implementing the solution in the best possible way. In the example of reconfiguring routers, you could log on to the routers and apply configurations from a remote office, but in some cases this creates additional security concerns. You might prefer instead to visit the offices and apply the changes yourself or talk a local IT employee who can make the changes on site.

Test the Result

After implementing your solution, you must test its result and verify that you have solved the problem properly. Obviously, the type of testing you perform depends on your solution. For example, if you replaced a patch cable between a switch port and a patch panel, a quick test of your solution would be to determine whether you could connect to the network from the device that relies on that patch cable. If the device does not successfully connect to the network, you may have to try another cable or reconsider whether the problem stems from physical or logical connectivity or some other cause. In that case, using the hardware and software troubleshooting tools discussed later in this chapter might lead to a more efficient evaluation of your solution.

Testing the results of your solution will also depend on the area affected by the problem. Suppose you replaced a switch that served four different departments in an organization. To test the result of your solution, you would need to verify connectivity from workstations in each of the four departments.

You may not be able to test your solution immediately after implementing it. In some cases, you may have to wait days or weeks before you know for certain whether it worked. For example, you may have discovered that a server was sometimes running out of processor capacity when handling clients' database queries, causing users to experience unacceptably slow response times. To solve this problem, you might add two processors and enable the server's symmetric multiprocessing capabilities. The timing of the database usage may be unpredictable, however. As a result, you may not find out whether the added processors eliminated the problem until a certain number of users attempt the operations that push the server to its peak processor usage.

 NOTE

A copy of all questions included in the preceding sections appears on a form in Appendix D, "Standard Networking Forms." You might want to create your own form based on these questions but tailored to your particular networking environment. Take your form along whenever you set out on a troubleshooting mission. It will help remind you of possibilities that you might otherwise forget to investigate.

NET+
4.9

Identify the Results and Effects of the Solution

Upon testing your solution, you should be able to determine how and why the solution was successful and what effects it had on users and functionality. For example, suppose you identified a symptom of excessively slow performance when saving and retrieving files to and from a server on your LAN. You determined that all users were affected by the problem and that it had worsened steadily in the past month. Your proposed solution was to replace the server with one that contained a faster processor, more memory, greater hard disk capacity, and dual NICs. You implemented the solution and then tested its outcome to make sure all users could save and retrieve files to and from the new server. If all went well, the effect of the solution might be an 80% increase in performance between clients and the server.

Most importantly, you want to avoid creating unintended, negative consequences as a result of your solution. For example, in the process of diagnosing a problem with a user's access to a mail directory, you might have reconfigured his mail settings to log on with your own user name to rule out the possibility of a physical connectivity error. After discovering that the problem was actually due to an IP addressing conflict, you might fix the IP addressing problem but forget that you changed the user's e-mail configuration. Having the user test your solution would reveal this oversight—and prevent you from having to return to the workstation to solve another problem.

After you have implemented and tested your solution and identified its results and effects, communicate your solution to your colleagues, thus adding to the store of knowledge about your network. The next section discusses how best to document your troubleshooting efforts and notify others of changes you've made.

Document the Solution and Process

Whether you are a one-person network support team or one of 100 network technicians at your organization, you should always record the symptoms and cause (or causes) of a problem and your solution. Given the volume of problems you and other analysts will troubleshoot, it will be impossible to remember the circumstances of each incident. In addition, networking personnel frequently change jobs, and everyone appreciates clear, thorough documentation. An effective way to document problems and solutions is in a centrally located database to which all networking personnel have online access.

Staff Involved in Troubleshooting

Many staff members may contribute to troubleshooting a network problem. Often the division of duties is formalized, with a help desk acting as the first, single point of contact for users to call in regarding errors. A help desk is typically staffed with help desk analysts—people proficient in basic (but not usually advanced) workstation and network troubleshooting. Larger organizations may group their help desk analysts into teams based on their expertise. For example, a company that provides users with word-processing, spreadsheet, project planning, scheduling, and graphics software might assign different technical support personnel at the help desk to answer questions pertaining to each application.

NET+
4.9

The help desk analysts are often considered first-level support, because they provide the first level of troubleshooting. When a user calls with a problem, a help desk analyst typically creates a record for the incident and attempts to diagnose the problem. The help desk analyst may be able to solve a common problem over the phone within minutes by explaining something to the user. On other occasions, the problem may be rare or complex. In such cases, the first-level support analyst will refer the problem to a second-level support analyst. A second-level support analyst is someone who has specialized knowledge in one or more aspects of a network. For example, if a user complains that she can't connect to a server, and the first-level support person narrows down the problem to a failed file server, that first-level support analyst would then refer the problem to the second-level support person.

In addition to having first- and second-level support analysts, most help desks include a help desk coordinator. The help desk coordinator ensures that analysts are divided into the correct teams, schedules shifts at the help desk, and maintains the infrastructure to enable analysts to better perform their jobs. They may also serve as third-level support personnel, taking responsibility for troubleshooting a problem when the second-level support analyst is unable to solve it.

Record Problems and Resolutions

For documenting problems, some organizations use a software program known as a **call tracking system** (also informally known as help desk software). Such programs provide user-friendly graphical interfaces that prompt the user for every piece of information associated with the problem. They assign unique identifying numbers to each problem, in addition to identifying the caller, the nature of the problem, the time necessary to resolve it, and the nature of the resolution.

Most call tracking systems are highly customizable, so you can tailor the form fields to your particular computing environment. For example, if you work for an oil refinery, you might add fields for identifying problems with the plant's flow-control software. In addition, most call tracking systems allow you to enter free-form text explanations of problems and solutions. Some also offer Web-based interfaces.

If your organization does not have a call tracking system, you should at least keep records in a simple electronic form. You can find an example of a network problem record in Appendix D. A typical problem record form should include at least the following fields:

◆ The name, department, and phone number of the problem originator (the person who first noticed the problem)
◆ Information regarding whether the problem is software- or hardware-related
◆ If the problem is software-related, the package to which it pertains; if the problem is hardware-related, the device or component to which it pertains
◆ Symptoms of the problem, including when it was first noticed
◆ The name and telephone number of the network support contact
◆ The amount of time spent troubleshooting the problem
◆ The resolution of the problem

As discussed earlier in this chapter, many organizations operate a help desk staffed with personnel who have only basic troubleshooting expertise and who record problems called in by users. To effectively field network questions, an organization's help desk staff must maintain current and accurate records for network support personnel. Your department should take responsibility for managing a supported services list that help desk personnel can use as a reference. A **supported services list** is a document (preferably online) that lists every service and software package supported within an organization, plus the names of first- and second-level support contacts for those services or software packages. Anything else you or your department can do to increase communication and availability of support information will expedite troubleshooting.

In addition to communicating problems and solutions to your peers whenever you work on a network problem, you should follow up with the user who reported the problem. Make sure that the client understands how or why the problem occurred, what you did to resolve the problem, and whom to contact should the problem recur. This type of education helps your clients make better decisions about the type of support or training they need, and also improves their understanding of and respect for your department.

Notify Others of Changes

After solving a particularly thorny network problem, you should record its resolution in your call tracking system, and also notify others of your solution and what, if anything, you needed to change to fix the problem. This communication serves two purposes: (1) It alerts others about the problem and its solution, and (2) it notifies others of network changes you made, in case they affect other services.

The importance of recording changes cannot be overemphasized. Imagine that you are the network manager for a group of five network technicians who support a WAN consisting of three different offices and 150 users. One day, the company's CEO travels from headquarters to a branch office for a meeting with an important client. At the branch office, she needs to print a financial statement, but encounters a printing problem. Your network technician discovers that her user account does not have rights to that office's printer, because users on your WAN do not have rights to printers outside the office to which they belong. The network technician quickly takes care of the problem by granting all users rights to all printers across the WAN. What are the implications of this change? If your technician tells no one about this change, at best users may incorrectly print to a printer in Duluth from the St. Paul office. In a worst-case scenario, a "guest" user account may gain rights to a networked printer, potentially creating a security hole in your network.

Large organizations often implement change management systems to methodically track changes on the network. A **change management system** is a process or program that provides support personnel with a centralized means of documenting changes to the network. In smaller organizations, a change management system may be as simple as one document on the network to which networking personnel continually add entries to mark their changes. In larger organizations, the system may consist of a database package complete with graphical interfaces

NET+

4.9

and customizable fields tailored to the computing environment. Whatever form your change management system takes, the most important element is participation. If networking personnel do not record their changes, even the most sophisticated software is useless.

The types of changes that network personnel should record in a change management system include the following:

◆ Adding or upgrading software on network servers or other devices

◆ Adding or upgrading hardware components on network servers or other devices

◆ Adding new hardware on the network (for example, a new server)

◆ Changing the network properties of a network device (for example, changing the IP address or host name of a server)

◆ Increasing or decreasing rights for a group of users

◆ Physically moving networked devices

◆ Moving user accounts and their files and directories from one server to another

◆ Making changes in processes (for example, a new backup schedule or a new contact for DNS support)

◆ Making changes in vendor policies or relationships (for example, a new hard disk supplier)

It is generally not necessary to record minor modifications, such as changing a user's password, creating a new group for users, creating new directories, or changing a network drive mapping for a user. Each organization will have unique requirements for its change management system, and analysts who record change information should clearly understand these requirements.

Help to Prevent Future Problems

If you review the troubleshooting questions and examples in this chapter, you can predict how some network problems can be averted by network maintenance, documentation, security, or upgrades. Although not all network problems are preventable, many can be avoided. Just as with your body's health, the best prescription for network health is prevention.

For example, to avoid problems with users' access levels for network resources, you can comprehensively assess users' needs, set policies for groups, use a variety of groups, and communicate to others who support the network why those groups exist. To prevent overusing network segments, you should perform regular network health checks—perhaps even continual network monitoring (discussed in the next section), with filters that isolate anomalous occurrences—and ensure that you have the means to either redesign the network to distribute traffic or purchase additional bandwidth well before utilization reaches critical levels. With experience, you will be able to add more suggestions for network problem prevention. When planning or upgrading a network, you should consciously think about how good network designs and policies can prevent later problems—not to mention, make your job easier and more fun.

Troubleshooting Tools

You have already learned about some utilities that can help you troubleshoot network problems. For example, you can learn many things about a user's workstation connection by attempting to ping different hosts on the network from that workstation. However, in some cases, the most efficient troubleshooting approach is to use a tool specifically designed to analyze and isolate network problems. Several tools are available, ranging from simple continuity testers that indicate whether a cable is faulty, to sophisticated protocol analyzers that capture and interpret all types of data traveling over the network. The tool you choose depends on the particular problem you need to investigate and the characteristics of your network.

The following sections describe a variety of network troubleshooting tools, their functions, and their relative costs.

NET+
3.3
4.8

Crossover Cable

As you have learned, in a crossover cable the transmit and receive wire pairs in one of the connectors are reversed. This reversal enables you to use a crossover cable to directly interconnect two nodes without using an intervening connectivity device. A crossover cable is useful for quickly and easily verifying that a node's NIC is transmitting and receiving signals properly. For example, suppose you are a network technician on your way to fix urgent network problems. A user flags you down and says that over the last week he occasionally had problems connecting to the network and as of this morning, he hasn't been able to connect at all. He's very frustrated, so you kindly say that if you can help him in 10 minutes, you will; otherwise, he'll have to call the help desk. You follow him to his workstation and, by asking around, you determine that he is the only one suffering this problem. Thus, you can probably narrow the problem down to his workstation (either hardware or software) or his cabling (or less likely, his port on the hub in the telecommunications closet). Because you have your laptop and troubleshooting gear in your bag, you quickly connect one plug of the crossover cable to his workstation's network adapter and the other plug to your laptop's network adapter. You then try logging on to your laptop from his workstation. Because this process is successful, you suggest that the problem lies with his network cable, and not with his workstation's software or hardware. You quickly hand him a new patch cable to replace his old one and rush off to your original destination.

Tone Generator and Tone Locator

Ideally, you and your networking colleagues would label each port and wire termination in a telecommunications closet so that problems and changes can be easily managed. However, because of personnel changes and time constraints, a telecommunications closet often is disorganized and poorly documented. If this is the case where you work, you may need a tone generator and a tone locator to determine where one pair of wires (out of possibly hundreds) terminates.

NET+
3.3
4.8

A **tone generator** is a small electronic device that issues a signal on a wire pair. A **tone locator** is a device that emits a tone when it detects electrical activity on a wire pair. By placing the tone generator at one end of a wire and attaching a tone locator to the other end, you can verify the location of the wire's termination. Figure 12-4 depicts the use of a tone generator and a tone locator. Of course, you must work by trial and error, guessing which termination corresponds to the wire over which you've generated a signal until the tone locator indicates the correct choice. This combination of devices is also known as a **fox and hound**, because the locator (the hound) chases the generator (the fox).

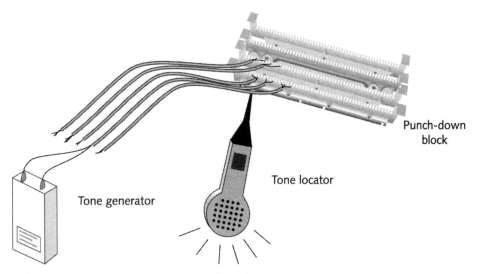

Punch-down block

Tone locator

Tone generator

FIGURE 12-4 *Use of a tone generator and tone locator*

Tone generators and tone locators cannot be used to determine any characteristics about a cable, such as whether it has defects or whether its length exceeds IEEE standards for a certain type of network. They are only used to determine where a wire pair terminates.

 CAUTION

A tone generator should never be used on a wire that's connected to a device's port or network adapter. Because a tone generator transmits electricity over the wire, it may damage the device or network adapter.

NET+
3.3
4.8

Multimeter

Cable testing tools are essential for both cable installers and network troubleshooters, as faulty cables are often the cause of network problems. Symptoms of cabling problems can be as elusive as occasional lost packets or as obvious as a break in network connectivity. You can easily test cables for faults with specialized tools. In this section and in the ones following, you will learn about different tools that can help isolate problems with network cables. The first device you will learn about is a **multimeter**, a simple instrument that can measure many characteristics of an electric circuit, including its resistance and voltage.

If you have taken an introductory electronics class, you are probably familiar with a **voltmeter**, the instrument that measures the pressure, or voltage, of an electric current. Recall that voltage is used to create signals over a network wire. Thus, every time data travels over a wire, the wire carries a small voltage. In addition, each wire has a certain amount of resistance, or opposition to electric current. Resistance is a fundamental property of wire that depends on a wire's molecular structure and size. Every type of wire has different resistance characteristics. Resistance is measured in ohms, and the device used to measure resistance is called an **ohmmeter**. Another characteristic of electrical circuits is impedance—the resistance that contributes to controlling the signal. Impedance is also measured in ohms. Impedance is the telltale factor for ascertaining where faults in a cable lie. A certain amount of impedance is required for a signal to be properly transmitted and interpreted. However, very high or low levels of impedance can signify a damaged wire, incorrect pairing, or a termination point. In other words, changes in impedance can indicate where current is stopped or inhibited.

Although you could use separate instruments for measuring impedance, resistance, and voltage on a wire, it is more convenient to have one instrument that accomplishes all of these functions. The multimeter is such an instrument. Figure 12-5 shows a multimeter.

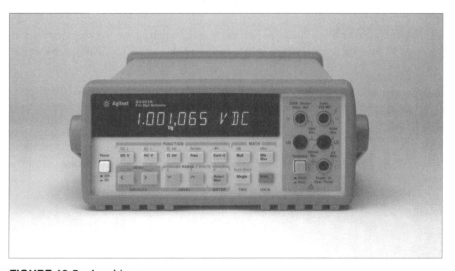

FIGURE 12-5 *A multimeter*

NET+
3.3
4.8

As a network professional, you might use a multimeter to:

- Verify that a cable is properly conducting electricity—that is, whether its signal can travel unimpeded from one node on the network to another
- Check for the presence of noise on a wire (by detecting extraneous voltage)
- Verify that the amount of resistance presented by terminators on coaxial cable networks is appropriate, or whether terminators are actually present and functional
- Test for short or open circuits in the wire (by detecting unexpected resistance or loss of voltage)

Multimeters vary in their degree of sophistication and features. Some merely show voltage levels, for example, whereas others can measure the level of noise on a circuit at any moment with extreme precision. Costs for multimeters also vary; some, such as those available at any home electronics store, cost as little as $30, while others cost as much as $4000. Multimeters capable of the greatest accuracy are most useful to electronics engineers. As a network technician, you won't often need to know the upper limit of noise on a cable within a small fraction of a decibel, for example. However, you do need to know how to check whether a cable is conducting current. Another instrument that can perform such a test is a continuity tester, which is discussed next.

Cable Continuity Testers

In troubleshooting a Physical layer problem, you may find the cause of a problem by simply testing whether your cable is carrying a signal to its destination. Tools used to make this determination are said to be testing the continuity of the cable and may be called **cable checkers** or **continuity testers**. They may also be called cable testers. The term **cable tester**, however, is a general term that also includes more sophisticated tools that can measure cable performance, as discussed in the following section.

When used on a copper-based cable, a continuity tester applies a small amount of voltage to each conductor at one end of the cable, and then checks whether that voltage is detectable at the other end. That means that a continuity tester consists of two parts: the base unit that generates the voltage and the remote unit that detects the voltage. Most cable checkers provide a series of lights that signal pass/fail. Some also indicate a cable pass/fail with an audible tone. A pass/fail test provides a simple indicator of whether a component can perform its stated function.

In addition to checking cable continuity, some continuity testers will verify that the wires in a UTP or STP cable are paired correctly and that they are not shorted, exposed, or crossed. Recall that different network models use specific wire pairings and follow cabling standards set forth in TIA/EIA 568. Make sure that the cable checker you purchase can test the type of network you use—for example, 10BASE-T, 100BASE-TX, or 1000BASE-T Ethernet.

Continuity testers for fiber-optic networks also exist. Rather than issuing voltage on a wire, however, these testers issue light pulses on the fiber and determine whether they reached the other end of the fiber. Some continuity testers offer the ability to test both copper and fiber-optic cable.

Figure 12-6 depicts a basic continuity tester and a more sophisticated continuity tester.

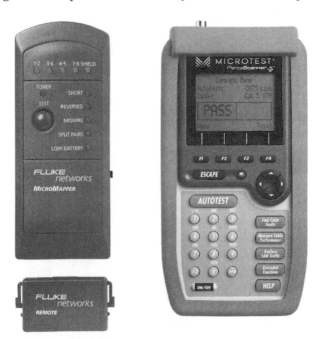

FIGURE 12-6 *Cable continuity testers*

Whether you make your own cables or purchase cabling from a reputable vendor, test the cable to ensure that it meets your network's required standards. Just because a cable is labeled "CAT 6," for example, does not necessarily mean that it will live up to that standard. Testing cabling before installing it may save many hours of troubleshooting after the network is in place.

CAUTION

Do not use a continuity tester on a live network cable. Disconnect the cable from the network, and then test its continuity.

For convenience, most continuity testers are portable and lightweight, and typically use one 9-volt battery. A simple continuity tester can cost between $100 and $300, and it may save many hours of work. Popular manufacturers of these cable testing devices include Belkin, Fluke, Microtest, and Paladin.

Cable Performance Testers

If you need to know more than whether a cable is simply carrying current, you can use a **cable performance tester**. The difference between continuity testers and performance testers lies in their sophistication and price. A performance tester accomplishes the same continuity and fault tests as a continuity tester, but can also perform the following tasks:

◆ Measure the distance to a connectivity device, termination point, or cable fault

◆ Measure attenuation along a cable

◆ Measure near-end crosstalk between wires

◆ Measure termination resistance and impedance

◆ Issue pass/fail ratings for CAT 3, CAT 5, CAT 5e, CAT 6, or CAT 7 standards

◆ Store and print cable testing results or directly save data to a computer database

◆ Graphically depict a cable's attenuation and crosstalk characteristics over the length of the cable

A sophisticated performance tester will include a **TDR (time domain reflectometer)**. A TDR issues a signal on a cable and then measures the way the signal bounces back (or reflects) to the TDR. Connectors, crimps, bends, short circuits, cable mismatches, or other defects modify the signal's amplitude before it returns to the TDR, thus changing the way it reflects. The TDR then accepts and analyzes the return signal, and based on its condition and the amount of time the signal took to return, determines cable imperfections. In the case of a coaxial cable network, a TDR can indicate whether terminators are properly installed and functional. A TDR can also indicate the distance between nodes and segments.

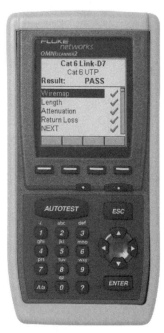

In addition to performance testers for coaxial and twisted-pair networks, you can also find performance testers for fiber-optic networks. Such performance testers use **OTDRs (optical time domain reflectometers)**. Rather than issue an electrical signal over the cable as twisted-pair cable testers do, an OTDR transmits light-based signals of different wavelengths over the fiber. Based on the type of return light signal, the OTDR can accurately measure the length of the fiber, determine the location of faulty splices, breaks, connectors, or bends, and measure attenuation over the cable.

Because of their sophistication, performance testers for both copper and fiber-optic cables cost significantly more than continuity testers. A high-end unit may cost from $5000 to $8000, and a low-end unit may cost between $1000 and $4000. Popular performance tester manufacturers include Fluke and Microtest. Figure 12-7 shows an example of a high-end performance tester that is capable of measuring the characteristics of both copper and fiber-optic cables.

FIGURE 12-7 *A performance tester*

Network Monitors

A **network monitor** is a software-based tool that continually monitors network traffic from a server or workstation attached to the network. Network monitors typically can interpret up to Layer 3 of the OSI Model. They can determine the protocols passed by each frame, but can't interpret the data inside the frame. By capturing data, they can provide either a snapshot of network activity at one point in time or a historical record of network activity over a period of time.

Some NOSs come with network monitoring tools. Microsoft **Network Monitor** is the tool that ships with Windows Server 2003 as well as with Windows NT and Windows 2000 Server. Novell **NETMON**, an NLM (NetWare Loadable Module), comes with NetWare 5.x and 6.x. In addition, you can purchase or download for free network monitoring tools written by other software companies. Hundreds of such programs exist. After you have worked with one network monitoring tool, you will find that other products work in much the same way. Most even use very similar graphical interfaces.

 NOTE

To take advantage of network monitoring and analyzing tools, the network adapter installed in the machine running the software must support promiscuous mode. In **promiscuous mode**, a device driver directs the NIC to pick up all frames that pass over the network—not just those destined for the node served by the card. You can determine whether your network adapter supports promiscuous mode by reading its manual or checking with the manufacturer. Some network monitoring software vendors may even suggest which network adapters to use with their software.

Network monitoring tools can perform at least the following functions:

◆ Continuously monitor network traffic on a segment

◆ Capture network data transmitted on a segment

◆ Capture frames sent to or from a specific node

◆ Reproduce network conditions by transmitting a selected amount and type of data

◆ Generate statistics about network activity (for example, what percentage of the total frames transmitted on a segment are broadcast frames)

Some network monitoring tools can also:

◆ Discover all network nodes on a segment

◆ Establish a **baseline**, or a record of how the network operates under normal conditions, including its performance, collision rate, utilization rate, and so on

NET+
4.2
4.8

◆ Store traffic data and generate reports

◆ Trigger alarms when traffic conditions meet preconfigured conditions (for example, if usage exceeds 50% of capacity)

How can capturing data help you solve a problem? Imagine that traffic on a segment of the network you administer suddenly grinds to a halt one morning at about 8:00. You no sooner step in the door than everyone from the help desk calls to tell you how slowly the network is running. Nothing has changed on the network since last night, when it ran normally, so you can think of no obvious reasons for problems.

At the workstation where you have previously installed a network monitoring tool, you capture all data transmissions for approximately five minutes. You then sort the frames in the network monitoring software, arranging the nodes in order based on the volume of traffic each has generated. You might find that one workstation appears at the top of the list with an inordinately high number of bad transmissions. Or, you might discover that a server has been compromised by a hacker and is generating a flood of data over the network.

Before adopting a network monitor or protocol analyzer, you should be aware of some of the data errors that these tools can distinguish. The following list defines some commonly used terms for abnormal data patterns and packets, along with their characteristics:

◆ **Local collisions**—Collisions that occur when two or more stations are transmitting simultaneously. A small number of collisions are normal on an Ethernet network. Excessively high collision rates within the network usually result from cable or routing problems.

◆ **Late collisions**—Collisions that take place outside the window of time in which they would normally be detected by the network and redressed. Late collisions are usually caused by one of two problems: (1) a defective station (for example, a card or transceiver) that is transmitting without first verifying line status, or (2) failure to observe the configuration guidelines for cable length, which results in collisions being recognized too late.

◆ **Runts**—Packets that are smaller than the medium's minimum packet size. For instance, any Ethernet packet that is smaller than 64 bytes is considered a runt. Runts are often the result of collisions.

◆ **Giants**—Packets that exceed the medium's maximum packet size. For example, an Ethernet packet larger than 1518 bytes is considered a giant.

◆ **Jabber**—A device that handles electrical signals improperly, usually affecting the rest of the network. A network analyzer will detect a jabber as a device that is always retransmitting, effectively bringing the network to a halt. A jabber usually results from a bad NIC. Occasionally, it can be caused by outside electrical interference.

◆ **Negative frame sequence checks**—The result of the CRC (Cyclic Redundancy Check) generated by the originating node not matching the checksum calculated from the data received. It usually indicates noise or transmission problems on the

LAN interface or cabling. A high number of negative CRCs usually result from excessive collisions or a station transmitting bad data.

◆ **Ghosts**—Frames that are not actually data frames, but aberrations caused by a device misinterpreting stray voltage on the wire. Unlike true data frames, ghosts have no starting delimiter.

Protocol Analyzers

A **protocol analyzer** (or **network analyzer**) is another tool that can capture traffic. But a protocol analyzer can also analyze frames, typically all the way to Layer 7 of the OSI Model. For example, it can identify that a frame uses TCP/IP and, more specifically, that it is an ARP request from one particular workstation to a server. Analyzers can also interpret the payload portion of frames, translating from binary or hexadecimal code to human-readable form. As a result, network analyzers can capture passwords going over the network, if their transmission is not encrypted. Some protocol analyzer software packages can run on a standard PC, but others require PCs equipped with special network adapters and operating system software.

As with network monitoring software, a variety of protocol analyzer software is available. One popular example is the free program called Ethereal. Essentially, a protocol analyzer performs the same features as the network monitor software discussed previously, plus a few extras. It can also generate traffic in an attempt to reproduce a network problem and monitor multiple network segments simultaneously. Its graphical interface makes this product very easy to use, readily revealing the traffic flow across the network. In addition, protocol analyzer software typically supports a multitude of protocols and network topologies.

Some protocol analyzers are not merely software tools, but hardware tools as well. Sniffer Technologies has led the way in developing hardware-based protocol analyzers, under the Sniffer brand name. (Following the popularity of the Sniffer Technologies product, some networking professionals generically refer to any hardware-based protocol analyzer as a "sniffer.") Hardware-based protocol analyzers usually resemble regular laptops, but are equipped with a special network adapter and network analysis software. The sole job of this device is to identify and assess network problems. Unlike laptops that have a network monitoring tool installed, hardware-based protocol analyzers typically cannot be used for other purposes, because they don't depend on a familiar desktop operating system such as Windows. They have their own proprietary operating system. Because they do not rely on a desktop operating system such as Windows, hardware-based network analyzers have an advantage over network monitoring software. They do not rely on Windows device drivers (for the NIC), for example, so they can capture information that the NIC would automatically discard, such as runt packets. Figure 12-8 illustrates how Sniffer Portable software can display network data. In this case, the screen depicts the distribution of traffic captured by protocol type.

Hardware-based protocol analyzers are tailored to a particular type of network. For example, one may be able to analyze both Ethernet and Token Ring networks, but another may be necessary to analyze fiber-optic networks. Still others are designed especially for analyzing

NET+
4.2
4.8

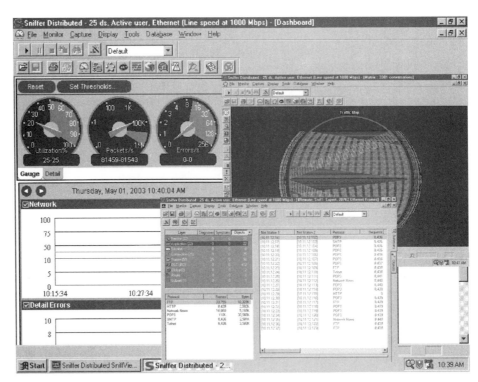

FIGURE 12-8 *Traffic displayed by protocol type*

wireless network traffic. A hardware-based protocol analyzer represents a significant investment, with costs ranging from $10,000 to $30,000.

Protocol analyzers offer a great deal of versatility in the type and depth of information they can reveal. The danger in using this type of tool is that it may collect more information than you or the machine can reasonably process, thus rendering your exercise futile. To avoid this problem, you should set filters on the data gathered. For example, if you suspect that a certain workstation is causing a traffic problem, you should filter the data collection to accept only frames to or from that workstation's MAC address. If you suspect that you have a gateway-related TCP/IP problem, you would set a filter to capture only TCP/IP frames and to ignore other protocols from the gateway's MAC address.

Before using a network monitor or protocol analyzer on a network, it's important to know what traffic on your network normally looks like. To obtain this information, you can run the program and capture data for a period of time on a regular basis—for example, every weekday between 8:00 A.M. and noon. You'll generate a lot of data, but you'll also learn a lot about your network. From this data, you can establish a baseline to use as a comparison with future traffic analyses.

NET+
4.2
4.8

 NOTE

Recall that using a switch logically separates a network into different segments. If a network is fully switched (that is, if every node is connected to its own switch port), your protocol analyzer can capture only frames destined for the port to which your node is connected. The increasing use of switches has made network monitoring more difficult, but not impossible. One solution to this problem is to reconfigure the switch to reroute the traffic so that your network analyzer can pick up all traffic. Obviously, you would want to weigh the disruptive effects of this reconfiguration against the potential benefits from being able to analyze the network traffic and solve a problem.

NET+
4.8

Wireless Network Testers

Cable continuity testers and performance testers, of course, will tell you nothing about the wireless connections, stations, or APs (access points) on a network. For that, you need tools that contain wireless NICs and run wireless protocols. In fact, you can learn some things about a wireless environment by viewing the wireless network connection properties on your workstation. For example, after establishing a wireless connection in Windows XP, right-click the wireless connection icon in your system tray, and then click Status in the shortcut menu. The Wireless Network Connection Status dialog box opens. The General tab in this dialog box shows you the duration of your connection, the speed and strength of your signal, and the number of packets that have been exchanged, as shown in Figure 12-9.

However, viewing the status of the wireless connection on your workstation tells you only a little about your wireless environment—and this information only applies to one workstation. Many programs exist that can scan for wireless signals over a certain geographical range

FIGURE 12-9 *Wireless Network Connection Status dialog box*

and discover all the APs and wireless stations transmitting in the area. This is useful for determining whether an AP is functioning properly, whether it is positioned correctly so that all the stations it serves are within its range, and whether stations and APs are communicating over the proper channels within a frequency band. Some programs can also capture the data transmitted between stations and APs. This information is useful for troubleshooting wireless connection problems (for example, poor performance or intermittent faults) after you've verified that connectivity is present. And some programs contain a **spectrum analyzer**, a tool that can assess the quality of the wireless signal. Spectrum analysis is useful, for example, to ascertain where noise (or interference) is greatest.

Software that can perform wireless network assessment is often available for free and may be provided by the AP's manufacturer. Following is a list of specific capabilities common to wireless network testing tools:

◆ Identify transmitting APs and stations and the channels over which they are communicating

◆ Measure signal strength from and determine the range of an access point

◆ Indicate the effects of attenuation, signal loss, and noise

◆ Interpret signal strength information to rate potential AP locations (from "very good" to "poor")

◆ Ensure proper association and reassociation when moving between APs

◆ Capture and interpret traffic exchanged between wireless APs and stations

◆ Measure throughput and assess data transmission errors

◆ Analyze the characteristics of each channel within a frequency band to indicate the clearest channels

Some companies have created testing instruments whose sole purpose is to assess the status of wireless networks. These tools can perform the same detection, data capture, and spectrum analysis functions as the software tools described previously. One advantage to using such devices, however, is that they are typically more portable than a laptop or desktop workstation. Second, they come installed with all the wireless network analysis tools you'll need, and these are usually accessible from one simple, graphical interface. A third advantage is that most wireless testing tools contain more powerful antennas than a workstation NIC. A more powerful antenna could mean the difference between assessing the wireless network for an entire building from your desk versus walking around to each floor with your laptop. Figure 12-10 shows one example of such a wireless network testing tool.

 NOTE

Wireless testing tools—both software- and hardware-based—are not only used for troubleshooting, but are also critical for wireless **site selection**, or determining the optimal placement for APs on a wireless LAN.

NET+
4.8

FIGURE 12-10 *Wireless network testing tool*

Chapter Summary

◆ The key to solving network problems is to approach them methodically and logically, using your experience to inform your decisions, and knowing when to ask for someone else's help.

◆ The first step in troubleshooting is identifying the symptoms and potential causes for a problem. Symptoms may include error messages, the inability to perform certain functions on the network, or the inability to connect to a network. Record what you learn about symptoms.

◆ Next identify the affected area. In general, a network problem may be limited to one user; all users on a segment; all users on a network; certain types of users, departments, or locations; or certain times of the day or week.

◆ At each point in the troubleshooting process, stop to consider what kind of changes have occurred on the network that might have created a problem. Changes pertaining to hardware may include the addition of a new device, the removal of an old device, a component upgrade, a cabling upgrade, or an equipment move. Changes pertaining to software may include an operating system upgrade, a device driver upgrade, a new application, or a changed configuration.

◆ Based on an analysis of the symptoms and how changes might have affected the network, select a probable cause for the problem. First ensure that the user is performing all functions correctly, then attempt to reproduce the problem's symptoms, check the physical connectivity of clients and devices involved in the problem, and determine whether software and hardware are configured correctly.

◆ After you have identified the probable cause, implement an action plan and your solution, while considering the potential effects of the solution. Consider the number of users affected, costs, potential down time, and scalability of your solution. Collect documentation about the hardware or software configuration you are working with and keep this handy while implementing your solution.

◆ After implementing your solution, test your result to ensure that you solved the problem and haven't created new problems. The type of testing you perform will depend on your solution. Enlist the help of users to test the solution. If the solution required significant network changes, revisit the solution a day or two after you implement it to verify that it has truly worked and not caused additional problems.

◆ Next identify the effects and results of your solution. Verify that you have solved the problem you set out to solve and that you have not created any new problems inadvertently as a result.

◆ Finally, document the solution and the process of solving the problem. Some organizations use a software program for documenting problems, known as a call tracking system (or help desk software). These programs provide a user-friendly graphical interface that prompts the user for every piece of information associated with the problem.

◆ When troubleshooting, record the following details about a problem: the originator's name, department, and phone number; whether the problem is software- or hardware-related; if the problem is software-related, the package to which it pertains; if the problem is hardware-related, the device or component to which it pertains; the symptoms of the problem, including when it was first noticed; the name and telephone number of the network support contact; the amount of time spent troubleshooting the problem; and the resolution of the problem.

◆ A tone generator and tone locator are used to identify the terminating location of a wire pair. This combination of devices may also be known as a fox and hound.

◆ A multimeter is a simple device that can measure the voltage, resistance, impedance, and other characteristics of an electrical circuit.

◆ Basic cable continuity testers determine whether your cabling can provide connectivity. In the case of copper-based cables, they apply a small voltage to each conductor at one end of the cable, and then check whether that voltage is detectable at the other end. They may also verify that voltage cannot be detected on other conductors in the cable. A good cable checker will also verify that the wires are paired correctly and that they are not shorted, exposed, or crossed.

◆ A cable performance tester accomplishes the same continuity and fault tests as a continuity tester, but also ensures that the cable length is not too long, measures the distance to a cable fault, measures attenuation along a cable, measures near-end crosstalk between wires, measures termination resistance and impedance, issues pass/fail ratings for CAT 3, CAT 5, CAT 6, and CAT 7 standards, and stores and prints test results.

◆ A network monitor is a software-based tool that monitors network traffic from a server or workstation attached to the network. Network monitors typically can interpret up to Layer 3 of the OSI Model. They can determine the protocols passed by each packet, but can't interpret the data inside the packet.

◆ Network Monitor is the name of the network monitoring software that comes with Windows Server 2003 (and earlier versions of the Windows NOS). NETMON is the network monitoring NLM provided with the NetWare NOS. Many other types of network monitoring software are available.

◆ Protocol analyzers can typically interpret data up to Layer 7 of the OSI Model. They can also interpret the payload portion of packets, translating from binary or hexadecimal code to human-readable form. Protocol analyzers may be software programs or devices dedicated to protocol analysis.

◆ Wireless network testing tools can be dedicated instruments or software that runs on a workstation (usually a laptop). They can: discover wireless APs and stations, measure signal strength and interference, capture and interpret wireless data, measure throughput and identify data errors, and ensure proper association and reassociation between stations and APs.

Key Terms

baseline—A record of how a network operates under normal conditions (including its performance, collision rate, utilization rate, and so on). Baselines are used for comparison when conditions change.

cable checker—See *continuity tester*.

cable performance tester—A troubleshooting tool that tests cables for continuity, but can also measure crosstalk, attenuation, and impedance; identify the location of faults; and store or print cable testing results.

cable tester—A device that tests cables for one or more of the following conditions: continuity, segment length, distance to a fault, attenuation along a cable, near-end crosstalk, and termination resistance and impedance. Cable testers may also issue pass/fail ratings for wiring standards or store and print cable testing results.

call tracking system—A software program used to document technical problems and how they were resolved (also known as help desk software).

change management system—A process or program that provides support personnel with a centralized means of documenting changes made to the network.

continuity tester—An instrument that tests whether voltage (or light, in the case of fiber-optic cable) issued at one end of a cable can be detected at the opposite end of the cable. A continuity tester can indicate whether the cable will successfully transmit a signal.

fox and hound—Another term for the combination of devices known as a tone generator and a tone locator. The tone locator is considered the hound because it follows the tone generator (the fox).

ghost—A frame that is not actually a data frame, but rather an aberration caused by a device misinterpreting stray voltage on the wire. Unlike true data frames, ghosts have no starting delimiter.

giant—A packet that exceeds the medium's maximum packet size. For example, any Ethernet packet that is larger than 1518 bytes is considered a giant.

jabber—A device that handles electrical signals improperly, usually affecting the rest of the network. A network analyzer will detect a jabber as a device that is always retransmitting, effectively bringing the network to a halt. A jabber usually results from a bad NIC. Occasionally, it can be caused by outside electrical interference.

late collision—A collision that takes place outside the normal window in which collisions are detected and redressed. Late collisions are usually caused by a defective station (such as a card, or transceiver) that is transmitting without first verifying line status or by failure to observe the configuration guidelines for cable length, which results in collisions being recognized too late.

local collision—A collision that occurs when two or more stations are transmitting simultaneously. Excessively high collision rates within the network can usually be traced to cable or routing problems.

multimeter—A simple instrument that can measure multiple characteristics of an electric circuit, including its resistance and voltage.

negative frame sequence check—The result of the CRC (cyclic redundancy check) generated by the originating node not matching the checksum calculated from the data received. It usually indicates noise or transmission problems on the LAN interface or cabling. A high number of (nonmatching) CRCs usually results from excessive collisions or a station transmitting bad data.

NETMON—Novell's network monitoring NLM. NETMON is included in NetWare 5.x and 6.x.

network analyzer—See *protocol analyzer*.

network monitor—A software-based tool that monitors traffic on the network from a server or workstation attached to the network. Network monitors typically can interpret up to Layer 3 of the OSI Model.

Network Monitor—A network monitoring program that comes with Windows Server 2003 (as well as with Windows NT and Windows 2000 Server).

ohmmeter—A device used to measure resistance in an electrical circuit.

optical time domain reflectometer—See *OTDR*.

OTDR (optical time domain reflectometer)—A performance testing device for use with fiber-optic networks. An OTDR works by issuing a light-based signal on a fiber-optic cable and measuring the way in which the signal bounces back (or reflects) to the OTDR. By measuring the length of time it takes the signal to return, an OTDR can determine the location of a fault.

promiscuous mode—The feature of a network adapter that allows it to pick up all frames that pass over the network—not just those destined for the node served by the card.

protocol analyzer—A software package or hardware-based tool that can capture and analyze data on a network. Protocol analyzers are more sophisticated than network monitoring tools, as they can typically interpret data up to Layer 7 of the OSI Model.

runt—A packet that is smaller than the medium's minimum packet size. For instance, any Ethernet packet that is smaller than 64 bytes is considered a runt.

site selection—The process of determining optimal locations for access points on a wireless network.

spectrum analyzer—A tool that assesses the characteristics (for example, frequency, amplitude, and the effects of interference) of wireless signals.

supported services list—A document that lists every service and software package supported within an organization, plus the names of first- and second-level support contacts for those services or software packages.

TDR (time domain reflectometer)—A high-end instrument for testing the qualities of a cable. It works by issuing a signal on a cable and measuring the way in which the signal bounces back (or reflects) to the TDR. Many performance testers rely on TDRs.

time domain reflectometer—See *TDR*.

tone generator—A small electronic device that issues a signal on a wire pair. When used in conjunction with a tone locator, it can help locate the termination of a wire pair.

tone locator—A small electronic device that emits a tone when it detects electrical activity on a wire pair. When used in conjunction with a tone generator, it can help locate the termination of a wire pair.

voltmeter—A device used to measure voltage (or electrical pressure) on an electrical circuit.

Review Questions

1. _____ assign unique identifying numbers to each problem, in addition to identifying the caller, the nature of the problem, the time necessary to resolve it, and the nature of the resolution.

   a. Call tracking systems

   b. Jabbers

   c. NETMONs

   d. TDRs

2. A _____ is a software-based tool that continually monitors network traffic from a server or workstation attached to the network.

   a. change management system

   b. jabber

   c. network monitor

   d. call tracking system

3. A _____ is a record of how the network operates under normal conditions.

   a. ghost

   b. runt

   c. fox and hound

   d. baseline

4. Which of the following is a device that handles electrical signals improperly, usually affecting the rest of the network?

   a. Runt

   b. Ghost

   c. Jabber

   d. Giant

5. A _____ is a tool that can be used to assess the quality of a wireless signal.

   a. runt

   b. spectrum analyzer

   c. jabber

   d. protocol analyzer

6. True or false? The time frequency with which a problem occurs can reveal subtle network problems.

7. True or false? An excellent way to learn more about the causes of a problem is to recreate the symptoms.

8. True or false? Physical connectivity problems typically result in software application anomalies, the inability to use a single application, poor network performance, and software licensing errors.

9. True or false? Whether you are a one-person network support team or one of 100 network technicians, you should always record the symptoms and cause (or causes) of a problem and your solution.

10. True or false? Any Ethernet packet that is larger than 64 bytes is considered a runt.

11. A(n) _____ is a document that lists every service and software package supported within an organization, plus the names of first- and second-level support contacts for those services or software packages.

12. A(n) _____ is a process or program that provides support personnel with a centralized means of documenting changes to the network.

13. A(n) _____ cable is useful for quickly and easily verifying that a node's NIC is transmitting and receiving signals properly.

14. A(n) _____ is a device that emits a tone when it detects electrical activity on a wire pair.

15. Resistance is measured in _____.

Chapter 13

Ensuring Integrity and Availability

After reading this chapter and completing the exercises, you will be able to:

- Identify the characteristics of a network that keep data safe from loss or damage

- Protect an enterprise-wide network from viruses

- Explain network- and system-level fault-tolerance techniques

- Discuss issues related to network backup and recovery strategies

- Describe the components of a useful disaster recovery plan and the options for disaster contingencies

As networks take on more of the burden of transporting and storing a day's work, you must pay increasing attention to the risks involved. You can never assume that data is safe on the network until you have taken explicit measures to protect the information. In this book, you have learned about building scalable, reliable enterprise-wide networks as well as selecting the most appropriate hardware and network operating systems to operate your network. But all the best equipment and software cannot ensure that server hard drives will never fail or that a malicious employee won't sabotage your network.

Methods for protecting data evolve quickly as networks change and new threats, such as computer viruses, are released. This chapter provides a broad overview of measures that you can take to ensure that your data remain safe. The far-reaching topic of network security is covered in the next chapter.

What Are Integrity and Availability?

Before learning how to ensure integrity and availability, you should fully understand what these terms mean. **Integrity** refers to the soundness of a network's programs, data, services, devices, and connections. To ensure a network's integrity, you must protect it from anything that might render it unusable. Closely related to the concept of integrity is availability. **Availability** of a file or system refers to how consistently and reliably it can be accessed by authorized personnel. For example, a server that allows staff to log on and use its programs and data 99.99% of the time is considered to be highly available, whereas one that is functional only 98% of the time is less available. To ensure high availability, you need a well-planned and well-configured network, as well as data backups, redundant devices, and protection from malicious intruders who could potentially immobilize the network.

A number of phenomena may compromise both integrity and availability, including security breaches, natural disasters (such as tornadoes, floods, hurricanes, and ice storms), malicious intruders, power flaws, and human error. Every network administrator should consider these possibilities when designing a sound network. You can readily imagine the importance of integrity and availability of data in a hospital, for example, in which the network stores patient records and also provides quick medical reference material, video displays for surgical cameras, and perhaps even control of critical care monitors.

If you have ever supported computer users, you know that they sometimes unintentionally harm data, applications, software configurations, or even hardware. Networks may also be intentionally harmed by users unless network administrators take precautionary measures and pay regular, close attention to systems and networks so as to protect them. This section reminds you of commonsense approaches to data integrity and availability. Later in this chapter, you will learn about more specific or formal (and potentially more expensive) approaches to data protection.

NET+
3.11

Although you can't predict every type of vulnerability, you can take measures to guard against most damaging events. Following are some general guidelines for protecting your network:

◆ *Allow only network administrators to create or modify NOS and application system files.* Pay attention to the rights assigned to regular users (including the groups "users" or "everyone" and the user name "guest"). Bear in mind that the worst consequence of applying overly stringent file restrictions is an inconvenience to users. In contrast, the worst consequence of applying overly lenient file restrictions could be a failed network.

◆ *Monitor the network for unauthorized access or changes.* You can install programs that routinely check whether and when the files you've specified (for example, server.exe on a NetWare server) have changed. Such monitoring programs are typically inexpensive and easy to customize. They may even enable the system to page or e-mail you when a system file changes.

◆ *Record authorized system changes in a change management system.* You have learned about the importance of change management when troubleshooting networks. Routine changes should also be documented in a change management system. Recording system changes enables you and your colleagues to understand what's happening to your network and protect it from harm. For example, suppose that the remote access service on a Linux server has stopped accepting connections. Before taking troubleshooting steps that may create more problems and further reduce the availability of the system, you could review the change management log. It might indicate that a colleague recently installed an update to the Linux NOS. With this information in hand, you could focus on the update as a likely source of the problem.

◆ *Install redundant components.* The term **redundancy** refers to an implementation in which more than one component is installed and ready to use for storing, processing, or transporting data. Redundancy is intended to eliminate single points of failure. To maintain high availability, you should ensure that critical network elements, such as your connection to the Internet or your file server's hard disk, are redundant. Some types of redundancy—for example, redundant sources of electrical power for a building—require large investments, so your organization should weigh the risks of losing connectivity or data against the cost of adding duplicate components.

◆ *Perform regular health checks on the network.* Prevention is the best weapon against network downtime. By establishing a baseline and regular network monitoring, you can anticipate problems before they affect availability or integrity. For example, if your network monitor alerts you to rapidly rising utilization on a critical network segment, you can analyze the network to discover where the problem lies and perhaps fix it before it takes down the segment.

◆ *Check system performance, error logs, and the system log book regularly.* By keeping track of system errors and trends in performance, you have a better chance of correcting problems before they cause a hard disk failure and potentially damage your system files. By default, all NOSs keep error logs (on a Linux server, for example, a file

NET+
3.11

called "messages" located in the /var/log directory collects error messages from system services, such as DNS, and other programs also save log files in the /var/log directory). It's important that you know where these error logs reside on your server and understand how to interpret them.

◆ *Keep backups, boot disks, and emergency repair disks current and available.* If your file system or critical boot files become corrupted by a system crash, you can use the emergency or boot disks to recover the system. Otherwise, you may need to reinstall the software before you can start the system. If you ever face the situation of recovering from a system loss or disaster, you must recover in the quickest manner possible. For this effort, you need backup devices and also a backup strategy tailored to your environment.

◆ *Implement and enforce security and disaster recovery policies.* Everyone in your organization should know what she is allowed to do on the network. For example, if you decide that it's too risky for employees to download games off the Internet because of the potential for virus infection, you should inform them of a ban on downloading games. You might enforce this policy by restricting users' ability to create or change files (such as executable files) that are copied to the workstation during the downloading of games. Making such decisions and communicating them to staff should be part of your IT policy. Likewise, key personnel in your organization should be familiar with your disaster recovery plan, which should detail your strategy for restoring network functionality in case of an unexpected failure. Although such policies take time to develop and may be difficult to enforce, they can directly affect your network's availability and integrity.

These measures are merely first steps to ensuring network integrity and availability, but they are essential. The following sections describe what types of policies, hardware, and software you can implement to achieve availability and integrity, beginning with virus detection and prevention.

Viruses

NET+
3.10

Strictly speaking, a **virus** is a program that replicates itself with the intent to infect more computers, either through network connections or through the exchange of external storage devices (such as floppy disks, CD-ROMs, or CompactFlash cards). Viruses are typically copied to a computer's storage device without the user's knowledge. A virus may damage files or systems, or it may simply annoy users by flashing messages or pictures on the screen or by causing the computer to beep. In fact, some viruses cause no harm and can remain unnoticed on a system indefinitely.

Many other unwanted and potentially destructive programs are called viruses, but technically do not meet the criteria used to define a virus. For example, a program that disguises itself as something useful but actually harms your system is called a **Trojan horse** (or simply, **Trojan**), after the famous wooden horse in which soldiers were hidden. Because Trojan horses do not replicate themselves, they are not considered viruses. An example of a Trojan horse is an executable file that someone

NET+
3.10

sends you over the Internet, promising that the executable will install a great new game, when in fact it erases data on your hard disk or mails spam to all the users in your e-mail program's address book.

In this section, you will learn about the different viruses and other malicious programs that may infect your network, their methods of distribution, and, most important, protection against them. Viruses can infect computers running any type of operating system—Macintosh, Net-Ware, Windows, Linux, or UNIX—at any time. As a network administrator, you must take measures to guard against them.

Types of Viruses

Many thousands of viruses exist, although only a relatively small number cause the majority of virus-related damage. Viruses can be classified into different categories based on where they reside on a computer and how they propagate themselves. Often, creators of viruses apply slight variations to existing viruses to make their version undetectable by antivirus programs. The result is a host of related, albeit different, viruses. The makers of antivirus software must then update their programs to recognize the new variations, and the virus creators may again alter their viruses to render them undetectable. This cycle continues, ad infinitum. No matter what their variation, all viruses belong to one of the following categories:

◆ *Boot sector viruses*—**Boot sector viruses** position their code in the boot sector of a computer's hard disk so that when the computer boots up, the virus runs in place of the computer's normal system files. Boot sector viruses are commonly spread from external storage devices to hard disks. This may happen, for example, if a floppy disk is left in the drive when a computer boots up and the computer is configured to boot first from a floppy disk when a floppy disk is present (rather than from the hard disk). Boot sector viruses vary in their destructiveness. Some merely display a screen advertising the virus's presence when you boot the infected computer. Others do not advertise themselves, but stealthily destroy system files or make it impossible for the file system to access at least some of the computer's files. Examples of boot sector viruses include "POLYBOOT-B" (also known as "WYX.B" or "WYX-B"), "Michelangelo," and the "Stoned" virus, which was widespread in the early 1990s (in fact, it disabled U.S. military computers during the 1991 Persian Gulf War), and persists today in many variations. Until you disinfect a computer that harbors a boot sector virus, the virus propagates to every external disk to which that computer writes information. Removing a boot sector virus first requires rebooting the computer from an uninfected, write-protected disk with system files on it. Only after the computer is booted from a source other than the infected hard disk can you run software to remove the boot sector virus.

◆ *Macro viruses*—**Macro viruses** take the form of a macro (such as the kind used in a word processing or spreadsheet program), which may be executed as the user works with a program. For example, you might send a WordPerfect document as an attachment to an e-mail message. If that document contains a macro virus, when the recipient opens the document, the macro runs, and all future documents created or saved by that program are infected. Macro viruses were the first type of virus to infect data files rather than executable files. They are quick to emerge and spread because they are easy to write, and because users share data files more frequently than executable files. Although the earliest versions of macro viruses were annoying but not harmful, currently circulating macro viruses may threaten data files. Examples of macro viruses include "Corner.A" and its variants, "Jerk.A" and its variants, and "Tristate.A" and its variants. Symptoms of macro virus infection vary widely but may include missing options from application menus; damaged, changed, or missing data files; or strange pop-up messages that appear when you use an application.

◆ *File-infected viruses*—**File-infected viruses** attach themselves to executable files. When an infected executable file runs, the virus copies itself to memory. Later, the virus attaches itself to other executable files. Some file-infected viruses attach themselves to other programs even while their "host" executable runs a process in the background, such as a printer service or screen saver program. Because they stay in memory while you continue to work on your computer, these viruses can have devastating consequences, infecting numerous programs and requiring that you disinfect your computer, as well as reinstall virtually all software. Symptoms of virus infection may include damaged program files, inexplicable file size increases, changed icons for programs, strange messages that appear when you attempt to run a program, or the inability to run a program. Examples of file-infected viruses include "Vacsina" and "WoodGoblin" (both of which are dangerous because they overwrite files on a computer's hard disk), and "Harmony.A," which is harmless but increases the size of and adds a message to all executable files on a hard disk installed with a Windows operating system.

◆ *Worms*—**Worms** are not technically viruses, but rather programs that run independently and travel between computers and across networks. They may be transmitted by any type of file transfer, including e-mail attachments. Worms do not alter other programs in the same way that viruses do, but they may carry viruses. Because they can transport (and hide) viruses, you should be concerned about picking up worms when you exchange files from the Internet, via e-mail, or through disks. Examples of worms include W32/Klez (and its variants), which spreads via e-mail attachments, and W32Lovesan.worm, which spreads through unprotected TCP and UDP ports on Windows computers when a user is connected to a network. Symptoms of worm infection may include almost any type of anomaly, ranging from strange pop-up messages to file damage.

◆ *Trojan horse*—As mentioned earlier, a Trojan horse (or Trojan) is not actually a virus, but rather a program that claims to do something useful but instead harms the computer or system. Trojan horses range from being nuisances to causing significant system destruction. Virus detection programs recognize known Trojan horses and eradicate them. Examples of Trojan Horses include JS/NoClose, which runs a JavaScript routine to generate HTML windows or applications that the user cannot close, and "Helvis," which collects all the e-mails in a user's inbox and outbox and sends them to an address associated with the virus writer. The best way to guard

NET+
3.10

against Trojan horses is to refrain from downloading an executable file whose origins you can't confirm. Suppose, for example, that you needed to download a new driver for a NIC on your network. Rather than going to a generic "network support site" on the Internet, you should download the file from the NIC manufacturer's Web site. Most important, never run an executable file that was sent to you over the Internet as an attachment to a mail message whose sender or origins you cannot verify.

◆ *Network viruses*—**Network viruses** propagate themselves via network protocols, commands, messaging programs, and data links. Although all viruses can theoretically travel across network connections, network viruses are specially designed to take advantage of network vulnerabilities. For example, a network virus may attach itself to FTP transactions to and from your Web server. Another type of network virus may spread through Microsoft Outlook messages only. Because network viruses are characterized by their transmission method, their symptoms may include almost any type of anomaly, ranging from strange pop-up messages to file damage.

◆ *Bots*—Another virus category defined by its propagation method is a bot. In networking, the term **bot** (short for robot) means a program that runs automatically, without requiring a person to start or stop it. One type of bot is a virus that propagates itself automatically between systems. It does not require an unsuspecting user to download and run an executable file or to boot from an infected disk, for example. Many bots spread through the **IRC (Internet Relay Chat)**, a protocol that enables users running IRC client software to communicate instantly with other participants in a chat room on the Internet. Chat rooms require an IRC server, which accepts messages from an IRC client and either broadcasts the messages to all other chat room participants (in an open chat room) or sends the message to select users (in a restricted chat room). Virus bots take advantage of IRC to transmit data, commands, or executable programs from one infected participant to others. (Consequently, a virus-spreading bot can also be considered a worm or Trojan.) After a bot has copied files on a client's hard disk, these files can be used to damage or destroy a computer's data or system files, issue objectionable content, and further propagate the virus. Bots are especially difficult to contain because of their fast, surreptitious, and distributed dissemination.

Virus Characteristics

Viruses that belong to any of the preceding categories may have additional characteristics that make them harder to detect and eliminate. Some of these characteristics include the following:

◆ *Encryption*—Some viruses are encrypted to prevent detection. Most virus-scanning software searches files for a recognizable string of characters that identify the virus. However, an encrypted virus may thwart the antivirus program's attempts to detect it.

◆ *Stealth*—Some viruses hide themselves to prevent detection. Typically, **stealth viruses** disguise themselves as legitimate programs or replace part of a legitimate program's code with their destructive code.

◆ *Polymorphism*—**Polymorphic viruses** change their characteristics (such as the arrangement of their bytes, size, and internal instructions) every time they are transferred to a new system, making them harder to identify. Some polymorphic viruses use complicated algorithms and incorporate nonsensical commands to achieve their changes. Polymorphic viruses are considered the most sophisticated and potentially dangerous type of virus.

◆ *Time-dependence*—**Time-dependent viruses** are programmed to activate on a particular date. These types of viruses, also known as "time bombs," can remain dormant and harmless until their activation date arrives. Like any other virus, time-dependent viruses may have destructive effects or may cause some innocuous event periodically. For example, viruses in the "Time" family cause a PC's speaker to beep approximately once per hour.

A virus may exhibit more than one of the preceding characteristics. The "Natas" virus, for example, combines polymorphism and stealth techniques to create a very destructive virus.

Hundreds of new viruses are unleashed on the world's computers each month. Although it is impossible to keep abreast of every virus in circulation, you should at least know where you can find out more information about viruses. An excellent resource for learning about new viruses, their characteristics, and ways to get rid of them is McAfee's Virus Information Library at *us.mcafee.com/virusInfo/default.asp*.

Virus Protection

You may think that you can simply install a virus-scanning program on your network and move to the next issue. In fact, virus protection involves more than just installing antivirus software. It requires choosing the most appropriate antivirus program for your environment, monitoring the network, continually updating the antivirus program, and educating users.

Antivirus Software

Even if a user doesn't immediately notice a virus on her system, the virus generally leaves evidence of itself, whether by changing the operation of the machine or by announcing its signature characteristics in the virus code. Although the latter can be detected only via antivirus software, users can typically detect the operational changes without any special software. For example, you may suspect a virus on your system if any of the following symptoms appear:

◆ Unexplained increases in file sizes

◆ Significant, unexplained decline in system performance (for example, a program takes much longer than usual to launch or to save a file)

◆ Unusual error messages appearing without probable cause

◆ Significant, unexpected loss of system memory

◆ Periodic, unexpected rebooting

◆ Fluctuations in display quality

NET+
3.10

Often, however, you don't notice a virus until it has already damaged your files.

Although virus programmers have become more sophisticated in disguising their viruses (for example, using encryption and polymorphism), antivirus software programmers have kept pace with them. The antivirus software you choose for your network should at least perform the following functions:

◆ Detect viruses through **signature scanning**, a comparison of a file's content with known virus signatures (that is, the unique identifying characteristics in the code) in a signature database. This signature database must be frequently updated so that the software can detect new viruses as they emerge. Updates can be downloaded from the antivirus software vendor's Web site. Alternatively, you can configure such updates to be copied from the Internet to your computer automatically, with or without your consent.

◆ Detect viruses through **integrity checking**, a method of comparing current characteristics of files and disks against an archived version of these characteristics to discover any changes. The most common example of integrity checking involves using a checksum, though this tactic may not prove effective against viruses with stealth capabilities.

◆ Detect viruses by monitoring unexpected file changes or virus-like behaviors.

◆ Receive regular updates and modifications from a centralized network console. The vendor should provide free upgrades on a regular (at least monthly) basis, plus technical support.

◆ Consistently report only valid viruses, rather than reporting "false alarms." Scanning techniques that attempt to identify viruses by discovering "virus-like" behavior, also known as **heuristic scanning**, are the most fallible and most likely to emit false alarms. On the other hand, heuristic scanning successfully detected the "SoBig" worm that affected thousands of users in 2003 before the worm could be added to vendors' signature databases. Heuristic scanning worked in this case because of the way "SoBig" propagated itself.

 NOTE

Occasionally, shrink-wrapped, off-the-shelf software ships with viruses on its disks. Therefore, it is always a good idea to scan authorized software from known sources just as you would scan software from unknown sources.

Your implementation of antivirus software depends on your computing environment's needs. For example, you may use a desktop security program on every computer on the network that prevents users from copying executable files to their hard disks or to network drives. In this case, it may be unnecessary to implement a program that continually scans each machine; in fact, this approach may be undesirable because the continual scanning adversely impacts performance. On the other hand, if you are the network administrator for a student computer lab

NET+
3.10

where potentially thousands of different users bring their own disks for use on the computers, you will want to scan the machines thoroughly at least once a day and perhaps more often.

When implementing antivirus software on a network, one of your most important decisions is where to install the software. If you install antivirus software only on every desktop, you have addressed the most likely point of entry, but ignored the most important files that might be infected—those on the server. If the antivirus software resides on the server and checks every file and transaction, you will protect important files but slow your network performance considerably. To find a balance between sufficient protection and minimal impact on performance, you must examine your network's vulnerabilities and critical performance needs.

Obviously, the antivirus package you choose should be compatible with your network and desktop operating systems. Popular antivirus packages include F-Secure's Anti-Virus, McAfee's VirusScan, Computer Associates' eTrust Antivirus Scanner, Trend Micro's PC-cillin, and Symantec's (Norton's) AntiVirus.

 NOTE

In addition to using specialized antivirus software to guard against virus infection, you may find that your applications can help identify viruses. Microsoft Word and Excel programs, for example, warn you when you attempt to open a file that contains macros. You then have the option of disabling the macros (thereby preventing any macro viruses from working when you open the file) or allowing the macros to remain usable. In general, it's a good idea to disable the macros in a file that you have received from someone else, at least until after you have checked the file for viruses with your virus scanning software.

Antivirus Policies

Antivirus software alone will not keep your network safe from viruses. Because most computer viruses can be prevented by applying a little technology and forethought, it's important that all network users understand how to prevent viruses. An antivirus policy provides rules for using antivirus software and policies for installing programs, sharing files, and using floppy disks. To be most effective, it should be authorized and supported by the organization's management. Suggestions for antivirus policy guidelines include the following:

◆ Every computer in an organization should be equipped with virus detection and cleaning software that regularly scans for viruses. This software should be centrally distributed and updated to stay current with newly released viruses.

◆ Users should not be allowed to alter or disable the antivirus software.

◆ Users should know what to do in case their antivirus program detects a virus. For example, you might recommend that the user stop working on his computer, and instead call the help desk to receive assistance in disinfecting the system.

NET+
3.10

◆ An antivirus team should be appointed to focus on maintaining the antivirus measures. This team would be responsible for choosing antivirus software, keeping the software updated, educating users, and responding in case of a significant virus outbreak.

◆ Users should be prohibited from installing any unauthorized software on their systems. This edict may seem extreme, but in fact users downloading programs (especially games) from the Internet are a common source of viruses. If your organization permits game playing, you might institute a policy in which every game must be first checked for viruses and then installed on a user's system by a technician.

◆ Systemwide alerts should be issued to network users notifying them of a serious virus threat and advising them how to prevent infection, even if the virus hasn't been detected on your network yet.

When drafting an antivirus policy, bear in mind that these measures are not meant to restrict users' freedom, but rather to protect the network from damage and downtime. Explain to users that the antivirus policy protects their own data as well as critical system files. If possible, automate the antivirus software installation and operation so that users barely notice its presence. Do not rely on users to run their antivirus software each time they insert a disk or download a new program, because they will quickly forget to do so.

Virus Hoaxes

As in any other community, rumors spread through the Internet user community. One type of rumor consists of a false alert about a dangerous, new virus that could cause serious damage to your workstation. Such an alert is known as a **virus hoax**. Virus hoaxes usually have no realistic basis and should be ignored, as they merely attempt to create panic. Virus hoaxes also typically demand that you pass the alert to everyone in your Internet address book, thus propagating the rumor. However, virus hoaxes should not be passed on. If you receive a message that you suspect is a virus hoax, you can confirm your suspicion by looking up the message on a Web page that lists virus hoaxes. A good resource for verifying virus hoaxes is *www.icsalabs.com/html/communities/antivirus/hoaxes.shtml.* This Web site also teaches you more about the phenomenon of virus hoaxes.

If you receive a virus hoax, simply ignore it. Educate your colleagues to do the same, explaining why virus hoaxes should not cause alarm. Remember, however, that even a virus hoax message could potentially contain an *attached* file that does cause damage if executed. Once again, the best policy is to refrain from running any program whose origins you cannot verify.

Fault Tolerance

NET+
3.11

Besides guarding against viruses, another key factor in maintaining the availability and integrity of data is fault tolerance. You have learned that fault tolerance is the capacity for a system to continue performing despite an unexpected hardware or software malfunction. To better understand the issues related to fault tolerance, you must recognize the difference between failures and faults as they apply to networks. In broad terms, a **failure** is a deviation from a specified level of system performance for a given period of time. In other words, a failure occurs when something doesn't work as promised or as planned. For example, if your car breaks down on the highway, you can consider the breakdown to be a failure. A **fault**, on the other hand, involves the malfunction of one component of a system. A fault can result in a failure. For example, the fault that caused your car to break down might be a leaking water pump. The goal of fault-tolerant systems is to prevent faults from progressing to failures.

Fault tolerance can be realized in varying degrees; the optimal level of fault tolerance for a system depends on how critical its services and files are to productivity. At the highest level of fault tolerance, a system remains unaffected by even the most drastic problem, such as a regional power outage. In this case, a backup power source, such as an electrical generator, is necessary to ensure fault tolerance. However, less dramatic faults, such as a malfunctioning NIC on a router, can still cause network outages, and you should guard against them.

The following sections describe network aspects that must be monitored and managed to ensure fault tolerance.

Environment

As you consider sophisticated fault-tolerance techniques for servers, routers, and WAN links, remember to analyze the physical environment in which your devices operate. Part of your data protection plan involves protecting your network from excessive heat or moisture, break-ins, and natural disasters. For example, you should make sure that your telecommunications closets and equipment rooms have locked doors and are air-conditioned and maintained at a constant humidity, according to the hardware manufacturer's recommendations. You can purchase temperature and humidity monitors that trip alarms if specified limits are exceeded. These monitors can prove very useful because the temperature can rise rapidly in a room full of equipment, causing overheated equipment to function poorly or fail outright.

Power

No matter where you live, you have probably experienced a complete loss of power (a blackout) or a temporary dimming of lights (a brownout). Such fluctuations in power are frequently caused by forces of nature, such as hurricanes, tornadoes, or ice storms. They may also occur when a utility company performs maintenance or construction tasks. The following section describes the types of power fluctuations for which network administrators should prepare. The next two sections describe alternate power sources, such as a UPS (uninterruptible power supply) or an electrical generator, that can compensate for power loss.

Power Flaws

Whatever the cause, power loss or less than optimal power cannot be tolerated by networks. The following list describes power flaws that can damage your equipment:

◆ *Surge*—A momentary increase in voltage due to lightning strikes, solar flares, or electrical problems. Surges may last only a few thousandths of a second, but can degrade a computer's power supply. Surges are common. You can guard against surges by making sure every computer device is plugged into a **surge protector**, which redirects excess voltage away from the device to a ground, thereby protecting the device from harm. Without surge protectors, systems would be subjected to multiple surges each year.

◆ *Noise*—A fluctuation in voltage levels caused by other devices on the network or electromagnetic interference. Some noise is unavoidable on an electrical circuit, but excessive noise may cause a power supply to malfunction, immediately corrupting program or data files and gradually damaging motherboards and other computer circuits. When you turn on fluorescent lights or a laser printer and the lights dim, you have probably introduced noise into the electrical system. Power that is free from noise is called "clean" power. To make sure power is clean, a circuit must pass through an electrical filter.

◆ *Brownout*—A momentary decrease in voltage; also known as a **sag**. An overtaxed electrical system may cause brownouts, which you may recognize in your home as a dimming of the lights. Such decreases in voltage can cause significant problems for computer devices.

◆ *Blackout*—A complete power loss. A blackout may or may not cause significant damage to your network. For example, if you are performing an NOS upgrade when a blackout occurs and you have not protected the server, its NOS may be damaged so completely that the server cannot restart and its operating system must be reinstalled from scratch. If the file server is idle when a blackout occurs, however, it may recover very easily.

Each of these power problems can adversely affect network devices and their availability. It is not surprising then, that network administrators must spend a great deal of money and time ensuring that power remains available and problem-free. The following sections describe devices and ways of dealing with unstable power.

UPSs (Uninterruptible Power Supplies)

A popular way to ensure that a network device does not lose power is to install a **UPS (uninterruptible power supply)**. A UPS is a battery-operated power source directly attached to one or more devices and to a power supply (such as a wall outlet), which prevents undesired features of the wall outlet's A/C power from harming the device or interrupting its services.

UPSs vary widely in the type of power aberrations they can rectify, the length of time for which they can provide power, and the number of devices they can support. Of course, they also vary widely in price. Some UPSs are intended for home use, designed merely to keep your workstation running long enough for you to properly shut it down in case of a blackout. Other UPSs perform sophisticated operations such as line filtering, or conditioning (which includes the elimination of noise to ensure clean power), power supply monitoring, and error notification. The type of UPS you choose depends on your budget, the number and size of your systems, and the critical nature of those systems.

UPSs are classified into two general categories: standby and online. A **standby UPS** provides continuous voltage to a device by switching virtually instantaneously to the battery when it detects a loss of power from the wall outlet. Upon restoration of the power, the standby UPS switches the device back to A/C power. The problem with standby UPSs is that, in the brief amount of time that it takes the UPS to discover that power from the wall outlet has faltered, a device may have already detected the power loss and shut down or restarted. Technically, a standby UPS doesn't provide continuous power; for this reason, it is sometimes called an **offline UPS**. Nevertheless, standby UPSs may prove adequate even for critical network devices, such as servers, routers, and gateways. They cost significantly less than online UPSs.

An **online UPS** uses the A/C power from the wall outlet to continuously charge its battery, while providing power to a network device through its battery. In other words, a server connected to an online UPS always relies on the UPS battery for its electricity. Because the server never needs to switch from the wall outlet's power to the UPS's power, there is no risk of momentarily losing service. Also, because the UPS always provides the power, it can handle noise, surges, and sags before the power reaches the attached device. As you can imagine, online UPSs are more expensive than standby UPSs. Figure 13-1 shows standby and online UPSs.

FIGURE 13-1 *Standby and online UPSs*

How do you decide which UPS is right for your network? Consider a number of factors:

◆ *Amount of power needed*—The more power required by your device, the more power-ful the UPS must be. Suppose that your organization decides to cut costs and pur-chase a UPS that cannot supply the amount of power required by a device. If the power to your building ever fails, this UPS will not support your device—you might as well not have any UPS.

Electrical power is measured in volt-amps. A **volt-amp (VA)** is the product of the voltage and current (measured in amps) of the electricity on a line. To determine approximately how many VAs your device requires, you can use the following conversion: 1.4 volt-amps = 1 watt (W). A desktop computer, for example, may use a 200 W power supply, and therefore require a UPS capable of at least 280 VA to keep the CPU running in case of a blackout. If you want backup power for your entire home office, however, you must account for the power needs for your monitor and any peripherals, such as printers, when purchasing a UPS. A medium-sized server with a monitor and external tape drive may use 402 W, thus requiring a UPS capable of providing at least 562 VA power. Determin-ing your power needs can be a challenge. You must account for your existing equipment and consider how you might upgrade the supported device(s) over the next several years. You may want to consult with your equipment manufacturer to obtain recommendations on power needs.

◆ *Period of time to keep a device running*—The longer you anticipate needing a UPS to power your device, the more powerful your UPS must be. For example, the medium-sized server that relies on a 574 VA UPS to remain functional for 20 minutes needs a 1100 VA UPS to remain functional for 90 minutes. To determine how long your device might require power from a UPS, research the length of typical power out-ages in your area.

◆ *Line conditioning*—A UPS should also offer surge suppression to protect against surges and line conditioning, or filtering, to guard against line noise. Line condition-ers and UPS units include special noise filters that remove line noise. The manufac-turer's technical specifications should indicate the amount of filtration required for each UPS. Noise suppression is expressed in decibel levels (dB) at a specific fre-quency (KHz or MHz). The higher the decibel level, the greater the protection.

◆ *Cost*—Prices for good UPSs vary widely, depending on the unit's size and extra fea-tures. A relatively small UPS that can power one server for five to ten minutes might cost between $100 and $300. A large UPS that can power a sophisticated router for three hours might cost between $200 and $3000. Still larger UPSs, which can power an entire data center for several hours, can cost hundreds of thousands of dollars. On a critical system, you should not try to cut costs by buying an off-brand, potentially unreliable, or weak UPS.

NET+
3.11

As with other large purchases, research several UPS manufacturers and their products before reaching a decision. Also ensure that the manufacturer provides a warranty and lets you test the UPS with your equipment. Testing UPSs with your equipment is an important part of the decision-making process. Popular UPS manufacturers are APC, Deltec, MGE, Powerware, and Tripp Lite.

Generators

If your organization cannot withstand a power loss of any duration, either because of its computer services or other electrical needs, you might consider investing in an electrical generator for your building. Generators can be powered by diesel, liquid propane gas, natural gas, or steam. They do not provide surge protection, but they do provide electricity that's free from noise. In highly available environments, such as an ISP's or telecommunications carrier's data center, generators are common. In fact, in those environments, they are typically combined with large UPSs to ensure that clean power is always available. In the event of a power failure, the UPS supplies electricity until the generator starts and reaches its full capacity, typically no more than three minutes. If your organization relies on a generator for backup power, be certain to check fuel levels and quality regularly. Figure 13-2 illustrates the power infrastructure of a network (such as a data center's) that uses both a generator and dual UPSs.

When choosing a generator, you should calculate your organization's crucial electrical demands to determine the generator's optimal size. Also estimate how long the generator may be required to power your building. Depending on the amount of power draw, a high-capacity generator can supply power for several days. Gas or diesel generators may cost between $10,000 and $3,000,000 (for the largest industrial types). For a company such as a network service provider that stands to lose up to $1,000,000 per minute if its data facilities fail completely, a multi-million-dollar investment to ensure available power is a wise choice. Smaller businesses, however, might choose the more economical solution of renting an electrical generator. To find out more about options for renting or purchasing generators in your area, contact your local electrical utility.

Topology and Connectivity

You read about topology and architecture fault tolerance in previous chapters of this book. Recall that each physical topology inherently assumes certain advantages and disadvantages, and you need to assess your network's needs before designing your data links.

The key to fault tolerance in network design is supplying multiple paths data can use to travel from any one point to another. Therefore, if one connection fails, data can be rerouted over an alternate path. On a LAN, a star topology and a parallel backbone provide the greatest fault tolerance. On a WAN, a full mesh topology offers the best fault tolerance. A partial mesh topology offers some redundancy, but is not as fault-tolerant as a full mesh WAN, because it offers fewer alternate routes for data. Refer to Figure 7-5 to refresh your memory on the comparison between partial mesh and full mesh WAN topologies.

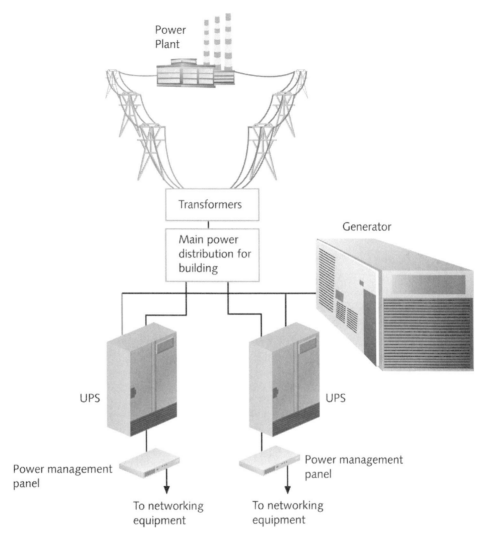

FIGURE 13-2 *UPSs and a generator in a network design*

Another highly fault-tolerant network is one based on SONET technology, which relies on a dual, fiber-optic ring for its transmission. Recall that because it uses two fiber rings for every connection, a SONET network can easily recover from a fault in one of its links. Refer to Figure 7-18 to refresh your memory on SONET's dual-ring topology.

Mesh topologies and SONET rings are good choices for highly available enterprise networks. But what about connections to the Internet or data backup connections? You may need to establish more than one of these links.

NET+
3.11

As an example, imagine that you work for a data services firm called PayNTime that processes payroll checks for a large oil company in the Houston area. Every day, you receive updated payroll information over a T1 link from your client, and every Thursday you compile this information and then cut 2000 checks that you ship overnight to the client's headquarters. What would happen if the T1 link between PayNTime and the oil company suffered damage in a flood and became unusable on a Thursday morning? How would you ensure that the employees received their pay? If no redundant link to the oil company existed, you would probably need to gather and input the data into your system at least partially by hand. Even then, chances are that you wouldn't process the payroll checks in time to be shipped overnight.

In this type of situation, you would want a duplicate connection between PayNTime and the oil company's site for redundancy. You might contract with two different service carriers to ensure the redundancy. Alternatively, you might arrange with one service carrier to provide two different routes. However you provide redundancy in your network topology, you should make sure that the critical data transactions can follow more than one possible path from source to target.

Redundancy in your network offers the advantage of reducing the risk of lost functionality, and potentially lost profits, from a network fault. As you might guess, however, the main disadvantage of redundancy is its cost. If you subscribed to two different service providers for two T1 links in the PayNTime example, you would probably double your monthly leasing costs of approximately $700. Multiply that amount times 12 months, and then times the number of clients for which you need to provide redundancy, and the extra layers of protection quickly become expensive. Redundancy is like a homeowner's insurance policy: You may never need to use it, but if you don't get it, the cost when you do need it can be much higher than your premiums. As a general rule, you should invest in connection redundancies where they are absolutely necessary.

Now suppose that PayNTime provides services not only to the oil company, but also to a temporary agency in the Houston area. Both links are critical because both companies need their payroll checks cut each week. To address concerns of capacity and scalability, the company may want to consider partnering with an ISP and establishing secure VPNs (virtual private networks) with its clients. With a VPN, PayNTime could shift the costs of redundancy and network design to the service provider and concentrate on the task it does best—processing payroll. Figure 13-3 illustrates this type of arrangement.

But what about the devices that connect one segment of a LAN or WAN to another? What happens when they experience a fault? Previously, you learned how connectivity devices work and how dedicated lines terminate at a customer's premises and in a service provider's data center. Next, you consider how to fundamentally increase the fault tolerance of connectivity devices and a LAN's or WAN's connecting links.

To understand how to increase the fault tolerance of not just the topology, but also the network's connectivity, let's return to the example of PayNTime. Suppose that the company's network administrator decides to establish a VPN agreement with a national ISP. PayNTime's bandwidth analysis indicates that a T1 link is sufficient to transport the data of five customers from the ISP's office to PayNTime's data room. Figure 13-4 provides a detailed representation of this arrangement.

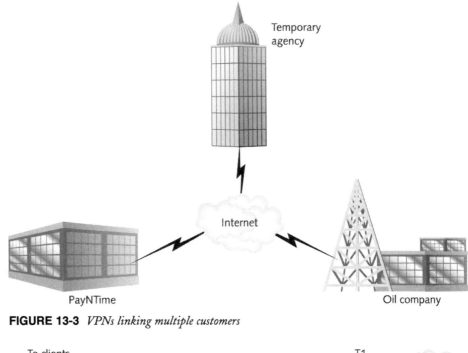

FIGURE 13-3 *VPNs linking multiple customers*

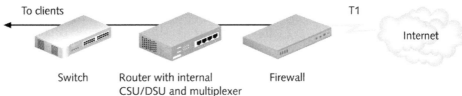

FIGURE 13-4 *Single T1 connectivity*

Notice the many single points of failure in the arrangement depicted in Figure 13-4. As mentioned earlier, the T1 connection could incur a fault. In addition, the firewall, router, CSU/DSU, multiplexer, or switch might suffer faults in their power supplies, NICs, or circuit boards. In a critical component such as a router or switch, the utmost fault tolerance necessitates the use of redundant NICs, power supplies, cooling fans, interfaces, and I/O modules, all of which should ideally be able to immediately assume the duties of an identical component, a capability known as automatic **fail-over**. Even if one router's NIC fails, for example, fail-over ensures that the router's other NIC can automatically handle the first server's responsibilities.

In cases in which it's impractical to have fail-over capable components, you can provide some level of fault tolerance by using hot swappable parts. The term **hot swappable** refers to identical components that can be changed (or swapped) while a machine is still running (hot). A hot swappable component assumes the functions of its counterpart if one suffers a fault. When you purchase switches or routers to support critical links, look for those that contain fail-over capable or hot swappable components. As with other redundancy provisions, these features add to the cost of your device purchase.

Purchasing connectivity devices with hot swappable or fail-over capable components does not address all faults that may occur on a connection. Faults may also affect the connecting links. For example, if you connect two offices with a dedicated T1 connection and the T1 cable is severed during a construction mishap, it doesn't matter whether your router has redundant NICs. The connection will still be down. Because a fault in the T1 link has the same effect as a bad T1 interface in a router, a fully redundant system might be a better option. Such a system is depicted in Figure 13-5.

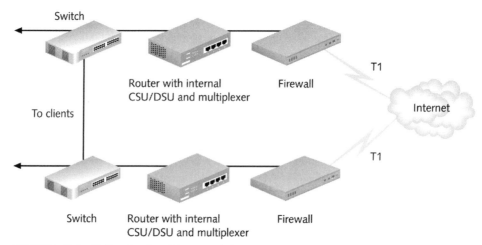

FIGURE 13-5 *Fully redundant T1 connectivity*

The preceding scenario utilizes the most reliable option for providing network redundancy for PayNTime. In addition, leasing redundant T1s allows for **load balancing**, or an automatic distribution of traffic over multiple links or processors to optimize response. Load balancing would maximize the throughput between PayNTime and its ISP, because the aggregate traffic flowing between the two points could move over either T1 link, avoiding potential bottlenecks on a single T1 connection. Although one company might be willing to pay for such complete redundancy, another might prefer a less expensive solution. A less expensive redundancy option might be to use a dial-back WAN link. For example, a company that depends on a Frame Relay WAN might also have an access server with a DSL or dial-up link that automatically connects to the remote site when it detects a failure of the primary link.

Servers

As with other devices, you can make servers more fault-tolerant by supplying them with redundant components. Critical servers (such as those that perform user authentication for an entire LAN, or those that run important, enterprise-wide applications such as an electronic catalog in a library) often contain redundant NICs, processors, and hard disks. These redundant

NET+
3.11

failed disk. Users do not even notice the failure. After repairing the failed disk, the network administrator must perform a resynchronization to return the disk to the array. Because the failed disk's twin has been saving all of its data while it was out of service, this task is rarely difficult.

The advantages of RAID Level 1 derive from its simplicity and its automatic and complete data redundancy. On the other hand, because it requires two identical disks instead of just one, RAID Level 1 is somewhat costly. In addition, it is not the most efficient means of protecting data, as it usually relies on system software to perform the mirroring, which taxes CPU resources. Figure 13-7 depicts a 128-KB file being written to a disk array using RAID Level 1.

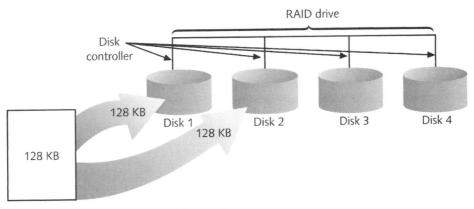

FIGURE 13-7 *RAID Level 1—disk mirroring*

> ### NOTE
>
> Although they are not covered in this chapter, RAID levels 2, 4, and higher also exist, in addition to RAID installations that combine multiple RAID levels. These versions of RAID are rarely used, however, because they are less reliable, less economical, or less efficient than Levels 0, 1, 3, and 5.

The concept of disk duplexing is related to disk mirroring. In **disk duplexing**, data is continually copied from one disk to another when it is saved, just as in disk mirroring. In duplexing, however, a separate disk controller is used for each different disk. This provides added fault tolerance, because a disk controller failure will not render data inaccessible. Conversely, if a RAID 1 disk controller fails, all of the data on the storage device becomes inaccessible.

RAID Level 3—Disk Striping with Parity ECC

RAID Level 3 involves disk striping with a special **ECC (error correction code)**, or algorithm used to detect and correct errors, known as parity error correction code. The term **parity** refers to the mechanism used to verify the integrity of data by making the number of bits in a byte

NET+
3.11

sum to either an odd or even number. To accomplish parity, a parity bit (equal to either 0 or 1) is added to the bits' sum. Table 13-1 expresses how the sums of many bits achieve even parity through a parity bit. Notice that the numbers in the fourth column are all even. If the summed numbers in the fourth column were odd, an odd parity would be used. A system may use either even parity or odd parity, but not both.

Table 13-1 The use of parity bits to achieve parity

Original Data	Sum of Data Bits	Parity Bit	Sum of Data Plus Parity Bits
01110010	4	0	4
00100010	2	0	2
00111101	5	1	6
10010100	3	1	4

Parity tracks the integrity of data on a disk. It does not reflect the data type, protocol, transmission method, or file size. A parity bit is assigned to each data byte when it is transmitted or written to a disk. When data is later read from the disk, the data's bits plus the parity bit are summed again. If the parity does not match (for example, if the end sum is odd but the system uses even parity), then the system assumes that the data has suffered some type of damage. The process of comparing the parity of data read from disk with the type of parity used by the system is known as **parity error checking**.

In RAID Level 3, parity error checking takes place when data is written across the disk array. If the parity error checking indicates an error, the RAID Level 3 system can automatically correct it. The advantage of using RAID 3 is that it provides a high data transfer rate when reading from or writing to the disks. This quality makes RAID 3 particularly well suited to applications that require high speed in data transfers, such as video editing. A disadvantage of RAID 3 is that the parity information appears on a single disk, which represents a potential single point of failure in the system. Figure 13-8 illustrates how RAID Level 3 works.

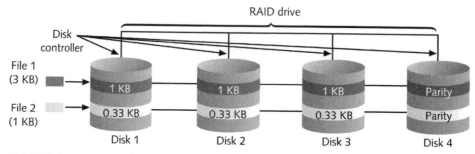

FIGURE 13-8 *RAID Level 3—disk striping with parity ECC*

NET+
3.11

RAID Level 5—Disk Striping with Distributed Parity

The highly fault-tolerant **RAID Level 5** is the most popular data storage technique in use today. In RAID Level 5, data is written in small blocks across several disks. At the same time, parity error checking information is distributed among the disks. Figure 13-9 depicts two files being written over several disks via RAID Level 5.

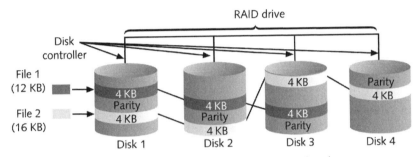

FIGURE 13-9 *RAID Level 5—disk striping with distributed parity*

NET+
3.11
3.12

RAID Level 5 is similar to, but has several advantages over, RAID Level 3. First, it can write data more rapidly because the parity information can be written by any one of the several disk controllers in the array. Unlike RAID Level 3, RAID Level 5 uses several disks for parity information, making it more fault-tolerant. Also, RAID Level 5 allows you to replace a failed disk with a good one with little interruption of service. This is because, using parity information and the parts of a file that remain on the good disks, RAID controlling software can regenerate the parts of the file that were on the failed disk after that disk is replaced. To take advantage of this feature, some network administrators equip their RAID 5 systems with a **hot spare**, a disk or partition that is part of the array, but used only in case one of the RAID disks fails. More generally, the term hot spare is used as a synonym for a hot swappable component, which, as you learned earlier, is a duplicate component installed in a device that can assume the original component's functions in case that component fails. In contrast, **cold spare** refers to a duplicate component that is not installed, but can be installed in case of a failure. Replacing a component with a cold spare requires an interruption of service.

NET+
3.11

NAS (Network Attached Storage)

NAS (network attached storage) is a specialized storage device or group of storage devices that provides centralized fault-tolerant data storage for a network. NAS differs from RAID in that it maintains its own interface to the LAN rather than relying on a server to connect it to the network and control its functions. In fact, you can think of NAS as a unique type of server dedicated to data sharing. The advantage to using NAS over a typical file server is that a NAS device contains its own file system that is optimized for saving and serving files (as opposed to also managing printing, authenticating logon IDs, and so on). Because of this optimization, NAS reads and writes from its disk significantly faster than other types of servers could.

Another advantage to using NAS is that it can be easily expanded without interrupting service. For instance, if you purchased a NAS device with 400 GB of disk space, then six months later realized you need three times as much storage space, you could add the new 800 GB of disk space to the NAS device without requiring users to log off the network or taking down the NAS device. After physically installing the new disk space, the NAS device would recognize the added storage and add it to its pool of available reading and writing space. Compare this process to adding hard disk space to a typical server, for which you would have to take the server down, install the hardware, reformat the drive, integrate it with your NOS, and then add directories, files, and permissions as necessary.

Although NAS is a separate device with its own file system, it still cannot communicate directly with clients on the network. When using NAS, the client requests a file from its usual file server over the LAN. The server then requests the file from the NAS device on the network. In response, the NAS device retrieves the file and transmits it to the server, which transmits it to the client. Figure 13-10 depicts how a NAS device physically connects to a LAN.

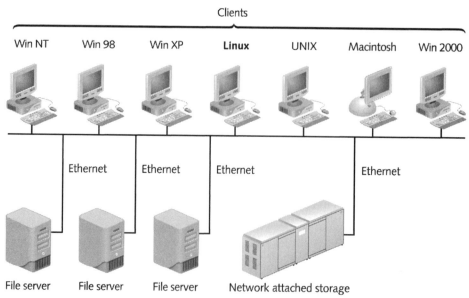

FIGURE 13-10 *Network attached storage on a LAN*

NAS is appropriate for enterprises that require not only fault tolerance, but also fast access for their data. For example, an ISP might use NAS to host its customers' Web pages. Because NAS devices can store and retrieve data for any type of client (providing it can run TCP/IP), NAS is also appropriate for organizations that use a mix of different operating systems on their desktops.

The two major vendors of network attached storage are Network Appliance, Inc., and EMC Corporation. In addition, computer manufacturers such as Hewlett-Packard and Dell offer their own NAS solutions.

NET+
3.11

Large enterprises that require even faster access to data and larger amounts of storage might prefer storage area networks over NAS. You will learn about storage area networks in the following section.

SANs (Storage Area Networks)

As you have learned, NAS devices are separate storage devices, but they still require a file server to interact with other devices on the network. In contrast, **SANs (storage area networks)** are distinct networks of storage devices that communicate directly with each other and with other networks. In a typical SAN, multiple storage devices are connected to multiple, identical servers. This type of architecture is similar to the mesh topology in WANs, the most fault-tolerant type of topology possible. If one storage device within a SAN suffers a fault, data is automatically retrieved from elsewhere in the SAN. If one server in a SAN suffers a fault, another server steps in to perform its functions.

Not only are SANs extremely fault-tolerant, but they are also extremely fast. Much of their speed can be attributed to the use of a special transmission method that relies on fiber-optic media and its own, proprietary protocols. One popular SAN transmission method is called **Fibre Channel**. Fibre Channel connects devices within the SAN and also connects the SAN to other networks. Fibre Channel is capable of up to 2-Gbps throughput. Because it depends on Fibre Channel, and not on a traditional network transmission method (for example, 100BASE-TX), a SAN is not limited to the speed of the client/server network for which it provides data storage. In addition, because the SAN does not belong to the client/server network, it does not have to contend with the normal overhead of that network, such as broadcasts and acknowledgments. Likewise, a SAN frees the client/server network from the traffic-intensive duties of backing up and restoring data.

Figure 13-11 shows a SAN connected to a traditional Ethernet network.

Another advantage to using SANs is that a SAN can be installed in a location separate from the LAN it serves. Being in a separate location provides added fault tolerance. For example, if an organization's main offices suffered a fire or flood, the SAN and the data it stores would still be safe. Remote SANs can be kept in an ISP's data center, which can provide greater security and fault tolerance and also allows an organization to outsource the management of its storage, in case its own staff don't have the time or expertise.

Like NAS, SANs provide the benefit of being highly scalable. After establishing a SAN, you can easily add further storage and new devices to the SAN without disrupting client/server activity on the network. Finally, SANs use a faster, more efficient method of writing data than do both NAS devices and typical client/server networks.

SANs are not without drawbacks, however. One noteworthy disadvantage to implementing SANs is their high cost. A small SAN can cost $100,000, while a large SAN costs several millions of dollars. In addition, because SANs are more complex than NAS or RAID systems, investing in a SAN means also investing in long hours of training for technical staff before

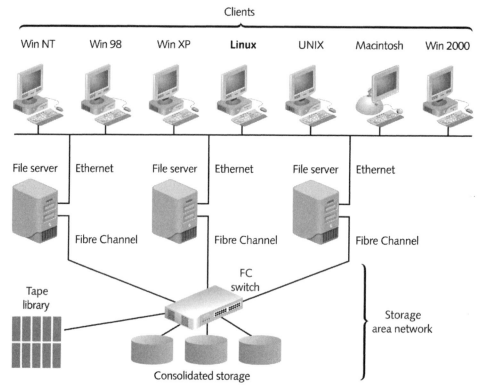

FIGURE 13-11 *A storage area network*

installation, plus significant administration efforts to keep the SAN functional (that is, unless an organization outsources its storage management).

Due to their very high fault tolerance, massive storage capabilities, and speedy data access, SANs are best suited to environments with huge quantities of data that must always be quickly available. Usually, such an environment belongs to a very large enterprise. A SAN is typically used to house multiple databases—for example, inventory, sales, safety specifications, payroll, and employee records for an international manufacturing company.

Data Backup

You have probably heard or even spoken the axiom, "Make regular backups!" A **backup** is a copy of data or program files created for archiving or safekeeping. Without backing up your data, you risk losing everything through a hard disk fault, fire, flood, or malicious or accidental erasure or corruption. No matter how reliable and fault-tolerant you believe your server's hard disk (or disks) to be, you still risk losing everything unless you make backups on separate media and store them off-site.

NOTE

Elsewhere in this book, the term "media" refers to the elements, physical or atmospheric, that make up a path for data transmission (for example, fiber-optic cable). In the context of data backups, "media" refers to the objects on which data is stored (for example, CD-ROMs).

To fully appreciate the importance of backups, imagine coming to work one morning to find that everything disappeared from the server: programs, configurations, data files, user IDs, passwords, and the network operating system. It doesn't matter how it happened. What matters is how long it will take to reinstall the network operating systems; how long it will take to duplicate the previous configuration; and how long it will take to figure out which IDs should reside on the server, in which groups they should belong, and which rights each group should have. What will you say to your colleagues when they learn that all of the data that they have worked on for the last year is irretrievably lost? When you think about this scenario, you quickly realize that you can't afford *not* to perform regular backups.

Many different options exist for making backups. They can be performed by different types of software and hardware combinations and use different types of media for storage. They can be controlled by NOS utilities or third-party software. In this section, you will learn about the most common backup media, methods of performing data backups, ways to schedule them, and methods for determining what you must back up.

Backup Media and Methods

When selecting backup media and methods, you can choose from several approaches, each of which comes with certain advantages and disadvantages. To select the appropriate solution for your network, consider the following questions:

◆ Does the backup drive or media provide sufficient storage capacity?

◆ Are the backup software and hardware proven to be reliable?

◆ Does the backup software use data error checking techniques?

◆ Is the system efficient enough to complete the backup process before daily operations resume?

◆ How much do the hardware, software, and media cost, relative to the amount of data they can store?

◆ Will the backup hardware and software be compatible with existing network hardware and software?

◆ Does the backup system require frequent manual intervention? (For example, must staff members become involved in inserting media or filing it in a library?)

◆ Will the backup hardware, software, and media accommodate your network's growth?

NET+
3.12

To help you answer these questions for your own situation, the following sections compare the most popular backup media and methods available today.

Optical Media

A simple way to save data is by copying it to **optical media**, which is a type of media capable of storing digitized data and that uses a laser to write data to it and read data from it. Examples of optical media include all types of CD-ROMs and DVDs. Backing up data to optical media requires only a computer with the appropriate recordable CD or DVD (digital versatile disc) drive and a utility for writing data to the media. Such utilities often come with a computer's operating system. If not, they are inexpensive and easy to find. A **CD-R (compact disc -recordable)** can be written to once and can store up to 650 MB of data. A **CD-RW (compact disc - rewriteable)** also stores up to 650 MB of data, but can be used more than once for backing up data. Besides being simple to create, CD backups are simple to restore from, because their formats are standard and can be read by any computer with a matching drive. However, they suffer from a relatively low storage capacity.

A **recordable DVD** can hold up to 4.7 GB on one single-layered side, and both sides of the disc can be used. In addition, each side can have up to two layers. Thus, in total, a double-layered, two-sided DVD can store up to 17 GB of data. Recordable DVDs, which are not the same as the video DVD that you rent from a movie store, come in several different formats. DVD manufacturers, such as Dell, Hewlett-Packard, Hitachi, Panasonic, Philips, Pioneer, and Sony, are competing to make their version of the recordable DVD format the most popular. Therefore, if you decide to back up media to DVDs, be sure to standardize on one manufacturer's equipment.

One potential disadvantage to using CD-R and recordable DVDs for backups is that writing your data to these optical media usually takes longer than saving your data to another type of media, such as a tape or disk drive. In addition, this method requires more human intervention than other backup methods, such as tape backups, which are discussed next.

Tape Backups

In the early days of networking, the most popular method for backing up networked systems was **tape backup**, or copying data to a magnetic tape. Now this method, which is relatively simple, capable of storing very large amounts of data, and at least partially automated, is making a comeback. Tape backups require the use of a tape drive connected to the network (via a system such as a file server or dedicated, networked workstation), software to manage and perform backups, and, of course, backup media. The tapes used for tape backups resemble small cassette tapes, but they are a higher quality, specially made to reliably store data. Figure 13-12 depicts typical tape backup media.

On a relatively small network, standalone tape drives may be attached to each server. On a large network, one large, centralized tape backup device may manage all of the subsystems' backups. This tape backup device usually is connected to a computer other than a busy file server to reduce the possibility that backups might cause traffic bottlenecks. Extremely large environments (for example, global manufacturers with several terabytes of inventory and product information to safeguard) may require robots to retrieve and circulate tapes from a tape storage library, also known as a **vault**, that may be as large as a warehouse.

NET+
3.12

FIGURE 13-12 *Example of tape backup media*

Examples of tape backup software include Computer Associates' ARCserve, Dantz Development Corporation's Retrospect, Hewlett-Packard's Colorado and OmniBack, NovaStor Corporation's NovaBACKUP, and Veritas Software Corporation's Backup Exec. Popular tape drive manufacturers include Exabyte, Hewlett-Packard, IBM, Quantum, Seagate, and Sony. Consult the software and hardware specifications to determine whether a particular backup system is compatible with your network.

External Disk Drives

Another option for backing up data is to use an **external disk drive**, a storage device that can be attached temporarily to a computer via its USB, PCMCIA, FireWire, or CompactFlash port. External disk drives are also known as **removable disk drives**. Small external disk drives are frequently used by laptop or desktop computer users to save and share data. These contain circuit boards with attached chips that can store up to 4 GB of data. After being connected to the computer, the external disk drives appear as any other drive, and the user can copy files directly to them. For backing up large amounts of data, however, network administrators are likely to use an external disk drive with backup control features, higher storage capacity, and faster read-write access. One example is the Iomega REV drive, which uses a cartridge containing a small hard disk that can hold up to 90 GB of data. The REV drive operates faster than tape backups or optical media. It can connect to a computer via several bus types and comes with proprietary software that automates the backup, manages the backup schedule, identifies data to be backed up, compresses files, and verifies that the backup completed successfully. Another disk manufacturer, LaCie, makes external drives that can hold up to 500 GB of data.

One advantage to using external disk drives is that they are simple to use. Also, they provide faster data transfer rates than optical media or tape backups. However, on most networks, backing up data to a fixed disk elsewhere on the network, as explained in the next section, is faster.

NET+

3.12

Network Backups

Instead of saving data to a removable disk or media, you might choose to save data to another place on the network. For example, you could copy all the user data from your organization's mail server to a different server on the network. If you choose this option, be certain to back up data to a different disk than where it was originally stored, because if the original disk fails, you will lose both the original data and its backup. (Although disk locations on workstations are typically obvious, on a network they might not be.) If your organization operates a WAN, it's best to back up data to disks at another location. That way, if one location suffers an outage or catastrophe, the data will remain safe at the other location on the WAN. A sophisticated network backup solution would use software to automate and manage backups and save data to a SAN or NAS storage device. Most network operating systems provide utilities for automating and managing network backups.

If your organization does not have a WAN or a high-end storage solution, you might consider online backups. An **online backup** saves data across the Internet to another company's storage array. Usually, online backup providers require you to install their client software. You also need a (preferably high-speed) connection to the Internet. Online backups implement strict security measures to protect the data in transit, as the information must traverse public carrier links. Most online backup providers allow you to retrieve your data at any time of day or night, without calling a technical support number. Both the backup and restoration processes are entirely automated. In case of a disaster, the online backup company may offer to create CD-ROMs containing your servers' data. When evaluating an online backup provider, you should test its speed, accuracy, security, and, of course, the ease with which you can recover the backed-up data. Be certain to test the service before you commit to a long-term contract for online backups.

Backup Strategy

After selecting the appropriate tool for performing your servers' data backups, devise a backup strategy to guide you and your colleagues in performing reliable backups that provide maximum data protection. This strategy should be documented in a common area where all IT staff can access it. The strategy should address at least the following questions:

- What data must be backed up?
- What kind of rotation schedule will backups follow?
- At what time of day or night will the backups occur?
- How will you verify the accuracy of the backups?
- Where and for how long will backup media be stored?
- Who will take responsibility for ensuring that backups occurred?
- How long will you save backups?
- Where will backup and recovery documentation be stored?

Different backup methods provide varying levels of certainty and corresponding labor and cost. An important concept to understand before learning about different backup methods is the

NET+
3.12

archive bit. An **archive bit** is a file attribute that can be checked (or set to "on") or unchecked (or set to "off") to indicate whether the file must be archived. When a file is created or changed, the operating system automatically sets the file's archive bit to "on." Various backup methods use the archive bit in different ways to determine which files should be backed up, as described in the following list:

♦ **Full backup**—All data on all servers is copied to storage media, regardless of whether the data is new or changed. After backing up the files, a full backup unchecks—or turns "off"—the files' archive bits.

♦ **Incremental backup**—Only data that has changed since the last full or incremental backup is copied to a storage medium. An incremental backup saves only files whose archive bit is checked. After backing up files, an incremental backup unchecks the archive bit for every file it has saved.

♦ **Differential backup**—Only data that has changed since the last backup is copied to a storage medium, and that information is then marked for subsequent backup, regardless of whether it has changed. In other words, a differential backup does not uncheck the archive bits for files it backs up.

When managing network backups, you need to determine the best possible **backup rotation scheme**—you need to create a plan that specifies when and how often backups will occur. The aim of a good backup rotation scheme is to provide excellent data reliability without overtaxing your network or requiring a lot of intervention. For example, you might think that backing up your entire network's data every night is the best policy because it ensures that everything is completely safe. But what if your network contains 2 TB of data and is growing by 100 GB per month? Would the backups even finish by morning? How many tapes would you have to purchase? Also, why should you bother backing up files that haven't changed in three weeks? How much time will you and your staff need to devote to managing the tapes? How would the transfer of all of the data affect your network's performance? All of these considerations point to a better alternative than the "tape-a-day" solution—that is, an option that promises to maximize data protection but reduce the time and cost associated with backups.

When planning your backup strategy, you can choose from several standard backup rotation schemes. The most popular of these schemes, called **grandfather-father-son**, uses daily (son), weekly (father), and monthly (grandfather) backup sets. As depicted in Figure 13-13, in the grandfather-father-son scheme, three types of backups are performed each month: daily incremental (every Monday through Thursday), weekly full (every Friday), and monthly full (last day of the month).

In this scheme, backup tapes are reused regularly. For example, week 1's Monday tape also serves as week 2's and week 3's Monday tape. One day each week, a full backup, called "father," is recorded in place of an incremental one and labeled for the week to which it corresponds—for example, "week 1," "week 2," and so on. This "father" tape is reused monthly—for example, October's week 1 tape is reused for November's week 1 tape. The final set of media is labeled "month 1," "month 2," and so on, according to which month of the quarter the tapes are used. This "grandfather" medium records full backups on the last business day of each month and is

NET+
3.12

	Monday	Tuesday	Wednesday	Thursday	Friday
Week 1	A	A	A	A	B
Week 2	A	A	A	A	B
Week 3	A	A	A	A	B
Week 4	A	A	A	A	B
Week 5	A	A	C		

One month of backups

A = Incremental "son" backup (daily)
B = Full "father" backup (weekly)
C = Full "grandfather" backup (monthly)

FIGURE 13-13 *The "grandfather-father-son" backup rotation scheme*

reused quarterly. Each of these media may consist of a single tape or a set of tapes, depending on the amount of data involved. A total of 12 media sets are required for this basic rotation scheme, allowing for a history of two to three months.

After you have determined your backup rotation scheme, you should ensure that backup activity is recorded in a backup log. Information that belongs in a backup log includes the backup date, tape identification (day of week or type), type of data backed up (for example, Accounting Department spreadsheets or a day's worth of catalog orders), type of the backup (full, incremental, or differential), files that were backed up, and site at which the tape is stored. Having this information available in case of a server failure greatly simplifies data recovery.

Finally, after you begin to back up network data, you should establish a regular schedule of verification. From time to time (depending on how often your data change and how critical the information is), you should attempt to recover some critical files from your backup media. Many network administrators attest that the darkest hour of their career was when they were asked to retrieve critical files from a backup tape, and found that no backup data existed because their backup system never worked in the first place!

Disaster Recovery

NET+
3.12

Disaster recovery is the process of restoring your critical functionality and data after an enterprise-wide outage that affects more than a single system or a limited group of users. Disaster recovery must take into account the possible extremes, rather than relatively minor outages, failures, security breaches, or data corruption.

NET+
3.12

Disaster Recovery Planning

A disaster recovery plan accounts for the worst-case scenarios, from a far-reaching hurricane to a military or terrorist attack. It should identify a disaster recovery team (with an appointed coordinator) and provide contingency plans for restoring or replacing computer systems, power, telephony systems, and paper-based files. Sections of the plan related to computer systems should include the following:

- ◆ Contact names and phone and pager numbers for emergency coordinators who will execute the disaster recovery response in case of disaster, as well as roles and responsibilities of other staff.

- ◆ Details on which data and servers are being backed up, how frequently backups occur, where backups are kept (off-site), and, most important, how backed up data can be recovered in full.

- ◆ Details on network topology, redundancy, and agreements with national service carriers, in case local or regional vendors fall prey to the same disaster.

- ◆ Regular strategies for testing the disaster recovery plan.

- ◆ A plan for managing the crisis, including regular communications with employees and customers. Consider the possibility that regular communications modes (such as phone lines) might be unavailable.

Having a comprehensive disaster recovery plan lessens the risk of losing critical data in case of extreme situations, and also makes potential customers and your insurance providers look more favorably on your organization.

Disaster Recovery Contingencies

An organization can choose from several options for recovering from a disaster. The options vary by the amount of employee involvement, hardware, software, planning, and investment each involves. They also vary according to how quickly they will restore network functionality in case a disaster occurs. As you would expect, every contingency necessitates a site other than the building where the network's main components normally reside. An organization might maintain its own disaster recovery sites—for example, by renting office space in a different city—or contract with a company that specializes in disaster recovery services to provide the site. Disaster recovery contingencies are commonly divided into three categories: cold site, warm site, and hot site.

A **cold site** is a place where the computers, devices, and connectivity necessary to rebuild a network exist, but they are not appropriately configured, updated, or connected. Therefore, restoring functionality from a cold site could take a long time. For example, suppose your small business network consists of a file and print server, mail server, backup server, Internet gateway/DNS/DHCP server, twenty-five clients, four printers, a router, a switch, two access points, and a connection to your local ISP. At your cold site, you might store four server computers on

NET+
3.12

which your company's NOS is not installed, and that do not possess the appropriate configurations and data necessary to operate in your environment. The twenty-five client machines stored there might be in a similar state. In addition, you might have a router, a switch, and two access points at the cold site, but these might also require configuration to operate in your environment. Finally, the cold site would not necessarily have Internet connectivity, or at least not the same type as your network used. Supposing you followed good backup practices and stored your backup media at the cold site, you would then need to restore operating systems, applications, and data to your servers and clients, reconfigure your connectivity devices, and arrange with your ISP to have your connectivity restored to the cold site. Even for a small network, this process could take weeks.

A **warm site** is a place where the computers, devices, and connectivity necessary to rebuild a network exist, with some appropriately configured, updated, or connected. For example, a service provider that specializes in disaster recovery might maintain for you a duplicate of each of your servers in its data center. You might arrange to have the service provider update those duplicate servers with your backed-up data on the first of each month, because updating the servers daily is much more expensive. In that case, if a disaster occurs in the middle of the month, you would still need to update your duplicate servers with your latest weekly or daily backups before they could stand in for the downed servers. Recovery from a warm site can take hours or days, compared to the weeks a cold site might require. Maintaining a warm site costs more than maintaining a cold site, but not as much as maintaining a hot site.

A **hot site** is a place where the computers, devices, and connectivity necessary to rebuild a network exist, and all are appropriately configured, updated, and connected to match your network's current state. For example, you might use server mirroring to maintain identical copies of your servers at two WAN locations. In a hot site contingency plan, both locations would also contain identical connectivity devices and configurations, and thus be able to stand in for the other at a moment's notice. As you can imagine, hot sites are expensive and potentially time consuming to maintain. For organizations that cannot tolerate downtime, however, hot sites provide the best disaster recovery option.

Chapter Summary

♦ Integrity refers to the soundness of your network's files, systems, and connections. To ensure their integrity, you must protect them from anything that might render them unusable, such as corruption, tampering, natural disasters, and viruses. Availability of a file or system refers to how consistently and reliably it can be accessed by authorized personnel.

♦ Several basic measures can be employed to protect data and systems on a network: (1) Prevent anyone other than a network administrator from opening or changing the system files; (2) monitor the network for unauthorized access or changes; (3) record authorized system changes in a change management system; (4) use redundancy for critical servers, cabling, routers, hubs, gateways, NICs, hard disks, power supplies, and other components; (5) perform regular health checks on the network; (6) monitor system performance, error logs, and the system log book regularly; (7) keep backups, boot disks, and emergency repair disks current and available; and (8) implement and enforce security and disaster recovery policies.

◆ A virus is a program that replicates itself so as to infect more computers, either through network connections or through external storage devices passed among users. Viruses may damage files or systems, or simply annoy users by flashing messages or pictures on the screen or by causing the computer to beep.

◆ Any type of virus may have additional characteristics that make it harder to detect and eliminate. Such viruses may be encrypted, stealth, polymorphic, or time-dependent.

◆ A good antivirus program should be able to detect viruses through signature scanning, integrity checking, and heuristic scanning. It should also be compatible with your network environment, centrally manageable, easy to use (transparent to users), and not prone to false alarms.

◆ Antivirus software is merely one piece of the puzzle in protecting your network from viruses. An antivirus policy is another essential component. It should provide rules for using antivirus software and policies for installing programs, sharing files, and using floppy disks.

◆ A failure is a deviation from a specified level of system performance for a given period of time. A fault, on the other hand, is the malfunction of one component of a system. A fault can result in a failure. The goal of fault-tolerant systems is to prevent faults from progressing to failures.

◆ Fault tolerance is a system's capacity to continue performing despite an unexpected hardware or software malfunction. It can be achieved in varying degrees. At the highest level of fault tolerance, a system is unaffected by even a drastic problem, such as a power failure.

◆ As you consider sophisticated fault-tolerance techniques for servers, routers, and WAN links, remember to address the environment in which your devices operate. Protecting your data also involves protecting your network from excessive heat or moisture, break-ins, and natural disasters.

◆ Networks cannot tolerate power loss or less than optimal power and may suffer downtime or reduced performance due to blackouts, brownouts (sags), surges, and line noise.

◆ A UPS is a battery power source directly attached to one or more devices and to a power supply, which prevents undesired features of the power source from harming the device or interrupting its services. UPSs vary in the type of power aberrations they can rectify, the length of time they can provide power, and the number of devices they can support.

◆ A standby UPS provides continuous voltage to a device by switching virtually instantaneously to the battery when it detects a loss of power from the wall outlet. Upon restoration of the power, the standby UPS switches the device to use A/C power again.

◆ An online UPS uses the A/C power from the wall outlet to continuously charge its battery, while providing power to a network device through its battery. In other words, a server connected to an online UPS always relies on the UPS battery for its electricity.

◆ For utmost fault tolerance in power supply, a generator is necessary. Generators can be powered by diesel, liquid propane gas, natural gas, or steam. They do not provide surge protection, but they do provide noise-free electricity.

◆ Network topologies such as a full mesh WAN or a star-based LAN with a parallel backbone offer the greatest fault tolerance. A SONET ring also offers high fault tolerance, because of its dual-ring topology.

◆ When components are hot swappable, they have identical functions and can automatically assume the functions of their counterpart if it suffers a fault. They can be changed (or swapped) while a machine is still running (hot). Hot swappable components are sometimes called hot spares.

◆ Critical servers often contain redundant NICs, processors, and/or hard disks to provide better fault tolerance. These redundant components provide assurance that if one fails, the whole system won't fail, and they enable load balancing.

◆ A fault-tolerance technique that involves utilizing a second, identical server to duplicate the transactions and data storage of one server is called server mirroring. Mirroring can take place between servers that are either side by side or geographically distant. Mirroring requires not only a link between the servers, but also software running on both servers to enable the servers to continually synchronize their actions and to permit one to take over in case the other fails.

◆ Clustering is a fault-tolerance technique that links multiple servers together to act as a single server. In this configuration, clustered servers share processing duties and appear as a single server to users. If one server in the cluster fails, the other servers in the cluster automatically take over its data transaction and storage responsibilities.

◆ An important storage redundancy feature is a RAID (Redundant Array of Independent (or Inexpensive) Disks). All types of RAID use shared, multiple physical or logical hard disks to ensure data integrity and availability; some designs also increase storage capacity and improve performance. RAID is either hardware- or software-based. Software RAID can be implemented through operating system utilities.

◆ RAID Level 0 is a simple version of RAID in which data is written in 64-KB blocks equally across all of the disks in the array, a technique known as disk striping. Disk striping is not a fault-tolerant method, because if one disk fails, the data contained in it will be inaccessible.

◆ RAID Level 1 provides redundancy through a process called disk mirroring, in which data from one disk is automatically copied to another disk as the information is written. This option is considered a dynamic data backup. If one disk in the array fails, the disk array controller automatically switches to the disk that was mirroring the failed disk.

◆ RAID Level 3 involves disk striping with parity error correction code. Parity refers to the integrity of the data as expressed in the number of 1s contained in each group of correctly transmitted bits. In RAID Level 3, parity error checking takes place when the data is written across the disk array.

◆ RAID Level 5 is the most popular fault-tolerant data storage technique in use today. In RAID Level 5, data is written in small blocks across several disks; parity error checking information is also distributed among the disks.

◆ NAS (network attached storage) is a dedicated storage device attached to a client/server network. It uses its own file system but relies on a traditional network transmission method such as Ethernet to interact with the rest of the client/server network.

◆ A SAN (storage area network) is a distinct network of multiple storage devices and servers that provides fast, highly available, and highly fault-tolerant access to large quantities of data for a client/server network. A SAN uses a proprietary network transmission method (such as Fibre Channel) rather than Ethernet.

◆ A backup is a copy of data or program files created for archiving or safekeeping. If you do not back up your data, you risk losing everything through a hard disk fault, fire, flood, or malicious or accidental erasure or corruption. Backups should be stored on separate media (other than the backed-up server), and these media should be stored off-site.

◆ Backups can be saved to optical media (such as CDs and DVDs), tapes, external disk drives, or to another location on a network. Of these, tape backups remain popular because of their reliability, storage capacity, and speed. Tape backups require a tape drive connected to the network, software to manage and perform backups, and backup media.

◆ A full backup copies all data on all servers to a storage medium, regardless of whether the data is new or changed. An incremental backup copies only data that has changed since the last full or incremental backup, and unchecks the archive bit for files it backs up. A differential backup copies only data that has changed since the last full or incremental backup, but does not uncheck the archive bit for files it backs up.

◆ The aim of a good backup rotation scheme is to provide excellent data reliability but not to overtax your network or require much intervention. The most popular backup rotation scheme is called "grandfather-father-son." This scheme combines daily (son), weekly (father), and monthly (grandfather) backup sets.

◆ Disaster recovery is the process of restoring your critical functionality and data after an enterprise-wide outage that affects more than a single system or a limited group of users. It must account for the possible extremes, rather than relatively minor outages, failures, security breaches, or data corruption. In a disaster recovery plan, you should consider the worst-case scenarios, from a hurricane to a military or terrorist attack.

◆ Every organization should have a disaster recovery team (with an appointed coordinator) and a disaster recovery plan. The plan should address not only computer systems, but also power, telephony, and paper-based files.

◆ To prepare for recovery after a potential disaster, you can maintain (or a hire a service to maintain for you) a cold site, warm site, or hot site. A cold site contains the elements necessary to rebuild a network, but none are appropriately configured and connected. Therefore, restoring functionality from a cold site can take a long time. A warm site contains the elements necessary to rebuild a network, and only some of them are appropriately configured and connected. A hot site is a precise duplicate of the network's elements, all properly configured and connected. This allows an organization to regain network functionality almost immediately.

Key Terms

archive bit—A file attribute that can be checked (or set to "on") or unchecked (or set to "off") to indicate whether the file needs to be archived. An operating system checks a file's archive bit when it is created or changed.

array—A group of hard disks.

availability—How consistently and reliably a file, device, or connection can be accessed by authorized personnel.

backup—A copy of data or program files created for archiving or safekeeping.

backup rotation scheme—A plan for when and how often backups occur, and which backups are full, incremental, or differential.

blackout—A complete power loss.

boot sector virus—A virus that resides on the boot sector of a floppy disk and is transferred to the partition sector or the DOS boot sector on a hard disk. A boot sector virus can move from a floppy to a hard disk only if the floppy disk is left in the drive when the machine starts.

bot—A program that runs automatically. Bots can spread viruses or other malicious code between users in a chat room by exploiting the IRC protocol.

brownout—A momentary decrease in voltage, also known as a *sag*. An overtaxed electrical system may cause brownouts, recognizable as a dimming of the lights.

CD-R (compact disc - recordable)—A type of compact disc that can be written to only once. It can store up to 650 MB of data.

CD-RW (compact disc - rewriteable)—A type of compact disc that can be written to more than once. It can store up to 650 MB of data.

clustering—A fault-tolerance technique that links multiple servers to act as a single server. In this configuration, clustered servers share processing duties and appear as a single server to users. If one server in the cluster fails, the other servers in the cluster automatically take over its data transaction and storage responsibilities.

cold site—A place where the computers, devices, and connectivity necessary to rebuild a network exist, but they are not appropriately configured, updated, or connected to match the network's current state.

cold spare—A duplicate component that is not installed, but can be installed in case of a failure.

compact disc, recordable—See *CD-R*.

compact disc, rewriteable—See *CD-RW*.

differential backup—A backup method in which only data that has changed since the last full or incremental backup is copied to a storage medium, and in which that same information is marked for subsequent backup, regardless of whether it has changed. In other words, a differential backup does not uncheck the archive bits for files it backs up.

disaster recovery—The process of restoring critical functionality and data to a network after an enterprise-wide outage that affects more than a single system or a limited group of users.

disk duplexing—A storage fault-tolerance technique in which data is continually copied from one disk to another when it is saved, just as in disk mirroring. In duplexing, however, a separate disk controller is used for each different disk.

disk mirroring—A RAID technique in which data from one disk is automatically copied to another disk as the information is written.

disk striping—A simple implementation of RAID in which data is written in 64-KB blocks equally across all disks in the array.

ECC (error correction code)—An algorithm used to detect and correct errors. In RAID Levels 3 and 5, for example, a type of ECC known as parity error checking is used.

encrypted virus—A virus that is encrypted to prevent detection.

error correction code—See *ECC*.

external disk drive—A storage device that can be attached temporarily to a computer.

fail-over—The capability for one component (such as a NIC or server) to assume another component's responsibilities without manual intervention.

failure—A deviation from a specified level of system performance for a given period of time. A failure occurs when something doesn't work as promised or as planned.

fault—The malfunction of one component of a system. A fault can result in a failure.

Fibre Channel—A distinct network transmission method that relies on fiber-optic media and its own, proprietary protocol. Fibre Channel is capable of up to 2-Gbps throughput.

file-infected virus—A virus that attaches itself to executable files. When the infected executable file runs, the virus copies itself to memory. Later, the virus attaches itself to other executable files.

full backup—A backup in which all data on all servers is copied to a storage medium, regardless of whether the data is new or changed. A full backup unchecks the archive bit on files it has backed up.

grandfather-father-son—A backup rotation scheme that uses daily (son), weekly (father), and monthly (grandfather) backup sets.

hardware RAID—A method of implementing RAID that relies on an externally attached set of disks and a RAID disk controller, which manages the RAID array.

heuristic scanning—A type of virus scanning that attempts to identify viruses by discovering "virus-like" behavior.

hot site—A place where the computers, devices, and connectivity necessary to rebuild a network exist, and all are appropriately configured, updated, and connected to match your network's current state.

hot spare—In the context of RAID, a disk or partition that is part of the array, but used only in case one of the RAID disks fails. More generally, "hot spare" is used as a synonym for a hot swappable component.

hot swappable—A characteristic that enables identical components to be interchanged (or swapped) while a machine is still running (hot). After being installed, a hot swappable component automatically assumes the functions of its counterpart.

incremental backup—A backup in which only data that has changed since the last full or incremental backup is copied to a storage medium. After backing up files, an incremental backup unchecks the archive bit for every file it has saved.

integrity—The soundness of a network's files, systems, and connections. To ensure integrity, you must protect your network from anything that might render it unusable, such as corruption, tampering, natural disasters, and viruses.

integrity checking—A method of comparing the current characteristics of files and disks against an archived version of these characteristics to discover any changes. The most common example of integrity checking involves a checksum.

Internet Relay Chat—See *IRC*.

IRC (Internet Relay Chat)—A protocol that enables users running special IRC client software to communicate instantly with other participants in a chat room on the Internet.

load balancing—An automatic distribution of traffic over multiple links, hard disks, or processors intended to optimize responses.

macro virus—A virus that takes the form of an application (for example, a word-processing or spreadsheet) program macro, which may execute when the program is in use.

mirroring—A fault-tolerance technique in which one component or device duplicates the activity of another.

NAS (network attached storage)—A device or set of devices attached to a client/server network, dedicated to providing highly fault-tolerant access to large quantities of data. NAS depends on traditional network transmission methods such as Ethernet.

network attached storage—See *NAS*.

network virus—A virus that takes advantage of network protocols, commands, messaging programs, and data links to propagate itself. Although all viruses could theoretically travel across network connections, network viruses are specially designed to attack network vulnerabilities.

offline UPS—See *standby UPS*.

online backup—A technique in which data is backed up to a central location over the Internet.

online UPS—A power supply that uses the A/C power from the wall outlet to continuously charge its battery, while providing power to a network device through its battery.

optical media—A type of media capable of storing digitized data, which uses a laser to write data to it and read data from it.

parity—The mechanism used to verify the integrity of data by making the number of bits in a byte sum equal to either an odd or even number.

parity error checking—The process of comparing the parity of data read from a disk with the type of parity used by the system.

polymorphic virus—A type of virus that changes its characteristics (such as the arrangement of its bytes, size, and internal instructions) every time it is transferred to a new system, making it harder to identify.

RAID (Redundant Array of Independent (or Inexpensive) Disks)—A server redundancy measure that uses shared, multiple physical or logical hard disks to ensure data integrity and availability. Some RAID designs also increase storage capacity and improve performance. See also *disk mirroring* and *disk striping*.

RAID Level 0—An implementation of RAID in which data is written in 64-KB blocks equally across all disks in the array.

RAID Level 1—An implementation of RAID that provides redundancy through disk mirroring, in which data from one disk is automatically copied to another disk as the information is written.

RAID Level 3—An implementation of RAID that uses disk striping for data and writes parity error correction code on a separate parity disk.

RAID Level 5—The most popular fault-tolerant data storage technique in use today, RAID Level 5 writes data in small blocks across several disks. At the same time, it writes parity error checking information among several disks.

recordable DVD—An optical storage medium that can hold up to 4.7 GB on one single-layered side. Both sides of the disc can be used, and each side can have up to two layers. Thus, in total, a double-layered, two-sided DVD can store up to 17 GB of data. Recordable DVDs come in several different formats.

redundancy—The use of more than one identical component, device, or connection for storing, processing, or transporting data. Redundancy is the most common method of achieving fault tolerance.

Redundant Array of Independent (or Inexpensive) Disks—See *RAID*.

removable disk drive—See *external disk drive*.

replication—A fault-tolerance technique that involves dynamic copying of data (for example, an NOS directory or an entire server's hard disk) from one location to another.

sag—See *brownout*.

SAN (storage area network)—A distinct network of multiple storage devices and servers that provides fast, highly available, and highly fault-tolerant access to large quantities of data for a client/server network. A SAN uses a proprietary network transmission method (such as Fibre Channel) rather than a traditional network transmission method such as Ethernet.

server mirroring—A fault-tolerance technique in which one server duplicates the transactions and data storage of another, identical server. Server mirroring requires a link between the servers and software running on both servers so that the servers can continually synchronize their actions and one can take over in case the other fails.

signature scanning—The comparison of a file's content with known virus signatures (unique identifying characteristics in the code) in a signature database to determine whether the file is a virus.

software RAID—A method of implementing RAID that uses software to implement and control RAID techniques over virtually any type of hard disk(s). RAID software may be a third-party package or utilities that come with an operating system NOS.

standby UPS—A power supply that provides continuous voltage to a device by switching virtually instantaneously to the battery when it detects a loss of power from the wall outlet. Upon restoration of the power, the standby UPS switches the device to use A/C power again.

stealth virus—A type of virus that hides itself to prevent detection. Typically, stealth viruses disguise themselves as legitimate programs or replace part of a legitimate program's code with their destructive code.

storage area network—See *SAN*.

surge—A momentary increase in voltage due to distant lightning strikes or electrical problems.

surge protector—A device that directs excess voltage away from equipment plugged into it and redirects it to a ground, thereby protecting the equipment from harm.

tape backup—A relatively simple and economical backup method in which data is copied to magnetic tapes.

time-dependent virus—A virus programmed to activate on a particular date. This type of virus, also known as a "time bomb," can remain dormant and harmless until its activation date arrives.

Trojan—See *Trojan horse*.

Trojan horse—A program that disguises itself as something useful, but actually harms your system.

uninterruptible power supply—See *UPS*.

UPS (uninterruptible power supply)—A battery-operated power source directly attached to one or more devices and to a power supply (such as a wall outlet), which prevents undesired features of the power source from harming the device or interrupting its services.

vault—A large tape storage library.

virus—A program that replicates itself to infect more computers, either through network connections or through floppy disks passed among users. Viruses may damage files or systems, or simply annoy users by flashing messages or pictures on the screen or by causing the keyboard to beep.

virus hoax—A rumor, or false alert, about a dangerous, new virus that could supposedly cause serious damage to your workstation.

volt-amp (VA)—A measure of electrical power. A volt-amp is the product of the voltage and current (measured in amps) of the electricity on a line.

warm site—A place where the computers, devices, and connectivity necessary to rebuild a network exist, though only some are appropriately configured, updated, or connected to match the network's current state.

worm—An unwanted program that travels between computers and across networks. Although worms do not alter other programs as viruses do, they may carry viruses.

Review Questions

1. _____ refers to the soundness of a network's programs, data, services, devices, and connections.

    a. Availability

    b. Heuristic scanning

    c. Disk duplexing

    d. Integrity

2. The term _____ refers to an implementation in which more than one component is installed and ready to use for storing, processing, or transporting data.

   a. disk mirroring

   b. redundancy

   c. hot swappable

   d. load balancing

3. Which of the following terms implies a fluctuation in voltage levels caused by other devices on the network or electromagnetic interference?

   a. Noise

   b. Brownout

   c. Surge

   d. Cold spare

4. _____ is a specialized storage device or group of storage devices that provides centralized fault-tolerant data storage for a network.

   a. Software RAID

   b. Offline UPS

   c. Network attached storage

   d. A Trojan horse

5. A _____ is a place where the computers, devices, and connectivity necessary to rebuild a network exist, but they are not appropriately configured, updated or connected.

   a. cold site

   b. hot spare

   c. vault

   d. warm site

6. True or false? A recordable DVD can hold up to 4.7 GB on one single-layered side, and both sides of the disc can be used.

7. True or false? A Trojan horse is a program that replicates itself with the intent to infect more computers, either through network connections or through the exchange of external storage devices.

8. True or false? Boot sector viruses are commonly spread from external storage devices to hard disks.

9. True or false? Fault tolerance is the capacity for a system to continue performing despite an unexpected hardware or software malfunction.

10. True or false? Clustering is a fault tolerance technique in which one device or component duplicates the transactions and data storage of another.

11. _____ viruses propagate themselves via network protocols, commands, messaging programs, and data links.

12. A momentary decrease in voltage is known as a(n) _____.

13. The term _____ refers to identical components that can be changed while a machine is still running.

14. _____ is a fault-tolerance technique that links multiple servers together to act as a single server.

15. _____ is the process of restoring your critical functionality and data after an enterprise-wide outage that affects more than a single system or a limited group of users.

Chapter 14

Network Security

After reading this chapter and completing the exercises, you will be able to:

■ Identify security risks in LANs and WANs and design security policies that minimize risks

■ Explain how physical security contributes to network security

■ Discuss hardware- and design-based security techniques

■ Use network operating system techniques to provide basic security

■ Understand methods of encryption, such as SSL and IPSec, that can secure data in storage and in transit

■ Describe how popular authentication protocols, such as RADIUS, TACACS, Kerberos, PAP, CHAP, and MS-CHAP, function

■ Understand wireless security protocols, such as WEP, WPA, and 802.11i

In the early days of computing, when secured mainframes acted as central hosts and data repositories that were accessed only by dumb terminals with limited rights, network security was all but unassailable. As networks have become more geographically distributed and heterogeneous, however, the risk of their misuse has also increased. Consider the largest, most heterogeneous network in existence: the Internet. Because it contains millions of points of entry, millions of servers, and millions of miles of transmission paths, it is vulnerable to millions of break-ins. Because so many networks connect to the Internet, the threat of an outsider accessing an organization's network via the Internet, and then stealing or destroying data, is very real. In this chapter, you will learn how to assess your network's risks, how to manage those risks, and, perhaps most important, how to convey the importance of network security to the rest of your organization through an effective security policy.

Security Audits

Before spending time and money on network security, you should examine your network's security risks. As you learn about each risk facing your network, consider the effect that a loss of data, programs, or access would have on your network. The more serious the potential consequences, the more attention you need to pay to the security of your network.

Different types of organizations have different levels of network security risk. For example, if you work for a large savings and loan institution that allows its clients to view their current loan status online, you must consider a number of risks associated with data and access. If someone obtained unauthorized access to your network, all of your customers' personal financial data could be vulnerable. On the other hand, if you work for a local car wash that is not connected to the Internet and uses its internal LAN only to track assets and sales, you may be less concerned if someone gains access to your network, because the implications of unauthorized access to your data are less dire. When considering security risks, the fundamental questions are: "What is at risk?" and "What do I stand to lose if it is stolen, damaged, or eradicated?"

Every organization should assess its security risks by conducting a **security audit**, which is a thorough examination of each aspect of the network to determine how it might be compromised. Security audits should be performed at least annually and preferably quarterly. They should also be performed after making any significant changes to the network. For each threat listed in the following sections, your security audit should rate the severity of its potential effects, as well as its likelihood. A threat's consequences may be severe, potentially resulting in a network outage or the dispersal of top-secret information, or it may be mild, potentially resulting in a lack of access for one user or the dispersal of a relatively insignificant piece of corporate data. The more devastating a threat's effects and the more likely it is to happen, the more rigorously your security measures should address it. Appendix D provides a sample checklist you can use to perform a fundamental security audit.

If your IT Department has sufficient skills and time for routine security audits, they can be performed in-house. A qualified consulting company can also conduct security audits for your network. The advantage of having an objective third party, such as a consultant, analyze your network is that he might find risks that you overlooked because of your familiarity with your environment. Third-party audits may seem expensive, but if your network hosts confidential and critical data, they are well worth their cost.

In the next section, you will learn about security risks associated with people, hardware, software, and Internet access.

Security Risks

As you have learned, natural disasters, viruses, and power faults can damage a network's data, programs, and hardware. A security breach, however, can harm a network just as easily and quickly. To understand how to manage network security, you should first recognize the types of threats that your network may suffer. Not all security breaches result from a manipulation of network technology. Instead, some occur when staff members purposely or inadvertently reveal their passwords; others result from undeveloped security policies.

 NOTE

Many terms are used to describe those who break into data networks. A **hacker**, in the original sense of the word, is someone who masters the inner workings of computer hardware and software in an effort to better understand them. To be called a hacker used to be a compliment, reflecting extraordinary computer skills. Those who use their computer skills to destroy data or systems are technically considered **crackers**. Today, many people use the words hacker and cracker interchangeably, and many networking professionals have settled on "hacker" as a general term for hackers and crackers alike. For simplicity's sake, this chapter uses "hacker" to describe individuals who gain unauthorized access to voice or data networks, with or without malicious intent.

As you read about each security threat, think about how it could be prevented, whether it applies to your network (and if so, how damaging it might be), and how it relates to other security threats. Keep in mind that malicious and determined intruders may use one technique, which then allows them to use a second technique, which then allows them to use a third technique, and so on. For example, a hacker might discover someone's user name by watching her log on to the network; the hacker might then use a password-cracking program to access the network, where he might plant a program that generates an extraordinary volume of traffic that essentially disables the network's connectivity devices.

Risks Associated with People

By some estimates, human errors, ignorance, and omissions cause more than half of all security breaches sustained by networks. One of the most common methods by which an intruder gains access to a network is to simply ask a user for his password. For example, the intruder might pose as a technical support analyst who needs to know the password to troubleshoot a problem. This strategy is commonly called **social engineering**, because it involves manipulating social relationships to gain access. This and other risks associated with people are included in the following list:

- Intruders or attackers using social engineering or snooping to obtain user passwords
- An administrator incorrectly creating or configuring user IDs, groups, and their associated rights on a file server, resulting in file and logon access vulnerabilities
- Network administrators overlooking security flaws in topology or hardware configuration
- Network administrators overlooking security flaws in the operating system or application configuration
- Lack of proper documentation and communication of security policies, leading to deliberate or inadvertent misuse of files or network access
- Dishonest or disgruntled employees abusing their file and access rights
- An unused computer or terminal being left logged on to the network, thereby providing an entry point for an intruder
- Users or administrators choosing easy-to-guess passwords
- Authorized staff leaving computer room doors open or unlocked, allowing unauthorized individuals to enter
- Staff discarding disks or backup tapes in public waste containers
- Administrators neglecting to remove access and file rights for employees who have left the organization
- Users writing their passwords on paper, then placing the paper in an easily accessible place (for example, taping it to their monitor or keyboard)

Human errors account for so many security breaches because taking advantage of them is the easiest way to circumvent network security. Imagine a man named Kyle, who was recently fired from his job at a local bank. Kyle felt he was unfairly treated, so he wants to take revenge on his employer. He still has a few friends at the bank. Even though the bank's network administrator was wise enough to deactivate Kyle's user account upon his termination, and even though the bank has a policy prohibiting employees from sharing their passwords, Kyle knows his friends' user names and passwords. Nevertheless, the bank's policy prevents former employees from walking into its offices.

How might Kyle attain his goal of deleting a month's worth of client account activity statements? Although the bank has a network security policy, employees such as Kyle's friends probably don't pay much attention to it. Kyle might walk into the bank's offices, ostensibly to meet one of his friends for lunch. While in the offices, Kyle could either sit down at a machine where his friend was still logged on or log on as his friend because he knows his friend's password. Once in the system, he could locate the account activity statements and delete them. Alternatively, if the bank allows employees to access the network remotely, Kyle might use a friend's user name and password to log on to the bank's LAN from home.

Risks Associated with Transmission and Hardware

This section describes security risks inherent in the Physical, Data Link, and Network layers of the OSI Model. Recall that the transmission media, NICs, hubs, network access methods (for example, Ethernet), bridges, switches, and routers reside at these layers. At these levels, security breaches require more technical sophistication than those that take advantage of human errors. For instance, to eavesdrop on transmissions passing through a switch, an intruder must use a device such as a sniffer, connected to one of the switch's ports. In the middle layers of the OSI Model, it is somewhat difficult to distinguish between hardware and software techniques. For example, because a router acts to connect one type of network to another, an intruder might take advantage of the router's security flaws by sending a flood of TCP/IP transmissions to the router, thereby disabling it from carrying legitimate traffic. You will learn about software-related risks in the following section.

The following risks are inherent in network hardware and design:

◆ Transmissions can be intercepted (spread-spectrum wireless and fiber-based transmissions are more difficult to intercept).

◆ Networks that use leased public lines, such as T1 or DSL connections to the Internet, are vulnerable to eavesdropping at a building's demarcation point (demarc), at a remote switching facility, or in a central office.

◆ Network hubs broadcast traffic over the entire segment, thus making transmissions more widely vulnerable to sniffing. (By contrast, switches provide logical point-to-point communications, which limit the availability of data transmissions to the sending and receiving nodes.)

◆ Unused hub, router, or server ports can be exploited and accessed by hackers if they are not disabled. A router's configuration port, accessible by Telnet, may not be adequately secured.

◆ If routers are not properly configured to mask internal subnets, users on outside networks (such as the Internet) can read the private addresses.

◆ Modems attached to network devices may be configured to accept incoming calls, thus opening security holes if they are not properly protected.

◆ Dial-in access servers used by telecommuting or remote staff may not be carefully secured and monitored.

◆ Computers hosting very sensitive data may coexist on the same subnet with computers open to the general public.

◆ Passwords for switches, routers, and other devices may not be sufficiently difficult to guess, changed frequently, or worse, may be left at their default value.

Imagine that a hacker wants to bring a library's database and mail servers to a halt. Suppose also that the library's database is public and can be searched by anyone on the Web. The hacker might begin by scanning ports on the database server to determine which have no protection. If she found an open port on the database server, the hacker might connect to the system and deposit a program that would, a few days later, damage operating system files. Or, she may launch a heavy stream of traffic that overwhelms the database server and prevents it from functioning. She might also use her newly discovered access to determine the root password on the system, gain access to other systems, and launch a similar attack on the library's mail server, which is attached to the database server. In this way, even a single mistake on one server (not protecting an open port) can open vulnerabilities on multiple systems.

Risks Associated with Protocols and Software

Like hardware, networked software is only as secure as you configure it to be. This section describes risks inherent in the higher layers of the OSI Model, such as the Transport, Session, Presentation, and Application layers. As noted earlier, the distinctions between hardware and software risks are somewhat blurry because protocols and hardware operate in tandem. For example, if a router has not been properly configured, a hacker may exploit the openness of TCP/IP to gain access to a network. Network operating systems and application software present different risks. In many cases, their security is compromised by a poor understanding of file access rights or simple negligence in configuring the software. Remember—even the best encryption, computer room door locks, security policies, and password rules make no difference if you grant the wrong users access to critical data and programs.

The following are some risks pertaining to networking protocols and software:

◆ TCP/IP contains several security flaws. For example, IP addresses can be falsified easily, checksums can be thwarted, UDP requires no authentication, and TCP requires only weak authentication.

◆ Trust relationships between one server and another may allow a hacker to access the entire network because of a single flaw.

◆ NOSs may contain "back doors" or security flaws that allow unauthorized users to gain access to the system. Unless the network administrator performs regular updates, a hacker may exploit these flaws.

◆ If the NOS allows server operators to exit to a command prompt, intruders could run destructive command-line programs.

◆ Administrators might accept the default security options after installing an operating system or application. Often, defaults are not optimal. For example, the default user name that enables someone to modify anything in Windows Server 2003 is called "Administrator." This default is well known, so if you leave the default user name as "Administrator," you have given a hacker half the information he needs to access and obtain full rights to your system.

◆ Transactions that take place between applications, such as databases and Web-based forms, may be open to interception.

To understand the risks that arise when an administrator accepts the default settings associated with a software program, consider the following scenario. Imagine that you have invited a large group of computer science students to tour your IT Department. While you're in the computer room talking about subnetting, a bored student standing next to a Windows XP workstation that is logged on to the network decides to find out which programs are installed on the workstation. He discovers that this workstation has the SQL Server administrator software installed. Your organization uses a SQL Server database to hold all of your employees' salaries, addresses, and other confidential information. The student knows a little about SQL Server, including the facts that the default administrator user ID is called "sa," and that, by default, no password is created for this ID when someone installs SQL Server. He tries connecting to your SQL Server database with the "sa" user ID and no password. Because you accepted the defaults for the program during its installation, within seconds the student is able to gain access to your employees' information. He could then change, delete, or steal any of the data.

Risks Associated with Internet Access

Although the Internet has brought computer crime, such as hacking, to the public's attention, network security is more often compromised "from the inside" than from external sources. Nevertheless, the threat of outside intruders is very real, and it will only grow as more people gain access to the Internet.

Users need to be careful when they connect to the Internet. Even the most popular Web browsers sometimes contain bugs that permit scripts to access their systems while they're connected to the Internet, potentially for the purpose of causing damage. Users must also be careful about providing information while browsing the Web. Some sites will capture that information to use when attempting to break into systems. Bear in mind that hackers are creative and typically revel in devising new ways of breaking into systems. As a result, new Internet-related security threats arise frequently. By keeping software current, staying abreast of emerging security threats, and designing your Internet access wisely, users can prevent most of these threats. Common Internet-related security issues include the following:

◆ A firewall may not be adequate protection, if it is configured improperly. For example, it may allow outsiders to obtain internal IP addresses, then use those addresses to pretend that they have authority to access your internal network from the Internet—a process called **IP spoofing**. Alternately, a firewall may not be configured correctly to perform even its simplest function—preventing unauthorized packets from entering the LAN from outside. (You will learn more about firewalls later in this chapter.) Correctly configuring a firewall is one of the best means to protect your internal LAN from Internet-based attacks.

◆ When a user Telnets or FTPs to your site over the Internet, his user ID and password are transmitted in plain text—that is, unencrypted. Anyone monitoring the network (that is, running a network monitor program or a hacking program specially designed to capture logon data) can pick up the user ID and password and use it to gain access to the system.

◆ Hackers may obtain information about your user ID from newsgroups, mailing lists, or forms you have filled out on the Web.

◆ While users remain logged on to Internet chat sessions, they may be vulnerable to other Internet users who might send commands to their machines that cause the screen to fill with garbage characters and require them to terminate their chat sessions. This type of attack is called **flashing**.

◆ After gaining access to your system through the Internet, a hacker may launch denial-of-service attacks. A **denial-of-service attack** occurs when a system becomes unable to function because it has been deluged with data transmissions or otherwise disrupted. This incursion is a relatively simple attack to launch (for example, a hacker could create a looping program that sends thousands of e-mail messages to your system per minute). The easiest resolution of this problem is to bring down the attacked server, then reconfigure the firewall to deny service (in return) to the attacking machine. Denial-of-service attacks may also result from malfunctioning software. Regularly upgrading software is essential to maintaining network security.

An Effective Security Policy

As you have learned, network security breaches can be initiated from within an organization, and many take advantage of human errors. This section describes how to minimize the risk of break-ins by communicating with and managing the users in your organization via a thoroughly planned security policy. A **security policy** identifies your security goals, risks, levels of authority, designated security coordinator and team members, responsibilities for each team member, and responsibilities for each employee. In addition, it specifies how to address security breaches. It should not state exactly which hardware, software, architecture, or protocols will be used to ensure security, nor how hardware or software will be installed and configured. These details change from time to time and should be shared only with authorized network administrators or managers.

Security Policy Goals

Before drafting a security policy, you should understand why the security policy is necessary and how it will serve your organization. Typical goals for security policies are as follows:

◆ Ensure that authorized users have appropriate access to the resources they need.

◆ Prevent unauthorized users from gaining access to the network, systems, programs, or data.

◆ Protect sensitive data from unauthorized access, both from within and from outside the organization.

◆ Prevent accidental damage to hardware or software.

◆ Prevent intentional damage to hardware or software.

◆ Create an environment in which the network and systems can withstand and, if necessary, quickly respond to and recover from any type of threat.

◆ Communicate each employee's responsibilities with respect to maintaining data integrity and system security.

 NOTE

A company's security policy may not pertain exclusively to computers or networks. For example, it might state that each employee must shred paper files that contain sensitive data or that each employee is responsible for signing in his visitors at the front desk and obtaining a temporary badge for them. Non-computer-related aspects of security policies are beyond the scope of this chapter, however.

After defining the goals of your security policy, you can devise a strategy to attain them. First, you might form a committee composed of managers and interested parties from a variety of departments, in addition to your network administrators. The more decision-making people you can involve, the more supported and effective your policy will be. This committee can assign a security coordinator, who will then drive the creation of a security policy.

 TIP

To increase the acceptance of your security policy in your organization, tie security measures to business needs and clearly communicate the potential effects of security breaches. For example, if your company sells clothes over the Internet and a two-hour outage (as could be caused by a hacker who uses IP spoofing to gain control of your systems) could cost the company $1 million in lost sales, make certain that users and managers understand this fact. If they do, they are more likely to embrace the security policy.

A security policy must address an organization's specific risks. To understand your risks, you should conduct a security audit that identifies vulnerabilities and rates both the severity of each threat and its likelihood of occurring, as described earlier in this chapter. After risks are identified, the security coordinator should assign one person the responsibility for addressing that threat.

Security Policy Content

After your risks are identified and responsibilities for managing them are assigned, the policy's outline should be generated with those risks in mind. Some subheadings for the policy might include the following: Password policy; Software installation policy; Confidential and sensitive data policy; Network access policy; E-mail use policy; Internet use policy; Modem use policy; Remote access policy; Policies for connecting to remote locations, the Internet, and customers' and vendors' networks; Policies for use of laptops and loaner machines; and Computer room access policy. Although compiling all of this information might seem daunting, the process ensures that everyone understands the organization's stance on security and the reasons it is so important.

The security policy should explain to users what they can and cannot do and how these measures protect the network's security. Clear and regular communication about security policies make them more acceptable and better understood. One idea for making security policies more sustainable is to distribute a "security newsletter" that keeps security issues fresh in everyone's mind. Perhaps the newsletter could highlight industry statistics about significant security breaches and their effect on the victimized organizations.

Another tactic is to create a separate section of the policy that applies only to users. Within the users' section, divide security rules according to the particular function or part of the network to which they apply. This approach makes the policy easier for users to read and understand; it also prevents them from having to read through the entire document. For example, in the "Passwords" section, guidelines might include: "Users may not share passwords with friends or relatives"; "users must choose passwords that exceed six characters and are composed of both letters and numbers"; and "users should choose passwords that bear no resemblance to a spouse's name, pet's name, birth date, anniversary, or other widely available information."

A security policy should also define what "confidential" means to the organization. In general, information is confidential if it could be used by other parties to impair an organization's functioning, decrease customers' confidence, cause a financial loss, damage an organization's status, or give a significant advantage to a competitor. However, if you work in an environment such as a hospital, where most data is sensitive or confidential, your security policy should classify information in degrees of sensitivity that correspond to how strictly its access is regulated. For example, "top-secret" data may be accessible only by the organization's CEO and vice presidents, whereas "confidential" data may be accessible only to those who must modify or create it (for example, doctors or hospital accountants).

Response Policy

Finally, a security policy should provide for a planned response in the event of a security breach. The response policy should identify the members of a response team, all of whom should clearly understand the security policy, risks, and measures in place. Each team member should be assigned a role and responsibilities. Like a disaster recovery response team, the security response team should regularly rehearse their defense by participating in a security threat drill. Some suggestions for team roles are the following:

◆ *Dispatcher*—The person on call who first notices or is alerted to the problem. The dispatcher notifies the lead technical support specialist and then the manager. She creates a record for the incident, detailing the time it began, its symptoms, and any other pertinent information about the situation. The dispatcher remains available to answer calls from clients or employees or to assist the manager.

◆ *Manager*—This team member coordinates the resources necessary to solve the problem. If in-house technicians cannot handle the break-in, the manager finds outside assistance. The manager also ensures that the security policy is followed and that everyone within the organization is aware of the situation. As the response ensues, the manager continues to monitor events and communicate with the public relations specialist.

◆ *Technical support specialist*—This team member focuses on only one thing: solving the problem as quickly as possible. After the situation has been resolved, the technical support specialist describes in detail what happened and helps the manager find ways to avert such an incident in the future. Depending on the size of the organization and the severity of the incident, this role may be filled by more than one person.

◆ *Public relations specialist*—If necessary, this team member learns about the situation and the response, then acts as official spokesperson for the organization to the public.

After resolving a problem, the team reviews what happened, determines how it might have been prevented, then implements those measures to prevent future problems. A security policy alone can't guard against intruders. Network administrators must also attend to physical, network design, and network operating system vulnerabilities, as described in the following sections.

Physical Security

An important element in network security is restricting physical access to its components. At the very least, only authorized networking personnel should have access to computer rooms. If computer rooms are not locked, intruders may easily steal equipment or sabotage software and hardware. For example, a malicious visitor could slip into an unsecured computer room and take control of a NetWare server where an administrator is logged on, then steal data or reformat the server's hard disk. Although a security policy defines who has access to the computer room, locking the computer room is necessary to keep unauthorized individuals out.

It isn't only the computer room that must be secured. Think of all the points at which your systems or data could be compromised: hubs or switches in a wiring closet, an unattended workstation at someone's desk, an equipment room or entrance facility where your leased line to the Internet terminates, or a storage room for archived data and backup tapes. If a wiring closet is left unlocked, for example, a prankster could easily enter, grab a handful of wires, and pull them out of the patch panels.

Locks may be either physical or electronic. Many large organizations require authorized employees to wear electronic access badges. These badges can be programmed to allow their owner access to some, but not all, rooms in a building. Figure 14-1 depicts a typical badge access security system.

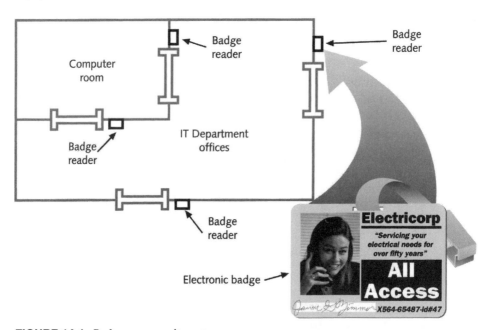

FIGURE 14-1 *Badge access security system*

A less expensive alternative to the electronic badge access system consists of locks that require entrants to punch a numeric code to gain access. For added security, these electronic locks can be combined with key locks. A more expensive solution involves **bio-recognition access**, in which a device scans an individual's unique physical characteristics, such as the color patterns in her iris or the geometry of her hand, to verify her identity. On a larger scale, organizations may regulate entrance through physical barriers to their campuses, such as gates, fences, walls, or landscaping.

Many IT departments also use closed-circuit TV systems to monitor activity in secured rooms. Surveillance cameras may be placed in computer rooms, telco rooms, supply rooms, and data storage areas, as well as facility entrances. A central security office may display several camera views at once, or it may switch from camera to camera. The video footage generated from these cameras is usually saved for a time in case it's needed in a security breach investigation or prosecution.

As with other security measures, the most important way to ensure physical security is to plan for it. You can begin your planning by asking questions related to physical security checks in your security audit. Relevant questions include the following:

◆ Which rooms contain critical systems or data and must be secured?

◆ Through what means might intruders gain access to the facility, computer room, telecommunications room, wiring closet, or data storage areas (including doors, windows, adjacent rooms, ceilings, temporary walls, hallways, and so on)?

◆ How and to what extent are authorized personnel granted entry? (Do they undergo background or reference checks? Is their need for access clearly justified? Are their hours of access restricted? Who ensures that lost keys or ID badges are reported?)

◆ Are employees instructed to ensure security after entering or leaving secured areas (for example, by not propping open doors)?

◆ Are authentication methods (such as ID badges) difficult to forge or circumvent?

◆ Do supervisors or security personnel make periodic physical security checks?

◆ Are all combinations, codes, or other access means to computer facilities protected at all times, and are these combinations changed frequently?

◆ Do you have a plan for documenting and responding to physical security breaches?

Also consider what you might stand to lose if someone salvaged computers you discarded. To guard against the threat of information being stolen from a decommissioned hard disk, you can run a specialized disk sanitizer program to not only delete the hard drive's contents but also make file recovery impossible. Alternatively, you can remove the disk from the computer and erase its contents using a magnetic hard disk eraser. Some security professionals even advise physically destroying a disk by pulverizing or melting it to be certain data is unreadable.

Security in Network Design

Addressing physical access to hardware and connections is just one part of a comprehensive security approach. Even if you restrict access to computer rooms, teach employees how to select secure passwords, and enforce a security policy, breaches may still occur due to poor LAN or WAN design. In this section, you will learn how to address some security risks via intelligent network design.

The optimal way to prevent external security breaches from affecting your LAN is not to connect your LAN to the outside world at all. This option is impractical in today's business environment, however. The next best protection is to restrict access at every point where your LAN connects to the rest of the world. This principle forms the basis of hardware- and design-based security.

NET+
3.5

Firewalls

A firewall is a specialized device, or a computer installed with specialized software, that selectively filters or blocks traffic between networks. A firewall typically involves a combination of hardware and software and may reside between two interconnected private networks or, more typically, between a private network and a public network (such as the Internet), as shown in Figure 14-2. Many types of firewalls exist, and they can be implemented in many different ways. To understand secure network design and to qualify for Network+ certification, you should recognize which functions firewalls can provide, where they can appear on a network, and how to decide what features you need in a firewall. Figure 14-3 depicts a firewall designed for use in a business with many users.

The simplest form of a firewall is a **packet-filtering firewall**, which is a router (or a computer installed with software that enables it to act as a router) that examines the header of every packet of data it receives to determine whether that type of packet is authorized to continue to its destination. If a packet does not meet the filtering criteria, the firewall prevents the packet

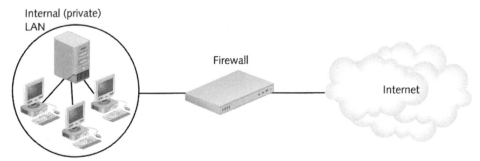

FIGURE 14-2 *Placement of a firewall between a private network and the Internet*

FIGURE 14-3 *Firewall*

NET+

3.5

from continuing. However, if a packet does meet filtering criteria, the firewall allows that packet to pass through to the network connected to the firewall. Packet-filtering firewalls are also called **screening firewalls**. (In fact, nearly all routers can be configured to act as packet-filtering firewalls.) Examples of software that enables a computer to act as a packet-filtering firewall include IP Tables (for Linux systems), Checkpoint Firewall Technologies' Firewall-1, McAfee Firewall, and Symantec.

NET+

3.5
3.7

In addition to blocking traffic on its way *into* a LAN, packet-filtering firewalls can block traffic attempting to *exit* a LAN. One reason for blocking outgoing traffic is to stop worms from spreading. For example, if you are running a Web server, which in most cases only needs to respond to incoming requests and does not need to initiate outgoing requests, you could configure a packet-filtering firewall to block certain types of outgoing transmissions initiated by the Web server. In this way, you help prevent spreading worms that are designed to attach themselves to Web servers and propagate themselves to other computers on the Internet.

Often, firewalls ship with a default configuration designed to block the most common types of security threats. In other words, the firewall may be preconfigured to accept or deny certain types of traffic. However, many network administrators choose to customize the firewall settings, for example, blocking additional ports or adding criteria for the type of traffic that may travel in or out of ports. Some common criteria a packet-filtering firewall might use to accept or deny traffic include the following:

- ◆ Source and destination IP addresses
- ◆ Source and destination ports (for example, ports that supply TCP/UDP connections, FTP, Telnet, ARP, ICMP, and so on)
- ◆ Flags set in the IP header (for example, SYN or ACK)
- ◆ Transmissions that use the UDP or ICMP protocols
- ◆ A packet's status as the first packet in a new data stream or a subsequent packet
- ◆ A packet's status as inbound to or outbound from your private network

Based on these options, a network administrator could configure his firewall, for example, to prevent any IP address that does not begin with "196.57," the network ID of the addresses on his network, from accessing the network's router and servers. Furthermore, he could disable—or block—certain well-known ports, such as the FTP ports (20 and 21), through the router's configuration. Blocking ports prevents *any* user from connecting to and completing a transmission through those ports. This technique is useful to further guard against unauthorized access to the network. In other words, even if a hacker could spoof an IP address that began with "196.57," he could not access the FTP ports (which are notoriously insecure) on the firewall. Ports can be blocked not only on firewalls, but also on routers, servers, or any device that uses ports. For example, if you established a Web server for testing but did not want anyone in your organization to connect to your Web pages through his or her browsers, you could block port 80 on that server.

NET+

3.5

For greater security, you can choose a firewall that performs more complex functions than simply filtering packets. Among the factors to consider when making your decision are the following:

◆ Does the firewall support encryption? (You will learn more about encryption later in this chapter.)

◆ Does the firewall support user authentication?

◆ Does the firewall allow you to manage it centrally and through a standard interface (for example, by using SNMP)?

◆ How easily can you establish rules for access to and from the firewall?

◆ Does the firewall support filtering at the highest layers of the OSI Model, not just at the Data Link and Transport layers?

◆ Does the firewall provide logging and auditing capabilities, or alert you to possible intrusions?

◆ Does the firewall protect the identity of your internal LAN's addresses from the outside world?

NET+

3.5

3.7

You will recognize examples of firewall placement in most VPN architectures. For example, you might design a VPN that uses the Internet to connect your Houston and Denver offices. To ensure that only traffic from Houston can access your Denver LAN through an external connection, you could install a packet-filtering firewall between the Denver LAN and the Internet. Further, you could configure the firewall to accept incoming traffic only from IP addresses that match the IP addresses on your Houston LAN. In a way, the firewall acts like a bouncer at a private club who checks everyone's ID and ensures that only club members enter through the door. In the case of the Houston-Denver VPN, the firewall will discard any data packets that arrive at the Denver firewall and *do not* contain source IP addresses that match those of Houston's LAN.

Because you must tailor a firewall to your network's needs, you cannot simply purchase one, install it between your private LAN and the Internet, and expect it to offer much security. Instead, you must first consider what type of traffic you want to filter, then configure the firewall accordingly. It may take weeks to achieve the best configuration—not so strict that it prevents authorized users from transmitting and receiving necessary data, yet not so lenient that you risk security breaches. Further complicating the matter is that you may need to create exceptions to the rules. For example, suppose that your human resources manager is working from a conference center in Salt Lake City while recruiting new employees and needs to access the Denver server that stores payroll information. In this instance, the Denver network administrator might create an exception to allow transmissions from the human resources manager's workstation's IP address to reach that server. In the networking profession, creating an exception to the filtering rules is called "punching a hole" in the firewall.

Because packet-filtering firewalls operate at the Network layer of the OSI Model and examine only network addresses, they cannot distinguish between a user who is trying to breach the firewall and a user who is authorized to do so. For example, your organization might host a

NET+

3.5

3.7
Web server, which necessitates accepting requests for port 80 on that server. In this case, a packet-filtering firewall, because it only examines the packet header, could not distinguish between a harmless Web browser and a hacker attempting to manipulate his way through the Web site to gain access to the network. For higher-layer security, a firewall that can analyze data at higher layers is required. The next section describes this kind of device.

Proxy Servers

NET+

3.6
One approach to enhancing the security of the Network and Transport layers provided by firewalls is to combine a packet-filtering firewall with a proxy service. A **proxy service** is a software application on a network host that acts as an intermediary between the external and internal networks, screening all incoming and outgoing traffic. The network host that runs the proxy service is known as a **proxy server**. (A proxy server may also be called an **Application layer gateway**, an **application gateway**, or simply, a **proxy**.) Proxy servers manage security at the Application layer of the OSI Model. To understand how they work, think of the secure data on a server as the president of a country and the proxy server as the secretary of state. Rather than have the president risk her safety by leaving the country, the secretary of state travels abroad, speaks for the president and gathers information on the president's behalf. In fact, foreign leaders may never actually meet the president. Instead, the secretary of state acts as her proxy. In a similar way, a proxy server represents a private network to another network (usually the Internet).

NET+

3.6

3.7
Although a proxy server appears to the outside world as an internal network server, in reality it is merely another filtering device for the internal LAN. One of its most important functions is preventing the outside world from discovering the addresses of the internal network. For example, suppose your LAN uses a proxy server, and you want to send an e-mail message from your workstation to your mother via the Internet. Your message would first go to the proxy server (depending on the configuration of your network, you may or may not have to log on separately to the proxy server first). The proxy server would repackage the data frames that make up the message so that, rather than your workstation's IP address being the source, the proxy server inserts its own IP address as the source. Next, the proxy server passes your repackaged data to the packet-filtering firewall. The firewall verifies that the source IP address in your packets is valid (that it came from the proxy server) and then sends your message to the Internet. Examples of proxy server software include Squid (for use on UNIX-type of systems), Novell BorderManager, and Microsoft Internet Security and Acceleration (ISA) Server 2000, an optional service for Windows 2000 Server and Windows Server 2003 servers. Figure 14-4 depicts how a proxy server might fit into a WAN design.

Proxy servers can also improve performance for users accessing resources external to their network by caching files. For example, a proxy server situated between a LAN and an external Web server can be configured to save recently viewed Web pages. The next time a user on the LAN wants to view one of the saved Web pages, content is provided by the proxy server. This eliminates the time required to travel over a WAN and retrieve the content from the external Web server.

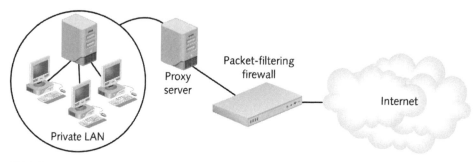

FIGURE 14-4 *A proxy server used on a WAN*

 NOTE

Often, firewall and proxy server features are combined in one device. In other words, you might purchase a firewall and be able to configure it not only to block certain types of traffic from entering your network, but also to modify the addresses in the packets leaving your network.

Remote Access

As you have learned, many companies supply traveling employees, telecommuters, or distant vendors with remote access to their private LANs or WANs. When working with remote access, you must remember that any entry point to a LAN or WAN creates a potential security risk. In other words, if an employee can get to your network in New York from his hotel room in Rome, a smart hacker can likely do the same. You can, however, take advantage of techniques designed to minimize the possibility of such unauthorized remote access. In this section, you will learn about security measures tailored to remote access solutions, such as remote control and dial-up networking.

Remote Control

Remote control systems enable a user to connect to a host system on a network from a distance and use that system's resources as if the user were sitting in front of it. Although such remote control systems can be convenient, they can also present serious security risks. Most remote control software programs (for example, Symantec Corporation's pcAnywhere) offer features that increase the security of remote control systems. If you intend to allow remote control access to a host on your LAN, you should investigate these security features and know how to implement them correctly. Important security features that you should seek in a remote control program include the following:

NET+
3.7

◆ A user name and password requirement for gaining access to the host system.

◆ The ability of the host system to call back. This feature enables a remote user to dial into the network, enter a user name, and hang up. The host system then calls the user back at a predetermined number (the authorized user's modem number), thus preventing a hacker from taking over a system even if he obtains the correct user ID and password for the host system.

◆ Support for data encryption on transmissions between the remote user and the system.

◆ The ability to leave the host system's screen blank while a remote user works on it. This feature prevents people walking by from seeing potentially confidential data.

◆ The ability to disable the host system's keyboard and mouse. This feature turns the host system into a terminal that responds only to remote users.

◆ The ability to restart the host system when a remote user disconnects from the system. This feature prevents anyone from reviewing what happened during the remote user's session or gaining access if the session was accidentally terminated before the remote user could properly log off.

Dial-Up Networking

Another method for remote access, dial-up networking, requires users to dial into a remote access server attached to the network. Dial-up networking differs from remote control in that it effectively turns a remote workstation into a node on the network, through a remote access server. When choosing a remote access software package, you should evaluate its security. A secure remote access server package includes at least the following features:

◆ User name and password authentication

◆ The ability to log all dial-up connections, their sources, and their connection times

◆ The ability to perform callbacks to users who initiate connections

◆ Centralized management of dial-up users and their rights on the network

Dial-up network security depends on strict verification of a user's credentials. Methods of achieving this verification are discussed later in the "Authentication Protocols" section of this chapter.

Network Operating System Security

NET+
3.1

Regardless of whether you run your network on a Novell, Microsoft, Macintosh, Linux, or UNIX network operating system, you can implement basic security by restricting what users are authorized to do on a network. Every network administrator should understand which resources on the server all users need to access. The rights conferred to all users are called public rights, because anyone can have them and exercising them presents no security threat to the

NET+
3.1

network. In most cases, public rights are very limited. They may include privileges to view and execute programs from the server and to read, create, modify, delete, and execute files in a shared data directory.

In addition, network administrators need to group users according to their security levels and assign additional rights that meet the needs of those groups. As you know, creating groups simplifies the process of granting rights to users. For example, if you work in the IT Department at a large college, you will most likely need more than one person to create new user IDs and passwords for students and faculty. Naturally, the staff in charge of creating new user IDs and passwords need the rights to perform this task. You could assign the appropriate rights to each staff member individually, but a more efficient approach is to put all of the personnel in a group, and then assign the appropriate rights to the group as a whole.

Logon Restrictions

In addition to restricting users' access to files and directories on the server, a network administrator can constrain the ways in which users can access the server and its resources. The following is a list of additional restrictions that network administrators can use to strengthen the security of their networks:

◆ *Time of day*—Some user accounts may be valid only during specific hours—for example, between 8:00 A.M. and 5:00 P.M. Specifying valid hours for an account can increase security by preventing any account from being used by unauthorized personnel after hours.

◆ *Total time logged on*—Some user accounts may be restricted to a specific number of hours per day of logged-on time. Restricting total hours in this way can increase security in the case of temporary user accounts. For example, suppose that your organization offers a WordPerfect training class to a group of high school students one afternoon, and the WordPerfect program and training files reside on your staff server. You might create accounts that could log on for only four hours on that day.

◆ *Source address*—You can specify that user accounts can log on only from certain workstations or certain areas of the network (that is, domains or segments). This restriction can prevent unauthorized use of user names from workstations outside the network.

◆ *Unsuccessful logon attempts*—Hackers may repeatedly attempt to log on under a valid user name for which they do not know the password. As the network administrator, you can set a limit on how many consecutive unsuccessful logon attempts from a single user ID the server will accept before blocking that ID from even attempting to log on.

Another security technique that can be enforced by a network administrator through the NOS is the selection of secure passwords. The following section discusses the importance and characteristics of choosing a secure password.

Passwords

Choosing a secure password is one of the easiest and least expensive ways to guard against unauthorized access. Unfortunately, too many people prefer to use an easy-to-remember password. If your password is obvious to you, however, it may also be easy for a hacker to figure out. The following guidelines for selecting passwords should be part of your organization's security policy. It is especially important for network administrators to choose difficult passwords, and also to keep passwords confidential and to change them frequently.

Tips for making and keeping passwords secure include the following:

- ◆ Always change system default passwords after installing new programs or equipment. For example, after installing a router, the default administrator's password on the router might be set by the manufacturer to be "1234" or the router's model number.

- ◆ Do not use familiar information, such as your name, nickname, birth date, anniversary, pet's name, child's name, spouse's name, user ID, phone number, address, or any other words or numbers that others might associate with you.

- ◆ Do not use any word that might appear in a dictionary. Hackers can use programs that try a combination of your user ID and every word in a dictionary to gain access to the network. This is known as a **dictionary attack**, and it is typically the first technique a hacker uses when trying to guess a password (besides asking the user for her password).

- ◆ Make the password longer than eight characters—the longer, the better. Some operating systems require a minimum password length (often, eight characters), and some may also restrict the password to a maximum length.

- ◆ Choose a combination of letters and numbers; add special characters, such as exclamation marks or hyphens, if allowed. Also, if passwords are case sensitive, use a combination of uppercase and lowercase letters.

- ◆ Do not write down your password or share it with others.

- ◆ Change your password at least every 60 days, or more frequently, if desired. If you are a network administrator, establish controls through the network operating system to force users to change their passwords at least every 60 days. If you have access to sensitive data, change your password even more frequently.

- ◆ Do not reuse passwords.

Password guidelines should be clearly communicated to everyone in your organization through your security policy. Although users may grumble about choosing a combination of letters and numbers and changing their passwords frequently, you can assure them that the company's financial and personnel data is safer as a result. No matter how much your colleagues protest, do not back down from your password requirements. Many companies mistakenly require employees only to use a password, and don't help them choose a good one. This oversight increases the risk of security breaches.

Encryption

NET+
3.7

Encryption is the use of an algorithm to scramble data into a format that can be read only by reversing the algorithm—that is, by decrypting the data. The purpose of encryption is to keep information private. Many forms of encryption exist, with some being more secure than others. Even as new forms of encryption are developed, new ways of cracking their codes emerge, too.

Encryption is the last means of defense against data theft. In other words, if an intruder has bypassed all other methods of access, including physical security (for instance, he has broken into the telecommunications room) and network design security (for instance, he has defied a firewall's packet-filtering techniques), data may still be safe if it is encrypted. Encryption can protect data stored on a medium, such as a hard disk, or in transit over a communications channel. To protect data, encryption provides the following assurances:

◆ Data was not modified after the sender transmitted it and before the receiver picked it up.

◆ Data can only be viewed by its intended recipient (or at its intended destination).

◆ All of the data received at the intended destination was truly issued by the stated sender and not forged by an intruder.

The following sections describe data encryption techniques used to protect data stored on or traveling across networks.

Key Encryption

The most popular kind of encryption algorithm weaves a **key** (a random string of characters) into the original data's bits—sometimes several times in different sequences—to generate a unique data block. The scrambled data block is known as **ciphertext**. The longer the key, the less easily the ciphertext can be decrypted by an unauthorized system. For example, a 128-bit key allows for 2^{128} possible character combinations, whereas a 16-bit key allows for 2^{16} possible character combinations. Hackers may attempt to crack, or discover, a key by using a **brute force attack**, which means simply trying numerous possible character combinations to find the key that will decrypt encrypted data. (Typically a hacker runs an application to carry out the attack.) Through a brute force attack, a hacker could discover a 16-bit key quickly and without using sophisticated computers, but would have difficulty discovering a 128-bit key.

 NOTE

Adding 1 bit to an encryption key makes it twice (2^1 times) as hard to crack. For example, a 129-bit key would be twice as hard to crack than a 128-bit key. Similarly, a 130-bit key would be four (2^2) times harder to crack than a 128-bit key.

NET+
3.7

The process of key encryption is similar to what happens when you finish a card game, place your five-card hand into the deck, and then shuffle the deck numerous times. After shuffling, it might take you a while to retrieve your hand. If you shuffled your five cards into four decks of cards at once, it would be even more difficult to find your original hand. In encryption, theoretically only the user or program authorized to retrieve the data knows how to unshuffle the ciphertext and compile the data in its original sequence. Figure 14-5 provides a simplified view of key encryption and decryption. Note that actual key encryption does not simply weave a key into the data once, but rather inserts the key, shuffles the data, shuffles the key, inserts another copy of the shuffled key into the shuffled data, shuffles the data again, and so on for several iterations.

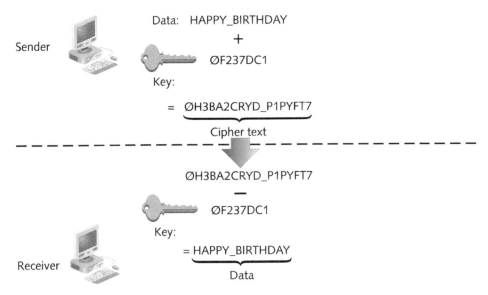

FIGURE 14-5 *Key encryption and decryption*

Keys are randomly generated, as needed, by the software that manages the encryption. For example, an e-mail program or a Web browser program may be capable of generating its own keys to encrypt data. In other cases, special encryption software is used to generate keys. This encryption software works with other types of software, such as word-processing or spreadsheet programs, to encrypt data files before they are saved or transmitted.

Private Key Encryption

Key encryption can be separated into two categories: private key and public key encryption. In **private key encryption**, data is encrypted using a single key that only the sender and the receiver know. Private key encryption is also known as **symmetric encryption**, because the same key is used during both the transmission and reception of the data.

Suppose John wants to send a secret message to Mary via private encryption. Assume he has chosen a private key. Next, he must share his private key with Mary, as shown in Step 1 of Figure 14-6. Then, John runs a program that encrypts his message by combining it with his private key, as shown in Step 2. Next, John sends Mary the encrypted message, as shown in Step 3. After Mary receives John's encrypted message, she runs a program that uses John's private key to decrypt the message, as shown in Step 4. The result is that Mary can read the original message John wrote.

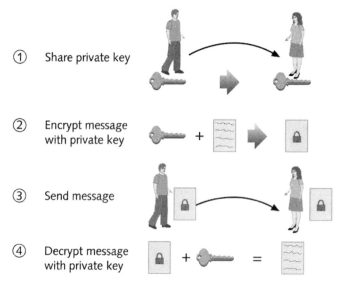

FIGURE 14-6 *Private key encryption*

The most popular private, or symmetric, key encryption is based on **DES** (pronounced "dez"), which stands for **Data Encryption Standard**. DES, which uses a 56-bit key, was developed by IBM in the 1970s. When DES was released, a 56-bit key was secure; however, now such a key could be cracked within days, given sufficient computer power. For greater security, the modern implementation of DES weaves a 56-bit key through data three times, using two or three different keys. This implementation is known as **Triple DES (3DES)**.

A more recent private key encryption standard is the **AES (Advanced Encryption Standard)**, which weaves keys of 128, 160, 192, or 256 bits through data multiple times. The algorithm used in the most popular form of AES is known as **Rijndael**, after its two Belgian inventors, Dr. Vincent Rijmen and Dr. Joan Daemen. AES is considered more secure than DES and much faster than Triple DES. AES has replaced DES in situations such as military communications, which must have the highest level of security.

The problem with private key encryption is that the sender must somehow share his key with the recipient. For example, John could call Mary and tell her his key, or he could send it to her in an e-mail message. But neither of these methods is very secure. To overcome this potential vulnerability, a method of associating publicly available keys with private keys was developed. This method is called public key encryption.

NET+
3.7

Public Key Encryption

In **public key encryption**, data is encrypted using two keys: One is a key known only to a user (that is, a private key), and the other is a public key associated with the user. A user's public key can be obtained the old-fashioned way—by asking that user—or it can be obtained from a third-party source, such as a public key server. A **public key server** is a publicly accessible host (such as a server on the Internet) that freely provides a list of users' public keys, much as a telephone book provides a list of peoples' phone numbers.

Figure 14-7 illustrates the process of public key encryption.

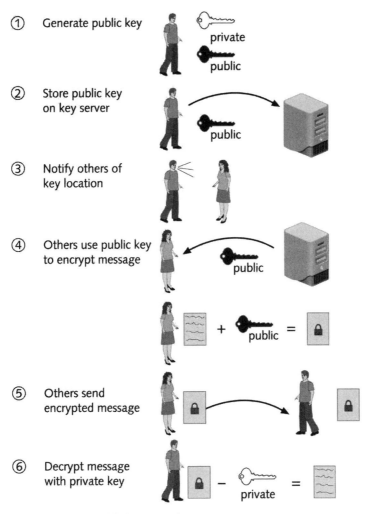

1. Generate public key
2. Store public key on key server
3. Notify others of key location
4. Others use public key to encrypt message
5. Others send encrypted message
6. Decrypt message with private key

FIGURE 14-7 *Public key encryption*

NET+

3.7

For example, suppose that Mary wants to use public key encryption to send John a message via the Internet. Assume John already established a private and a public key, as shown in Step 1 of Figure 14-7. He stores his public key on a key server on the Internet, as shown in Step 2, and keeps his private key to himself. Before Mary can send John a message, she must know his public key. John tells Mary where she can find his public key, as shown in Step 3. Next, Mary writes John a message, retrieves his public key from the public key server, and then uses her encryption software to scramble her message with John's public key, as shown in Step 4. Mary sends her encrypted message to John over the Internet, as shown in Step 5. When John receives the message, his software recognizes that the message has been encrypted with his public key. In other words, the public key has an association with the private key. A message that has been encrypted with John's public key can only be decrypted with his private key. The program then prompts John for his private key to decrypt the message, as shown in Step 6. To respond to Mary in a publicly encrypted message, John must obtain Mary's public key. Then, the steps illustrated in Figure 14-7 are repeated, with John and Mary's roles reversed.

The combination of a public key and a private key is known as a **key pair**. In the private key encryption example discussed previously, John has a key pair, but only he knows his private key, whereas the public key is available to people, like Mary, who want to send him encrypted messages. Because public key encryption requires the use of two different keys, it is also known as **asymmetric encryption**.

Due to their semipublic nature, public keys are more vulnerable than private keys and therefore, public key algorithms generally use longer keys. The first public, or asymmetric, key algorithm, called **Diffie-Hellman**, was released in 1975 by its creators, Whitfield Diffie and Martin Hellman. However, the most popular public key algorithm in use today is **RSA** (named after its creators, Ronald Rivest, Adi Shamir, and Leonard Adleman), which was made public in 1977. In RSA, a key is created by first choosing two large prime numbers (numbers that cannot be divided evenly by anything but 1 or themselves) and multiplying them together. RSA is routinely used to secure e-commerce transactions. RSA may be used in conjunction with **RC4**, a key encryption technique that weaves a key with data multiple times, as a computer issues the stream of data. RC4 keys can be as long as 2048 bits. In addition to being highly secure, RC4 is fast. It is used with many e-mail and browser programs, including Lotus Notes and Netscape.

With the abundance of private and public keys, not to mention the number of places where each may be kept, users need easier key management. One answer to this problem is using digital certificates. A **digital certificate** is a password-protected and encrypted file that holds an individual's identification information, including a public key. In the context of digital certificates, the individual's public key verifies the sender's digital signature. For example, on the Internet, certificate authorities such as VeriSign will, for a fee, keep your digital certificate on their server and ensure to all who want to send encrypted messages to you (for example, an order via your e-commerce site) that the certificate is indeed yours.

The following sections detail specific methods of encrypting data as it is transmitted over a network. These methods use one or more of the encryption algorithms discussed in this section.

PGP (Pretty Good Privacy)

You have probably exchanged e-mail messages over the Internet without much concern for what happens with your message between the time you send it and when your intended recipient picks it up. In addition, you have probably picked up e-mails from friends without thinking that they might *not* be from your friends, but rather from other users who are impersonating your friends over the Internet. In fact, typical e-mail communication is a highly insecure form of data exchange. The contents of a message are usually sent in clear (that is, unencrypted) text, which makes it readable by anyone who can capture the message on its way from you to your recipient. In addition, a person with malicious intentions can easily pretend he is someone else. For example, if your e-mail address is joe@trinketmakers.com, someone else could assume your address and send messages that appear to be sent by joe@trinketmakers.com. To secure e-mail transmissions, a computer scientist named Phil Zimmerman developed PGP in the early 1990s. **PGP (Pretty Good Privacy)** is a public key encryption system that can verify the authenticity of an e-mail sender and encrypt e-mail data in transmission. PGP, which is now administered at MIT, is freely available as both an open source and a proprietary software package. Since its release, it has become the most popular tool for encrypting e-mail. However, PGP can also be used to encrypt data on storage devices (for example, a hard disk) or with applications other than e-mail (for example, IP telephony).

SSL (Secure Sockets Layer)

NET+
2.17

SSL (Secure Sockets Layer) is a method of encrypting TCP/IP transmissions—including Web pages and data entered into Web forms—en route between the client and server using public key encryption technology. If you trade stocks or purchase goods on the Web, for example, you are most likely using SSL to transmit your order information. SSL is popular and used widely. The most recent versions of Web browsers, such as Netscape and Internet Explorer, include SSL client support in their software.

If you have used the Web, you have probably noticed that URLs for most Web pages begin with the HTTP prefix, which indicates that the request is handled by TCP/IP port 80 using the HTTP protocol. When Web page URLs begin with the prefix **HTTPS** (which stands for **HTTP over Secure Sockets Layer** or **HTTP Secure**) they require that their data be transferred from server to client and vice versa using SSL encryption. HTTPS uses the TCP port number 443, rather than port 80. After an SSL connection has been established between a Web server and client, the client's browser indicates this by showing a padlock in the lower-right corner of the screen in the browser's status bar. (Some older browser versions might not display the padlock, but almost all popular contemporary browsers do.)

Each time a client and server establish an SSL connection, they also establish a unique **SSL session**, or an association between the client and server that is defined by an agreement on a specific set of encryption techniques. An SSL session allows the client and server to continue to exchange data securely as long as the client is still connected to the server. An SSL session is created by the SSL handshake protocol, one of several protocols within SSL, and perhaps the most significant. As its name implies, the **handshake protocol** allows the client and server to authenticate (or introduce) each other and establishes terms for how they will securely

NET+
2.17

exchange data. For example, when you are connected to the Web and you decide to open your bank's account access URL, your browser initiates an SSL connection with the handshake protocol. The handshake protocol sends a special message to the server, called a **client_hello** message, which contains information about what level of security your browser is capable of accepting and what type of encryption your browser can decipher (for example, RSA or Diffie-Hellman). The client_hello message also establishes a randomly generated number that uniquely identifies your client and another number that identifies your SSL session. The server responds with a **server_hello** message that confirms the information it received from your client and agrees to certain terms of encryption based on the options your client supplied. Depending on the Web server's preferred encryption method, the server may choose to issue your browser a public key or a digital certificate at this time. After the client and server have agreed on the terms of encryption, they begin exchanging data.

SSL was originally developed by Netscape. Since that time, the IETF has attempted to standardize SSL in a protocol called **TLS (Transport Layer Security)**. Besides standardizing SSL for use with software from multiple vendors, IETF also aims to create a version of SSL that encrypts UDP as well as TCP transmissions. TLS, which is supported by new Web browsers (such as Internet Explorer version 5.0 and higher and Netscape version 6.0 and higher), uses slightly different encryption algorithms than SSL, but otherwise is very similar to the most recent version of SSL.

SSH (Secure Shell)

NET+
2.10

Earlier in this book, you learned about Telnet, the TCP/IP utility that provides remote connections to hosts. For example, if you were a network administrator working at one of your company's satellite offices and had to modify the configuration on a router at the home office, you could telnet to the router (over a VPN, for example) and run commands to modify its configuration. However, Telnet provides little security for establishing a connection (authenticating) and no security for transmitting data (encryption). **SSH (Secure Shell)** is a collection of protocols that does both. With SSH, you can securely log on to a host, execute commands on that host, and copy files to or from that host. SSH encrypts data exchanged throughout the session. It guards against a number of security threats, including: unauthorized access to a host, IP spoofing, interception of data in transit (even if it must be transferred via intermediate hosts), and **DNS spoofing**, in which a hacker forges name server records to falsify his host's identity. Depending on the version, SSH may use DES, Triple DES, RSA, Kerberos, or another, less common encryption algorithm or method.

SSH was developed by SSH Communications Security, and use of their SSH implementation requires paying for a license. However, open source versions of the protocol suite, such as **OpenSSH**, are available for most computer platforms. To form a secure connection, SSH must be running on both the client and server. Like Telnet, the SSH client is a utility that can be run at the shell prompt on a UNIX-type of system or at the command prompt on a Windows-based system. Other versions of the program come with a graphical interface. The SSH suite of protocols is included with all modern UNIX and Linux distributions and with Mac OS X Server and Mac OS X client operating systems. For Windows-based computers, you must download a freeware GUI SSH client, such as PuTTy or Tectia.

NET+
2.10

Before you can establish a secure SSH connection, you must first generate a public key and a private key on your client workstation by running the `ssh keygen` command (or by choosing the correct menu options in a graphical SSH program). The keys are saved in two different, encrypted files on your hard disk. Next, you must transfer the public key to an authorization file on the host to which you want to connect. Finally, you are ready to connect to the host via SSH. On a UNIX-type of computer, this is accomplished by running the `slogin -l` *username hostname* command, where *username* is your client user name and *hostname* is the name of the host to which you are trying to connect. The client and host then exchange public keys, and if both can be authenticated, the connection is completed. On a Windows-based computer, follow the menu options in the SSH client application.

SSH is highly configurable. For example, it can be configured to use one of several types of encryption for data en route between the client and host. It can be configured to require that the client enter a password in addition to a key. It can also be configured to perform **port forwarding**, which means it can redirect traffic that would normally use an insecure port (such as FTP) to an SSH-secured port. This allows you to use SSH for more than simply logging on to a host and manipulating files. With port forwarding you could, for example, exchange HTTP traffic with a Web server via a secured SSH connection.

SCP (Secure CoPy) and SFTP (Secure File Transfer Protocol)

An extension to OpenSSH is the **SCP (Secure CoPy)** utility, which allows you to copy files from one host to another securely. SCP replaces insecure file copy protocols such as FTP, which do not encrypt user names, passwords, or data while transferring them. Most modern OpenSSH packages, such as those supplied with the UNIX, Linux, and Macintosh OS X (client and server version) operating systems, include the SCP utility. Not all freeware SSH programs available for Windows include SCP, but separate, freeware SCP applications, such as WinSCP, exist.

SCP is simple to use. At the shell prompt of a UNIX-type of system, type `scp` *filename1 filename2*, where *filename1* is the name of the file on the source host and *filename2* is the name of the file on the target host. Suppose you are copying a file from a server to your client workstation. In that case, you also need to include your user name on the server and the server's host name in the command, as follows:

```
scp userid@hostname:filename1 filename2
```

In this command, *userid* is your user name on the server, *hostname* is the server's fully qualified host name, *filename1* is the name of the file on the server, and *filename2* is what you want to call the file on your client workstation. On a Windows-based system, follow the menu options in your SSH or SCP client for copying files with SCP.

If your system uses the proprietary version of SSH, available from SSH Communications Security, you need to use **SFTP (Secure File Transfer Protocol)** to copy files rather than SCP. SFTP is slightly different from SCP, in that it does more than copy files. Like FTP, SFTP first establishes a connection with a host and then allows a remote user to browse directories, list files, and copy files. To open an SFTP connection from a UNIX-type of system, type `sftp` *hostname* at a shell prompt, where *hostname* is the fully qualified host name of the computer to which you want to connect. To copy a file, type `get` *filename1 filename2*, where *filename1* is the name of the file on the source computer and *filename2* is what you want to call the file on the target computer. To close the SFTP connection, type `quit` and then press Enter. On a Windows-based system, follow the menu options in the SSH or SFTP client for copying files with SFTP.

The following section describes another technique for encrypting data in transit on a network.

IPSec (Internet Protocol Security)

IPSec (Internet Protocol Security) protocol defines encryption, authentication, and key management for TCP/IP transmissions. It is an enhancement to IPv4 and is native to the newer IPv6 standard. IPSec is somewhat different from other methods of securing data in transit. Rather than apply encryption to a stream of data, IPSec actually encrypts data by adding security information to the header of all IP packets. In effect, IPSec transforms the data packets. To do so, IPSec operates at the Network layer (Layer 3) of the OSI Model.

IPSec accomplishes authentication in two phases. The first phase is key management, and the second phase is encryption. **Key management** refers to the way in which two nodes agree on common parameters for the keys they will use. IPSec relies on **IKE (Internet Key Exchange)** for its key management. IKE is a service that runs on UDP port 500. After IKE has established the rules for the type of keys two nodes will use, IPSec invokes its second phase, encryption. In this phase, two types of encryption may be used: **AH (authentication header)** and **ESP (Encapsulating Security Payload)**. It is not important to know the inner workings of these services to qualify for Network+ certification, but you should be aware that both types of encryption provide authentication of the IP packet's data payload through public key techniques. In addition, ESP encrypts the entire IP packet for added security.

IPSec can be used with any type of TCP/IP transmission. However, it most commonly runs on routers or other connectivity devices in the context of VPNs. As you learned in Chapter 7, VPNs are used to transmit private data over public networks. Therefore, they require strict encryption and authentication to ensure that data is not compromised.

Authentication Protocols

You have learned that authentication is the process of verifying a user's credentials (typically a user name and password) to grant the user access to secured resources on a system or network. **Authentication protocols** are the rules that computers follow to accomplish authentication. Several types of authentication protocols exist. They vary according to which encryption schemes they rely on and the steps they take to verify credentials. The following sections describe some common authentication protocols in more detail.

NET+
2.18

RADIUS and TACACS

In environments in which many simultaneous dial-up connections must be supported and their user IDs and passwords managed, a service called **RADIUS (Remote Authentication Dial-In User Service)** might be used to authenticate users. RADIUS is a service defined by the IETF that runs over UDP and provides centralized network authentication and accounting for multiple users. RADIUS can operate as a software application on a remote access server or on a computer dedicated to this type of authentication, called a **RADIUS server**. A RADIUS server does not replace functions performed by the remote access server, but communicates with the access server to manage user logons. RADIUS is frequently used with dial-up networking connections.

RADIUS servers are highly scalable, as they can attach to pools containing hundreds of modems. Many Internet service providers use a RADIUS server to allow their subscribers to dial into their network and gain access to the Internet. Other organizations employ it as a central authentication point for mobile or remote users. RADIUS is also more secure than a simple remote access solution because its method of authentication prevents users' IDs and passwords from traveling across the connection in clear text format.

Figure 14-8 illustrates these two methods for allowing remote users to connect using RADIUS authentication. RADIUS can run on UNIX, Linux, Windows, Macintosh, or NetWare networks. A similar, but earlier version of a centralized authentication system is **TACACS (Terminal Access Controller Access Control System)**.

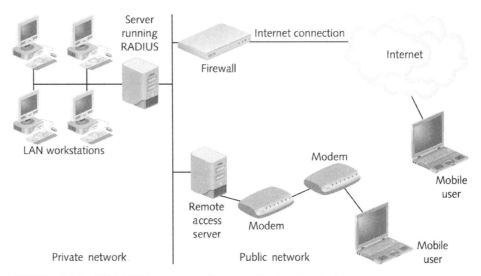

FIGURE 14-8 *A RADIUS server providing centralized authentication*

PAP (Password Authentication Protocol)

In Chapter 7's discussion of remote access protocols, you were introduced to PPP (Point-to-Point Protocol), which belongs to the Data Link layer of the OSI Model and provides the foundation for connections between remote clients and hosts. PPP alone, however, does not secure connections. For this it requires an authentication protocol.

In fact, several types of authentication protocols can work over PPP. One is **PAP (Password Authentication Protocol)**. After establishing a link with a server through PPP, a client uses PAP to send an authentication request that includes its credentials—usually a user name and password. The server compares the credentials to those in its user database. If the credentials match, the server responds to the client with an acknowledgment of authentication and grants the client access to secured resources. If the credentials do not match, the server denies the request to authenticate. Figure 14-9 illustrates PAP's two-step authentication process.

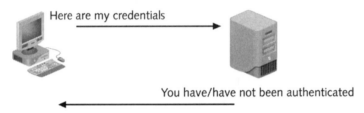

Here are my credentials

You have/have not been authenticated

FIGURE 14-9 *Two-step authentication used in PAP*

Thus, PAP is a simple authentication protocol, but it is not very secure. It sends the client's credentials in clear text, without encryption, and this opens the way for eavesdroppers to capture a user name and password. In addition, PAP does not protect against the possibility of a malicious intruder attempting to guess a user's password through a brute force attack. For these reasons, PAP is rarely used on modern networks. Instead, more sophisticated protocols, such as those described in the following sections, are preferred.

CHAP and MS-CHAP

CHAP (Challenge Handshake Authentication Protocol) is another authentication protocol that operates over PPP. Unlike PAP, CHAP encrypts user names and passwords for transmission. It also differs from PAP in that it requires three steps to complete the authentication process. Together, these steps are known as a **three-way handshake**.

In CHAP, the authenticating device (for example, the remote access server in a dial-up scenario) takes the first step in authentication after PPP establishes a connection between it and the computer requesting authentication (for example, a dial-up client). The server sends the client a randomly generated string of characters called the **challenge**. In the second step, the client adds its password to the challenge and encrypts the new string of characters. It sends this new string of characters in a response to the server. Meanwhile, the server also concatenates the user's password with the challenge and encrypts the new character string, using the

NET+
2.18

same encryption scheme the client used. In the third step of the three-way handshake, the server compares the encrypted string of characters it received from the client with the encrypted string of characters it has generated. If the two match, it authenticates the client. But if the two differ, it rejects the client's request for authentication. Figure 14-10 illustrates the three-way handshake used in CHAP.

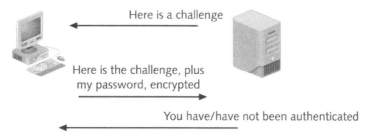

FIGURE 14-10 *Three-way handshake used in CHAP*

The benefit of CHAP over PAP is that in CHAP, a password is never transmitted alone, and never as clear text. This same type of security is offered in **MS-CHAP (Microsoft Challenge Authentication Protocol),** a similar authentication protocol from Microsoft used with Windows-based computers. One potential flaw in CHAP and MS-CHAP authentication is that someone eavesdropping on the network could capture the string of characters that is encrypted with the password, decrypt that string, and obtain the client's password. To address this, Microsoft released **MS-CHAPv2 (Microsoft Challenge Authentication Protocol, version 2),** which uses stronger encryption, does not use the same encryption strings for transmission and reception, and requires mutual authentication. In **mutual authentication,** both computers verify the credentials of the other—for example, the client authenticates the server just as the server authenticates the client. This is more secure than requiring only one of the communicating computers to authenticate the other.

NET+
2.18
3.4

MS-CHAPv2 is available for use with VPN connections in the Windows 98, NT 4.0, 2000, XP, and Server 2003 operating systems. Only Windows 2000, XP, and Server 2003 support MS-CHAPv2 for dial-up connections. And by default, Windows XP clients are configured to support PAP, CHAP, MS-CHAP, and MS-CHAPv2 when making dial-up connections.

To modify the dial-up connection's supported authentication protocols on a Windows XP client:

1. Click **Start**, and then click **My Network Places**. The My Network Places window opens.

2. Under Network Tasks, click **View Network Connections**. The Network Connections window opens.

3. Right-click the dial-up connection and choose **Properties** from the shortcut menu. The dial-up connection's Properties dialog box opens.

4. Click the **Security** tab to view security options for this connection.

5. Click the **Advanced (custom settings)** option, and then click the **Settings** button. The Advanced Security Settings dialog box opens, as shown in Figure 14-11.

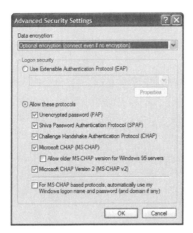

FIGURE 14-11 *Advanced Security Settings dialog box*

6. Notice that, by default, the Data encryption variable is set to "Optional encryption (connect even if no encryption)" and under Allow these protocols, all available authentication protocols are selected. In this dialog box, you could choose, for example, to require encryption for your dial-up connection by selecting "Require encryption (disconnect if server declines)" under the Data encryption heading. Or, you could choose to support only certain authentication protocols by deselecting some of the protocols listed under the Allow these protocols heading.

7. Click **OK** to save your changes if you made any. If you chose to require encryption and did not deselect PAP, SPAP (the Shiva Password Authentication Protocol, which is used with remote access servers using the Shiva software), or CHAP, you will receive a message alerting you that if one of these authentication protocols is selected, data encryption will not occur. Click **Yes** to continue. Thereafter, you will not be able to connect to a server that supports only PAP, SPAP, or CHAP. If you deselected MS-CHAP and did not select EAP, you will receive a message telling you that you must chose one of these. In that case, click **OK** to return to the Advanced Security Settings dialog box, select at least one of the more secure authentication protocols, and then click **OK** to continue.

8. Click **OK** to close the dial-up connection Properties dialog box.

An authentication protocol that is more secure than CHAP or MS-CHAP and is supported by multiple operating systems is EAP, discussed next.

NET+
2.18

EAP (Extensible Authentication Protocol)

EAP (Extensible Authentication Protocol) is another extension to the PPP protocol suite. It differs from the authentication protocols discussed previously in that it is only a mechanism for authenticating clients and servers; it does not perform encryption or authentication on its own. Instead, it works with other encryption and authentication schemes to verify the credentials of clients and servers.

Like CHAP, EAP requires the authenticator (for example, the server) initiate the authentication process by asking the connected computer (for example, the client) to verify itself. In EAP, the server usually sends more than one request. In its first request, it asks the client's identity and indicates what type of authentication to use. In subsequent requests, it asks the client for authentication information to prove the client's identity. The client responds to each of the servers' requests in the required format. If the responses match what the server expects, the server authenticates the client.

One of EAP's advantages is its flexibility. It is supported by nearly all modern operating systems and can be used with any authentication method. For example, although the typical network authentication involves a user ID and password, EAP also works with bio-recognition methods, such as retina or hand scanning. EAP is also adaptable to new technology. Therefore, no matter what future wireless encryption schemes are developed, EAP will support them.

In the case of wireless LANs, EAP is used with older encryption and authentication protocols to form a new, more secure method of connecting to networks from wireless stations. You will learn more about wireless security protocols—and how EAP is used with these—later in this chapter.

Kerberos

Kerberos is a cross-platform authentication protocol that uses key encryption to verify the identity of clients and to securely exchange information after a client logs on to a system. It is an example of a private key encryption service. Kerberos provides significant security advantages over simple network operating system authentication. Whereas an NOS client/server logon process assumes that clients are who they say they are and only verifies a user's name against the password in the NOS database, Kerberos does not automatically trust clients. Instead, it requires a client to prove its identity through a third party. This is similar to what happens when you apply for a passport. The government does not simply believe that you are "Leah Torres," but instead requires you to present proof, such as your birth certificate. In addition to checking the validity of a client, Kerberos communications are encrypted and unlikely to be deciphered by any device on the network other than the client. Contrast this type of transmission to the normally unencrypted and vulnerable communication between an NOS and a client.

To understand specifically how a client uses Kerberos, you need to understand some of the terms used when discussing this protocol. In Kerberos terminology, the server that issues keys to clients during initial client authentication is known as the **KDC (Key Distribution Center)**. To authenticate a client, the KDC runs an **AS (authentication service)**. An AS issues a **ticket**, which is a temporary set of credentials that a client uses to prove that its identity has been validated (note that a ticket is not the same as a key, which is used to initially validate its identity). A Kerberos client, or user, is known as a **principal**.

Now that you have learned the terms used by Kerberos, you can follow the process it requires for client/server communication. Bear in mind that the purpose of Kerberos is to connect a valid user with the *service* that user wants to access. To accomplish this, both the user and the service must register their keys with the authentication service. Suppose the principal is Jamal Sayad and the service is called "inventory." Jamal first logs on to his network as usual. Next, he attempts to log on to the "inventory" service with his Kerberos principal name and password. (On a Windows 2000 Server or Windows Server 2003 network, the KDC is, by default, the user's domain controller, and therefore, a user may not need to separately log on to a Kerberos-authenticated service.) The KDC confirms that Jamal Sayad is in its database and that he has provided the correct password. Then, the AS running on the KDC randomly generates two copies of a new key, called the **session key**. The AS issues one copy to Jamal's computer and the other copy to the inventory service. Further, it creates a ticket that allows Jamal to use the inventory service. This ticket contains the inventory service key and can only be decrypted using Jamal Sayad's key. The AS sends the ticket to Jamal Sayad. Jamal's computer decrypts the session key with Jamal's personal key. It then creates a time stamp associated with his request, and encrypts this time stamp with the session key. The encrypted time stamp is known as the **authenticator**. This time stamp helps the service verify that the ticket is indeed associated with Jamal Sayad's request to use the inventory service. Next, Jamal's computer sends his ticket and authenticator to the service. The service decrypts the ticket using its own key and decrypts the authenticator using its session key. Finally, the service verified that the principal requesting its use is truly Jamal Sayad as the KDC indicated.

The preceding events illustrate the original version of the Kerberos authentication process. The problem with the original version was that a user had to request a separate ticket each time he wanted to use a different service. To alleviate this inconvenience, Kerberos developers created the **TGS (Ticket-granting service)**, an application separate from the AS that also runs on the KDC. So that the client does not need to request a new ticket from the TGS each time it wants to use a different service on the network, the TGS issues the client a **TGT (ticket-granting ticket)**. After receiving the TGT, any time that the user wants to contact a service, he requests a ticket not from the AS, but from the TGS. Furthermore, the reply is encrypted not with the user's personal key, but with the session key that the AS provided for use with the TGS. Inside that reply is the new session key for use with the regular service. The rest of the exchange continues as described previously.

NOTE

Kerberos, which is named after the three-headed dog in Greek mythology who guarded the gates of Hades, was designed at MIT (Massachusetts Institute of Technology). MIT still provides free copies of the Kerberos code. In addition, many software vendors have developed their own versions of Kerberos.

Wireless Network Security

Wireless transmissions are particularly susceptible to eavesdropping. For example, a hacker could search for unprotected wireless networks by driving around with a laptop configured to receive and capture wireless data transmissions—a practice known as **war driving**. (The term is derived from the term "war dialing," which is a similar tactic involving modems.) War driving is surprisingly effective for obtaining private information. Recently, the hacker community publicized the vulnerabilities of a well-known store chain, which were discovered while war driving. The retailer used wireless cash registers to help customers make purchases when the regular, wire-bound cash registers were busy. However, the wireless cash registers transmitted purchase information, including credit card numbers and customer names, to network APs (access points) in clear text. By chance, a person in the parking lot who was running a protocol analyzer program on his laptop obtained several credit card numbers in a very short time. The person alerted the retailer to the security risk (rather than exploiting the information he gathered). Needless to say, after the retailer discovered its error, it abandoned the use of wireless cash registers until after a thorough evaluation of its data security.

WEP (Wired Equivalent Privacy)

As you have learned, most organizations use one of the 802.11 protocol standards on their WLANs. By default, the 802.11 standard does not offer any security. In addition, most APs do not require a client to authenticate before it can communicate with the AP. The client only needs to know the AP's SSID, which most APs broadcast. Smart network administrators prevent their APs from broadcasting the SSIDs, making them harder to detect. However, this does not provide true security.

For some measure of security, 802.11 allows for optional encryption using the **WEP (Wired Equivalent Privacy)** standard. WEP uses keys both to authenticate network clients and to encrypt data in transit. When configuring WEP, you establish a character string required to associate with the AP, also known as the **network key**. When the client detects the presence of the AP, the user is prompted to provide a network key before the client can gain access to a network via the AP. On a Windows XP computer, the network key can be saved as part of the wireless connection's properties.

To edit or add a WEP key for a wireless connection on your Windows XP client:

1. Click **Start**, and then click **My Network Places**. The My Network Places window opens.

2. Under Network Tasks, click **View network connections**. The Network Connections window opens.

3. Right-click the **Wireless Network Connection** icon, and then choose **Properties** from the shortcut menu. The Wireless Network Connection Properties dialog box opens.

4. Select the **Wireless Networks** tab.

5. Under Preferred networks, click the network (or the SSID) for which you want to establish a WEP key, then click **Properties**. Your wireless network's properties dialog box opens, with the Association tab selected by default.

6. In the drop-down menu next to Data encryption, choose **WEP**.

7. Enter your WEP key in the Network key text box. You must enter precisely the same key that your AP is configured to use, in either ASCII or hexadecimal form.

8. Enter your WEP key again in the Confirm network key text box. As shown in Figure 14-12, the network key will not appear on the screen, so that anyone peering over your shoulder cannot discover it.

FIGURE 14-12 *Entering a WEP key in the wireless network properties dialog box*

9. Click **OK** to save your changes and close the wireless network properties dialog box.

10. Click **OK** again to close the Wireless Network Connection Properties dialog box.

The first implementation of WEP allowed for 64-bit network keys, which, as you know, are not highly secure. Consequently, many early wireless networks were susceptible to brute force attacks, even though they used the best possible encryption. Current versions of WEP allow for more secure, 128-bit network keys. Still, WEP's use of the shared key for authenticating all users and for exchanging data makes it more susceptible to discovery than a dynamically

NET+
2.17

generated, random, or single-use key. Moreover, because WEP operates in the Physical and Data Link layers of the OSI Model, it does not offer end-to-end data transmission security. A better wireless security technique is 802.11i, which is discussed next.

IEEE 802.11i and WPA (Wi-Fi Protected Access)

Because of WEP's relative insecurity, IEEE devised a new wireless security protocol, called **802.11i**, that uses EAP (discussed previously in this chapter) with a strong encryption scheme and that dynamically assigns every transmission its own key. As you can imagine, EAP makes logging on to a wireless network more complex than it is with WEP. In 802.11i, a wireless station first issues a request to the AP. The AP acts as a proxy between the remote access server and station until the station has successfully authenticated with a remote access server. Meanwhile, the AP prevents any direct exchange of data between the two. After obtaining data from an unknown station, the AP repackages the data and then transmits it to the remote access server. It also repackages data from the remote access server before issuing it to the station. Thus, 802.11i requires mutual authentication—the station authenticates with the remote access server, and also, the remote access server authenticates with the station. After mutual authentication, the remote access server instructs the AP to allow traffic from the client into the network without first having to be repackaged. Next, the client and server agree on the encryption key that they will use with the encryption scheme. Following that, they exchange data that has been encrypted through the mutually agreed-upon method. 802.11i specifies the AES encryption method and mixes each packet in a data stream with a different key. Because of its impressive security, 802.11i is poised to replace the less-secure WEP as the preferred means for protecting wireless transmissions from intruders.

WPA (Wi-Fi Protected Access) is a subset of the 802.11i standard endorsed by the **Wi-Fi Alliance**, an international nonprofit organization dedicated to ensuring the interoperability of 802.11-capable devices. In fact, the Wi-Fi Alliance released WPA before 802.11i was ratified to quickly provide a more secure alternative to WEP. In WPA, authentication follows the same mechanism specified in 802.11i. The main difference is that WPA specifies RC4 encryption rather than AES. Since the 802.11i standard was approved, the Wi-Fi Alliance has released an updated version called **WPA2**. WPA2 includes support for the previously released WPA protocol. In all other ways, it is identical to 802.11i.

To support 802.11i, WPA, and WPA2, most currently installed APs and wireless NICs require driver, if not firmware, upgrades.

Chapter Summary

◆ Every organization should assess its security risks by conducting a security audit, at least annually and preferably quarterly. For each threat, your security audit should rate the severity of its potential consequences, as well as its likelihood.

◆ One of the most common methods by which an intruder gains access to a network is to simply ask a user for his password. This strategy is commonly called social engineering because it involves manipulating social relationships to gain access.

◆ Security risks that a network administrator must guard against include: incorrectly configuring user accounts or groups, and their privileges; overlooking security flaws in topology or hardware configuration; overlooking security flaws in operating system or application configuration; improperly documenting or communicating security policies; and leaving system settings (such as a program's administrator user name or the administrator's password on a router) at their default values.

◆ Some risks inherent in network transmission and design include: leased public lines that may allow for eavesdropping; hubs that broadcast traffic over the entire segment, making transmissions more vulnerable to sniffing; unused hub, router, or server ports that can be exploited and accessed by hackers if not disabled; a router's configuration port, accessible by Telnet, that may not be adequately secured; routers that may not be properly configured to mask internal subnets; modems attached to network devices that may be configured to accept incoming calls; and dial-in access servers used by telecommuting or remote staff that may not be carefully secured and monitored.

◆ Some risks pertaining to networking protocols and software include the following: inherent TCP/IP security flaws; trust relationships between one server and another; NOS "back doors" or security flaws; an NOS that allows server operators to exit to a command prompt; administrators who accept default operating system security; and transactions that take place between applications left open to interception.

◆ A security policy identifies an organization's security goals, risks, levels of authority, designated security coordinator and team members, responsibilities for each team member, responsibilities for each employee, and strategies for addressing security breaches.

◆ A security policy should: ensure that authorized users have appropriate access to the resources they need; prevent unauthorized users from gaining access to the network and its resources; protect sensitive data from unauthorized access; prevent accidental damage to hardware or software; prevent intentional damage to hardware or software; create an environment in which the network and systems can withstand and quickly recover from any type of threat; and communicate each employee's responsibilities with respect to maintaining data integrity.

◆ At the very least, computer rooms should allow access only to authorized networking personnel. If computer rooms or wiring closets remain unlocked, intruders may easily enter and steal equipment, or sabotage software and hardware.

◆ A firewall is a specialized device (typically a router, but possibly only a desktop computer running special software) that selectively filters or blocks traffic between networks. It may be placed between two interconnected private networks or, more typically, between a private network and a public network (such as the Internet).

◆ The most common form of firewall is a packet-filtering firewall, which examines the header of every packet of data that it receives to determine whether that type of packet is authorized to continue to its destination.

◆ A proxy service is a software application on a network host that acts as an intermediary between the external and internal networks, screening all incoming and outgoing traffic. The host that runs the proxy service is known as a proxy server. A proxy server appears to external machines as a network server, but it is actually another filtering device for the internal LAN.

◆ A secure remote access server package includes at least the following features: user name and password authentication; the ability to log all dial-up connections, their sources, and their connection times; the ability to perform callbacks to users who initiate connections; and centralized management of dial-up users and their rights on the network.

◆ Every NOS provides at least some security by allowing you to limit users' access to files and directories on the network. In addition, network administrators can constrain how those with different types of user IDs can use the network by setting restrictions on, for example, time of day, total time logged on, source address, and number of unsuccessful logon attempts.

◆ Choosing secure passwords is one of the easiest and least expensive ways to guard against unauthorized access. The following guidelines for selecting passwords should be part of your organization's security policy: Do not use the familiar types of passwords; do not use any word that can be found in a dictionary; make the password longer than eight characters; choose a combination of letters and numbers; add special characters, such as exclamation marks or hyphens, if allowed; use uppercase and lowercase letters, if the password is case sensitive; do not write down your password or share it with others; do not reuse passwords; and change your password at least every 60 days.

◆ Encryption is the use of an algorithm to scramble data into a format that can be read only by reversing the algorithm—or decrypting the data—to keep the information private. Many forms of encryption exist, with some being more secure than others.

◆ The most popular kind of encryption algorithm weaves a key (a random string of characters) into the original data's bits, sometimes several times in different sequences, to generate a unique data block. The longer the key, the less easily the encrypted data can be decrypted by an unauthorized system.

◆ Key encryption comes in two forms: public and private key encryption. Popular private (symmetric) key encryption algorithms include DES (Data Encryption Standard), Triple DES (3DES), and AES (Advanced Encryption Standard). Popular public (asymmetric) key encryption algorithms include Diffie-Hellman, RSA, and RC4.

◆ Popular methods of encryption include PGP (Pretty Good Privacy), SSL (Secure Sockets Layer), SSH (Secure Shell) and OpenSSH, and IPSec (Internet Protocol Security). IPSec is the protocol used on many modern VPNs.

◆ SCP (Secure CoPy) and SFTP (Secure File Transfer Protocol) are ways of copying files securely via SSH or OpenSSH.

◆ Authentication protocols used with PPP connections include RADIUS (Remote Authentication Dial-In User Service), TACACS (Terminal Access Controller Access Control System), PAP (Password Authentication Protocol), CHAP (Challenge Handshake Authentication Protocol), and MS-CHAP (Microsoft Challenge Handshake Authentication Protocol). Other authentication protocols include EAP (Extensible Authentication Protocol) and Kerberos.

◆ Wireless networks can use the WEP (Wired Equivalent Privacy) method of encrypting data in transit between stations and APs. WEP allows for keys as long as 128 bits. However, because WEP uses the same key for all stations attaching to an AP and for all transmissions, it is not very secure.

◆ A better wireless security solution than WEP is provided by IEEE's 802.11i standard. In 802.11i, the EAP authentication method is combined with AES encryption. Also, each 802.11i transmission is dynamically assigned its own key for encryption.

◆ The Wi-Fi Alliance has released two wireless security standards: WPA and WPA2. WPA follows the same authentication and encryption processes as 802.11i, but uses RC4 encryption. WPA2 is identical to 802.11i, but provides backward compatibility for clients running WPA.

Key Terms

3DES—See *Triple DES*.

802.11i—The IEEE standard for wireless network encryption and authentication that uses the EAP authentication method, strong encryption, and dynamically assigned keys, which are different for every transmission. 802.11i specifies AES encryption and weaves a key into each packet.

Advanced Encryption Standard—See *AES*.

AES (Advanced Encryption Standard)—A private key encryption algorithm that weaves keys of 128, 160, 192, or 256 bits through data multiple times. The algorithm used in the most popular form of AES is known as Rijndael. AES has replaced DES in situations such as military communications, which require the highest level of security.

AH (authentication header)—In the context of IPSec, a type of encryption that provides authentication of the IP packet's data payload through public key techniques.

application gateway—See *proxy server*.

Application layer gateway—See *proxy server*.

AS (authentication service)—In Kerberos terminology, the process that runs on a KDC (key distribution center) to initially validate a client who's logging on. The authentication service issues session keys to the client and the service the client wants to access.

asymmetric encryption—A type of encryption (such as public key encryption) that uses a different key for encoding data than is used for decoding the ciphertext.

authentication header—See *AH*.

authentication protocol—A set of rules that governs how servers authenticate clients. Several types of authentication protocols exist.

authentication service—See *AS*.

authenticator—In Kerberos authentication, the user's time stamp encrypted with the session key. The authenticator is used to help the service verify that a user's ticket is valid.

bio-recognition access—A method of authentication in which a device scans an individual's unique physical characteristics (such as the color patterns in his iris or the geometry of his hand) to verify the user's identity.

brute force attack—An attempt to discover an encryption key or password by trying numerous possible character combinations. Usually, a brute force attack is performed rapidly by a program designed for that purpose.

challenge—A random string of text issued from one computer to another in some forms of authentication. Used, along with the password (or other credential), in a response to verify the computer's credentials.

Challenge Handshake Authentication Protocol—See *CHAP*.

CHAP (Challenge Handshake Authentication Protocol)—An authentication protocol that operates over PPP and that requires the authenticator to take the first step by offering the other computer a challenge. The requestor responds by combining the challenge with its password, encrypting the new string of characters and sending it to the authenticator. The authenticator matches to see if the requestor's encrypted string of text matches its own encrypted string of characters. If so, the requester is authenticated and granted access to secured resources.

ciphertext—The unique data block that results when an original piece of data (such as text) is encrypted (for example, by using a key).

client_hello—In the context of SSL encryption, a message issued from the client to the server that contains information about what level of security the client's browser is capable of accepting and what type of encryption the client's browser can decipher (for example, RSA or Diffie-Hellman). The client_hello message also establishes a randomly generated number that uniquely identifies the client, plus another number that identifies the SSL session.

cracker—A person who uses his knowledge of operating systems and utilities to intentionally damage or destroy data or systems.

Data Encryption Standard—See *DES.*

denial-of-service attack—A security attack caused by a deluge of traffic that disables the victimized system.

DES (Data Encryption Standard)—A popular private key encryption technique that was developed by IBM in the 1970s.

dictionary attack—A technique in which attackers run a program that tries a combination of a known user ID and, for a password, every word in a dictionary to attempt to gain access to a network.

Diffie-Hellman—The first commonly used public, or asymmetric, key algorithm. Diffie-Hellman was released in 1975 by its creators, Whitfield Diffie and Martin Hellman.

digital certificate—A password-protected and encrypted file that holds an individual's identification information, including a public key and a private key. The individual's public key is used to verify the sender's digital signature, and the private key allows the individual to log on to a third-party authority who administers digital certificates.

DNS spoofing—A security attack in which an outsider forges name server records to falsify his host's identity.

EAP (Extensible Authentication Protocol)—A Data Link layer protocol defined by the IETF that specifies the dynamic distribution of encryption keys and a pre-authentication process in which a client and server exchange data via an intermediate node (for example, an access point on a wireless LAN). Only after they have mutually authenticated can the client and server exchange encrypted data. EAP can be used with multiple authentication and encryption schemes.

Encapsulating Security Payload—See *ESP.*

encryption—The use of an algorithm to scramble data into a format that can be read only by reversing the algorithm—decrypting the data—to keep the information private. The most popular kind of encryption algorithm weaves a key into the original data's bits, sometimes several times in different sequences, to generate a unique data block.

ESP (Encapsulating Security Payload)—In the context of IPSec, a type of encryption that provides authentication of the IP packet's data payload through public key techniques. In addition, ESP also encrypts the entire IP packet for added security.

Extensible Authentication Protocol—See *EAP.*

flashing—A security attack in which an Internet user sends commands to another Internet user's machine that cause the screen to fill with garbage characters. A flashing attack causes the user to terminate her session.

hacker—A person who masters the inner workings of operating systems and utilities in an effort to better understand them. A hacker is distinguished from a cracker in that a cracker attempts to exploit a network's vulnerabilities for malicious purposes.

handshake protocol—One of several protocols within SSL, and perhaps the most significant. As its name implies, the handshake protocol allows the client and server to authenticate (or introduce) each other and establishes terms for how they securely exchange data during an SSL session.

HTTP over Secure Sockets Layer—See *HTTPS*.

HTTP Secure—See *HTTP over Secure Sockets Layer*.

HTTPS (HTTP over Secure Sockets Layer)—The URL prefix that indicates that a Web page requires its data to be exchanged between client and server using SSL encryption. HTTPS uses the TCP port number 443, rather than port 80 (the port that normal HTTP uses).

IKE (Internet Key Exchange)—The first phase of IPSec authentication, which accomplishes key management. IKE is a service that runs on UDP port 500. After IKE has established the rules for the type of keys two nodes use, IPSec invokes its second phase, encryption.

Internet Key Exchange—See *IKE*.

Internet Protocol Security—See *IPSec*.

IPSec (Internet Protocol Security)—A Layer 3 protocol that defines encryption, authentication, and key management for TCP/IP transmissions. IPSec is an enhancement to IPv4 and native to IPv6. IPSec is unique among authentication methods in that it adds security information to the header of all IP packets.

IP spoofing—A security attack in which an outsider obtains internal IP addresses, then uses those addresses to pretend that he has authority to access a private network from the Internet.

KDC (Key Distribution Center)—In Kerberos terminology, the server that runs the authentication service and the Ticket-granting service to issue keys and tickets to clients.

Kerberos—A cross-platform authentication protocol that uses key encryption to verify the identity of clients and to securely exchange information after a client logs on to a system. It is an example of a private key encryption service.

key—A series of characters that is combined with a block of data during that data's encryption. To decrypt the resulting data, the recipient must also possess the key.

Key Distribution Center—See *KDC*.

key management—The method whereby two nodes using key encryption agree on common parameters for the keys they will use to encrypt data.

key pair—The combination of a public and private key used to decipher data that was encrypted using public key encryption.

Microsoft Challenge Handshake Authentication Protocol—See *MS-CHAP*.

Microsoft Challenge Handshake Authentication Protocol, version 2—See *MS-CHAPv2*.

MS-CHAP (Microsoft Challenge Handshake Authentication Protocol)—An authentication protocol offered by Microsoft with its Windows clients and servers. Similar to CHAP, MS-CHAP uses a three-way handshake to verify a client's credentials and encrypts passwords with a challenge text.

MS-CHAPv2 (Microsoft Challenge Authentication Protocol, version 2)—An authentication protocol provided with Windows XP, 2000, and Server 2003 operating systems that follows the CHAP model, but uses stronger encryption, uses different encryption keys for transmission and reception, and requires mutual authentication between two computers.

mutual authentication—An authentication scheme in which both computers verify the credentials of each other.

network key—A key (or character string) required for a wireless station to associate with an access point using WEP.

OpenSSH—An open source version of the SSH suite of protocols.

packet-filtering firewall—A router that operates at the Data Link and Transport layers of the OSI Model, examining the header of every packet of data that it receives to determine whether that type of packet is authorized to continue to its destination. Packet-filtering firewalls are also called screening firewalls.

PAP (Password Authentication Protocol)—A simple authentication protocol that operates over PPP. Using PAP, a client issues its credentials in a request to authenticate, and the server responds with a confirmation or denial of authentication after comparing the credentials to those in its database. PAP is not very secure and is therefore rarely used on modern networks.

Password Authentication Protocol—See *PAP*.

PGP (Pretty Good Privacy)—A key-based encryption system for e-mail that uses a two-step verification process.

port forwarding—The process of redirecting traffic from its normally assigned port to a different port, either on the client or server. In the case of using SSH, port forwarding can send data exchanges that are normally insecure through encrypted tunnels.

Pretty Good Privacy—See *PGP*.

principal—In Kerberos terminology, a user or client.

private key encryption—A type of key encryption in which the sender and receiver use a key to which only they have access. DES (data encryption standard), which was developed by IBM in the 1970s, is a popular example of a private key encryption technique. Private key encryption is also known as symmetric encryption.

proxy—See *proxy server*.

proxy server—A network host that runs a proxy service. Proxy servers may also be called gateways.

proxy service—A software application on a network host that acts as an intermediary between the external and internal networks, screening all incoming and outgoing traffic and providing one address to the outside world, instead of revealing the addresses of internal LAN devices.

public key encryption—A form of key encryption in which data is encrypted using two keys: One is a key known only to a user, and the other is a key associated with the user and can be obtained from a public source, such as a public key server. Some examples of public key algorithms include RSA (named after its creators, Rivest, Shamir, and Adleman), Diffie-Hellman, and Elliptic-curve cryptography. Public key encryption is also known as asymmetric encryption.

public key server—A publicly available host (such as an Internet host) that provides free access to a list of users' public keys (for use in public key encryption).

RADIUS (Remote Authentication Dial-In User Service)—A protocol that runs over UDP and provides centralized network authentication and accounting for multiple users. RADIUS is commonly used with dial-up networking, VPNs, and wireless connections.

RADIUS server—A server that offers centralized authentication services to a network's access server, VPN server, or wireless access point via the RADIUS protocol.

RC4—An asymmetric key encryption technique that weaves a key with data multiple times as a computer issues the stream of data. RC4 keys can be as long as 2048 bits. In addition to being highly secure, RC4 is fast.

Remote Authentication Dial-In User Service—See *RADIUS*.

Rijndael—The algorithm used for AES encryption.

RSA—An encryption algorithm that creates a key by randomly choosing two large prime numbers and multiplying them together. RSA is named after its creators, Ronald Rivest, Adi Shamir, and Leonard Adleman. RSA was released in 1977, but remains popular today for e-commerce transactions.

SCP (Secure CoPy)—A method for copying files securely between hosts. SCP is part of the OpenSSH package, which comes with most modern UNIX-type of operating systems. Third-party SCP applications are available for Windows-based computers.

screening firewall—See *packet-filtering firewall*.

Secure CoPy—See *SCP*.

Secure Shell—See *SSH*.

Secure Sockets Layer—See *SSL*.

security audit—An assessment of an organization's security vulnerabilities. A security audit should be performed at least annually and preferably quarterly—or sooner if the network has undergone significant changes. For each risk found, it should rate the severity of a potential breach, as well as its likelihood.

security policy—A document or plan that identifies an organization's security goals, risks, levels of authority, designated security coordinator and team members, responsibilities for each team member, and responsibilities for each employee. In addition, it specifies how to address security breaches.

server_hello—In the context of SSL encryption, a message issued from the server to the client that confirms the information the server received in the client_hello message. It also agrees to certain terms of encryption based on the options the client supplied. Depending on the Web server's preferred encryption method, the server may choose to issue your browser a public key or a digital certificate at this time.

session key—In the context of Kerberos authentication, a key issued to both the client and the server by the authentication service that uniquely identifies their session.

SFTP (Secure File Transfer Protocol)—A protocol available with the proprietary version of SSH that copies files between hosts securely. Like FTP, SFTP first establishes a connection with a host and then allows a remote user to browse directories, list files, and copy files. Unlike FTP, SFTP encrypts data before transmitting it.

social engineering—The act of manipulating personal relationships to circumvent network security measures and gain access to a system.

SSH (Secure Shell)—A connection utility that provides authentication and encryption. With SSH, you can securely log on to a host, execute commands on that host, and copy files to or from that host. SSH encrypts data exchanged throughout the session.

SSL (Secure Sockets Layer)—A method of encrypting TCP/IP transmissions—including Web pages and data entered into Web forms—en route between the client and server using public key encryption technology.

SSL session—In the context of SSL encryption, an association between the client and server that is defined by an agreement on a specific set of encryption techniques. An SSL session allows the client and server to continue to exchange data securely as long as the client is still connected to the server. SSL sessions are established by the SSL handshake protocol.

symmetric encryption—A method of encryption that requires the same key to encode the data as is used to decode the ciphertext.

TACACS (Terminal Access Controller Access Control System)—A centralized authentication system for remote access servers that is similar to, but older than, RADIUS.

Terminal Access Controller Access Control System—See *TACACS*.

TGS (Ticket-granting service)—In Kerberos terminology, an application that runs on the KDC that issues ticket-granting tickets to clients so that they need not request a new ticket for each new service they want to access.

TGT (ticket-granting ticket)—In Kerberos terminology, a ticket that enables a user to be accepted as a validated principal by multiple services.

three-way handshake—An authentication process that involves three steps.

ticket—In Kerberos terminology, a temporary set of credentials that a client uses to prove that its identity has been validated by the authentication service.

Ticket-granting service—See *TGS*.

ticket-granting ticket—See *TGT*.

TLS (Transport Layer Security)—A version of SSL being standardized by the IETF (Internet Engineering Task Force). With TLS, IETF aims to create a version of SSL that encrypts UDP as well as TCP transmissions. TLS, which is supported by new Web browsers, uses slightly different encryption algorithms than SSL, but otherwise is very similar to the most recent version of SSL.

Transport Layer Security—See *TLS*.

Triple DES (3DES)—The modern implementation of DES, which weaves a 56-bit key through data three times, each time using a different key.

war driving—The act of driving while running a laptop configured to detect and capture wireless data transmissions.

WEP (Wired Equivalent Privacy)—A key encryption technique for wireless networks that uses keys both to authenticate network clients and to encrypt data in transit.

Wi-Fi Alliance—An international, nonprofit organization dedicated to ensuring the interoperability of 802.11-capable devices.

Wi-Fi Protected Access—See *WPA*.

Wired Equivalent Privacy—See *WEP*.

WPA (Wi-Fi Protected Access)—A wireless security method endorsed by the Wi-Fi Alliance that is considered a subset of the 802.11i standard. In WPA, authentication follows the same mechanism specified in 802.11i. The main difference between WPA and 802.11i is that WPA specifies RC4 encryption rather than AES.

WPA2—The name given to the 802.11i security standard by the Wi-Fi Alliance. The only difference between WPA2 and 802.11i is that WPA2 includes support for the older WPA security method.

Review Questions

1. Which of the following terms refers to a thorough examination of each aspect of a network to determine how it might be compromised?

    a. Symmetric encryption

    b. Application gateway

    c. Security audit

    d. Social engineering

2. The use of an algorithm to scramble data into a format that can be read only by reversing the algorithm is known as _____.

    a. encryption

    b. bio-recognition

    c. DNS spoofing

    d. flashing

3. Trying a number of possible character combinations to find the key that will decrypt encrypted data is known as a _____.

    a. denial-of-service attack

    b. dictionary attack

    c. social engineering

    d. brute force attack

4. A _____ is a password-protected and encrypted file that holds an individual's identification information, including a public key.

    a. network key

    b. digital certificate

    c. key pair

    d. session key

5. _____ occurs when a hacker forges name server records to falsify his host's identity.

    a. DNS spoofing

    b. Port forwarding

    c. Public key encryption

    d. Social engineering

6. True or false? Networks that use leased public lines, such as T1 or DSL connections to the Internet, are vulnerable to eavesdropping at a building's demarcation point, at a remote switching facility, or in a central office.

7. True or false? Proxy servers manage security at the Network layer of the OSI Model.

8. True or false? The Password Authentication Protocol (PAP) encrypts usernames and passwords for transmission.

9. True or false? If routers are not configured to mask internal subnets, users on outside networks can read the private addresses.

10. True or false? Dial-up networking turns a remote workstation into a node on the network, through a remote access server.

11. A(n) _____ occurs when a system becomes unable to function because it has been deluged with data transmissions or otherwise disrupted data.

12. A(n) _____ identifies your security goals, risks, levels of authority, designated security coordinator and team members, responsibilities for each team member, and responsibilities for each employee.

13. A(n) _____ is a router that examines the header of every packet of data it receives to determine whether that type of packet is authorized to continue to its destination.

14. In _____ encryption, data is encrypted using a single key that only the sender and the receiver know.

15. The _____ protocol defines encryption, authentication, and key management for TCP/IP transmissions.

Chapter 15

Implementing and Managing Networks

After reading this chapter and completing the exercises, you will be able to:

■ Describe the elements and benefits of project management

■ Manage a network implementation project

■ Understand network management and the importance of baselining to assess a network's health

■ Plan and follow regular hardware and software maintenance routines

■ Describe the steps involved in upgrading network software and hardware

In this book, you have learned the technologies and techniques necessary to design an efficient, secure network. In this chapter, you will learn how to put those elements together to plan a network implementation or improve an existing network from start to finish. One of the first steps in implementing a network is devising a plan. Before you can create such a plan, however, you must learn some project management fundamentals. After a network is in place, it requires continual review and adjustment. Therefore, a network, like any other complex system, is in a constant state of flux. Whether the changes are due to internal factors, such as increased demand on the server's processor, or external factors, such as the obsolescence of a router, you should count on spending a significant amount of time investigating, performing, and verifying changes to your network. In this chapter, you will build on this knowledge to learn about changes dictated by immediate needs as well as those required to enhance the network's functionality, growth, performance, or security.

Project Management

Whether you are designing a network from scratch or making significant changes to an existing network, it's important to plan carefully before purchasing hardware or software or committing staff time. Project management provides a framework for planning and implementing significant undertakings.

Project management is the practice of managing staff, budget, timelines, and other resources and variables to achieve a specific goal within given bounds. The project might be constrained by time, money, or the number of developers who can help you with the project. In the networking field, for example, you might employ project management when upgrading your servers to Solaris version 10, or when replacing the CAT 3 wiring in your organization's building with CAT 6 wiring. This section describes some project management techniques that apply specifically to network and other technology implementations.

Different project managers have differing philosophies about the best way to ensure that project goals are met. However, most would agree that project management attempts to answer at least the following questions in roughly the following order:

- ◆ Is the proposed project feasible?
- ◆ What needs must the project address?
- ◆ What are the project's goals? (What are the standards for success?)
- ◆ What tasks are required to meet the goals?
- ◆ How long should tasks take, and in what order should they be undertaken?
- ◆ What resources are required to accomplish the tasks, and how much will they cost?

◆ Who will be involved and what skills must they possess?

◆ How will staff communicate with others about the project?

◆ After completion, did the project meet the stated need?

Most projects can be divided into phases, each of which addresses some of the questions in the preceding list. For example, you might divide a project into four phases: initiation, specification, implementation, and resolution. In that case, the initiation phase would include determining whether the project is feasible, assessing needs, and determining which staff will be involved. Identifying goals and answering questions about tasks, timelines, costs, resources, staff requirements, and communication methods would occur during the specification phase. Next comes implementation, when the work of the project would take place. Finally, the completion of a project and the analysis of its success would be considered the project's resolution. Figure 15-1 illustrates how a project can be divided into these four phases. In fact, there are many different ways to depict a project's progress over time, and in many cases the phases overlap.

At several points during a project the team might stop to assess its progress. In project planning, a **milestone** is a reference point that marks the completion of a major task or group of tasks in the project and contributes to measuring the project's progress. For example, if you were in charge of establishing an e-commerce server, you might designate the completion of the software installation on your server as being a milestone. Milestones are particularly useful in large projects that have high visibility within the organization. They provide a quick indication of a project's relative success or failure.

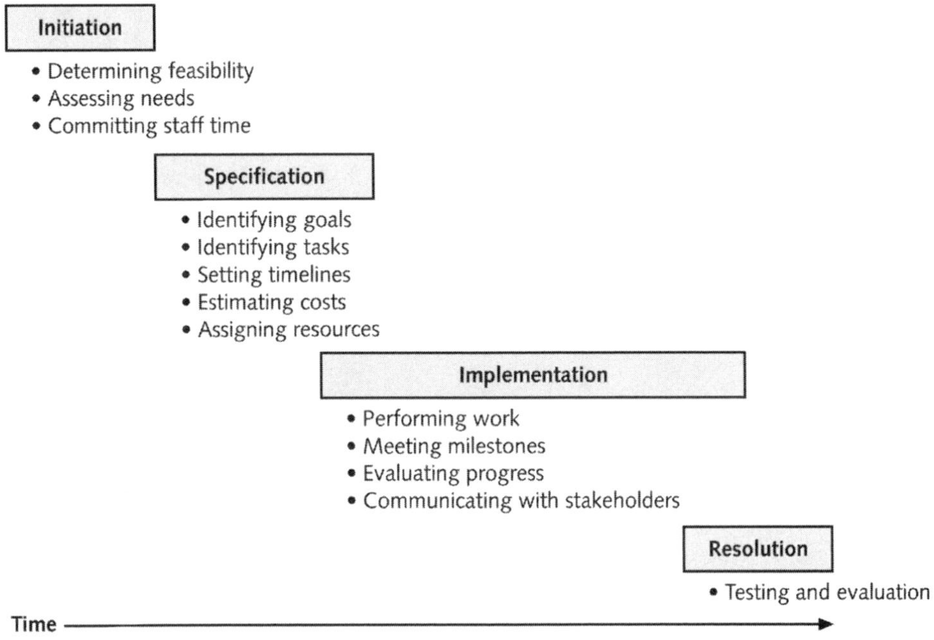

Initiation
- Determining feasibility
- Assessing needs
- Committing staff time

Specification
- Identifying goals
- Identifying tasks
- Setting timelines
- Estimating costs
- Assigning resources

Implementation
- Performing work
- Meeting milestones
- Evaluating progress
- Communicating with stakeholders

Resolution
- Testing and evaluation

Time ――――――――――――――――――――――――――――→

FIGURE 15-1 *Project phases*

The following sections discuss project management steps in more detail. Throughout these sections, the example of a comprehensive network upgrade is used to illustrate project management concepts as they relate to networking.

Determining Project Feasibility

Before committing money and time to a project, you must decide whether the proposed project is possible—that is, whether it's feasible. Often, and especially in technology-based companies, staff become so enamored with gadgetry and the desire for faster network access that they push a project through without realistically assessing its costs and benefits. To formalize the process of determining whether a proposed project makes sense, you can conduct a feasibility study. A **feasibility study** outlines the costs and benefits of the project and attempts to predict whether it will result in a favorable outcome (for example, whether it will achieve its goals without imposing excessive cost or time burdens on the organization). A feasibility study should be performed for any large-scale project before resources are committed to that project.

 NOTE

Often, organizations hire business consultants to help them develop a feasibility study. The advantage to outsourcing this work is that consultants do not make the same assumptions that internal staff might make when weighing the costs and benefits of a proposed project.

Suppose you are the network manager for the Wyndham School District, which consists of nine buildings: one administration building, one high school, two middle schools, and five elementary schools. Some staff have complained to you about the slow performance of the LAN, slow access to the Internet, and client computers that are barely powerful enough to run learning software. You, too, recognize that the district's technology is outdated. You and other staff perceive that a comprehensive upgrade seems necessary. However, you don't know whether the school board has sufficient money to allocate to the project, if it's a priority compared to other expenses, or if students' and staff productivity will be significantly hampered during such an upgrade. Your feasibility study might consist of rough estimates for the following:

◆ Costs of equipment, connectivity, consulting services
◆ Required staff time for project participation, training, and evaluation
◆ Duration of project
◆ Decrease in productivity due to disruption versus increase in future productivity due to better network and client performance
◆ A conclusion that addresses whether the costs (equipment, staff, decreased productivity) justify the benefits (increased ongoing productivity)

If you conclude that the project is feasible, you can move to the next step of project planning: assessing needs.

Assessing Needs

All the staff in the Wyndham School District might agree that the current e-mail system is too slow and needs to be replaced, or numerous users might complain that the connection between their classroom computers and the LAN's servers is unreliable. Often a network change project begins with a group of people identifying a need. Before you concur with popular opinion about what portions of the network must be upgraded and how changes must occur, as a responsible network administrator you should perform a thorough, objective needs assessment. A **needs assessment** is the process of clarifying the reasons and objectives underlying a proposed change. It involves interviewing users and comparing perceptions to factual data. It probably also involves analyzing network baseline data (discussed later in this chapter). Your goal in performing a needs assessment is to determine the appropriate scope and nature of the proposed changes.

A needs assessment may address the following questions:

◆ Is the expressed need valid, or does it mask a different need?

◆ Can the need be resolved?

◆ Is the need important enough to allocate resources to its resolution? Will meeting the need have a measurable effect on productivity?

◆ If fulfilled, will the need result in additional needs? Will fulfilling the need satisfy other needs?

◆ Do users affected by the need agree that change is a good answer? What kind of resolution will satisfy them?

A network's needs and requirements should be investigated as they relate to users, network performance, availability, scalability, integration, and security. Although only one or a few of these needs may constitute driving forces for your project, you should consider each aspect before drafting a project plan. A project based solely on user requirements may result in unforeseen, negative consequences on network performance, if performance needs are not considered as well.

A good way to start clarifying user requirements is to interview as many users as possible. Just as if you were a reporter, you should ask pointed questions. If the answer is not complete or sufficiently specific, follow up your original question with additional questions. The more narrowly focused the answers, the easier it is to suggest how a project might address those needs. Besides asking the user what he needs, you may also want to ask why the need should be addressed, what ways he suggests the need can be addressed, what kind of priority he would place on the need being met, and whether it takes precedence over other needs.

In the process of interviewing users, you may recognize that not all users have the same needs. In fact, the needs of one group of users may conflict with the needs of another group. In such cases, you must sort out which needs have a greater priority, which needs were expressed by the majority of users, whether the expressed needs have anything in common, and how to address needs that do not fall into the majority.

In the case of the Wyndham School District, you have identified a broad need for improving network performance. The performance of different segments and the network as a whole can be measured over time. However, performance goals and the steps necessary to improve performance may be subjective. One of the district's network engineers might believe that upgrading the network to a fully switched 100BASE-TX solution is the best way to improve performance, whereas the technical manager might think it critical to replace all of the network's CAT 5 with fiber-optic cable. The choice of which solution to pursue (if not both) might depend on budgetary constraints, ease of installation, technical research that favors one solution, or results from preliminary tests.

Suppose that after interviewing key Wyndham School District staff you discover that the top need for elementary school teaching staff is to improve performance between workstations in the classrooms and servers, which are currently housed in the district's small data center at the high school. For example, students currently wait between 30 seconds and a minute for popular applications to load over the WAN. Ideally, that time would be cut to 10 seconds. The primary need for middle school and high school teaching staff is improving response time between computers on the LAN and the Internet. For example, using the current fractional T1 to the Internet, students in the foreign language lab wait an average of 15 seconds before a Web-based training tool refreshes its screens. Ideally, teachers want this wait reduced to no more than five seconds. At the same time, technical staff have identified specific WAN performance and security improvements and administrators have established specific budget limits.

Now that you have collected a list of project requirements, you are ready to turn those requirements into project goals.

Setting Project Goals

Project goals help keep a project on track. They are also necessary later when evaluating whether a project was successful. A popular technique for setting project goals is to begin with a broad goal, then narrow it down into specific goals that contribute to the larger goal. For example, one of the Wyndham School District's goals is to improve performance between its network and the Internet. Beneath that goal, you may insert several smaller goals, such as increasing the throughput of its current Internet connection, connecting to a nationwide ISP, and using a proxy server to cache frequently accessed Web pages.

In addition to being specific, project goals should be attainable. The feasibility study should help determine whether you can achieve the project goals within the given time, budgetary, and staffing constraints. If project goals are not attainable from the outset, you risk losing backing from the project participants, the users, and the managers who agree with the project's goals and who will strive to help you achieve them. Managers and others who oversee resource allocation are called **sponsors**. In the Wyndham School District upgrade example, the high school principal and key members of the school board might act as sponsors. Although sponsors do not necessarily participate in project tasks or supervise project teams, they can lobby for the funding necessary to complete the project, appeal to a group of managers to extend a project's deadline, assist with negotiating vendor contracts, and so on. And if you lose backing, chances are good that the project will fail. Sponsors belong to a larger group of interested parties known as stakeholders. A **stakeholder** is any person who is affected by the project. For example, in the Wyndham School District upgrade project, stakeholders include teachers, administrators, technical staff, and even students, because students are also network users.

Projects without clear goals suffer from inefficiencies. A lack of well-defined goals can result in misunderstandings between project participants, lack of focus among team members, lack of proper resource allocation, and an uncertainty about whether the project's outcomes constituted success. After you have worked with project participants and sponsors to clearly identify the project's goals, you are ready to develop a project plan.

Project Planning

A **project plan** organizes the details (for example, the timeline and the significant tasks) of a managed project. Plans for small projects may take the form of a simple text or spreadsheet document. For larger projects, however, you typically take advantage of project management software such as Microsoft Project or PrimaVera Project Planner. Project management software facilitates project planning by providing a framework for inputting tasks, timelines, resource assignments (identifying which staff are responsible for each task), completion dates, and so on. Such software is also highly customizable, so you can use only a small portion or all of its features, depending on the scope of your project and your project management skills. Figure 15-2 shows a list of tasks as they might appear in Microsoft Project.

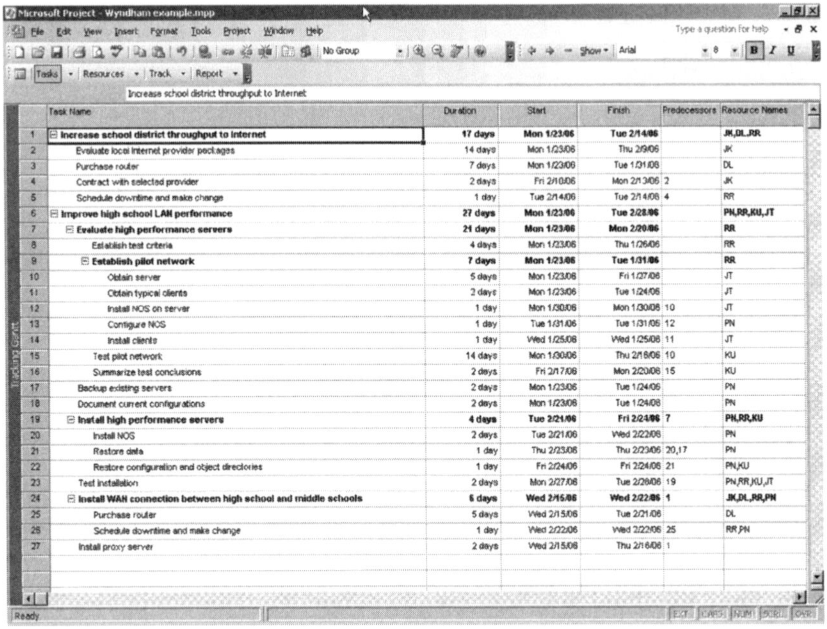

FIGURE 15-2 *A project plan in Microsoft Project*

Tasks and Timelines

A project should be divided into specific tasks. Larger tasks are then broken into even smaller subtasks. For example, upgrading the Wyndham School District's backbone from CAT 5 to fiber-optic cabling represents a large task with numerous subtasks: documenting the current cable plant, obtaining the fiber-optic cable, obtaining the connectivity devices compatible with fiber-optic connections, scheduling network downtime during which the upgrade can occur, removing the CAT 5 cabling, installing the fiber-optic cabling, testing the changes, and so on.

After you have identified tasks, you can assign a duration, start date, and finish date to each task and subtask in the project plan. You can also designate milestones, task priority, and how the timeline might change depending on resource availability or dependencies. Timelines are not always easy to predict. Seasoned professionals may be able to gauge how long a particular task might take based on their previous experience with similar tasks. However, every project may entail conditions that affect a timeline differently. When creating a timeline, you should allow extra time for any especially significant tasks. A **Gantt chart** is a popular method for depicting when projects begin and end along a horizontal timeline. Figure 15-3 illustrates a simple Gantt chart.

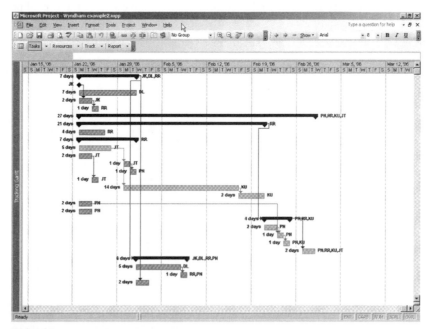

FIGURE 15-3 *A simple Gantt chart*

TIP

You may be asked to plan a project with seemingly impossible deadlines. One technique for making the project fit into a tight time frame is to work backward to create the timeline. Begin at the project's predetermined endpoint and move toward the beginning of the project, allowing the normal time requirements for tasks. This method highlights which tasks may delay the project and therefore need to be dropped or modified, at least temporarily.

In addition to these elements, project plans may provide information on the amount of flexibility in the timeline, task dependencies, links to other project plans, and so on. With most project planning software, you can add your own columns to the plan and insert any type of information you deem appropriate. For example, if you are managing a very large network design project, you might create a Web site with links to documentation for each phase of the project. In the project plan, you might include a column to list the URLs of the documents for each task or group of tasks.

Communication

Without clear and regular communication, a project will falter. Communication is necessary to ensure that all participants understand the project's goals, help keep a project's budget and timeline on track, encourage teamwork, avoid duplicate efforts, and allow learning from previous mistakes. The project manager is responsible for facilitating regular, effective communication among project participants. In addition, the project manager must ensure consistent communication with all project stakeholders.

No matter how small and insignificant your network change appears, if it could potentially affect the way that users accomplish their daily work, you must prepare users for the change. In some cases, the likelihood of a change affecting users is plainly evident. For example, if you upgrade the version of NetWare used by your file servers and therefore must upgrade the Novell networking client version used by clients, every user will see a slightly different screen when she starts up the computer and logs on to the network. If you replace a segment of CAT 3 cabling with CAT 6 cabling, however, users might not notice the difference.

For a major network change, you definitely must inform users. Among other things, explain to users:

◆ How their access to the network will be affected

◆ How their data will be protected during the change (even if you are confident that the data will remain unaffected by the change, explain how the protection works)

◆ Whether you will provide any means for users to access the network during the change

◆ Whether the change will require users to learn new skills

Although providing all of this information may seem burdensome, it lessens the possibility that your project might be stymied by negative reaction. To minimize the amount of time spent communicating with users, you might convene company-wide meetings or send mass e-mail distributions. If a network implementation has the potential to drastically change the way that users perform their work, you might want to form a committee of user representatives who can attend project meetings and provide input from the users' point of view.

Contingency Planning

Even the most meticulously planned project may be derailed by unforeseen circumstances. For instance, a key team participant may quit, your budget may be unexpectedly cut, or a software package may not work as promised. Each of these conditions may threaten to delay your project's completion. To prepare for such circumstances, you must create a contingency plan at the beginning of the project. **Contingency planning** is the process of identifying steps that minimize the risk of unforeseen events that could affect the quality or timeliness of the project's goals.

For example, suppose that as the Wyndham School District network manager, you have only one week—while students are on spring break—to replace older servers with new, high-performance servers. Long before that week, you have established an excellent relationship with your hardware vendor. You order the servers two months in advance. However, after six weeks, they still haven't arrived, due to a quality control problem at the manufacturer. Spring break is nearing, so you arrange with your hardware vendor to ship a slightly different, but similar model of server that's in stock in case the new servers don't appear in the coming week. This change may require a modification in your installation process, but it ensures that the upgrade can still occur.

Using a Pilot Network

One of the best ways to evaluate a large-scale network or systems implementation is to first test it in your environment on a small scale. A small-scale network that stands in for the larger network is sometimes called a **pilot network**. Although a pilot network is much smaller than the enterprise-wide network, it should be similar enough to closely mimic the larger network's hardware, software, connectivity, unique configurations, and load. If possible, you should establish the pilot network in the same location or environment in which the final network will exist.

The following tips will help you create a more realistic and useful pilot network:

◆ Include at least one of each type of device (whether a critical router or a client workstation) that might be affected by the change.

◆ Use the same transmission methods and speeds as employed on your network.

◆ Try to emulate the number of segments, protocols, and addressing schemes in your network. And, although it is impractical to emulate the same number of nodes, if possible, try to generate a similar amount of traffic.

◆ Implement the same server and client software and configurations on your pilot network as found in your current network (unless they are part of the change you're testing).

◆ After you have established the pilot network, test it for at least two weeks to verify that its performance, security, availability, or other characteristics meet your criteria.

TIP

As the pilot network is intended for testing only, do not connect the pilot network to your live network. By keeping the two networks separate, you ensure that experimental changes do not inadvertently harm your functioning network.

The pilot network offers you opportunities to both educate yourself and test your implementation goals. Use your time with the pilot network to become familiar with any new features in the hardware or software. Be certain to document what you learn about the new technology's features and idiosyncrasies. As you evaluate your results against your predefined test criteria, note where your results show success or failure. All of this documentation provides valuable information for your final implementation and for future baselining.

Testing and Evaluation

After completing each major step in a project, you should assess whether the tasks you've completed have achieved their goals. To successfully test your implementation, you must establish a testing plan that includes relevant methods and criteria. For example, your method of testing the network performance may be to use the Windows Server 2003 Network Monitor application from a server. For each performance test you run, you will want to use Network Monitor with the same configuration so that you can compare your results across the various tests. In this case, the criteria you use to measure network performance may be the number of bytes that travel from one particular workstation to the server every five minutes. Testing should help determine whether a change was successful, partially successful, or unsuccessful. It should also reveal any unintended consequences of the change or whether the change revealed the need for additional changes.

In addition, as part of a project's resolution, you should perform testing to determine whether the project was successful. For example, in the case of Wyndham School District, performance testing should occur after the servers, backbone, and Internet connectivity have been upgraded. Teachers in the elementary schools can time how long they now wait for applications to load from the LAN server. Teachers at the high school can measure how long it takes for a Web-based learning tool to load. IT staff can use network monitoring tools to measure how quickly routers and switches receive and respond to requests. Such quantitative evaluations are necessary to gauge the success of a project. They may also reveal errors introduced during a project, such as an improper switch configuration that causes network congestion.

In the following section, you will learn how networks are managed to ensure the best possible performance and availability over time.

Network Management

Network management is a general term that means different things to different networking professionals. At its broadest, **network management** refers to the assessment, monitoring, and maintenance of all aspects of a network. On some large networks, administrators run network management applications that continually check devices and connections to make certain they respond within an expected performance threshold. If a device doesn't respond quickly enough or at all, the application automatically issues an alert that pages the network administrator responsible for that device. On a small network, however, comprehensive network management might not be economically feasible. Instead, such a network might run an inexpensive application that periodically tests devices and connections to determine only whether they are still functioning.

Several disciplines fall under the heading of network management (including topics discussed in previous chapters, such as security audits and change management), but all share the primary goal of preventing costly downtime or loss. Ideally, network management accomplishes this by helping the administrator predict problems before they occur. For example, a trend in network usage could indicate when a switch will be overwhelmed with traffic. In response, the network administrator could increase the switch's processing capabilities (or replace the switch) before users begin experiencing slow or dropped connections. Before you can assess and make predictions about a network's health, however, you must first measure its baseline status.

Obtaining Baseline Measurements

As you learned in Chapter 12, a baseline is a report of the network's current state of operation. Baseline measurements might include the utilization rate for your network backbone, number of users logged on per day or per hour, number of protocols that run on your network, statistics about errors (such as runts, collisions, jabbers, or giants), frequency with which networked applications are used, or information regarding which users take up the most bandwidth. The graph in Figure 15-4 shows an example baseline for daily network traffic over a six-week period.

Baseline measurements allow you to compare future performance increases or decreases caused by network changes with past network performance. Obtaining baseline measurements is the only way to know for certain whether a pattern of usage has changed (and requires attention) or, later, whether a network upgrade made a difference. Each network requires its own approach. The elements you measure depend on which functions are most critical to your network and its users.

For instance, suppose that your network currently serves 500 users and that your backbone traffic exceeds 50% at 10:00 A.M. and 2:00 P.M. each business day. That pattern constitutes your baseline. Now suppose that your company decides to add 200 users who perform the same types

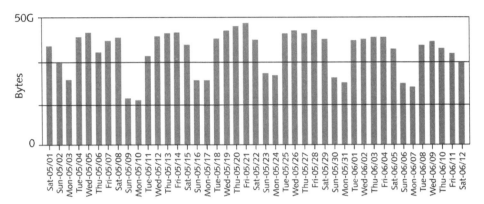

FIGURE 15-4 *Baseline of daily network traffics*

of functions on the network. The added number of users equals 40% of the current number of users (200/500). Therefore, you can estimate that your backbone's capacity should increase by approximately 40% to maintain your current service levels.

The more data you gather while establishing your network's baseline (in other words, the longer you gather data), the more accurate your prediction will be. Network traffic patterns might be difficult to forecast, because you cannot predict users' habits, effects of new technology, or changes in demand for resources over a given period of time. For instance, the preceding example assumed that all new users would share the same network usage habits as the current users. In fact, however, the new users may generate a great deal more, or a great deal less, network traffic.

How do you gather baseline data on your network? Although you could theoretically use a network monitor or network analyzer and record its output at regular intervals, several software applications can perform the baselining for you. These applications range from freeware available on the Internet to expensive, customizable hardware and software combination products. Before choosing a network baselining tool, you should determine how you will use it. If you manage a small network that provides only one critical application to users, an inexpensive tool may suffice. If you work on a WAN with several critical links, however, you should investigate purchasing a more comprehensive package. The baseline measurement tool should also be capable of collecting the statistics needed. For example, only a sophisticated tool can measure traffic generated by each node on a network, filter traffic according to types of protocols and errors, and simultaneously measure statistics from several different network segments.

A baseline assessment should address the following questions:

◆ *Physical topology*—Which types of LAN and WAN topologies does your network use: bus, star, ring, hybrid, mesh, or a combination of these? Which type of backbone does your network use—collapsed, distributed, parallel, serial, or a combination of these? Which type and grade of cabling does your network use?

◆ *Access method*—Does your network use Ethernet, Token Ring, wireless, or a mix of transmission methods? What transmission speed does it provide? Is it switched?

◆ *Protocols*—Which protocols are used by servers, nodes, and connectivity devices?

◆ *Devices*—How many of the following devices are connected to your network—switches, routers, hubs, gateways, firewalls, access points, servers, UPSs, printers, backup devices, and clients? Where are they physically located? What are their model numbers and vendors?

◆ *Operating systems*—Which network and desktop operating systems appear on the network? Which versions of these operating systems are used by each device? Which type and version of operating systems are used by connectivity devices such as routers?

◆ *Applications*—Which applications are used by clients and servers? Where do you store the applications? From where do they run?

If you have not already collected and centrally stored this information, it may take the efforts of several people and several weeks to compile it, depending on the size and complexity of your network. This evaluation involves visits to the telecommunications and equipment rooms, an examination of servers and desktops, a review of receipts for software and hardware purchases, and, potentially, the use of a protocol analyzer or network monitoring software package. A baseline assessment may take a great deal of time and effort to complete, but it promises to save work in the future. After you have compiled the information, organize it into a format (such as a database) that can be easily updated, allowing your staff to keep the baseline current.

Performance and Fault Management

NET+
2.13

After establishing a baseline, you are ready to implement an application that assesses your network's status on an ongoing basis. This process includes both **performance management** (monitoring how well links and devices are keeping up with the demands placed on them) and **fault management** (the detection and signaling of device, link, or component faults).

To accomplish both performance and fault management, organizations often use enterprise-wide network management software. Some popular applications include HP's Openview, IBM's NetView, and Cisco's CiscoWorks, but hundreds of other such tools exist. All rely on a similar architecture, in which at least one network management console (which may be a server or workstation, depending on the size of the network) collects data from multiple networked devices at regular intervals, in a process called **polling**. Each managed device runs a network management **agent**, a software routine that collects information about the device's operation and provides it to the network management application running on the console. So as not to affect the performance of a device while collecting information, agents do not demand significant processing resources.

A managed device may contain several objects that can be managed, including components such as processor, memory, hard disk, NIC, or intangibles such as performance or utilization.

NET+

2.13

For example, on a server, an agent can measure how many users are connected to the server or what percentage of the processor's resources are used at any time. The definition of managed devices and their data are collected in a **MIB (management information base)**.

Agents communicate information about managed devices via any one of several Application layer protocols. On modern networks, most agents use **SNMP (Simple Network Management Protocol)**. SNMP is part of the TCP/IP suite of protocols and typically runs over UDP on port 161 (though it can be configured to run over TCP).

Figure 15-5 illustrates the relationship between a network management application and managed devices on a network.

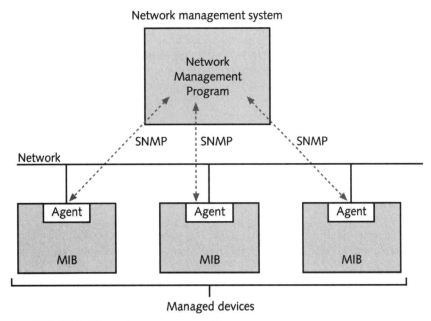

FIGURE 15-5 *Network management architecture*

After data is collected, the network management application can present an administrator with several ways to view and analyze the data. For example, a popular way to view data is in the form of a map that shows fully functional links or devices in green, partially (or less than optimally) functioning links or devices in yellow, and failed links or devices in red. One type of network status map generated by Solarwinds.net's Orion network management software is shown in Figure 15-6.

Because of their flexibility, sophisticated network management applications are also challenging to configure and fine-tune. You have to be careful to collect only useful data and not an excessive amount of routine information. For example, on a network with dozens of routers, collecting SNMP-gener-

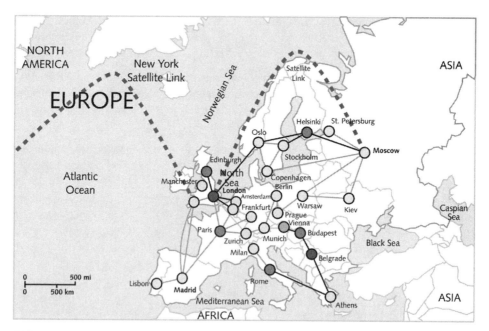

FIGURE 15-6 *Map showing network status*

ated messages that essentially say "I'm still here" every five seconds would result in massive amounts of insignificant data. A glut of information would make it difficult to ascertain when the router in fact requires attention. Instead, when configuring a network management application to poll a router, you might choose to generate an SNMP-based message only when the router's processor is operating at 75% of its capacity or to measure only the amount of traffic passing through a NIC every five minutes.

Performance and fault management monitoring does not necessarily require a complex application. One of the most common network management tools used on WANs is **MRTG (Multi Router Traffic Grapher)**. MRTG is a command-line utility that uses SNMP to poll devices, collects data in a log file, then generates HTML-based views of the data. MRTG is freely distributed software originally written by Tobias Oetiker, a networking professional who in the early 1990s saw a need for a tool to regularly measure the status of his organization's WAN link. The software has undergone many enhancements since then, but retains its simple interface. MRTG can be used with UNIX- and Windows-based operating systems and can collect and graph data from any type of device that uses SNMP. Figure 15-7 provides examples of two MRTG-generated graphs. One shows the amount of traffic traversing a WAN link in one day, and the other shows the amount of traffic on the same WAN link over eight days' time.

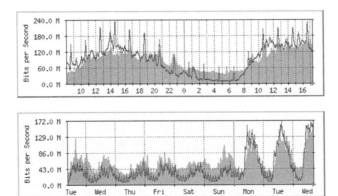

FIGURE 15-7 *Graphs generated by MRTG*

Asset Management

Another key component in network evaluation is identifying and tracking the hardware and software on your network, a process called **asset management**. The first step in asset management is to take an inventory of each node on the network. This inventory should include the total number of components on the network, and also each device's configuration files, model number, serial number, location on the network, and technical support contact. You will also want to keep records of every piece of software purchased by your organization, its version number, vendor, licensing, and technical support contact.

As with a baselining tool, the asset management tool you choose depends on your organization's needs. You may purchase an application that can automatically discover all devices on the network and then save that information in a database, or you may use a simple spreadsheet to save the data. In either case, your asset management records should be comprehensive and accessible to all personnel who may become involved in maintaining or troubleshooting the network. In addition, you should ensure that the asset management database is regularly updated, either manually or automatically, as changes to network hardware and software occur. The information you retain is useful only while it is current.

Asset management simplifies maintaining and upgrading the network chiefly because you know what the system includes. For example, if you discover that a router purchased two years ago requires an upgrade to its operating system software to fix a security flaw, you need to know how many routers are installed, where they are installed, and whether any have already received the software upgrade. An up-to-date asset management system allows you to avoid searching through old invoices and troubleshooting records to answer these questions.

In addition, asset management provides network administrators with information about the costs and benefits of certain types of hardware or software. For example, if you conclude that 50% of your staff's troubleshooting time is spent on one flawed brand of NIC, an asset management system can reveal how many NICs you would need to replace if you chose to replace those cards, and whether it would make sense to replace the entire installed base. Some asset management applications can even track the length of equipment leases and alert network managers when leases will expire.

 NOTE

The term "asset management" originally referred to an organization's system for keeping tabs on every piece of equipment it owned. This function was usually handled through the Accounting Department. Some of the accounting-related tasks included under the original definition for asset management, such as managing the depreciation on network equipment or tracking the expiration of leases, apply to asset management in networking as well.

Software Changes

If you have ever supported desktop computers professionally or even maintained your own computer at home, you know that an important part of keeping a system running optimally is upgrading its software.

You are most likely to implement the following types of software changes on your network: patches (improvements or enhancements to a particular piece of a software application), upgrades (major changes to the existing code), and revisions (a general term for minor or major changes to the existing code). Although the specifics vary for each type of software change, the general steps involved can be summarized as follows:

1. Determine whether the change (whether it be a patch, revision, or upgrade) is necessary.
2. Research the purpose of the change and its potential effects on other applications. Also determine whether and how the change can be reversed, in case troubles arise.
3. Determine whether the change should apply to some or all users and whether it will be distributed centrally or machine-by-machine.
4. If you decide to implement the change, notify system administrators, help desk personnel, and users. Schedule the change for completion during off-hours (unless it is an emergency).
5. Back up the current system or software before making any modifications.
6. Prevent users from accessing the system or part of the system being altered (for example, disable logons).
7. Keep the upgrade instructions handy and follow them during installation of the patch or revision.
8. Make the change.
9. Test the system fully after the change, preferably exercising the software as a typical user would. Note any unintended or unanticipated consequences of the modification.

10. If the change was successful, re-enable access to the system. If it was unsuccessful, revert to the previous version of the software.

11. Inform system administrators, help desk personnel, and users when the change is complete. If you had to reverse it, explain why.

12. Record your change in the change management system.

As a general rule, upgrading or patching software according to a vendor's recommendations is a good idea and can often prevent network problems. For example, a vendor may issue an alert to its customers regarding a security flaw in its Web browser product. To fix this flaw, it may supply a patch. At other times, you may have to search for product upgrades on your own. Whatever your means of finding patches and upgrades, you should take responsibility for this task and make the necessary changes to your network's software. Bear in mind, however, that such changes can sometimes create new troubles on your system. You should therefore be prepared to reverse software upgrades or patches, just in case.

In the following sections, you will learn about the types of software changes associated with sensible network maintenance. You also will see the best way to approach these changes.

Patches

A **patch** is a correction, improvement, or enhancement to a particular piece of a software application. It differs from a revision or software upgrade in that it changes only part of an application, leaving most of the code untouched. Patches are often distributed at no charge by software vendors in an attempt to fix a bug in their code or to add slightly more functionality.

You'll encounter patches in all areas of routine networking maintenance. Among other things, network maintenance sometimes entails patching the server's NOS. For example, if your server runs NetWare 6.5, you may need to patch it to enable it to back up clustered servers.

 NOTE

Microsoft calls its significant patches for its Windows operating systems **service packs**. You may see them abbreviated as "SP1" and "SP2" for Service Pack 1 and Service Pack 2, respectively.

 NOTE

Keep in mind that a patch is not a replacement for an entire software package; instead, a patch is installed on top of the existing software. Patches apply to more than just NOS software. For example, you might have to patch the software on your Cisco switch to allow it to handle IP multicasts over a Token Ring network. Alternatively, you might patch the application that allows you to centrally control your printers across the network

TIP

If you install new hardware on a Windows Server 2003 server after installing a service pack, you are prompted to insert your original Windows Server 2003 installation CD to obtain the device driver and support files for that hardware. By doing so, however, you may overwrite some of the files that were updated by the service pack. Therefore, it is a good idea to upgrade your server's hardware *before* applying service packs. If you do upgrade the server's hardware after installing a service pack, you may have to implement the service pack a second time.

Patch installations are no more difficult than installations of new software applications. The patch itself should come with installation instructions and a description of its purpose, at the very least, in the form of a text file. As with any significant system change, you should back up the system before installing a patch. Although patches ought to be fully tested by the vendor before release, you cannot assume that they will work flawlessly on your system. This consideration is especially important when you patch an NOS. Some patch installation utilities automatically make a backup of the system before installation begins, but you should not rely on this method. Always make sure you have a way to reverse a software change if it does more harm than good.

In addition, try to perform software patches during a time when users cannot and will not attempt to access the network. Even if you suspect that a patch can be implemented quickly and without adverse effects on current users, don't take a chance by applying it during normal business hours. If the patch does create problems, you will need extra time to reverse the process. Depending on how complicated or comprehensive the patch is, you may want to alert users to stay off the system for only a few hours or perhaps overnight.

After applying the patch, test the system to verify that its desired enhancements have taken effect. At this time, you should review the vendor's documentation to ensure that you correctly understood the patch's purpose and installed it correctly. For some patches to take effect, you have to change system configuration files and restart the system. Test the software to verify that the patch hasn't caused any unintentional, undesired effects. After you are certain that the patch worked successfully, you can allow users to access the system again.

To stay apprised of patches released by your vendors, you should regularly check the vendor's technical support Web site or subscribe to its mailing list. Manufacturers usually attempt to bundle a number of bug fixes into one large patch; if you're a registered user, they will alert you about the release of significant patches. News about patches from vendors as large as Novell, Microsoft, Sun, Apple, and Red Hat will also probably appear in trade magazines. Smaller vendors may need to release a patch that fixes a single problem with their application only occasionally.

Make it a policy to keep informed about patches to your network software, whether it involves the operating system, an application, or the client software. If you work in a large organization with several servers, routers, and other devices, you may want to assign one network administrator to manage patches for the servers, one to manage patches for the printers, and so on.

Client Upgrades

A software **upgrade** is a major change to a software package's existing code. It may or may not be offered free from a vendor and may or may not be comprehensive enough to substitute for the original application. In general, upgrades are designed to add functionality and fix bugs in the previous version of the client. For example, an upgrade to a newer version of Netscape may provide stronger SSL encryption services. The scope and purpose of client upgrades vary widely, depending on whether the upgrade is a redesign or simply a bug fix.

 NOTE

The term **bug** is frequently used to describe a flaw in a software application that causes some part of the application to malfunction. Less frequently, this term may also be used to describe a hardware defect. Legend has it that the term originated when a moth became trapped inside the electrical workings of the first digital computer.

Before upgrading client software, carefully read the documentation accompanying the upgrade. It should reveal how best to install the software, whether the upgrade requires you to install any previous upgrades first, whether the upgrade requires any special preparation, and how its changes will affect users.

A client upgrade may be transparent to users, or it may completely change the appearance of the network logon interface. Client upgrades typically overwrite some system files on the workstation, so their installation may affect other applications adversely. They may even prevent other applications from working as they did in the past. For example, a user who receives an upgrade to his Windows XP Dial-up Networking client may later experience problems with an older version of AOL software that worked perfectly for the last two years. In this case, the best solution may be to upgrade the AOL software as well.

As with all upgrades, you should test a client upgrade on a single workstation before distributing it to all users. Also, you should prepare a way to reverse the process. Because most client upgrades do not back up the previous version automatically, you should keep the old client software close at hand, either on the network or on disk, in case you need to reinstall it.

You may either perform client upgrades on a workstation-by-workstation basis or use a software distribution application to upgrade multiple workstations simultaneously from the network. Although the latter approach is more efficient, it may not be appropriate in all situations.

Consider a network of 500 users who have different software, hardware, and usage requirements. Can you be certain that the client upgrade will be compatible with each workstation's hardware and software? Can you be certain that the client upgrade will not adversely affect any user's current software setup? Can you be certain that every user will log on to the network to receive his upgrade? (For instance, what happens if many users are mobile?)

In general, you need to plan carefully and become familiar with your client characteristics before allowing a software distribution application to upgrade client software. In addition, you should notify clients about the upgrade and explain how their workstation might change as a result. If you don't, users may become alarmed at the changes and flood the help desk with questions.

Shared Application Upgrades

Like client upgrades, application upgrades represent modifications to all or part of an application that are designed to enhance functionality or fix problems related to software. Shared application upgrades, however, apply to software shared by clients on the network. Bear in mind that changes to shared applications affect all users at once. You should therefore take extra precautions to ensure that the application upgrade does not cause unanticipated problems. It's essential to test it fully before allowing users to access the new version.

The principles underlying the modification of shared applications on the network are the same as those for the modification of client software. Before applying the change, you should determine the need for it and its potential effects. Also back up the current software before upgrading it, prevent users from accessing the software during the implementation process, and keep users and system administrators informed of all changes.

Applications are usually designed to enhance the application's functionality. For this reason, an application upgrade may be more a matter of convenience than necessity. Therefore, the time, cost, and effort involved in application upgrades should be weighed against the necessity of performing operating system or client upgrades. This consideration is especially important if a networking professional's time is limited (as it usually is). For example, users may urge a network administrator to upgrade the company's version of Adobe Photoshop. If the only advantage in doing so is to allow users to enter text along curved lines, the upgrade may be a waste of time and money. On the other hand, if the application upgrade adds a necessary feature, such as integration with an animation application used by the company for its Web development, it may be well worth the effort.

For a significant application upgrade, you may also need to provide (or suggest classes for) user training. If you choose to refer your users to an outside training facility, make sure they will learn about the particulars of the application in your networking environment. For instance, if you make it a policy never to install the foreign language support for a word-processing application, make sure your users know about this constraint. Likewise, if you have limited the functionality of an application (for example, preventing users from posting the Web pages they create in Microsoft FrontPage to the server), you should publicize this policy. The better you prepare and inform your users, the fewer support calls your help desk will have to field.

Network Operating System Upgrades

Perhaps the most critical type of software upgrade you'll perform is an upgrade to your network operating system. It usually involves significant, potentially drastic, changes to the way your servers and clients operate. As such, it requires plenty of forethought, product research, and rigorous testing before you implement it. In fact, for any network with more than a few users, you should create and follow a project plan for this undertaking. This plan should include all of the precautions typically associated with other software upgrades. In addition, you should consider the following in your project plan:

- ◆ How will the upgrade affect user IDs, groups, rights, and policies?
- ◆ How will the upgrade affect file, printer, and directory access on the server?
- ◆ How will the upgrade affect applications or client interactions on the server?
- ◆ How will the upgrade affect configuration files, protocols, and services running on the server?
- ◆ How will the upgrade affect the server's interaction with other devices on the network?
- ◆ How accurately can you test the upgrade software in a simulated environment?
- ◆ How can you take advantage of the new operating system to make your system more efficient?
- ◆ What is your technical support arrangement with the operating system's manufacturer if you need help in the midst of the upgrade?
- ◆ Have you allotted enough time to perform the upgrade? (For example, would it be more appropriate to do it over a weekend rather than overnight?)
- ◆ During the upgrade will old NOS files be saved, and can you reverse the installation if troubles arise?
- ◆ Have you ensured that the users, help desk personnel, and system administrators understand how the upgrade will affect their daily operations and support burdens?

The preceding items are only some of the critical questions you need to ask before embarking on an NOS upgrade. Your networking environment may warrant additional considerations. For example, suppose that you are the network administrator for a company that is merging with a second company. Your two companies may use dissimilar network operating systems, and the IT director may ask you to upgrade your NOS to match the other company's version. In this situation, you would have not only the previous list of questions to consider, but also a list of questions pertaining to the other company's operating system—for instance, how its NOS directories are organized. By addressing these questions before you upgrade your own NOS, you ensure that the merger of the two networks goes more smoothly.

An NOS upgrade is a complex and far-reaching change. It should not be undertaken with severe budgetary, resource, or time constraints. The following steps demonstrate how careful planning and a methodical process can help you accomplish an NOS upgrade. (Depending on your situation, the order and complexity of the steps may vary.)

1. *Research*—Gather information about the NOS from the manufacturer and from other sources, including reputable Internet bulletin boards, reputable magazines, and other networking professionals. Evaluate the costs involved in upgrading. Also list the benefits and risks involved in embarking on this NOS upgrade.

2. *Project plan*—Before you have committed significant time and money to the project, devise a project plan. This plan should include the following steps, the task assignments for staff, and a rough budget and timeline. Even if you decide not to upgrade the NOS after all, you have to commit resources to proposing and evaluating the option.

3. *Proposal*—Write a proposal to evaluate the product, including a plan to purchase and implement it if the proposal is accepted. A proposal should include the following elements:

   ◆ Questions to answer during evaluation (for example, "Will the NOS work with my current network monitoring software?")

   ◆ Names of personnel who will assist with evaluation and final approval

   ◆ A rough timeline and plan for implementing the change if it is approved

   ◆ A rough project plan for implementing the change if it is approved

   ◆ Cost considerations

   ◆ A review of the short- and long-term benefits and risks of the upgrade

   ◆ A recommendation for or against performing the upgrade

   ◆ A plan for purchasing the software and implementing the change

4. *Evaluation*—Assuming that the proposal indicates that you should proceed with an upgrade and that your superiors approve your recommendation, you are ready to begin the evaluation phase. First order an evaluation copy of the NOS. Then install the software on an unused server whose hardware is similar to the hardware of your production servers (making sure that the test server meets the NOS manufacturer's recommended hardware requirements). On the test system, create several mock user IDs and groups to simulate the real network environment. Also install the applications and services that the server will support if it goes into production.

   Next, as part of your evaluation, distribute updated client software to a team of technical staff and project stakeholders and ask them to use the mock IDs and groups to test the system. Over a given time period, they can test the system and keep notes on how the system meets the requirements specified in your proposal. The test team should pay particular attention to the new user interface for clients, the way in which your company's applications operate, the system's response time, and any new features provided by the upgrade. Meet regularly with the team during the evaluation period to discuss and compare experiences.

5. *Training*—If the results of the initial stages of evaluation lead you to decide to purchase the upgrade, make sure you and other networking staff get trained on the new NOS. Schedule training to take place only weeks before the anticipated implementation date so that your new skills are fresh when you begin the conversion.

6. *Pre-implementation*—Before implementing the change, expand on the rough project plan for the upgrade. Ensure that your plan for transferring user accounts, groups, and their rights to the new system is sound. Decide how you want to reorganize the NOS directory, if necessary, and what types of volumes to create. In addition, review the existing servers to determine which applications, files, and directories should be transferred and which can be archived.

   Weeks before upgrading, inform users, help desk personnel, and other networking staff of the timeline and explain what changes to expect. Recommend that users clean up their data directories on the server and discard any unnecessary files. Similarly, ask networking staff to remove any nonessential applications or services they have installed on the server. If necessary, arrange to upgrade the client software on all workstations that will be affected by the operating system upgrade. A few days before the upgrade, issue a final warning to staff specifying when and for how long the server will be down to accomplish the upgrade.

7. *Implementation*—Perform the upgrade when few or no users will be on the network. Before beginning the upgrade, gather the software documentation and your project plan, along with the software CDs or DVDs and a bootable disk for the server (making certain that the CD-ROM or DVD-ROM device driver is on the bootable disk). Just before taking the system down, broadcast a warning to all users on the network that the server is going down soon. Then disable all logons to the network. Next, back up the entire server's hard disk. When the backup is complete, use your backup software to verify that critical files were successfully copied. Finally, perform the upgrade according to the manufacturer's instructions and your network's specifications.

8. *Post-implementation*—Test functions and applications on the upgraded server to verify the success of your upgrade. After you are satisfied that the upgrade is successful, re-enable logons to the network and inform staff that the system is running again. Later, you can review the upgrade process with other networking staff to find out whether you learned any lessons that could make future server upgrades more efficient and less troublesome. Work with the help desk personnel to understand the kinds of support calls generated by the upgrade. Also continue testing the new operating system, fine-tuning when necessary, to fix problems or find errors before they become problems for users.

Reversing a Software Upgrade

If the software upgrade you perform creates problems in your existing system, you should be prepared to reverse the process. The process of reverting to a previous version of software after attempting to upgrade it is known as **backleveling**. Every network professional has been forced to backlevel at some point in her career. The steps that constitute this process differ, depending on the complexity of the upgrade and the network environment involved.

Although no hard-and-fast rules for backleveling exist, Table 15-1 summarizes some basic suggestions. Bear in mind that you must always refer to the software vendor's documentation to reverse an upgrade. If you must backlevel a network operating system upgrade, you should also consult with experienced professionals about the best approach for your network environment.

Table 15-1 Reversing a software upgrade

Type of Upgrade	Options for Reversing
Operating system patch	Use the patch's automatic uninstall utility.
Client software upgrade	Use the upgrade's automatic uninstall utility or reinstall the previous version of the client on top of the upgrade.
Shared application upgrade	Use the application's automatic uninstall utility or maintain a complete copy of the previous installation of the application and reinstall it over the upgrade.
Operating system upgrade	Prior to the upgrade, make a complete backup of the system; to back-level, restore entire system from the backup; uninstall an operating system upgrade only as a last resort.

Hardware and Physical Plant Changes

Hardware and physical plant changes may be required when a network component fails or malfunctions, but more often they are performed as part of an upgrade to increase capacity, improve performance, or add functionality to the network. In this section, you will learn about the simplest and most popular form of hardware change—adding more of what you already use, such as adding four more switches to the backbone or adding 10 new networked printers. You also learn about more complex hardware changes, such as replacing the entire network backbone with a more robust system.

Many of the same issues apply to hardware changes as apply to software changes. In particular, proper planning is the key to a successful upgrade. When considering a change to your network hardware, use the following steps as a guide:

1. Determine whether the change is necessary.
2. Research the upgrade's potential effects on other devices, functions, and users.
3. If you decide to implement the change, notify system administrators, help desk personnel, and users, and schedule it during off-hours (unless it is an emergency).
4. If possible, back up the current hardware's configuration. Most hardware (for example, routers, switches, and servers) has a configuration that you can easily copy to a disk. In other cases (for example, networked printers), you may have to print the hardware's configuration.
5. Prevent users from accessing the system or the part of the system that you are changing.

6. Keep the installation instructions and hardware documentation handy.

7. Implement the change.

8. Test the hardware fully after the change, preferably putting a higher load on the device than it would incur during normal use in your organization. Note any unintended or unanticipated consequences of the change.

9. If the change was successful, re-enable access to the device. If it was unsuccessful, isolate the device or reinsert the old device, if possible.

10. Inform system administrators, help desk personnel, and users when the change is complete. If it was not successful, explain why.

11. Record your change in the change management system.

Adding or Upgrading Equipment

The difficulty involved in adding or upgrading hardware on your network depends largely on whether you have used the hardware in the past. For instance, if your organization always uses Cisco switches, adding one more Cisco switch to your second-floor telecommunications closet may take only a few minutes and cause absolutely no disruption of service to your users. On the other hand, even if your company uses Cisco switches, adding a Cisco VPN router to your network may be an entirely new experience. You should research, evaluate, and test any unfamiliar piece of equipment that you intend to add or upgrade on your network, even if it is manufactured by a vendor that supplies much of your other hardware.

With the rapid changes in the hardware industry, you may not be able to purchase identical hardware even from one quarter to the next. If consistency is a concern—for example, if your technical staff is familiar with only one brand and model of printer, and you do not have the time or money to retrain personnel—you would be wise to purchase as much hardware as possible in a single order. If this approach is not feasible, purchase equipment from vendors with familiar products and solid reputations.

Each type of device that you add or upgrade on the network will have different preparation and implementation requirements. Knowing exactly how to handle the changes requires not only a close reading of the manufacturer's instructions, but also some experience with the type of networking equipment at hand. The following list provides a very general overview of how you might approach adding or upgrading devices on the network, from the least disruptive to the most complex types of equipment. The devices at the bottom of the list are not only the most disruptive and complex to add or upgrade, but also the most difficult to remove or backlevel.

◆ *Networked workstation*—A networked workstation is perhaps the simplest device to add. It directly affects only a few users, and does not alter network access for anyone else. If your organization has a standard networked workstation configuration (for example, a disk image—a compressed snapshot of the workstation's contents—on the server), adding a networked workstation will be a quick operation as well. You can successfully add a networked workstation without notifying users or support staff and without worrying about downtime.

◆ *Networked printer*—A networked printer is easy to add to your network, too. Adding this equipment is slightly more complex than adding a networked workstation, however, because of its unique configuration process and because it is shared. Although it affects multiple users, a networked printer does not typically perform a mission-critical function in an organization, so the length of time required to install one does not usually affect productivity. Thus, although you should notify the affected users of a networked printer addition, you do not need to notify all users and support staff. Likewise, you do not need to restrict access to the network or worry about downtime in this instance.

◆ *Hub or access point*—A single hub or access point might service as few as one or as many as 64 users. You do not have to worry about downtime or notifying users when *adding* a new hub or access point, because it cannot affect anyone until it is actually in use. However, if you are upgrading or swapping out an existing hub or access point, you must notify the affected users, because the upgrade or swap will create downtime. In addition, you must consider the traffic and addressing implications of adding or upgrading a hub or access point. For example, if you need to expand the capacity of a TCP/IP-based network segment from 24 users to 60 users, you can easily enough swap your 24-port hub with a 64-port hub. But before doing so, make sure that the segment has been allotted enough free IP addresses to service 60 users; otherwise, these users will not be able to access the network.

◆ *Server*—A server addition or upgrade can be tricky. Typically, this type of change (unless it is the replacement of a minor component) requires a great deal of foresight and planning. Before installing a new server, you need to consider the hardware and connectivity implications of the change, as well as issues relating to the NOS. Even if you are adding a server that will not be used immediately, you still need to plan for its installation. It's preferable to add the server while network traffic is low or nonexistent. You should also restrict access to the new server; otherwise, one of your users could find the server while browsing the network and try to save files to it or run an application from it.

Upgrading the hardware (such as a NIC or memory) on an existing server may require nearly as much planning as adding an entirely new server. Schedule upgrades to an existing server for off-hours, so that you can shut down the server without inconveniencing any users who rely on it.

◆ *Switches and routers*—Changing or adding switches or routers to a network design is more complicated for several reasons. First, this type of change can be physically disruptive—for example, it might require the installation of new racks or other support frames in your telecommunications room. Second, switches and routers usually affect many users—and might affect all users—on the network. For instance, if you must replace the Internet gateway for your organization's headquarters, you will cut every user's access to the Internet in the process (unless you have redundant gateways, which is the optimal setup if you rely on the Internet for mission-critical services). You should notify all users on the network about the impending change, even if you don't think they will be affected—sometimes a router or switch may have unintended effects on segments of the network other than the one it services. In addition, you should plan at least weeks in advance for switch or router changes and expect at least several hours of downtime. Because switches and routers are expensive, take extraordinary care when handling and configuring the equipment. Also, because switches and routers serve different purposes, you should rely on the manufacturer's documentation to guide you through the installation process.

CAUTION

Bear in mind that adding a new processor to a server, a new NIC to a router, or more memory to a printer may affect your service or warranty agreement with the manufacturer. Before purchasing any components to add or replace in your network devices, check your agreement for stipulations that might apply. You may be allowed to add only components made by the same manufacturer, or risk losing all support from that manufacturer.

Above all, keep safety in mind when you upgrade or install hardware on a network. Never tinker with the insides of a device that is turned on. Make sure that all cords and devices are stowed safely out of the way and cannot cause trips or falls. Avoid wearing jewelry, scarves, or very loose clothing when you work on equipment; if you have long hair, tie it back. Not only will you prevent injury this way, but you will also be less distracted. By removing metal jewelry, you may prevent damage to the equipment caused by a short if the metal touches a circuit. If the equipment is heavy (such as a large switch or server), do not try to lift it by yourself. Finally, to protect the equipment from damage, follow the manufacturer's temperature, ventilation, antistatic, and moisture guidelines.

Cabling Upgrades

Cabling upgrades (unless they involve the replacement of a single faulty patch cable) may require significant planning and time to implement, depending on the size of your network. Remember from Chapter 12 that troubleshooting cabling problems may be difficult because the cable layout may be undocumented and poorly planned, particularly if it was installed years before and survived intact despite building changes and network growth. For the same reason, an enterprise-wide cabling upgrade is complex. The best way to ensure that future upgrades go smoothly is to carefully document the existing cable *before* making any upgrades. If this assessment is not possible, you may have to compile your documentation as you upgrade the existing cabling.

Because a change of this magnitude affects all users on the network, you should upgrade the network cabling in phases. Perhaps you can schedule an upgrade of the first-floor east wing of your building one weekend, then the first-floor west wing of your building the next, and so on. Weigh the importance of the upgrade against its potential for disruption. For example, if the Payroll Department is processing end-of-month checks and having no difficulties other than somewhat slow response time, it is not critical to take away its access to install CAT 6 wiring. On the other hand, if the building maintenance staff needs a 1-Gbps connection to run a new HVAC control system, you will probably make it a priority to take down this access temporarily and replace the wiring. In this case, not only must you replace the wiring, but you may also need to replace hubs and NICs.

For the most part, only organizations that run very small networks are able to upgrade or install their own network cabling. Most other organizations rely on contractors who specialize in this service. Nevertheless, as a networking professional you should know how to run a cable across a room, either under a raised floor or through a ceiling plenum, in order to connect a device to the network.

Backbone Upgrades

The most comprehensive and complex upgrade involving network hardware is a backbone upgrade. Recall that the network backbone represents the main conduit for data on LANs and WANs, connecting major routers, servers, and switches. A backbone upgrade requires not only a great deal of planning, but also the efforts of several personnel (and possibly contractors) and a significant investment. You may upgrade parts of the backbone—a NIC in a router or a section of cabling, for example—at any time, but upgrading the entire backbone changes the whole network.

Examples of backbone upgrades include migrating from Token Ring to Ethernet, migrating from a slower technology to a faster one, and replacing routers with switches (to make use of VLANs, for example). Such upgrades may satisfy a variety of needs: a need for faster throughput, a physical move or renovation, a more reliable network, greater security, more consistent standards, support of a new application, or greater cost-effectiveness. For example, the need for faster throughput may prompt an upgrade from an older Ethernet technology to Gigabit Ethernet. Likewise, the need to support videoconferencing may require a backbone upgrade from CAT 5 to fiber-optic cable.

If you recall the cabling and hardware required for different networking technologies (as explained in Chapters 3 and 6), you get an idea of how far-reaching a backbone upgrade can be. For example, to convert from Token Ring to Ethernet, you must replace or upgrade connectivity equipment such as hubs (or MAUs), switches, and routers. In addition, you must replace the NIC in every workstation and printer on the network and change the configuration for each device so that it works with Ethernet rather than Token Ring. For a small network, this effort may not be more than a weekend's work. For a network of thousands of users, such an upgrade requires the services of a dedicated team.

Because backbone upgrades are expensive and time-consuming, the first step in approaching such a project is to justify it. Will the benefits outweigh the costs? Can the upgrade wait a year or more? If so, you might be wise to wait and find out whether a cheaper or better technical solution becomes available later. Don't try to wait until the technology "settles down," because networking progress never stands still. On the other hand, do wait to implement brand-new technology until you can find out how it has worked on other networks similar to your own or until the manufacturer eliminates most of the bugs.

The second step is to determine which kind of backbone design to implement. To make this decision, you must analyze the future capacity needs of your network, decide whether you want a distributed or collapsed backbone, determine whether you want to rely on switches or routers, decide whether to use subnetting and to what extent, and so on. Although some of these predictions will be guesswork, you can minimize the variables by examining the history of your organization's growth and needs.

After designing your backbone upgrade, develop a project plan to accomplish the upgrade. Given that you don't upgrade your backbone every day, you might want to contract this work to a firm that specializes in network design and upgrades. In that case, you will draft an RFP (request for proposal) to specify what that contractor should do. Regardless of whether you employ specialists, your project plan should include a logical process for upgrading the backbone one section at a time (if possible). Because this process causes network outages, determine how best to proceed based on users' needs. Choose a time when usage is low (such as over a holiday) to perform your upgrade.

Reversing Hardware Changes

As with software changes, you should provide a way to reverse the hardware upgrade and reinstall the old hardware if necessary. If you are replacing a faulty component or device, this restoration, of course, is not possible. If you are upgrading a component in a device, on the other hand, you should keep the old component safe (for example, keep NICs in static-resistant containers) and nearby. Not only might you need to put it back in the device, but you might also need to refer to it for information. For example, if you have not documented the necessary jumper settings for an interface card in a switch, the old card might indicate the jumper settings needed on your new card. Even if the device seems to be operating well with the new component, keep the old component for a while, especially if it is the only one of its kind at your organization.

Chapter Summary

- ◆ Project management is the practice of managing staff, budget, timelines, and other resources and variables so as to complete a specific goal within given bounds. The person who designs the project plan and oversees the project is the project manager. A project needs a plan, and also participants, funding, a specific means of communication, definitive processes, contingency plans, and a testing and evaluation phase.
- ◆ The first step in project management is to conduct a feasibility study. A feasibility study determines whether a proposed project fits within an organization's budget, time, and staff restrictions. It also attempts to weigh the benefits and costs of undertaking a project.
- ◆ A needs assessment is the process of clarifying the reasons and objectives for a proposed change. It involves interviewing users and other stakeholders and comparing their perceptions to factual data. In addition, it may involve analyzing network

baseline data. Your goal in performing a needs assessment is to decide whether the change is worthwhile and necessary and to determine the appropriate scope and nature of the change.

◆ Project goals help keep a project on track. They are also necessary later for evaluating whether a project was successful. Project managers typically begin with a broad goal, then narrow it down into specific goals that contribute to the larger goal.

◆ A project plan describes how the details of a managed project are organized. It divides tasks and subtasks, dependencies, resource allocation, timelines, and milestones. Project plans may take the form of a simple text or spreadsheet document for small projects. Larger projects, however, often require the use of project management software (such as Microsoft Project).

◆ When implementing a major network change, communicate with users about how their access to the network will be affected; for how long their access to the network will be affected; how their data will be protected during the change; whether you will provide any means for users to access the network during the change; and whether the change requires them to learn new skills.

◆ The best way to evaluate a large-scale network or systems implementation is to first test it on a small scale on a pilot network. Although a pilot network differs from the enterprise-wide network, it should mimic it closely enough to represent the larger network's hardware, software, connectivity, unique configurations, and load.

◆ Network management involves assessing, monitoring, and maintaining network devices and connections.

◆ Baselining includes keeping a history of network performance, the physical topology, logical topology, number of devices on the network, operating systems and protocols in use, and number and type of applications in use. In other words, it provides a complete picture of the network's current state. Baselining provides the basis for determining what types of changes might improve the network and for later evaluating how successful the improvements were.

◆ Assessing a network's status on an ongoing basis includes performance management, or monitoring how well links and devices are keeping up with the demands placed on them, and fault management, or the detection and signaling of device, link, or component faults.

◆ Network management applications typically use SNMP (Simple Network Management Protocol) to communicate with agents running on managed devices. Agents may report information on a device's components or status (such as utilization or performance).

◆ An asset management system includes an inventory of the total number of components on the network as well as each device's configuration files, model number, serial number, location on the network, and technical support contact. In addition, it records every piece of software purchased by your organization, its version number, vendor, and technical support contact.

◆ A patch is an enhancement or improvement to a part of a software application, often distributed at no charge by software vendors to fix a bug in their code or to add slightly more functionality. Patches differ from revisions and software upgrades because they change only part of the software application, leaving most of the code untouched.

◆ Make it a policy to keep informed about patches to your network software, whether they involve the operating system, an application, or a client software. If you work in a large organization with several servers, routers, and other devices, you may want to assign one network administrator to manage patches for the servers, another to manage patches for the printers, and so on.

◆ A software upgrade represents a major change to the existing code, which may or may not be offered free from a vendor and may or may not be comprehensive enough to substitute for the original application. An upgrade to the client software replaces the existing client software so as to add functionality and fix bugs found in the previous version.

◆ Before upgrading client software, carefully read the instructions that accompany the upgrade to find out how best to apply it, whether it depends on any previous upgrades, whether it requires any special preparation, and how its changes will affect users. Client upgrades typically overwrite some system files on the workstation, so their installation may affect other applications adversely.

◆ Like client upgrades, application upgrades consist of modifications to all or part of an application that are designed to enhance functionality or fix problems with the software. Application upgrades, however, affect software applications shared by clients on the network.

◆ Perhaps the most critical type of software upgrade you'll perform comprises an upgrade to your network operating system. This effort usually involves significant, potentially drastic, changes to the operation of your servers and clients. As such, it requires plenty of forethought, product research, and rigorous testing before you implement it. In fact, for any network with more than a few users, you should create and follow a project plan for this undertaking.

◆ The process of upgrading an NOS should include research, proposal, evaluation, training, pre-implementation, implementation, and post-implementation phases.

◆ You should plan for the possibility that a software upgrade might harm your existing system (or systems), and be prepared to reverse the process. The restoration of a previous version of software after an attempted upgrade is known as backleveling.

◆ Hardware and physical plant changes may be required when your network has problems. More often, however, they are performed as part of a move to increase capacity, improve performance, or add functionality to the network.

◆ Research, evaluate, and test any unfamiliar piece of equipment you intend to add or upgrade on your network, even if it is manufactured by a vendor that supplies much of your other hardware. The process of implementing a hardware upgrade is very similar to that of carrying out a software upgrade, including notifying users and preparing to bring the system down during the change.

◆ Cabling upgrades are simpler and less error-prone if a network's cable plant is well documented. Also make sure to document new cable infrastructure after making changes. When embarking on a major cabling upgrade, such as a backbone replacement, it is advisable to upgrade the infrastructure in phases.

◆ The most comprehensive and complex upgrade involving network hardware is a backbone upgrade. The network backbone serves as the main conduit for data on LANs and WANs, connecting major routers, servers, and/or switches. A backbone upgrade not only requires a great deal of time to plan, but also the efforts of several staff members (and possibly contractors) and a significant investment.

◆ You should provide a way to reverse a hardware upgrade and replace it with the old hardware. If you are upgrading a component in a device, keep the old component safe (for example, keep NICs in static-resistant containers) and nearby. Not only might you need to put it back in the device, but you might also need to refer to it for information.

Key Terms

agent—A software routine that collects data about a managed device's operation and provides it to the network management application running on the console.

asset management—The process of identifying and tracking an organization's assets, such as hardware and software.

backleveling—The process of reverting to a previous version of a software application after attempting to upgrade it.

bug—A flaw in software or hardware that causes it to malfunction.

contingency planning—The process of identifying steps that minimize the risk of unforeseen circumstances endangering the quality or timeliness of the project's goals.

fault management—The detection and signaling of device, link, or component faults.

feasibility study—A study that determines the costs and benefits of a project and attempts to predict whether the project will result in a favorable outcome (for example, whether it will achieve its goal without imposing excessive cost or time burdens on the organization).

Gantt chart—A popular method of depicting when projects begin and end along a horizontal timeline.

Management Information Base—See *MIB*.

MIB (Management Information Base)—A database used in network management that contains a device's definitions of managed objects and their data.

milestone—A reference point that marks the completion of a major task or group of tasks in a project and contributes to measuring the project's progress.

MRTG (Multi Router Traffic Grapher)—A command-line utility that uses SNMP to poll devices, collects data in a log file, and then generates HTML-based views of the data. MRTG is freely distributed software originally written by Tobias Oetiker, a networking professional who in the early 1990s saw a need for a tool to regularly measure the status of his organization's WAN link.

Multi Router Traffic Grapher—See *MRTG*.

needs assessment—The process of clarifying the reasons and objectives for a proposed change to determine whether the change is worthwhile and necessary, and to elucidate the scope and nature of the proposed change.

network management—The assessment, monitoring, and maintenance of the devices and connections on a network.

patch—A correction, improvement, or enhancement to part of a software application, often distributed at no charge by software vendors to fix a bug in their code or to add slightly more functionality.

performance management—The ongoing assessment of how well network links, devices, and components keep up with demands on them.

pilot network—A small-scale network that stands in for the larger network. A pilot network may be used to evaluate the effects of network changes or additions.

polling—A network management application's regular collection of data from managed devices.

predecessor—A task in a project that must be completed before other tasks can begin.

project management—The practice of managing staff, budget, timelines, and other resources and variables to complete a specific goal within given bounds.

project plan—The way in which details of a managed project (for example, the timeline and the significant tasks) are organized. Some project plans are created via special project planning software, such as Microsoft Project.

service pack—A significant patch to one of the Microsoft Windows operating systems.

Simple Network Management Protocol—See *SNMP*.

SNMP (Simple Network Management Protocol)—An Application layer protocol in the TCP/IP suite used to convey data regarding the status of managed devices on a network.

sponsor—A person in a position of authority who supports a project and who can lobby for budget increases necessary to complete the project, appeal to a group of managers to extend a project's deadline, and assist with negotiating vendor contracts.

stakeholder—Any person who may be affected by a project, for better or for worse. A stakeholder may be a project participant, user, manager, or vendor.

upgrade—A major change to the existing code in a software application, which may or may not be offered free from a vendor, and may or may not be comprehensive enough to substitute for the original application.

Review Questions

1. A _____ is the process of clarifying the reasons and objectives underlying a proposed change.

   a. patch assessment

   b. needs assessment

   c. milestone

   d. feasibility study

2. Which of the following refers to the correction, improvement, or enhancement to a particular piece of a software application?

   a. Milestone

   b. Service pack

   c. Gantt chart

   d. Patch

3. _____ represent modifications to all or part of an application that are designed to enhance functionality or fix problems related to software.

   a. Application upgrades

   b. Shared application upgrades

   c. Project plans

   d. Feasibility studies

4. _____ is necessary to ensure that all participants understand the project's goals, encourage teamwork, avoid duplicate efforts, and allow learning from prior mistakes.

   a. Contingency planning

   b. Testing and evaluation

   c. Communication

   d. Setting timelines

5. _____ involves identifying and tracking the hardware and software on your network.

   a. Needs assessment

   b. Contingency planning

   c. Fault management

   d. Asset management

6. True or false? Migrating from a Token Ring network to Ethernet is an example of a backbone upgrade.

7. True or false? A contingency plan is a popular method for depicting when projects begin and end along a horizontal timeline.

8. True or false? You do not have to worry about downtime or notifying users when adding a new hub or access point, because it cannot affect anyone until it is actually in use.

9. True or false? The detection and signaling of device, link, or component faults is known as performance management.

10. True or false? A small-scale network that stands in for a larger network is sometimes called a pilot network.

11. A(n) _____ is a reference point that marks the completion of a major task or group of tasks in the project and contributes to measuring the project's progress.

12. A(n) _____ outlines the costs and benefits of the project and attempts to predict whether it will result in a favorable outcome.

13. _____ is the process of identifying steps that minimize the risk of unforeseen events that could affect the quality or timeliness of the project's goals.

14. The process of reverting to a previous version of software after attempting to upgrade is known as _____.

15. _____ is the practice of managing staff, budget, timelines, and other resources and variables to achieve a specific goal within given bounds.

Appendix A

Network+ Examination Objectives

This book covers all of the Network+ examination objectives, which were released by CompTIA (the Computing Technology Industry Association) in 2005. The official list of objectives is available at CompTIA's Web site, *www.comptia.org*. For your reference, the following table lists each exam objective and the chapter of this book that explains the objective, plus the amount of the exam that will cover each certification domain. Each objective belongs to one of four domains (or main topics) of networking expertise. For example, the objective of recognizing an RJ-45 connector belongs to the "Media and Topologies" domain, which accounts for 20% of the exam's content.

Domain 1.0 Media and Topologies— 20% of Examination

Table A-1 Network+ Examination Objectives—Media and Topologies

Objective	Chapter
1.1 Recognize the following logical or physical network topologies given a diagram, schematic or description:	
Star	1, 6, 7
Bus	1, 6, 7
Mesh	7
Ring	1, 6, 7
1.2 Specify the main features of 802.2 (Logical Link Control), 802.3 (Ethernet), 802.5 (token ring), 802.11 (wireless), and FDDI (Fiber Distributed Data Interface) networking technologies, including:	
Speed	3, 6
Access method (CSMA / CA (Carrier Sense Multiple Access / Collision Avoidance) and CSMA / CD (Carrier Sense Multiple Access / Collision Detection))	3, 6
Topology	6
Media	3, 6
1.3 Specify the characteristics (For example: speed, length, topology, and cable type) of the following cable standards:	
10BASE-T and 10BASE-FL	3
100BASE-TX and 100BASE-FX	3
1000BASE-T, 1000BASE-CX, 1000BASE-SX and 1000BASE-LX	3
10 GBASE-SR, 10 GBASE-LR and 10 GBASE-ER	3
1.4 Recognize the following media connectors and describe their uses:	
RJ-11 (Registered Jack)	3, Appendix C
RJ-45 (Registered Jack)	3, Appendix C
F-Type	3, Appendix C
ST (Straight Tip)	3, Appendix C

Table A-1 Continued

Objective	Chapter
SC (Subscriber Connector or Standard Connector)	3, Appendix C
IEEE 1394 (FireWire)	5, Appendix C
Fiber LC (Local Connector)	3, Appendix C
MT-RJ (Mechanical Transfer Registered Jack)	3, Appendix C
USB (Universal Serial Bus)	5, Appendix C
1.5 Recognize the following media types and describe their uses:	
Category 3, 5, 5e, and 6	3
UTP (Unshielded Twisted Pair)	3
STP (Shielded Twisted Pair)	3
Coaxial cable	3
SMF (Single Mode Fiber) optic cable	3
MMF (Multimode Fiber) optic cable	3
1.6 Identify the purposes, features and functions of the following network components:	
Hubs	3, 5
Switches	5, 7
Bridges	5
Routers	5, 11, 14
Gateways	5, 11, 14
CSU / DSU (Channel Service Unit / Data Service Unit)	7
NICs (Network Interface Cards)	1, 5
ISDN (Integrated Services Digital Network) adapters	7
WAPs (Wireless Access Points)	3, 5, 6
Modems	3, 7
Transceivers (media converters)	3
Firewalls	5, 14
1.7 Specify the general characteristics (For example: carrier speed, frequency, transmission type and topology) of the following wireless technologies:	
802.11 (Frequency hopping spread spectrum)	3, 6
802.11x(Direct sequence spread spectrum)	3, 6
Infrared	3, 6
Bluetooth	3, 6
1.8 Identify factors which affect the range and speed of wireless service (For example: interference, antenna type and environmental factors).	3

Domain 2.0 Protocols and Standards— 20% of Examination

Table A-2 Network+ Examination Objectives—Protocols and Standards

Objective	Chapter
2.1 Identify a MAC (Media Access Control) address and its parts.	2
2.2 Identify the seven layers of the OSI (Open Systems Interconnect) model and their functions.	2
2.3 Identify the OSI (Open Systems Interconnect) layers at which the following network components operate:	
Hubs	2, 5
Switches	5
Bridges	5
Routers	2, 5
NICs (Network Interface Cards)	2, 5
WAPs (Wireless Access Points)	3, 5
2.4 Differentiate between the following network protocols in terms of routing, addressing schemes, interoperability and naming conventions:	
IPX / SPX (Internetwork Packet Exchange / Sequence Packet Exchange)	4
NetBEUI (Network Basic Input / Output System Extended User Interface)	4
AppleTalk / AppleTalk over IP (Internet Protocol)	4
TCP / IP (Transmission Control Protocol / Internet Protocol)	4, 11
2.5 Identify the components and structure of IP (Internet Protocol) addresses (IPv4, IPv6) and the required setting for connections across the Internet.	4, 11
2.6 Identify classful IP (Internet Protocol) ranges and their subnet masks (For example: Class A, B and C).	4, 11
2.7 Identify the purpose of subnetting.	4, 11
2.8 Identify the differences between private and public network addressing schemes.	11
2.9 Identify and differentiate between the following IP (Internet Protocol) addressing methods:	
Static	3
Dynamic	3
Self-assigned (APIPA (Automatic Private Internet Protocol Addressing))	3

Table A-2 Continued

Objective	Chapter
2.10 Define the purpose, function and use of the following protocols used in the TCP/IP (Transmission Control Protocol/Internet Protocol) suite:	
TCP (Transmission Control Protocol)	2, 4
UDP (User Datagram Protocol)	2, 4
FTP (File Transfer Protocol)	4
SFTP (Secure File Transfer Protocol)	14
TFTP (Trivial File Transfer Protocol)	4
SMTP (Simple Mail Transfer Protocol)	11
HTTP (Hypertext Transfer Protocol)	2, 4
HTTPS (Hypertext Transfer Protocol Secure)	14
POP3 / IMAP4 (Post Office Protocol version 3 / Internet Message Access Protocol version 4)	11
Telnet	4
SSH (Secure Shell)	14
ICMP (Internet Control Message Protocol)	4
ARP / RARP (Address Resolution Protocol/Reverse Address Resolution Protocol)	4
NTP (Network Time Protocol)	4
NNTP (Network News Transport Protocol)	4
SCP (Secure Copy Protocol)	14
LDAP (Lightweight Directory Access Protocol)	8
IGMP (Internet Group Multicast Protocol)	4
LPR (Line Printer Remote)	9
2.11 Define the function of TCP / UDP (Transmission Control Protocol / User Datagram Protocol) ports.	4
2.12 Identify the well-known ports associated with the following commonly used services and protocols:	4
20 FTP (File Transfer Protocol)	4
21 FTP (File Transfer Protocol)	4
22 SSH (Secure Shell)	4
23 Telnet	4
25 SMTP (Simple Mail Transfer Protocol)	4
53 DNS (Domain Name Service)	4
69 TFTP (Trivial File Transfer Protocol)	4
80 HTTP (Hypertext Transfer Protocol)	4
110 POP3 (Post Office Protocol version 3)	4
119 NNTP (Network News Transport Protocol)	4

Table A-2 Continued

Objective	Chapter
123 NTP (Network Time Protocol)	4
143 IMAP4 (Internet Message Access Protocol version 4)	4
443 HTTPS (Hypertext Transfer Protocol Secure)	4
2.13 Identify the purpose of network services and protocols (For example: DNS (Domain Name Service), NAT (Network Address Translation), ICS (Internet Connection Sharing), WINS (Windows Internet Name Service), SNMP (Simple Network Management Protocol), NFS (Network File System), Zeroconf (Zero configuration), SMB (Server Message Block), AFP (Apple File Protocol), LPD (Line Printer Daemon) and Samba).	4, 8, 9, 11, 14, 15
2.14 Identify the basic characteristics (For example: speed, capacity and media) of the following WAN (Wide Area Networks) technologies:	
Packet switching	6
Circuit switching	6
ISDN (Integrated Services Digital Network)	7
FDDI (Fiber Distributed Data Interface)	6
T1 (T Carrier level 1) / E1 / J1	7
T3 (T Carrier level 3) / E3 / J3	7
OCx (Optical Carrier)	7
X.25	7
2.15 Identify the basic characteristics of the following internet access technologies:	
xDSL (Digital Subscriber Line)	7
Broadband Cable (Cable modem)	7
POTS / PSTN (Plain Old Telephone Service / Public Switched Telephone Network)	7
Satellite	7
Wireless	7
2.16 Define the function of the following remote access protocols and services:	
RAS (Remote Access Service)	7
PPP (Point-to-Point Protocol)	7
SLIP (Serial Line Internet Protocol)	7
PPPoE (Point-to-Point Protocol over Ethernet)	7
PPTP (Point-to-Point Tunneling Protocol)	7
VPN (Virtual Private Network)	7
RDP (Remote Desktop Protocol)	7

Table A-2 Continued

Objective	Chapter
2.17 Identify the following security protocols and describe their purpose and function:	
IPSec (Internet Protocol Security)	14
L2TP (Layer 2 Tunneling Protocol)	7
SSL (Secure Sockets Layer)	14
WEP (Wired Equivalent Privacy)	14
WPA (Wi-Fi Protected Access)	14
802.1x	14
2.18 Identify authentication protocols (For example: CHAP (Challenge Handshake Authentication Protocol), MS-CHAP (Microsoft Challenge Handshake Authentication Protocol), PAP (Password Authentication Protocol), RADIUS (Remote Authentication Dial-In User Service), Kerberos and EAP (Extensible Authentication Protocol)).	14

Domain 3.0 Network Implementation— 25% of Examination

Table A-3 Network+ Examination Objectives—Network Implementation

Objective	Chapter
3.1 Identify the basic capabilities (For example: client support, interoperability, authentication, file and print services, application support and security) of the following server operating systems to access network resources:	
UNIX / Linux / Mac OS X Server	9
Netware	10
Windows	8
Appleshare IP (Internet Protocol)	9
3.2 Identify the basic capabilities needed for client workstations to connect to and use network resources (For example: media, network protocols and peer and server services).	3, 4, 8
3.3 Identify the appropriate tool for a given wiring task (For example: wire crimper, media tester / certifier, punch down tool or tone generator).	3

Table A-3 Network+ Examination Objectives—Network Implementation

Objective	Chapter
3.4 Given a remote connectivity scenario comprised of a protocol, an authentication scheme, and physical connectivity, configure the connection. Includes connection to the following servers:	
UNIX / Linux / MAC OS X Server	4, 8, 9, 10
Netware	4, 8, 9, 10
Windows	4, 8, 9, 10
Appleshare IP (Internet Protocol)	4, 8, 9, 10
3.5 Identify the purpose, benefits and characteristics of using a firewall.	14
3.6 Identify the purpose, benefits and characteristics of using a proxy service.	14
3.7 Given a connectivity scenario, determine the impact on network functionality of a particular security implementation (For example: port blocking/filtering, authentication and encryption).	14
3.8 Identify the main characteristics of VLANs (Virtual Local Area Networks).	5
3.9 Identify the main characteristics and purpose of extranets and intranets.	11
3.10 Identify the purpose, benefits and characteristics of using antivirus software.	13
3.11 Identify the purpose and characteristics of fault tolerance:	
Power	13
Link redundancy	13
Storage	13
Services	13
3.12 Identify the purpose and characteristics of disaster recovery:	
Backup / restore	13
Offsite storage	13
Hot and cold spares	13
Hot, warm and cold sites	13

Domain 4.0 Network Support— 35% of Examination

Table A-4 Network+ Examination Objectives—Network Support

Objective	Chapter
4.1 Given a troubleshooting scenario, select the appropriate network utility from the following:	
Tracert / traceroute	11
ping	4, 11
arp	4
netstat	11
nbtstat	11
ipconfig / ifconfig	4, 11
winipcfg	11
nslookup / dig	11
4.2 Given output from a network diagnostic utility (For example: those utilities listed in objective 4.1), identify the utility and interpret the output.	4, 11
4.3 Given a network scenario, interpret visual indicators (For example: link LEDs (Light Emitting Diodes) and collision LEDs (Light Emitting Diodes)) to determine the nature of a stated problem.	5
4.4 Given a troubleshooting scenario involving a client accessing remote network services, identify the cause of the problem (For example: file services, print services, authentication failure, protocol configuration, physical connectivity and SOHO (Small Office / Home Office) router).	7, 12
4.5 Given a troubleshooting scenario between a client and the following server environments, identify the cause of a stated problem:	
UNIX / Linux / Mac OS X Server	9, 12
Netware	10, 12
Windows	8, 12
Appleshare IP (Internet Protocol)	8, 12
4.6 Given a scenario, determine the impact of modifying, adding or removing network services (For example: DHCP (Dynamic Host Configuration Protocol), DNS (Domain Name Service) and WINS (Windows Internet Name Service)) for network resources and users.	4, 12

Table A-4 Continued

Objective	Chapter
4.7 Given a troubleshooting scenario involving a network with a particular physical topology (For example: bus, star, mesh or ring) and including a network diagram, identify the network area affected and the cause of the stated failure.	6, 12
4.8 Given a network troubleshooting scenario involving an infrastructure (For example: wired or wireless) problem, identify the cause of a stated problem (For example: bad media, interference, network hardware or environment).	4, 12
4.9 Given a network problem scenario, select an appropriate course of action based on a logical troubleshooting strategy. This strategy can include the following steps:	
1. Identify the symptoms and potential causes	12
2. Identify the affected area	12
3. Establish what has changed	12
4. Select the most probable cause	12
5. Implement an action plan and solution including potential effects	12
6. Test the result	12
7. Identify the results and effects of the solution	12
8. Document the solution and process	12

Appendix B

Network+
Practice Exam

The following exam contains questions similar in content and format to what you will encounter on CompTIA's Network+ certification exam. The exam consists of 65 questions, all of which are multiple choice. Some questions have more than one answer, and some questions require that you study a figure to determine the right answer. The questions are in no particular order. The number of questions on each topic reflects the weighting that CompTIA assigned to these topics in their 2005 exam objectives. If you want to simulate taking the CompTIA Network+ certification exam, you should allow yourself 90 minutes to answer all of the questions.

1. What TCP/IP utility would you use to determine the number of hops between two routers?

    a. FTP

    b. Nslookup

    c. Nbtstat

    d. Tracert

    e. Telnet

2. You are the network administrator for a NetWare 6.5 network that runs the TCP/IP protocol. A new user in your organization can log on to the NetWare server, but cannot retrieve her spreadsheet files. Which two of the following situations could be the cause of her problem?

    a. She has entered the wrong user name or password.

    b. She does not have permission to read files in the directory where the spreadsheets are stored.

    c. Her network cable is not inserted into her workstation's NIC.

    d. She does not have permission to view files on the volume where the spreadsheets are stored.

    e. The DHCP settings in her workstation's TCP/IP configuration are incorrect.

3. Which of the following figures reflects the type of physical topology commonly used on a 100BASE-TX network?

    a.

    b.

c.

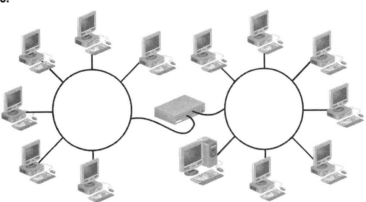

d.

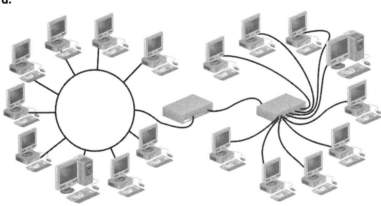

e.

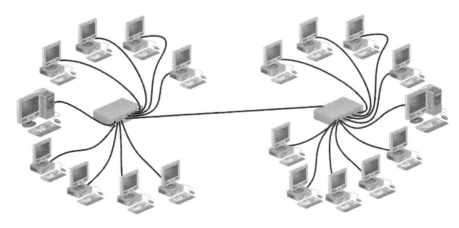

4. You have connected to your bank's home page. Its URL begins with "https://." Based on this information, what type of security can you assume the bank employs for receiving and transmitting data to and from its Web server?

   a. Kerberos

   b. SSL

   c. IPSec

   d. L2TP

   e. packet-filtering firewall

5. You are a support technician for an ISP (Internet service provider) called Alpha Enterprises. A new customer calls to ask why his dial-up connection to your company's RADIUS access server won't work. After the user double-clicks the ISP dial-up networking connection icon on his Windows XP desktop, you can hear his modem dialing. And even though another machine seems to answer, his connection never gets established. You verify that his phone line is connected properly and that he has entered the correct phone number. You also make sure he is using the correct, case-sensitive user name and password that he just received from your Customer Service Department. What do you ask him to check next to get closer to solving his problem?

   a. the type of server specified in his Alpha Enterprises Properties dialog box

   b. the version of Windows XP his system uses

   c. whether the "Save Password" check box is checked in his Connect to Alpha Enterprises dialog box

   d. whether he has disabled the call waiting feature in his Alpha Enterprises Properties dialog box

   e. the maximum baud rate his modem can handle

6. Which of the following protocols is not routable?

   a. RIP

   b. NetBEUI

   c. TCP/IP

   d. IPX/SPX

   e. AppleTalk

7. Which of the following best describes the function(s) of the MAC sublayer?

   a. It performs data compression, reformatting, and encryption.

   b. It appends a node's physical address to frames before they're transmitted.

   c. It interprets program requests and requirements to provide an interface between applications and the network.

   d. It manages flow control, and issues requests for retransmission of data that has suffered errors.

   e. It translates network addresses into their physical counterparts and determines routing.

8. You are a networking technician in a radiology clinic, where physicians use the network to transmit and store patients' diagnostic results. Shortly after a new wing, which contains X-ray and magnetic resonance imaging (MRI) machines, is added to the building, computers in that area begin having intermittent problems saving data to the file server. After you have identified the symptoms, what is your next step in troubleshooting this problem?

   a. Determine the number of workstations affected, to which segment the affected workstations belong, and which area of workstations is affected.

   b. Notify colleagues in the clinic's IT Department about a change you are going to make while attempting to resolve the problem.

   c. Research the problem on your NOS vendor's technical support Web site.

   d. Identify recent changes to the network to determine whether a hardware or software change may be responsible for the problem.

   e. Identify the potential effects of the solution you are about to apply, to make sure that you do not inadvertently create new problems.

9. Which two of the following media are capable of providing the foundation for a Fast Ethernet network?

   a. Level 1 UTP

   b. CAT 2 UTP

   c. CAT 5 UTP

   d. RG-58A/U coaxial cable

   e. fiber-optic cable

10. In which of the following situations would a crossover cable be useful for troubleshooting a network connectivity problem with a workstation?

   a. to connect the workstation to a hub

   b. to connect the workstation's hub port to a punch-down block

   c. to connect the workstation to another workstation

   d. to connect the workstation's switch port to its hub port

   e. to connect between the workstation's wall plate and its hub port

11. Which of the following WAN topologies is the most fault-tolerant?
    a. full mesh
    b. bus
    c. peer-to-peer
    d. ring
    e. hierarchical

12. Which of the following is a valid MAC address?
    a. C3000000FFFF
    b. 111.111.111.111
    c. ::9F53
    d. AEFFG0930110
    e. D0000000

13. What type of network could use the type of connector shown below?

    a. 100BASE-FX
    b. 100BASE-TX
    c. 10BASE-T
    d. 10BASE-5
    e. 10BASE-2

14. Your organization has just ordered its first T1 connection to the Internet. Prior to that, your organization relied on a DSL connection. Which of the following devices must you now have that your DSL connection didn't require?
    a. modem
    b. CSU/DSU
    c. switch
    d. hub
    e. MAU

15. What type of addresses do bridges read, and to which layer of the OSI Model do bridges belong?

    a. IP addresses; the Network layer

    b. IP addresses; the Transport layer

    c. MAC addresses; the Network layer

    d. MAC addresses; the Data Link layer

    e. IP addresses; the Data Link layer

16. You have been asked to provide a connectivity solution for a small, locally owned franchise of a national restaurant chain. The owners of the franchise want to send their confidential sales figures, personnel information, and inventory updates to the national office, which is 1200 miles away, once per week. Their total monthly data transfer will amount to almost 50 megabytes. The franchise owners do not plan to use the connection for any other purposes, and they do not have any IT staff to support the connection. Also, they do not want to spend more than $75 per month, nor more than $500 to install their connection. Considering cost, speed, reliability, technical expertise, distance, security, and the nature of their environment, what is the best solution for this client?

    a. a T1 that connects to the national office via a router at the local franchise and a router at the national office and that uses IPSec to ensure the security of the data en route

    b. a PSTN connection to a local Internet service provider that uses PPP to dial into an access server, then sends data via e-mail to the national office

    c. a DSL connection to a local telephone and Internet service provider that uses IPSec to encrypt the data before it is sent to the national office's file server over the Internet

    d. a private SONET ring to connect with two local telephone and Internet service providers that connects to the national office's T3 and sends data via TCP/IP over ATM

    e. an ISDN connection to a local Internet service provider that allows you to copy files to the national office's anonymous FTP site

17. IEEE's Physical layer standards for wireless networking are established by which IEEE committee?

    a. 802.3

    b. 802.5

    c. 802.11

    d. 802.2

    e. 802.7

18. You are a software programmer using a development Web server at your office to test your programs. Although your Web server is connected to the Internet for test purposes, you want to ensure that no one on the Internet can access your Web files. To make it more difficult for someone to connect to your Web server from the Internet, which TCP/IP default port number would you change in your Web server software configuration?

    a. 21

    b. 22

    c. 65

    d. 80

    e. 90

19. What is the maximum segment length on a 10BASE-T network?

    a. 85 meters

    b. 100 meters

    c. 185 meters

    d. 200 meters

    e. 1000 meters

20. You are the network administrator for a large college whose network contains nearly 10,000 workstations, over 100 routers, 80 switches, and 2000 printers. You are researching a proposal to both upgrade the routers and switches on your network and at the same time improve the management of your network. What type of protocol should you ensure that the new routers and switches can accept in order to more easily automate your network management?

    a. TFTP

    b. SMTP

    c. NNTP

    d. ICMP

    e. SNMP

21. In the process of troubleshooting an intermittent performance problem with your network's Internet connection, you attempt to run a traceroute test to *www.microsoft.com*. The traceroute response displays the first 12 hops in the route, but then presents several "Request timed out" messages in a row. What is the most likely reason for this?

    a. Your network's ISP is experiencing connectivity problems.

    b. The Internet backbone is experiencing traffic congestion.

    c. Your client's TCP/IP service limits the traceroute command to a maximum of 12 hops.

   d. Your IP gateway failed while you were attempting the traceroute test.

   e. Microsoft's network is bounded by firewalls that do not accept incoming ICMP traffic.

22. What is the network ID for a network that contains the group of IP addresses from 194.73.44.1 through 194.73.44.254 and is not subnetted?

   a. 194.1.1.1

   b. 194.73.0.0

   c. 194.73.44.1

   d. 194.73.44.255

   e. 194.73.44.0

23. Which of the following disaster recovery contingencies is the most expensive to maintain?

   a. hot spare

   b. warm spare

   c. hot site

   d. warm site

   e. cold site

24. What type of device is typically used to create a VLAN?

   a. hub

   b. bridge

   c. switch

   d. router

   e. firewall

25. In NAT, how does an IP gateway ensure that outgoing traffic can traverse public networks?

   a. It modifies each outgoing frame's Type field to indicate that the transmission is destined for a public network.

   b. It assigns each outgoing packet a masked ID via the Options field.

   c. It interprets the contents of outgoing packets to ensure that they contain no client-identifying information.

   d. It replaces each outgoing packet's Source address field with a valid IP address.

   e. It modifies the frame length to create uniformly sized frames, called cells, which are required for public network transmission.

26. You have purchased an access point capable of exchanging data via the 802.11b or 802.11g wireless standard. According to these standards, what is the maximum distance from the access point that wireless stations can travel and still exchange data with the access point at the maximum potential throughput?

    a. 10 feet

    b. 50 feet

    c. 80 feet

    d. 100 feet

    e. 175 feet

27. Which of the following RAID levels uses parity error checking? (Choose all that apply.)

    a. RAID Level 0

    b. RAID Level 1

    c. RAID Level 3

    d. RAID Level 5

    e. RAID Level 11

28. Which of the following is used to resolve NetBIOS names with IP addresses?

    a. DNS

    b. SMTP

    c. DHCP

    d. WINS

    e. hosts file

29. Which of the following figures (See choices a through e.) illustrates a VPN WAN?

    a.

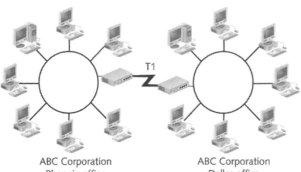

    ABC Corporation
    Phoenix office

    ABC Corporation
    Dallas office

b.

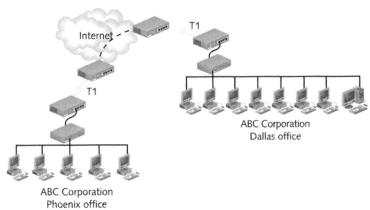

ABC Corporation
Dallas office

ABC Corporation
Phoenix office

c.

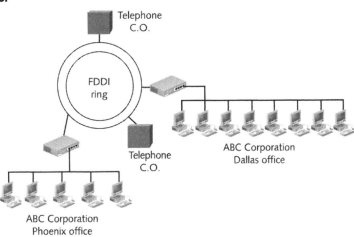

Telephone
C.O.

FDDI
ring

Telephone
C.O.

ABC Corporation
Dallas office

ABC Corporation
Phoenix office

d.

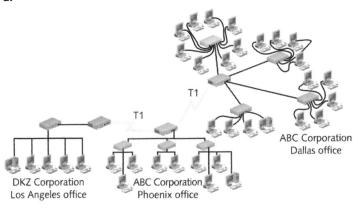

ABC Corporation
Dallas office

DKZ Corporation
Los Angeles office

ABC Corporation
Phoenix office

e.

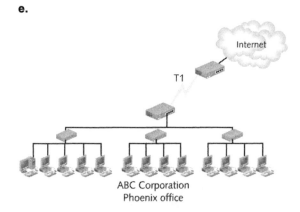

ABC Corporation
Phoenix office

30. Suppose you want to copy files from a Linux server at the office to your home computer, which also runs Linux, across a VPN. Both computers run OpenSSH. Which utility would you use to make sure these files are copied securely?

a. SCP

b. SFTP

c. FTP

d. TFTP

e. HTTP

31. What security measure verifies that your user name and password are contained in the NOS directory when you attempt to log on to a server?

a. remapping

b. encryption

c. authentication

d. caching

e. redirection

32. You are a network administrator for a WAN that connects two regional insurance company offices—one main office and one satellite office—to each other by a T1. The main office is also connected to the Internet using a T1. This T1 provides Internet access for both offices. To ensure that your private network is not compromised by unauthorized access through the Internet connection, you install a firewall between the main office and the Internet. Shortly thereafter, users in your satellite office complain that they cannot access the file server in the main office, but users in the main office can still access the Internet. What two things should you check?

a. whether the firewall has been configured to run in promiscuous mode

b. whether the firewall is placed in the appropriate location on the network

   c. whether the firewall has been configured to allow access from IP addresses in the satellite office

   d. whether the firewall has been configured to receive and transmit UDPbased packets

   e. whether the firewall has been configured to allow Internet access over the main office's T1

33. What TCP/IP utility was used to generate the following output, and what piece of information does it tell you about the machine on which the utility shown below was used?

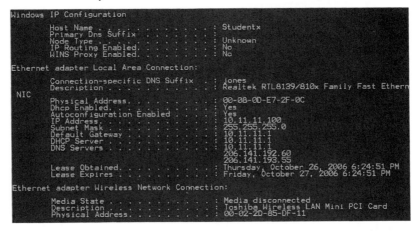

   a. Ipconfig; the output indicates that the machine has a MAC address of 00080DE72F0C

   b. PING; the output indicates that the machine cannot communicate with any external hosts

   c. ARP; the output indicates that the machine resolves to a name of Studentx

   d. Ifconfig; the output indicates that the machine does not rely on DHCP

   e. Nbtstat; the output indicates that it is currently connected to the machine with a NetBIOS name of Studentx

34. While troubleshooting a workstation connectivity problem, you type the following command: ping*f*127.0.0.1. The response indicates that the test failed. What can you determine about that workstation?

   a. Its network cable is faulty or not connected to the wall jack.

   b. Its TCP/IP protocol is not installed properly.

   c. Its IP address has been prevented from transmitting data past the default gateway.

   d. Its DHCP settings are incorrect.

   e. Its DNS name server specification is incorrect.

35. You are a support technician working in a telecommunications closet in a remote office. You suspect that a connectivity problem is related to a broken RJ-45 plug on a patch cable that connects a hub's uplink port to a router. You need to replace that connection, but you forgot to bring an extra patch cable. You decide to install a new RJ-45 connector to replace the broken RJ-45 connector. What two tools should you have to successfully accomplish this?

    a. punch-down tool

    b. crimping tool

    c. wire stripper

    d. cable tester

    e. multimeter

36. In the IP version 6 addressing scheme, which of the following IP addresses equals the loopback address?

    a. 1.0.0.1

    b. 127:0:0:0:0:0:0:1

    c. 0.0.0.0.0.1

    d. ::1

    e. 127.0.0.1

37. Which two of the following devices operate only at the Physical layer of the OSI Model?

    a. hub

    b. switch

    c. router

    d. bridge

    e. repeater

38. Which of the following is a reason for using subnetting or supernetting?

    a. to facilitate easier migration from IPv4 to IPv6 addressing

    b. to enable a network to use DHCP

    c. to make more efficient use of limited numbers of legitimate IP addresses

    d. to reduce the likelihood for user error when modifying TCP/IP properties

    e. to limit the number of addresses that can be assigned to one network interface

39. In which two of the following switching techniques must multiple data packets that make up the same transmission use identical paths to reach their destination?

    a. circuit switching

    b. layer 2 switching

    c. packet switching

    d. message switching

    e. layer 3 switching

40. Which of the following wireless networking technologies can make use of WPA to improve the security of data in transit?

    a. 802.11b

    b. 802.5

    c. Infrared

    d. Bluetooth

    e. 802.3

41. In the following network diagram, which network nodes belong to a private network?

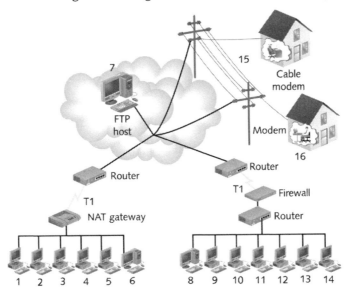

    a. nodes 1 through 6 and nodes 8 through 14

    b. nodes 1 through 6

    c. nodes 8 through 14

    d. nodes 1 through 7, plus 15 and 16

    e. all of the nodes

42. You are the network administrator for a law firm whose two primary offices are located five blocks apart in the center of a large city. The two offices have different specialties, and therefore keep separate file servers. Each file server runs the Windows Server 2003 NOS. A T1 connects the two offices so employees at each office can communicate and share files. To protect the lawyers' records, you currently make regular backups of all the data on both file servers and store the backup tapes in an off-site warehouse. However, one of the firm's partners asked you to do more than simply back up data. In addition, she requests that you implement this added measure within the next week. Which of the following solutions is the best choice to ensure greater data protection in the given time frame?

    a. Contract with an online backup provider to back up data over the Internet using the T1.

    b. Add a UNIX server to the network so that you can establish clustering between all the servers.

    c. Establish mirroring between the two servers using the T1.

    d. Add a RAID Level 5 device to one of the file servers.

    e. Connect the T1 to a third office across town and back up files from the two other locations to the third location.

43. By default, an IPX address contains what other type of address?

    a. IP address

    b. SPX address

    c. MAC address

    d. logical address

    e. NetBIOS address

44. Which transport protocol and TCP/IP port does the Telnet utility use?

    a. UDP, port 23

    b. TCP, port 21

    c. UDP, port 22

    d. TCP, port 23

    e. UDP, port 21

45. Which two of the following guarantee that a server continually has power, even if a building's electrical service is interrupted?

    a. RAID Level 3

    b. RAID Level 5

    c. online UPS

    d. standby UPS

    e. gas-powered generator

46. What protocol is used to transfer mail between a Sendmail server and a Microsoft Exchange server?

   a. SMTP

   b. SNMP

   c. IMAP4

   d. POP3

   e. TFTP

47. What is the function of RARP?

   a. to associate a host name with a given IP address

   b. to associate a MAC address with a given IP address

   c. to associate an IP address with a given MAC address

   d. to associate a NetBIOS name with a given MAC address

   e. to associate a MAC address with a given host name

48. Your 100BASE-T network is wired following the TIA/EIA 568-A standard. As you make your own patch cable, which wires do you crimp into pins 1 and 2 of the RJ-45 connector?

   a. white with green stripe and green

   b. white with brown stripe and brown

   c. white with blue stripe and blue

   d. white with red stripe and red

   e. white with orange stripe and orange

49. You are a support technician at an organization that uses a NetWare 6.5 LAN with a mixture of Windows 98, Windows 2000, and Windows XP workstations. You are asked to help a user in the Accounting Department who can retrieve files from the network, but suddenly can't print to the same printer he uses every day. You have determined that he is the only person in his area affected by this problem. Further, if you log on to the LAN with his user name and password, you can successfully print to the same printer. Which of the following might be the cause of this user's problem?

   a. He inadvertently deleted the network printer object from his workstation's Printers window.

   b. His network password expired.

   c. His user name was accidentally deleted from the group that has rights to print to that printer.

   d. His workstation's operating system requires an update before it can print to that printer.

   e. His network adapter is loose or improperly installed.

50. What is the function of the Network layer of the OSI Model?

    a. to manage the flow of communications over a channel

    b. to add segmentation and assembly information

    c. to encode and encrypt data

    d. to add logical addresses and properly route data

    e. to apply electrical pulses to the wire

51. Which of the following utilities could you use to log on to a UNIX host?

    a. NTP

    b. ARP

    c. PING

    d. Telnet

    e. SNMP

52. On your UNIX workstation, what command would you type at the shell prompt to send a file to the printer queue?

    a. prn *file*

    b. lpr *file*

    c. lpd *file*

    d. ftp *file*

    e. ps *file*

53. What is the default subnet mask for the following IP address: 154.13.44.87?

    a. 255.255.255.255

    b. 255.255.255.0

    c. 255.255.0.0

    d. 255.0.0.0

    e. 0.0.0.0

54. Which of the following diagrams illustrates a FDDI network?

a.

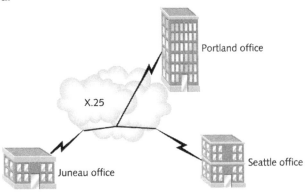

b.

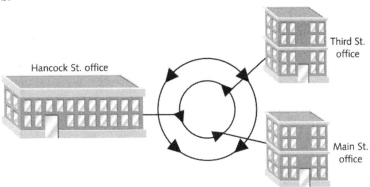

c.

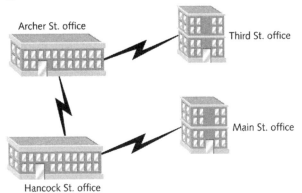

d.

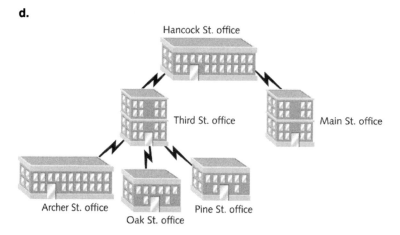

e.

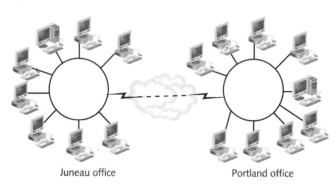

55. You are a support technician installing 13 new Windows XP workstations on your company's network, which relies on several Windows Server 2003 servers for authentication and file sharing, one Fedora Core Linux e-mail server, and one Fedora Core Linux proxy server. The network runs the TCP/IP protocol over 100BASE-TX Ethernet technology. It also uses DHCP and NAT. Which of the following settings must you manually specify on each workstation so that their users can pick up their Internet e-mail from the Linux e-mail server?

    a. DNS server address

    b. IP address

    c. WINS server name

    d. NTP server address

    e. SMTP server name

56. Which of the following IEEE committees designs standards for Token Ring networks?

    a. 802.2

    b. 802.3

    c. 802.5

    d. 802.7

    e. 802.11

57. You have decided to create two separate VLANs in your office: one for computers on the first floor of your building and one for computers on the second floor. What type of device will you need in order for clients on the first floor to communicate with clients on the second floor?

    a. router

    b. switch

    c. bridge

    d. hub

    e. repeater

58. Which application on the Mac OS X Server allows the administrator to create new users and groups?

    a. Console One

    b. Workgroup Manager

    c. MMC

    d. User Manager

    e. Monitor

59. What types of files does an incremental backup save?

    a. data that changed prior to the previous incremental backup

    b. data that changed since the previous full or incremental backup

    c. all data, regardless of whether it has changed

    d. data that was backed up exactly a week previously

    e. data that users have flagged for backup since the last backup occurred

60. You are setting up a new Windows XP client to connect with your LAN, which relies on DHCP. You made certain that the client has the TCP/IP protocol installed and bound to its NIC. Which of the following must you do next to ensure that the client obtains correct TCP/IP information via DHCP?

    a. Make certain the client's computer name and host name are identical.

    b. Enter the client's MAC address in the DHCP server's ARP table.

    c. Make sure the Client for Microsoft Networks service is bound to the client's NIC.

    d. Enter the DHCP server address in the Windows XP TCP/IP configuration.

    e. Nothing; in Windows XP the DHCP option is selected by default and the client will obtain IP addressing information upon connecting to the network.

61. You are a support technician installing a new NIC on a Windows XP workstation. After physically installing the NIC, then installing the appropriate device driver for the NIC, you restart the workstation. Upon restarting, an error indicates that the NIC is attempting to use an IRQ already in use by another device. The workstation's Device Manager window indicates that both the NIC and the sound card are attempting to use IRQ 11. Of the following IRQs, which one could you most likely assign to the new NIC so that it will not conflict with another device?

    a. 4

    b. 6

    c. 9

    d. 13

    e. 15

62. Which three of the following components must be installed on a Windows XP workstation for it to successfully connect to a Windows Server 2003 file server over the network?

    a. NIC

    b. Client for Microsoft Networks

    c. file-sharing services

    d. protocol(s)

    e. Microsoft Family Logon

63. Which one of the following media is most resistant to EMI?

    a. coaxial cable

    b. UTP cable

    c. STP cable

    d. fiber-optic cable

    e. microwaves

64. In the following figure, if router B suffers a failure, how will this failure affect nodes 1 through 9?

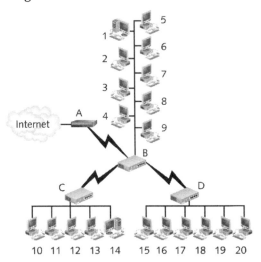

a. They will only be unable to access the Internet.

b. They will be unable to access the Internet and either nodes 10 through 14 or 15 through 20.

c. They will be unable to access the Internet, other nodes on the WAN, and other nodes on the LAN.

d. They will be unable to access the Internet and nodes 10 through 20.

e. Their connectivity will not be affected.

65. Which of the following specifies standards for naming and accessing objects in an NOS's directory and thereby improves interoperability?

a. ANSI

b. LDAP

c. AFP

d. OSPF

e. WINS

Appendix C

Visual Guide to Connectors

Throughout this book, you learned about several different cabling and connector options that may be used on networks. Some, such as RJ-45, are very common, whereas others, such as Fiber LC connectors, are used only on newer high-speed networks. So that you can compare such connectors and ensure that you understand their differences, this Appendix compiles drawings of the connectors and a brief summary of their application in a simple table. You must be familiar with the most popular types of connectors to qualify for Network+ certification. You can find more detail about these connectors and the networks on which they are used in Chapters 3 and 5.

Table C-1 Network connectors and their uses

Specification	Male Connector (front view)	Male Connector (side view)	Female Receptacle (front view)	Application
RJ-11 (Registered Jack 11)				Used on twisted-pair cabling for telephone systems (and some older twisted-pair networks)
RJ-45 (Registered Jack 45)				Used on twisted-pair cabling for modern networks
F-Type				Used on coaxial cable suitable for use with broadband video and data applications
ST (Straight Tip)				Used on fiber-optic cabling (for example, on 100BASE-X, Gigabit, and 10-GB Ethernet networks)
SC (Subscriber Connector or Standard Connector)				Used on fiber-optic cabling (for example, on 100BASE-X, Gigabit, and 10-GB Ethernet networks)
IEEE 1394 (FireWire), 4-pin				Used to connect a variety of peripherals, including digital cameras and external storage devices; also used to network computers in a bus topology
IEEE 1394 (FireWire), 6-pin				Used to connect a variety of peripherals, including digital cameras and external storage devices; also used to network computers in a bus topology
Fiber LC (Local Connector), Single-mode				Used on fiber-optic cabling (for example, on 100BASE-FX, Gigabit, and 10-GB Ethernet networks)

Table C-1 Continued

Specification	Male Connector (front view)	Male Connector (side view)	Female Receptacle (front view)	Application
MT-RJ (Mechanical Transfer-Registered Jack)				Used on fiber-optic cabling (for example, on 100BASE-FX, Gigabit, and 10-GB Ethernet networks)
USB (universal serial bus)				Used to connect external peripherals, such as modems, mice, audio players, and NICs
Type 1 IBM Data Connector				Used on older Token Ring networks; has been replaced by RJ-45 connectors on newer Token Ring networks
DB-9				Used on older Token Ring networks; has been replaced by RJ-45 connectors on newer Token Ring networks

Appendix D

Standard Networking Forms

Throughout this book, you have learned about various operating procedures and policies that help your IT operations, upgrades, and installations run more smoothly. This appendix offers examples of forms you can use when planning and maintaining a network. Recognize that you may need to change the forms slightly to suit your environment. However, having a form template can help you remember steps you may otherwise have forgotten.

This appendix provides the following forms:

- Server Installation Checklist—Windows Server 2003
- Server Installation Checklist—NetWare 6.5
- Server Installation Checklist—Red Hat Enterprise Linux ES
- User Account Creation Form
- Technical Support Contacts Form
- Incident Report Form
- Network Security Checklist

Server Installation Form – Windows Server 2003

Installer: _____ Date: _____

Model and Serial Number: _____

RAM: _____ Processor: _____ Hard Disk: _____

Server is a: ☐ Domain Controller   ☐ Member Server   ☐ Other (specify): _____

Server Name: _____

Domain Name: _____

NIC 1 Type: _____ IRQ: _____ Base I/O: _____ DMA: _____

NIC 2 Type: _____ IRQ: _____ Base I/O: _____ DMA: _____

Protocols:

    ☐ TCP/IP   ☐ NWLink IPX/SPX Compatible Protocol

        IP Address: _____   ☐ Other: _____

        Gateway: _____

        DNS Server: _____

Disk Controller type(s): _____

Partitions:

    1:    Type: Size: Name:

    2:    Type: Size: Name:

    3:    Type: Size: Name:

    4:    Type: Size: Name:

Registration Key: _____

Licensing mode: ☐ Per Server   ☐ Per Seat

Number of Users: _____

Server Installation Checklist – NetWare 6.5

Installer: _____   Date: _____

Model and Serial Number: _____

RAM: _____   Processor: _____   Hard Disk: _____

Server is a: ☐ File Server   ☐ Customized NetWare Server   ☐ Pre-migration Server   ☐ Other: _____

Server Name: _____

Disk Controller type(s): _____

NIC 1 Type: _____   IRQ: _____   Base I/O: _____   DMA: _____

NIC 2 Type: _____   IRQ: _____   Base I/O: _____   DMA: _____

Volumes:

      1:    Name: Size:

      2:    Name: Size:

      3:    Name: Size:

      4:    Name: Size:

eDirectory Tree: _____   eDirectory Container: _____

Protocols:

    ☐ TCP/IP   ☐ IPX/SPX

         IP Address: _____   ☐ Other: _____

         Gateway: _____

         DNS Server: _____

License Number: _____

Licensing mode: ☐ Per Site   ☐ Per Server   ☐ Per User

Number of Users: _____

Server Installation Checklist – Red Hat Linux

Installer: _____   Date: _____

Model and Serial Number: _____

RAM: _____   Processor: _____   Hard Disk: _____

Keyboard type: _____   Monitor: _____

Packages to Install: _____

_____

Mouse type: _____

Video Card type: _____

TCP/IP Settings:

     IP Address: _____   Netmask: _____

     Default Gateway: _____   Primary Name Server _____

     Domain Name: _____   Host Name: _____

Other Protocols: _____

User Account Creation Form

User Name: _____

Department/location: _____ Phone: _____

Date Created: _____ By: _____

Requested by: _____

Approved by: _____

User ID: _____

Context (NetWare) or Domain/Workgroup (Windows): _____

Group memberships: _____

Home Directory: _____

Password restrictions:

      Minimum password length: _____   Require unique passwords? ☐ Yes   ☐ No

      Days before password expires: _____   Grace logins: _____

      Password History limit: _____

Logon restrictions:

      Valid logon times: _____   Maximum connections: _____

      Address restrictions: _____   Location restrictions: _____

Technical Support Contacts Form

Vendor Name: _____

Address: _____

General phone number: _____   Tech. support phone number: _____

General Web page: _____   Tech. support Web page: _____

Contact name: _____

Products supported:

      Product name: _____   Product license number: _____

      Product name: _____   Product license number: _____

      Product name: _____   Product license number: _____

      Product name: _____   Product license number: _____

Support agreement specifics:

Support experiences with vendor:

Date:	Reason for call:	Resolution:
Date:	Reason for call:	Resolution:
Date:	Reason for call:	Resolution:
Date:	Reason for call:	Resolution:
Date:	Reason for call:	Resolution:

Incident Report Form

User name: _____

User ID: _____

Location: _____ Phone: _____

Date: _____ Time: _____

Received by: _____

Nature of the problem:

Resolution:

    Date: _____ By: _____

    Notes:

Follow-up Call:

    Date: _____ By: _____

    Notes:

Network Security Checklist

- ❏ Write and enforce security policy
- ❏ Communicate security policy to all employees
- ❏ Identify vulnerabilities
- ❏ Enforce use of passwords
- ❏ Require minimum password length
- ❏ Require frequent password changes
- ❏ Disable Administrator user account on servers (use another ID with equivalent privileges)
- ❏ Implement virus scanning on servers and workstations
- ❏ Implement firewalls between private and public networks
- ❏ Properly configure firewall and router access
- ❏ Review remote access links for security threats
- ❏ Implement enterprise-wide intrusion detection
- ❏ Restrict logons to TCP/IP ports
- ❏ Encrypt sensitive data in transit (e.g., use digital certificates)
- ❏ Implement automated, enterprise-wide virus detection
- ❏ Implement badge access for equipment and telecommunications rooms
- ❏ Use security cameras to monitor entrances and equipment rooms
- ❏ Perform background checks on prospective employees
- ❏ Plan for security breaches by having a trained response team

Appendix E

Answers to Chapter Review Questions

Chapter 1

1. a
2. d
3. c
4. b
5. d
6. True
7. True
8. False
9. False
10. True
11. Mail services
12. Web server
13. soft skills
14. Certification
15. File services

Chapter 2

1. b
2. a
3. d
4. c
5. a
6. True
7. False
8. True
9. True
10. False
11. Connection-oriented
12. segments
13. virtual addresses, logical addresses
14. physical layer
15. Presentation

Chapter 3

1. d
2. b
3. a
4. b
5. c
6. True
7. False
8. True
9. True
10. False
11. wavelength
12. Overhead
13. Crosstalk
14. Shielded twisted-pair, STP manual
15. Fault tolerance

Chapter 4

1. a
2. c
3. d
4. b
5. c
6. False
7. True
8. False
9. True
10. False
11. Multicasting
12. subnet mask
13. Resolvers
14. Telnet
15. Network Time Protocol, NTP

Chapter 5

1. a
2. b
3. d
4. c
5. a
6. False
7. True
8. False
9. True
10. True
11. jumper
12. interrupt request, IRQ
13. memory range
14. loopback plug, loopback adapter
15. collision domain

Chapter 6

1. c
2. a
3. d
4. b
5. d
6. False
7. True
8. True
9. False
10. True
11. bus
12. distributed backbone
13. access method
14. Switched Ethernet
15. token passing

Chapter 7

1. a
2. c
3. b
4. d
5. a
6. False
7. False
8. True
9. True
10. True
11. Wide Area Network, WAN
12. X.25
13. terminal adapter, TA
14. uplink
15. Integrated Services Digital Network, ISDN

Chapter 8

1. c
2. a
3. d
4. b
5. b
6. True
7. True
8. False
9. True
10. False
11. Mapping
12. Administrator
13. physical memory
14. Hardware Compatibility List, HCL
15. trust relationship

Chapter 9

1. c
2. a
3. d
4. b
5. a
6. True
7. True
8. False
9. True
10. False
11. kernel
12. kernel module
13. HFS+
14. command interpreter
15. pipeline

Chapter 10

1. b
2. a
3. d
4. c
5. a
6. True
7. True
8. False
9. True
10. False
11. kernel
12. Netware loadable modules, NLMs
13. X Server
14. DOS
15. eDirectory

Chapter 11

1. b
2. a
3. d
4. c
5. a
6. True
7. True
8. False
9. False
10. True
11. ANDing
12. intranet
13. whois
14. traceroute, tracert
15. ifconfig

Chapter 12

1. a
2. c
3. d
4. c
5. b
6. True
7. True
8. False
9. True
10. False
11. supported services list
12. change management system
13. crossover
14. tone locator
15. ohms

Chapter 13

1. d
2. b
3. a
4. c
5. a
6. True
7. False
8. True
9. True
10. False
11. Network
12. brownout
13. hot swappable
14. Clustering
15. Disaster recovery

Chapter 14

1. c
2. a
3. d
4. b
5. a
6. True
7. False
8. False
9. True
10. True
11. denial-of-service attack
12. security policy
13. packet-filtering firewall
14. private key, symmetric
15. IPSec, Internet Protocol Security

Chapter 15

1. b
2. d
3. a
4. c
5. d
6. True
7. False
8. True
9. False
10. True
11. milestone
12. feasibility study
13. Contingency planning
14. backleveling
15. Project management

Glossary

1 gigabit per second (Gbps)—1,000,000,000 bits per second.

1 kilobit per second (Kbps)—1000 bits per second.

1 megabit per second (Mbps)—1,000,000 bits per second.

1 terabit per second (Tbps)—1,000,000,000,000 bits per second.

1000BASE-CX—A Physical layer standard for achieving 1-Gbps throughput over twinaxial copper wire. 1000BASE-CX segments are limited to 25 meters, and are useful mainly to connect devices such as servers or switches.

1000BASE-LX—A Physical layer standard for networks that specifies 1-Gbps transmission over fiber-optic cable using baseband transmission. 1000BASE-LX can run on either single-mode or multimode fiber. The "LX" represents its reliance on "long wavelengths" of 1300 nanometers. 1000BASE-LX can extend to 5000-meter segment lengths using single-mode, fiber-optic cable. 1000BASE-LX networks can use one repeater between segments.

1000BASE-SX—A Physical layer standard for networks that specifies 1-Gbps transmission over fiber-optic cable using baseband transmission. 1000BASE-SX runs on multimode fiber. Its maximum segment length is 550 meters. The "SX" represents its reliance on "short wavelengths" of 850 nanometers. 1000BASE-SX can use one repeater.

1000BASE-T—A Physical layer standard for achieving 1 Gbps over UTP. 1000BASE-T achieves its higher throughput by using all four pairs of wires in a CAT 5 or higher twisted-pair cable to both transmit and receive signals. 1000BASE-T also uses a different data encoding scheme than that used by other UTP Physical layer specifications.

100BASE-FX—A Physical layer standard for networks that specifies baseband transmission, multimode fiber cabling, and 100-Mbps throughput. 100BASE-FX networks have a maximum segment length of 2000 meters. 100BASE-FX may also be called Fast Ethernet.

100BASE-T—A Physical layer standard for networks that specifies baseband transmission, twisted-pair cabling, and 100-Mbps throughput. 100BASE-T networks have a maximum segment length of 100 meters and use the star topology. 100BASE-T is also known as Fast Ethernet.

100BASE-TX—A type of 100BASE-T network that uses two wire pairs in a twisted-pair cable, but uses faster signaling to achieve 100-Mbps throughput. It is capable of full-duplex transmission and requires CAT 5 or higher twisted-pair media.

10BASE-2—See *Thinnet*.

10BASE-5—See *Thicknet*.

10BASE-F—A Physical layer standard for achieving 10-Mbps throughput over multimode fiber-optic cable. Three different kinds of 10BASE-F exist. All require two strands of multimode fiber, in which one strand is used for data transmission and one strand is used for reception, making 10BASE-F a full-duplex technology.

10BASE-FL—The most popular version of the 10BASE-F standard. 10BASE-FL is designed to connect workstations to a LAN or two repeaters and can take advantage of fiber-optic repeating technology to reach its maximum segment length of 2000 meters. 10BASE-FL makes use of the star topology, with its repeaters connected through a bus.

10BASE-T—A Physical layer standard for networks that specifies baseband transmission, twisted-pair media, and 10-Mbps throughput. 10BASE-T networks have a maximum segment length of 100 meters and rely on a star topology.

10GBASE-ER—A Physical layer standard for achieving 10-Gbps data transmission over _single-mode, fiber-optic cable. In 10GBASE-ER the "ER" stands for "extended reach." This standard specifies a star topology and segment lengths up to 40 kilometers.

10GBASE-LR—A Physical layer standard for achieving 10-Gbps data transmission over _single-mode, fiber-optic cable using wavelengths of 1310 nanometers. In 10GBASE-LR, the "LR" stands for "long reach." This standard specifies a star topology and segment lengths up to 10 kilometers.

10GBASE-SR—A Physical layer standard for achieving 10-Gbps data transmission over multimode fiber using wavelengths of 850 nanometers. The maximum segment length for 10GBASE-SR can reach up to 300 meters, depending on the fiber core diameter and modal bandwidth used.

2.4-GHz band—The range of radiofrequencies from 2.4- to 2.4835-GHz. The 2.4-GHz band is often used for wireless network transmissions.

3DES—See *Triple DES*.

3-tier architecture—A client/server environment that uses middleware to translate requests between the client and server.

5-4-3 rule—A guideline for 10-Mbps Ethernet networks stating that between two communicating nodes, the network cannot contain more than five network segments connected by four repeating devices, and no more than three of the segments may be populated.

802.11a—The IEEE standard for a wireless networking technique that uses multiple frequency bands in the 5-GHz frequency range and provides a theoretical maximum throughput of 54 Mbps. 802.11a's high throughput, compared with 802.11b, is attributable to its use of higher frequencies, its unique method of encoding data, and more available bandwidth.

802.11b—The IEEE standard for a wireless networking technique that uses DSSS (direct sequence spread spectrum) signaling in the 2.4–2.4835-GHz frequency range (also called the 2.4-GHz band). 802.11b separates the 2.4-GHz band into 14 overlapping 22-MHz channels and provides a theoretical maximum of 11-Mbps throughput. 802.11b is also known as Wi-Fi.

802.11g—The IEEE standard for a wireless networking technique designed to be compatible with 802.11b while using different encoding techniques that allow it to reach a theoretical maximum capacity of 54 Mbps. 802.11g, like 802.11b, uses the 2.4-GHz frequency band.

802.11i—The IEEE standard for wireless network encryption and authentication that uses the EAP authentication method, strong encryption, and dynamically assigned keys, which are different for every transmission. 802.11i specifies AES encryption and weaves a key into each packet.

802.11—The IEEE standard for wireless networking.

802.15.1—The IEEE standard for wireless personal area network (WPAN) technology, including Bluetooth.

802.16a—An IEEE standard for wireless MANs that specifies the use of the frequency ranges between 2 and 11 GHz. In IEEE 802.16a, antennas do not require a line-of-sight path between them and can exchange signals with multiple stations at once. 802.16a is capable of achieving up to 70-Mbps throughput and its range is 50 kilometers (or approximately 30 miles).

802.16—An IEEE standard for wireless MANs that specifies the use of frequency ranges between 10 and 66 GHz and requires line-of-sight paths between antennas. 802.16 antennas can cover 50 kilometers (or approximately 30 miles) and connections can achieve a maximum throughput of 70 Mbps.

802.2—The IEEE standard for error and flow control in data frames.

802.3ab—The IEEE standard that describes 1000BASE-T, a 1-Gigabit Ethernet technology that runs over four pairs of CAT 5 or better cable.

802.3ae—The IEEE standard that describes 10-Gigabit Ethernet technologies, including 10GBASE-SR, 10GBASE-ER, and 10GBASE-LR.

802.3af—The IEEE standard that specifies a way of supplying electrical power over Ethernet (PoE). 802.3af requires CAT 5 or better UTP or STP cabling and uses power sourcing equipment to supply current over a wire pair to powered devices. PoE is compatible with existing 10BASE-T, 100BASE-TX, and 1000BASE-T implementations.

802.3—The IEEE standard for Ethernet networking devices and data handling.

802.3u—The IEEE standard that describes Fast Ethernet technologies, including 100BASE-TX, 100BASE-T4, and 100BASE-FX.

802.3z—The IEEE standard that describes 1000Base (or 1-Gigabit) Ethernet technologies, including 1000BASE-LX, 1000BASE-SX, and 1000BASE-CX.

802.5—The IEEE standard for Token Ring networking devices and data handling.

A+—The professional certification established by CompTIA that verifies knowledge about PC operation, repair, and management.

access method—A network's method of controlling how nodes access the communications channel. CSMA/CD (Carrier Sense Multiple Access with Collision Detection) is the access method specified in the IEEE 802.3 (Ethernet) standard. CSMA/CA (Carrier Sense Multiple Access with Collision Avoidance) is the access method specified by IEEE 802.11 (wireless LAN) standards.

access point—See *AP*.

access server—See *remote access server*.

account—A record of a user that contains all of her properties, including rights to resources, password, user name, and so on.

ACK (acknowledgment)—A response generated at the Transport layer of the OSI Model that confirms to a sender that its frame was received. The ACK packet is the third of three in the three-step process of establishing a connection.

acknowledgment—See *ACK*.

Active Directory—The Windows Server 2003 method for organizing and managing objects associated with the network.

active monitor—On a Token Ring network, the workstation that maintains timing for token passing, monitors token and frame transmission, detects lost tokens, and corrects problems when a timing error or other disruption occurs. Only one workstation on the ring can act as the active monitor at any given time.

active scanning—A method used by wireless stations to detect the presence of an access point. In active scanning, the station issues a probe to each channel in its frequency range and waits for the access point to respond.

active topology—A topology in which each workstation participates in transmitting data over the network.

ad hoc—A type of wireless LAN in which stations communicate directly with each other (rather than using an access point).

address—A number that uniquely identifies each workstation and device on a network. Without unique addresses, computers on the network could not reliably communicate.

address management—The process of centrally administering a finite number of network addresses for an entire LAN. Usually this task can be accomplished without touching the client workstations.

Address Resolution Protocol—See *ARP*.

address resource record—A type of DNS data record that maps the IP address of an Internet-connected device to its domain name.

addressing—The scheme for assigning a unique identifying number to every workstation and device on the network. The type of addressing used on a network depends on its protocols and network operating system.

Administrator—A user account that has unlimited privileges to resources and objects managed by a server or domain. The Administrator account is created during NOS installation.

Advanced Encryption Standard—See *AES*.

AES (Advanced Encryption Standard)—A private key encryption algorithm that weaves keys of 128, 160, 192, or 256 bits through data multiple times. The algorithm used in the most popular form of AES is known as Rijndael. AES has replaced DES in situations such as military communications, which require the highest level of security.

AFP (AppleTalk Filing Protocol or Apple File Protocol)—The native file access protocol used by Macintosh computers.

agent—A software routine that collects data about a managed device's operation and provides it to the network management application running on the console.

AH (authentication header)—In the context of IPSec, a type of encryption that provides authentication of the IP packet's data payload through public key techniques.

AIX—A proprietary implementation of the UNIX system distributed by IBM.

alias—A nickname for a node's host name. Aliases can be specified in a local host file.

AM (amplitude modulation)—A modulation technique in which the amplitude of the carrier signal is modified by the application of a data signal.

American National Standards Institute—See *ANSI*.

amplifier—A device that boosts, or strengthens, an analog signal.

amplitude—A measure of a signal's strength.

amplitude modulation—See *AM*.

analog—A signal that uses variable voltage to create continuous waves, resulting in an inexact transmission.

ANDing—A logical process of combining bits. In ANDing, a bit with a value of 1 plus another bit with a value of 1 results in a 1. A bit with a value of 0 plus any other bit results in a 0.

ANSI (American National Standards Institute)—An organization composed of more than 1000 representatives from industry and government who together determine standards for the electronics industry in addition to other fields, such as chemical and nuclear engineering, health and safety, and construction.

anycast address—A type of address specified in IPv6 that represents a group of interfaces, any one of which (and usually the first available of which) can accept a transmission. At this time, anycast addresses are not designed to be assigned to hosts, such as servers or workstations, but rather to routers.

AP (access point)—A device used on wireless LANs that transmits and receives wireless signals to and from multiple nodes and retransmits them to the rest of the network segment. Access points can connect a group of nodes with a network or two networks with each other. They may use directional or omnidirectional antennas.

API (application program interface)—A set of routines that make up part of a software _application.

Apple File Protocol—See *AFP*.

AppleShare IP—A proprietary network operating system from Apple Computer that offers file, print, Web, DNS, and mail services. AppleShare IP was the predecessor to Mac OS X Server.

AppleTalk—The protocol suite used to interconnect Macintosh computers. Although AppleTalk was originally designed to support peer-to-peer networking among Macintoshes, it can now be routed between network segments and integrated with NetWare- or Microsoft-based networks.

AppleTalk Filing Protocol—See *AFP*.

AppleTalk network number—A unique 16-bit number that identifies the network to which an AppleTalk node is connected.

AppleTalk node ID—A unique 8-bit or 16-bit number that identifies a computer on an AppleTalk network.

AppleTalk zone—A logically defined group of computers on an AppleTalk network.

application gateway—See *proxy server*.

Application layer—The seventh layer of the OSI Model. Application layer protocols enable software programs to negotiate formatting, procedural, security, synchronization, and other requirements with the network.

Application layer gateway—See *proxy server*.

application program interface—See *API*.

application switch—Another term for a Layer 3 or Layer 4 switch.

archive bit—A file attribute that can be checked (or set to "on") or unchecked (or set to "off") to indicate whether the file needs to be archived. An operating system checks a file's archive bit when it is created or changed.

ARP (Address Resolution Protocol)—A core protocol in the TCP/IP suite that belongs in the Network layer of the OSI Model. ARP obtains the MAC (physical) address of a host, or node, and then creates a local database that maps the MAC address to the host's IP (logical) address.

ARP cache—See *ARP table*.

ARP table—A database of records that map MAC addresses to IP addresses. The ARP table is stored on a computer's hard disk where it is used by the ARP utility to supply the MAC addresses of network nodes, given their IP addresses.

array—A group of hard disks.

AS (authentication service)—In Kerberos terminology, the process that runs on a KDC (key distribution center) to initially validate a client who's logging on. The authentication service issues session keys to the client and the service the client wants to access.

asset management—The process of collecting and storing data on the number and types of software and hardware assets in an organization's network. The data collection is automated by electronically examining each network client from a server.

association—In the context of wireless networking, the communication that occurs between a station and an access point to enable the station to connect to the network via that access point.

asymmetric encryption—A type of encryption (such as public key encryption) that uses a different key for encoding data than is used for decoding the ciphertext.

asymmetric multiprocessing—A multiprocessing method that assigns each subtask to a specific processor.

asymmetrical—The characteristic of a transmission technology that affords greater bandwidth in one direction (either from the customer to the carrier, or vice versa) than in the other direction.

asymmetrical DSL—A variation of DSL that offers more throughput when data travels downstream, downloading from a local carrier's switching facility to the customer, than when it travels upstream, uploading from the customer to the local carrier's switching facility.

asynchronous—A transmission method in which data being transmitted and received by nodes does not have to conform to any timing scheme. In asynchronous communications, a node can transmit at any time and the destination node must accept the transmission as it comes.

Asynchronous Transfer Mode—See *ATM*.

ATM (Asynchronous Transfer Mode)—A Data Link layer technology originally conceived in 1983 at Bell Labs, and standardized by the ITU in the mid-1990s. It relies on fixed packets, called cells, that each consist of 48 bytes of data plus a 5-byte header. ATM relies on virtual circuits and establishes a connection before sending data. Having a reliable connection therefore allows network managers to specify QoS levels for certain types of traffic.

attenuation—The extent to which a signal has weakened after traveling a given distance.

attribute—A variable property associated with a network object. For example, a restriction on the time of day a user can log on is an attribute associated with that user object.

authentication—The process of comparing and matching a client's credentials with the credentials in the NOS user database to enable the client to log on to the network.

authentication header—See *AH*.

authentication protocol—A set of rules that governs how servers authenticate clients. Several types of authentication protocols exist.

authentication service—See *AS*.

authenticator—In Kerberos authentication, the user's time stamp encrypted with the session key. The authenticator is used to help the service verify that a user's ticket is valid.

availability—How consistently and reliably a file, device, or connection can be accessed by authorized personnel.

B channel—In ISDN, the "bearer" channel, so named because it bears traffic from point to point.

backbone—The part of a network to which segments and significant shared devices (such as routers, switches, and servers) connect. A backbone is sometimes referred to as "a network of networks," because of its role in interconnecting smaller parts of a LAN or WAN.

backleveling—The process of reverting to a previous version of a software application after attempting to upgrade it.

back up—The process of copying critical data files to a secure storage area. Often, backups are performed according to a formulaic schedule.

backup—A copy of data or program files created for archiving or safekeeping.

backup rotation scheme—A plan for when and how often backups occur, and which backups are full, incremental, or differential.

bandwidth—A measure of the difference between the highest and lowest frequencies that a medium can transmit.

base I/O port—A setting that specifies, in hexadecimal notation, which area of memory will act as a channel for data traveling between the NIC and the CPU. Like its IRQ, a device's base I/O port cannot be used by any other device.

base schema—The standard set of object classes and attributes installed as the default schema for NetWare's eDirectory. The base schema can be extended through NetWare utilities.

baseband—A form of transmission in which digital signals are sent through direct current pulses applied to a wire. This direct current requires exclusive use of the wire's capacity, so baseband systems can transmit only one signal, or one channel, at a time. Every device on a baseband system shares a single channel.

baseline—A record of how a network operates under normal conditions (including its performance, collision rate, utilization rate, and so on). Baselines are used for comparison when conditions change.

basic input/output system—See *BIOS*.

Basic Rate Interface—See *BRI*.

beacon frame—In the context of wireless networking, a frame issued by an access point to alert other nodes of its existence.

bend radius—The radius of the maximum arc into which you can loop a cable before you will cause data transmission errors. Generally, a twisted-pair cable's bend radius is equal to or greater than four times the diameter of the cable.

Berkeley Software Distribution—See *BSD*.

best path—The most efficient route from one node on a network to another. Under optimal network conditions, the best path is the most direct path between two points. However, when traffic congestion, segment failures, and other factors create obstacles, the most direct path may not be the best path.

BGP (Border Gateway Protocol)—A complex routing protocol used on border and exterior routers. BGP is the routing protocol used on Internet backbones.

binary—A system founded on using 1s and 0s to encode information.

binding—The process of assigning one network component to work with another.

bio-recognition access—A method of authentication in which a device scans an individual's unique physical characteristics (such as the color patterns in his iris or the geometry of his hand) to verify the user's identity.

BIOS (basic input/output system)—The firmware attached to a computer's motherboard that controls the computer's communication with its devices, among other things.

bit (binary digit)—A bit equals a single pulse in the digital encoding system. It may have only one of two values: 0 or 1.

blackout—A complete power loss.

Block ID—The first set of six characters that make up the MAC address and that are unique to a particular manufacturer.

Bluetooth—A wireless networking standard that uses FHSS (frequency hopping spread spectrum) signaling in the 2.4-GHz band to achieve a maximum throughput of either 723 Kbps or 2.1 Mbps, depending on the version. Bluetooth was designed for use primarily with small office or home networks in which multiple devices (including cordless phones, computers, and pagers) are connected.

Bluetooth Special Interest Group (SIG)—A consortium of companies, including Sony Ericsson, Intel, Nokia, Toshiba, and IBM, that formally banded together in 1998 to refine and standardize Bluetooth technology.

bonding—The process of combining more than one bearer channel of an ISDN line to increase throughput. For example, BRI's two 64-Kbps B channels are bonded to create an effective throughput of 128 Kbps.

boot partition—A partition on a computer's hard disk from which the operating system software is launched.

boot sector virus—A virus that resides on the boot sector of a floppy disk and is transferred to the partition sector or the DOS boot sector on a hard disk. A boot sector virus can move from a floppy to a hard disk only if the floppy disk is left in the drive when the machine starts.

BOOTP (Bootstrap Protocol)—An Application layer protocol in the TCP/IP suite that uses a central list of IP addresses and their associated devices' MAC addresses to assign IP addresses to clients dynamically. BOOTP was the precursor to DHCP.

Bootstrap Protocol—See *BOOTP*.

Border Gateway Protocol—See *BGP*.

border router—A router that connects an autonomous LAN with an exterior network—for example, the router that connects a business to its ISP.

BorderManager—An application from Novell that provides proxy and firewall services on NetWare servers.

bot—A program that runs automatically. Bots can spread viruses or other malicious code between users in a chat room by exploiting the IRC protocol.

braiding—A braided metal shielding used to insulate some types of coaxial cable.

branch—A part of the organizational structure of an operating system's directory that contains objects or other organizational units.

BRI (Basic Rate Interface)—A variety of ISDN that uses two 64-Kbps bearer channels and one 16-Kbps data channel, as summarized by the notation 2B+D. BRI is the most common form of ISDN employed by home users.

bridge—A connectivity device that operates at the Data Link layer (Layer 2) of the OSI Model and reads header information to forward packets according to their MAC addresses. Bridges use a filtering database to determine which packets to discard and which to forward. Bridges contain one input and one output port and separate network segments.

bridge router (brouter)—A router capable of providing Layer 2 bridging functions.

broadband—A form of transmission in which signals are modulated as radiofrequency analog pulses with different frequency ranges. Unlike baseband, broadband technology does not involve binary encoding. The use of multiple frequencies enables a broadband system to operate over several channels and therefore carry much more data than a baseband system.

broadband cable—A method of connecting to the Internet over a cable network. In broadband cable, computers are connected to a cable modem that modulates and demodulates signals to and from the cable company's head-end.

broadcast—A transmission that involves one transmitter and multiple receivers.

broadcast domain—A combination of ports on a switch (or multiple switches) that make up a Layer 2 segment. To be able to exchange data with each other, broadcast domains must be connected by a Layer 3 device, such as a router or Layer 3 switch. A VLAN is one type of broadcast domain.

brouter—See *bridge router*.

brownout—A momentary decrease in voltage, also known as a *sag*. An overtaxed electrical system may cause brownouts, recognizable as a dimming of the lights.

brute force attack—An attempt to discover an encryption key or password by trying numerous possible character combinations. Usually, a brute force attack is performed rapidly by a program designed for that purpose.

BSD (Berkeley Software Distribution)—A UNIX distribution that originated at the University of California at Berkeley. The BSD suffix differentiates these distributions from AT&T distributions. No longer being developed at Berkeley, the last public release of BSD UNIX was version 4.4.

bug—A flaw in software or hardware that causes it to malfunction.

bus topology—A topology in which a single cable connects all nodes on a network without intervening connectivity devices.

bus topology WAN—A WAN in which each location is connected to no more than two other locations in a serial fashion.

bus—The single cable connecting all devices in a bus topology.

bus—The type of circuit used by a computer's motherboard to transmit data to components. Most new Pentium computers use buses capable of exchanging 32 or 64 bits of data. As the number of bits of data a bus handles increases, so too does the speed of the device attached to the bus.

byte—Eight bits of information. In a digital signaling system, broadly speaking, one byte carries one piece of information.

cable checker—See *continuity tester*.

cable drop—A fiber-optic or coaxial cable that connects a neighborhood cable node to a customer's house.

cable modem—A device that modulates and demodulates signals for transmission and reception via cable wiring.

cable modem access—See *broadband cable*.

cable performance tester—A troubleshooting tool that tests cables for continuity, but can also measure crosstalk, attenuation, and impedance; identify the location of faults; and store or print cable testing results.

cable plant—The hardware that constitutes the enterprise-wide cabling system.

cable tester—A device that tests cables for one or more of the following conditions: continuity, segment length, distance to a fault, attenuation along a cable, near-end crosstalk, and termination resistance and impedance. Cable testers may also issue pass/fail ratings for wiring standards or store and print cable testing results.

call tracking system—A software program used to document technical problems and how they were resolved (also known as help desk software).

capacity—See *throughput*.

CardBus—A PCMCIA standard that specifies a 32-bit interface running at 33 MHz, similar to the PCI expansion board standard. Most modern laptops are equipped with CardBus slots for connecting external modems and NICs, among other things.

Carrier Sense Multiple Access with Collision Avoidance—See *CSMA/CA*.

Carrier Sense Multiple Access with Collision Detection—See *CSMA/CD*.

CAT 3 (Category 3)—A form of UTP that contains four wire pairs and can carry up to 10 Mbps, with a possible bandwidth of 16 MHz. CAT 3 has typically been used for 10-Mbps Ethernet or 4-Mbps Token Ring networks. Network administrators are gradually replacing CAT 3 cabling with CAT 5 to accommodate higher throughput. CAT 3 is less expensive than CAT 5.

CAT 4 (Category 4)—A form of UTP that contains four wire pairs and can support up to 16-Mbps throughput. CAT 4 may be used for 16-Mbps Token Ring or 10-Mbps Ethernet networks. It is guaranteed for data transmission up to 20 MHz and provides more protection against crosstalk and attenuation than CAT 1, CAT 2, or CAT 3.

CAT 5 (Category 5)—A form of UTP that contains four wire pairs and supports up to 100-Mbps throughput and a 100-MHz signal rate.

CAT 5e (Enhanced Category 5)—A higher-grade version of CAT 5 wiring that contains high-quality copper, offers a high twist ratio, and uses advanced methods for reducing crosstalk. Enhanced CAT 5 can support a signaling rate of up to 350 MHz, more than triple the capability of regular CAT 5.

CAT 6 (Category 6)—A twisted-pair cable that contains four wire pairs, each wrapped in foil insulation. Additional foil insulation covers the bundle of wire pairs, and a fire-resistant plastic sheath covers the second foil layer. The foil insulation provides excellent resistance to crosstalk and enables CAT 6 to support a signaling rate of 250 MHz and at least six times the throughput supported by regular CAT 5.

CAT 6e (Enhanced Category 6)—A higher-grade version of CAT 6 wiring that further reduces attenuation and crosstalk and allows for potentially exceeding traditional network segment length limits. CAT 6e is capable of a 550-MHz signaling rate and can reliably transmit data at multi-Gigabit per second rates.

CAT 7 (Category 7)—A twisted-pair cable that contains multiple wire pairs, each separately shielded then surrounded by another layer of shielding within the jacket. CAT 7 can support up to a 1-GHz signal rate. But because of its extra layers, it is less flexible than other forms of twisted-pair wiring.

CAT—Abbreviation for the word "category" when describing a type of twisted-pair cable. For example, Category 3 unshielded twisted-pair cable may also be called CAT 3.

Category 3—See *CAT 3*.

Category 4—See *CAT 4*.

Category 5—See *CAT 5*.

Category 6—See *CAT 6*.

Category 7—See *CAT 7*.

CDFS (CD-ROM File System)—The read-only file system used to access resources on a CD. Windows Server 2003 supports this file system to allow CD-ROM file sharing.

CD-R (compact disc - recordable)—A type of compact disc that can be written to only once. It can store up to 650 MB of data.

CD-ROM File System—See *CDFS*.

CD-RW (compact disc - rewriteable)—A type of compact disc that can be written to more than once. It can store up to 650 MB of data.

cell—A packet of a fixed size. In ATM technology, a cell consists of 48 bytes of data plus a 5-byte header.

central office—The location where a local or long-distance telephone service provider terminates and interconnects customer lines.

certification—The process of mastering material pertaining to a particular hardware system, operating system, programming language, or other software program, then proving your mastery by passing a series of exams.

Certified NetWare Engineer—See *CNE*.

challenge—A random string of text issued from one computer to another in some forms of authentication. Used, along with the password (or other credential), in a response to verify the computer's credentials.

Challenge Handshake Authentication Protocol—See *CHAP*.

change management system—A process or program that provides support personnel with a centralized means of documenting changes made to the network.

channel—A distinct communication path between two or more nodes, much like a lane is a distinct transportation path on a freeway. Channels may be separated either logically (as in multiplexing) or physically (as when they are carried by separate wires).

channel service unit—See *CSU*.

CHAP (Challenge Handshake Authentication Protocol)—An authentication protocol that operates over PPP and that requires the authenticator to take the first step by offering the other computer a challenge. The requestor responds by combining the challenge with its password, encrypting the new string of characters and sending it to the authenticator. The authenticator matches to see if the requestor's encrypted string of text matches its own encrypted string of characters. If so, the requester is authenticated and granted access to secured resources.

checksum—A method of error checking that determines if the contents of an arriving data unit match the contents of the data unit sent by the source.

child domain—A domain established within another domain in a Windows Server 2003 domain tree.

CIDR (Classless Inter-domain Routing)—An IP addressing and subnetting method in which network and host information is manipulated without adhering to the limitations imposed by traditional network class distinctions. CIDR is also known as classless routing or supernetting. Older routing protocols, such as RIP, are not capable of interpreting CIDR addressing schemes.

CIDR block—In CIDR notation, the number of bits used for an extended network prefix. For example, the CIDR block for 199.34.89.0/22 is /22.

CIDR notation—In CIDR, a method of denoting network IDs and their subnet boundaries. Slash notation takes the form of the network ID followed by a /, followed by the number of bits that are used for the extended network prefix.

CIFS (Common Internet File System)—A file access protocol. CIFS runs over TCP/IP and is the standard file access protocol used by Windows operating systems.

ciphertext—The unique data block that results when an original piece of data (such as text) is encrypted (for example, by using a key).

CIR (committed information rate)—The guaranteed minimum amount of bandwidth selected when leasing a Frame Relay circuit. Frame Relay costs are partially based on CIR.

circuit switching—A type of switching in which a connection is established between two network nodes before they begin transmitting data. Bandwidth is dedicated to this connection and remains available until users terminate the communication between the two nodes.

cladding—The glass or plastic shield around the core of a fiber-optic cable. Cladding reflects light back to the core in patterns that vary depending on the transmission mode. This reflection allows fiber to bend around corners without impairing the light-based signal.

class—A type of object recognized by an NOS directory and defined in an NOS schema. Printers and users are examples of object classes.

classful addressing—An IP addressing convention that adheres to network class distinctions, in which the first 8 bits of a Class A address, the first 16 bits of a Class B address, and the first 24 bits of a Class C address are used for network information.

Classless Inter-domain Routing—See *CIDR*.

classless routing—See *CIDR*.

client—A computer on the network that requests resources or services from another computer on a network. In some cases, a client could also act as a server. The term "client" may also refer to the user of a client workstation or a client software application installed on the workstation.

Client Services for NetWare (CSNW)—A Microsoft program that can be installed on Windows clients to enable them to access NetWare servers and make full use of NetWare's eDirectory, its objects, files, directories, and permissions.

client/server architecture—A network design in which clients (typically desktop or laptop computers) use a centrally administered server to share data, data storage space, and devices.

client/server network—A network that uses centrally administered computers, known as servers, to enable resource sharing for and facilitate communication between the other computers on the network.

client_hello—In the context of SSL encryption, a message issued from the client to the server that contains information about what level of security the client's browser is capable of accepting and what type of encryption the client's browser can decipher (for example, RSA or Diffie-Hellman). The client_hello message also establishes a randomly generated number that uniquely identifies the client, plus another number that identifies the SSL session.

clustering—A fault-tolerance technique that links multiple servers to act as a single server. In this configuration, clustered servers share processing duties and appear as a single server to users. If one server in the cluster fails, the other servers in the cluster automatically take over its data transaction and storage responsibilities.

CMOS (complementary metal oxide semiconductor)—A type of microchip that requires very little energy to operate. In a PC, the CMOS stores settings pertaining to a computer's devices, among other things.

CN (common name)—In LDAP naming conventions, the name of an object.

CNE (Certified NetWare Engineer)—The professional certification established by Novell that demonstrates an in-depth understanding of Novell's networking software, including NetWare.

coaxial cable—A type of cable that consists of a central copper core surrounded by an insulator, a braided metal shielding, called braiding, and an outer cover, called the sheath or jacket. Coaxial cable, called "coax" for short, was the foundation for Ethernet networks in the 1980s and remained a popular transmission medium for many years.

cold site—A place where the computers, devices, and connectivity necessary to rebuild a network exist, but they are not appropriately configured, updated, or connected to match the network's current state.

cold spare—A duplicate component that is not installed, but can be installed in case of a _failure.

collapsed backbone—A type of backbone that uses a router or switch as the single central connection point for multiple subnetworks.

collision—In Ethernet networks, the interference of one network node's data transmission with another network node's data transmission.

collision domain—A portion of a LAN encompassing devices that may cause and detect collisions among their group. Bridges and switches can logically separate collision domains.

command interpreter—A (usually text-based) program that accepts and executes system programs and applications on behalf of users. Often, it includes the ability to execute a series of instructions that are stored in a file.

committed information rate—See *CIR*.

Common Internet File System—See *CIFS*.

common name—See *CN*.

communications server—See *access server*.

compact disc, recordable—See *CD-R*.

compact disc, rewriteable—See *CD-RW*.

CompactFlash—The standard for an ultra-small removable data and input/output device capable of connecting many kinds of external peripherals to workstations, PDAs, and other computerized devices. CompactFlash was designed by the CompactFlash Association (CFA), a consortium of computer manufacturers.

complementary metal oxide semiconductor—See *CMOS*.

CompTIA (Computing Technology Industry Association)—An association of computer resellers, manufacturers, and training companies that sets industry-wide standards for computer professionals. CompTIA established and sponsors the A+ and Network+ (Net+) certifications.

Computing Technology Industry Association—See *CompTIA*.

conduit—The pipeline used to contain and protect cabling. Conduit is usually made from metal.

connectionless—A type of Transport layer protocol that services a request without requiring a verified session and without guaranteeing delivery of data.

connection-oriented—A type of Transport layer protocol that requires the establishment of a connection between communicating nodes before it will transmit data.

connectivity device—One of several types of specialized devices that allows two or more networks or multiple parts of one network to connect and exchange data.

connectors—The pieces of hardware that connect the wire to the network device, be it a file server, workstation, switch, or printer.

console—The interface to a NetWare server and its kernel operations.

ConsoleOne—The graphical interface to NetWare server administration tasks. ConsoleOne can be used at the server or from another workstation connected to the same network.

container—See *organizational unit*.

context—The characteristic that indicates where an object belongs in an eDirectory tree. A context is made up of an object's organizational unit names, arranged from most specific to most general, plus the organization name. Periods separate the organizational unit names in context.

contingency planning—The process of identifying steps that minimize the risk of unforeseen circumstances endangering the quality or timeliness of the project's goals.

continuity tester—An instrument that tests whether voltage (or light, in the case of fiber-optic cable) issued at one end of a cable can be detected at the opposite end of the cable. A continuity tester can indicate whether the cable will successfully transmit a signal.

convergence—The use of packet-switched networks to carry data, plus video and voice signals.

convergence time—The time it takes for a router to recognize a best path in the event of a change or network outage.

core—The central component of a cable designed to carry a signal. The core of a fiber-optic cable, for example, consists of one or several glass or plastic fibers. The core of a coaxial copper cable consists of one large or several small strands of copper.

core gateway—A gateway that operates on the Internet backbone.

cracker—A person who uses his knowledge of operating systems and utilities to intentionally damage or destroy data or systems.

CRC (Cyclic Redundancy Check)—An algorithm (or mathematical routine) used to verify the accuracy of data contained in a data frame.

credentials—A user's unique identifying characteristics that enable him to authenticate with a server and gain access to network resources. The most common type of credentials are a user name and password.

crossover cable—A twisted-pair patch cable in which the termination locations of the transmit and receive wires on one end of the cable are reversed.

crosstalk—A type of interference caused by signals traveling on nearby wire pairs infringing on another pair's signal.

CSMA/CA (Carrier Sense Multiple Access with Collision Avoidance)—A network access method used on 802.11 wireless networks. In CSMA/CA, before a node begins to send data it checks the medium. If it detects no transmission activity, it waits a brief, random amount of time, and then sends its transmission. If the node does detect activity, it waits a brief period of time before checking the channel again. CSMA/CA does not eliminate, but minimizes, the potential for collisions.

CSMA/CD (Carrier Sense Multiple Access with Collision Detection)—A network access method specified for use by IEEE 802.3 (Ethernet) networks. In CSMA/CD, each node waits its turn before transmitting data, to avoid interfering with other nodes' transmissions. If a node's NIC determines that its data has been involved in a collision, it immediately stops transmitting. Next, in a process called jamming, the NIC issues a special 32-bit sequence that indicates to the rest of the network nodes that its previous transmission was faulty and that those data frames are invalid. After waiting, the NIC determines if the line is again available; if it is available, the NIC retransmits its data.

CSU (channel service unit)—A device used with T-carrier technology that provides termination for the digital signal and ensures connection integrity through error correction and line monitoring. Typically, a CSU is combined with a DSU in a single device, a CSU/DSU.

CSU/DSU—A combination of a CSU (channel service unit) and a DSU (data service unit) that serves as the connection point for a T1 line at the customer's site. Most modern CSU/DSUs also contain a multiplexer. A CSU/DSU may be a separate device or an expansion card in another device, such as a router.

cut-through mode—A switching mode in which a switch reads a frame's header and decides where to forward the data before it receives the entire packet. Cut-through mode is faster, but less accurate, than the other switching method, store and forward mode.

Cyclic Redundancy Check—See *CRC*.

D channel—In ISDN, the "data" channel is used to carry information about the call, such as session initiation and termination signals, caller identity, call forwarding, and conference calling signals.

daisy chain—A group of connectivity devices linked together in a serial fashion.

Data Encryption Standard—See *DES*.

Data Link layer—The second layer in the OSI Model. The Data Link layer bridges the networking media with the Network layer. Its primary function is to divide the data it receives from the Network layer into frames that can then be transmitted by the Physical layer.

data packet—A discrete unit of information sent from one node on a network to another.

data port—A port on a connectivity device to which network nodes are connected.

data propagation delay—The length of time data takes to travel from one point on the segment to another point. On Ethernet networks, CSMA/CD's collision detection routine cannot operate accurately if the data propagation delay is too long.

data service unit—See *DSU*.

DB-9 connector—A connector containing nine pins that is used on STP-based Token Ring networks.

DC (domain component)—In LDAP naming conventions, the name of any one of the domains to which an object belongs.

dedicated—A continuously available link or service that is leased through another carrier. Examples of dedicated lines include ADSL, T1, and T3.

default gateway—The gateway that first interprets a device's outbound requests, and then interprets its inbound requests to and from other subnets. In a Postal Service analogy, the default gateway is similar to a local post office.

default router—See *default gateway*.

demarcation point (demarc)—The point of division between a telecommunications service carrier's network and a building's internal network.

demultiplexer (demux)—A device that separates multiplexed signals once they are received and regenerates them in their original form.

denial-of-service attack—A security attack caused by a deluge of traffic that disables the victimized system.

dense wavelength division multiplexing—See *DWDM*.

DES (Data Encryption Standard)—A popular private key encryption technique that was developed by IBM in the 1970s.

device driver—The software that enables an attached device to communicate with the computer's operating system.

Device ID—The second set of six characters that make up a network device's MAC address. The Device ID, which is added at the factory, is based on the device's model and manufacture date.

DHCP (Dynamic Host Configuration Protocol)—An Application layer protocol in the TCP/IP suite that manages the dynamic distribution of IP addresses on a network. Using DHCP to assign IP addresses can nearly eliminate duplicate-addressing problems.

dial return—A satellite Internet access connection in which a subscriber receives data from the Internet via the satellite link, but sends data to the satellite via an analog modem (dial-up) connection. With dial return, downstream throughputs are rated for 400–500 Kbps, whereas upstream throughputs are practically limited to 53 Kbps and are usually lower. Therefore, dial return satellite Internet access is an asymmetrical technology.

dial-up—A type of connection in which a user connects to a distant network from a computer and stays connected for a finite period of time.

dial-up networking—The process of dialing into a remote access server to connect with a network, be it private or public.

dictionary attack—A technique in which attackers run a program that tries a combination of a known user ID and, for a password, every word in a dictionary to attempt to gain access to a network.

differential backup—A backup method in which only data that has changed since the last full or incremental backup is copied to a storage medium, and in which that same information is marked for subsequent backup, regardless of whether it has changed. In other words, a differential backup does not uncheck the archive bits for files it backs up.

Diffie-Hellman—The first commonly used public, or asymmetric, key algorithm. Diffie-Hellman was released in 1975 by its creators, Whitfield Diffie and Martin Hellman.

diffraction—In the context of wireless signal propagation, the phenomenon that occurs when an electromagnetic wave encounters an obstruction and splits into secondary waves. The secondary waves continue to propagate in the direction in which they were split. If you could see wireless signals being diffracted, they would appear to be bending around the obstacle. Objects with sharp edges—including the corners of walls and desks—cause diffraction.

dig (domain information groper)—A TCP/IP utility that queries the DNS database and provides information about a host given its IP address or vice versa. Dig is similar to the nslookup utility, but provides more information, even in its simplest form, than nslookup can.

digital—As opposed to analog signals, digital signals are composed of pulses that can have a value of only 1 or 0.

digital certificate—A password-protected and encrypted file that holds an individual's identification information, including a public key and a private key. The individual's public key is used to verify the sender's digital signature, and the private key allows the individual to log on to a third-party authority who administers digital certificates.

digital PBX—See *IP-PBX*.

digital subscriber line—See *DSL*.

digital versatile disc—See *DVD*.

DIP (dual inline package) switch—A small plastic toggle switch on a circuit board that can be flipped to indicate either an "on" or "off" status, which translates into a parameter setting.

direct sequence spread spectrum—See *DSSS*.

directional antenna—A type of antenna that issues wireless signals along a single direction, or path.

directory—In general, a listing that organizes resources and correlates them with their properties. In the context of network operating systems, a method for organizing and managing objects.

DirXML—A Novell tool for integrating eDirectory and Windows Active Directory or Windows NT domain data.

disaster recovery—The process of restoring critical functionality and data to a network after an enterprise-wide outage that affects more than a single system or a limited group of users.

disk duplexing—A storage fault-tolerance technique in which data is continually copied from one disk to another when it is saved, just as in disk mirroring. In duplexing, however, a separate disk controller is used for each different disk.

disk mirroring—A RAID technique in which data from one disk is automatically copied to another disk as the information is written.

disk striping—A simple implementation of RAID in which data is written in 64-KB blocks equally across all disks in the array.

diskless workstation—A workstation that doesn't contain a hard disk, but instead relies on a small amount of read-only memory to connect to a network and to pick up its system files.

distinguished name—See *DN*.

distributed backbone—A type of backbone in which a number of connectivity devices (usually hubs) are connected to a series of central connectivity devices, such as hubs, switches, or routers, in a hierarchy.

DN (distinguished name)—A long form of an object's name in Active Directory that explicitly indicates the object name, plus the names of its containers and domains. A distinguished name includes a DC (domain component), OU (organizational unit), and CN (common name). A client uses the distinguished name to access a particular object, such as a printer.

DNS (Domain Name System or **Domain Name Service)**—A hierarchical way of tracking domain names and their addresses, devised in the mid-1980s. The DNS database does not rely on one file or even one server, but rather is distributed over several key computers across the Internet to prevent catastrophic failure if one or a few computers go down. DNS is a TCP/IP service that belongs to the Application layer of the OSI Model.

DNS spoofing—A security attack in which an outsider forges name server records to falsify his host's identity.

domain—A group of users, servers, and other resources that share account and security policies through a Windows Server 2003 network operating system.

domain account—A type of user account on a Windows Server 2003 network that has privileges to resources across the domain onto which it is logged.

domain component—See *DC*.

domain controller—A Windows Server 2003 computer that contains a replica of the Active Directory database.

domain information groper—See *dig*.

domain local group—A group on a Windows Server 2003 network that allows members of one domain to access resources within that domain only.

domain model—In Microsoft terminology, the type of client/server network that relies on domains, rather than workgroups.

domain name—The symbolic name that identifies a domain. Usually, a domain name is associated with a company or other type of organization, such as a university or military unit.

Domain Name Service—See *DNS*.

Domain Name System—See *DNS*.

domain tree—A group of hierarchically arranged domains that share a common namespace in the Windows Server 2003 Active Directory.

dotted decimal notation—The shorthand convention used to represent IP addresses and make them more easily readable by humans. In dotted decimal notation, a decimal number between 0 and 255 represents each binary octet. A period, or dot, separates each decimal.

downlink—A connection from an orbiting satellite to an earth-based receiver.

downstream—A term used to describe data traffic that flows from a carrier's facility to the customer. In asymmetrical communications, downstream throughput is usually much higher than upstream throughput. In symmetrical communications, downstream and upstream throughputs are equal.

driver—See *device driver*.

DS0 (digital signal, level 0)—The equivalent of one data or voice channel in T-carrier technology, as defined by ANSI physical layer standards. All other signal levels are multiples of DS0.

DSL (digital subscriber line)—A dedicated WAN technology that uses advanced data modulation techniques at the Physical layer to achieve extraordinary throughput over regular phone lines. DSL comes in several different varieties, the most common of which is asymmetric DSL (ADSL).

DSL access multiplexer—See *DSLAM*.

DSL modem—A device that demodulates an incoming DSL signal, extracting the information and passing it to the data equipment (such as telephones and computers) and modulates an outgoing DSL signal.

DSLAM (DSL access multiplexer)—A connectivity device located at a telecommunications carrier's office that aggregates multiple DSL subscriber lines and connects them to a larger carrier or to the Internet backbone.

DSSS (direct sequence spread spectrum)—A transmission technique in which a signal's bits are distributed over an entire frequency band at once. Each bit is coded so that the receiver can reassemble the original signal upon receiving the bits.

DSU (data service unit)—A device used in T-carrier technology that converts the digital signal used by bridges, routers, and multiplexers into the digital signal used on cabling. Typically, a DSU is combined with a CSU in a single device, a CSU/DSU.

duplex—See *full-duplex*.

DVD (digital versatile disc)—A type of optical disk capable of storing large amounts of data, including audio and video files. Several DVD standards exist, but all have a minimum storage capacity of 4.7 GB.

DWDM (dense wavelength division multiplexing)—A multiplexing technique used over single-mode or multimode fiber-optic cable in which each signal is assigned a different wavelength for its carrier wave. In DWDM, little space exists between carrier waves, in order to achieve extraordinary high capacity.

dynamic address—An IP address that is assigned to a device through DHCP and may change when the DHCP lease expires or is terminated.

dynamic ARP table entry—A record in an ARP table that is created when a client makes an ARP request that cannot be satisfied by data already in the ARP table.

Dynamic Host Configuration Protocol—See *DHCP*

dynamic IP address—An IP address that is assigned to a device upon request and may change over time. BOOTP and DHCP are two ways of assigning dynamic IP addresses.

Dynamic Ports—TCP/IP ports in the range of 49152 through 65535, which are open for use without requiring administrative privileges on a host or approval from IANA.

dynamic routing—A method of routing that automatically calculates the best path between two nodes and accumulates this information in a routing table. If congestion or failures affect the network, a router using dynamic routing can detect the problems and reroute data through a different path. Modern networks primarily use dynamic routing.

E1—A digital carrier standard used in Europe that offers 30 channels and a maximum of 2.048-Mbps throughput.

E3—A digital carrier standard used in Europe that offers 480 channels and a maximum of 34.368-Mbps throughput.

EAP (Extensible Authentication Protocol)—A Data Link layer protocol defined by the IETF that specifies the dynamic distribution of encryption keys and a pre-authentication process in which a client and server exchange data via an intermediate node (for example, an access point on a wireless LAN).

Only after they have mutually authenticated can the client and server exchange encrypted data. EAP can be used with multiple authentication and encryption schemes.

ECC (error correction code)—An algorithm used to detect and correct errors. In RAID Levels 3 and 5, for example, a type of ECC known as parity error checking is used.

echo reply—The response signal sent by a device after another device pings it.

echo request—The request for a response generated when one device pings another device.

eDirectory—The database of objects and their attributes in NetWare 6.x.

EEPROM (electrically erasable programmable read-only memory)—A type of ROM that is found on a circuit board and whose configuration information can be erased and rewritten through electrical pulses.

EIA (Electronic Industries Alliance)—A trade organization composed of representatives from electronics manufacturing firms across the United States that sets standards for electronic equipment and lobbies for legislation favorable to the growth of the computer and electronics industries.

EIGRP (Enhanced Interior Gateway Routing Protocol)—A routing protocol developed in the mid-1980s by Cisco Systems that has a fast convergence time and a low network overhead, but is easier to configure and less CPU-intensive than OSPF. EIGRP also offers the benefits of supporting multiple protocols and limiting unnecessary network traffic between routers.

electrically erasable programmable read-only memory—See *EEPROM*.

electromagnetic interference—See *EMI*.

Electronic Industries Alliance—See *EIA*.

EMI (electromagnetic interference)—A type of interference that may be caused by motors, power lines, televisions, copiers, fluorescent lights, or other sources of electrical activity.

encapsulate—The process of wrapping one layer's PDU with protocol information so that it can be interpreted by a lower layer. For example, Data Link layer protocols encapsulate Network layer packets in frames.

Encapsulating Security Payload—See *ESP*.

encrypted virus—A virus that is encrypted to prevent detection.

encryption—The use of an algorithm to scramble data into a format that can be read only by reversing the algorithm—decrypting the data—to keep the information private. The most popular kind of encryption algorithm weaves a key into the original data's bits, sometimes several times in different sequences, to generate a unique data block.

enhanced Category 5—See *CAT 5e*.

enhanced Category 6—See *CAT 6e*.

Enhanced Interior Gateway Routing Protocol—See *EIGRP*.

enterprise—An entire organization, including local and remote offices, a mixture of computer systems, and a number of departments. Enterprise-wide computing takes into account the breadth and diversity of a large organization's computer needs.

error correction code—See *ECC*.

ESP (Encapsulating Security Payload)—In the context of IPSec, a type of encryption that provides authentication of the IP packet's data payload through public key techniques. In addition, ESP also encrypts the entire IP packet for added security.

Ethernet—A networking technology originally developed at Xerox in the 1970s and improved by Digital Equipment Corporation, Intel, and Xerox. Ethernet, which is the most common form of network transmission technology, follows the IEEE 802.3 standard.

Ethernet_II—The original Ethernet frame type developed by Digital, Intel, and Xerox, before the IEEE began to standardize Ethernet. Ethernet_II contains a 2-byte type field to identify the upper-layer protocol contained in the frame. It supports TCP/IP, AppleTalk, IPX/SPX, and other higher-layer protocols.

expansion board—A circuit board used to connect a device to a computer's motherboard.

expansion card—See *expansion board*.

expansion slot—A receptacle on a computer's motherboard that contains multiple electrical contacts into which an expansion board can be inserted.

explicit one-way trust—A type of trust relationship in which two domains that belong to different NOS directory trees are configured to trust each other.

ExpressCard—A PCMCIA standard that allows external devices to connect to portable computers through a 26-pin interface, with data transfer rates of 250 MBps in each direction (for a total of 500 MBps), similar to the PCI Express expansion board specification. ExpressCard modules come in two sizes: 34 mm and 54 mm wide. Over time, PCMCIA expects the ExpressCard standard to replace the CardBus standard.

ext3—The name of the primary file system used in most Linux distributions.

extended network prefix—The combination of an IP address's network ID and subnet information. By interpreting the address's extended network prefix, a device can determine the subnet to which an address belongs.

extended schema—In NetWare, a set of object classes and attributes that is different from the base schema.

Extensible Authentication Protocol—See *EAP*.

exterior router—A router that directs data between nodes outside a given autonomous LAN, for example, routers used on the Internet's backbone.

external disk drive—A storage device that can be attached temporarily to a computer.

external network number—Another term for the network address portion of an IPX/SPX address.

extranet—A network that uses browser-based services to exchange information within an organization *and* with certain, authorized users outside of that organization.

fading—A change in a wireless signal's strength as a result of some of the electromagnetic energy being scattered, reflected, or diffracted after being issued by the transmitter.

fail-over—The capability for one component (such as a NIC or server) to assume another component's responsibilities without manual intervention.

failure—A deviation from a specified level of system performance for a given period of time. A failure occurs when something doesn't work as promised or as planned.

Fast Ethernet—A type of Ethernet network that is capable of 100-Mbps throughput. 100BASE-T and 100BASE-FX are both examples of Fast Ethernet.

FAT (file allocation table)—The original PC file system designed in the 1970s to support floppy disks and, later, hard disks. FAT is inadequate for most server operating systems because of its partition size limitations, naming limitations, and fragmentation and speed issues.

FAT16 (16-bit file allocation table)—A file system designed for use with early DOS- and Windows-based computers that allocates file system space in 16-bit units. Compared to FAT32, FAT16 is less desirable because of its partition size, file naming, fragmentation, speed, and security limitations.

FAT32 (32-bit file allocation table)—An enhanced version of FAT that accommodates the use of long filenames and smaller allocation units on a disk. FAT32 makes more efficient use of disk space than the original FAT.

fault—The malfunction of one component of a system. A fault can result in a failure.

fault management—The detection and signaling of device, link, or component faults.

fault tolerance—The capability for a component or system to continue functioning despite damage or malfunction.

FCS (Frame Check Sequence)—The field in a frame responsible for ensuring that data carried by the frame arrives intact. It uses an algorithm, such as CRC, to accomplish this verification.

FDDI (Fiber Distributed Data Interface)—A networking standard originally specified by ANSI in the mid-1980s and later refined by ISO. FDDI uses a dual fiber-optic ring to transmit data at speeds of 100 Mbps. It was commonly used as a backbone technology in the 1980s and early 1990s, but lost favor as Fast Ethernet technologies emerged in the mid-1990s. FDDI provides excellent reliability and security.

feasibility study—A study that determines the costs and benefits of a project and attempts to predict whether the project will result in a favorable outcome (for example, whether it will achieve its goal without imposing excessive cost or time burdens on the organization).

Fedora Core—A popular version of the Linux operating system packaged and distributed by Red Hat, Inc.

ferrule—A short tube within a fiber-optic cable connector that encircles the fiber strand and keeps it properly aligned.

FHSS (frequency hopping spread spectrum)—A wireless signaling technique in which a signal jumps between several different frequencies within a band in a synchronization pattern known to the channel's receiver and transmitter.

Fiber Distributed Data Interface—See *FDDI*.

fiber-optic cable—A form of cable that contains one or several glass or plastic fibers in its core. Data is transmitted via pulsing light sent from a laser or light-emitting diode (LED) through the central fiber (or fibers). Fiber-optic cables offer significantly higher throughput than copper-based cables. They may be single-mode or multimode and typically use wave-division multiplexing to carry multiple signals.

Fibre Channel—A distinct network transmission method that relies on fiber-optic media and its own, proprietary protocol. Fibre Channel is capable of up to 2-Gbps throughput.

file access protocol—A protocol that enables one system to access files on another system.

file allocation table—See *FAT*.

File and Print Services for NetWare—The Microsoft application that, when installed on a Windows Server 2003 server, makes the server's file and print resources appear to NetWare-attached clients as NetWare directory resources. File and Print Services for NetWare is part of the Microsoft Windows Services for NetWare software package.

file globbing—A form of filename substitution, similar to the use of wildcards in Windows and DOS.

file server—A specialized server that enables clients to share applications and data across the network.

file services—The functions of a file server that allow users to share data files, applications, and storage areas.

file system—An operating system's method of organizing, managing, and accessing its files through logical structures and software routines.

File Transfer Protocol—See *FTP*.

file-infected virus—A virus that attaches itself to executable files. When the infected executable file runs, the virus copies itself to memory. Later, the virus attaches itself to other executable files.

filtering database—A collection of data created and used by a bridge that correlates the MAC addresses of connected workstations with their locations. A filtering database is also known as a forwarding table.

firewall—A device (either a router or a computer running special software) that selectively filters or blocks traffic between networks. Firewalls are commonly used to improve data security.

FireWire—A peripheral bus standard developed by Apple Computer and codified by the IEEE as the IEEE 1394 standard. Traditional FireWire connections support a maximum throughput of 400 Mbps, but a newer version supports potential throughput rates of over 3 Gbps. In addition to connecting peripherals, FireWire can be used to network computers directly in a bus fashion.

firmware—A combination of hardware and software. The hardware component of firmware is a ROM (read-only memory) chip that stores data established at the factory and possibly changed by configuration programs that can write to ROM.

fixed—A type of wireless system in which the locations of the transmitter and receiver are static. In a fixed connection, the transmitting antenna focuses its energy directly toward the receiving antenna. This results in a point-to-point link.

flashing—A security attack in which an Internet user sends commands to another Internet user's machine that cause the screen to fill with garbage characters. A flashing attack causes the user to terminate her session.

flavor—The term used to refer to the different implementations of a particular UNIX-type of system. For example, different flavors of Linux include Red Hat's Fedora Core, SUSE, and Mandrake.

flow control—A method of gauging the appropriate rate of data transmission based on how fast the recipient can accept data.

FM (frequency modulation)—A method of data modulation in which the frequency of the carrier signal is modified by the application of the data signal.

forest—In the context of Windows Server 2003, a collection of domain trees that use different namespaces. A forest allows for trust relationships to be established between trees.

Format Prefix—A variable-length field at the beginning of an IPv6 address that indicates what type of address it is (for example, unicast, anycast, or multicast).

forwarding table—See *filtering database.*

fox and hound—Another term for the combination of devices known as a tone generator and a tone locator. The tone locator is considered the hound because it follows the tone generator (the fox).

fractional T1—An arrangement that allows a customer to lease only some of the channels on a T1 line.

fragmentation—A Network layer service that subdivides segments it receives from the Transport layer into smaller packets.

frame—A package for data that includes not only the raw data, or "payload," but also the sender's and recipient's addressing and control information. Frames are generated at the Data Link layer of the OSI Model and are issued to the network at the Physical layer.

Frame Check Sequence—See *FCS.*

Frame Relay—A digital, packet-switched WAN technology whose protocols operate at the Data Link layer. The name is derived from the fact that data is separated into frames, which are then relayed from one node to another without any verification or processing. Frame Relay offers throughputs between 64 Kbps and 45 Mbps. A Frame Relay customer chooses the amount of bandwidth he requires and pays for only that amount.

freely distributable software—See *open source software.*

frequency—The number of times that a signal's amplitude changes over a fixed period of time, expressed in cycles per second, or hertz (Hz).

frequency hopping spread spectrum—See *FHSS.*

frequency modulation—See *FM.*

FTP (File Transfer Protocol)—An Application layer protocol used to send and receive files via TCP/IP.

F-Type connector—A connector used to terminate coaxial cable used for transmitting television and broadband cable signals.

full backup—A backup in which all data on all servers is copied to a storage medium, regardless of whether the data is new or changed. A full backup unchecks the archive bit on files it has backed up.

full mesh WAN—A version of the mesh topology WAN in which every site is directly connected to every other site. Full mesh WANs are the most fault-tolerant type of WAN.

full-duplex—A type of transmission in which signals may travel in both directions over a medium simultaneously. May also be called, simply, "duplex."

Gantt chart—A popular method of depicting when projects begin and end along a horizontal timeline.

gateway—A combination of networking hardware and software that connects two dissimilar kinds of networks. Gateways perform connectivity, session management, and data translation, so they must operate at multiple layers of the OSI Model.

gateway router—See *border router*.

GEO (geosynchronous orbit or **geostationary orbit)**—The term used to refer to a satellite that maintains a constant distance from a point on the equator at every point in its orbit. Geosynchronous satellites are the type used to provide satellite Internet access.

geostationary orbit—See *GEO*.

geosynchronous—See *GEO*.

ghost—A frame that is not actually a data frame, but rather an aberration caused by a device misinterpreting stray voltage on the wire. Unlike true data frames, ghosts have no starting delimiter.

giant—A packet that exceeds the medium's maximum packet size. For example, any Ethernet packet that is larger than 1518 bytes is considered a giant.

Gigabit Ethernet—A type of Ethernet network that is capable of 1000 Mbps, or 1 Gbps, throughput. Examples of Gigabit Ethernet include 1000BASE-T and 1000BASE-CX.

global group—A group on a Windows Server 2003 network that allows members of one domain to access resources within that domain as well as resources from other domains in the same forest.

globally unique identifier—See *GUID*.

GNU—The name given to the public software project to implement a complete, free source code implementation of UNIX. It also refers to the collection of UNIX-inspired utilities and tools that are included with Linux distributions. The term "GNU" is an acronym within an acronym that stands for "GNU's Not UNIX."

grandfather-father-son—A backup rotation scheme that uses daily (son), weekly (father), and monthly (grandfather) backup sets.

graphical user interface—See *GUI*.

group—A means of collectively managing users' permissions and restrictions applied to shared resources. Groups form the basis for resource and account management for every type of network operating system, not just Windows Server 2003. Many network administrators create groups according to department or, even more specifically, according to job function within a department.

GroupWise—An application from Novell that runs on NetWare servers and provides e-mail, messaging, scheduling, and collaboration services.

Guest—A user account with very limited privileges that is created during the installation of a network operating system.

GUI (graphical user interface)—A pictorial representation of computer functions and elements that, in the case of network operating systems, enables administrators to more easily manage files, users, groups, security, printers, and other issues.

GUID (globally unique identifier)—A 128-bit number generated and assigned to an object upon its creation in the Windows Server 2003 Active Directory. Network applications and services use an object's GUID to communicate with it.

hacker—A person who masters the inner workings of operating systems and utilities in an effort to better understand them. A hacker is distinguished from a cracker in that a cracker attempts to exploit a network's vulnerabilities for malicious purposes.

half-duplex—A type of transmission in which signals may travel in both directions over a medium, but in only one direction at a time.

handshake protocol—One of several protocols within SSL, and perhaps the most significant. As its name implies, the handshake protocol allows the client and server to authenticate (or introduce) each other and establishes terms for how they securely exchange data during an SSL session.

hardware address—See *MAC address*.

Hardware Compatibility List—See *HCL*.

hardware RAID—A method of implementing RAID that relies on an externally attached set of disks and a RAID disk controller, which manages the RAID array.

HCL (Hardware Compatibility List)—A list of computer components proven to be compatible with Windows Server 2003. The HCL appears on the same CD as your Windows Server 2003 software and on Microsoft's Web site.

head-end—A cable company's central office, which connects cable wiring to many nodes before it reaches customers' sites.

hertz (Hz)—A measure of frequency equivalent to the number of amplitude cycles per second.

heuristic scanning—A type of virus scanning that attempts to identify viruses by discovering "virus-like" behavior.

HFC (hybrid fiber-coax)—A link that consists of fiber cable connecting the cable company's offices to a node location near the customer and coaxial cable connecting the node to the customer's house. HFC upgrades to existing cable wiring are required before current TV cable systems can provide Internet access.

HFS+—The primary file system used in Mac OS X Server.

hierarchical file system—The organization of files and directories (or folders) on a disk in which directories may contain files and other directories. When displayed graphically, this organization resembles a treelike structure.

High-Speed Token Ring—See *HSTR*.

home directory—A directory on a server associated with a particular user account. A user has full access privileges to files and subdirectories within his home directory.

hop—A term used to describe each trip a unit of data takes from one connectivity device to another. Typically, "hop" is used in the context of router-to-router communications.

host—A computer that enables resource sharing by other computers on the same network.

host file—A text file that associates TCP/IP host names with IP addresses.

host name—A symbolic name that describes a TCP/IP device.

hosts—Name of the host file used on UNIX, Linux, and Windows systems. On a UNIX- or Linux-based computer, hosts is found in the /etc directory. On a Windows-based computer, it is found in the %systemroot%\system32\drivers\etc folder.

hot site—A place where the computers, devices, and connectivity necessary to rebuild a network exist, and all are appropriately configured, updated, and connected to match your network's current state.

hot spare—In the context of RAID, a disk or partition that is part of the array, but used only in case one of the RAID disks fails. More generally, "hot spare" is used as a synonym for a hot swappable component.

hot spot—An area covered by a wireless access point that provides visitors with wireless services, including Internet access.

hot swappable—A characteristic that enables identical components to be interchanged (or swapped) while a machine is still running (hot). After being installed, a hot swappable component automatically assumes the functions of its counterpart.

HSTR (High-Speed Token Ring)—A standard for Token Ring networks that operate at 100 Mbps.

HTML (Hypertext Markup Language)—The language that defines formatting standards for Web documents.

HTTP (Hypertext Transfer Protocol)—An Application layer protocol that formulates and interprets requests between Web clients and servers.

HTTP over Secure Sockets Layer—See *HTTPS*.

HTTP Secure—See *HTTP over Secure Sockets Layer*.

HTTPS (HTTP over Secure Sockets Layer)—The URL prefix that indicates that a Web page requires its data to be exchanged between client and server using SSL encryption. HTTPS uses the TCP port number 443, rather than port 80 (the port that normal HTTP uses).

hub—A connectivity device that retransmits incoming data signals to its multiple ports. Typically, hubs contain one uplink port, which is used to connect to a network's backbone.

hybrid fiber-coax—See *HFC*.

hybrid topology—A physical topology that combines characteristics of more than one simple physical topology.

Hypertext Markup Language—See *HTML*.

Hypertext Transfer Protocol—See *HTTP*.

IAB (Internet Architecture Board)—A technical advisory group of researchers and professionals interested in overseeing the Internet's design, growth, standards, and management.

IANA (Internet Assigned Numbers Authority)—A nonprofit, U.S. government-funded group that was established at the University of Southern California and charged with managing IP address allocation and the domain name system. The oversight for many of IANA's functions was given to ICANN in 1998; however, IANA continues to perform Internet addressing and domain name system administration.

ICA (Independent Computing Architecture) client—The software from Citrix Systems, Inc. that, when installed on a client, enables the client to connect with a remote access server and exchange keystrokes, mouse clicks, and screen updates. Citrix's ICA client can work with virtually any operating system or application.

ICANN (Internet Corporation for Assigned Names and Numbers)—The nonprofit corporation currently designated by the U.S. government to maintain and assign IP addresses.

ICMP (Internet Control Message Protocol)—A core protocol in the TCP/IP suite that notifies the sender that something has gone wrong in the transmission process and that packets were not delivered.

ICS (Internet Connection Sharing)—A service provided with Windows 98, Me, 2000 and 32-bit versions of XP operating systems that allows one computer, the ICS host, to share its Internet connection with other computers on the same network.

ICS host—On a network using the Microsoft Internet Connection Sharing service, the computer whose Internet connection other computers share. The ICS host must contain two network interfaces: one that connects to the Internet and one that connects to the LAN.

IEEE (Institute of Electrical and Electronics Engineers)—An international society composed of engineering professionals. Its goals are to promote development and education in the electrical engineering and computer science fields.

IEEE 1394—See *FireWire*.

IETF (Internet Engineering Task Force)—An organization that sets standards for how systems communicate over the Internet (for example, how protocols operate and interact).

ifconfig—A utility that establishes and allows management of TCP/IP settings on UNIX-type of systems.

IGMP (Internet Group Management Protocol or Internet Group Multicast Protocol)—A TCP/IP protocol used to manage multicast transmissions. Routers use IGMP to determine which nodes use IGMP to join or leave a multicast group.

IKE (Internet Key Exchange)—The first phase of IPSec authentication, which accomplishes key management. IKE is a service that runs on UDP port 500. After IKE has established the rules for the type of keys two nodes use, IPSec invokes its second phase, encryption.

iManager—A browser-based tool for managing eDirectory in NetWare 6.x.

IMAP (Internet Message Access Protocol)—A mail retrieval protocol that improves on the shortcomings of POP. The single biggest advantage IMAP4 has relative to POP is that it allows users to store messages on the mail server, rather than always having to download them to the local machine. The most current version of IMAP is version 4 (IMAP4).

IMAP4 (Internet Message Protocol, version 4)—The most commonly used form of the Internet Message Access Protocol (IMAP).

impedance—The resistance that contributes to controlling an electrical signal. Impedance is measured in ohms.

incremental backup—A backup in which only data that has changed since the last full or incremental backup is copied to a storage medium. After backing up files, an incremental backup unchecks the archive bit for every file it has saved.

Industry Standard Architecture—See *ISA.*

information node—See *i-node.*

infrared—A type of data transmission in which infrared light signals are used to transmit data through space, similar to the way a television remote control sends signals across the room. Networks may use two types of infrared transmission: direct or indirect.

Infrared Data Association—See *IrDA.*

infrastructure WLAN—A type of WLAN in which stations communicate with an access point and not directly with each other.

inherited—A type of permission, or right, that is passed down from one group (the parent) to a group within that group (the child).

i-node (information node)—A UNIX-type file system information storage area that holds all details about a file. This information includes the size, the access rights, the date and time of creation, and a pointer to the actual contents of the file.

Institute of Electrical and Electronics Engineers—See *IEEE.*

Integrated Services Digital Network—See *ISDN.*

integrity—The soundness of a network's files, systems, and connections. To ensure integrity, you must protect your network from anything that might render it unusable, such as corruption, tampering, natural disasters, and viruses.

integrity checking—A method of comparing the current characteristics of files and disks against an archived version of these characteristics to discover any changes. The most common example of integrity checking involves a checksum.

intelligent hub—A hub that possesses processing capabilities and can therefore monitor network traffic, detect packet errors and collisions, poll connected devices for information, and gather the data in database format.

interior router—A router that directs data between nodes on an autonomous LAN.

International Organization for Standardization—See *ISO.*

International Telecommunication Union—See *ITU.*

Internet—A complex WAN that connects LANs and clients around the globe.

Internet Architecture Board—See *IAB.*

Internet Assigned Numbers Authority—See *IANA.*

Internet Connection Sharing—See *ICS.*

Internet Control Message Protocol—See *ICMP.*

Internet Corporation for Assigned Names and Numbers—See *ICANN.*

Internet Engineering Task Force—See *IETF.*

Internet Group Management Protocol—See *IGMP.*

Internet Group Multicast Protocol—See *IGMP.*

Internet Key Exchange—See *IKE*.

Internet Message Access Protocol—See *IMAP*.

Internet Message Access Protocol, version 4—See *IMAP4*.

Internet Protocol—See *IP*.

Internet Protocol address—See *IP address*.

Internet Protocol Security—See *IPSec*.

Internet Relay Chat—See *IRC*.

Internet Service Provider—See *ISP*.

Internet services—The services that enable a network to communicate with the Internet, including World Wide Web servers and browsers, file transfer capabilities, Internet addressing schemes, security filters, and a means for directly logging on to other computers.

Internet Society—See *ISOC*.

Internet telephony—The provision of telephone service over the Internet.

internetwork—To traverse more than one LAN segment and more than one type of network through a router.

Internetwork Packet Exchange—See *IPX*.

Internetwork Packet Exchange/Sequenced Packet Exchange—See *IPX/SPX*.

interrupt—A circuit board wire through which a device issues voltage, thereby signaling a request for the processor's attention.

interrupt request—See *IRQ*.

interrupt request number—See *IRQ number*.

intranet—A network or part of a network that uses browser-based services to exchange information within an enterprise. Intranets may be contained within a LAN or may be accessible via a WAN or the Internet.

intraNetWare—Another term for NetWare version 4.11, the version in which support for Internet services was first introduced.

IP (Internet Protocol)—A core protocol in the TCP/IP suite that operates in the Network layer of the OSI Model and provides information about how and where data should be delivered. IP is the subprotocol that enables TCP/IP to internetwork.

IP address (Internet Protocol address)—The Network layer address assigned to nodes to uniquely identify them on a TCP/IP network. IP addresses consist of 32 bits divided into four octets, or bytes.

IP datagram—The IP portion of a TCP/IP frame that acts as an envelope for data, holding information necessary for routers to transfer data between subnets.

IP next generation—See *IPv6*.

IP phone—See *IP telephone*.

IP spoofing—A security attack in which an outsider obtains internal IP addresses, then uses those addresses to pretend that he has authority to access a private network from the Internet.

IP telephone—A telephone used for VoIP on a TCP/IP-based network. IP telephones are designed to transmit and receive only digital signals.

IP telephony—See *Voice over IP*.

ipconfig—The utility used to display TCP/IP addressing and domain name information in the Windows NT, Windows 2000, and Windows XP operating systems.

IPng—See *IPv6*.

IP-PBX—A private switch that accepts and interprets both analog and digital voice signals (although some IP-PBXs do not accept analog lines). It can connect with both traditional PSTN lines and data networks. An IP-PBX transmits and receives IP-based voice signals to and from other network connectivity devices, such as a router or gateway.

IPSec (Internet Protocol Security)—A Layer 3 protocol that defines encryption, authentication, and key management for TCP/IP transmissions. IPSec is an enhancement to IPv4 and native to IPv6. IPSec is unique among authentication methods in that it adds security information to the header of all IP packets.

IPv4 (IP version 4)—The current standard for IP addressing that specifies 32-bit addresses composed of four octets.

IPv4LL (IP version 4 Link Local)—A protocol that manages automatic address assignment among locally connected nodes. IPv4LL is part of the Zeroconf group of protocols.

IPv6 (IP version 6)—A newer standard for IP addressing that will replace the current IPv4 (IP version 4). Most notably, IPv6 uses a newer, more efficient header in its packets and allows for 128-bit source and destination IP addresses. The use of longer addresses will allow for many more IP addresses to be in circulation.

IPX (Internetwork Packet Exchange)—A core protocol of the IPX/SPX suite that operates at the Network layer of the OSI Model and provides routing and internetwork services, similar to IP in the TCP/IP suite.

IPX address—An address assigned to a device on an IPX/SPX-based network.

IPX/SPX (Internetwork Packet Exchange/Sequenced Packet Exchange)—A protocol originally developed by Xerox, then modified and adopted by Novell in the 1980s for the NetWare network operating system.

IRC (Internet Relay Chat)—A protocol that enables users running special IRC client software to communicate instantly with other participants in a chat room on the Internet.

IrDA (Infrared Data Association)—A nonprofit organization founded in 1994 to develop and promote standards for wireless communication using infrared signals. IrDA is also used to denote the type of wireless technology this group has developed.

IRQ (interrupt request)—A message sent to the computer that instructs it to stop what it is doing and pay attention to something else. IRQ is often used (informally) to refer to the interrupt request number.

IRQ number—The unique number assigned to each interrupt in a computer. Interrupt request numbers range from 0 to 15, and many PC devices reserve specific numbers for their use alone.

ISA (Industry Standard Architecture)—The original PC bus type, developed in the early 1980s to support an 8-bit and later 16-bit data path and a 4.77-MHz clock speed.

ISDN (Integrated Services Digital Network)—An international standard that uses PSTN lines to carry digital signals. It specifies protocols at the Physical, Data Link, and Transport layers of the OSI Model. ISDN lines may carry voice and data signals simultaneously. Two types of ISDN connections are used in North America: BRI (Basic Rate Interface) and PRI (Primary Rate Interface). Both use a combination of bearer channels (B channels) and data channels (D channels).

ISO (International Organization for Standardization)—A collection of standards organizations representing 146 countries with headquarters located in Geneva, Switzerland. Its goal is to establish international technological standards to facilitate the global exchange of information and barrier-free trade.

ISOC (Internet Society)—A professional organization with members from more than 180 countries that helps to establish technical standards for the Internet.

ISP (Internet Service Provider)—A business that provides organizations and individuals with Internet access and often other services, such as e-mail and Web hosting.

ITU (International Telecommunication Union)—A United Nations agency that regulates international telecommunications and provides developing countries with technical expertise and equipment to advance their technological bases.

J1—A digital carrier standard used in Japan that offers 24 channels and 1.544-Mbps throughput.

J3—A digital carrier standard used in Japan that offers 480 channels and 32.064-Mbps throughput.

jabber—A device that handles electrical signals improperly, usually affecting the rest of the network. A network analyzer will detect a jabber as a device that is always retransmitting, effectively bringing the network to a halt. A jabber usually results from a bad NIC. Occasionally, it can be caused by outside electrical interference.

jamming—A part of CSMA/CD in which, upon detecting a collision, a station issues a special 32-bit sequence to indicate to all nodes on an Ethernet segment that its previously transmitted frame has suffered a collision and should be considered faulty.

Java System Directory Server Enterprise Edition—The Sun Microsystems implementation of LDAP.

jumper—A small, removable piece of plastic that contains a metal receptacle that fits over a pair of pins on a circuit board to complete a circuit between those two pins. By moving the jumper from one set of pins to another set of pins, you can modify the board's circuit, thereby giving it different instructions on how to operate.

KDC (Key Distribution Center)—In Kerberos terminology, the server that runs the authentication service and the Ticket-granting service to issue keys and tickets to clients.

Kerberos—A cross-platform authentication protocol that uses key encryption to verify the identity of clients and to securely exchange information after a client logs on to a system. It is an example of a private key encryption service.

kernel—The core of a UNIX-type of system and a NetWare NOS. This part of the operating system is loaded and run when you turn on your computer. It mediates between user programs and the computer hardware.

kernel module—A portion of the kernel that you can load and unload to add or remove functionality on a running UNIX or Linux system.

key—A series of characters that is combined with a block of data during that data's encryption. To decrypt the resulting data, the recipient must also possess the key.

Key Distribution Center—See *KDC*.

key management—The method whereby two nodes using key encryption agree on common parameters for the keys they will use to encrypt data.

key pair—The combination of a public and private key used to decipher data that was encrypted using public key encryption.

L2TP (Layer 2 Tunneling Protocol)—A protocol that encapsulates PPP data, for use on VPNs. L2TP is based on Cisco technology and is standardized by the IETF. It is distinguished by its compatibility among different manufacturers' equipment, its ability to connect between clients, routers, and servers alike, and also by the fact that it can connect nodes belonging to different Layer 3 networks.

label—A character string that represents a domain (either top-level, second-level, or third-level).

LAN (local area network)—A network of computers and other devices that is confined to a relatively small space, such as one building or even one office.

LAN Emulation—See *LANE*.

LANE (LAN Emulation)—A method for transporting Token Ring or Ethernet frames over ATM networks. LANE encapsulates incoming Ethernet or Token Ring frames, then converts them into ATM cells for transmission over an ATM network.

last mile—See *local loop*.

late collision—A collision that takes place outside the normal window in which collisions are detected and redressed. Late collisions are usually caused by a defective station (such as a card, or transceiver) that is transmitting without first verifying line status or by failure to observe the configuration guidelines for cable length, which results in collisions being recognized too late.

latency—The delay between the transmission of a signal and its receipt.

Layer 2 Tunneling Protocol—See *L2TP*.

Layer 3 switch—A switch capable of interpreting data at Layer 3 (Network layer) of the OSI Model.

Layer 4 switch—A switch capable of interpreting data at Layer 4 (Transport layer) of the OSI Model.

LC (Local Connector)—A connector used with single-mode or multimode fiber-optic cable.

LDAP (Lightweight Directory Access Protocol)—A standard protocol for accessing network directories.

leaf object—An object in an operating system's directory, such as a printer or user, that does not contain other objects.

lease—The agreement between a DHCP server and client on how long the client can use a DHCP-assigned IP address. DHCP services can be configured to provide lease terms equal to any amount of time.

LEO (low earth orbiting)—A type of satellite that orbits the earth with an altitude between 700 and 1400 kilometers, closer to the earth's poles than the orbits of either GEO or MEO satellites. LEO satellites cover a smaller geographical range than GEO satellites and require less power.

Level 1—A form of UTP that contains two wire pairs. Level 1 is the type of wire used for older voice networks and is unsuitable for transmitting data.

license tracking—The process of determining the number of copies of a single application that are currently in use on the network and whether the number in use exceeds the authorized number of licenses.

Lightweight Directory Access Protocol—See *LDAP*.

line printer daemon—See *lpd*.

line-of-sight—See *LOS*.

link segment—See *unpopulated segment*.

Linux—A freely distributable implementation of a UNIX-type of system. Finnish computer scientist Linus Torvalds originally developed it.

LLC (Logical Link Control) sublayer—The upper sublayer in the Data Link layer. The LLC provides a common interface and supplies reliability and flow control services.

load balancing—An automatic distribution of traffic over multiple links, hard disks, or processors intended to optimize responses.

local account—A type of user account on a Windows Server 2003 network that has rights to the resources managed by the server the user has logged on to.

local area network—See *LAN*.

local collision—A collision that occurs when two or more stations are transmitting simultaneously. Excessively high collision rates within the network can usually be traced to cable or routing problems.

Local Connector—See *LC*.

local loop—The part of a phone system that connects a customer site with a telecommunications carrier's switching facility.

logical address—See *network address*.

Logical Link Control layer—See *LLC (Logical Link Control) sublayer*.

logical topology—A characteristic of network transmission that reflects the way in which data is transmitted between nodes (which may differ from the physical layout of the paths that data takes). The most common logical topologies are bus and ring.

loopback adapter—See *loopback plug*.

loopback address—An IP address reserved for communicating from a node to itself (used mostly for troubleshooting purposes). The loopback address is always cited as 127.0.0.1, although in fact, transmitting to any IP address whose first octet is "127" will contact the originating device.

loopback plug—A connector used for troubleshooting that plugs into a port (for example, a serial, parallel, or RJ-45 port) and crosses over the transmit line to the receive line, allowing outgoing signals to be redirected back into the computer for testing.

loopback test—An attempt to contact one's own machine for troubleshooting purposes. In TCP/IP-based networking, a loopback test can be performed by communicating with an IP address that begins with an octet of 127. Usually, this means pinging the address 127.0.0.1.

LOS (line-of-sight)—A wireless signal or path that travels directly in a straight line from its transmitter to its intended receiver. This type of propagation uses the least amount of energy and results in the reception of the clearest possible signal.

low earth orbiting—See *LEO*.

lpd (line printer daemon)—A UNIX service responsible for printing files placed in the printer queue by the lpr command.

lpr—The UNIX command. This command simply places files in the printer queue. The files are subsequently printed with lpd, the print service.

MAC (Media Access Control) sublayer—The lower sublayer of the Data Link layer. The MAC appends the physical address of the destination computer onto the frame.

MAC address—A 12-character string that uniquely identifies a network node. The manufacturer hardcodes the MAC address into the NIC. This address is composed of the Block ID and Device ID.

Mac OS X Server—A proprietary network operating system from Apple Computer that is based on a version of UNIX.

Mach—A UNIX-type of operating system kernel developed by researchers at Carnegie Mellon University in Pittsburgh, PA. Mach is the basis for the kernel in Mac OS X Server.

macro virus—A virus that takes the form of an application (for example, a word-processing or spreadsheet) program macro, which may execute when the program is in use.

mail server—A server that manages the storage and transfer of e-mail messages.

mail services—The network services that manage the storage and transfer of e-mail between users on a network. In addition to sending, receiving, and storing mail, mail services can include filtering, routing, notification, scheduling, and data exchange with other mail servers.

main bus—See *bus*.

MAN (metropolitan area network)—A network that is larger than a LAN, typically connecting clients and servers from multiple buildings, but within a limited geographic area. For example, a MAN could connect multiple city government buildings around a city's center.

man pages—See *manual pages*.

managed hub—See *intelligent hub*.

Management Information Base—See *MIB*.

management services—The network services that centrally administer and simplify complicated management tasks on the network. Examples of management services include license tracking, security auditing, asset management, address management, software distribution, traffic monitoring, load balancing, and hardware diagnosis.

manual pages—The online documentation for any variety of the UNIX operating system. This documentation describes the use of the commands and the programming interface.

map—The action of associating a disk, directory, or device with a drive letter.

MAU (Multistation Access Unit)—A device on a Token Ring network that regenerates signals; equivalent to a hub.

maximum transmission unit—See *MTU*.

MCSE (Microsoft Certified Systems Engineer)—A professional certification established by Microsoft that demonstrates in-depth knowledge about Microsoft products, including Windows 2000, Windows XP, and Windows Server 2003.

Mechanical Transfer Registered Jack—See *MT-RJ*.

Media Access Control sublayer—See *MAC (Media Access Control) sublayer*.

media converter—A device that enables networks or segments using different media to interconnect and exchange signals.

medium earth orbiting—See *MEO*.

member server—A type of server on a Windows Server 2003 network that does not hold directory information and therefore cannot authenticate users.

memory range—A hexadecimal number that indicates the area of memory that the NIC and CPU will use for exchanging, or buffering, data. As with IRQs, some memory ranges are reserved for specific devices—most notably, the motherboard.

MEO (medium earth orbiting)—A type of satellite that orbits the earth 10,390 kilometers above its surface, positioned between the equator and the poles. MEO satellites can cover a larger area of the earth's surface than LEO satellites while using less power and causing less signal delay than GEO satellites.

mesh topology WAN—A type of WAN in which several sites are directly interconnected. Mesh WANs are highly fault-tolerant because they provide multiple routes for data to follow between any two points.

message switching—A type of switching in which a connection is established between two devices in the connection path; one device transfers data to the second device, then breaks the connection. The information is stored and forwarded from the second device after a connection between that device and a third device on the path is established.

Metaframe—A software package from Citrix Systems, Inc. that supplies terminal services to remote clients.

metropolitan area network—See *MAN*.

MIB (Management Information Base)—A database used in network management that contains a device's definitions of managed objects and their data.

Microsoft Certified Systems Engineer—See *MCSE*.

Microsoft Challenge Handshake Authentication Protocol—See *MS-CHAP*.

Microsoft Challenge Handshake Authentication Protocol, version 2—See *MS-CHAPv2*.

Microsoft Directory Synchronization Services—See *MSDSS*.

Microsoft Management Console—See *MMC*.

Microsoft Windows Services for NetWare—A suite of tools for integrating Windows 2000 Server or Windows Server 2003 servers with NetWare servers. The suite includes a tool for synchronizing data from NetWare directories with Active Directory, a tool for migrating files from a NetWare server to a Windows Server 2003 server, and File and Print Services for NetWare, which allows a Windows Server 2003 computer to appear as a NetWare server to NetWare clients.

middleware—The software that sits between the client and server in a 3-tier architecture. Middleware may be used as a messaging service between clients and servers, as a universal query language for databases, or as means of coordinating processes between multiple servers that need to work together in servicing clients.

milestone—A reference point that marks the completion of a major task or group of tasks in a project and contributes to measuring the project's progress.

MIME (Multipurpose Internet Mail Extensions)—A standard for encoding and interpreting binary files, images, video, and non-ASCII character sets within an e-mail message.

mirroring—A fault-tolerance technique in which one component or device duplicates the activity of another.

MMC (Microsoft Management Console)—A customizable, graphical network management interface used with Windows Server 2003.

MMF (multimode fiber)—A type of fiber-optic cable that contains a core with a diameter between 50 and 100 microns, through which many pulses of light generated by a light-_emitting diode (LED) travel at different angles.

mobile—A type of wireless system in which the receiver can be located anywhere within the transmitter's range. This allows the receiver to roam from one place to another while continuing to pick up its signal.

modal bandwidth—A measure of the highest frequency of signal a multimode fiber-optic cable can support over a specific distance. Modal bandwidth is measured in MHz-km.

modem—A device that modulates analog signals into digital signals at the transmitting end for transmission over telephone lines, and demodulates digital signals into analog signals at the receiving end.

modular router—A router with multiple slots that can hold different interface cards or other devices so as to provide flexible, customizable network interoperability.

modulation—A technique for formatting signals in which one property of a simple carrier wave is modified by the addition of a data signal during transmission.

Monitor—A NetWare NLM that provides a text-based menu for viewing and modifying server parameters, such as protocols, bindings, system resources, and loaded modules.

motherboard—The main circuit board that controls a computer.

mount—The process of making a disk partition available.

MRTG (Multi Router Traffic Grapher)—A command-line utility that uses SNMP to poll devices, collects data in a log file, and then generates HTML-based views of the data. MRTG is freely distributed software originally written by Tobias Oetiker, a networking professional who in the early 1990s saw a need for a tool to regularly measure the status of his organization's WAN link.

MS-CHAP (Microsoft Challenge Handshake Authentication Protocol)—An authentication protocol offered by Microsoft with its Windows clients and servers. Similar to CHAP, MS-CHAP uses a three-way handshake to verify a client's credentials and encrypts passwords with a challenge text.

MS-CHAPv2 (Microsoft Challenge Authentication Protocol, version 2)—An authentication protocol provided with Windows XP, 2000, and Server 2003 operating systems that follows the CHAP model, but uses stronger encryption, uses different encryption keys for transmission and reception, and requires mutual authentication between two computers.

MSDSS (Microsoft Directory Synchronization Services)—An application that, when installed on a Windows Server 2003 server, can synchronize information between an Active Directory database and a NetWare eDirectory database.

MT-RJ (Mechanical Transfer Registered Jack)—A connector used with single-mode or multimode fiber-optic cable.

MTU (maximum transmission unit)—The largest data unit a network (for example, Ethernet or Token Ring) will accept for transmission.

Multi Router Traffic Grapher—See *MRTG*.

multicast address—A type of address in the IPv6 that represents multiple interfaces, often on multiple nodes. An IPv6 multicast address begins with the following hexadecimal field: FF0*x*, where *x* is a character that identifies the address's group scope.

multicasting—A means of transmission in which one device sends data to a specific group of devices (not necessarily the entire network segment) in a point-to-multipoint fashion. Multicasting can be used for videoconferencing over the Internet, for example.

multimeter—A simple instrument that can measure multiple characteristics of an electric circuit, including its resistance and voltage.

multimode fiber—See *MMF*.

multipath—The characteristic of wireless signals that follow a number of different paths to their destination (for example, because of reflection, diffraction, and scattering).

multiplexer (mux)—A device that separates a medium into multiple channels and issues signals to each of those subchannels.

multiplexing—A form of transmission that allows multiple signals to travel simultaneously over one medium.

multiprocessing—The technique of splitting tasks among multiple processors to expedite the completion of any single instruction.

multiprotocol network—A network that uses more than one protocol.

Multipurpose Internet Mail Extensions—See *MIME*.

Multistation Access Unit—See *MAU*.

multitasking—The ability of a processor to perform multiple activities in a brief period of time (often seeming simultaneous to the user).

mutual authentication—An authentication scheme in which both computers verify the credentials of each other.

name server—A server that contains a database of TCP/IP host names and their associated IP addresses. A name server supplies a resolver with the requested information. If it cannot resolve the IP address, the query passes to a higher-level name server.

namespace—The complete database of hierarchical names (including host and domain names) used to resolve IP addresses with their hosts.

narrowband—A type of wireless transmission in which signals travel over a single frequency or within a specified frequency range.

NAS (network attached storage)—A device or set of devices attached to a client/server network, dedicated to providing highly fault-tolerant access to large quantities of data. NAS depends on traditional network transmission methods such as Ethernet.

NAT (Network Address Translation)—A technique in which IP addresses used on a private network are assigned a public IP address by a gateway when accessing a public network.

nbtstat—A TCP/IP troubleshooting utility that provides information about NetBIOS names and their addresses. If you know the NetBIOS name of a workstation, you can use nbtstat to determine its IP address.

NDS (NetWare Directory Services)—In NetWare 4.x and 5.x, the system of managing multiple servers and their resources, including users, volumes, groups, profiles, and printers, used with NetWare versions 4.x and 5.x. The NDS model was the precursor to eDirectory.

needs assessment—The process of clarifying the reasons and objectives for a proposed change to determine whether the change is worthwhile and necessary, and to elucidate the scope and nature of the proposed change.

negative frame sequence check—The result of the CRC (cyclic redundancy check) generated by the originating node not matching the checksum calculated from the data received. It usually indicates noise or transmission problems on the LAN interface or cabling. A high number of (nonmatching) CRCs usually results from excessive collisions or a station transmitting bad data.

net mask—See *subnet mask*.

NetBEUI (NetBIOS Enhanced User Interface)—The Microsoft adaptation of the IBM NetBIOS protocol. NetBEUI expands on NetBIOS by adding a Transport layer component. NetBEUI is a fast and efficient protocol that consumes few network resources, provides excellent error correction, and requires little configuration.

NetBIOS (Network Basic Input Output System)—A protocol designed by IBM to provide Transport and Session layer services for applications running on small, homogeneous networks.

NetBIOS Enhanced User Interface—See *NetBEUI*.

NetDrive—The client software that enables Windows workstations to connect to a NetWare 6.5 server using standard Internet protocols, such as FTP and HTTP. After connecting through NetDrive, a user can navigate the server's directories and manage files as if navigating a Windows hard disk.

NETMON—Novell's network monitoring NLM. NETMON is included in NetWare 5.x and 6.x.

netstat—A TCP/IP troubleshooting utility that displays statistics and the state of current TCP/IP connections. It also displays ports, which can signal whether services are using the correct ports.

NetStorage—A TCP/IP-based tool from Novell that allows users to navigate directories and manage files on a NetWare 6.x server.

NetWare 3.x—The group of NetWare versions that includes versions 3.0, 3.1, and 3.2.

NetWare 4.x—The group of NetWare versions that includes versions 4.0, 4.1, and 4.11.

NetWare 5.x—The group of NetWare versions that includes versions 5.0, 5.1, and 5.11.

NetWare 6.x—The group of NetWare versions that includes versions 6.0 and 6.5.

NetWare Directory Services—See *NDS*.

NetWare Integrated Kernel—The core of NetWare 6.x's operating system. The NetWare Integrated Kernel manages multiprocessing, multithreading, and access to the server's interrupts, memory, and I/O address space.

NetWare loadable module—See *NLM*.

network—A group of computers and other devices (such as printers) that are connected by and can exchange data via some type of transmission media, such as a cable, a wire, or the atmosphere.

network access method—See *access method*.

network adapter—See *NIC*.

network address—A unique identifying number for a network node that follows a hierarchical addressing scheme and can be assigned through operating system software. Network addresses are added to data packets and interpreted by protocols at the Network layer of the OSI Model.

Network Address Translation—See *NAT*.

network analyzer—See *protocol analyzer*.

network attached storage—See *NAS*.

Network Basic Input Output System—See *NetBIOS*.

network class—A classification for TCP/IP-based networks that pertains to the network's potential size and is indicated by an IP address's network ID and subnet mask. Network classes A, B, and C are commonly used by clients on LANs; network classes D and E are reserved for special purposes.

Network File System—See *NFS*.

network ID—The portion of an IP address common to all nodes on the same network or subnet.

network interface card—See *NIC*.

network key—A key (or character string) required for a wireless station to associate with an access point using WEP.

Network layer—The third layer in the OSI Model. Protocols in the Network layer translate network addresses into their physical counterparts and decide how to route data from the sender to the receiver.

Network layer address—See *network address*.

network management—The assessment, monitoring, and maintenance of the devices and connections on a network.

Network Monitor—A network monitoring program that comes with Windows Server 2003 (as well as with Windows NT and Windows 2000 Server).

network monitor—A software-based tool that monitors traffic on the network from a server or work-station attached to the network. Network monitors typically can interpret up to Layer 3 of the OSI Model.

Network News Transport Protocol—See *NNTP*.

network number—See *network ID*.

network operating system—See *NOS*.

network prefix—See *network ID*.

network service provider—See *NSP*.

network services—The functions provided by a network.

Network Termination 1—See *NT1*.

Network Termination 2—See *NT2*.

Network Time Protocol—See *NTP*.

network virus—A virus that takes advantage of network protocols, commands, messaging programs, and data links to propagate itself. Although all viruses could theoretically travel across network connections, network viruses are specially designed to attack network vulnerabilities.

Network+ (Net+)—The professional certification established by CompTIA that verifies broad, vendor-independent networking technology skills such as an understanding of protocols, topologies, networking hardware, and network troubleshooting.

New Technology File System—See *NTFS*.

newsgroup—An Internet-based forum for exchanging messages on a particular topic. Newsgroups rely on NNTP for the collection and dissemination of messages.

NFS (Network File System)—A popular remote file system created by Sun Microsystems, and available for UNIX-type of systems.

NIC (network interface card)—The device that enables a workstation to connect to the network and communicate with other computers. NICs are manufactured by several different companies and come with a variety of specifications that are tailored to the workstation's and the network's requirements. NICs are also called network adapters.

NLM (NetWare loadable module)—A routine associated with a particular NetWare application or ser-vice. Each NLM consumes some of the server's memory and processor resources (at least temporarily). The kernel requires many NLMs to run NetWare's core operating system.

NNTP (Network News Transport Protocol)—An Application layer protocol in the TCP/IP suite which facilitates the exchange of newsgroup messages, or articles, between multiple servers and users.

node—A computer or other device connected to a network, which has a unique address and is capable of sending or receiving data.

noise—The unwanted signals, or interference, from sources near network cabling, such as electrical motors, power lines, and radar.

NOS (network operating system)—The software that runs on a server and enables the server to manage data, users, groups, security, applications, and other networking functions. The most popular network operating systems are Microsoft Windows NT, Windows 2000 Server, and Windows Server 2003, UNIX, Linux, and Novell NetWare.

Novell Storage Services—See *NSS*.

nslookup—A TCP/IP utility that allows you to look up the DNS host name of a network node by specifying its IP address, or vice versa. This ability is useful for verifying that a host is configured correctly and for troubleshooting DNS resolution problems.

NSP (network service provider)—A carrier that provides long-distance (and often global) connectivity between major data-switching centers across the Internet. AT&T, PSINet, Sprintlink, and UUNET (MCI Worldcom) are all examples of network service providers. Customers, including ISPs, can lease dedicated private or public Internet connections from an NSP.

NSS (Novell Storage Services)—The 64-bit file access and storage system installed by default and preferred for use on NetWare 6.x servers. NSS offers several benefits over traditional file systems such as FAT, including faster access, more efficient use of memory, support for files or directories as large as 8 TB, and up to a trillion files in a single directory.

NT1 (Network Termination 1)—A device used on ISDN networks that connects the incoming twisted-pair wiring with the customer's ISDN terminal equipment.

NT2 (Network Termination 2)—An additional connection device required on PRI to handle the multiple ISDN lines between the customer's network termination connection and the local phone company's wires.

Nterprise Linux Services—A group of tools and programs for integrating Linux computers into a NetWare 6.5 network. Nterprise Linux Services consists of client tools for accessing eDirectory, development tools for use with DirXML, plus browser-based file and print services.

NTFS (New Technology File System)—A file system developed by Microsoft for use with its Windows NT, Windows 2000 Server, and Windows Server 2003 operating systems. NTFS integrates reliability, compression, the ability to handle massive files, system security, and fast access. Most Windows Server 2003 partitions employ NTFS.

NTP (Network Time Protocol)—A simple Application layer protocol in the TCP/IP suite used to synchronize the clocks of computers on a network. NTP depends on UDP for Transport layer services.

object—A representation of a thing or person associated with the network that belongs in the NOS directory. Objects include users, printers, groups, computers, data files, and applications.

object class—See *class*.

OC (Optical Carrier)—An internationally recognized rating that indicates throughput rates for SONET connections.

octet—One of the four 8-bit bytes that are separated by periods and together make up an IP address.

offline UPS—See *standby UPS*.

ohmmeter—A device used to measure resistance in an electrical circuit.

omnidirectional antenna—A type of antenna that issues and receives wireless signals with equal strength and clarity in all directions. This type of antenna is used when many different receivers must be able to pick up the signal, or when the receiver's location is highly mobile.

on-board NIC—A NIC that is integrated into a computer's motherboard, rather than connected via an expansion slot or peripheral bus.

on-board port—A port that is integrated into a computer's motherboard.

online backup—A technique in which data is backed up to a central location over the Internet.

online UPS—A power supply that uses the A/C power from the wall outlet to continuously charge its battery, while providing power to a network device through its battery.

Open Directory—The version of OpenLDAP by Apple Computer that is included with Mac OS X Server.

Open Shortest Path First—See *OSPF*.

open source software—The term used to describe software that is distributed with few restrictions and whose source code is freely available.

Open Systems Interconnection Model—See *OSI (Open Systems Interconnection) Model*.

OpenLDAP—A popular open source application included with many Linux distributions that implements LDAP.

OpenSSH—An open source version of the SSH suite of protocols.

Optical Carrier—See *OC*.

optical loss—The degradation of a light signal on a fiber-optic network.

optical media—A type of media capable of storing digitized data, which uses a laser to write data to it and read data from it.

optical time domain reflectometer—See *OTDR*.

organizational unit—See *OU*.

OSI (Open Systems Interconnection) Model—A model for understanding and developing computer-to-computer communication developed in the 1980s by ISO. It divides networking functions among seven layers: Physical, Data Link, Network, Transport, Session, Presentation, and Application.

OSPF (Open Shortest Path First)—A routing protocol that makes up for some of the limitations of RIP and can coexist with RIP on a network.

OTDR (optical time domain reflectometer)—A performance testing device for use with fiber-optic networks. An OTDR works by issuing a light-based signal on a fiber-optic cable and measuring the way in which the signal bounces back (or reflects) to the OTDR. By measuring the length of time it takes the signal to return, an OTDR can determine the location of a fault.

OU (organizational unit)—A logical receptacle for holding objects with similar characteristics or privileges in an NOS directory. Containers form the branches of the directory tree.

overhead—The nondata information that must accompany data in order for a signal to be properly routed and interpreted by the network.

P2P network—See *peer-to-peer network*.

Packet Internet Groper—See *PING*.

packet switching—A type of switching in which data is broken into packets before it is transported. In packet switching, packets can travel any path on the network to their destination, because each packet contains a destination address and sequencing information.

packet-filtering firewall—A router that operates at the Data Link and Transport layers of the OSI Model, examining the header of every packet of data that it receives to determine whether that type of packet is authorized to continue to its destination. Packet-filtering firewalls are also called screening firewalls.

padding—The bytes added to the data (or information) portion of an Ethernet frame to ensure this field is at least 46 bytes in size. Padding has no effect on the data carried by the frame.

page file—A file on the hard disk that is used for virtual memory.

paging—The process of moving blocks of information, called pages, between RAM and into a page file on disk.

paging file—See *page file*.

PAN (personal area network)—A small (usually home) network composed of personal communications devices.

PAP (Password Authentication Protocol)—A simple authentication protocol that operates over PPP. Using PAP, a client issues its credentials in a request to authenticate, and the server responds with a confirmation or denial of authentication after comparing the credentials to those in its database. PAP is not very secure and is therefore rarely used on modern networks.

parallel backbone—A type of backbone that consists of more than one connection from the central router or switch to each network segment.

parity—The mechanism used to verify the integrity of data by making the number of bits in a byte sum equal to either an odd or even number.

parity error checking—The process of comparing the parity of data read from a disk with the type of parity used by the system.

partial mesh WAN—A version of a mesh topology WAN in which only critical sites are directly interconnected and secondary sites are connected through star or ring topologies. Partial mesh WANs are less expensive to implement than full mesh WANs.

partition—An area of a computer's hard disk that is logically defined and acts as a separate disk drive.

passive hub—A hub that simply retransmits signals over the network.

passive scanning—In the context of wireless networking, the process in which a station listens to several channels within a frequency range for a beacon issued by an access point.

Password Authentication Protocol—See *PAP*.

patch—A correction, improvement, or enhancement to part of a software application, often distributed at no charge by software vendors to fix a bug in their code or to add slightly more functionality.

patch cable—A relatively short section (usually between 3 and 25 feet) of cabling with connectors on both ends.

patch panel—A wall-mounted panel of data receptors into which cross-connect patch cables from the punch-down block are inserted.

pattern—In the context of installing the NetWare NOS, a choice of server type to install (for example, Basic NetWare File Server). Based on the pattern, the installation program will include files necessary for specific services or, if the Customized NetWare Server pattern is selected, prompt the user to select which services should be installed.

PBX (private branch exchange)—A telephone switch used to connect calls within a private organization.

PC Card—A PCMCIA standard that specifies a 16-bit interface running at 8 MHz for externally attached devices. PC Cards' characteristics match those of the ISA expansion card. And like the ISA standard, the PC Card standard suffered from its lower data transfer rates, compared to other PCMCIA standards.

PCI (Peripheral Component Interconnect)—A 32 or 64-bit bus that can run at 33 or 66 MHz, introduced in its original form in the 1990s. The PCI bus is the NIC connection type used for nearly all new PCs. It's characterized by a shorter length than ISA or EISA cards, but has a much faster data transmission capability.

PCI Express—A 64-bit bus standard capable of transferring data at up to 500 MBps in full-duplex transmission. PCI Express was introduced in 2002. It follows a new type of bus design and offers several advantages over the old PCI, and its expansion cards can fit into older PCI slots, with some modifications to the motherboard. Manufacturers predict PCI Express will replace PCI in the coming years.

PCIe—See *PCI Express*.

PCIx—See *PCI Express*.

PCMCIA (Personal Computer Memory Card International Association)—A group of computer manufacturers who developed an interface for connecting any type of device to a portable computer. PCMCIA slots may hold memory, modem, network interface, external hard disk, or CD-ROM cards. PCMCIA-standard cards include PC Card, CardBus, and the newest, ExpressCard.

PD (powered device)—On a network using Power over Ethernet, a node that receives power from power sourcing equipment.

PDA (personal digital assistant)—A handheld computer. PDAs normally use a stylus for user input and often communicate via infrared or another wireless signaling method.

PDU (protocol data unit)—A unit of data at any layer of the OSI Model.

peer-to-peer network—A network in which every computer can communicate directly with every other computer. By default, no computer on a peer-to-peer network has more authority than another. However, each computer can be configured to share only some of its resources and keep other resources inaccessible to other nodes on the network.

per seat—In the context of applications, a licensing mode that limits access to an application to specific users or workstations. In the context of Microsoft's Windows Server 2003, a licensing mode that requires a license for every client capable of connecting to the Windows Server 2003 server.

per server—A Windows Server 2003 licensing mode that allows a limited number of clients to access the server simultaneously. (The number is determined by your Windows Server 2003 purchase agreement.) The restriction applies to the number of concurrent connections, rather than specific clients. Per server mode is the most popular choice for installing Windows Server 2003.

per user—A licensing mode that allows a fixed quantity of clients to use one software package simultaneously.

performance management—The ongoing assessment of how well network links, devices, and components keep up with demands on them.

Peripheral Component Interconnect—See *PCI*.

permanent virtual circuit—See *PVC*.

personal area network—See *PAN*.

Personal Computer Memory Card International Association—See *PCMCIA*.

personal digital assistant—See *PDA*.

PGP (Pretty Good Privacy)—A key-based encryption system for e-mail that uses a two-step verification process.

phase—A point or stage in a wave's progress over time.

physical address—See *MAC address*.

Physical layer—The lowest, or first, layer of the OSI Model. Protocols in the Physical layer generate and detect voltage so as to transmit and receive signals carrying data over a network medium. These protocols also set the data transmission rate and monitor data error rates, but do not provide error correction.

physical memory—The RAM chips installed on the computer's system board that provide dedicated memory to that computer.

physical topology—The physical layout of a network. A physical topology depicts a network in broad scope; it does not specify devices, connectivity methods, or addresses on the network. Physical topologies are categorized into three fundamental geometric shapes: bus, ring, and star. These shapes can be mixed to create hybrid topologies.

piconet—A PAN (personal area network) that relies on Bluetooth transmission technology.

pilot network—A small-scale network that stands in for the larger network. A pilot network may be used to evaluate the effects of network changes or additions.

PING (Packet Internet Groper)—A TCP/IP troubleshooting utility that can verify that TCP/IP is installed, bound to the NIC, configured correctly, and communicating with the network. PING uses ICMP to send echo request and echo reply messages that determine the validity of an IP address.

ping—To send an echo request signal from one node on a TCP/IP-based network to another, using the PING utility. See also *PING*.

pipe—A character that enables you to combine existing commands to form new commands. The pipe symbol is the vertical bar ("|").

pipeline—A series of two or more commands in which the output of prior commands is sent to the input of subsequent commands.

plain old telephone service (POTS)—See *PSTN*.

plenum—The area above the ceiling tile or below the subfloor in a building.

PoE (Power over Ethernet)—A method of delivering current to devices using Ethernet connection cables.

Point-to-Point Protocol—See *PPP*.

Point-to-Point Protocol over Ethernet—See *PPPoE*.

Point-to-Point Tunneling Protocol—See *PPTP*.

point-to-point—A data transmission that involves one transmitter and one receiver.

polling—A network management application's regular collection of data from managed devices.

polymorphic virus—A type of virus that changes its characteristics (such as the arrangement of its bytes, size, and internal instructions) every time it is transferred to a new system, making it harder to identify.

pool—A collection of storage objects in NetWare 6.x.

POP (Post Office Protocol)—An Application layer protocol used to retrieve messages from a mail server. When a client retrieves mail via POP, messages previously stored on the mail server are downloaded to the client's workstation, and then deleted from the mail server.

POP3 (Post Office Protocol, version 3)—The most commonly used form of the Post Office Protocol.

populated segment—A network segment that contains end nodes, such as workstations.

port forwarding—The process of redirecting traffic from its normally assigned port to a different port, either on the client or server. In the case of using SSH, port forwarding can send data exchanges that are normally insecure through encrypted tunnels.

port number—The address on a host where an application makes itself available to incoming data.

Post Office Protocol—See *POP*.

Post Office Protocol, version 3—See *POP3*.

POTS—See *PSTN*.

Power over Ethernet—See *PoE*.

power sourcing equipment—See *PSE*.

powered device—See *PD*.

PowerPC—The brand of computer central processing unit invented by Apple Computer, IBM, and Motorola, Inc., and used in Apple computers and IBM servers.

PPP (Point-to-Point Protocol)—A communications protocol that enables a workstation to connect to a server using a serial connection. PPP can support multiple Network layer protocols and can use both asynchronous and synchronous communications. It performs compression and error correction and requires little configuration on the client workstation.

PPPoE (Point-to-Point Protocol over Ethernet)—PPP running over an Ethernet network.

PPTP (Point-to-Point Tunneling Protocol)—A Layer 2 protocol developed by Microsoft that encapsulates PPP data for transmission over VPN connections. PPTP operates with Windows RRAS access services and can accept connections from multiple different clients. It is simple, but less secure than other modern tunneling protocols.

preamble—The field in an Ethernet frame that signals to the receiving node that data is incoming and indicates when the data flow is about to begin.

predecessor—A task in a project that must be completed before other tasks can begin.

preemptive multitasking—The type of multitasking in which tasks are actually performed one at a time, in very brief succession. In preemptive multitasking, one program uses the processor for a certain period of time, then is suspended to allow another program to use the processor.

Presentation layer—The sixth layer of the OSI Model. Protocols in the Presentation layer translate between the application and the network. Here, data are formatted in a schema that the network can understand, with the format varying according to the type of network used. The Presentation layer also manages data encryption and decryption, such as the scrambling of system passwords.

Pretty Good Privacy—See *PGP*.

PRI (Primary Rate Interface)—A type of ISDN that uses 23 bearer channels and one 64-Kbps data channel, represented by the notation 23B+D. PRI is less commonly used by individual subscribers than BRI, but it may be used by businesses and other organizations needing more throughput.

principal—In Kerberos terminology, a user or client.

print services—The network service that allows printers to be shared by several users on a network.

printer queue—A logical representation of a networked printer's functionality. To use a printer, clients must have access to the printer queue.

private branch exchange – See *PBX*.

private key encryption—A type of key encryption in which the sender and receiver use a key to which only they have access. DES (data encryption standard), which was developed by IBM in the 1970s, is a popular example of a private key encryption technique. Private key encryption is also known as symmetric encryption.

probe—In 802.11 wireless networking, a type of frame issued by a station during active scanning to find nearby access points.

process—A routine of sequential instructions that runs until it has achieved its goal. For example, a spreadsheet program is a process.

project management—The practice of managing staff, budget, timelines, and other resources and variables to complete a specific goal within given bounds.

project plan—The way in which details of a managed project (for example, the timeline and the significant tasks) are organized. Some project plans are created via special project planning software, such as Microsoft Project.

promiscuous mode—The feature of a network adapter that allows it to pick up all frames that pass over the network—not just those destined for the node served by the card.

proprietary UNIX—Any implementation of UNIX for which the source code is either unavailable or available only by purchasing a licensed copy from The SCO Group (costing as much as millions of dollars). Redistribution of proprietary UNIX versions requires paying royalties to The SCO Group.

protocol—A standard method or format for communication between network devices. Protocols ensure that data are transferred whole, in sequence, and without error from one node on the network to another.

protocol analyzer—A software package or hardware-based tool that can capture and analyze data on a network. Protocol analyzers are more sophisticated than network monitoring tools, as they can typically interpret data up to Layer 7 of the OSI Model.

protocol data unit—See *PDU*.

proxy—See *proxy server*.

proxy server—A network host that runs a proxy service. Proxy servers may also be called gateways.

proxy service—A software application on a network host that acts as an intermediary between the external and internal networks, screening all incoming and outgoing traffic and providing one address to the outside world, instead of revealing the addresses of internal LAN devices.

PSE (power sourcing equipment)—On a network using Power over Ethernet, the device that supplies power to end nodes.

PSTN (Public Switched Telephone Network)—The traditional telephone network, from the lines that connect homes and businesses to the network centers that connect different regions of a country. Now, except for the local loop, nearly all of the PSTN uses digital transmission. Its traffic is carried by fiber-optic and copper twisted-pair cable, microwave, and satellite connections.

public key encryption—A form of key encryption in which data is encrypted using two keys: One is a key known only to a user, and the other is a key associated with the user and can be obtained from a public source, such as a public key server. Some examples of public key algorithms include RSA (named after its creators, Rivest, Shamir, and Adleman), Diffie-Hellman, and Elliptic-curve cryptography. Public key encryption is also known as asymmetric encryption.

public key server—A publicly available host (such as an Internet host) that provides free access to a list of users' public keys (for use in public key encryption).

Public Switched Telephone Network—See *PSTN*.

punch-down block—A panel of data receptors into which horizontal cabling from the workstations is inserted.

PVC (permanent virtual circuit)—A point-to-point connection over which data may follow any number of different paths, as opposed to a dedicated line that follows a predefined path. X.25, Frame Relay, and some forms of ATM use PVCs.

quality of service (QoS)—The result of standards for delivering data within a certain period of time after their transmission. For example, ATM networks can supply four QoS levels, from a "best effort" attempt for noncritical data to a guaranteed, real-time transmission for time-sensitive data.

radiation pattern—The relative strength over a three-dimensional area of all the electromagnetic energy an antenna sends or receives.

radiofrequency interference—See *RFI*.

RADIUS (Remote Authentication Dial-In User Service)—A protocol that runs over UDP and provides centralized network authentication and accounting for multiple users. RADIUS is commonly used with dial-up networking, VPNs, and wireless connections.

RADIUS server—A server that offers centralized authentication services to a network's access server, VPN server, or wireless access point via the RADIUS protocol.

RAID (Redundant Array of Independent (or Inexpensive) Disks)—A server redundancy measure that uses shared, multiple physical or logical hard disks to ensure data integrity and availability. Some RAID designs also increase storage capacity and improve performance. See also *disk mirroring* and *disk striping*.

RAID Level 0—An implementation of RAID in which data is written in 64-KB blocks equally across all disks in the array.

RAID Level 1—An implementation of RAID that provides redundancy through disk mirroring, in which data from one disk is automatically copied to another disk as the information is written.

RAID Level 3—An implementation of RAID that uses disk striping for data and writes parity error correction code on a separate parity disk.

RAID Level 5—The most popular fault-tolerant data storage technique in use today, RAID Level 5 writes data in small blocks across several disks. At the same time, it writes parity error checking information among several disks.

range—The geographical area in which signals issued from an antenna or wireless system can be consistently and accurately received.

RARP (Reverse Address Resolution Protocol)—A core protocol in the TCP/IP suite that belongs in the Network layer of the OSI Model. RARP relies on a RARP table to associate the IP (logical) address of a node with its MAC (physical) address. RARP can be used to supply IP addresses to diskless workstations.

RAS (Remote Access Service)—The dial-up networking software provided with Microsoft Windows 95, 98, NT, and 2000 client operating systems and Windows NT and 2000 network operating systems. RAS requires software installed on both the client and server, a server configured to accept incoming clients, and a client with sufficient privileges (including user name and password) on the server to access its resources. In more recent versions of Windows, RAS has been incorporated into the RRAS (Routing and Remote Access Service).

RC4—An asymmetric key encryption technique that weaves a key with data multiple times as a computer issues the stream of data. RC4 keys can be as long as 2048 bits. In addition to being highly secure, RC4 is fast.

RDN (relative distinguished name)—An attribute of an object that identifies the object separately from its related container(s) and domain. For most objects, the relative distinguished name is the same as its common name (CN) in the distinguished name convention.

RDP (Remote Desktop Protocol)—An Application layer protocol that uses TCP/IP to transmit graphics and text quickly over a remote client-host connection. RDP also carries session, licensing, and encryption information.

reassembly—The process of reconstructing data units that have been segmented.

reassociation—In the context of wireless networking, the process of a station establishing a connection (or associating) with a different access point.

recordable DVD—An optical storage medium that can hold up to 4.7 GB on one single-layered side. Both sides of the disc can be used, and each side can have up to two layers. Thus, in total, a double-layered, two-sided DVD can store up to 17 GB of data. Recordable DVDs come in several different formats.

redirector—A service that runs on a client workstation and determines whether the client's request should be handled by the client or the server.

redundancy—The use of more than one identical component, device, or connection for storing, processing, or transporting data. Redundancy is the most common method of achieving fault tolerance.

Redundant Array of Independent (or Inexpensive) Disks—See *RAID*.

reflection—In the context of wireless, the phenomenon that occurs when an electromagnetic wave encounters an obstacle and bounces back toward its source. A wireless signal will bounce off objects whose dimensions are large compared to the signal's average wavelength.

regeneration—The process of retransmitting a digital signal. Regeneration, unlike amplification, repeats the pure signal, with none of the noise it has accumulated.

Regional Internet Registry—See *RIR*.

Registered Ports—TCP/IP ports in the range of 1024 to 49151. These ports are accessible to network users and processes that do not have special administrative privileges. Default assignments of these ports must be registered with IANA.

relative distinguished name—See *RDN*.

release—The act of terminating a DHCP lease.

remote access—A method for connecting and logging on to a LAN from a workstation that is remote, or not physically connected, to the LAN. Remote access can be accomplished by one of many ways, including dial-up connections, terminal services, remote control, or Web portals.

remote access server—A server that runs communications services that enable remote users to log on to a network. Also known as a communications server or access server.

Remote Access Service—See *RAS*.

Remote Authentication Dial-In User Service—See *RADIUS*.

remote control—A remote access method in which the remote user dials into a workstation that is directly attached to a LAN. Software running on both the remote user's computer and the LAN computer allows the remote user to "take over" the LAN workstation. Only keystrokes, mouse clicks, and screen updates are exchanged between the two computers.

Remote Desktop—An optional feature in Windows XP operating systems that allows a Windows XP computer to be remotely controlled from a client running the Windows 95, 98, Me, NT, XP, 2000, or

Server 2003 operating system. Remote Desktop is also the program Windows XP clients use to connect with computers using Windows Terminal Server.

Remote Desktop Protocol—See *RDP*.

Remote Manager—A browser-based tool that enables network administrators to perform server and object management in NetWare 6.5.

remote user—A person working on a computer on a different network or in a different geographical location from the LAN's server.

removable disk drive—See *external disk drive*.

Rendezvous—Apple Computer's implementation of the Zeroconf group of protocols.

repeater—A device used to regenerate a signal.

replication—The process of copying Active Directory data to multiple domain controllers. This ensures redundancy so that in case one of the domain controllers fails, clients can still log on to the network, be authenticated, and access resources.

Request to Send/Clear to Send—See *RTS/CTS*.

resolver—Any host on the Internet that needs to look up domain name information.

resource record—The element of a DNS database stored on a name server that contains information about TCP/IP host names and their addresses.

resources—The devices, data, and data storage space provided by a computer, whether standalone or shared.

restore—The process of retrieving files from a backup. It is necessary to restore files if the original files are lost or deleted.

Reverse Address Resolution Protocol—See *RARP*.

RFI (radiofrequency interference)—A kind of interference that may be generated by broadcast signals from radio or TV towers.

RG-6—A type of coaxial cable used for television, satellite, and broadband cable connections.

Rijndael—The algorithm used for AES encryption.

ring topology—A network layout in which each node is connected to the two nearest nodes so that the entire network forms a circle. Data is transmitted unidirectionally around the ring. Each workstation accepts and responds to packets addressed to it, then forwards the other packets to the next workstation in the ring.

ring topology WAN—A type of WAN in which each site is connected to two other sites so that the entire WAN forms a ring pattern.

RIP (Routing Information Protocol)—The oldest routing protocol that is still widely used, RIP does not work in very large network environments in which data may have to travel through more than 15 routers to reach their destination (for example, on the Internet). And, compared to other routing protocols, RIP is slower and less secure.

RIR (Regional Internet Registry)—A not-for-profit agency that manages the distribution of IP addresses to private and public entities. ARIN is the RIR for North, Central, and South America and sub-Saharan Africa. APNIC is the RIR for Asia and the Pacific region. RIPE is the RIR for Europe and North Africa.

risers—The backbone cabling that provides vertical connections between floors of a building.

RJ-11 (Registered Jack 11)—The standard connector used with unshielded twisted-pair cabling (usually CAT 3 or Level 1) to connect analog telephones.

RJ-45 (Registered Jack 45)—The standard connector used with shielded twisted-pair and unshielded twisted-pair cabling.

root—A highly privileged user ID that has all rights to create, delete, modify, move, read, write, or execute files on a system. This term may also refer to the network administrator.

root domain—In Windows Server 2003 networking, the single domain from which child domains branch out in a domain tree.

root server—A DNS server maintained by ICANN and IANA that is an authority on how to contact the top-level domains, such as those ending with .com, .edu, .net, .us, and so on. ICANN oversees the operation of 13 root servers around the world.

round trip time—See *RTT*.

routable—Protocols that can span more than one LAN because they carry Network layer and addressing information that can be interpreted by a router.

route—To direct data intelligently between networks based on addressing, patterns of usage, and availability of network segments.

router—A multiport device that operates at Layer 3 of the OSI Model and uses logical addressing information to direct data between networks or segments. Routers can connect dissimilar LANs and WANs running at different transmission speeds and using a variety of Network layer protocols. They determine the best path between nodes based on traffic congestion, available versus unavailable routes, load balancing targets, and other factors.

Routing and Remote Access service (RRAS)—The software included with Windows NT, Windows 2000 Server, and Windows Server 2003 that enables a server to act as a router, firewall, and remote access server. Using RRAS, a server can provide network access to multiple remote clients.

Routing Information Protocol—See *RIP*.

routing protocols—The means by which routers communicate with each other about network status. Routing protocols determine the best path for data to take between nodes.

routing switch—See *Layer 3 switch*.

RRAS—See *Routing and Remote Access Service*.

RSA—An encryption algorithm that creates a key by randomly choosing two large prime numbers and multiplying them together. RSA is named after its creators, Ronald Rivest, Adi Shamir, and Leonard Adleman. RSA was released in 1977, but remains popular today for e-commerce transactions.

RTS/CTS (Request to Send/Clear to Send)—An exchange in which a wireless station requests the exclusive right to communicate with an access point and the access point confirms that it has granted that request.

RTT (round trip time)—The length of time it takes for a packet to go from sender to receiver, then back from receiver to sender. RTT is usually measured in milliseconds.

runt—A packet that is smaller than the medium's minimum packet size. For instance, any Ethernet packet that is smaller than 64 bytes is considered a runt.

sag—See *brownout*.

Samba—An open source software package that provides complete Windows-style file- and printer-sharing capabilities.

SAN (storage area network)—A distinct network of multiple storage devices and servers that provides fast, highly available, and highly fault-tolerant access to large quantities of data for a client/server network. A SAN uses a proprietary network transmission method (such as Fibre Channel) rather than a traditional network transmission method such as Ethernet.

satellite return—A type of satellite Internet access service in which a subscriber sends and receives data to and from the Internet over the satellite link. This is a symmetrical technology, in which both upstream and downstream throughputs are advertised to reach 400–500 Kbps; in reality, throughput is often higher.

SC (Subscriber Connector or Standard Connector)—A connector used with single-mode or multimode fiber-optic cable.

scalable—The property of a network that allows you to add nodes or increase its size easily.

scanning—The process a wireless station undergoes to find an access point. See also *active scanning* and *passive scanning*.

scattering—The diffusion of a wireless signal that results from hitting an object that has smaller dimensions compared to the signal's wavelength. Scattering is also related to the roughness of the surface a wireless signal encounters. The rougher the surface, the more likely a signal is to scatter when it hits that surface.

scatternet—A network composed of multiple piconets using Bluetooth transmission technology.

schema—The description of object types, or classes, and their required and optional attributes that are stored in an NOS's directory.

SCP (Secure CoPy)—A method for copying files securely between hosts. SCP is part of the OpenSSH package, which comes with most modern UNIX-type of operating systems. Third-party SCP applications are available for Windows-based computers.

screening firewall—See *packet-filtering firewall*.

SDH (Synchronous Digital Hierarchy)—The international equivalent of SONET.

Secure CoPy—See *SCP*.

Secure Shell—See *SSH*.

Secure Sockets Layer—See *SSL*.

security audit—An assessment of an organization's security vulnerabilities. A security audit should be performed at least annually and preferably quarterly—or sooner if the network has undergone significant changes. For each risk found, it should rate the severity of a potential breach, as well as its likelihood.

security policy—A document or plan that identifies an organization's security goals, risks, levels of authority, designated security coordinator and team members, responsibilities for each team member, and responsibilities for each employee. In addition, it specifies how to address security breaches.

segment—A part of a network. Usually, a segment is composed of a group of nodes that share the same communications channel for all their traffic.

segmentation—The process of decreasing the size of data units when moving data from a network that can handle larger data units to a network that can handle only smaller data units.

self-healing—A characteristic of dual-ring topologies that allows them to automatically reroute traffic along the backup ring if the primary ring becomes severed.

Sequenced Packet Exchange—See *SPX*.

sequencing—The process of assigning a placeholder to each piece of a data block to allow the receiving node's Transport layer to reassemble the data in the correct order.

serial backbone—A type of backbone that consists of two or more internetworking devices connected to each other by a single cable in a daisy-chain fashion. Hubs are often connected in this way to extend a network.

Serial Line Internet Protocol—See *SLIP*.

server—A computer on the network that manages shared resources. Servers usually have more processing power, memory, and hard disk space than clients. They run network operating software that can manage not only data, but also users, groups, security, and applications on the network.

Server Message Block—See *SMB*.

server mirroring—A fault-tolerance technique in which one server duplicates the transactions and data storage of another, identical server. Server mirroring requires a link between the servers and software running on both servers so that the servers can continually synchronize their actions and one can take over in case the other fails.

server_hello—In the context of SSL encryption, a message issued from the server to the client that confirms the information the server received in the client_hello message. It also agrees to certain terms of encryption based on the options the client supplied. Depending on the Web server's preferred encryption method, the server may choose to issue your browser a public key or a digital certificate at this time.

service pack—A significant patch to one of the Microsoft Windows operating systems.

Service Set Identifier—See *SSID*.

session—A connection for data exchange between two parties. The term "session" may be used in the context of Web, remote access, or terminal and mainframe communications, for example.

session key—In the context of Kerberos authentication, a key issued to both the client and the server by the authentication service that uniquely identifies their session.

Session layer—The fifth layer in the OSI Model. The Session layer establishes and maintains communication between two nodes on the network. It can be considered the "traffic cop" for network communications.

SFD (start-of-frame delimiter)—A 1-byte field that indicates where the data field begins in an Ethernet frame.

SFTP (Secure File Transfer Protocol)—A protocol available with the proprietary version of SSH that copies files between hosts securely. Like FTP, SFTP first establishes a connection with a host and then allows a remote user to browse directories, list files, and copy files. Unlike FTP, SFTP encrypts data before transmitting it.

shared Ethernet—A version of Ethernet in which all the nodes share a common channel and a fixed amount of bandwidth.

sheath—The outer cover, or jacket, of a cable.

shell—Another term for the UNIX command interpreter.

shielded twisted-pair—See *STP*.

signal bounce—A phenomenon, caused by improper termination on a bus-topology network, in which signals travel endlessly between the two ends of the network, preventing new signals from getting through.

signal level—An ANSI standard for T-carrier technology that refers to its Physical layer electrical signaling characteristics. DS0 is the equivalent of one data or voice channel. All other signal levels are multiples of DS0.

signature scanning—The comparison of a file's content with known virus signatures (unique identifying characteristics in the code) in a signature database to determine whether the file is a virus.

Simple Mail Transfer Protocol—See *SMTP*.

Simple Network Management Protocol—See *SNMP*.

simplex—A type of transmission in which signals may travel in only one direction over a medium.

single point of failure—A device or connection on a network that, were it to fail, could cause the entire network to stop functioning.

single-mode fiber—See *SMF*.

site license—A type of software license that, for a fixed price, allows any number of users in one location to legally access a program.

site selection—The process of determining optimal locations for access points on a wireless network.

slash notation—See *CIDR notation*.

SLIP (Serial Line Internet Protocol)—A communications protocol that enables a workstation to connect to a server using a serial connection. SLIP can support only asynchronous communications and IP traffic, and requires some configuration on the client workstation. SLIP has been made obsolete by PPP.

SMB (Server Message Block)—A protocol for communications and resource access between systems, such as clients and servers. SMB originated at IBM and then was adopted and further developed by

Microsoft for use on its Windows operating systems. The current version of SMB is known as the CIFS (Common Internet File System) protocol.

SMF (single-mode fiber)—A type of fiber-optic cable with a narrow core that carries light pulses along a single path data from one end of the cable to the other end. Data can be transmitted faster and for longer distances on single-mode fiber than on multimode fiber. However, single-mode fiber is more expensive.

SMTP (Simple Mail Transfer Protocol)—The Application layer TCP/IP subprotocol responsible for moving messages from one e-mail server to another.

snap-in—An administrative tool, such as Computer Management, that can be added to the MMC (Microsoft Management Console).

sneakernet—A way of exchanging data between computers that are not connected on a network. Sneakernet requires that data be copied from a computer to a removable storage device such as a floppy disk, carried (presumably by someone wearing sneakers) to another computer, then copied from the storage device onto the second computer.

SNMP (Simple Network Management Protocol)—An Application layer protocol in the TCP/IP suite used to convey data regarding the status of managed devices on a network.

social engineering—The act of manipulating personal relationships to circumvent network security measures and gain access to a system.

socket—A logical address assigned to a specific process running on a computer. Some sockets are reserved for operating system functions.

soft skills—The skills such as customer relations, leadership ability, and dependability, which are not easily measured, but are nevertheless important in a networking career.

softphone—A computer programmed to act like an IP telephone. Softphones present the caller with a graphical representation of a telephone dial pad and can connect to a network via a LAN, WAN, PPP dial-up connection, or leased line.

software distribution—The process of automatically transferring a data file or installing a software application from the server to a client on the network.

software RAID—A method of implementing RAID that uses software to implement and control RAID techniques over virtually any type of hard disk(s). RAID software may be a third-party package or utilities that come with an operating system NOS.

SOHO (small office-home office) router—A router designed for use on small office or home office networks. SOHO routers typically have no more than eight data ports and do not offer advanced features such as traffic prioritization, network management, or hardware redundancy.

Solaris—A proprietary implementation of the UNIX operating system by Sun Microsystems.

SONET (Synchronous Optical Network)—A high-bandwidth WAN signaling technique that specifies framing and multiplexing techniques at the Physical layer of the OSI Model. It can integrate many other WAN technologies (for example, T-carriers, ISDN, and ATM technology) and allows for simple link additions and removals. SONET's topology includes a double ring of fiber-optic cable, which results in very high fault tolerance.

source code—The computer instructions written in a programming language that is readable by humans. Source code must be translated into a form that is executable by the machine, typically called binary code (for the sequence of zeros and ones) or target code.

spam—An unsolicited, unwanted e-mail.

SPARC—The brand of computer central processing unit invented by and used in Sun Microsystems servers.

spectrum analyzer—A tool that assesses the characteristics (for example, frequency, amplitude, and the effects of interference) of wireless signals.

sponsor—A person in a position of authority who supports a project and who can lobby for budget increases necessary to complete the project, appeal to a group of managers to extend a project's deadline, and assist with negotiating vendor contracts.

spread spectrum—A type of wireless transmission in which lower-level signals are distributed over several frequencies simultaneously. Spread spectrum transmission is more secure than narrowband.

SPX (Sequenced Packet Exchange)—One of the core protocols in the IPX/SPX suite. SPX belongs to the Transport layer of the OSI Model and works in tandem with IPX to ensure that data are received whole, in sequence, and error free.

SSH (Secure Shell)—A connection utility that provides authentication and encryption. With SSH, you can securely log on to a host, execute commands on that host, and copy files to or from that host. SSH encrypts data exchanged throughout the session.

SSID (Service Set Identifier)—A unique character string used to identify an access point on an 802.11 network.

SSL (Secure Sockets Layer)—A method of encrypting TCP/IP transmissions—including Web pages and data entered into Web forms—en route between the client and server using public key encryption technology.

SSL session—In the context of SSL encryption, an association between the client and server that is defined by an agreement on a specific set of encryption techniques. An SSL session allows the client and server to continue to exchange data securely as long as the client is still connected to the server. SSL sessions are established by the SSL handshake protocol.

ST (Straight Tip)—A connector used with single-mode or multimode fiber-optic cable.

stackable hub—A type of hub designed to be linked with other hubs in a single telecommunications closet. Stackable hubs linked together logically represent one large hub to the network.

stakeholder—Any person who may be affected by a project, for better or for worse. A stakeholder may be a project participant, user, manager, or vendor.

standalone computer—A computer that uses applications and data only from its local disks and that is not connected to a network.

standalone hub—A type of hub that serves a workgroup of computers that are separate from the rest of the network, also known as a workgroup hub.

standard—A documented agreement containing technical specifications or other precise criteria that are used as guidelines to ensure that materials, products, processes, and services suit their intended purpose.

Standard Connector—See *SC*.

standby UPS—A power supply that provides continuous voltage to a device by switching virtually instantaneously to the battery when it detects a loss of power from the wall outlet. Upon restoration of the power, the standby UPS switches the device to use A/C power again.

star topology—A physical topology in which every node on the network is connected through a central device, such as a hub. Any single physical wire on a star network connects only two devices, so a cabling problem will affect only two nodes. Nodes transmit data to the hub, which then retransmits the data to the rest of the network segment where the destination node can pick it up.

star topology WAN—A type of WAN in which a single site acts as the central connection point for several other points. This arrangement provides separate routes for data between any two sites; however, if the central connection point fails, the entire WAN fails.

start-of-frame delimiter (SFD)—See *SFD*.

star-wired bus topology—A hybrid topology in which groups of workstations are connected in a star fashion to hubs that are networked via a single bus.

star-wired ring topology—A hybrid topology that uses the physical layout of a star and the token-passing data transmission method.

static ARP table entry—A record in an ARP table that someone has manually entered using the ARP utility. Static ARP table entries remain the same until someone manually modifies them with the ARP utility.

static IP address—An IP address that is manually assigned to a device and remains constant until it is manually changed.

static routing—A technique in which a network administrator programs a router to use specific paths between nodes. Because it does not account for occasional network congestion, failed connections, or device moves, static routing is not optimal.

station—An end node on a network; used most often in the context of wireless networks.

statistical multiplexing—A method of multiplexing in which each node on a network is assigned a separate time slot for transmission, based on the node's priority and need.

stealth virus—A type of virus that hides itself to prevent detection. Typically, stealth viruses disguise themselves as legitimate programs or replace part of a legitimate program's code with their destructive code.

storage area network—See *SAN*.

store and forward mode—A method of switching in which a switch reads the entire data frame into its memory and checks it for accuracy before transmitting it. Although this method is more time-consuming than the cut-through method, it allows store and forward switches to transmit data more accurately.

STP (shielded twisted-pair)—A type of cable containing twisted-wire pairs that are not only individually insulated, but also surrounded by a shielding made of a metallic substance such as foil.

Straight Tip—See *ST*.

straight-through cable—A twisted-pair patch cable in which the wire terminations in both connectors follow the same scheme.

structured cabling—A method for uniform, enterprise-wide, multivendor cabling systems specified by the TIA/EIA 568 Commercial Building Wiring Standard. Structured cabling is based on a hierarchical design using a high-speed backbone.

subchannel—One of many distinct communication paths established when a channel is multiplexed or modulated.

subnet—A part of a network in which all nodes shares a network addressing component and a fixed amount of bandwidth.

subnet mask—A 32-bit number that, when combined with a device's IP address, indicates what kind of subnet the device belongs to.

subnetting—The process of subdividing a single class of network into multiple, smaller networks.

subprotocols—Small, specialized protocols that work together and belong to a protocol suite.

Subscriber Connector—See *SC*.

supernet—A type of subnet that is created using bits that normally would be reserved for network class information—by moving the subnet boundary to the left.

supernet mask—A 32-bit number that, when combined with a device's IP address, indicates the kind of supernet to which the device belongs.

supernetting—See *CIDR*.

supported services list—A document that lists every service and software package supported within an organization, plus the names of first- and second-level support contacts for those services or software packages.

surge—A momentary increase in voltage due to distant lightning strikes or electrical problems.

surge protector—A device that directs excess voltage away from equipment plugged into it and redirects it to a ground, thereby protecting the equipment from harm.

SVC (switched virtual circuit)—A logical, point-to-point connections that relies on switches to determine the optimal path between sender and receiver. ATM technology uses SVCs.

swap file—See *page file*.

switch—A connectivity device that logically subdivides a network into smaller, individual collision domains. A switch operates at the Data Link layer of the OSI Model and can interpret MAC address information to determine whether to filter (discard) or forward packets it receives.

switch—The letters or words added to a command that allow you to customize a utility's output. Switches are usually preceded by a hyphen or forward slash character.

switched Ethernet—An Ethernet model that enables multiple nodes to simultaneously transmit and receive data and individually take advantage of more bandwidth because they are assigned separate logical network segments through switching.

switched virtual circuit—See *SVC*.

switching—A component of a network's logical topology that manages how packets are filtered and forwarded between nodes on the network.

symmetric encryption—A method of encryption that requires the same key to encode the data as is used to decode the ciphertext.

symmetric multiprocessing—A method of multiprocessing that splits all operations equally among two or more processors. Windows Server 2003 supports this type of multiprocessing.

symmetrical—A characteristic of transmission technology that provides equal throughput for data traveling both upstream and downstream and is suited to users who both upload and download significant amounts of data.

symmetrical DSL—A variation of DSL that provides equal throughput both upstream and downstream between the customer and the carrier.

SYN (synchronization)—The packet one node sends to request a connection with another node on the network. The SYN packet is the first of three in the three-step process of establishing a connection.

SYN-ACK (synchronization-acknowledgment)—The packet a node sends to acknowledge to another node that it has received a SYN request for connection. The SYN-ACK packet is the second of three in the three-step process of establishing a connection.

synchronization—See *SYN*.

synchronization-acknowledgement—See *SYN-ACK*.

synchronous—A transmission method in which data being transmitted and received by nodes must conform to a timing scheme.

Synchronous Digital Hierarchy—See *SDH*.

Synchronous Optical Network—See *SONET*.

system bus—See *bus*.

System V—The proprietary version of UNIX that comes from Bell Labs.

T1—A digital carrier standard used in North America and most of Asia that provides 1.544-Mbps throughput and 24 channels for voice, data, video, or audio signals. T1s rely on time division multiplexing and may use shielded or unshielded twisted-pair, coaxial cable, fiber-optic, or microwave links.

T3—A digital carrier standard used in North America and most of Asia that can carry the equivalent of 672 channels for voice, data, video, or audio, with a maximum data throughput of 44.736 Mbps (typically rounded up to 45 Mbps for purposes of discussion). T3s rely on time division multiplexing and require either fiber-optic or microwave transmission media.

TA (terminal adapter)—A device used to convert digital signals into analog signals for use with ISDN phones and other analog devices. TAs are sometimes called ISDN modems.

TACACS (Terminal Access Controller Access Control System)—A centralized authentication system for remote access servers that is similar to, but older than, RADIUS.

tape backup—A relatively simple and economical backup method in which data is copied to magnetic tapes.

T-carrier—The term for any kind of leased line that follows the standards for T1s, fractional T1s, T1Cs, T2s, T3s, or T4s.

TCP (Transmission Control Protocol)—A core protocol of the TCP/IP suite. TCP belongs to the Transport layer and provides reliable data delivery services.

TCP/IP (Transmission Control Protocol/Internet Protocol)—A suite of networking protocols that includes TCP, IP, UDP, and many others. TCP/IP provides the foundation for _data exchange across the Internet.

TCP/IP core protocols—The major subprotocols of the TCP/IP suite, including IP, TCP, and UDP.

TDM (time division multiplexing)—A method of multiplexing that assigns a time slot in the flow of communications to every node on the network and, in that time slot, carries data from that node.

TDR (time domain reflectometer)—A high-end instrument for testing the qualities of a cable. It works by issuing a signal on a cable and measuring the way in which the signal bounces back (or reflects) to the TDR. Many performance testers rely on TDRs.

TE (terminal equipment)—The end nodes (such as computers and printers) served by the same connection (such as an ISDN, DSL, or T1 link).

Telecommunications Industry Association—See *TIA*.

Telnet—A terminal emulation protocol used to log on to remote hosts using the TCP/IP protocol. Telnet resides in the Application layer of the OSI Model.

terminal—A device with little (if any) of its own processing or disk capacity that depends on a host to supply it with applications and data-processing services.

Terminal Access Controller Access Control System—See *TACACS*.

terminal adapter—See *TA*.

terminal equipment—See *TE*.

terminal server—A computer that runs specialized software to act as a host and supply applications and resource sharing to remote clients.

terminal services—A remote access method in which a terminal server acts as a host for multiple remote clients. Terminal services requires specialized software on both the client and server. After connecting and authenticating, a client can access applications and data just as if it were directly attached to the LAN.

Terminal Services—The Microsoft software that enables a server to supply centralized and secure network connectivity to remote clients.

terminator—A resistor that is attached to each end of a bus-topology network and that causes the signal to stop rather than reflect back toward its source.

TFTP (Trivial File Transfer Protocol)—A TCP/IP Application layer protocol that enables file transfers between computers. Unlike FTP, TFTP relies on UDP at the Transport layer and does not require a user to log on to the remote host.

TGS (Ticket-granting service)—In Kerberos terminology, an application that runs on the KDC that issues ticket-granting tickets to clients so that they need not request a new ticket for each new service they want to access.

TGT (ticket-granting ticket)—In Kerberos terminology, a ticket that enables a user to be accepted as a validated principal by multiple services.

The Open Group—A nonprofit industry association that owns the UNIX trademark.

The SCO Group—The company that owns the rights to the UNIX source code.

Thicknet—An IEEE Physical layer standard for achieving a maximum of 10-Mbps throughput over coaxial copper cable. Thicknet is also known as 10BASE-5. Its maximum segment length is 500 meters, and it relies on a bus topology.

thickwire Ethernet—See *Thicknet*.

thin client—A client that relies on another host for the majority of processing and hard disk resources necessary to run applications and share files over the network.

thin Ethernet—See *Thinnet*.

Thinnet—An IEEE Physical layer standard for achieving 10-Mbps throughput over coaxial copper cable. Thinnet is also known as10BASE-2. Its maximum segment length is 185 meters, and it relies on a bus topology.

thread—A well-defined, self-contained subset of a process. Using threads within a process enables a program to efficiently perform related, multiple, simultaneous activities. Threads are also used to enable processes to use multiple processors on SMP systems.

three-way handshake—An authentication process that involves three steps.

throughput—The amount of data that a medium can transmit during a given period of time. Throughput is usually measured in megabits (1,000,000 bits) per second, or Mbps. The physical nature of every transmission media determines its potential throughput.

TIA (Telecommunications Industry Association)—A subgroup of the EIA that focuses on standards for information technology, wireless, satellite, fiber optics, and telephone equipment. Probably the best known standards to come from the TIA/EIA alliance are its guidelines for how network cable should be installed in commercial buildings, known as the "TIA/EIA 568-B Series."

ticket—In Kerberos terminology, a temporary set of credentials that a client uses to prove that its identity has been validated by the authentication service.

Ticket-granting service—See *TGS*.

ticket-granting ticket—See *TGT*.

tiered topology WAN—A type of WAN in which sites that are connected in star or ring formations are interconnected at different levels, with the interconnection points being organized into layers to form hierarchical groupings.

time division multiplexing—See *TDM*.

time domain reflectometer—See *TDR*.

Time to Live—See *TTL*.

time-dependent virus—A virus programmed to activate on a particular date. This type of virus, also known as a "time bomb," can remain dormant and harmless until its activation date arrives.

time-sharing—See *preemptive multitasking*.

TLD (top-level domain)—The highest-level category used to distinguish domain names—for example, .org, .com, .net. A TLD is also known as the domain suffix.

TLS (Transport Layer Security)—A version of SSL being standardized by the IETF (Internet Engineering Task Force). With TLS, IETF aims to create a version of SSL that encrypts UDP as well as TCP transmissions. TLS, which is supported by new Web browsers, uses slightly different encryption algorithms than SSL, but otherwise is very similar to the most recent version of SSL.

token—A special control frame that indicates to the rest of the network that a particular node has the right to transmit data.

token passing—A means of data transmission in which a 3-byte packet, called a token, is passed around the network in a round-robin fashion.

Token Ring—A networking technology developed by IBM in the 1980s. It relies upon direct links between nodes and a ring topology, using tokens to allow nodes to transmit data.

toll bypass—A cost-savings benefit that results from organizations completing long-distance telephone calls over their packet-switched networks, thus bypassing tolls charged by common carriers on comparable PSTN calls.

tone generator—A small electronic device that issues a signal on a wire pair. When used in conjunction with a tone locator, it can help locate the termination of a wire pair.

tone locator—A small electronic device that emits a tone when it detects electrical activity on a wire pair. When used in conjunction with a tone generator, it can help locate the termination of a wire pair.

top-level domain—See *TLD*.

topology—The physical layout of computers on a network.

traceroute (tracert)—A TCP/IP troubleshooting utility that uses ICMP to trace the path from one networked node to another, identifying all intermediate hops between the two nodes. Traceroute is useful for determining router or subnet connectivity problems. On Windows-based systems, the utility is known as tracert.

traffic—The data transmission and processing activity taking place on a computer network at any given time.

traffic monitoring—The process of determining how much data transfer activity is taking place on a network or network segment and notifying administrators when a segment becomes overloaded.

transceiver—A device that transmits and receives signals.

transmission—In networking, the application of data signals to a medium or the progress of data signals over a medium from one point to another.

Transmission Control Protocol/Internet Protocol—See *TCP/IP*.

Transmission Control Protocol—See *TCP*.

transmission media—The means through which data are transmitted and received. Transmission media may be physical, such as wire or cable, or atmospheric (wireless), such as radio waves.

transmit—To issue signals to the network medium.

transponder—The equipment on a satellite that receives an uplinked signal from earth, amplifies the signal, modifies its frequency, then retransmits it (in a downlink) to an antenna on earth.

Transport Layer Security—See *TLS*.

Transport layer—The fourth layer of the OSI Model. In the Transport layer, protocols ensure that data are transferred from point A to point B reliably and without errors. Transport layer services include flow control, acknowledgment, error correction, segmentation, reassembly, and sequencing.

tree—A logical representation of multiple, hierarchical levels in a directory. It is called a tree because the whole structure shares a common starting point (the root), and from that point extends branches (or containers), which may extend additional branches, and so on.

tree object—In NetWare terminology, the object that represents the root of an eDirectory tree.

Triple DES (3DES)—The modern implementation of DES, which weaves a 56-bit key through data three times, each time using a different key.

Trivial File Transfer Protocol—See *TFTP*.

Trojan—See *Trojan horse*.

Trojan horse—A program that disguises itself as something useful, but actually harms your system.

trust relationship—The relationship between two domains on a Windows Server 2003 network that allows a domain controller from one domain to authenticate users from the other domain.

TTL (Time to Live)—A number that indicates the maximum time that a datagram or packet can remain on the network before it is discarded. Although this field was originally meant to represent units of time, on modern networks it represents the number of router hops a datagram has endured. The TTL for datagrams is variable and configurable, but is usually set at 32 or 64. Each time a datagram passes through a router, its TTL is reduced by 1. When a router receives a datagram with a TTL equal to 1, the router discards that datagram.

tunnel—A secured, virtual connection between two nodes on a VPN.

tunneling—The process of encapsulating one type of protocol in another. Tunneling is the way in which higher-layer data is transported over VPNs by Layer 2 protocols.

twinaxial cable—A type of cable that consists of two copper conductors at its center surrounded by an insulator, a braided metal shielding, called braiding, and an outer cover, called the sheath or jacket.

twist ratio—The number of twists per meter or foot in a twisted-pair cable.

twisted-pair—A type of cable similar to telephone wiring that consists of color-coded pairs of insulated copper wires, each with a diameter of 0.4 to 0.8 mm, twisted around each other and encased in plastic coating.

two-way transitive trust—The security relationship between domains in the same domain tree in which one domain grants every other domain in the tree access to its resources and, in turn, that domain can access other domains' resources. When a new domain is added to a tree, it immediately shares a two-way trust with the other domains in the tree.

type 1 IBM connector—A type of Token Ring connector that uses interlocking tabs that snap into an identical connector when one is flipped upside-down, making for a secure connection. Type 1 IBM connectors are used on STP-based Token Ring networks.

typeful—A way of denoting an object's context in which the organization and organizational unit designators ("O=" and "OU=," respectively) are included. For example, OU=Inv.OU=_Ops.OU=Corp. O=Sutkin.

typeless—A way of denoting an object's context in which the organization and organizational unit designators ("O=" and "OU=," respectively) are omitted. For example, Inv.Ops.Corp._Sutkin.

UDF (Universal Disk Format)—A file system used on CD-ROMs and DVD (digital video disc) media.

UDP (User Datagram Protocol)—A core protocol in the TCP/IP suite that sits in the Transport layer of the OSI Model. UDP is a connectionless transport service.

UFS—The primary file system used in the Solaris operating system.

unicast address—A type of IPv6 address that represents a single interface on a device. An IPv6 unicast address begins with either FFC0 or FF80.

uninterruptible power supply—See *UPS*.

Universal Disk Format—See *UDF*.

universal group—A group on a Windows Server 2003 network that allows members from one domain to access resources in multiple domains and forests.

unpopulated segment—A network segment that does not contain end nodes, such as workstations. Unpopulated segments are also called link segments.

unshielded twisted-pair—See *UTP*.

upgrade—A major change to the existing code in a software application, which may or may not be offered free from a vendor, and may or may not be comprehensive enough to substitute for the original application.

uplink—A connection from an earth-based transmitter to an orbiting satellite.

uplink port—A port on a connectivity device, such as a hub or switch, used to connect it to another connectivity device.

UPN (user principal name) suffix—The portion of a universal principal name (in Windows Server 2003 Active Directory's naming conventions) that follows the @ sign.

UPN (user principal name)—The preferred Active Directory naming convention for objects when used in informal situations. This name looks like a familiar Internet address, including the positioning of the domain name after the @ sign. UPNs are typically used for e-mail and related Internet services.

UPS (uninterruptible power supply)—A battery-operated power source directly attached to one or more devices and to a power supply (such as a wall outlet), which prevents undesired features of the power source from harming the device or interrupting its services.

upstream—A term used to describe data traffic that flows from a customer's site to a carrier's facility. In asymmetrical communications, upstream throughput is usually much lower than downstream throughput. In symmetrical communications, upstream and downstream throughputs are equal.

USB (universal serial bus) port—A standard external bus that can be used to connect multiple types of peripherals, including modems, mice, and NICs, to a computer. Two USB standards exist: USB 1.1 and USB 2.0. Most modern computers support the USB 2.0 standard.

user—A person who uses a computer.

User Datagram Protocol—See *UDP*.

user principal name—See *UPN*.

UTP (unshielded twisted-pair)—A type of cabling that consists of one or more insulated wire pairs encased in a plastic sheath. As its name implies, UTP does not contain additional shielding for the twisted pairs. As a result, UTP is both less expensive and less resistant to noise than STP.

vault—A large tape storage library.

virtual address—See *network address*.

virtual circuit—A connection between network nodes that, although based on potentially disparate physical links, logically appears to be a direct, dedicated link between those nodes.

virtual local area network—See *VLAN*.

virtual memory—The memory that is logically carved out of space on the hard disk and added to physical memory (RAM).

virtual private network—See *VPN*.

virus—A program that replicates itself to infect more computers, either through network connections or through floppy disks passed among users. Viruses may damage files or systems, or simply annoy users by flashing messages or pictures on the screen or by causing the keyboard to beep.

virus hoax—A rumor, or false alert, about a dangerous, new virus that could supposedly cause serious damage to your workstation.

VLAN (virtual local area network)—A network within a network that is logically defined by grouping its devices' switch ports in the same broadcast domain. A VLAN can consist of any type of network node in any geographic location and can incorporate nodes connected to different switches.

Voice over IP (VoIP)—The provision of telephone service over a packet-switched network running the TCP/IP protocol suite. One form of VoIP (pronounced "voyp") is Internet telephony, though VoIP is frequently used over private networks to circumvent long-distance toll charges.

VoIP – See *voice over IP*.

volt—The measurement used to describe the degree of pressure an electrical current exerts on a conductor.

voltage—The pressure (sometimes informally referred to as the strength) of an electrical current.

volt-amp (VA)—A measure of electrical power. A volt-amp is the product of the voltage and current (measured in amps) of the electricity on a line.

voltmeter—A device used to measure voltage (or electrical pressure) on an electrical _circuit.

VPN (virtual private network)—A logically constructed WAN that uses existing public transmission systems. VPNs can be created through the use of software or combined software and hardware solutions. This type of network allows an organization to carve out a private WAN through the Internet that serves only its offices, while keeping the data secure and isolated from other (public) traffic.

WAN (wide area network)—A network that spans a long distance and connects two or more LANs.

WAN link—A point-to-point connection between two nodes on a WAN.

WAP (wireless access point)—See *AP*.

war driving—The act of driving while running a laptop configured to detect and capture wireless data transmissions.

warm site—A place where the computers, devices, and connectivity necessary to rebuild a network exist, though only some are appropriately configured, updated, or connected to match the network's current state.

wavelength—The distance between corresponding points on a wave's cycle. Wavelength is inversely proportional to frequency.

wavelength division multiplexing—See *WDM*.

WDM (wavelength division multiplexing)—A multiplexing technique in which each signal on a fiber-optic cable is assigned a different wavelength, which equates to its own subchannel. Each wavelength is modulated with a data signal. In this manner, multiple signals can be simultaneously transmitted in the same direction over a length of fiber.

Web portal—A secure, Web-based interface to an application or group of applications.

Web server—A computer that manages Web site services, such as supplying a Web page to multiple users on demand.

Webcasting—A broadcast transmission from one Internet-attached node to multiple other Internet-attached nodes.

Well Known Ports—TCP/IP port numbers 0 to 1023, so named because they were long ago assigned by Internet authorities to popular services (for example, FTP and Telnet), and are therefore well known and frequently used.

WEP (Wired Equivalent Privacy)—A key encryption technique for wireless networks that uses keys both to authenticate network clients and to encrypt data in transit.

whois—The utility that allows you to query ICANN's DNS registration database and find the information as a domain.

wide area network—See *WAN*.

Wi-Fi—See *802.11b*.

Wi-Fi Alliance—An international, nonprofit organization dedicated to ensuring the interoperability of 802.11-capable devices.

Wi-Fi Protected Access—See *WPA*.

WiMAX—See *802.16a*.

Windows Internet Naming Service—See *WINS*.

Windows Services for UNIX—A suite of applications designed to integrate Windows Server 2003 servers with UNIX-type of servers and clients. One application in this suite enables Windows and UNIX-type of servers to share directory information (when the UNIX-type of server has a directory installed). Another application enables UNIX-type of clients to view resources on a Windows Server 2003 server as if they were resources on a UNIX-type of server.

winipcfg—The TCP/IP configuration and management utility for use with Windows 9x and Me systems. Winipcfg differs from ipconfig in that it supplies a graphical user interface.

WINS (Windows Internet Naming Service)—A service that resolves NetBIOS names with IP addresses. WINS is used exclusively with systems that use NetBIOS—therefore, it is found on Windows-based systems.

wire-bound—A type of signal that relies on a physical medium, such as a cable, for its transmission.

Wired Equivalent Privacy—See *WEP*.

wireless—The signals made of electromagnetic energy that travel through the atmosphere.

wireless access point—See *WAP*.

wireless broadband—The term used to describe the recently released standards for high-throughput, long-distance digital data exchange over wireless connections. WiMAX (IEEE 802.16a) is one example of a wireless broadband technology.

wireless LAN—See *WLAN*.

wireless personal area network—See *WPAN*.

wireless spectrum—A continuum of electromagnetic waves used for data and voice communication. The wireless spectrum (as defined by the FCC, which controls its use) spans frequencies between 9 KHz and 300 GHz. Each type of wireless service can be associated with one area of the wireless spectrum.

WLAN (wireless LAN)—A LAN that uses wireless connections for some or all of its transmissions.

workgroup—A group of interconnected computers that share each others' resources without relying on a central file server.

workgroup hub—See *standalone hub*.

Workgroup Manager—The application in Mac OS X Server that enables a network administrator to manage users and groups.

workstation—A computer that runs a desktop operating system and connects to a network.

Worldwide Interoperability for Microwave Access (WiMAX)—See *802.16a*.

worm—An unwanted program that travels between computers and across networks. Although worms do not alter other programs as viruses do, they may carry viruses.

WPA (Wi-Fi Protected Access)—A wireless security method endorsed by the Wi-Fi Alliance that is considered a subset of the 802.11i standard. In WPA, authentication follows the same mechanism specified in 802.11i. The main difference between WPA and 802.11i is that WPA specifies RC4 encryption rather than AES.

WPA2—The name given to the 802.11i security standard by the Wi-Fi Alliance. The only difference between WPA2 and 802.11i is that WPA2 includes support for the older WPA security method.

WPAN (wireless personal area network)—A small office or home network in which devices such as mobile telephones, PDAs, laptops, and computers are connected via wireless transmission.

X Server—A NetWare 6.x server's graphical desktop. X Server loads by default when the server starts.

X Window system—The GUI environment for UNIX-type of systems.

X.25—An analog, packet-switched WAN technology optimized for reliable, long-distance data transmission and standardized by the ITU in the mid-1970s. The X.25 standard specifies protocols at the Physical, Data Link, and Network layers of the OSI Model. It provides excellent flow control and ensures data reliability over long distances by verifying the transmission at every node. X.25 can support a maximum of only 2-Mbps throughput.

xDSL—The term used to refer to all varieties of DSL.

XNU—The Mach-based kernel in Mac OS X.

Xserve—The enterprise-class of server computer by Apple Computer, which is based on the PowerPC processor and which runs Mac OS X Server.

Zeroconf (Zero Configuration)—A collection of protocols designed by the IETF to simplify the setup of nodes on a TCP/IP network. Zeroconf assigns a node an IP address, resolves the node's host name and IP address without requiring a DNS server, and discovers services, such as print services, available to the node, also without requiring a DNS server.

Index

A

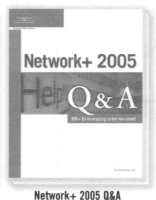